Editor in Chief **Dana L. Blatt, J.D., Esq.**

Managing Editor **Marie H. Stedman**

Written By **John M. Huberty, J.D., Esq.**
Alex Vinnitsky, J.D., Esq.
Annette L. Anderson, J.D., Esq.
Steven H. Blum, J.D., Esq.
Sunil Gupta, J.D., Esq.
Phillip J. Valdivia, J.D., Esq.
Xavier Tan-Sanchez, J.D., Esq.
Jennifer L. Peters, J.D., Esq.

Memory Graphics **Norman Vance**

Page Design **Terri Asher**

Chief Administrator **Richard A. Strober**

Adaptable to Courses Utilizing Burton's Casebook on Contracts 2nd Edition

Published by **WEST GROUP**
610 Opperman Drive
Eagan, MN
55123

610 Opperman Drive
P.O. Box 64526
St. Paul, MN 55164-0526

ISBN 0-314-14168-5

Printed in the United States of America

1st reprint 2004

A Message from Dana L. Blatt, J.D., Editor In Chief West Group High Court Case Summaries

As Editor in Chief of West Group's High Court Case Summaries, I am pleased to be associated with West Group and its tradition of providing the highest quality law student study aids such as Nutshells, Hornbooks, the Black Letter Series, and Sum and Substance products. I am also pleased that West Group, as the new publisher of High Court Case Summaries, will continue its tradition of providing students with the best quality student briefs available today. When you use these High Court Case Summaries, you will know that you have the advantage of using the best-written and most comprehensive student briefs available, with the most thorough analyses. Law students cannot afford to waste a minute of their time. That's why you need High Court Case Summaries. You'll find that with High Court you not only save time, but also have the competitive edge with our exclusive features such as memory graphics, "party lines," overview outlines, and case vocabulary. The following two pages will introduce you to the format of a High Court Brief.

Dana L. Blatt, J.D., Editor In Chief

FORMAT FOR A HIGH COURT BRIEF

THE HEADNOTE

Like a headline in a newspaper, the headnote provides you with a brief statement highlighting the importance of the case to the course.

"PARTY" LINE

A quick memory aid. For instantaneous recollection of the names of the parties and their relationship to each other.

MEMORY GRAPHIC

"A picture is worth a thousand words." Our professional cartoonists have created an entertaining "picture of the facts." To assist you in remembering what a particular case is about, simply glance at the picture.

INSTANT FACTS

Another great memory aid. A quick scan of a single sentence will instantly remind you of all of the facts of the case.

BLACK LETTER RULE

This section contains the single most important rule of the case (determined by reference to the chapter of the casebook where the case can be found). Read together with instant facts, you have a perfect mini brief.

CASE VOCABULARY

Every new or unusual legal, Latin or English word found in the original case is briefly defined in this section. This timesaver eliminates constant references to separate dictionaries.

PROCEDURAL BASIS

In a single sentence we summarize what happened, procedurally, to cause the case to be on appeal.

FACTS

"Just the facts ma'am..." Our facts are clearer and easier to understand than the original case. In fact, you can have a complete understanding of the original case without ever having to read it. Just read our brief.

ISSUE

Utilizing our I.R.A.C. format (Issue, Rule, Application, Conclusion), we put it all in focus by simply stating the single most important question of every case.

DECISION AND RATIONALE

We know you need to understand the rationale of every case to learn the law. In a clear, concise, and meticulous fashion we lay it all out for you. We do the work of separating what is important from what is not. Yet, we provide you with a thorough summary of every essential element of every case. Every concurrence and dissent is summarized as well.

ANALYSIS

We provide you with an extensive analysis of every single case. Here you will learn what you want to know about every case. What is the history or background of the litigation? What do authorities say about the opinion? How does it fit in with the course? How does each case compare with others in the casebook? Is it a majority or minority opinion? What is the importance of the case and why did the casebook author choose to include it as a major opinion in the casebook? What types of things will the professor be asking about the case? What will be said about the opinion in class? Will people criticize or applaud it? What would you want to say about the case if called upon in class to brief it? In other words, what are the "secret" essential things that one must know and understand about each case in order to do well in the course? We answer these and many other questions for you. Nobody else comes close to giving you the in-depth analysis that we give!

A Great All-Around Study Aid!

IMPLIED WARRANTIES OF MERCHANTABILITY SURVIVE EXPRESS CONTRACTUAL PROVISIONS TO THE CONTRARY

Henningsen v. Bloomfield Motors, Inc.

(Auto Purchaser) v. (Auto Dealer)

32 N.J. 358, 161 A.2d 69 (N.J. 1960)

MEMORY GRAPHIC

Instant Facts

An automobile purchaser sued the dealer and manufacturer for breach of an implied warranty of merchantability, although the express contractual terms of the sale disclaimed all implied warranties.

Black Letter Rule

A contract of adhesion does not trump statutory implied warranties of merchantability.

Case Vocabulary

CAVEAT EMPTOR: Let the buyer beware.

CONTRACT OF ADHESION: A contract between parties of unequal bargaining position, where the buyer must "take it or leave it."

IMPLIED WARRANTY OF MERCHANTABILITY: A warranty that means that the thing sold must be reasonably fit for the general purpose for which it is manufactured and sold.

Procedural Basis: Certification to New Jersey Supreme Court of appeal of judgment awarding damages for breach of implied warranty.

Facts: Mr. Henningsen purchased a car from Bloomfield Motors Inc. (D), a retail dealer. The car had been manufactured by Chrysler Corporation (D). Mr. Henningsen gave the car to his wife for Christmas. Mrs. Henningsen (P) was badly injured a few days later when the steering gear failéd and the car turned right into a wall. When he purchased the car, Mr. Henningsen signed a contract without reading the fine print. The fine print contained a "warranty" clause which disclaimed all implied warranties and which granted an express warranty for all defects within 90 days or 4000 miles, whichever came first. Mrs. Henningsen (P) sued Bloomfield (D) and Chrysler (D). The trial court dismissed her negligence counts but ruled for Mrs. Henningsen (P) based on the implied warranty of merchantability. Bloomfield (D) and Chrysler (D) appealed.

Issue: Does a contract of adhesion trump statutory implied warranties of merchantability?

Decision and Rationale: (Francis, J.) No. A contract of adhesion does not trump statutory implied warranties of merchantability. In order to ameliorate the harsh effects of the doctrine of caveat emptor, most states have imposed an implied warranty of merchantability on all sales transactions. This warranty simply means that the thing sold must be reasonably fit for the general purpose for which it is manufactured and sold. The warranty extends to all foreseeable users of the product, not merely those in privity of contract with the seller. In order to avoid the implied warranty obligations, many manufacturers, including Chrysler (D) and all other automobile manufacturers, include an express warranty provision which disclaims all statutory implied warranties. We must determine what effect to give this express warranty. Under traditional principles of freedom of contract, the law allows parties to contract away obligations. However, in the auto sales context, the fine-print disclaimer of implied warranties is a contract of adhesion. It is a standardized form contract, and the purchaser has no opportunity to bargain for different terms. He must "take it or leave it," and he cannot shop around to different dealers because all of them use the same standard contract. Because the purchaser and seller occupy grossly inequal bargaining positions, we feel that justice must trump the principle of freedom of contract. Chrysler's (D) attempted disclaimer of an implied warranty of merchantability is so inimical to the public good as to compel an adjudication of its invalidity. Affirmed.

Analysis:

This well-written opinion presents an excellent exegesis of several areas of law, ranging from products liability to various contract principles. The opinion notes several conflicting interests and principles which the court must weigh. First, the traditional principle of caveat emptor faces the modern doctrine of implied warranties of merchantability. The court has little difficulty in holding that modern commercial transactions require protection for purchasers. An implied warranty of merchantability is imposed in all auto sales transactions in order to protect the buyer. Second, the requirement of privity of contract is weighed against an implied warranty. The court notes that, in modern sales transactions, a warranty safeguards all consumers of a product, not merely those in direct contractual privity with the seller. Third, the principle of freedom of contract is weighed against this implied warranty. Freedom of contract is one of the fundamental tenets of the law. Parties should be free to contract for any provisions, and generally parties are bound by the terms of their contract. However, an important exception exists when a contract is one of adhesion. Contracts of adhesion typically involve terms in fine print, written by a powerful seller to limit liabilities or impose responsibilities upon an unsuspecting buyer. No bargaining occurs for these terms, and indeed the buyer is in no position to bargain. If the buyer attempts to change the terms of the contract, the seller simply will not complete the transaction. In order for a contract to be considered "adhesive" or "unconscionable," the buyer usually has nowhere else to go. As in the case at bar, all sellers of a particular type of goods may include similar terms in their adhesive contracts. Weighing all of these factors, a court may rule that the express contractual terms are invalid, notwithstanding the principle of freedom of contract. The arguments for and against this approach are easy to see. On one hand, a buyer should not be allowed to benefit from his failure to read the terms of a contract or to attempt to change some unwanted terms. On the other hand, social justice requires that the buyer be protected from an all-powerful seller, especially where the buyer has no other option but to accept the contract as written. All in all, public policy, and not traditional law, shapes this court's opinion.

Table of Contents

Alphabetical Table of Cases

Alphabetical Table of Cases

Perspective
The Autonomy and Security Principles

Chapter 1

To learn about the law of contracts is to learn about the every day interactions of people in society. Whether we recognize it or not, contracts affect virtually every aspect of our lives. The light that allows you to read these words, unless you are outside, is provided under the terms of a contractual agreement. The insurance on our cars is provided pursuant to a contract. Contracts provide a basis for the ordering of our lives.

By enforcing contracts, the law promotes economic prosperity. Why? Because contracts allow us to have certain expectations for the future. They allow merchants to deal with each other under the same rules, removing from the equation of business, as much as possible, the chance of unscrupulous and dishonest dealing. It is thus no surprise that the advancement, or modernization if you prefer, of western civilization closely corresponds to the advent of a practical system of laws, including quite prominently the law of contracts.

The freedom to contract was not always taken for granted. During medieval times in England, the courts rarely enforced contracts. This left merchants and others to their own devices—often their very own courts, and even arbitration. Some trace the reasons for this to the stratification of English society. Similar to the caste system of India, English citizens were assigned different societal statuses, something that hampered any attempts to contractually mandate how they dealt with each other and what they're legal expectations could be. However, as we all know, England did not stay this way. Instead, it became the world's foremost commercial center. As you may have guessed, the law changed with it, promoting England's evolution into a capitalist Mecca. The most important change, from our perspective, was the idea of freedom to contract, enhanced and sped up by the great thinkers of the era, Jeremy Bentham, Adam Smith, John Stuart Mill, and others.

As you will no doubt learn, the freedom to contract as applied in the days of Bentham and Smith is no longer a reality. Since those days, our freedom to contract has been restricted more and more by the legislative branches. When it comes to lawful endeavors, our freedom to contract is still a bedrock of modern law. In some areas, those that were perversely vulnerable to market distortions and unfair dealing, contracts are governed by more restrictive laws designed to protect the rights of the parties. One such area is employment contracts. The minimum wage laws are a restriction on our freedom to contract, a result of a public policy judgment that employees should be paid at least the bare minimum needed to survive.

Most legal commentators see the law of contracts moving toward more restrictions. This is a result of the view that the modern bargaining process is becoming more distorted, with one side having more power than the other. Standard form contracts used by the vast majority of merchants are one main cause. This practice skews one of the main premises of contract law—that the parties are roughly equal in the mix. When one party is able to force the other to deal on his terms and his terms only, the door for unfair dealing is opened wide. When this opportunity is taken advantage of, one party is left embittered by the process, a result that bodes no good will for future economic progress. However, as it has done in the past, the law of contracts will evolve to meet this new challenge.

Chapter Overview Outline
The Autonomy and Security Principles

Chapter 1

NOTE: THE PURPOSE OF THIS OUTLINE IS TO ORGANIZE THE CASES SO THAT ONE CAN QUICKLY UNDERSTAND THE RELEVANCE OF EACH CASE TO THE COURSE. NO ATTEMPT IS MADE IN THIS OVERVIEW TO ADDRESS EVERY CONCEPT THAT MUST BE STUDIED. BE SURE TO READ THE ENTIRE CASEBOOK AND/OR OTHER MATERIALS TO GAIN A FULL UNDERSTANDING OF ALL CONCEPTS.

I. Promises
  A. Promises made between members of society that society is prepared to enforce are "contracts."
    1. Contracts enforceable according to principles set forth at law are a vital part of the economy.
  B. The law of contracts allows people to obligate themselves while conferring legally enforceable rights on others.
  C. In order to make a promise, there must be at least two parties—a promisor and a promisee.
  D. A promise must be definite enough, as determined from the promise itself and all the surrounding circumstances, so that a reasonable person would understand it as imposing an obligation upon the promisor. *Hawkins v. McGee.*
  E. Promises have the effect of creating interests, rights, and duties in the parties to the promise.
    1. Only some interests receive the protection of law.
  F. There are three general interests at law—expectation, reliance, and restitution.
    1. The correct measure of damages for a failure to perform a contract as promised can be the difference between the result that was promised and what was actually provided. This is termed 'expectation damages.' *Hawkins v. McGee.*
    2. Reliance interests are those given rise to by a party's changing their position due to a promise from another. The party has "relied" on the promise.
    3. The restitution interest is the interest a party has in having the consideration given in exchange for a performance returned when the performance does not meet the valid expectations of the party.
  G. The Restatements of Contracts.
    1. The Restatements are the result of the American Law Institute's research into numerous cases throughout the nation, extraction of legal rules from those cases, and a final gathering of those rules in book form.
    2. The American Law Institute is an organization made up of the Supreme Court justices, numerous other judges from throughout the nation, along with the deans of the law schools and many other recognized experts in the legal profession.
    3. The Restatement, while widely accepted by the courts, is not the law, but merely a convenient statement of the modern view of the law, and thus serves as persuasive authority.

II. Promissory Agreements
  A. Intent of the Parties
    1. Where a party's actions and statements could reasonably be seen as manifesting an intent to enter into a contract, the party will be bound to the contract, even if the party had no subjective intent to enter into the agreement. *Lucy v. Zehmer.*
      a. Most contract scholars agree that mutual assent should be viewed from an objective standpoint, i.e. from the outward manifestations of the parties.
      b. Some commentators criticize the objective approach because it has the potential to take consent well beyond what the parties consciously intended.
    2. Where two parties come to an objective agreement, but subjectively attach different meanings to the manifestations of the other

and these meanings are reasonable under the circumstances, a contract has not been formed. This is called mutual mistake.

3. Both parties to a contract need not subjectively intend to enter into a contract in order to find that a contract has been validly formed. *Embry v. Hargadine, McKittrick Dry Goods Co.*
4. When a term or terms used to express an agreement is/are ambiguous and the parties understand it in different ways, a contract cannot exist unless one party is aware of the other party's understanding. *Oswald v. Allen.*

B. Offers
1. Every contract must start with an offer. An offer is a promise from the offeror that manifests a party's commitment to take some action in exchange for a return promise or performance from the other party—the offeree.
    a. Once an offer has been made, a power of acceptance has been created in the offeree.
    b. An offeree may do one of the following:
        (1) Accept the offer as is, with no material changes.
        (2) Reject the offer outright.
        (3) Propose different terms, thus terminating the power of acceptance and making a counteroffer.
2. A solicitation for an order or other expression of agreement to purchase, clearly specifying that no contract exists until ratification or assent by the party soliciting the order, is not itself an offer; it is a request for an offer or an invitation to deal. *Mesaros v. United States.*
3. Advertisements are generally not considered offers, but are rather invitations to make an offer. However, when an advertisement is clear, definite, and explicit, and leaves nothing open for negotiation, it may be construed as an offer. *Lefkowitz v. Great Minneapolis Surplus Store.*

C. The Power of Acceptance
1. An offer creates a legal power in the offeree. By accepting, the offeree exercises the legal power, which has the effect of changing the legal relations between the parties, e.g. the rights and duties of the offeror.
2. Offers always expire if not accepted. The expiration point will be expressed in the terms of the offer itself, or it will be at a reasonable time after the offer is made.
    a. An offer made during the course of a face-to-face conversation expires either by its terms or at the end of the conversation if no express expiration is provided. *Akers v. J.B. Sedberry, Inc.*
3. When acceptance of an offer is accompanied by further demands, the offeree makes a counter-offer, thus terminating the original power of acceptance. *Ardente v. Horan.*
    a. Sometimes, instead of viewing a purported acceptance that changes the terms of an offer as a rejection and counter-offer, a court may view it as an unconditional acceptance along with an offer to modify.
4. There are two basic types of contracts: Unilateral and Bilateral.
    a. A unilateral contract is where the offeror invites acceptance by performance. For example, if A were to offer B $10 if B mows A's lawn, A has invited B to accept by mowing the lawn, rather than by a promise to mow the lawn.
    b. A bilateral contract is simply a promise in exchange for a promise. If A instead offered B $10 in exchange for a promise to mow the lawn, A has invited acceptance by a return promise, rather than by performance.
5. An offer to enter into a unilateral contract may be withdrawn right up until the very moment performance is begun. *Petterson v. Pattberg.*
6. Partial performance of a unilateral contract creates a conditional contract that may not

be revoked by the offeror before the allotted time for completion of performance has run, or a reasonable time if the offer is silent as to the time allowed for complete performance. *Marchiondo v. Schenk.*

D. Acceptance
   1. Acceptance can only follow an offer, and once given, a binding contract is formed. By accepting an offer, the offeree has manifested assent and an intent to fulfill the requirements of the agreement.
      a. A valid acceptance must conform to the mode and manner of acceptance specified in the offer.
      b. There are default rules for dealing with situations where the offer does not adequately specify the manner of acceptance. For instance, when an offer fails to specify when the offer will expire, the law will operate to make the offer expire after a reasonable time.
      c. Contracting parties may get around default rules by making sure the contract covers all material terms and conditions, such that default rules are not needed. In this way, the autonomy of the parties is preserved.
   2. When the intent and circumstances surrounding an offer to contract are ambiguous with respect to whether the offer is for a bilateral or unilateral contract, there is a presumption that the offer was for a bilateral contract. *Davis v. Jacoby.*
   3. An acceptance of an offer that has expired by its own terms acts instead as a counter offer that must be accepted by the original offeror in order to form a binding contract. *Houston Dairy, Inc. v. John Hancock Mutual Life Ins. Co.*
   4. When the subject of a contract, either in its nature or by virtue of the conditions of the market, will become unmarketable by delay, the offeree's delay in notifying the offeror of rejection or acceptance will amount to acceptance by the offeree. *Cole-McIntyre-Norfleet Co. v. Holloway.*
   5. When a party purchases property with knowledge that the property is subject to certain conditions of ownership, the party consents to or manifests an acceptance of, and must conform to, said conditions of the implied-in-fact contract. *Seaview Ass'n of Fire Island, N.Y., Inc. v. Williams.*
      a. Some commentators prefer to premise a party's obligation on the principle of fair play as an alternative to consent.

E. Contract Formation Pursuant to the Uniform Commercial Code (UCC)
   1. Most contracting in the modern world is done as part of the normal course of business, over and over again, usually with the same or substantially similar terms, between the same parties.
      a. This nature of commercial contracting provides an incentive for parties to deal honestly and fairly with each other, with the parties often relying on implicit understandings between them.
      b. To promote autonomy and streamline contracting in the commercial sphere, contracts in this sphere are often governed by statute rather than by the common law rules. This statute is the UCC.
      c. The UCC allows for more flexible and reasonable interpretations of commercial contracts, thus promoting greater commercial activity through flexibility and uniformity.
      d. Forty-nine states follow the UCC, with only very small differences among the states.
      e. The UCC is, by its terms, to be "liberally construed and applied to promote its underlying purposes and policies" of simplifying the law of commercial transactions; promoting expansion of commerce through customary practices and usage; and to provide for uniform laws in the states.
   2. Article 2 of the UCC covers transactions in "goods," with goods being defined as "all things which are movable at the time of

identification to the contract for sale other than the money in which the price is to be paid...."

a. A contract for sale of goods may be made in any manner sufficient to show agreement, including conduct by both parties which recognizes the existence of such a contract. UCC § 2-204(1); *ProCD, Inc. v. Zeidenberg*.
   (1) Thus, a statement on the outside of a product's packaging that makes purchase and use subject to certain licensing restrictions contained inside the package is binding on the purchaser if the product may be returned if the purchaser does not wish to comply with the conditions. *ProCD, Inc. v. Zeidenberg*.
b. Conduct by an offeree tending to indicate acceptance may create a binding contract notwithstanding the offeree's failure to accept in the manner prescribed by the offeror. *Empire Machinery Co. v. Litton Business Telephone Systems*.
   (1) This is an exception to the common law "mirror image rule" that requires an acceptance to exactly match the terms of the offer. Strict adherence to this rule has the potential to restrict commercial transactions where the high volume of business allows little time to mull over the fine print in every one's business forms.
   (2) UCC § 2-207 put an end to the mirror image rule as applied to commercial transactions under UCC Article 2.
c. When contracting parties express assent conditional on the other party's acceptance of new terms, and subsequently conduct themselves in a manner that indicates the existence of a contract, U.C.C. § 207 operates to nullify the new terms to the extent they contradict any new terms added by the other party, or the terms of the original offer. *Ionics, Inc. v. Elmwood Sensors, Inc.*

F. Incomplete Contracts
   1. A court may not revise a contract that is incomplete because it lacks material elements; such a contract is unenforceable. *Sun Printing & Publishing Ass'n v. Remington Paper & Power Co., Inc.*
   2. Often, parties will negotiate contracts point-by-point, especially when the contract is complex. Agreements on the individual points or elements making up an entire contract are not contracts themselves, and should not be enforced as such. In this way, parties can avoid the problem of indefiniteness and retain maximum autonomy in contracting.
      a. A preliminary agreement by parties to a contract may be enforced as a binding contract itself if it covers all essential and material terms. *Shann v. Dunk*.
      b. The terms of a letter of intent or preliminary agreement may impose a duty to conduct further negotiations in good faith. *A/S Apothekernes Laboratorium for Specialpraeparater v. I.M.C. Chemical Group, Inc.*
      c. The full extent of a party's obligation to negotiate in good faith can only be determined from the terms of the letter of intent or the preliminary agreement. *A/S Apothekernes Laboratorium for Specialpraeparater v. I.M.C. Chemical Group, Inc.*
      d. The provisions of a preliminary letter of intent imposing a duty to negotiate in good faith must be read and construed from the entire text of the letter, not in isolation from the other provisions. *Itek Corp. v. Chicago Aerial Indus., Inc.*
   3. The autonomy principle is also reflected by the fact that the American legal system does not impose a requirement to negotiate in good faith. This does not mean, however, that parties are free to employ fraudulent practices and deception in negotiations.

Chapter Overview Outline
The Autonomy and Security Principles

III. The Requirement That A Contract Be In Writing: Statute of Frauds

A. In 1677, the English Parliament passed the Statute of Frauds for the purpose of obviating perjury, promoting certainty, deliberation, seriousness, and to show that an act was a genuine act of volition.

B. Forty-seven states have a Statute of Frauds, generally providing that certain agreements must be in written form to be enforceable.

C. The three most important categories of contracts covered by the various statutes of frauds are:

1. Contracts where one party agrees to be responsible for the debt of another
2. Contracts for the sale of land or interests therein
3. Contracts that cannot be performed in one year from the time of finalization.

D. Land and Goods:

1. The Statute of Frauds requires that a contract for the sale of lands, including any changes or modifications to the contract, be in written form to be enforceable. *Chomicky v. Buttolph.*
2. Section 2-201(1) of the U.C.C. requires contracts for the sale of goods valued at $500 or more to be memorialized in writing(s), signed by the party against whom enforcement is sought, and sufficient to indicate that a contract for sale has been made. *Nebraska Builders Prods. Co. v. Industrial Erectors, Inc.*

E. The general requirements of a contract to satisfy the Statute are:

1. Identification of the parties
2. A showing that the parties have made a contract
3. Identification of the subject matter of the contract
4. A statement of the essential terms
5. The signatures of the parties.

F. A fair criticism of the Statute of Frauds is that instead of making fraud more difficult, it sometimes promotes it by allowing a party to an oral contract to escape the contract by pleading the Statute. Exceptions to the Statute, along with crafty judicial decision-making, have mitigated some of this concern.

1. An oral contract, normally required to be in writing, may be given effect, if supported by clear and uncontradicted written documentary evidence, such that doing so comports with public policies against fraud and perjury. *Radke v. Brenon.*
2. U.C.C. section 2-201(3)(b) allows enforcement of a contract not meeting the requirements of § 2-201(1) if the party against whom enforcement is sought admits in court that a contract was made. *Nebraska Builders Prods. Co. v. Industrial Erectors, Inc.*
3. Notwithstanding the requirement of a written contract, the doctrine of promissory estoppel requires enforcement (*Warder & Lee Elevator, Inc. v. Britten*) where (all of the following):
   a. A party makes an oral contract
   b. Expecting the other party to rely on it
   c. The other party does rely on it to their detriment
   d. Failure to enforce the oral contract would be inequitable.

Hawkins v. McGee

(Boy with Mangled Hand) v. (Surgeon)

84 N.H. 114, 146 A. 641 (1929)

M E M O R Y G R A P H I C

Instant Facts

A young boy went to a surgeon to repair his scarred hand, and came away with a hand that was even more damaged.

Black Letter Rule

The correct measure of damages for a failure to perform a contract as promised is the difference between the result that was promised and what was actually provided. This is termed 'expectation damages.'

Case Vocabulary

ASSUMPSIT: A common law form of action which lies for the recovery of damages for the non-performance of a contract.

CHARGE TO THE JURY: The final address by the judge to the jury before the verdict, in which he sums up the case, and instructs the jury as to the rules of law which apply to the various issues, and which they must observe.

CHATTELS: Articles of personal property, as distinguished from real property.

EXCEPTIONS: Objections to an order or ruling of the trial court.

NEGLIGENCE: The failure to use such care as a reasonably prudent and careful person would use under similar circumstances.

NONSUIT: Type of judgment rendered against a party in a legal proceeding when he is unable to maintain his cause in court.

PREJUDICIAL: The probative value of the evidence is substantially outweighed by the danger of an undue tendency to move the jury to decide on an improper basis.

SET ASIDE THE VERDICT: To reverse, vacate, cancel, annul, or revoke a judgment or order.

WARRANTY: A promise that certain facts are truly as they are represented to be.

Procedural Basis: Both the plaintiff and the defendant filed exceptions to the jury's verdict for the plaintiff, and the trial court's subsequent setting aside of the verdict.

Facts: Hawkins (P) and his father went to a surgeon to have a considerable amount of scar tissue removed from the palm of his hand, and the grafting of skin taken from his chest in place thereof [a hairy palm - ick!]. The scar tissue was the result of a severe burn which Hawkins (P) had received nine years earlier. Hawkins (P) claims that Dr. McGee (D) promised him a perfect hand [who could *ever* believe something like that?] after the operation; and that he said, "I will guarantee to make the hand a hundred per cent perfect hand" or "a hundred per cent good hand." Prior to the operation, Hawkins' (P) hand was "a practical, useful hand," but as a result of the operation, the motion of his hand had become so restricted that the hand was useless to him [the price of vanity!]. Hawkins (P) brought a suit in assumpsit against the surgeon, Dr. McGee (D), for breach of the alleged warranty of the success of the operation. There was a trial by a jury, which rendered a verdict in favor of Hawkins (P), and awarded $3,000 in damages. McGee (D) moved to have the verdict set aside, and the trial court ordered that the verdict be set aside unless Hawkins (P) would remit all damages in excess of $500. Hawkins (P) refused, thus the trial court set aside the verdict as being "excessive and against the weight of the evidence." Hawkins (P) excepted to this ruling; his exception and numerous exceptions taken by McGee (D) were transferred to the Supreme Court.

Issue: Did the trial court err in instructing the jury to consider pain and suffering due to the operation and for injury sustained over and above what injury the plaintiff had before the operation?

Decision and Rationale: (Branch, J.) Yes. The only substantial basis for Hawkins' (P) claim is the testimony that McGee (D) also said before the operation was decided upon, "I will guarantee to make the hand a hundred per cent perfect hand" or "a hundred per cent good hand." Hawkins (P) was present when these words were alleged to have been spoken, and, if they are to be taken at their face value, it seems obvious that proof of their utterance would establish the giving of a warranty in accordance with his contention. McGee (D) argues, however, that even if these words were utttered by him, no reasonable man would understand that they were used with the intention of entering into any contractual relation whatsoever, and that they could reasonably be understood only as his expression in strong language that he believed and expected that as a result of the operation he would give Hawkins (P) a very good hand. It is unnecessary to determine at this time whether the argument of McGee (D), based upon common knowledge of the uncertainty which attends all surgical operations, and the improbability that a surgeon would ever contract to make a damaged part of the human body "one hundred per cent perfect," would, in the absence of countervailing considerations, be regarded as conclusive, for there were other factors in the present case which tended to support the contention of Hawkins (D). There was evidence that McGee (D) repeatedly solicited from Hawkins' (P) father the opportunity to perform this operation, and the theory was advanced by Hawkins' (P) counsel that McGee (D) sought an opportunity to experiment on skin grafting, in which he had little previous experience. If the jury accepted this part of Hawkins' contention, there would be a reasonable basis for the further conclusion that, if McGee (D) spoke the words attributed to him, he did so with the intention that they should be accepted at their face value, as an inducement for the granting of consent to the operation by Hawkins (P) and his father, and there was ample evidence that they were so accepted by them. The question of the making of the alleged contract was properly submitted to the jury. The jury was permitted to consider two elements of damage: pain and suffering due to the operation, and positive ill effects of the operation on Hawkins' (P) hand. Authority for any specific rule of damages in cases of this kind seems to be lacking, but when tested by general principles and by analogy, it appears that the instruction was erroneous. We conclude that the true measure of Hawkins' (P) damage in the present case is the difference between the value to him of a perfect hand or a good hand, such as the jury found McGee (D) promised him, and the value of his hand in its present condition, including any incidental consequences fairly within the contemplation of the parties when they made their contract. Damages not thus limited, although naturally resulting, are not to be given. The extent of Hawkins' (P) suffering does not measure this difference in value. The pain necessarily incident to a serious surgical operation was a part of the contribution which Hawkins (P) was willing to make to his joint undertaking with McGee (D) to produce a good hand. It was a legal detriment suffered by him which constituted a part of the consideration given by him for the contract. It represented a part of the price which he was willing to pay for a good hand, but it furnished no test of the value of a good hand or the difference between the value of the hand which McGee (D) promised and the one which resulted from the operation. It was also erroneous and misleading to submit to the jury as a separate element of damage any change for the worse in the condition of Hawkins' (P) hand resulting from the operation, although this error was probably more prejudicial to Hawkins (P) than to McGee (D). Any such ill effect from the operation would be included under the true rule of damages, but damages might properly be assessed for McGee's (D) failure to improve the condition of the hand, even if there were no evidence that its condition was made worse as a result of the operation. Finally, McGee's (D) requests for instructions were loosely drawn and were properly denied. A considerable number of issues of fact were raised by the evidence, and the standard by which McGee's (D) conduct is judged is not internal, but external. New trial.

Analysis:

The term "damages," as used in the law of contracts, is intended compensation for a breach, measured in the terms of the contract. The purpose of the law is to put the plaintiff in as good a position as he would have been in had the defendant kept his contract. The measure of recovery is based upon what the defendant should have given the plaintiff, not what the plaintiff has given the defendant or otherwise expended. The only losses that can be said fairly to come within the terms of a contract are such as the parties must have had in mind when the contract was made, or such as they either knew or should have known would probably result from a failure to comply with its terms. The present case is closely analogous to one in which a machine is built for a certain purpose and warranted to do certain work. In such cases, the usual rule of damages for breach of warranty in the sale of chattels is applied and it is held that the measure of damages is the difference between the value of the machine if it had corresponded with the warranty and its actual value, together with such incidental losses as the parties knew or should have known would probably result from the failure to comply with its terms.

A PARTY'S OUTWARD MANIFESTATIONS OF AN INTENT TO CONTRACT TRUMP A SUBJECTIVE INTENT NOT TO CONTRACT

Lucy v. Zehmer

(Farm Buyer) v. (Alleged Farm Seller)

(1954) 196 Va. 493; 84 S.E.2d 516

M E M O R Y   G R A P H I C

Instant Facts

Asserting that he had entered into a valid contract to purchase a farm, a buyer sued to enforce the alleged contract over the objections of the farm's owner who claimed to have been joking when he signed the sales contract with the buyer.

Black Letter Rule

Where a party's actions and statements could reasonably be seen as manifesting an intent to enter into a contract, the party will be bound to the contract, even if the party had no subjective intent to enter into the agreement.

Case Vocabulary

SPECIFIC PERFORMANCE: A legal remedy under which a court orders a party to perform the exact terms which he agreed to perform under a contract. It is often applied in real estate disputes because a parcel of land is considered unique and monetary damages are considered an inadequate substitute for the specific piece of land at issue.

Procedural Basis: Appeal from a state trial court's dismissal of a suit to obtain specific performance of an alleged contract to sell land.

Facts: W.O. Lucy ("Lucy") (P) and A.H. Zehmer ("Zehmer") (D) had been drinking at Zehmer's (D) restaurant. Lucy (P) offered Zehmer (D) $50,000 for Zehmer's (D) farm. Zehmer (D) took the back of a restaurant check and wrote down that he agreed to sell the farm to Lucy (P) for $50,000. Lucy (P), however, insisted that the contract be changed to include Zehmer's (D) wife as a party and also to be made conditional upon Lucy's (P) satisfactory examination of the title to the land. Zehmer (D) tore up the first draft and wrote a second draft that included the provisions Lucy (P) wanted. After signing the new document, Zehmer (D) walked over to his wife in the restaurant and, after whispering to her outside of Lucy's (P) hearing that the sale was a joke, had her sign the document. Zehmer (D) then gave the document to Lucy (P), who began financing the purchase the next day and soon after arranged for a title examination. Subsequently, Zehmer (D) refused to sell the farm and Lucy (P) sued Zehmer (D) and his wife seeking specific performance of the contract for the sale of the farm. At trial, Zehmer (D) and his wife asserted that they believed that Lucy's (P) offer to buy the farm had been made in jest and that they had signed the contract as a joke, with no real intention of selling the farm. The trial court ruled in favor of Zehmer (D) and Lucy (P) appealed.

Issue: Is a party bound to a contract if the party has no subjective intent to enter into the contract, but the party's actions and statements could reasonably be seen as manifesting an intent to enter the contract?

Decision and Rationale: (Buchanan, J.) Yes. Not only did Lucy (P) actually believe that the contract represented a serious business transaction, but the evidence shows that he was warranted in believing as such. In the field of contracts, we must look to the outward expression of a person as manifesting his intention rather than to his secret and unexpressed intention. The law imputes to a person an intention corresponding to the reasonable meaning of his words and acts. The mental assent of both the parties is not necessary for the formation of a contract. A party's undisclosed intent is immaterial, except where it is specifically known to the other party to the contract. A person cannot avoid a contract merely by claiming to have been joking when his conduct and words would cause a reasonable person to believe he intended a real agreement. Here, the facts suggest that a reasonable person would have understood the contract to be a serious business transaction rather than a casual, jesting matter. The parties discussed the contract for forty minutes before it was signed. They discussed what was to be included in the sale including the provision for the examination of title. The parties drafted one version of the contract and then, upon objection by Lucy (P) of the failure to include Zehmer's (D) wife as a party in the contract, drafted a second version which Zehmer's (D) wife signed. Whether the contract was the result of a serious offer and serious acceptance or a serious offer and an acceptance that was a secret joke, in either event it constituted a binding contract of sale between the parties. We find that Lucy (P) is entitled to specific performance. Reversed.

Analysis:

Although the litigants in this case seem like characters taken from an episode of *Hee Haw* or the *Dukes of Hazzard*, this classic case demonstrates the objective approach of the common law to the interpretation of contracts. The case shows that a joke can constitute a valid offer that can be validly accepted where the party upon whom the joke is being played is not aware of the joker's intent and it appears reasonable to believe that the offer is valid under all of the facts and circumstances involved in the case. If, however, the apparent offer is obviously a joke from the perspective of the party hearing it, the offer would not be valid and could not be validly accepted by the person hearing it. While virtually all common law courts would adopt this objective approach to the decision of whether a valid contract had been formed, some modern commentators have criticized this view, arguing that, in light of the costs to individual freedom that can result from a finding that a contract has been made, the objective test should only be utilized where the promisor carelessly used language that induced actual and justifiable reliance by the promisee. In the absence of such reliance, these critics argue that if there has been no harm, there should be no foul.

COURT HOLDS THAT BOTH PARTIES NEED NOT SUBJECTIVELY INTEND TO CONTRACT IN ORDER TO FIND THAT A CONTRACT HAS BEEN VALIDLY FORMED

Embry v. Hargadine, McKittrick Dry Goods Co.

(Employee) v. (Employer)
(1907) 127 Mo.App. 383; 105 S.W. 777

MEMORY GRAPHIC

Instant Facts

A fired employee sued his former employer alleging that his firing breached a contract to employ him for one year, a contract which the employer denied ever making with the former employee.

Black Letter Rule

Both parties need not subjectively intend to enter into a contract in order to find that a contract has been validly formed.

Case Vocabulary

REASONABLE MAN: An everyday person acting according to the dictates of logic and reason under all of the facts and circumstances.

Procedural Basis: Suit for breach of an alleged employment contract in state court.

Facts: Charles R. Embry ("Embry") (P) was employed by the Hargadine, McKittrick Dry Goods Co. ("Hargadine") (D) under a written annual contract as head of Hargadine's (D) sample department. His job was to select samples of the company's goods for Hargardine's (D) traveling salesmen to use in selling to retail merchants. After having made several attempts to get his contract renewed for another year, on December 23, 1903, eight days after his contract for the year had expired, Embry (P) went to the office of Hargadine's (P) president and told him that, with only a few days left in the year to seek employment with other companies, if Hargadine (D) wanted to retain his services it would have to agree to another contract or he would quit immediately. Hargadine's (D) president asked Embry (P) how he was getting along in his department. After Embry (P) responded that the department was busy and in the height of the selling season, Hargadine's (D) president said "Go ahead, you're all right. Get your men out, and don't let that worry you." Believing that this meant that the company was renewing his contract for another year, Embry (P) continued working for Hargadine (D) until February 15, 1904. On that date, Embry (P) was told that his services would be discontinued on March 1. Embry (P) sued, claiming breach of contract. Hargadine (D) asserted that it never intended to contract with Embry (P) for another year and that no contract existed. Following a trial, the judge instructed the jury that an employment contract existed only if the jury found that both parties intended one to be formed. The jury found for Hargadine (D) and Embry (P) appealed, arguing that the judge's instruction was in error.

Issue: In order to find that a contract has been validly formed, must both parties subjectively intend to enter into the contract?

Decision and Rationale: (Goode, J.) No. The inner intention of parties to a conversation that is subsequently alleged to create a contract cannot itself create a contract. It is the words the parties actually use that determine if a contract has been formed. Despite a party's real intent, a contract is formed if the party acts in such a way that a reasonable man would believe he is assenting to the terms proposed by another party and that other party believes he is agreeing to those terms. The party is bound to a contract just as if he had actually intended to agree to the other party's terms. Here, Embry (P) was demanding renewal of his contract, saying that he had been put off before and only had a few days before the end of the year to seek other employment. Embry (P) threatened to quit if his contract was not immediately renewed. Hargadine's (D) president inquired about Embry's (P) department, was told that the department was very busy, and said to Embry (P): "Go ahead, you're all right. Get your men out, and don't let that worry you." Even though Hargadine's (D) president may not have subjectively intended to employ Embry (P) for another year, a reasonable man listening to the conversation that occurred in the context in which it took place would have understood Hargadine's (D) president to be renewing the contract. Embry (P) so understood it. The trial court was wrong to instruct that the formation of a contract depended on a finding that both parties intended to contract. Reversed.

Analysis:

This case is another example of the classical objective theory of contracts which holds that the existence and terms of a contract are determined from the words and acts of the parties rather than by the parties' subjective intent. Here, the court's focus is on the language used by Hargadine's (D) president. The president used the words "don't let that worry you." Taken by itself, the phrase hardly seems like an acceptance of an offer to contract. The court, however, emphasizes the context in which the president's statement is made. Given that Embry (P) had just told the president that he only had a few days to look for work elsewhere, would quit immediately if the contract was not renewed, and, in response to the president's question, had indicated that his department was in the middle of its busy season, the court concludes that a reasonable person would have understood the president's response to mean that Embry's (P) demand had been accepted. The context controls as much as the actual words used by the president. This is very much like the tort law reasonable person standard for determining negligence. Note, though that the court does not completely ignore the subjective intent of the parties. It emphasizes that there is a contract only if Embry (P) subjectively intended to enter into one and could reasonably believe that Hargadine (D) also intended to contract.

NO CONTRACT EXISTS BETWEEN PARTIES WHO EACH HOLD REASONABLE BUT ERRONEOUS UNDERSTANDINGS OF THE BARGAIN

Oswald v. Allen

(Coin Collector) v. (Coin Seller)
417 F.2d 43 (2d Cir. 1969)

M E M O R Y   G R A P H I C

Instant Facts

Oswald (P) thought that he'd struck a bargain to buy all of Allen's (D) Swiss coins, while Allen (D) understood that only the coins in what she calls her "Swiss Coin Collection" were being sold, not all of her Swiss coins.

Black Letter Rule

When a term or terms used to express an agreement is/are ambiguous and the parties understand it in different ways, a contract cannot exist unless one party is aware of the other party's understanding.

Case Vocabulary

ASSENT: Agreement.

Procedural Basis: Appeal of a contract action based on diversity jurisdiction to the federal circuit court after the district court ruled that no contract existed.

Facts: Allen (D) kept two separate coin collections—her 'Swiss Coin Collection' (SCC) and her 'Rarity Coin Collection' (RCC). The SCC contained only Swiss coins, while the RCC contained some Swiss coins along with other coins. Both collections were kept in separate vault boxes at the bank. Oswald (P) was interested in Allen's (D) collection of Swiss coins and arranged to see the coins while in the United States. The parties went to the bank where the coins were kept and Oswald (P) examined the coins and took notes on the coins in the SCC. When Oswald (P) was done he was shown several Swiss coins from the RCC which he also took notes on and later testified that he did not know they were in a separate "collection." Each collection had a different key number and was housed in labeled cigar boxes. Oswald (P) spoke very little English and relied on his brother to make the transaction. A price of $50,000 was negotiated with the parties apparently never realizing that the references to "Swiss Coins" and the "Swiss Coin Collection" were ambiguous. The trial court found that Oswald (P) thought he was buying all the Swiss coins, while Allen (D) thought she was selling only the SCC and not the Swiss coins in the RCC. A short time after the negotiations, Oswald (P) sent a letter to Allen (D) to "confirm my purchase of all your Swiss coins (gold, silver and copper) at the price of $50,000. In response, Allen (D) wrote that she and Mr. Cantarella (Oswald's (P) agent in the transaction) would be going to Newburgh in short order. Allen's (D) letter does not otherwise mention the alleged contract or the quantity of coins sold. A few days later, after Allen (D) realized her estimation of the quantity of coins in the SCC was erroneous, she offered to allow a reexamination of the SCC and to undertake not to sell to another buyer. Oswald (P) decided to proceed as planned and had his agent send Allen (D) a letter stating Oswald's (P) understanding of the deal and requesting Allen (D) to sign it as a "mere formality." Allen (D) did not sign and return the letter. A few days later, Allen's (D) husband told Oswald's (P) agent that Allen (D) no longer wished to proceed with the bargain because her children did not want her to.

Issue: Can a valid contract be formed between parties who have different, but reasonable, understandings of the purported contract's terms?

Decision and Rationale: (Moore, CJ) No. The trial court concluded, based on the facts as it adduced them, that Oswald (P) believed he'd offered to buy all Swiss coins owned by Allen (D), while Allen (D) reasonably understood the offer which she accepted to relate to those of her Swiss coins as had been segregated in the 'Swiss Coin Collection.' There was ample evidence to justify the trial court's conclusion in this regard. In such factual situations the law is well settled that no contract exists. Professor Young states the rule as follows: "when any of the terms used to express an agreement is ambivalent and the parties understand it in different ways, there cannot be a contract unless one of them should have been aware of the other's understanding." Even though the mental assent of the parties is not required for the formation of a contract, the facts found by the trial judge clearly place this case within the small group of exceptional cases in which there is "no sensible basis for choosing between conflicting understandings. Affirmed.

Analysis:

There has been much commentary offered on the subject of assent, and whether actual mental assent, or a "meeting of the minds," should be required for a contract, or whether assent should be a purely objective inquiry relying on outward displays and manifestations. The objective theory of contracts has dominated the equation ever since the rules of evidence were changed to allow a person to testify on his own behalf in the mid-nineteenth century. When applying the objective theory, the mental assent and intent of a party is of no consequence. Those who espouse the objective theory also assert that a party's manifestations should be judged from the vantagepoint of a reasonable person in the position of the other party. This not only imputes to a party all the knowledge that a reasonable person would hold, but also what the party actually knows or should know as a result of superior knowledge. This is similar to the doctrine in tort law that not only imputes the knowledge and standard of care possessed by the elusive 'reasonable person,' but sets a higher standard for persons who possess a level of knowledge above and beyond that of the average reasonable person by virtue of their position or special skill. Thus a race car driver is expected to possess and exercise a greater level of skill while driving the streets than you or I are expected to exercise, and will be held to the greater standard should he be involved in a fender bender.

AN ADVERTISEMENT TO SELL GOODS AT A CERTAIN PRICE IS GENERALLY NOT AN OFFER

Mesaros v. United States

(Prospective Purchaser) v. (Coin Seller)
845 F.2d 1576 (Fed. Cir. 1988)

M E M O R Y G R A P H I C

Instant Facts

Mesaros (P) ordered a number of commemorative Statue of Liberty Coins. Demand for the coins was so high that the order could not be filled. Mesaros (P) is suing under breach of contract.

Black Letter Rule

A solicitation for an order or other expression of agreement to purchase, clearly specifying that no contract exists until ratification or assent by the party soliciting the order, is not itself an offer; it is a request for an offer or an invitation to deal.

Case Vocabulary

SOLICITATION: An invitation to negotiate or make an offer.

Procedural Basis: Appeal to the Federal Circuit of a breach of contract action dismissed by the district court, with jurisdiction resting on the Tucker Act (providing original jurisdiction to the federal courts over contractual suits against the United States).

Facts: In July 1985, Congress passed the Statue of Liberty-Ellis Island Commemorative Coin Act (Act), with the purpose of providing funds through the sale of a limited number of commemorative coins for the restoration of the Statute of Liberty and Ellis Island. A provision of the Act provided that prepaid orders for coins would be accepted prior to the issuance of the coins, with such prepaid orders getting a special discount. A related provision allowed discount bulk sales of the coins. Pursuant to these provisions, in November and December of 1985, the Federal Mint mailed certain advertising materials to pre-selected persons, including Mesaros (P). These materials described the coins being minted and encouraged potential purchasers to forward early payment for the coins. Payment could be made by check, money order, or credit card. The Mint had never dealt with credit card orders and contracted the handling of these orders to the Mellon Bank of Pittsburgh. The materials included an order form with the following located directly above the space provided for the customer's signature: "VERY IMPORTANT—PLEASE READ: YES, Please accept my order for the U.S. Liberty Coins I have indicated. I understand that all sales are final and not subject to refund. Verification of my order will be made by the Department of the Treasury, U.S. Mint. My coins will be delivered in multiple shipments. If my order is received by December 31, 1985, I will be entitled to purchase the coins at the Pre-Issue Discount price shown. I have read, understand and agree to the above." Demand for the coins far exceeded the Mint's expectations. There was an insufficient quantity of five-dollar gold coins with which to fill the orders of many of those who responded to the Mint's promotional materials. According to the Mint, the last order for gold coins was filled between December 31, 1985, and January 6, 1986, exhausting the supply of the 500,000 gold coins provided for under the Act. Mesaros (P) alleges that on November 26, 1985, she sent the Mint an order for certain Statue of Liberty coins. Credit card information was included on the order form, allowing for the cost of the coins to be charged. Subsequently, on December 30, 1985, Mesaros (P) forwarded orders for an additional eighteen gold coins, paid for with nine separate checks. On February 18, 1986, Mesaros (P) received a form letter from the Mint saying that it "had tried but was unable" to process Mesaros' (P) November 26, 1985, credit card order. The letter directed the recipient to contact their financial institution for details about the rejection of their order. Investigation by Mesaros (P) revealed that there was no problem with the credit account and that the charges had been authorized. Around May 1986, Mesaros (P) received the eighteen coins ordered in late December and paid for by checks. During this period, the gold coins appreciated in value by at least 200%, a development that greatly discouraged those who did not receive their entire order of gold coins. Mesaros (P) filed this breach of contract action on May 23, 1986.

Issue: Does an advertisement soliciting an order for goods at a certain price constitute an offer, the acceptance of which forms a binding contract?

Decision and Rationale: (Skelton, Sr. CJ) No. Mesaros (P) contends that the materials sent by the Mint, including the order form, constituted an offer that when accepted created a binding contract that obligated the government (D) to deliver the coins ordered. The great weight of authority is against this assertion. It is well established that materials such as those mailed to prospective customers by the Mint are no more than advertisements or invitations to deal. Williston on Contracts states it: "Thus, if goods are advertised for sale at a certain price, it is not an offer, and no contract is formed by the statement of an intending purchaser that he will take a specified quantity of the goods at that price." Such advertisements are viewed as "a mere invitation to enter into a bargain rather than an offer." It is generally considered unreasonable for a person to believe that an advertisement or solicitation is an offer that binds the advertiser. Otherwise the advertiser could be bound by an excessive number of contracts requiring delivery of goods far in excess of amounts available. Such is true in this case, where the number of gold coins was limited to 500,000 by the Act. A thorough reading, construction, and interpretation of the materials sent out by the Mint makes clear that it is unreasonable as a matter of law for Mesaros (P) to have thought the materials were intended as an offer. This is especially true in view of the words "YES, Please accept my order ..." that were printed on the credit card form, which showed that the credit card order was an offer from Mesaros (P) to the Mint to buy the coins, which offer might or might not have been accepted by the Mint. The Mint's materials were merely solicitations of offers subject to acceptance by the Mint before a contract could be formed. Mesaros' (P) assertion that *Lefkowitz v. Greater Minneapolis Surplus Store* requires the opposite result is erroneous. There a store advertised a fur stole on a first-come, first-served basis when the store opened at 9:00 a.m. The plaintiff arrived first, but the store refused to sell him the stole. The court held that the advertisement was an offer because of the way it was worded; that it stated the merchandise would be available if the customer showed up first, which Lefkowitz did. The Mint's advertisement contained no such statement about a first-come, first-served basis. Since the coins could be paid for with checks, credit cards or money orders, it would have been impossible to process the orders on such a basis. The situation in *Lefkowitz* was so different that it is of no help to Mesaros (P). We therefore hold that the Mint advertisement materials were not an offer of sale of the coins that could be accepted by Mesaros (P) to create a contract. Affirmed.

Analysis:

Ads normally do not state a quantity and do not contain statements of commitment, and thus are merely statements of intention to sell or invitations for offers. The reasonable person test is used to resolve cases of first impression that are then used as precedents in later cases and eventually refined into hard and fast legal rules. In this case, the rule goes against Mesaros (P), who may or may not have been justified in thinking a contract had been formed. Most non-lawyers don't know that such advertisements are almost exclusively held to be invitations to deal rather than offers. This may lead to abuse of the rule by unscrupulous merchants looking to exploit the average consumer's ignorance of contract law. But then again, most non-lawyers don't even know what the terms "offer" and "acceptance" are or how a binding contract is formed. Right or wrong, it has been established that advertisements like the one in this case are not offers. One possible justification for this rule is that a contrary rule would deter merchants from publishing what may be valuable market information, something that greatly aids consumers in deciding what to purchase. In the instant case, there were elements of the coin advertisement that would lead a reasonable person to believe that once the money was sent in, the deal was done. As the court pointed out, however, there were elements that would lead in the opposite direction, something that, when combined with the presumption the rule establishes, dictates the result obtained. As you will see in *Lefkowitz*, however, ads can be offers.

UNDER CERTAIN CIRCUMSTANCES, AN ADVERTISEMENT CAN CONSTITUTE A LEGAL OFFER

Lefkowitz v. Great Minneapolis Surplus Store

(Customer) v. (Store)
251 Minn. 188 (1957)

MEMORY GRAPHIC

Instant Facts

After it refused to sell to a male customer a fur piece at its advertised price, a retail store was sued for breach of a contract.

Black Letter Rule

When an advertisement is clear, definite, and explicit, and leaves nothing open for negotiation, it may be construed as an offer.

Procedural Basis: Appeal to the Supreme Court of Minnesota challenging an order of the trial court denying motions for amended findings and a new trial.

Facts: The Great Minneapolis Surplus Store (the Store) (D) advertised in a local newspaper that it was selling three fur coats and one stole, each for $1 and on a first come, first served basis. When Mr. Lefkowitz (P) was the first to appear at the store on two occasions, he was twice informed that by a "house rule" the offer was intended for women only. Mr. Lefkowitz (P) then filed suit, alleging that the newspaper ad was an offer, which he accepted when he tendered his dollar. The Store (D) countered with the argument that the ad was a unilateral offer which could be withdrawn at any time without notice and that advertisements are usually construed as invitations for an offer for sale.

Issue: May a newspaper advertisement constitute an offer for sale?

Decision and Rationale: (Murphy, J.) Yes. When an advertisement is clear, definite, and explicit, and leaves nothing open for negotiation, it may be construed as an offer. Moreover, an advertisement constitutes an offer if the facts show that some performance was promised in positive terms in return for something requested. The advertisement at issue meets all of these requirements. Therefore, having been the first to appear at the store, as requested by the advertisement, and having offered the stated purchase price, Lefkowitz (P) was entitled to performance on the part of the Store (D). The Store (D) cannot rely on its "house rule" because an offeror may not impose conditions on the offer after acceptance has been made.

Analysis:

This case represents a departure from the generally accepted rule that contracts are not formed when a willing customer responds to a particular advertisement. This rule notwithstanding, many courts have held that an advertisement can constitute a legally binding offer. These holdings have been reached on the theory that the advertisement is an offer for a unilateral contract. A unilateral contract is one where a promise is exchanged for the performance of some act. Accordingly, the court here requires that the advertisement contain promissory language. In this case that language was the use of "First Come, First Served," which the Restatement Second deems promissory in nature. The court also requires that for an advertisement to constitute an offer it must be definite, leaving little for negotiation. The advertisement here stated the items for sale, the quantity available and the exact price, all providing sufficient definiteness to constitute a legal offer. Thus, in keeping with the unilateral contract theory, the court's holding implies that the Store (D) promised to sell the fur items in exchange for being the first person to show. It is arguable, however, that the Store was promising to sell the fur in exchange for $1, which Lefkowitz (P) never tendered, his willingness to do so notwithstanding. Under this view, the Store (D) would not be liable because Lefkowitz (P) never performed the act sought by the Store (D).

AN OFFEREE WHO COMMUNICATES A DEFINITE REJECTION LOSES THE POWER OF ACCEPTANCE

Akers v. J.B. Sedberry, Inc.

(Employee) v. (Employer)
286 S.W.2d 617 (Tenn. 1955)

MEMORY GRAPHIC

Instant Facts

The owner of a manufacturing and distributing company sought to accept two employees' offers of resignation after rejecting the offers when she initially received them in a personal meeting with the employees.

Black Letter Rule

An offer made during the course of a face-to-face conversation expires either by its terms or at the end of the conversation if no express expiration is provided.

Procedural Basis: Appeal to the Court of Appeals of Tennessee challenging a decree of the Chancery Court awarding damages for breach of contract.

Facts: Concerned about the future of the company for which they worked, Mr. Akers (P) and Mr. Whitsitt (P) flew to Nashville to visit their employer Mrs. M.B. Sedberry (D), owner of J.B. Sedberry, Inc. At the commencement of the meeting both Akers (P) and Whitsitt (P) offered to tender their resignations on a ninety-day notice, as a sign of good faith for voicing concerns about their manager. At that time, Mrs. Sedberry (D) did not accept the resignations. She instead proceeded to discuss business matters with both of them for the rest of the day. Mrs. Sedberry (D) also gave the two men instructions to be followed upon their return to Texas. No further mention was made of the offers for resignation and Mrs. Sedberry (D) gave no other indication that she was leaving the matter up for consideration. The following Monday, Mrs. Sedberry (D) sent to Akers (P) and Whitsitt (P) telegrams stating that their resignations were accepted, effective immediately. The two men replied with a letter stating that they had no open or outstanding offer to resign and that they expected the remainder of their employment contracts to be honored.

Issue: Does an offer of resignation tendered and rejected in a face to face conversation remain open after the cessation of the conversation?

Decision and Rationale: (Felts, J.) No. When an offer for resignation is tendered in person and is silent as to the time allowed for acceptance, the employer has until the end of the conversation to accept. The evidence clearly establishes that Akers (P) and Whitsitt (P) expected an immediate answer to their offers to resign. There is nothing establishing the contrary. Even if the two men had intended their offers to extend beyond the conversation, the power to accept was extinguished upon Mrs. Sedberry's (D) initial rejection. Although she did not expressly reject either offer and she testified that she intended to take the matter under consideration, Mrs. Sedberry's (D) conduct did not disclose such an intent and led Akers (P) and Whitsitt (P) to believe she was rejecting the offers. As a result, Mrs. Sedberry's (D) attempt to terminate the two men was a breach of her contractual obligations, for which she is liable. Finally, we reject Mrs. Sedberry's (P) contention that Akers (P) and Whitsitt (P) may only avail themselves to recovery for the ninety-day period contained in their initial offers. As we have already established, after the end of the meeting between the parties, there ceased to exist any ninety-day offer upon which Mrs. Sedberry (P) could act. Affirmed.

Analysis:

This case illustrates two different ways in which the power to accept an offer can be extinguished. The first is upon the lapse of the offer. Some offers give the offeree a specific time limit to accept the offer. When the offer is silent as to the time for acceptance, the offeree has a reasonable time to accept. Despite the malleable nature of "reasonableness," there are some bright-line rules, one of which is discussed in this case. As the court points out, an offer made in a face to face conversation is valid until the end of the conversation. So when the meeting between Mrs. Sedberry (D) and Akers (P) and Whitsitt (P) ended without an express acceptance of the two men's resignations, Mrs. Sedberry's (D) power to accept was extinguished. The court also sets forth an alternate basis for its holding. Rejection of an offer will terminate the offeree's power to accept. The court here concluded that Mrs. Sedberry's conduct led the two men to believe she was rejecting the offer. This shows that, just as a contract can be based on the conduct of the parties, a contract can be rejected based on the conduct of the offeree. The reason that rejection terminates the power of acceptance is that the offeror is likely to act upon the belief that his offer has been rejected. Thus, the rule protects any reliance interest the offeror may have. Some have argued that the rule should not be applied when the offeror remains inactive and has not changed his position. However, this raised the question: why should the offeror be held at bay to the whims of the offeree?

A CONDITIONAL ACCEPTANCE IS A COUNTER-OFFER, WHICH TERMINATES THE POWER OF ACCEPTANCE

Ardente v. Horan

(Real Estate Buyer) v. (Real Estate Sellers)
117 R.I. 254 (1976)

MEMORY GRAPHIC

Instant Facts

After the buyer in a residential real estate transaction sent to the seller a signed purchase agreement accompanied by a letter addressing the buyer's concern that certain furnishings be included in the transaction, the sellers refused to sign the agreement.

Black Letter Rule

When acceptance is accompanied by further demands, the offeree makes a counter-offer, terminating his power of acceptance.

Procedural Basis: Appeal to the Supreme Court of Rhode Island challenging the judgment of the trial court granting the defendant's motion for summary judgment.

Facts: William A. and Katherine L. Horan (the Horans) (D) placed for sale residential property, for which Ernst Ardente (P) placed a bid of $250,000. The Horans (D) accepted this bid and had their attorney prepare and mail a sale agreement to Ardente (P). After investigating the title, Ardente (P) executed the agreement. Ardente's (P) attorney then forwarded to the Horans' (D) attorney the signed agreement and a letter stating, "My clients are concerned that the following items remain with the real estate: a) dining room set and tapestry wall covering in the dining room; b) fireplace fixtures throughout; c) the sun parlor furniture. I would appreciate you confirming that these items are part of the transaction, as they would be difficult to replace." The Horans (D) refused to include these items in the sale and did not sign the sale agreement. Ardente (P) filed suit for specific performance.

Issue: May acceptance of an offer to sell real estate include the offeree's requests to include items not contained in the offer?

Decision and Rationale: (Doris, J.) No. When acceptance is accompanied by further demands, the offeree makes a counter-offer, terminating his power of acceptance. Assuming that the agreement sent by the Horans' attorney to Ardente (P) constituted an offer, we must decided whether there was a valid acceptance. Acceptance of a bilateral contract must be communicated to the offeror. Accordingly, our decision must focus only on the signed agreement and accompanying letter, because those were the only communications made. To be valid, acceptance must be definite and unequivocal. If acceptance is conditioned or limited in some manner it becomes a counter-offer, requiring acceptance by the original offeror before a contract will be formed. This notwithstanding, conditional language that is independent of an acceptance will not serve to convert the acceptance into a counteroffer. The determination of whether collateral communications serve to qualify an acceptance or are merely inquiries is not any easy one to make. Nevertheless, we interpret the language used by Ardente (P) to have imposed a condition on his acceptance. First, the letter does not unequivocally state that acceptance is effective, notwithstanding the exclusion of the listed items from the transaction. In fact, the letter seeks confirmation of their inclusion. Moreover, Ardente (P) stressed the difficulty of replacing the items, indicating that he did not view their inclusion as merely a collateral matter. If additional conditions are to be added, the language of acceptance must be more definite. Affirmed.

Analysis:

There is no questioning the rule that a counter-offer terminates the offeree's power to accept and places that power in the hands of the offeror. The general issue presented was whether a counter-offer was actually made. The court here notes that a conditional acceptance is a counteroffer. The precise issue of whether an acceptance is conditioned or merely accompanied by collateral inquiries is determined on the particular facts and circumstances. It is difficult to tell from the language of Ardente's (P) letter whether he intended the items to form part of the bargain. The court here was willing to resolve the ambiguity in favor of the offeror. The holding is congruent with that of most courts, which require an offeree making inquiries or requests to clearly state his intent to accept, without regard to the collateral issues. If an offeree intends for additional conditions to be collateral to the acceptance, he should include language to the effect of, "I accept your offer, but would like to ask whether...." This should clearly communicate an intent to accept, but make further inquiries. As an aside, the court, in a footnote, states that this case could have been resolved based on the statute of frauds, which requires contracts for the sale of real estate to be in writing and signed by the party against whom enforcement is sought. Neither of these requirements were met in this case, but apparently the Horans' (D) attorney failed to notice this.

AN OFFER IN THE CONTEXT OF A UNILATERAL CONTRACT MAY BE REVOKED AT ANY TIME BEFORE PERFORMANCE IS BEGUN

Petterson v. Pattberg

(Landowner) v. (Mortgage Holder)
248 N.Y. 86, 161 N.E. 428 (N.Y. 1928)

M E M O R Y   G R A P H I C

Instant Facts

Pattberg (D) held a mortgage on Petterson's (P) land and offered to discount the total owed if Petterson (P) paid it off early. When Petterson (P) tried to comply, Pattberg (D) had already sold the mortgage note to someone else.

Black Letter Rule

An offer to enter into a unilateral contract may be withdrawn right up until the very moment performance is begun.

Case Vocabulary

UNILATERAL CONTRACT: A contract where only one of the parties makes a promise or tenders performance. Ex. A says to B, "I will pay you $10 if you mow my lawn." B's mowing of the lawn constitutes acceptance, or a tendering of performance, and activates A's promise to pay.

Procedural Basis: Appeal to the State's highest court after the Appellate Division affirmed the trial court's refusal to dismiss the suit.

Facts: Petterson (P) owned a parcel of land in Brooklyn. Pattberg (D) owned a bond executed by Petterson (P), which was secured by a third mortgage on the Brooklyn parcel. On April 4, 1924, $5,450 remained unpaid upon the principle. The remaining principal was payable in $250 installments with the first due on April 25, 1924, and the rest upon a like monthly date every third month thereafter. On April 4, 1924, Pattberg (D) wrote Petterson (P) that if the remaining principal was paid in cash "on or before May 31, 1924, and the regular quarterly payment due April 25, 1924, is paid when due" then Pattberg (D) would discount the total remaining principal by $780. Petterson (P) made the April 25 payment as scheduled. On a day in the latter part of May, Petterson (P) presented himself at Pattberg's (D) home and knocked on the door. When Pattberg (D) demanded the name of the caller, Petterson (P) replied, "It is Mr. Petterson. I have come to pay off the mortgage." Pattberg (P) answered that he had sold the mortgage. When Pattberg (D) opened the door, Petterson (P) showed him the cash, and said he was ready to pay off the mortgage according to the agreement. Pattberg (D) refused to take the cash. As it turns out, Petterson (P) had contracted to sell the land to a third person free and clear of the mortgage and was thus forced to pay the mortgage holder the full amount, including the $780 that was to be discounted for early payment. Petterson (P) is suing for the $780 plus interest.

Issue: May a party properly revoke an offer to enter into a unilateral contract just before performance is to be tendered, knowing that such tender is imminent?

Decision and Rationale: (Kellogg, J) Yes. Pattberg's (D) letter clearly proposed to Petterson (P) the making of a unilateral contract, the gift of a promise in exchange for the performance of an act. The thing conditionally promised was the reduction of the mortgage debt. The act requested, in consideration of the offered promise, was payment in full of the reduced principal of the debt prior to the due date thereof. It is settled that, "[i]n case of offers for a consideration, the performance of the consideration is always deemed a condition." Langdell's Summary of the Law of Contracts, § 4. "It is elementary that any offer to enter into a unilateral contract may be withdrawn before the act requested to be done has been performed." Williston on Contracts, § 60. An interesting question arises when, as here, the offeree approaches the offeror with the intention of proffering performance and, before actual tender is made, the offer is withdrawn. Williston says, "The offeror may see the approach of the offeree and know that an acceptance is contemplated. If the offeror can say 'I revoke' before the offeree accepts, however brief the interval of time between the two acts, there is no escape from the conclusion that the offer is terminated. Williston on Contracts. § 60b. Here, before Petterson (P) could tender the necessary moneys, Pattberg (D) informed Petterson (P) that he had sold the mortgage. That was a definite notice to Petterson (P) that Pattberg (D) could not perform his offered promise, and that a tender to Pattberg (D) would be ineffective to satisfy the debt. Thus it clearly appears that Pattberg's (D) offer was withdrawn before its acceptance had been tendered. Therefore, no contract was ever made. The complaint should be dismissed.

Dissent: (Lehman, J) Pattberg's (D) letter to Petterson (P) constituted a promise to accept payment at a discount on or before the set date. By the terms of this promise, Pattberg (D) made payment of the mortgage by the stipulated time a condition precedent to Pattberg's (D) own performance of his promise to accept payment at a discount. If the condition precedent has not been performed, it is because Pattberg (D) made performance impossible by refusing to accept payment. "It is a principle of fundamental justice that if a promisor is himself the cause of the failure of performance either of an obligation due him or of a condition upon which his own liability depends, he cannot take advantage of the failure." Williston on Contracts, § 677. The question is thus whether Pattberg (D), at the time he refused the offer of payment, had assumed any binding obligation, even though subject to condition. The promise made by Pattberg (D) lacked consideration when it was made, but the promise was not made as a gift or mere gratuity to Petterson (P). It was an offer which was to become binding whenever Petterson (P) should give exactly the consideration which Pattberg (D) requested. Until the act requested was performed, Pattberg (D) might undoubtedly revoke his offer. Our problem is to determine from the words of the letter what act Pattberg (D) requested as consideration for his promise. The majority takes the position that "the act requested to be performed was the completed act of payment, a thing incapable of performance, unless assented to by the person to be paid." So construed, Pattberg's (D) promise or offer, though intended to induce action by Petterson (P), is but a snare and delusion. This leaves everything up to Pattberg (D) and provides him with the ability to refuse to perform at any time, even if a tender had been made before the mortgage was sold. As Justice Cardozo stated in *Surace v. Danna*, "The thought behind the phrase proclaims itself misread when the outcome of the reading is injustice or absurdity." If such was the intent of Pattberg (D), he should have phrased his letter differently, to allow refusal of payment when tendered. Under a fair interpretation of the letter, I think Petterson (P) had done the act which Pattberg (D) requested as consideration for his promise. The judgment should be affirmed.

Analysis:

It seems unassailable that Pattberg (D) revoked his offer to enter into a unilateral contract before Petterson (P) tendered performance. Before Petterson (P) could physically give the money to Pattberg (D), he was told that the mortgage had been sold. The result is fairly cut and dried. Yet it leaves the reader with a bad feeling, like Petterson (P) was legally given the extreme short end of the stick even though he did nothing wrong and Pattberg (D) acted in bad faith. The simple truth is that is the only way it can be. A rule that would allow Petterson (P) to win because Pattberg (D) knew he was coming to tender performance and was thus sure to revoke his offer before such tender could take place would be extremely difficult to apply in an evenhanded manner. Such a rule would require courts to inquire into the mental goings-on of the offeror. What criteria could be applied to come up with consistent results? Courts are loath to delve into such subjective realms and do so with great reluctance. Instead, the hard and fast rule is utilized because it is easy to apply and offers a nice bright line with which to dispose of even complicated cases. One criticism of the majority that could be offered is that its assertion in dicta that Pattberg (D) could have properly refused to accept the money no matter whether he'd sold the mortgage goes against the whole idea of a unilateral contract, which the court quite clearly says is what Pattberg's (D) letter created. A unilateral contract is completed once the offeree tenders performance. To allow the offeror to refuse to assent to the performance takes it out of the realm of unilateral contracts.

Marchiondo v. Scheck

(Sales Agent) v. (Principal)
78 N.M. 440, 432 P.2d 405 (N.M. 1967)

M E M O R Y G R A P H I C

Instant Facts

Marchiondo (P) was given six days to find a buyer for Scheck's (D) real estate. Just before Marchiondo (P) closed the deal, Scheck (D) revoked the offer, causing Marchiondo (P) to lose his promised commission.

Black Letter Rule

Partial performance of a unilateral contract creates a conditional contract that may not be revoked by the offeror before the allotted time for complete performance has run, or a reasonable time if the offer is silent as to the time allowed for complete performance.

Procedural Basis: Appeal to the State's highest court of a breach of contract claim dismissed by the trial court.

Facts: Scheck (D), in writing, offered to sell real estate to a specified prospective buyer and agreed to pay a commission to Marchiondo (P) for brokering the deal. The offer set a six-day time limit for acceptance. On the morning of the sixth day, Scheck (D) sent a letter revoking the offer to Marchiondo (P), who did receive the revocation. Later in the day, Marchiondo (P) obtained the offeree's acceptance. Marchiondo (P) now sues Scheck (D) for the promised commission.

Issue: May an offer to enter into a unilateral contract be revoked at any time up until complete performance, even though performance has been partially completed at the time the offer is revoked?

Decision and Rationale: (Wood, J) No. Here we are only concerned with the revocation of Marchiondo's (P) agency, not the revocation of the offer as between Scheck (D) and the prospective buyer. When Scheck (D) made his offer to pay a commission upon sale of the property, he offered to enter a unilateral contract; the offer was for an act to be performed, a sale. Many courts hold that the principal has the right to revoke the broker's agency at any time before the broker has actually procured a purchaser because until there is performance, the offeror has not received consideration from the offeree and there is not a binding contract. Marchiondo (P) claims that this rule is not applicable where there has been partial performance of the offer. A majority of courts agree with this statement of the rule: that part performance of the consideration may make such an offer irrevocable. Scheck (D) asserts that the decisions giving effect to this rule were in cases where the offer was of an exclusive right to sell or of an exclusive agency, factors that are not present here. Because Scheck's (D) offer did not specifically state that it was exclusive, under State law it cannot be an exclusive agreement. But it is not the exclusiveness of the offer that deprives the offeror of the right to revoke. It is the action taken by the offeree which deprives the offeror of that right. Once partial performance is begun pursuant to the offer made, a contract with a condition, or an option contract results. Thus, "if an offer for a unilateral contract is made, and part of the consideration requested in the offer is given or tendered by the offeree in response thereto, the offeror is bound by a contract, the duty of immediate performance of which is conditional on the full consideration being given or tendered within the time stated in the offer, or, if no time is stated therein, within a reasonable time." Restatement of Contracts, § 45 (1932). Stated another way, an option contract is created when the offeree begins the invited performance or tenders part of it. The offeror's duty of performance under any option contract so created is conditional on completion or tender of the invited performance. The reason for this rule is that it avoids hardship to the offeree, and yet does not hold the offeror beyond the terms of his promise. It is implied in such a contract that the offeror will let performance be done; that the offer will remain open until the offeree who has begun can complete his performance. The offeree's partial performance furnishes the 'acceptance' and the 'consideration' for a binding subsidiary promise not to revoke the offer. We therefore hold that part performance by the offeree of an offer of a unilateral contract results in a contract with a condition. The condition is full performance by the offeree. Here, if Marchiondo (P) partially performed prior to receipt of Scheck's (D) revocation, such a contract was formed. This case is remanded for findings on the issue of Marchiondo's (P) partial performance of the offer prior to its revocation.

Analysis:

Should Marchiondo (P) have had to provide notice to Scheck (D) that he had begun performance by holding preliminary dealings with the prospective buyer before Scheck (D) should be required to leave the offer open in order to allow compete performance? The answer is obviously 'no.' Notice would enable the offeror to avoid having to contract with someone else for the identical performance. In credit guarantee cases, where A tells B that A will guarantee the credit of C in order to induce B to extend C credit, most courts hold that A must exercise reasonable diligence in providing B with notice that credit has been extended if he knows B has no adequate means of finding out. A failure by to provide such notice will have the effect of discharging B's obligations unless B otherwise learns of A's performance within a reasonable time, or the offer states that notice is not required. Another view of this situation is that, if notice is required, a contract will not be formed unless and until notice is provided. The majority view in both cases is that the offeror, B in the above example, has a duty of inquiry unless such inquiry is not reasonably feasible. A third, and more simple view, is that notice is not required unless specifically requested by the offeror. Requiring notice certainly takes the unilateral contract closer to the traditional contract in that notice acts like a promise to perform that will bind the offeror. Does this defeat the purpose of the unilateral contract?

AN OFFER TO CONTRACT IS PRESUMED TO BE BILATERAL RATHER THAN UNILATERAL WHEN THE OFFER IS AMBIGUOUS

Davis v. Jacoby

(Decedent's Niece) v. (Will Proponents)
1 Cal.2d 370, 34 P.2d 1026 (Cal. 1934)

M E M O R Y G R A P H I C

Instant Facts

Davis (P) accepted an offer to care for her aunt and uncle in exchange for a bequest of their estate. The wills of the aunt and uncle, however, were never changed to reflect the bargain struck and Davis (P) sues for specific performance.

Black Letter Rule

When the intent and circumstances surrounding an offer to contract are ambiguous with respect to whether the offer is for a bilateral or unilateral contract, there is a presumption that the offer was for a bilateral contract.

Case Vocabulary

SPECIFIC PERFORMANCE: A court ordered remedy requiring that a contract or other legal obligation be performed in full, applied when another remedy, such as money damages, will not be adequate.

Procedural Basis: Appeal to the California Supreme Court after the trial court refused to grant specific performance of an alleged contract to make a will.

Facts: Caro M. Davis (Caro) (P1) was the niece of Blanche Whitehead (Blanche) and Rupert Whitehead (Rupert) (collectively the Whiteheads). Prior to Caro's (P1) marriage to Frank M. Davis (Frank) (P2), she lived with the Whiteheads at their Piedmont home extensively and was treated as their daughter. In 1913, Caro (P1) married Frank (P2) at the Whitehead's residence before the two moved to Canada. From 1913 to 1931, the two families remained extremely close and often visited each other, often for long durations. In addition, the families corresponded frequently, the record being replete with letters showing the loving relationship. By 1930, Blanche had become seriously ill, had suffered several strokes, and her mind was failing so that Rupert had her placed in a private hospital. The doctors told Rupert that Blanche could die at any time or might linger for several months. Rupert had suffered severe financial setbacks, had had several sieges of sickness and was in poor health. In the early part of 1931, Rupert was in desperate need of help with Blanche and his business, and did not trust his friends in Piedmont. During this time, Rupert wrote several letters to Caro (P1) explaining Blanche's condition and telling her that the doctors felt it would help if she came to visit Blanche. On March 24, 1931, Frank (P2) wrote Rupert a letter offering his best wishes and asking if Caro (P2) should pay a visit. On March 30, 1931, Rupert wrote back explaining Blanche's health and also referring to his own poor health and dire financial straits, but offering the caveat that he retained considerable assets and needed someone he could trust to help manage these assets and suggesting that Frank (P2) could come to California and do so. On April 9, 1931, Rupert again wrote to Frank (P2) pointing out how badly he needed someone he could trust to assist him, and giving it as his belief that he could still save about $150,000 of his assets if properly handled. Rupert wrote Frank (P2) and Caro (P1) again on April 12, 1931, saying that Blanche's health outlook was not good and she would not last long and reiterating that $150,000 could be saved of his assets. Rupert also included that he himself did not have much longer to live either: "The next attack will be my end, I am 65 and my health has been bad for years, so, the Drs. don't give me much longer to live. So if you can come, Caro will inherit everything and you will make our lives happier and see Blanche is provided for to the end." Later on in the April 12 letter is the line "Will you let me hear from you as soon as possible, I know it will be a sacrifice but times are still bad and likely to be, so by settling down you can help me and Blanche and gain in the end." This letter was received by Frank (P2) in Windsor, Canada, on the morning of April 14, 1931 [yes, mail was faster then]. Frank (P2) read the letter to Caro (P1) and immediately wrote Rupert a letter unequivocally stating that he and Caro (P1) accepted the proposition and would leave Windsor for Piedmont on April 25th. This letter was sent via airmail and though it was lost, the trial court expressly found that it was received by Rupert, who acknowledged such receipt in a letter to Frank (P2) dated April 15. This letter was received by Frank (P2) on April 17. The same day, Frank (P2) telegraphed to Rupert: "Cheer up—we will soon be there, we will wire you from the train." Before Caro (P1) and Frank (P2) could get to Piedmont, Rupert committed suicide. Caro (P1) and Frank (P2) came at once to California where Caro (P1) cared for her aunt Blanche until she died on May 30, 1931. The trial record shows that after their arrival in California, Caro (P1) and Frank (P2) fully performed their side of the agreement. After Blanche died, it was discovered that the Whitehead's wills had never been changed and that they devised no property or other assets to Caro (P1), as had been promised by Rupert. Caro (P1) and Frank (P2) then brought his action for specific performance. The trial court held that Rupert had made an offer of a unilateral contract that was revoked upon his death, and thus could not be enforced.

Issue: Was an offer for a unilateral contract made in the April 12 letter?

Decision and Rationale: (Per Curiam) No. The distinction between unilateral and bilateral contracts is well settled. A unilateral contract is one in which no promisor receives a promise as consideration for his promise. A bilateral contract is one in which there are mutual promises between two parties to the contract, each party being both a promisor and a promisee. In the case of unilateral contracts no notice of acceptance by performance is required. Performance is acceptance. The difficulty in any particular case is to determine whether the offer is one to enter into a bilateral or unilateral contract. Some cases are clear-cut, others fall somewhere between. In this middle ground, the type of contract depends upon the intent of the offeror and the facts and circumstances of each case. The offer to contract involved herein falls within this middle category. The Restatement of Contracts, section 31, provides that in such situations there is a presumption that the offer is to enter into a bilateral contract, rather than the formation of one or more unilateral contracts by actual performance on the part of the offeree. The comment to section 31 states the reason for the presumption: "It is not always easy to determine whether an offerer requests an act or a promise to do the act. As a bilateral contract immediately and fully protects both parties, the interpretation is favored that a bilateral contract is proposed." Keeping these principles in mind, we are of the opinion that the offer of April 12 was an offer to enter into a bilateral contract. These parties were not dealing at arms length; in fact, they were very close. The record indisputably shows that Rupert had confidence in Caro (P1) and Frank (P2), in fact, that he had lost all confidence in everyone else. It also shows that Rupert had become desperate and that what he wanted was the promise of Caro (P1) and Frank (P2) that he could look to them for assistance. This is buttressed by the line "Will you let me hear from you as soon as possible" in Rupert's April 12 letter. This request for an immediate reply indicates the nature of the acceptance desired by Rupert, namely, Frank's (P2) and Caro's (P1) promise that they would come to California and do the things requested. This promise was immediately sent by Frank (P2) and Caro (P1) upon receipt of the offer, and was received by Rupert. It is elementary that when an offer has indicated the mode and means of acceptance, an acceptance in accordance with that mode or means is binding on the offeror. Under such circumstances it is well settled that specific performance will be granted. Reversed.

Analysis:

Did Rupert really give much thought to the type of contract he was offering? Did he think he was offering a contract at all? The answer to both of these questions is "probably not." Had Rupert really been thinking about the legal ramifications of his language he most assuredly would have preferred a unilateral contract, it being obvious that what he wanted was performance, not just a promise to perform. Deciding the offer was ambiguous allowed the Court to not only apply the presumption, but also to consider the facts and circumstances. The Court goes into the quality of the respective relationships with the Whiteheads of both the Plaintiffs and Defendants. From what is said, it seems clear the Court felt that Caro's (P1) and Frank's (P2) relationship with the Whiteheads was much more close and intimate than that of the Defendant's. Certainly if this were true, the Court made the decision that seems more appropriate. But should the quality of the relationships factor into the decision. In a strict legal sense, such a consideration should have nothing to do with the final disposition. This case applies the old Restatement of Contracts, which provides for the presumption of a bilateral contract. The reasoning behind the presumption, as the Court stated, is that the offeror wants the security of a promise that binds the offeree. This reasoning no longer prevails, however. The new rule is that unless it is crystal clear that the offeror has prescribed a certain mode of acceptance, the offer may be accepted in any reasonable way.

Houston Dairy, Inc. v. John Hancock Mutual Life Insurance Co.

(Prospective Borrower) v. (Prospective Lender)

643 F.2d 1185 (5th Cir. 1981)

M E M O R Y G R A P H I C

Instant Facts

Houston Dairy, Inc. (P) sought a loan from John Hancock (D), but failed to accept the loan offer in time. After sending a "good faith" deposit on the loan to John Hancock (D), Houston Dairy (P) found a better offer and seeks to recover the deposit.

Black Letter Rule

An acceptance of an offer that has expired by its own terms acts instead as a counter offer that must be accepted by the original offeror in order to form a binding contract.

Procedural Basis: Appeal of a diversity contract action to the federal circuit court after the district court ruled that a binding contract had been formed.

Facts: Houston Dairy, Inc. (Houston) (P) sought an $800,000 loan from John Hancock Mutual Life Insurance Company (Hancock) (D). Hancock (D) mailed a commitment letter to Houston (P) on December 30, 1977 in which it agreed to loan the sum at 9 ¼% interest provided that within seven days Houston (P) would return the commitment letter with a written acceptance and enclose either a letter of credit or a cashier's check for $16,000 as a "Good Faith Deposit" and the appropriate measure of liquidated damages if Houston (P) should default. Houston (P) did not comply until eighteen days later when it sent, along with the commitment letter, a cashier's check for $16,000. When Hancock (D) received the check and letter on January 23, it mailed the check to the John Hancock Depository and Service Center for deposit, and sent the loan-closing attorney, Henderson, the necessary information to close the loan. Hancock (D) also sent a copy of the commitment letter to Houston's (P) attorney and asked him to call Henderson about the loan-closing fee. On January 28, Henderson and Houston's (P) attorney talked and agreed on the method to be used in closing the loan, and the manner in which the fee would be charged. However, on January 30, Houston (P) was able to obtain a more favorable loan from a state bank. Houston (P) then requested a refund of the $16,000 from Hancock, which refused on the ground that a binding loan contract had been formed and the $16,000 was liquidated damages for Houston's (P) default. The district court held that Hancock (D) had both waived the seven-day time limit and validly accepted Houston's (P) counter offer.

Issue: Does a purported acceptance of an offer after the time limit for acceptance has run form a binding contract?

Decision and Rationale: (Ainsworth, CJ) No. It is clear in the instant case that upon expiration of the seven-day time period, Hancock's (D) offer terminated. Thus the action taken by Houston (P) in signing and returning the commitment letter subsequent to the termination of the offer constituted a counter offer which Hancock (D) could accept within a reasonable time. Courts have long recognized that for an acceptance to have effect, it must be communicated to the offeror. Hancock (D) asserts that depositing Houston's (P) check was itself sufficient to operate as communication of its acceptance of the counteroffer; that its silence and retention of the check were acceptance and notification. It is true that in some cases silence is equated with acceptance within the guidelines laid down in Restatement § 72. However, the present facts do not fit within these guidelines. Houston (P) neither had previous dealings nor had otherwise been led to understand that Hancock's (D) silence and temporary retention of its deposit would operate as acceptance. In addition, Houston (P) had no knowledge that its check had been deposited because it was a cashier's check. The mere depositing of a check is insufficient to constitute acceptance of an offer. Hancock (D) also contends that Houston (P) was notified of its acceptance in the conversation between the attorneys for both parties on January 28. However, a review of the testimony concerning that conversation shows no communication of acceptance. This conversation involved only information on the procedures for closing a loan should an agreement be reached. Houston (P) cannot be deemed to have knowledge of Hancock's (D) acceptance through that conversation. In summary, Houston (P) could not accept Hancock's (D) offer once the time period had lapsed. Thus, when Houston (P) executed and returned the commitment letter several days late, it was proposing a counter offer that Hancock (D) could either accept or reject. Since the actions and policies of Hancock (D) were unknown to Houston (P), mere silence was not operative as an acceptance of the counter offer, no communication of acceptance having been received. Houston (P) was therefore entitled to revoke its counter offer, which it did on January 31. Reversed.

Houston Dairy, Inc. v. John Hancock Mutual Life Insurance Co.
(Continued)

Analysis:

This case illustrates one of the ways the power of acceptance can be terminated: lapse of time. As it did in the instant case, some offers contain language indicating when an offer will come to an end. But including such limiting language is just the beginning of the inquiry. Say, for example, that an offer by letter is dated January 1st, received January 4th, and includes the language, "This offer is open for 10 days." When does the offer terminate? Professor Williston asserts that the time should be interpreted as starting on January 1st because the offeree should realize that the offer is ambiguous and that the limitation is included for the offeror's benefit. Professor Corbin takes the opposite approach, suggesting the ambiguity should be construed against the author, and thus the time limit should run from January 4th. This view comports with the rule that a contract should be construed against its author when ambiguous. Another problem is whether to include the day from which the time is reckoned. Thus, if January 1st is the limiting date, does January 1st count in calculating the 10 days? The majority rule is to exclude the date from which the time is reckoned. For an accomplished drafter of contracts, these questions should be moot. Knowing the possible ambiguities and the way in which they are interpreted, a drafter should always include language indicating the way in which any time limits are to be construed, thus trumping the established rules of contract law.

Cole-McIntyre-Norfleet Co. v. Holloway

(Seller) v. (Buyer)
141 Tenn. 679 (1919)

MEMORY GRAPHIC

Instant Facts

When one of his suppliers refused to fill a 60-day old order for 50 barrels of meal, the owner of a country store filed a suit for breach of contract, claiming that the supplier accepted his order when it failed to notify him of the rejection.

Black Letter Rule

When the subject of a contract, either in its nature or by virtue of the conditions of the market, will become unmarketable by delay, the offeree's delay in notifying the offeror of rejection or acceptance will amount to acceptance by the offeree.

Procedural Basis: Appeal to the Supreme Court of Tennessee challenging the finding of the circuit court, which inferred the existence of a contract from the defendant's unreasonable delay in notifying the plaintiff of rejection.

Facts: Through a traveling salesman, Holloway (P) placed an order for 50 barrels of meal for his country store from the Cole-McIntyre-Norfleet Co. (CMC) (D). The order form stated that it was to become a contract when accepted by CMC (D) at its office in Memphis. When Holloway (P) sought delivery of his order 60 days later, CMC (D) notified him that his order had not been accepted, and for that reason there was no contract. Although CMC (D) had weekly opportunities to notify Holloway (P) the rejection through its salesman, and daily opportunities to do so by wire or mail, no such notice was ever given. From the time of the order till the time delivery was sought, the price of the goods increased dramatically. The trial court found this delay to be unreasonable, and therefore, it inferred an acceptance from CMC's (D) silence.

Issue: May acceptance of an offer be inferred from an unreasonable delay in notifying an offeree of rejection?

Decision and Rationale: (Landsden, C.J.) Yes. When the subject of a contract, either in its nature or by virtue of the conditions of the market, will become unmarketable by delay, the offeree's delay in notifying the offeror of rejection or acceptance will amount to acceptance by the offeree. Otherwise, the offeree could place his goods on the market in search of a better offer, while at the same time holding the offeree to the contract. In this case, the only thing left to do was acceptance or rejection of the order. CMC (D) cannot argue that a seller of goods like these can wait indefinitely to decide whether he will accept or reject the offer of the buyer. Everything done was in the usual course of business, the items ordered were consumable in the use and would shortly become unfit to market. Writ denied.

Analysis:

In *Vogt v. Madden* [case involving an alleged sharecropper agreement] we say that acceptance can be inferred from silence when the parties' prior course of dealing makes such an inference reasonable. This case discusses another exception to the rule that acceptance cannot be inferred from silence on the part of the offeree. Actually, the exception in this case is more of an affirmative duty to speak. Courts will impose on an offeree the duty to expressly reject an offer when the facts indicate that the offeror had reason to expect such a rejection. The court here bases the duty on a theory of justified reliance. Holloway (P) was under the impression that he had a valid contract for 50 barrels of meal. Accordingly, he made no effort to place any other order in the face of rising prices. Thus, Holloway (P) had to be informed one way or the other so that he could make appropriate arrangements. When CMC (D) failed to provide any notice, it was reasonable for Holloway (P) to expect that his order had been accepted. The court also reasoned that it would be unfair for CMC (D) to wait for prices to climb and then reject the offer or accept the offer when the prices fell, all the while holding Holloway (P) to the contract.

PARTY THAT PURCHASED PROPERTY IN COOPERATIVE TYPE COMMUNITY HELD TO HAVE ENTERED CONTRACT TO PAY DUES ASSESSED COMMUNITY MEMBERS

Seaview Ass'n of Fire Island, N.Y., Inc. v. Williams

(Cooperative Association) v. (Property Owner)
69 N.Y.2d 987, 517 N.Y.S.2d 709, 510 N.E.2d 793 (N.Y. 1987)

MEMORY GRAPHIC

Instant Facts

Williams (D) purchased several homes with knowledge that the homes were part of the Seaview Association (P), a cooperative requiring payment of dues by member homeowners. Williams (D) refuses to pay the dues, so Seaview Association (P) sues to recover back dues.

Black Letter Rule

When a party purchases property with knowledge that the property is subject to certain conditions of ownership, the party manifests an acceptance of, and must conform with, said conditions of the implied-in-fact contract.

Case Vocabulary

IMPLIED-IN-FACT CONTRACT: A contract the parties to which are presumed to have intended because of an assumption or tacit understanding that it exists.

Procedural Basis: Appeal to the State's highest appellate court after the Appellate Division affirmed the findings of the trial court that the implied-in-fact contract had been breached.

Facts: The Seaview Association of Fire Island (Association) (P) is an association of homeowners formed over thirty years ago in Seaview, a Fire Island community of some 330 homes used largely for summer recreation. The Association (P) owns and maintains the streets, walkways and beaches of Seaview. The Association (P) also employs a community manager, provides a rent-free home for a resident doctor in the summers, maintains shelters for lifeguards and the police, and maintains various other amenities in the community. Seaview property owners are assessed a share of the Association's (P) annual costs for all services and facilities except the water company and tennis courts. Williams (husband, wife and son) (D) enjoys by deed easements providing the use of ocean beaches and walkways in Seaview. Prior to purchasing the first house in Seaview in 1963, Williams (D) lived in an adjoining community. Williams (D) now owns seven houses in Seaview, but refuses to pay any of the assessments on grounds that he is a nonmember of the Association (P) and a nonuser of the recreational facilities maintained by the Association (P). The Association (P) brought this action to recover assessments for the years 1976 through 1984. The trial court concluded that there is an implied contract arising out of Williams' (D) purchase of the Seaview property with knowledge of the nature of the community and the conditions imposed upon ownership there.

Issue: When a party purchases property with knowledge that ownership of the property entails certain obligations, does the party impliedly accept such conditions and become contractually bound to fulfill them?

Decision and Rationale: (Memorandum Opinion) Yes. Where there is knowledge that a private community homeowner's association provides facilities and services for the benefit of the community residents, the purchase of property there may manifest acceptance of conditions of ownership, among them payment for the facilities and services offered. An implied-in-fact contract results and includes the obligation to pay a proportionate share of the full cost of maintaining those facilities and services, not merely the reasonable value of those actually used. The trial court found that Williams (D) had adequate notice, gained from familiarity with the area, from signs or other sources, or from the Association (P). This finding is amply supported in the record that Williams (D) knew the nature of the community and by his purchase—indeed, successive purchases—impliedly accepted the conditions accompanying ownership of property in Seaview. Affirmed.

Analysis:

Here the court applies what is called an "implied-in-fact" contract. An implied-in-fact contract is formed where the parties manifest their agreement to contractual terms through conduct rather than words. Here, by purchasing several homes in Seaview, with knowledge of the conditions imposed by the members through their association, Williams (D) manifested an agreement to abide by the terms of the Association (P). This relates in a manner to the use of "terms of art" in contractual language. A contract implied in law is not a contract at all but an obligation imposed by law to do justice even though it is clear that no promise was ever made or intended. The principal function of this type of contract is generally said to be that of the prevention of unjust enrichment.

ProCD, Inc. v. Zeidenberg

(Software Seller) v. (Software Buyer)
86 F.3d 1447 (7th Cir. 1996)

MEMORY GRAPHIC

Instant Facts

A purchaser of a computer software database resold the database on the Internet in violation of the license included with the software.

Black Letter Rule

A license enclosed in a software package forms a binding contract between the software seller and buyer if the package provides notice that the purchase is subject to the license and the buyer can receive a refund if the buyer does not agree to the license's terms.

Case Vocabulary

LICENSE: Permission to do or omit an act, such as permission to use a copyrighted work for specific purposes.

Procedural Basis: Appeal of district court decision for defendant in breach of contract action seeking an injunction.

Facts: ProCD, Inc. (ProCD) (P) sells a CD-ROM disk set called SelectPhone that contains a database of information from more than 3000 telephone directories. The database cost ProCD (P) more than $10 million to compile and is expensive to keep current. ProCD (P) sold the database to the general public for about $150, and it sold a slightly different product to commercial buyers for a higher price. Every box containing its consumer product states that the software comes with restrictions in an enclosed license. The license is encoded on the CD-ROM disks, printed in the manual, and appears on the user's screen every time the software runs. The license limits the use of the program to non-commercial purposes. Zeidenberg (D) bought several consumer packages of SelectPhone from a retail outlet. He resold the SelectPhone database on the Internet for less than ProCD (P) charges its commercial customers. ProCD (P) sued Zeidenberg (D) seeking an injunction against further dissemination of the database in violation of the licenses. The district court held the licenses were ineffectual because their terms did not appear on the outside of the packages. The court held that a purchaser does not agree to and cannot be bound by terms that were undisclosed at the time of purchase.

Issue: Does a license enclosed in a software package form a binding contract between the software seller and buyer?

Decision and Rationale: (Easterbrook, J.) Yes, if the software package provides notice that the purchase is subject to a license and the buyer has the opportunity to return the software for a refund if the buyer does not agree to the license's terms. For purposes of this case, licenses are ordinary contracts governed by the UCC and the common law. Zeidenberg (D) argues that making the software package available for sale is an "offer," which the customer "accepts" by paying for the package. He argues that hidden terms inside the box cannot be part of the contract. However, the outside of the software box stated that the transaction was subject to a license. As a practical matter, ProCD (P) could not have included all the terms of the license on the outside of the box. However, providing notice of the license on the outside of the box, the terms of the license inside the box, and the right to return the software for a refund if the terms are unacceptable is an acceptable way to do business. Standardized agreements save time and are essential to a system of mass production and distribution. Transactions in which the exchange of money precedes the communication of the details of the contract are common. Examples include the sale of insurance, airline tickets, concert tickets, warranties on consumer goods, and drugs. Purchases of software are often made by phone or on the Internet, where there is no box setting forth the terms. On Zeidenberg's (D) argument, the seller has made a broad warranty and must pay consequential damages for any shortfalls in performance. This would drive the price of software through the ceiling. UCC §2-204(1) provides that "A contract for sale of goods may be made in any manner sufficient to show agreement, including conduct by both parties which recognizes the existence of such a contract." Here, ProCD (P) proposed a contract that a buyer accepts by using the software after having an opportunity to read the license. Zeidenberg (D) agreed to the terms by using the software. UCC §2-606 reinforces our opinion. It states that a buyer accepts goods when, after an opportunity to inspect, the buyer fails to reject the goods. Here, Zeidenberg (D) inspected the license and the software, and did not reject the goods. Reversed and remanded.

Analysis:

The court here distinguished a somewhat similar case, *Step-Saver Data Systems, Inc. v. Wyse Technology*. *Step-Saver* was a "battle-of-the-forms" case, similar to *Ionics, Inc. v. Elmwood Sensors, Inc.* discussed earlier in this chapter. In both *Ionics* and *Step-Saver*, the courts applied UCC § 2-207, which enforces those terms to which both parties agree. Here, there were not two forms and thus, § 2-207 does not apply. ProCD (P) offered its license as part of the sales contract and Zeidenberg (D) chose not to abide by its terms. Zeidenberg (D) never communicated his rejection of the license agreement, unless breach is the same as rejection. *Step-Saver* also involved a "box-top license" disclaiming certain warranties. The box-top license stated that opening the package constituted acceptance of the agreement. Here, on the other hand, a purchaser of the SelectPhone software was able to open the package, review the license agreement, and choose whether to abide by it. By using the software, Zeidenberg (D) was held to have accepted the license terms. Here the court relied on UCC §2-204(1) rather than on UCC §2-207. Section 2-204 provides that "A contract for sale of goods may be made in any manner sufficient to show agreement, including conduct by both parties which recognizes the existence of such a contract." This is also the rule at common law. It provides that a contract is implied where the parties' intention to contract is not manifested by explicit words but by their conduct. Thus, ProCD (P) did not require a buyer to write it a letter expressly agreeing to the terms of the license. It required a buyer to keep the software and not return it. It is common now for software not only to include a license agreement, but to require the user to click a box on the computer screen expressly stating that the user agrees to the license terms. If the user does not click the box, the user cannot access the software. Perhaps this is in response to cases like ProCD (P); software manufacturers are trying to avoid any question about whether users agree to the terms of their licenses.

Empire Machinery Co. v. Litton Business Telephone Systems

(Telephone Customer) v. (Telecommunications Company)
115 Ariz. 568, 566 P.2d 1044 (Ariz. Ct. App. 1977)

M E M O R Y G R A P H I C

Instant Facts

Empire Machinery Co. (P) entered into an agreement to purchase a phone system from Litton Business Telephone Systems (D). Difficulties arose and the deal fell through. Litton (D) now claims there was never a contract.

Black Letter Rule

Conduct by an offeree tending to indicate acceptance may create a binding contract notwithstanding the offeree's failure to accept in the manner prescribed by the offeror.

Case Vocabulary

CONVERSION: The wrongful use or retention of another's property without proper authorization.
QUASI CONTRACT: A contract imposed by law as a result of the conduct of the parties. Also called an "implied-in-law contract."

Procedural Basis: Appeal to the intermediate appeals court of a breach of contract action from the trial court's ruling in favor of Litton (D) on cross motions for summary judgment.

Facts: Empire Machinery Co. (Empire)(P), a dealer for Caterpillar Tractor Co., became interested in acquiring an "interconnect" telephone system. On April 12, 1973, Russell Murphy, National Accounts Manager for Litton Business Telephone Systems (Litton)(D), contacted Empire (P) about installing a system. Murphy visited Empire (P) on April 17, 1973, and explained that Litton (D) was developing a "Superplex" switching system that would be available in about a year. Ronald Mathis, Empire's (P) communications coordinator, expressed interest in the "Superplex." The parties negotiated until July 30, 1973, when Murphy submitted a letter to Empire (P) stating in pertinent part that Litton (D) would install a standard business telephone system in Empire's (P) premises and then replace it with a Superplex system when it came online, at no further expense. Following receipt of the July 30 letter, Jack Whitman, Empire's (P) president, signed an "Equipment Sales Agreement" (ESA) and delivered a check for $8,546.00 as the down payment to Murphy who acknowledged receipt. At issue in the ESA is clause number six, which read: "This agreement shall become effective and binding upon the Purchaser and BTS [Litton] only upon approval, acceptance, and execution hereof by BTS and its home office." There was a signature line for acceptance below this clause. Murphy never signed this portion of the contract. The estimated date for installation of the system was set for November 15, 1973. On August 9, 1973, Mathis, on Empire's (P) behalf, was requested by Murphy to send a form letter to Mountain Bell (the area telephone company) designating Litton (D) as Empire's (P) representative. This letter contained the following lead paragraph: We have this date entered into a contractual agreement with Litton BTS ... for the installation of the interconnect system." On August 30, 1973, John Parlett, National Systems Representative for Litton (D), wrote Mountain Bell with the details of the interconnect system. This letter contained the following lead paragraph: "We have this date entered into a contractual agreement with [Empire] for the installation of an 'interconnect' telephone system." Empire (P), at Litton's (D) request, purchased about $12,000 worth of electrical equipment to facilitate Litton's (D) equipment. On December 3, 1973, W. P. Scott, Litton's (D) service manager, requested that Mountain Bell supply Empire (P) with a new phone number as of December 21, 1973. Nothing further was done by either party in furtherance of the contract. Apparently Litton (D) had difficulties in perfecting its "Superplex" system and on January 10, 1974, Litton (D) tendered back Empire's (P) down payment. Subsequently, Empire (P) purchased another phone system from another company. This litigation then ensued.

Issue: May the conduct of an offeree that would be interpreted by a reasonable business person as acceptance constitute acceptance notwithstanding the offeree's failure to comply with the prescribed manner of acceptance?

Decision and Rationale: (Jacobson, PJ) Yes. Empire (P) contends that Litton's (D) letter of July 30, 1973, constituted an offer to sell that Empire (P) accepted by signing the ESA and delivering the deposit check to Murphy, thus binding Litton (D). The problem with this is it ignores the express language of clause six, stating that home office approval was required before the contract could be binding. Because Litton (D) clearly specified that there would be no contract until assent by the home office, the July 30 letter was an invitation to make an offer, not an offer itself. The execution of the ESA was itself an offer, that required Litton's (D) acceptance. We come now to the second issue: the offer having designated the manner in which it would be accepted (i.e. home office approval), is this the exclusive means by which that acceptance can occur? For the purposes of answering this question we assume that the ESA was never signed and

Empire Machinery Co. v. Litton Business Telephone Systems
(Continued)

executed by Litton (D) as prescribed. Empire (P) argues that clause six can be waived by it and assented to by Litton (D) and the conduct of Litton (D) subsequent to the submission of the ESA shows such assent, or at least a fact issue which would preclude summary judgment. Litton (D) argues that because the clause was not complied with, no contract was ever formed; and in the alternative, the conduct relied on by Empire (P) to show assent was performed by agents with no authority to bind Litton (D). Both parties rely on § 2-206 of the Uniform Commercial Code (UCC) as support for their contentions. Both parties miss the mark. As the comment to § 2-206 makes clear, this section was an attempt to simplify the common law rule that acceptance can only be made in the manner prescribed by the offer. This section did not attempt to change this common law rule. However, even under common law, a contract containing a clause that acceptance can only be made by approval of officers at the home office could be accepted in a different manner. We must therefore ask if the conduct of Litton (D) was directed toward the fulfilling of its obligations so as to sufficiently express its assent to the ESA and, if so, whether such conduct was performed by those authorized to bind Litton (D). As to Murphy's request that Empire (P) inform Mountain Bell of the contract between Litton (D) and Empire (P), such conduct could be considered by a trier of fact as constituting assent, if performed by an individual authorized to bind Litton (D). However, upon this record, Murphy had no such authority. The same is not true of Parlett and his letter of August 30, 1973, advising Mountain Bell of the contractual relationship. This presents a question of fact as to whether the letter constituted an assent by Litton (D), and whether Parlett had authority to bind Litton (D). The same can be said of Scott's letter to Mountain Bell concerning the new phone number. Empire's (P) purchase of equipment in reliance on this authority, if this be so, can also be considered by the trier of fact. Likewise, the cashing of Empire's (P) down payment. While Litton (D) is correct that the mere acceptance of the check does not constitute evidence of a binding conduct by Litton (D), the cashing of the check and retention of the funds for several months does give rise to factual inferences as to Litton's (D) intent to enter into a binding contract with Empire (P). All of this plays into the rule that if an offeree takes steps in furtherance of its contractual obligations which would lead a reasonable businessman to believe that the contract had been accepted, such conduct may, under the circumstances, constitute acceptance of the contract. We therefore hold that there are material questions of fact in this case that preclude summary judgment to either party. Reversed and remanded.

Analysis:

One of the things the Court says creates a question of material fact with respect to whether Litton (D) accepted Empire's (P) offer is the continued retention of the deposit. This illustrates the way in which the exercise of dominion over the property of another without permission can constitute conversion. For instance, when a party offers goods for sale and the offeree takes possession, but refuses to provide the requisite consideration, the offeree is a converter. Under traditional rules of estoppel, the offeror can treat the offeree's conduct as acceptance of the offer. This rule applies whenever the offeree's exercise of dominion is referable to the offeree's power of acceptance granted by the offeror. In such a situation, the offeror may bring an action in contract, quasi contract, or tort theory. Because there isn't really mutual assent, a requirement for a valid contract, the contract theory is actually a legal fiction. In this manner, a remedy based in contract rather than in tort (for conversion) can be utilized. However, if the exercise of dominion over the offeror's property is done with intent to accept the offer, an actual contract is formed, regardless of whether assent was communicated to the offeror. In the instant case, the rule applied by the Court keeps Litton (D) from intending to accept all along and then, when Litton (D) could not perform as promised, trying to use the "home office approval clause" as a way to escape liability.

Ionics, Inc. v. Elmwood Sensors, Inc.

(Thermostat Purchaser) v. (Thermostat Manufacturer)
110 F.3d 184 (1st Cir. 1997)

M E M O R Y G R A P H I C

Instant Facts

Ionics, Inc. (P) purchased defective thermostats from Elmwood Sensors, Inc. (D). In contracting, the parties both used forms that purported to set the contract terms, including the extent and bases of liability, many of which conflicted.

Black Letter Rule

When contracting parties express assent conditional on the other party's acceptance of new terms and subsequently conduct themselves in a manner that indicates the existence of a contract, U.C.C. § 207 operates to nullify the new terms to the extent they contradict any new terms added by the other party, or the terms of the original offer.

Procedural Basis: Certification of a question of law by the state district court (trial court) to the federal appeals court, after the district court denied a motion for partial summary judgment.

Facts: Elmwood Sensors, Inc. (Elmwood) (D) manufactures and sells thermostats. Ionics, Inc. (Ionics) (P) makes hot and cold water dispensers, which it leases to customers. Ionics (P) purchased thermostats from Elmwood (D) on three separate occasions, in order to use them in their water dispensers. Several of these dispensers caused fires allegedly resulting from defects in the thermostats. Ionics (P) filed suit against Elmwood (D) to recover costs incurred in the wake of the fires. Included with the orders from Ionics (P) were purchase order forms that contained various "conditions," two of which are relevant. Condition 18, titled "REMEDIES," stated, in summary, that all remedies provided Ionics (P) in the contract were "cumulative" and "in addition to any other remedies provided by law or equity." It also stated that "The laws of the state shown in Buyer's address printed on the masthead of this order shall apply in the construction hereof." Condition 19, titled "ACCEPTANCE," stated that "Acceptance by the Seller...shall be upon the terms and conditions set forth in items 1 to 17...and elsewhere in this order. Said order can be accepted only on the exact terms herein and set forth. No terms which are...different from those herein...shall become a part of...the terms and conditions herein set forth." When Ionics (P) placed its first order, it sent Elmwood (D) a letter stating that if [Elmwood (D)] objected to the terms in the purchase orders it was to inform Ionics (P) in writing, and that a failure to do so would constitute acceptance of the terms. Following receipt of each order, Elmwood (D) sent an "Acknowledgement" form stating that Elmwood (D) was willing to sell the goods ordered, but only upon the terms set forth therein as a counter offer, and that by failing to reject the counter offer within 10 days of receipt, the buyer would be accepting the terms contained therein and that any other terms were objected to by Elmwood (D) and would not be binding upon Elmwood (D). Among the terms and conditions set forth in Elmwood's (D) "Acknowledgement" was line 9, titled "WARRANTY." This "WARRANTY" contained language sharply limiting Elmwood's (D) liability to the repair of defective goods, repayment of the purchase price, or a reasonable allowance on account of any defects, at Elmwood's (D) discretion. The terms in each party's forms are diametrically opposed to each other on the issue of whether all warranties implied by law were reserved or waived. The only issue in dispute is the extent of Elmwood's (D) liability.

Issue: Under the U.C.C., should effect be given to provisions contained in an offeree's acceptance that purport to alter the terms of the original offer and are not objected to by the other party?

Decision and Rationale: (Torruella, CJ) No. What we face here is a battle of the forms. Our analysis begins with the statute.... [The court quoted U.C.C. § 2-207.] The dispute turns on whether the contract is governed by the language after the comma in § 2-207, according to the rule laid down in *Roto-Lith, Ltd. v. F.P. Bartlett & Co.*, or whether it is governed by subsection (3) of § 2-207. The same basic facts were at issue in *Roto-Lith*. There Roto-Lith sent a purchase order that was answered with an acknowledgment that included language purporting to limit Bartlett's liability. Roto-Lith did not object. We held that "a response which states a condition materially altering the obligation solely to the disadvantage of the offeror is an 'acceptance...expressly...conditional on assent to the additional...terms.'" This holding took the case outside of § 2-207 by applying the exception after the comma in subsection (1). In other words, the acceptance conditional on assent to the new terms was a counter offer rather than acceptance. When Roto-Lith accepted the goods without objecting to the new terms it accepted the counter offer along with the new terms. Elmwood (D) argues that *Roto-Lith* governs this case. Elmwood (D) is correct that this case is indistinguishable from *Roto-Lith*, but this does not end our inquiry. We must still look to § 2-207. A plain language reading of § 2-207 suggests that subsection (3) governs this case. Ionics (P) sent an initial offer to which Elmwood (D) responded with its "Acknowledgment." Thereafter, the conduct of the parties established the existence of a contract as required by § 2-207 (3). Comment 6 to § 2-207 buttresses this conclusion. Comment 6 says that where clauses on confirming forms sent by both parties conflict, each party is deemed to have objected to the new terms that conflict with its own terms. As a result, the requirement of subsection (2) that there be notice of objection is satisfied and the conflicting terms do not become part of the contract. The contract then consists of the terms originally expressly agreed to, terms on which the confirmations agree, and terms supplied by this act (§ 2-207). Comment 6 thus addresses the exact facts of this case, meaning that § 2-207 directly conflicts with *Roto-Lith*. We have, therefore, no choice but to overrule *Roto-Lith*. We hold, consistent with § 2-207 and Official Comment 6, that where the terms in two forms are contradictory, each party is assumed to object to the other party's conflicting clause. As a result, mere acceptance of the goods by the buyer is not sufficient to infer consent to the seller's terms under the language of subsection (1). Nor do such terms become part of the contract under subsection (2) because notice of objection has been given by the conflicting forms as required by subsection (2)(c). This is in accord with the purpose of § 2-207, which is to modify the strict principle that a response not in accord with the offer is a rejection and counter offer. Under *Roto-Lith*, virtually any response that added to or altered the terms of the offer would be a rejection and a counter offer. We do not think such a result is consistent with the intent of § 2-207 and we believe it to be expressly contradicted by Comment 6. We therefore conclude that § 2-207 (3) prevails and "the terms of the particular contract consist of those terms on which the writings of the parties agree, together with any supplementary terms incorporated under any other provisions provided for by law. Affirmed and remanded.

Analysis:

The common law rule is that a purported acceptance that varies from the terms of the offer is a rejection and counter offer, even if the new condition is purely trivial. Unyielding application of this rule harms the natural flow of commerce, especially since a lot of modern business is done using printed forms that frequently clash. Before § 2-207 took effect, the "last shot principle" governed the terms of the contract. When the reply to an offer to purchase was a counter offer, the purchaser's acceptance of the goods was deemed an acceptance of the seller's new terms. In this way, the last set of terms governed the terms of the contract. The reality, however, is that in such situations, parties frequently fail to read all of the conflicting forms, or simply let the conflict slide with the hope that nothing will come of it. The economies of scale inherent in the use of standardized forms compel such a result. Attempts to iron out the conflicts inevitably result in lost business and profit. This realization led to § 2-207. Life under § 2-207, however, has not been as happy as the authors had hoped. For example, many problems are run into concerning what should be done with "different terms" between merchants. When it is assumed that the writings of the parties form a contract, but the acceptance contains a term different from the offer, what should be done? Section 2-207 is silent as to what should be done in this situation. There are several differing views [as always] on what effect, if any, should be given to the different terms. Revision of § 2-207 is thus a major goal of the Article 2 revisers.

Sun Printing & Publishing Ass'n v. Remington Paper & Power Co.

(Newspaper) v. (Paper Supplier)
235 N.Y. 338, 139 N.E. 470 (N.Y. 1923)

M E M O R Y G R A P H I C

Instant Facts

Sun Printing (P) contracted for the supply of paper with Remington Paper (D), but the contract left out some material elements that were never settled, so Remington Paper (D) backed out.

Black Letter Rule

A court may not revise a contract that is incomplete because it lacks material elements; such a contract is unenforceable.

Case Vocabulary

INCHOATE: Incomplete; Imperfect.

Procedural Basis: Appeal of a certified question to the State's highest court after the Appellate Division reversed the ruling of the Special Term that no contract existed.

Facts: Sun Printing & Publishing Ass'n (Sun)(P) agreed to purchase paper from Remington Paper & Power Co., Inc. (Remington)(D). The contract called for the delivery of 1,000 tons of paper per month from September, 1919, to December, 1920, inclusive. The price for the first four months was set by the contract. For the year 1920, however, the contract specified that the price and length the price would apply was to be negotiated fifteen days before the previous price/duration agreement ended. Thus the first time a new price/duration agreement was needed was December 15. An additional clause said that whatever price was agreed upon, it would never "be higher than the contract price for news print charged by the Canadian Export Paper Company (Canadian) to the large consumers." All went as planned until the time came for a new price and duration to be agreed upon. Remington (D), in advance of this time, realized the contract was imperfect and disclaimed any obligation to deliver for the future. Sun (P) claimed that the price was to be ascertained from that charged the large consumers by Canadian and made a demand that during each month Remington (D) deliver 1,000 tons of paper at the Canadian price. This demand was renewed month by month until the contract was to expire. This action was then brought to recover damages.

Issue: May a contract that lacks material elements and is thus incomplete be revised by a court so as to make it enforceable against the parties?

Decision and Rationale: (Cardozo, J) No. Seller and buyer left two subjects to be settled in the middle of December and at unstated intervals thereafter. One was the price, the other was the length of time during which such price was to govern. Agreement as to one was insufficient without agreement as to the other. If all that was left open was price, then Sun (P) would have some force to its contention that it held an option contract to purchase paper at the maximum price—that set by Canadian for its large consumers. But the ascertainment of this price does not dispense with the necessity for agreement in respect of the term during which the price is to apply. This is so because the price charged the large consumers by Canadian is subject to fluctuation. While this would be fine if the successive terms were set, as the price charged by Canadian at the beginning of each term could be applied for the terms duration, without knowing these durations it is impossible to apply the Canadian price. In other words, while the term was unknown, the contract was inchoate. Sun (P) suggests that the contract amounts to the concession of an option to purchase the paper at the Canadian rate. However, without an agreement as to time, there would be not one option, but a dozen. The Canadian price today might be less than the Canadian price tomorrow. Election by the buyer to proceed with performance at the price prevailing in one month would not bind it to proceed at the price prevailing in another. Successive options to be exercised every month would thus be read into the contract. Nothing in the wording discloses an intent by Remington (D) to place itself to that extent at the mercy of Sun (P). The parties tried to guard against the contingency of failing to come together as to price. They did not guard against the contingency of failing to come together as to time. The result was nothing more than an agreement to agree. Remington (D) exercised its legal right when it insisted that there was need of something more. It does not matter what Remington's (D) motive was. Sun (P) asserts that Remington (D) was under a duty, in default of an agreement, to accept a term that would be reasonable in view of the nature of the transaction and the practice of the business. To hold it to such a standard is to make the contract over.

Remington (D) reserved the privilege of doing business in its own way, and did not undertake to conform to the practice and beliefs of others. We are not at liberty to revise while professing to construe. Reversed and the certified question answered in the negative.

Dissent: (Crane, J) I cannot take the view of this contract that has been adopted by the majority. The parties to this transaction unquestionably thought they were making a contract for the purchase and sale of 16,000 tons of newsprint. The contract was even written on Remington's (D) form, so we must suppose that it was intended to be what it states to be, and not a trick or device to defraud merchants. After the first four month's deliveries, Remington (D) refused to fix any price for the deliveries during the subsequent months, and refused to deliver any more paper. It has taken the position that this document was no contract; that it meant nothing; that it was formally executed for the purpose of permitting Remington (D) to furnish paper or not, as it pleased. It is a strain upon reason to imagine these two experienced companies formally executing a contract, drawn upon Remington's (D) prepared form, which was useless and amounted to nothing. We must at least start out by believing that they intended to make a binding contract. If this be so, the Court should spell out a binding contract if possible. There are several solutions to the failure to agree upon a period for which the agreed upon price would be effective. When December 15 came around Remington (D) failed to agree upon a price, made no attempt to agree upon a price, and deliberately broke its contract. Because of this, Remington (D) could readily be held to deliver the rest of the paper, 1,000 rolls a month, at the Canadian price. Or we can deal with this contract month by month, using the Canadian price charged on the 15th of every month, starting with December 15. Failing any other alternative, the law should do here what it has done in so many other cases—apply the rule of reason and compel the parties to contract in the light of fair dealing. It could hold Remington (D) to deliver its paper as it agreed to do, and take the Canadian price for a period which is reasonable under all the circumstances and conditions as applied in the paper trade. Instead, the Court lets Remington (D) escape from its formal obligations and gives the sanction of law to deliberate breach.

Analysis:

This case raises the issue of indefiniteness. There are three categories of problems that arise from indefiniteness: (1) where the parties think they have agreed as to a material term in the contract, but the meaning of the term is not reasonably certain; (2) where the parties are completely silent as to a material term; and (3) where the parties agree to agree as to a material term. The third type is presented here. The traditional rule for dealing with situations where the parties have agreed to agree is that such an agreement as to a material term doesn't create a valid contract. In other words, when a material term has been left up in the air for future negotiation, a contract is not created until the material term has been settled. In such a situation, the parties have left a gap in the contract to be filled at a later time. Because they have shown an intent to fill this gap themselves, the gap-filler mechanism doesn't have to be used by the court. On the other hand, if the parties have left a gap, but agreed to make reasonable efforts to fill the gap, there is a duty to negotiate in good faith. The more modern view takes the position that an agreement to agree has such a valuable commercial purpose that applying the traditional rule would result in unfairness where one party uses it to defeat an agreement that the parties fully intended to be binding. This is how Judge Crane would have preferred to look at this case. Some courts have done as Judge Crane would have done here and fill the gap when there is an agreement to agree. Other courts have applied a duty to negotiate in good faith, notwithstanding the agreement's lack of such a provision. The U.C.C. and Restatement (Second) of Contracts are mostly in accord with the modern approach to agreements to agree.

Shann v. Dunk

(Explosives Company Investor) v. (Explosives Company)
84 F.3d 73 (2nd Cir. 1996)

MEMORY GRAPHIC

Instant Facts

Shann (P) came to a preliminary agreement to purchase Dunk's (D) explosives company. The parties had disagreements over terms and could not finalize the contract. Shann (P) now seeks to enforce the preliminary agreement.

Black Letter Rule

A preliminary agreement by parties to a contract may be enforced as a binding contract itself if it covers all essential and material terms.

Case Vocabulary

PAROL EVIDENCE: Evidence that relates to a contract, but that comes from a separate source and thus does not appear in the contract. Not normally admissible to add to or contradict the terms of the contract.

Procedural Basis: Appeal to the Federal Circuit Court of a diversity action for breach of contract after the trial court consolidated the state and federal actions filed by the respective parties and ruled the agreement void after a court trial.

Facts: Shann (P) is a principal in the manufacture and sale of explosives for mining. Dunk (D) is the controlling shareholder of St. Lawrence Explosives Corp. (SLE), a manufacturer of low-grade explosives, and provider of drilling and blasting services. [A very EXPLOSIVE case!] Dunk (D) owns 242 of the 333 shares of SLE, with the remainder being owned by his daughter, son, and SLE's president, Julie Pecori. Dunk (D) had reached the age of 65 and wanted to retire. In the fall of 1992, Dunk's (D) son contacted Shann (P), proposing that Shann (P) purchase SLE. Shann (P) was receptive, but insisted that Dunk (D) commit himself to an option agreement obligating Dunk (D) to sell his shares. In the course of negotiating, Shann (P) apparently made clear to Dunk (D) that Shann (P) would undertake personal responsibility for any deferred payments. Once the option was agreed to, Shann (P) and his solicitor, Ashworth, came to the United States to work out the sale with Dunk (D). However, the option arrangement failed to result in a sale because of the parties' inability to secure financing, due to Shann's (P) refusal to give his personal guarantee. Shann (P) then left Ashworth to continue negotiations with Dunk (D). On the evening of November 24, 1992, Dunk (D) said to Ashworth, "I'm thinking about financing the deal for you," and the next morning proposed terms satisfactory to Ashworth. Ashworth put the terms down on paper, and secured Shann's (P) approval. Both Dunk (D) and Shann (P) signed the agreement. This "November 25th agreement" (or Agreement) contained provisions for a deposit of $50,000; payment at closing of $450,000; payment to Dunk of $2,352,000 as a consultant and pursuant to a non-compete agreement, along with 7% plus prime rate as interest on any outstanding payments; and payments and interest to Dunk's (D) daughter. Paragraph 10 of the Agreement provided that Shann (P) would pledge all shares acquired to Dunk (D) as security. Both sides agreed that they considered the November 25 Agreement to be binding, notwithstanding its expected replacement by a more elaborate, formal contract. Soon thereafter, Dunk's (D) attorney, Kissel, argued to Shann's (P) attorney, Chazen, that the allocations of the Agreement were inappropriate and unfair to Dunk (D) for tax reasons. Chazen was authorized to change the allocation. Chazen began to draft a more formal contract that made material changes to the Agreement. Shortly after receiving notice of these changes, Dunk (D) met with his advisers who took exception to the changes and expressed the view that the deal did not give Dunk (D) enough security, and that he should not go forward with it. Dunk (D) then contacted Shann (P) and told him that he required Shann's (P) personal guarantee of the deferred payments, or some other form of security. Dunk (D) and Chazen outlined a deal that would be acceptable. This proposal was in numerous respects very different from the November 25 Agreement and included the requirement that Shann (P) personal guarantee the purchase obligations. Shann (P) then sent Dunk (D) proposed closing documents, along with a draft for $450,000. Dunk (D) refused to go along, citing the departures from the terms of the November 25 Agreement and stating that he would not deal without the personal guarantee. Shann's (P) representative Ashworth then offered to eliminate any terms from the closing documents that were at variance with the November 25 Agreement—offering essentially to close on the November 25 Agreement, which Shann (P) insisted did not include a personally guarantee by Shann (P) of the deferred payments. Dunk (D) refused this offer. Dunk (D) then filed suit in state court seeking a declaratory judgment, while Shann (P) filed in federal court. Shann (P) removed Dunk's (D) suit to federal court where the two actions were consolidated. After a five-day bench trial, the court ruled that the November 25 Agreement was unenforceable because it lacked certain essential terms relating to the concult/noncompete clause.

Issue: May a preliminary agreement to a contract be given effect as a binding contract if all essential terms are outlined in the agreement?

Decision and Rationale: (Leval, CJ) Yes. Ordinarily, preliminary manifestations of assent that require further negotiation and further contracts do not create binding obligations. Nonetheless, we have recognized that in some rare instances, if a preliminary agreement clearly manifests such intention, it can create binding obligations. Such agreements fall into two categories: Type I is where all essential terms have been agreed upon and no disputed issues are perceived to remain, and a further contract is envisioned primarily to satisfy formalities. Type II is where the parties recognize the existence of open terms, even major ones, but agree to bind themselves to negotiate in good faith to work out the terms remaining open. It seems clear that, notwithstanding their intention to sign a more elaborate contract, the parties viewed themselves as having reached a complete agreement on all significant terms in the November 25 Agreement, and intended to be bound. Accordingly, the parties viewed their contract as either a binding Type I agreement with the only thing remaining being the need for lawyer's embellishments, or a binding Type II agreement in which all important terms were settled, with only questions of undrafted boilerplate to be settled through good faith negotiation. We now turn to the question of whether the November 25 Agreement lacked essential terms. The district court ruled that no binding contract had been formed because essential terms relating to the consult/noncompete clause were lacking. We disagree. The evidence suggests that the structure of the November 25 Agreement was a fiction inspired by the hope of securing tax benefits. As for the consulting, even Dunk (D) himself understood that any duties were to be extremely limited. It was clear to Dunk (D) that the "guts of the deal" was money in exchange for stock. At no time did Shann (P) negotiate for any commitment of the amount of time, or the degree of service, Dunk (D) would render. Neither side had an interest in the scope of the noncompete clause, because Dunk (D), entering retirement, had no intention to compete. Both sides testified that they considered the terms of the consult/noncompete agreement to be of little importance. We therefore hold that the consult/noncompete clause and the terms thereof were not important or essential. The district court reached the opposite conclusion by refusing to "look beyond the four corners of the agreement in order to determine whether the parties actually meant what they said." There is no legal doctrine that requires a court to restrict its examination to the "four corners" of a contract to determine whether omitted terms are essential. To the contrary, the law requires a court to consider the broad framework of a contract in determining whether missing terms are actually essential—that is, necessary to make the agreement binding. We conclude that the district court erred in finding the November 25 Agreement was void by reason of the absence of essential terms related to the consult/noncompete clause because neither side considered the consult/noncompete agreement significant. However, because of uncertainty regarding whether Shann (P) was personally obligated to with respect to the very substantial deferred payments, we are unable to conclude on the present record that the November 25 Agreement was sufficiently complete so as to make an enforceable contract. This issue was obviously of great importance to the parties. Without Shann's (P) guarantee, Dunk's (D) receipt of the deferred payments would depend on the sufficiency of SLE's future cash flow, something that would largely be dependent on how well Shann (P) ran the company. As for Shann (P), he was deeply committed to avoiding personal responsibility. Shann (P) believed that the purpose of the high interest rate provided under the Agreement was to compensate Dunk (D) for the risk that the future payments might not materialize. We therefore conclude that the issue of Shann's (P) responsibility for deferred payments was an "essential" term. It is clear that the November 25 Agreement is sufficiently ambiguous on this question of Shann's (P) personal responsibility for the deferred payments to justify consideration of all the extrinsic evidence of the parties' negotiations and conduct to determine the meaning of the contract. This admission of parol evidence is particularly warranted here because a court should find an agreement too indefinite to enforce when it is satisfied that the agreement cannot be rendered reasonably certain by reference to an extrinsic standard that makes its meaning clear. There is certainly much parol evidence available here for a court to consider and we remand the case for this task of determining whether Shann (P) did, or did not, undertake personal responsibility for the deferred payments, or, alternatively, whether the parties failed to reach an understanding on this question. If the parties failed to agree on this essential point, the district court will be required to void the contract for absence of an essential term. If, on the other hand, the parties had reached agreement on the question of Shann's (P) liability, then the district court must decide whether they had a Type I or Type II agreement. If a Type I, then the parties could have closed the deal on the November 25 Agreement, and either party's refusal would constitute an actionable breach. Alternatively, if the parties had agreed on Shann's (P) liability, the contract might be seen as a more limited agreement of the Type II variety, with only the remaining boilerplate to be negotiated in good faith. In sum, if the district court finds that the parties resolved the question of Shann's (P) liability for deferred payments, it will need to decide whether their agreement was Type I or Type II and whether either side breached. If the district court finds that the issue of liability for deferred payments was not resolved, then the parties failed to reach a binding contract. Remanded.

Analysis:

This case illustrates the modern view of agreements to agree. When elements of a contract are left open for future negotiations, the modern view takes the position that the parties must negotiate in good faith. A failure to negotiate in good faith may constitute a breach of the contract. Here the Court finds that the parties entered into either a "Type I" agreement or a "Type II" agreement. If a Type I, then all essential terms of the contract have been settled and the parties can go forward on the November 25 Agreement alone, with no further negotiations. On the other hand, if the agreement is of the Type II variety, then the parties must negotiate the remaining "boilerplate" in good faith, a failure to do so being breach of contract. In *Sun Printing*, we saw a case that applies the traditional rule that when a material term has been left open for future negotiations, no contract results and no requirement to negotiate in good faith exists unless it has been written into the agreement to agree. [Confused yet?] Here, if the agreement is of the Type II variety, the Court will read into the agreement a requirement that the parties negotiate in good faith. Another way a court may deal with an agreement to agree is by applying a "gap-filler." A gap-filler is a term supplied by a court because it is in keeping with community standards of fairness. In supplying a gap-filler, a court will rely primarily on the intent of the parties. However, when a court cannot find an objective standard on which to base the gap-filler, it may refuse to apply it.

A/S Apothekernes Laboratorium for Specialpraeparater v. I.M.C. Chemical Group, Inc.

(Chemical Company) v. (Chemical Company)
873 F.2d 155 (7th Cir. 1989)

M E M O R Y G R A P H I C

Instant Facts

Apothekernes Laboratorium (P) reached a preliminary agreement to purchase assets of I.M.C. (D) with final approval vested in the respective company boards. I.M.C.'s (D) board voted down the final agreement. Apothekernes Laboratorium (P) now sues for breach and other claims.

Black Letter Rule

1) The terms of a letter of intent or preliminary agreement may impose a duty to conduct further negotiations in good faith. 2) The full extent of a party's obligation to negotiate in good faith can only be determined from the terms of the letter of intent or the preliminary agreement.

Case Vocabulary

ESTOPPEL: A legally imposed preclusion against an assertion or denial regarding a fact, resulting from one's course of conduct.

Procedural Basis: Appeal of a diversity action in breach, fraud and estoppel from the federal district court's finding of no violations after a bench trial.

Facts: In March of 1997, A/S Apothekernes Laboratorium for Specialpraeparater (ALS) (P), through its president, E.W. Sissener, entered negotiations with I.M.C. Chemical Group, Inc. (IMC) (D) and its president and CEO, Dr. M.B. Gillis, for the purchase of various IMC (D) assets. On December 9, the parties signed a letter "intended to set forth the terms upon which we and/or our nominee intend to negotiate and consummate an Agreement of Sale relative to the purchase of certain assets of ... [IMC]." The letter set forth those matters that had been substantially agreed upon, as well as those that required further negotiation. The letter concluded that "[a]ll of the above is subject to our concluding an Agreement of Sale which shall be acceptable to the Boards of Directors of our respective corporations, whose discretion shall in no way be limited by this letter...." Included in the letter was a provision in which IMC (D) agreed not to negotiate with any others for the sale of the subject assets. Finally, the letter also provided for an Agreement of Sale to be executed within 60 days of December 9, 1977. Although negotiations proceeded in good faith, at the end of the 60 days a final deal had not been reached. The district court found that at the end of the 60 days, Gillis and IMC (D) were no longer obligated to continue negotiations. Nonetheless, Sissener and ALS (P) finally capitulated on the contested terms on February 24, 1978, at which time the district court found that the parties had a "meeting of the minds on all substantial terms." However, when Gillis presented the deal to Lenon, the president of IMC's (D) parent corporation, Lenon summarily rejected the deal and instructed the board of IMC (D) to vote it down, which it did. The district court found nothing wrong with this process and that therefore the deal was never consummated, and no contract resulted. ALS (P) then appealed the judgment of the district court.

Issue: 1) May the terms of a letter of intent or of a preliminary agreement impose a duty upon the parties thereto to conduct further negotiations in good faith? 2) Is the meaning of "good faith" as imposed by a preliminary agreement or letter of intent defined only by referencing the language of the preliminary agreement or letter of intent?

Decision and Rationale: (Coffey, CJ) 1) Yes. 2) Yes. ALS (P) asserts two arguments on appeal: First, that the February 24 meeting of the minds constituted a binding contract which IMC (D) breached. Second, in the alternative, that the December 9 letter of intent imposed a duty upon IMC (D) to negotiate in good faith, which IMC (D) breached when its board rejected the deal. The first argument fails because the absence of approval by IMC's (D) board prevents a finding that the parties intended to be bound by the February 24 agreement. The intent of the parties is paramount in considering whether an enforceable contract came in to being. Here, the December 9 letter of intent, as well as the circumstances surrounding the transaction itself, indicates that the deal was at all times subject to the approval of the parties' respective boards of directors. Without this final approval there was never any full intent to form a binding contract. As for ALS's (P) second argument, the district court found that the December 9 letter did not form a binding contract. This finding is in keeping with the principle that the purpose and function of a preliminary letter of intent is not to bind the parties, but instead is only to provide an initial framework from which the parties might later negotiate a final agreement. ALS (P) is, however, correct, and the district court so found, that the December 9 letter of intent did impose upon the parties a duty to negotiate in good faith. A number of courts, including this court, have held that the terms of a letter of intent may impose such a duty. ALS (P) asserts that IMC (D) violated this duty when its board rejected the deal. We disagree. The obligation to negotiate in good faith has been generally described as preventing one party from renouncing the deal, abandoning the negotiations, or insisting on conditions that do not conform to the preliminary agreement. The full extent of a party's duty to negotiate in good faith, however, can only be determined from the terms of the letter of intent itself. In the absence of any agreed upon terms or even a general framework within which to conduct the negotiations, the parties were free to insist on or reject any proposed terms to the contract that they wished. Here the letter of intent simply imposed the requirement that IMC (D) not negotiate with any other party for the assets at issue. In another case with very similar preliminary letter of intent language we stated, in general, that it was no great surprise that in business transactions both sides try to get the best of the deal; That one thus "cannot characterize self-interest as bad faith;" that "no particular demand in negotiations could be termed dishonest, even if it seemed outrageous...;" and that the "proper recourse is to walk away from the bargaining table, not sue for 'bad faith' in negotiations." Thus the scope of any obligation to negotiate in good faith can only be determined from the framework the parties have established for themselves in their letter of intent. ALS (P) doesn't argue that Gillis and IMC (D) were guilty of bad faith during the actual negotiations, but that IMC (D) was obligated to go ahead and approve the deal once the details had been hammered out. Here, ALS (P) misses the mark. A duty to negotiate in good faith does not encompass an automatic duty to approve the final deal. Nor does the duty encompass any requirement on the negotiator's part to advocate the deal to the ultimate decision-maker. The letter of intent said nothing of the sort. Indeed, it clearly stated that the deal was subject to board approval. How or why the board came to its decision has nothing to do with whether IMC (D) negotiated in good faith. Gillis and IMC (D) were therefore not guilty of bad faith. We thus hold that there was never any final and binding contract for sale. Affirmed.

Analysis:

The Court her lays down the rule that an obligation to negotiate in good faith can only be interpreted from the content of the preliminary agreement or letter of intent. When the negotiating parties decide on the language of this duty, what good can such a rule possibly have? A negotiating party can simply tailor the language to its intended course of dealing and then simply not violate the language while taking full advantage of what the language allows. An answer to this criticism may be that at least the parties have provided themselves with some framework from which to operate and from which to formulate expectations for further negotiation. In such a way, the parties at least have some idea of the ways in which the other party can and cannot conduct themselves. It might be said that some guidance, even if minimal, is better than none. All of this begs the question of why not just formulate a common law rule imposing a general duty to negotiate in good faith, with established criteria and benchmarks, and allow parties to opt out of the duty by agreement if they so desire? One might criticize this suggestion as a violation of the autonomy principle, which recognizes the desirability of letting people regulate their own affairs as much as reasonably possible, and to bind themselves by their expression of intention to be bound. However, the possibility for the contracting parties to opt out should preserve the autonomy principle, since the parties would be completely free to choose their own definition of "good faith," or simply to impose no duty at all. A failure to opt out could thus be viewed as an affirmative choice to abide by the common law good faith rule as interpreted by the courts.

Itek Corp. v. Chicago Aerial Indus., Inc.

(Stock Purchaser) v. (Bad-Faith Bargainer)
248 A.2d 625 (Del. 1968)

MEMORY GRAPHIC

Instant Facts

Itek (P) was attempting to purchase the stock of Chicago Aerial Industries (D). The parties signed a preliminary letter of intent requiring all reasonable efforts be made to close the deal. Chicago Aerial Industries (D) got a better offer and dumped the negotiations. Itek (P) sues.

Black Letter Rule

The provisions of a preliminary letter of intent imposing a duty to negotiate in good faith must be read and construed from the entire text of the letter, not in isolation from the other provisions.

Procedural Basis: Appeal to the State's highest court from a grant of summary judgment by the trial court in favor of Chicago Aerial Industries (D).

Facts: Both Itek (P) and Chicago Aerial Industries (CAI) (D) are producers of photographic equipment. Approximately 50% of the CAI (D) stock was owned by its president and by the estates of two of CAI's (D) founders. In early 1964, the beneficiaries of the estates (beneficiaries) formed a committee to explore selling the stock. In the spring of 1964, Itek (P) became interested in acquiring CAI's (D) assets. Negotiations between CAI (D) and Itek (P) reached a climax in the fall of 1964 with the conditional acceptance by CAI (D) of Itek's (P) offer to purchase all of CAI's (D) assets at a total price based upon $12.00 per share of CAI (D) stock plus one-twentieth of a share of Itek (P). The agreement of the principal CAI (D) stockholders was obtained and the CAI (D) board agreed to recommend acceptance of the offer to the other CAI (D) stockholders. Itek (P) arranged for the financing and, on January 15, 1965, the parties drafted a letter of intent [here we go again] that was signed by both parties. The letter confirmed the terms upon which the parties would go forward in trying to reach an ultimate deal. Paragraph 2 contained the following language: "Itek and CAI shall make every reasonable effort to agree upon and have prepared as quickly as possible a contract providing for the foregoing purchase by Itek and sale of CAI .... If the parties fail to agree upon and execute such a contract they shall be under no further obligation to one another." Thereafter, the parties commenced preparation of a formal agreement. While the two parties were ironing out the final details, one of the committee representing CAI (D), and its largest stockholders, succeeded in reviving an earlier interest in purchasing CAI (D) stock by Bourns, Inc. Bourns eventually offered to purchase the stock of the largest CAI (D) shareholders for $16.00 per share, a better offer than Itek's (P). After further productive negotiations with Itek (P), the formal offer from Bourns came through and on February 26, 1965, the principal stockholders of CAI (D) accepted the Bourns offer. On March 2, 1965, CAI (D) notified Itek (P) that it was terminating the transaction as a result of unforeseen circumstances and the failure of the parties to reach agreement. This lawsuit followed.

Issue: May a court interpret the requirements in a preliminary letter of intent by relying on a single provision in the letter, rather than construing the letter as a whole?

Decision and Rationale: (Wolcott, CJ) No. Itek (P) asserts that the preliminary letter of intent of January 15, 1965, is a binding contract breached by CAI (D) when it willfully refused to negotiate in good faith toward completion of the deal. To the contrary, CAI (D) argues that the letter was at most a statement of intent, not a binding contract, and points to the last sentence of paragraph 2: "If the parties fail to agree ... they shall be under no further obligation to one another," as evidence that they did not violate the letters terms. The question of whether a enforceable contract comes into being during the preliminary stages of negotiations depends on the intention of the parties. The fact that some matters are left for future agreement does not necessarily preclude the finding that a binding agreement was entered into. In making the determination, the trier of fact must look at the circumstances surrounding the negotiations and the actions of the principals at the time and subsequently. From all of these, the intention of the parties to be bound or not to be bound must be ascertained. The trial judge, however, made his decision by relying solely on the last sentence of paragraph 2. We think, however, that it was error to separate the last sentence of paragraph 2. All of its provisions must be read and considered together. If this is done, then it is apparent that the parties obligated themselves to "make every reasonable effort" to agree upon a formal contract, and only if such effort failed were they absolved from "further obligation" from having "failed" to agree upon and execute a formal contract. The first issue to be resolved is whether the January 15 letter of intent was an enforceable agreement. This decision is to be made after consideration of the surrounding circumstances and what the parties intended and believed to have been the result. There is evidence which, if accepted by the trier of fact, would support the conclusion that on January 15, both Itek (P) and CAI (D) intended to be bound. There is also evidence to support the conclusion that CAI (D) willfully failed to negotiate in good faith and to make "every reasonable effort" to agree upon a formal contract, as it was required to do. These are issues of material fact that preclude summary judgment for CAI (D). The ruling of the trial court is therefore reversed.

Analysis:

Is there a way in which CAI (D) could have (should have) conducted itself that would have avoided these legal troubles while still allowing its stockholders to get a better deal than Itek's (P) original offer? Look at the language of paragraph 2. It required "every reasonable effort" to agree upon a formal contract. At the time Bourns made its offer, Itek (P) and CAI (D) had not agreed to a formal contract. What would bar CAI (D) from simply approaching Itek (P) and letting it know there was a better offer on the table? Certainly no one can say that refusing to finalize the deal with Itek (P) in light of the Bourns offer would be unreasonable. Indeed, it would be unreasonable to fail to insist on a better deal from Itek (P). Rather than deal openly with Itek (P), CAI (D) made the improvident choice of attempting to pull the wool over Itek's (P) eyes and hope for the best. Further, the deal with Itek (P) was subject to approval by a majority of the CAI (D) stockholders. In proposing the deal to the CAI (D) stockholders, the CAI (D) board could have also informed them of the Bourns offer. It is highly unlikely that a majority of these stockholders would vote for a deal that would net them less money than the Bourns proposal. As an aside, how could the attorneys of CAI (D) argue in good faith that the last sentence of paragraph 2 absolved CAI (D) of any liability? [Well, they did get one judge to buy it.] If such was the correct construction of paragraph 2, why bother putting the "every reasonable effort" clause in? After all, a party that did not wish to negotiate in good faith would certainly rather end negotiations all together in reliance on the last sentence instead of wasting resources by continuing to negotiate in bad faith. What this case serves as an example of is poor executive decision-making by CAI (D). It reminds one of the old adage [oft repeated by Gomer Pyle]: "Oh what a tangled web we weave when we first practice to deceive."

Chomicky v. Buttolph

(Lake-Home Seeker) v. (Lake-Home Owner)
147 Vt. 128, 513 A.2d 1174 (Vt. 1986)

M E M O R Y G R A P H I C

Instant Facts

Chomicky (P) negotiated a contingent written contract to purchase a parcel of Buttolph's (D) land. The parties had a separate oral agreement should the contingency fail. The contingency did fail and Chomicky (P) now seeks specific performance of the oral agreement.

Black Letter Rule

The Statute of Frauds requires that a contract for the sale of lands, including any changes or modifications to the contract, be in written form to be enforceable.

Case Vocabulary

ASSUMPSIT: An action at common law for the breach of an express or implied promise not under seal.
SPECIFIC PERFORMANCE: A remedy requiring the fulfillment of a legal or contractual obligation, ordered by courts when monetary damages would be inadequate.

Facts: Buttolph (D) is a landowner of lakeside property with a desire to sell a parcel of that property. Chomicky (P) negotiated with Buttolph (D) and reached an agreement to buy some of the lakeside property. The agreement was written up by Chomicky's (P) attorney and signed by both parties. The contract was contingent, however, on Buttolph (D) obtaining a subdivision permit from the local Planning Commission. While the subdivision petition was pending, Chomicky (P) phoned Buttolph (D) and suggest that in the event the petition was not granted, that Buttolph (D) retain an easement granting them a 50 foot right-of-way leading to the lake (something a successful petition would have obviated). After discussing the option with his wife, Buttolph (D) phoned Chomicky (P) and told him that the right-of-way arrangement was acceptable in the event the petition was denied. The Planning Commission denied the petition, causing the failure of the written contract. The next day, Buttolph (D) phoned Chomicky (P) and told him "the deal was off," and that he wanted to sell the whole parcel or nothing. Chomicky (P) sued for specific performance on the oral contract concluded over the phone.

Issue: Is an oral contract involving the sale of land, or modifying a separate written contract for the sale of land, enforceable under the statute of frauds?

Decision and Rationale: (Hill, J) No. A contract involving the sale of land or interests therein is controlled by the Statute of Frauds. As a general rule, such contracts must be in writing to be enforceable. Moreover, any proposed changes or modifications are subjected to the same requirements of form as the original provisions. Chomicky (P) asserts that because Buttolph (D) admits to the existence of the oral contract, that he is precluded from setting up the Statute of Frauds as a defense. Even if there was an oral contract, we do not believe that such an admission removes the case from under the Statute of Frauds. While the writing requirement is imposed primarily as a shield against possible fraud, it also promotes deliberation, seriousness, certainty, and shows that the act was a genuine act of volition. It thus helps ensure that contracts for the sale of land or interests therein are not entered into improvidently. The fact that one admits to the sale of land by verbal contract does not bar him from pleading the Statute of Frauds as a defense. Chomicky (P) also asserts that the doctrine of part performance demands the case be resolved in his favor. This doctrine is properly invoked to give relief to those who substantially and irretrievably change their position in reliance on a oral agreement. Chomicky (P) points to his financing arrangements and title search in preparation for the closing as requiring the application of part performance. However, activities in preparation for a proposed transfer of title belong to that class of responsibilities that fall into the lot of any prospective seller or purchaser of real estate, and are not the kind of imposition supporting the equitable relief sought. Also, Chomicky's (P) downpayment of $5,000 does not warrant granting specific performance. Money payments on the purchase are not enough to give the oral agreement enforceable status, even coupled with possession, in the face of the Statute of Frauds. The judgment of the lower court's decree of specific performance is therefore reversed.

Analysis:

The early common law did not generally enforce oral promises. However, with the advent and proliferation of the action in assumpsit the courts began to enforce oral promises, a development that led to widespread perjury. In response to this development, the English Parliament enacted the Act for Prevention of Fraud and Perjuries in 1677. This Act imposed the requirement that many categories of contracts be in written form and signed by the parties to the contract. This is the forbear of the modern Statute of Frauds. While the main purpose of the Statute is to obviate perjury, there are other policies promoted by it as well, such as the promotion of certainty, deliberation, seriousness, and to show that an act was a genuine act of volition. These are certainly valid goals, but in the realization of them the Act sometimes imposes costs. Similar to the costs imposed by stringent application of the parol evidence rule, sometimes the Act requires courts to ignore what the parties orally agreed on. Thus when one party actually performs based on an oral agreement, the fact the agreement is covered by the Statute may allow an unscrupulous dealer to breach the agreement, leaving the other party with no remedy and unjustly enriching the unscrupulous dealer. In this way, the Statute may be said to promote the undesirable goals of fraud and unethical conduct. These concerns often lead courts to give a narrow construction to the coverage of the Statute of Frauds. Some courts have even developed ways in which to "take the contract outside" the Statute. Finally, as the instant case hinted at, a number of legal and equitable remedies have been developed by courts in order to provide relief to those who would otherwise be unjustly harmed by strict application of the Statute.

Radke v. Brenon

(Land Buyer) v. (Land Partitioner/Seller)
271 Minn. 35, 134 N.W.2d 887 (1965)

MEMORY GRAPHIC

Instant Facts

Radke (P) received an unsigned written offer from Brenon (D) to sell a parcel of land. Radke (P) orally accepted, but Brenon (D) decided not to sell. Radke (P) sued, citing the written offer as evidence of the deal.

Black Letter Rule

An oral contract, normally required to be in writing, may be given effect, if supported by clear and uncontradicted written documentary evidence, such that doing so comports with public policies against fraud and perjury.

Procedural Basis: Appeal to the State's highest court from a judgment of the trial court decreeing specific performance of a contract for real estate.

Facts: Radke (P) and Brenon (D) are neighbors, along with eight other homeowners, owning adjacent lots near a lake. None of the ten neighbors' lots extended all the way to the lake's shoreline. On December 1, 1959, Brenon (D) acquired ownership of the strip of land between the ten neighbors and the lake. After having the strip of land surveyed, Brenon (D) sent an identical letter to his nine neighbors, including Radke (P), offering to sell them the irregular parcels separating their lots from the lake. In the letter, Brenon (D) explained that he had "no desire to make a profit ... if everyone owning adjoining property is willing to buy their portion" and divide the cost "equally among all 10 including [him]self." Brenon (D) itemized the total cost at $2,120 and offered to sell each lot for $212 on any terms agreeable. The letter was not signed by Brenon (D), but his name was typewritten thereon, he having authorized this and considered such to be tantamount to his signature. About two weeks after Radke (P) received the written offer, he orally accepted it. Sometime later, Radke (P) learned that two of the neighbors declined to purchase, and thus the divided cost of each lot was increased to $262. Radke (P) was agreeable to pay the increase, but did not immediately so inform Brenon (D). The trial court found that Radke (P) accepted the offer on May 7, 1947, at which time he knew of the price increase. Brenon (D) testified that the parties did have an oral agreement. On August 14, 1947, Radke (P) delivered to his attorney a check for $262 payable to Brenon (D) for the purpose of completing the sale. This information was forwarded to Brenon (D) on August 16, along with instructions to proffer the deed upon payment. Sometime after August 16, Radke (P) received a letter from Brenon (D) dated August 16 informing him that the offer to sell was revoked.

Issue: Is a letter or memorandum offering land for sale sufficient to satisfy the requirements of the Statute of Frauds?

Decision and Rationale: (Rogosheske, J.) Yes. The Statute of Frauds (Statute) expresses a public policy of preventing the enforcement by means of fraud and perjury of contracts that were never in fact made. To inhibit perversion of this policy, the Statute permits enforcement of an oral contract if there exists a note or memorandum as evidence of the contract. As an aid in promoting this policy, the Statute lists some requisites of a memorandum and this court has added others, so that we have some indication of the content a memorandum normally must have in order to be sufficient evidence of a contract. Under the Statute, the writing must express the consideration and must be subscribed by the party making the sale or his lawful agent. In addition, this court has added the requirements that the memorandum state expressly or by necessary implication the parties to the contract, the lands involved, and the general terms and conditions of the sale. These latter elements are clearly present in the letter written by Brenon (D). The parties' names are included as well as the particular land to be sold. As to the terms of the contract, such as manner of payment, Brenon (D) merely held himself ready "to work out any kind of terms" with the purchasers. The elements expressly required by the Statute are not so obvious. First, the consideration of $212 as stated in the letter is not the same as the $262 tendered in accord with the oral understanding. Despite this, we think the letter sufficiently expresses the consideration because the $212 represented an equal share as divided by the ten parties. While the actual price was changed, the consideration was simply a mathematical computation according to the formula specified by the letter. This variation does not render the letter's expression of the consideration insufficient. The necessity of subscription is the final problem. A "subscription" is the same as a "signing" and it is clear that Brenon's (D) typewritten name, typed with the intent, according to his own testimony, that it be tantamount to a written signature, is sufficient. We by no means intend to hold that Brenon's (D) letter would be a sufficient memorandum in every case. We will overlook technical requirements only if proof of the oral contract is clear and uncontradicted, as in this case where Brenon (D) admitted a contract had been made. We will not blindly apply these technicalities if they lead to a conclusion repugnant to commonsense. As Professor Williston has said: "if after a consideration of the surrounding circumstances, the pertinent facts and all the evidence in a particular case, the court concludes that enforcement of the agreement will not subject the defendant to fraudulent claims, the purpose of the Statute will best be served by holding the note or memorandum sufficient even though it be ambiguous or incomplete. The policy of the Statute would be perverted if the admitted contract were not enforced. Affirmed.

Analysis:

As the Court stated, the memorandum must state with reasonable [there's that word again] certainty: (1) the identity of both contracting parties (if the memorandum sufficiently describes the party, then the party does not have to be named); (2) the subject matter of the contract for identification purposes (sufficient enough to allow identification from the writing alone or with the aid of extrinsic evidence); and (3) the essential terms and conditions of all promises that make up the contract along with the identities of the promisor and promisee. If payment has already been made, some courts will waive the consideration requirement. Remember that these essential terms need only be stated with reasonable certainty. This comports with the Court's holding that the terms and conditions of the sale need only be stated in "general." A memorandum that meets the Statute's requirements can be in any written form—a check, letter, receipt, notes on a napkin—so long as it amounts to acknowledgement by the party to be charged that he has assented to the contract that is asserted by the other party. Here, the Court resorts to a functional analysis of the purposes of the Statute of Frauds in order to determine whether they would be fulfilled by strictly applying the Statute. In this way, the Court avoids a probable miscarriage of justice by enforcing the written/oral agreement between the parties.

Nebraska Builders Prods. Co. v. Industrial Erectors, Inc.

(Construction Subcontractor) v. (Crane Supplier)
239 Neb. 744, 478 N.W.2d 257 (1992)

MEMORY GRAPHIC

Instant Facts

Industrial Erectors (D) contracted to supply some cranes and equipment to Nebraska Builders (P) for a construction project. Requirements for the project caused several changes to be made to the contract until Industrial Erectors (D) disavowed the contract altogether.

Black Letter Rule

1) Section 2-201(1) of the U.C.C. requires contracts for the sale of goods valued at $500 or more to be memorialized in writing(s), signed by the party against whom enforcement is sought, and sufficient to indicate that a contract for sale has been made. 2) U.C.C. Section 2-201(3)(b) allows enforcement of a contract not meeting the requirements of § 2-201(1) if the party against whom enforcement is sought admits in court that a contract was made.

Procedural Basis: Appeal of a breach of contract action to the State's highest court from the trial court's ruling that no contract existed.

Facts: Nebraska Builders Products Co. (NBP) (P) planned to submit a bid to supply the cranes for a new construction project. To this end, NBP's (P) representative, William Hawkins, held discussions with Timothy Brennan, representing Industrial Erectors, Inc. (Industrial) (D). On March 12 or 13, 1985, Brennan phoned Hawkins and said that Industrial (D) would provide all crane systems needed for $449,920. On March 26, Brennan wrote Hawkins confirming the phone conversation and "propos[ing] to furnish all Crane Systems, Jib Cranes and Monorail Systems...." Also in this letter was a list of the specific items to be supplied. The price was adjusted in further discussions. Hawkins testified that he phoned Brennan to accept Industrial's (D) offer, but Brennan denies such a conversation. The parties exchanged correspondence concerning details of the materials to be supplied, involving some confusion regarding the specifications for the project. Brennan requested several times that NBP (P) issue a purchase order, written contract, or letter of intent. NBP (P) held off, however, until it had a contract with the general contractor. Industrial (D), in turn, refrained from issuing any written contracts to its suppliers until it received one from NBP (P). Nonetheless, Brennan and Hawkins continued planning for the work. On July 23, Brennan sent Hawkins a letter confirming some verbal communications regarding some added costs and the reasons therefor. There were some more added costs due to the project specifications, until Hawkins finally said the additional costs were not acceptable, ending discussions. NBP (P) obtained performance of the contract at a cost of $136,135.11 more than what it would have cost under the contract with Industrial(D). NBP (P) sued to recover these added costs.

Issue: 1) May an oral contract for the sale of goods worth at least $500 be enforced if supported by written evidence of the contract? 2) May an oral contract for the sale of goods worth at least $500 be enforced absent any writing if the party against whom enforcement is sought admits in court that the contract was made?

Decision and Rationale: (Hastings, C.J.) 1) Yes. 2) Yes. [The Court first found that there was an oral contract.] Since the value of the cranes exceeds $500, the Statute of Frauds is applicable. Therefore, the question is whether the Statute's requirements have been met. This court has stated that a writing will be sufficient to avoid the Uniform Commercial Code (UCC) Statute of Frauds if the writing evidences a contract for the sale of goods, is signed by the party against whom enforcement is sought, and specifies a quantity. The writing need not include all the material terms, so long as, according to comment 1 to § 2-201, it affords a basis for believing that the offered oral evidence rests on a real transaction. Several writings can be pieced together to satisfy the requirement. In the case at bar, the proposal letter and the following letters indicate that a contract was formed. The proposal letter of March 26, 1985, states the quantity of goods to be furnished and lists them in detail. Also, after the alleged phone conversation in which NBP (P) accepted Industrial's (D) bid, a correspondence emerged concerning the materials to be furnished. This includes the letters of May 31, June 10, August 9, and August 15, all detailing and discussing the projects requirements and the attendant costs. The three requirements of the Statute of Frauds § 2-201 are satisfied when the five letters are read together. They clearly evidence a sale of goods. They are signed by the authorized agent of the party against whom enforcement is sought. Finally, the quantity of goods to be sold is indicated in the letter dated March 26, which describes in detail 14 cranes and one monorail. The agreement is also enforceable under the Statute of Frauds exception, § 2-201(3)(b). According to § 2-201(3)(b), oral contracts may be enforced absent a writing "if the party against whom enforcement is sought admits in his pleading, testimony or otherwise in court that a contract for sale was made...." Comment 7 to § 2-201 states that "it is no longer possible to admit the contract in court and still treat the statute as a defense." Brennan admitted the existence of the contract in court, while being cross-examined. This satisfies § 2-201(3)(b). We do not hereby hold that an admission is made whenever the defendant utters the magic words "contract" or "agreement," as laypeople often misuse legal terminology. If this happens, the court should look at the other evidence presented by the defendant. The record here shows that Brennan's actions indicate an agreement between the parties did in fact exist. The judgment of the district court is therefore reversed.

Analysis:

Before the Uniform Commercial Code was enacted it was the Uniform Sales Act that was generally applied in the United States. Because § 2-201 resembles quite closely the Sales Act provision, cases decided pursuant to the Sales Act are still valid authority. One of the provisions of the UCC applied here by the court is § 2-201(3)(b). This provision applies when the party against whom enforcement is sought admits, either in court or in court documents, that a contract was formed. One thing the court neglects to mention is that under this subsection, a contract is not enforceable beyond the quantity of goods admitted. This entire provision is new, probably the result of prior cases in which the defendant was allowed to raise the Statute of Frauds as a defense despite having admitted to the contract. Many courts expressed dissatisfaction with the rule allowing the Statute to be raised as a defense in the face of a defendant's admission of a contract. Such a rule does not comport with the main purpose of the Statute—to avoid fraudulent contracts—although it does with the Statute's purpose of promoting deliberation in contracting. The provision does raise at least one important question, however. This problem is whether the party against whom enforcement is sought may be forced to acknowledge the oral contract. Some commentators take the position that admission should not be compelled whenever the Statute is raised as a defense. Several, if not the majority of courts, however, refuse to dismiss a complaint founded on an oral contract covered by the Statute on the ground that a defendant may acknowledge the oral contract during the trial. Obviously, should a defendant or an authorized agent acknowledge the existence of an oral contract, the case would then fit within the § 2-201(3)(b) exception to the writing requirement. What this does is provide a defendant with a choice: admit to the oral contract and most likely lose the case, or risk perjury charges by denying the oral contract. [A classic Hobson's choice.]

AN ORAL CONTRACT THAT INDUCES RELIANCE MAY BE ENFORCEABLE NOTWITHSTANDING THE REQUIREMENT OF A WRITING

Warder & Lee Elevator, Inc. v. Britten

(Grain Elevator) v. (Grain Farmer)

274 N.W.2d 339 (Iowa 1979)

M E M O R Y   G R A P H I C

Instant Facts

Britten (D) orally agreed in the summer to sell grain at a set price to Ward & Lee Elevator (P) for delivery in the fall. Ward & Lee Elevator (P) sold grain in reliance on the deal. Grain prices went up making Britten (D) refuse to deliver on the oral contract.

Black Letter Rule

Notwithstanding the requirement of a written contract, the doctrine of promissory estoppel requires enforcement where (1) a party makes an oral contract, (2) expecting the other party to rely on it, (3) the other party does rely on it to their detriment, and (4) failure to enforce the oral contract would be inequitable.

Case Vocabulary

AD HOC: For a particular purpose; Case-by-case.

INTER ALIA: Among other things.

PROMISSORY ESTOPPEL: A doctrine that holds that a promise lacking consideration will still be binding where (1) the promisor knows, or should reasonably know, that the promise will induce reliance, (2) the promisee does rely on the promise, and (3) failure to enforce the promise will result in injury or injustice.

Procedural Basis: Appeal to the State's highest court after the trial court applied promissory estoppel to enforce an oral contract falling within the Statute of Frauds.

Facts: Warder & Lee Elevator, Inc. (W&L or the elevator) (P) operate a grain elevator. On July 4, 1974, John Britten (D), a local farmer, came to W&L's (P) offices to sell some grain. Britten (D) and W&L (P) had dealt with each other for several years. At Britten's (D) request, Francis Lee, president of W&L (P), quoted a price of $2.60 per bushel of corn and $5.70 per bushel of soybeans for fall delivery. The parties agreed on the sale of 4,000 bushels of corn and 2,000 bushels of soybeans at these prices for October-November delivery. The elevator (P) did not at the time require a seller to sign a memorandum or other writing to show the agreement. The only writing reflecting the agreement was some notes showing the terms of the sale for internal bookkeeping purposes. All of the elevator's (P) prior purchases from Britten (D) had been upon oral agreement and none were ever breached. In reliance on the oral contract with Britten (D), on July 5 the elevator (P) sold the same quantities of corn and soybeans that it purchased from Britten (D) for fall delivery to terminal elevators at Muscatine for a few cents more per bushel. Grain prices increased substantially during July and on July 29, 1974, Britten (D) phoned the elevator (P) and stated that he wished to "call the deal off." W&L (P) told Britten (D) he could not call the deal off as the grain had already been sold. Britten (D) reasserted that he would not deliver the grain. In an effort to makeup for the breach, the elevator (P) purchased appropriate quantities of corn and beans from other farmers on and shortly after July 29. That August, Britten (D) and James Lee, Francis Lee's son and future president of the elevator (P), met on the street [no, they did not duke it out] where Britten (D) offered to settle the issue with a payment of $500. Lee rejected the offer and told Britten (D) that the elevator (P) expected delivery according to the contract. Britten (D) sold his 1974 crop elsewhere. The elevator (P) brought this action for damages sustained in covering the delivery obligation.

Issue: May an oral contract covered by the Statute of Frauds be enforced where the contract has induced reliance by one of the parties thereto?

Decision and Rationale: (McCormick, J) Yes. The Iowa Statute of Frauds applicable to the sale of crops is § 554.2201. Under this statute an oral contract for the sale of goods is unenforceable, with certain stated exceptions. Promissory estoppel is not among them. Authority to use the doctrine of promissory estoppel to defeat the Statute of Frauds, if it exists, must be found under § 554.1103. This statute allows application of promissory estoppel "[u]nless displaced by the particular provisions of this chapter...," meaning § 554.2201 [U.C.C. § 2-201]. We have never had occasion to decide whether the provisions of § 554.2201 displace the doctrine of estoppel, otherwise available under § 554.1103. We have long recognized promissory estoppel as a means of defeating the general Statute of Frauds. We see nothing in § 554.2201 which purports to require a different rule under the Uniform Commercial Code (UCC). To hold otherwise would mean that an oral contract coming within the terms of § 554.2201 would be unenforceable despite fraud, deceit, misrepresentation, dishonesty or any other form of unconscionable conduct. No court has taken such an extreme position, nor will we. Indeed, courts uniformly hold "that the Statute of Frauds, having been enacted for the purpose of preventing fraud, shall not be made the instrument of shielding, protecting, or aiding the party who relies upon it in perpetration of a fraud or in the consummation of a fraudulent scheme." 3 Williston on Contracts § 553A at 796. The estoppel defense developed from this principle. We therefore hold that the provisions of § 554.2201 do not displace the doctrine of estoppel in relation to the sale of goods in Iowa. The elements of promissory estoppel are (1) a clear and definite oral agreement, (2) proof that th party urging the doctrine acted to his detriment in relying on the agreement, and (3) finding that the equities support enforcement of the agreement. In applying this doctrine it is immaterial whether the promise was unilateral or bilateral. This doctrine is aptly expressed in Restatement (2d) Contracts § 217A [now Restatement (2d) Contracts § 139]. Britten (D) contends the elevator (P) should not have the benefit of the doctrine because it was not proved that Britten (D) knew the elevator (P) would rely on the oral agreement. We find this argument lacks merit because there is substantial evidence supporting the inference that Britten (D) expected or reasonably should have expected the agreement to induce action by the elevator (P). Britten (P) should have known his prior dealings with elevator (P) gave it every reason to believe he would keep his word. Furthermore, it is reasonable to believe that a farmer who sells grain regularly to country elevators knows they may immediately sell the grain which they purchase. We therefore conclude that the elements of promissory estoppel were supported by substantial evidence and hold that injustice could be avoided only by enforcement of Britten's (D) promise. Affirmed.

Dissent: (Reynoldson, C.J.) The majority opinion misapprehends and misapplies our rules relating to promissory estoppel. Further, the facts of this case do not bring it within the new principles pioneered in this decision. Iowa follows the Uniform Sales Act and its successor since 1965, the Uniform Commercial Code—Sales. The UCC's Statute of Frauds, § 554.2201, was modified to clarify that its exceptions are limited to those contained in its provisions. Our general Statute of Frauds is embodied in § 622.32. The catchall exception of § 622.32 that had previously allowed for the application of promissory estoppel ceased to be applicable to sales of goods after the modification. Retained as applicable, however, were the "failure to deny" and "oral evidence of the maker" exceptions contained in § 622.34 and .35 respectively. Section 554.2201 limits exceptions to the writing requirement to those provided for in that section—the § 622.34 and .35 exceptions. These do not include promissory estoppel. Section 554.1103 permits application of estoppel "unless displaced by the particular provisions of this chapter." The limiting language of § 554.2201 constitutes such a displacement. Following this reasoning would not leave parties without a remedy. The victim of fraud who has no legal remedy because § 554.2201 prevents proof of the oral contract may rely on the equitable remedy of restitution because it is not dependent on proof of a contract. The basic elements of equitable estoppel and fraud are (1) intentional misrepresentation, (2) innocent, reasonable and foreseeable reliance, and (3) injury. These are not contract-dependent. Recovery is based on the injury suffered in the course of reliance. Liability is premised on the fraud, not a contract. Thus, a fraudulent party has little protection from the Statute of Frauds. The § 554.2201 Statute of Frauds is obviously designed to suffer some injustices in isolated oral contract cases in favor of the general public policy to reduce fraud and perjury, etc. Indeed, it is significant that by the time of trial the elevator (P) was using written sales contracts. The majority's opinion will frustrate the purpose of the Statute. Finally, it should be noted that the facts of this case would not warrant application of the rule the court lays down and as stated in § 217A of the Restatement.. Imposition of this rule requires proof that Britten (D) "should reasonably expect" that the elevator (P) would promptly resell the grain. There is no evidence in the transcript to show that Britten (D) either knew this was the elevator's (P) practice or that it was custom in the industry. The majority seeks to supply this crucial missing proof by asserting "it is reasonable to believe a farmer who sells grain regularly to country elevators knows they may immediately sell the grain...." I doubt these matters qualify for such judicial notice as being within common knowledge or capable of certain verification. I would therefore reverse and remand for a new trial, during which proof of the alleged contract would be regulated by § 554.2201undiluted by promissory estoppel.

Analysis:

Chief Justice Reynoldson seems to take exception to two points raised by the majority. First, the Chief Justice disagrees that promissory estoppel is an available remedy under the Statute of Frauds as enacted in Iowa. He may be correct on this point, but whether he is right or wrong, by his own admission, should not matter to the outcome of this case. This is because there are other remedies available to W&L (P), such as equitable estoppel, which, because it does not depend on the formation of a contract, either oral or written, does not fall within the bailiwick of the Statute of Frauds. This remedy, as Chief Justice Reynoldson aptly stated, is predicated on the fraud, not the existence of any contract. A failure to apply promissory estoppel would thus not, as the majority seemed to fear, leave a victim of fraud without any recourse. On the other hand, the purpose of the Statute of Frauds could still be carried out. Chief Justice Reynoldson's second point is that even if the majority's rule is correct, there is simply no proof that Britten (D) knew or reasonably should have known that the elevator (P) would rely on his promise. As a brief aside, the majority never expressly states that the promissory estoppel doctrine has such a requirement. The majority does, however, imply such a requirement by addressing whether it was met by the facts of the case and then concluding that it was. Chief Justice Reynoldson criticizes the majority for taking this judicial notice that Britten (D) should have known his promise would induce reliance. This criticism does seem to have some merit. The court cites Britten's (D) prior dealings with the elevator (P) and comes to the very quick conclusion that "a farmer who sells grain regularly to country elevators knows they may immediately sell the grain which they purchase." This conclusory statement is not supported by any real evidence—Britten (D) never even testified—and seems to assume that the average farmer concerns himself with the business practices of the elevator he sells his grain to. Is this a safe assumption?

Perspective
The Justification Principle

Chapter 2

The world is full of promises made and forgotten, yet the law will only assure the enforcement of a small set of those promises. The reason is that there must be a socially useful reason for the law to intervene by imposing itself upon two parties that disagree over a promise. Therefore, not only must a promise take place to be enforceable, but there also must be some justification for the law to enforce it.

Three of the primary legal justifications to enforce a contract are a bargained for exchange, reliance, and unjust enrichment. Each of these justifications has evolved separately, but oftentimes they have commingled with sometimes confusing results.

Bargained for promises are enforced because the parties are presumed to benefit through their exchange. The parties make an exchange because the other has something they deem more valuable than what they each give up. Furthermore, a bargained for exchange ensures that the promise was made with deliberation and thought, instead of on a whim.

Early contract law termed such deliberation "consideration." Relied upon promises are enforced because the promise, while not the result of bargaining, induced the person promised to incur some kind of injury or loss in anticipation of the promise being carried out. To not enforce a promise in such a situation would be unjust because the other party has suffered a loss.

The third category, unjust enrichment, does not necessarily concern a promise made. In fact, the doctrine of unjust enrichment evolved to deal with circumstances that did not meet the traditional promissory framework, but where an injustice required compensation. These cases often involve the situation where someone does something of value for another but is not compensated for it, and the recipient unjustly retains the value of what was given.

In the following cases, observe how the concepts of consideration develop and how some courts have expanded the definition of consideration to include doctrines involving reliance and unjust enrichment. As you read each of these cases, keep in mind the benefits and purposes for enforcing a particular promise or for requiring compensation.

Chapter 2

NOTE: THE PURPOSE OF THIS OUTLINE IS TO ORGANIZE THE CASES SO THAT ONE CAN QUICKLY UNDERSTAND THE RELEVANCE OF EACH CASE TO THE COURSE. NO ATTEMPT IS MADE IN THIS OVERVIEW TO ADDRESS EVERY CONCEPT THAT MUST BE STUDIED. BE SURE TO READ THE ENTIRE CASEBOOK AND/OR OTHER MATERIALS TO GAIN A FULL UNDERSTANDING OF ALL CONCEPTS.

I. The Bargained for Exchange
   A. The law will enforce a promise only where there are sufficient legal justifications to enforce the promise.
   B. It is against public policy to enforce an oral promise of a charitable donation if made without consideration or reliance. *Congregation Kadimah Toras-Moshe v. DeLeo.*
   C. Nominal consideration is consideration in form rather than in substance and will not create a legally enforceable contract. *Schnell v. Nell.*
   D. While the term consideration traditionally meant a "bargained for exchange", courts have sometimes also defined consideration to include concepts such as reliance and unjust enrichment.
   E. A waiver of a legal right at the request of another party is sufficient consideration for a promise. *Hamer v. Sidway.*
   F. Mere inadequacy of consideration will not void a contract. *Batsakis v. Demotsis.*
      1. In examining contractual rights, it is generally presumed that the parties are acting under their own free will and deliberation; however, some parties' free will may be hampered by their economic or social conditions as in *Batsakis v. Demotsis.*
      2. This raises the question of whether contract law should take into account those social conditions that may restrain a party's choices in entering a contract or whether contract law should avoid manipulating the doctrine of consideration in favor of enforcing promises regardless of social conditions.
   G. A transaction based on otherwise worthless consideration is not enforceable. *Newman & Snell's State Bank v. Hunter.*
   H. Forbearance to litigate a claim, even though invalid, may provide sufficient consideration to enforce a contract as long as there was a good faith belief in the claim. *Dyer v. National By-Products, Inc.*
   I. A contract of sale is not mutual where there is an obligation to sell, but no obligation to purchase. *Wickham & Burton Coal Co. v. Farmer's Lumber Co.*
   J. Exclusive dealing arrangements impose an obligation by the seller to use his best efforts to distribute and market goods. *Wood v. Lucy, Lady Duff-Gordon.*
   K. An accord and satisfaction must be supported by separate consideration. *Levine v. Blumenthal.*
      1. The modification of a contract for the sale of goods does not require consideration to be enforceable. *Gross Valentino Printing Co. v. Clarke.*
      2. The pre-existing duty rule does not prevent parties from modifying their contract when unexpected or unanticipated difficulties arise during the course of the performance of the contract, as long as the parties voluntarily agree. *Angel v. Murray.*

II. Reliance on a Promise
   A. If only promises that were the product of bargained for exchange were enforceable, then the law would inappropriately enforce the bargained for exchange where a carjacker demands of his victim, "Your car or your life."
      1. In addition, the law would also not enforce promises that lack consideration, but probably should be enforced.
   B. A burden borne by a party based on the promise of another provides sufficient consideration to enforce that promise. *Devecmon v. Shaw.*
   C. A promise that the maker knows is likely to be relied upon by the promisee, and is so relied

upon, is enforceable under a theory of promissory estoppel. *Feinberg v. Pfeiffer.*

D. Promissory estoppel is inapplicable where the promise does not actually induce reliance. *Hayes v. Plantations Steel Co.*

E. An offer may not be freely revocable if the offeree has substantially relied on the offer. *Drennan v. Star Paving Co.*

F. The listing of a subcontractor in the contractor's prime bid is not an implied acceptance of the subcontractor's bid. *Southern California Acoustics Co., Inc. v. C.V. Holder, Inc.*

III. Unjust Enrichment

A. The doctrine of unjust enrichment (also known as quasi-contract, implied-in-law contract, or restitution) is used to remedy situations where a party nongratuitously confers a benefit upon a second party and the second party unjustly retains that benefit.

1. This injustice generally requires one party to gain at the expense of the other.
2. This remedy is available whether or not a promise was actually made.

B. A person is unjustly enriched when he or she receives a benefit from another for services or goods for which one would normally expect to be paid. *Sparks v. Gustafson.*

C. A moral obligation is not always sufficient consideration to enforce a promise. *Mills v. Wyman.*

D. When a material benefit is conferred to another without request, the beneficiary's subsequent promise to pay for the benefit is sufficient consideration. *Webb v. McGowin.*

Congregation Kadimah Toras-Moshe v. DeLeo.

(Synagogue) v. (Estate Administrator)
405 Mass. 365, 540 N.E.2d 691 (1989)

M E M O R Y G R A P H I C

Instant Facts

A dying man promised to give a synagogue $25,000.

Black Letter Rule

It is against public policy to enforce an oral promise of a charitable donation if made without consideration or reliance.

Case Vocabulary

CHARITABLE SUBSCRIPTION: A donation of money or property to a charity.
CONSIDERATION: Something of value exchanged between parties in a contract.
DECEDENT: A deceased person.
DETRIMENT: Any loss or injury suffered by a person.
PROMISEE: The party that receives the promise.
PROMISOR: The party who makes a promise.
RELIANCE: Dependence or trust on the words or actions of another.

Procedural Basis: Appeal directly to the state supreme court after a municipal court and a superior court granted summary judgments against the plaintiff.

Facts: A dying man orally promised a rabbi, Abraham Halbfinger, that he would give his synagogue, Congregation Kadimah Toras-Moshe (P), $25,000. While this promise was never made in writing, it was made to Rabbi Halbfinger during four or five of several visits the rabbi made to the dying man throughout his prolonged illness. The promise was made in the presence of several witnesses. The Congregation (P) had planned to use the money to turn the synagogue's storage room into a library. However, the man eventually died, [becoming a "stiff" while also "stiffing" the Congregation (P)], leaving behind no will and survived only by his wife. The Congregation filed suit against the executor (D) in order to fulfill the oral promise. Both the local municipal and superior courts granted summary judgment in favor of the executor (D) of the deceased man.

Issue: Is an oral promise to give a charitable donation that is made without consideration or reliance enforceable?

Decision and Rationale: (Liacos, J.) No. There was no consideration in this case because no legal benefit was made to the promisor and the promisee suffered no detriment. There was no evidence that the Congregation (P) induced the decedent to make his donation by plans to name the library after him. The mere allocation of $25,000 in the Congregation's (P) budget is insufficient reliance to create an enforceable obligation. An expectation or hope does not establish legal detriment or reliance. This case is, therefore, distinguishable from other cases involving promises of charitable subscriptions since those cases involved substantial consideration or reliance. We decline to discard the rule requiring consideration or reliance in cases of charitable subscriptions. A moral obligation does not create a legal obligation. Enforcing such an oral promise against a state would be against public policy.

Analysis:

This case illustrates a fundamental rule of contracts: that donative promises are generally not enforced. There are a number of reasons why the law shies away from enforcing such promises. First, donative promises are often difficult to prove. A promise to give a gift is rarely ever put in a writing signed by both parties. After all, putting a promise to make a gift in writing would awkwardly dampen both the joys of giving and receiving. Second, donative promises, in general, are often made with little thought and no serious decision-making or, put in terms of contract law, without consideration. Often, a person may change their mind about giving a gift if the recipient does something to the dislike of the giver or for other reasons. Third, if the law were to enforce every donative promise, our courts would obviously infringe and become the arbiters of every dispute of a promise made between friends, spouses, and business persons. This is an area best relegated to the more flexible arena of social values and norms, and not the rigidity of the courts. In the case at hand, the deceased made a promise to a religious organization. The fact that the deceased wound up "stiffing" the rabbi and the synagogue seems abhorrent. However, as the court points out the promise was not induced by the Congregation (P), nor did the Congregation (P) detrimentally rely on the deceased's promise. As a result, absent such factors, it seems likely that the deceased made the promise with little deliberation, no doubt overly influenced by the knowledge of his impeding death. If, for example, the Congregation bargained for the $25,000 (e.g. give us the money and we'll name the library after you) then such bargaining would have provoked thought and consideration on the part of the deceased regarding his promise. Without such inducement, the promise may merely have been the delusional gratitude of a dying man. Moreover, even if delusional, the Congregation (P) suffered no financial harm from the promise. They expended no funds or did nothing to their disadvantage in reliance on the promise. As a result, the deceased's promise was neither a product of significant deliberation nor caused any real harm. Therefore, a court enforcing such a promise would simply be too much meddling in the world of give and take.

NOMINAL CONSIDERATION WILL NOT BE SUFFICIENT TO MAKE A CONTRACT LEGALLY ENFORCEABLE

Schnell v. Nell

(Disappointed Promisee) v. (Promisor of Money)
17 Ind. 29, 79 Am.Dec.453 (Supreme Court of Indiana, 1861).

M E M O R Y   G R A P H I C

Instant Facts

After Schnell's wife made an inoperative will giving $200 to each of three recipients, Schnell entered into an agreement with the three to pay each the $200 promised by his wife in her will. After he refused payment, one of the recipients brought suit to enforce the agreement.

Black Letter Rule

Nominal consideration is consideration in form rather than in substance and will not create a legally enforceable contract.

Case Vocabulary

DEMURRER: A formal means of stating that the other party has not alleged facts sufficient to support a legal claim—a way of disputing the legal sufficiency of a claim.
NOMINAL CONSIDERATION: Consideration in name only, or consideration that does not bear any real relationship to the value of the thing contracted for.

Procedural Basis: Appeal of a lower court decision sustaining a demurrer to the defendant's answer and finding in favor of the plaintiff.

Facts: Theresa Schnell was wife of Zach Schnell (D). Theresa made a will out that devised a sum of $200 to each of three recipients: J.B. Nell (P), Wendelin Lorenz and Donata Lorenz. At her death, Theresa did not own any property in her own name and all of the property held jointly by herself and her husband went to her husband. As a result, the provisions in the will devising the sums of money to the three recipients were void. Zach Schnell (D) later entered into an agreement with the three providing that he would pay the sums owed under his wife's inoperative will. The agreement listed three potential forms of consideration. One was a promise on the part of Nell (P) and the other recipients to pay Schnell (D) one cent. A second was the love and affection Schnell had born for his deceased wife, and the third was the fact that his wife had expressed her desire to pay the money to the recipients in the inoperative will. After the agreement was signed by all parties, Schnell (D) refused to pay the $600. Nell (P) brought suit to enforce the agreement. In his complaint, Nell (P) did not aver any consideration over and above those which were listed in the agreement, nor did he aver that he had ever actually paid the one cent due to Schnell (D) under the agreement's terms. Schnell (D) demurred but the demurrer was overturned. Thereafter, Schnell (D) answered the complaint and stated that the agreement was given for no consideration whatsoever. Nell (P) demurred after the answers and the court sustained the demurrer. Schnell (D) appealed.

Issue: Is nominal consideration sufficient to make a contract valid and enforceable?

Decision and Rationale: (Perkins, J.) No. It is true that, in general, the inadequacy of consideration will not vitiate a contract. Courts do not generally inquire into the adequacy of consideration. However, this rule does not apply to a mere exchange of sums of money whose value is exactly fixed. In this case, Nell (P) was supposed to give Schnell (D) one cent and in return, Schnell (D) was supposed to give Nell $200. There was no indication that the one cent specified was a particular coin, a keepsake, a family piece or was in any other way a remarkable coin. It did not have an indeterminable value. On the contrary, this was simply a promise to pay $200 in exchange for one cent. It was purely nominal consideration and was intended to be so. Theresa Schnell's will was legally inoperative. It imposed no legal obligation upon her husband to honor its provisions or to discharge her void bequests. A moral obligation will not itself provide consideration to support an agreement. Nor can Nell's (P) promise (in the agreement) to refrain from filing suit against Schnell (D) based on the voided will be adequate consideration. Giving up the right to file a legally groundless claim is not consideration for an agreement. The agreement admits that the will was legally inoperative and void. The past services of Schnell's (D) wife was also insufficient for two reasons. First, they are past considerations, and second, her services to Schnell (D) did not constitute consideration for Schnell's (D) promise to pay Nell (D). This was simply a promise to make a gift in accordance with Schnell's (D) deceased wife's wishes. There was no consideration for the agreement. The demurrer to the answer should have been overruled. Reversed.

Analysis:

Nominal consideration, also known sometimes as sham consideration, is almost always insufficient to make a contract enforceable. The rationale behind this rule is that nominal consideration is consideration in form only. There is no substantive component to the bargain being made. In other words, the agreement is basically one encompassing a donative promise or other legally unenforceable promise, and the nominal consideration is being added just to make it look like all of the elements of contract formation are present. In fact, if the consideration being proffered is essentially worthless, it is likely that it is no consideration at all. There are two important exceptions to the doctrine that nominal consideration is insufficient to make a legally enforceable contract. According to the Restatement Second of Contracts, nominal consideration will make a promise enforceable in two areas—option contracts and guaranties. However, case law decisions have sometimes refused to adopt the Restatement view and have held that a mere *recital* of nominal consideration is insufficient even to enforce an option contract. The cases vary in circumstances where the consideration for an option contract is clearly nominal, but has already been *paid*.

IT IS ENOUGH THAT SOMETHING IS PROMISED, DONE, FORBORNE, OR SUFFERED BY THE PARTY TO WHOM THE PROMISE IS MADE AS CONSIDERATION FOR THE PROMISE MADE TO HIM

Hamer v. Sidway

(Mesne Assignee) v. (Will Executor)
124 N.Y. 538, 27 N.E. 256 (1891)

MEMORY GRAPHIC

Instant Facts

An uncle promised to pay his nephew $5,000 to not smoke, swear or gamble until he was 21 years old.

Black Letter Rule

In general, a waiver of any legal right at the request of another party is a sufficient consideration for a promise.

Case Vocabulary

FORBEARANCE: Refraining from doing something that one has the legal right to do.
GENERAL TERM: A phrase used in some jurisdictions to denote the ordinary session of a court for the trial and determination of cases.
MESNE ASSIGNMENT: If A grants to B, and B assigns his interest to C, and C in turn assigns his interest to D, the assignments made by B and C would be termed mesne assignments; that is, they are assignments intervening between A's original grant and the vesting of D's interest under the last assignment.
SPECIAL TERM: That branch of the court which is held by a single judge for hearing and deciding motions and causes of equitable nature.
TESTATOR: One who makes or has made a will.

Procedural Basis: Appeal from an order of the general term of the supreme court, reversing a judgment entered at special term in favor of the plaintiff.

Facts: William Story promised his nephew that if he would refrain from drinking, using tobacco, swearing, and playing cards or billiards for money until he was 21 years old, he would pay him $5,000 [holy #@*%! – oops, lost it already!]. The nephew agreed, and fully performed the conditions inducing the promise. When the nephew turned 21, he wrote to his uncle, informing him that he had performed his part of the agreement , and was entitled to the $5,000. Story wrote back, agreeing that his nephew was entitled to the sum, but he offered to keep the money, plus interest, so as to prevent unwise spending [imagine that!] on the nephew's part. The nephew agreed to this, and Story kept the money for him until his death twelve years later. At the time of his death, Story had not paid over to his nephew any portion of the $5,000 and interest. Hamer (P) presented a claim to the executor (D) of Story's estate for the amount due plus interest. She had acquired the interest through several mesne assignments from Story's nephew. The claim was rejected by the executor (D) and Hamer (P) filed suit.

Issue: Must the promisor be benefited in order for consideration to be valid?

Decision and Rationale: (Parker, J.) No. Sidway (D) claims that the contract was without consideration because the nephew was not harmed but actually benefited by not engaging in the various vices. In addition, Sidway (D) claims the uncle received no benefit stemming from his nephew's refrainment from such activities. However, these contentions have no basis in law. Consideration is not simply defined as requiring one party to receive some profit or benefit while the other party incurs some responsibility or loss. Consideration may also include damage to, loss of, or forbearance of a legal right. Consideration does not necessarily mean that one party must profit from the other's suspension of a legal right, but merely requires that a promise induces another to give up a legal right. Here, the promisee clearly had a legal right to consume tobacco and liquor, frequently doing so in the past. However, he abandoned this right for years based on his uncle's promise. Regardless of the effort the nephew undertook, he definitely restricted his "lawful freedom of action" based on the uncle's promise. As a result, it is irrelevant whether the nephew's performance of the contract actually benefited the uncle. Judgment affirmed.

Analysis:

The executor (D) of Story's will contends that the contract was without consideration to support it, and therefore invalid. He asserts that the promisee, by refraining from the use of liquor and tobacco, was not harmed, but benefited. It was argued that what he did was best for him to do independent of his uncle's promise, and as such it follows that, unless the promisor was benefited, the contract was without consideration. He also argues that the decedent did not benefit in any way by Hamer's (P) conduct. If their contentions were well-founded, it would seem to leave open for controversy whether what the promisee did or omitted to do was in fact of benefit to anyone, so as to leave no consideration to support the enforcement of the promisor's agreement. However, a valuable consideration, in the sense of the law, may consist either in some right, interest, profit, or benefit accruing to the one party, or some forbearance, detriment, loss, or responsibility given, suffered, or undertaken by the other. Courts will not ask whether the thing which forms the consideration does in fact benefit the promisee or a third party, or is of any substantial value to anyone. It is enough that something is promised, done, forborne, or suffered by the party to whom the promise is made as consideration for the promise made to him.

A PLEA OF LACK OF CONSIDERATION AMOUNTS TO A CONTENTION THAT THE CONTRACT WAS NEVER VALID IN THE FIRST PLACE

Batsakis v. Demotsis

(Money Lender) v. (Money Borrower)

226 S.W.2d 673 (1949)

M E M O R Y G R A P H I C

Instant Facts

A man loaned $25 to a woman having financial difficulties, and made her sign a promissory note to repay him $2,000 plus interest.

Black Letter Rule

Mere inadequacy of consideration will not void a contract.

Case Vocabulary

AVER: To set out distinctly and formally; to allege.

BREACH: Exists where one party to a contract fails to carry out a term, promise or condition of the contract.

CROSS-ASSIGNED ERROR: Errors being assigned by the appellee.

ERROR ASSIGNMENT: A specification of the errors upon which the appellant will rely in seeking to have the judgment of the lower court reversed, vacated, modified, or a new trial ordered.

GENERAL DENIAL: A pleading which controverts all of the averments of the complaint.

JUDGMENT AFFIRMED: To declare the decision is valid and right and must stand as rendered in the lower court.

PER ANNUM: Each year.

PLEA: The answer which the defendant made to the plaintiff's declaration in which he sets up a matter of fact as a defense.

Procedural Basis: The plaintiff appeals from the trial court's judgment awarding the plaintiff $750 of a $2000 claim.

Facts: On April 2, 1942, Eugenia Demotsis (D) found herself and her family stranded in Greece during World War II and unable to access any of her funds in America. Demotsis (D) and George Batsakis (P) entered into a written contract where Demotsis (D) acknowledged the receipt of $2,000 in American money as a loan "during these difficult days" and promised to repay Batsakis (P) the $2,000 US when she could access her American funds. Demotsis (D) never repaid the money. Batsakis (P) sued Demotsis (D) to recover $2,000 with interest at a rate of 8% per year. At trial, the evidence indicated that Batsakis actually loaned Demotsis 500,000 Greek drachmas which was equivalent to only $25 US, [yup, she got ripped off]. At trial, Demotsis (D) claimed that Batsakis (P) knew that she was in financial distress, that she wished to return to America and "extracted of her" the written contract at issue in this case. She further testified that Batsakis (P) compelled her to sign the contract in exchange for the 500,000 drachmas. The trial court found inadequate consideration to enforce the contract but ruled in favor of Batsakis (P) in the amount of $1,163.83 ($750 principal plus interest at the rate of 8% per year until the date of judgment). Batsaksis (P) appealed.

Issue: Will inadequacy of consideration void a contract?

Decision and Rationale: (McGill, J.) No. Batsaksis (P) claims that the trial court erred because the evidence showed that there was sufficient consideration to merit payment of the entire principal of $2,000. The transaction was essentially a sale by Batsaksis (P) of the 500,000 drachmas in consideration of the performance of the written contract being sued upon. The drachmas had value, and the trial court, in fact, valued the 500,000 drachmas as $750 US. Therefore, there was sufficient consideration to enforce the contract. Mere inadequacy of consideration will not prevent the enforcement of a contract.

Analysis:

This case is a rather strict enforcement of the idea that courts will often not interfere in what the parties deemed valuable to them in making a contract. Absent any evidence of sham consideration, the court will enforce a contract even if the consideration given is meager. In this case, the court reasoned that there was a promise for Demotsis (D) to pay $2,000 and the consideration to enforce that promise was the 500,000 drachmas that Batsaksis (P) gave her. Thus, even though the drachmas only had a value of $25, it was nonetheless sufficient consideration to enforce the contract, requiring Demotsis (D) to pay the entire $2,000 plus seven years of interest. However, one cannot imagine why the court enforced this contract given that the facts clearly established that Batsaksis (P) either tricked or exploited Demotsis (D). In fact, the written contract states that Batsaksis (P) gave her $2,000, when she obviously did not receive this. In all likelihood, Demotsis' (D) attorney also got the best of Demotsis (D) by neglecting to argue that the contract be voided because it was unconscionable or the product of fraud or duress. Without raising these issues and only raising the claim of inadequacy of consideration, the court may have been forced to reach this seemingly unjust result.

Newman & Snell's State Bank v. Hunter

(Bank) v. (Widow)
243 Mich. 331, 220 N.W. 665, 59 A.L.R. 311(1928)

MEMORY GRAPHIC

Instant Facts

A widow entered into a contract with a bank to pay off a debt owed by her late husband.

Black Letter Rule

A transaction based on otherwise worthless consideration is not enforceable.

Case Vocabulary

COLLATERAL: Property that is promised as security for repayment of a debt.
INSOLVENT: The inability to pay one's debts.
NOTE: A written promise by one party to pay another.

Procedural Basis: Appeal to the state supreme court of a judgment awarded to the plaintiff.

Facts: Lee Hunter took a loan from Newman & Snell's State Bank (P) in the amount of $3,700. For collateral for the note, the bank held 50 shares of stock of Hunter's company. At Hunter's death, his estate and his company were insolvent making the debt impossible to collect. Just over a month after his death, Hunter's widow, Zennetta Hunter (D), [graciously but unwisely] took up her husband's debt at the bank (P) with her own note along with earned interest due on her husband's note. In exchange for Hunter's (D) note, the bank discharged her husband's loan. The bank (P) later tried to collect on the widow's (D) note, but the widow (D) [wised up and] took the bank (P) to court claiming lack of consideration. The trial court ruled in the bank's (P) favor. The widow (D) appealed.

Issue: Is a transaction based on worthless consideration enforceable?

Decision and Rationale: (Fellows, J.) No. Both parties have filed excellent briefs and made helpful arguments. Case law on this subject is in conflict. Plaintiff's strongest case is *Judy v. Louderman* [holding that a note taken up by a father on behalf of his deceased son was valid despite the fact the son died insolvent making the original note worthless to the bank.] Other cases, including this court, have found that the widow's note, given for the discharge of her husband's debt, was unenforceable where the husband's estate was insolvent, making the original note worthless and the widow's note based on insufficient consideration. In this case, the deceased's note was worthless. The deceased died insolvent. Moreover, because deceased's company was also insolvent, the shares that the bank (P) held as collateral were also worthless. Thus, it is irrelevant whether ownership of the stock passed over to the widow (D) as a result of her new note or remained in the bank's (P) possession. Judgment is reversed.

Analysis:

In order for a promise to be enforceable, the promise must induce legal detriment. In other words the promise must make the promisee do something that he or she was not otherwise legally obligated to do. For example, a buyer who leaves a deposit to secure a promise to buy the seller's automobile has induced the seller to incur a legal detriment. The buyer has promised to buy the automobile and has used a deposit to ensure that the promise is secured by consideration. As a result, by accepting the deposit, the seller has taken on a legal detriment. The seller cannot now renege on the buyer by selling the automobile to someone else. However, what if the deposit left by the buyer is worthless? Is the promise still enforceable? Courts have generally steered clear of evaluating the adequacy of consideration except where the consideration given is merely a sham to make an otherwise donative promise enforceable (see *Schnell v. Nell* above). The rationale is that courts should not infringe on the freedom of individuals to bargain for whatever they deem valuable. As the saying goes, one man's treasure is another man's garbage. The key is that the promisee suffered a legal detriment, no matter how slim its value. Nevertheless, in the case at hand, the court evaluated the consideration and found it insufficient to make the promise enforceable. This is questionable given that the bank did incur a legal detriment and there was no evidence of a "sham" consideration. While the claim against the husband was, in all practicality, worthless because he died insolvent, the legal claim still existed because a debt was still owed. As we will see below, forbearance of a legal claim can form the basis of consideration. Here, however, the insolvency and death of the husband merely made it impossible to collect any money on the legal claim. Still, it seems apparent that the widow, at the very least, thought that she was receiving something of value when she took her husband's note, and there is nothing to indicate that the bank knew it was cheating the widow. Thus, the facts seem to support an induced legal detriment based on a bargained for exchange. Yet, the court did not enforce the promise on the basis that the consideration given was worthless. The decision may have been more clear if it decided that the promise was valid but unenforceable because it was based on fraud (the bank knew the claim was worthless, but gave the widow the note anyway) or mistake (the bargain was defective because the parties thought the husband's debt could still be collected).

FORBEARANCE TO LITIGATE A CLAIM, EVEN THOUGH INVALID, MAY PROVIDE SUFFICIENT CONSIDERATION TO ENFORCE A CONTRACT AS LONG AS THERE WAS A GOOD FAITH BELIEF IN THE CLAIM

Dyer v. National By-Products, Inc.

(Employee) v. (Employer)
380 N.W.2d 732 (1982)

M E M O R Y G R A P H I C

Instant Facts

An employee, who was injured at work, claimed that he struck a deal with his employer to not sue the employer for the injury in exchange for lifetime employment.

Black Letter Rule

Forbearance to litigate a claim, even though invalid, may provide sufficient consideration to enforce a contract as long as there was a good faith belief in the claim.

Case Vocabulary

FORBEARANCE: The act of refraining from the enforcement of a legal right.
GOOD FAITH: A state of mind exhibiting honesty of belief.
RECIPROCAL: Mutual.

Procedural Basis: Appeal to the state supreme court of a district court summary judgment in favor of the defendant.

Facts: On October 29, 1981, Dale Dyer (P) lost his right foot while on the job for his employer, National By-Products (D). Dyer (P) was placed on leave of absence to recover but [eventually was back on his feet, (actually, more like his foot),] returning to his foreman position on August 16, 1982. On March 11, 1983 National (D) laid off Dyer (P). Dyer (P) claimed that he made an oral contract with National (D) to not sue his employer for the injury in exchange for a promise of lifetime employment. The district court granted summary judgment in favor of National (D) on the basis that: 1) there was no evidence of a reciprocal promise to work for the employer for life, and 2) the forbearance to assert the legal claim against National (D) had no value because worker's compensation was Dyer's (P) only available remedy. Dyer (P) appealed.

Issue: Can forbearance to litigate a claim, even though unfounded and invalid provide sufficient consideration to enforce a contract?

Decision and Rationale: (Schultz, J.) Yes. On appeal, Dyer (P) restricts his claim to the issue of whether the forbearance from pursuing a claim was sufficient consideration. Dyer argues that summary judgment was improper because the issue of whether he had a reasonable good faith belief in the validity of his claim was an unresolved factual issue. National (D), on the other hand, argues that state worker's compensation law prevents Dyer (P) from raising a claim against it, thereby making his forbearance from filing a claim unfounded and making any consideration worthless. [In other words, he didn't have a leg to stand on.] The law generally favors the settling of controversies without resort to the courts. As a result, our courts have held that the surrendering of even a doubtful legal right, if made in good faith, can provide sufficient consideration for a promise. However, our case concerns a claim that clearly has no validity under our law. Professor Corbin suggests that forbearance on an otherwise unfounded claim may be sufficient consideration as long as the claim is asserted in good faith. This is due to the possibility that the facts or operations of the law may not be what the claimant supposes them to be. There is some support in our own case law for this view. However, other jurisdictions take an opposing view and require that the claim must have some merit in fact or at law in order to provide sufficient consideration. In fact, some of our own case law supports this view. We believe however, that the better reasoned position is that held by the Restatement (Second) of Contracts § 74. Forbearance can provide sufficient consideration if the claim is made in good faith. This rule favors compromise and disencourages a party from attempting to test the validity of a compromise. We therefore overrule any of our holdings that were contrary to this view. Consequently, because the issue of Dyer's (P) good faith belief was not an issue brought out by the present record, there remains a material fact that has not been resolved. Accordingly, the summary judgment is reversed and remanded for further proceedings consistent with this opinion.

Analysis:

Much like the previous case, the issue here is whether forbearance of an otherwise worthless claim can constitute sufficient consideration to enforce a promise. This again deals with the adequacy of consideration. Clearly, the surrender or forbearance of a valid legal claim can form sufficient consideration. However, if the claim has no legal merit, this begs closer scrutiny. Courts have generally adopted the view the surrender or forbearance of an invalid legal claim can form sufficient consideration where the claim was made in good faith. This rule preserves the essential rule in contracts of preserving the expectancies of the parties. If a claim is made in good faith, but the parties mistakenly think the claim has a legal basis, then the parties have clearly made a mistake. Nevertheless, this mistake did not invalidate the fact that the parties bargained over the promise. The court did not invalidate the consideration, even though it was, in reality, worthless. While the mistake contaminated a fundamental assumption of the promise, a valid consideration took place because the parties thought a claim existed; therefore, the bargaining process, which is the hallmark of contracts, did take place with the parties considering their obligations. Of course the bargaining process would be defective and lopsided if the party asserting the claim knew that it has no legal basis. In the case at hand, there was no evidence in the record properly establishing whether Dyer (P) was making his compensation claim in good faith. Therefore, the court did not adopt an objective rule by throwing out the promise because the claim objectively had no legal basis. Instead, it ordered the trial court to investigate the issue of what Dyer (P) subjectively knew about the validity of his claim. In many ways, this is a better approach than the prior case (*Newman & Snell's State Bank v. Hunter*).

A CONTRACT OF SALE IS NOT MUTUAL WHERE THERE IS AN OBLIGATION TO SELL, BUT NO OBLIGATION TO PURCHASE

Wickham & Burton Coal Co. v. Farmers' Lumber Co.

(Coal Seller) v. (Coal Buyer)
189 Iowa 1183, 179 N.W. 417, 14 A.L.R. 1293 (1920)

MEMORY GRAPHIC

Instant Facts

A coal buyer is counterclaiming a coal seller, asserting that their contract is void for failure of mutuality and certainty.

Black Letter Rule

A contract of sale is void for want of mutuality if the quantity to be delivered is conditioned entirely on what the buyer may want to buy.

Case Vocabulary

ALLEGATION: The assertion, claim, declaration, or statement of a party to an action, made in a pleading, setting out what he expects to prove.
CITATIONS: The reading, or production of, or reference to, legal authorities and precedents to fortify the propositions advanced.
COUNTERCLAIM: A claim presented by a defendant in opposition to or deduction from the claim of the plaintiff.
ESTOPPEL: A party is prevented by his own acts from claiming a right to the detriment of the other party who was entitled to rely on such conduct and has acted accordingly.
SUSTAINED: Granted, as when a judge agrees with the objection and gives it effect.

Procedural Basis: The plaintiff appeals from the court's overruling of a demurrer to the counterclaim.

Facts: The counterclaim alleges that Farmers' Lumber Co. (D), through an agent, entered into an oral agreement whereby Wickham & Burton Coal Co. (P) agreed to furnish and deliver to Farmers' Lumber (D) orders given for carload shipments of coal at the price of $1.50 per ton on all orders up to September 1, 1916, and $1.65 per ton on all orders from then to April 1, 1917. It is further alleged that the coal would consist of lump, egg, or nut coal [ooh, the *good* stuff!]. It is next alleged that Farmers' Lumber (D) owns and operates a line of lumber yards and that it handles coal in carload lots, with purposes of selling the same at retail to its patrons. The basis of the counterclaim is the allegation that a stated amount of coal had to be purchased by Farmers' Lumber (D) in the open market at greater than the contract price.

Issue: Is a contract of sale void for want of mutuality if the quantity to be delivered is conditioned entirely on the want of the buyer?

Decision and Rationale: (Salinger, J.) Yes. The demurrer makes, in effect, three assertions: (a) That the arrangement between the parties is void for uncertainty; (b) that it lacks consideration; (c) that it lacks mutuality of obligation. We have given the argument and the citations on the first two propositions full consideration. However, we conclude that these first two are of no importance if mutuality is wanting. The question of first importance, then, is whether there is a lack of mutuality. The counterclaim is based on the allegation that Wickham & Burton (P) undertook to furnish Farmers' Lumber (D) such described coal as it would want to purchase. Farmers' Lumber (D) never "accepted." But concede, for argument's sake, that it did accept. What was the acceptance? At the utmost, it was a consent that Wickham & Burton (P) might ship it such coal as Farmers' Lumber (D) "would want to purchase from Wickham & Burton (P)." What obligation did this fasten upon Farmers' Lumber (D)? It did not bind itself to buy all it could sell. It did not bind itself to buy of Wickham & Burton (P) only. It merely "agreed" to buy what it pleased. It may have been ascertainable how much it would need to buy of some one, but there was no undertaking to buy that much, or indeed, any specified amount of coal of Wickham & Burton (P). The "contract" on part of Farmers' Lumber (D) is to buy if it pleased, when it pleased, to buy if it thought it advantageous, to buy much, little, or not at all, as it thought best. A contract of sale is void for want of mutuality if the quantity to be delivered is conditioned entirely on the want of the buyer. While Farmers's Lumber (D) argues that the three cars of coal that were actually delivered and received completed the contract and made it mutual, the reality is that there never was agreement to ship anything. Because there was no mutuality or consideration, the parties were not bound to deliver or bound to receive any goods. The defendant never agreed to order or pay any quantity of these goods, and, if he refused to accept them upon shipment, no cause of action would exist. A contract will only exist after the other declares how much he will buy. The demurrer should have been sustained. Reversed.

Analysis:

The asserted lack of consideration is bottomed on the claim that mutuality is lacking. Wickham & Burton (P) does not deny that a promise may be a consideration for a promise; its position is that this is true only of enforceable promises. That is the law. If, from lack of mutuality, the promise is not binding, it cannot form a consideration. While a promise may be a good consideration for another promise, this is not so unless there is an absolute mutuality of engagement, so that each party has the right at once to hold the other to a positive agreement. A contract of sale is mutual where it contains an agreement to sell on the one side, and an agreement to purchase on the other. But it is not mutual where there is an obligation to sell, but no obligation to purchase, or an obligation to purchase, but no obligation to sell.

COURT IMPLIES DUTY TO MAKE REASONABLE EFFORTS IN AN EXCLUSIVE DEALING ARRANGEMENT

Wood v. Lucy, Lady Duff-Gordon

(Distributor) v. (Fashion Designer)
228 N.Y. 88, 118 N.E. 214 (1917)

M E M O R Y   G R A P H I C

Instant Facts

A famous fashion designer attempts to invalidate an exclusive-dealing arrangement by arguing that the supplier never made any promise to market her goods.

Black Letter Rule

Exclusive dealing arrangements impose an obligation by the seller to use his best efforts to distribute and market goods.

Case Vocabulary

EXCLUSIVE DEALING ARRANGEMENT: An agreement whereby a distributor expressly or implicitly contracts to supply all of a seller's goods, using the distributor's best efforts.

Procedural Basis: Appeal from order reversing denial of demurrer to complaint for breach of contract.

Facts: Lucy, Lady Duff-Gordon (D) was a famous fashion designer. In order to profit from her fame, Lucy (D) employed Wood (P). Wood (P) was granted the exclusive right to endorse products using Lucy's (D) famous name for one year. In return, Wood (P) agreed to split the profits with Lucy (D). Wood (P) sued for breach of contract after he discovered that Lucy (D) had endorsed products without his knowledge and without splitting the profits. Lucy (D) demurred on the ground that a valid contract never existed between the parties. In granting the demurrer and dismissing the complaint, the Appellate division found that the contract lacked mutuality, as Wood (P) never promised to do anything. Wood (P) appeals.

Issue: May a court imply a promise to make reasonable efforts in an exclusive-dealing arrangement?

Decision and Rationale: (Cardozo, J.) Yes. A court may imply a promise to make reasonable efforts in an exclusive-dealing arrangement. Indeed, Wood (P) never expressly promised to use reasonable efforts to endorse Lucy's (D) products or to market her designs. However, such a promise may be fairly implied by the court. Lucy (D) gave an exclusive privilege to Wood (P), and his acceptance of the exclusive agency was an assumption of its duties. To hold otherwise would be to undermine the purpose of the agreement. Lucy's (D) sole compensation for the grant of exclusive agency was to receive one-half of all profits. He agreed to account monthly for all moneys received, and to take out the necessary patents, copyrights, and trademarks. Unless Wood (P) gave some reasonable effort, Lucy (D) could never get anything. In line with the intention of the parties, we determine that Wood (P) made an implied promise, and thus that the contract was not lacking in mutuality of obligation. Reversed.

Analysis:

One of the fundamental bases of contract law is that the parties should be free to establish the terms of the contract. Ordinarily a court should not interfere and create implied promises or duties. For this reason, the holding of the Court of Appeals of New York in this opinion is open to some criticism. Obligations should be created voluntarily by contracting parties, not imposed by courts. Wood (P) never promised to make any efforts whatsoever in marketing Lucy's (D) designs and endorsing products under her name. Ironically, however, Wood (P) is saved by the court imposing a reasonable-efforts duty on him! Without the court's imposition, no valid contract would have existed, and Lucy (D) could have endorsed any product without his knowledge or consent. An illusory promise is an expression cloaked in promissory terms, but which, on closer examination, reveals that the promisor is not committed to any act or forbearance. One of the methods of circumventing the illusory promise problem is interpolating into an agreement that otherwise seems illusory the requirement of good faith or reasonableness. The method of this case is to find a promise by inferences drawn from the facts. Under some circumstances the promise inferred is called an implied promise and in others it is referred to as a constructive promise. The UCC adopts the reasoning of *Wood v. Lucy, Lady Duff-Gordon*; indeed, the UCC goes even further. It provides in §2-306(2), (and the 1997 revision draft, §2-304, is substantially the same): "A lawful agreement by either the seller or the buyer for exclusive dealing in the kind of goods concerned imposes unless otherwise agreed an obligation by the seller to use best efforts to supply the goods and by the buyer to use best efforts to promote their sale." Of course the Code provision has reference only to exclusive dealings in "goods." Thus, it would not be applicable to an agreement such as was involved in the *Wood* case, but the UCC adopts and extends its rationale by imposing the obligation of best efforts as a matter of legislative fiat rather than as a matter of interpretation. The road opened by *Wood v. Lucy* has been much traveled. It is now common for courts to find a means of implying promises to give effect to the intent of the parties.

Levine v. Blumenthal

(Lessor) v. (Lessee)
117 N.J.L. 23, 186 A. 457 (1936)

M E M O R Y   G R A P H I C

Instant Facts

The operators of a retail business selling women's apparel tried to modify their lease with the lessor to reduce their rent.

Black Letter Rule

An accord and satisfaction must be supported by separate consideration.

Case Vocabulary

ACCORD AND SATISFACTION: An agreement to use a substituted performance to satisfy a pre-existing debt (accord) and the receipt of that performance fully discharges the pre-existing debt (satisfaction).

Procedural Basis: An appeal to the state supreme court of a district court decision in favor of the plaintiff.

Facts: In an agreement dated April 16, 1931, defendants (D) agreed to lease retail space from Levine (P) to run a women's apparel store. Originally, defendants (D) agreed to a two-year lease with rent being $2,100 for the first year and $2,400 for the second and with an option for renewal. Just before the expiration of the first year, in April 1932, defendants (D) advised Levine (P) that the collapse of their business, [thanks to the Great Depression,] made it difficult to pay the current rent. More importantly, defendants (D) indicated that it was "absolutely impossible" for them to pay the increased rent required in the second year and that the higher rent would put them out of business. The parties disputed whether Levine (P) agreed to accept the present rent of $175 per month to satisfy the rent in full during the second year or whether Levine merely took the $175 per month on account with the balance to be paid later. Defendants (D) continued to pay the $175 per month until their lease expired, at which time they moved out, failing to pay last month's rent and the balance of the rent required by the lease in the second year. Levine (P) brought suit for the last month's rent and the unpaid balance. The district court ruled in Levine's favor (P) finding that while an oral agreement had been made to change the lease agreement, this change was ineffective because it was not supported by consideration. Defendants (D) appealed.

Issue: Does an accord and satisfaction have to be supported by separate consideration?

Decision and Rationale: (Heher, J.) Yes. Defendants (D) put forward defenses that the economic depression created a special circumstance and that the Defendants executed the agreed upon substituted performance. Defendants also argue that the plaintiff accepted the payments in full, making any remaining balance a gift, if not an accord and satisfaction. However, it has been a long-held rule that the payment of only part of a debt, that is received in full satisfaction of the entire debt, does not discharge the entire debt unless the agreement to pay the lesser amount is supported by consideration. This rule is rooted in the principle that "a promise to do what the promisor is already legally bound to do is an unreal consideration." Even disastrous economic adversity is no justification to abrogate this principle. Also, the fact that the parties executed the agreed substituted performance, regardless of any separate consideration, has no relevance. The actual performance of what one is legally bound to do is the same as the promise to do what one can be legally compelled to do. Because it is clear that consideration is essential to a valid accord and satisfaction, the judgment is affirmed with costs.

Analysis:

This case is a classic example of the pre-existing duty rule. Early contract law recognized that if two parties have an existing agreement to do something, they are already legally compelled to carry out their respective responsibilities. A subsequent agreement in which a party merely promises to do what was already required of that party under the original contract does not impose a detriment on that party. Therefore, the subsequent agreement is essentially based on illusory consideration. The pre-existing duty rule is most often implicated when parties try to modify their prior contract. These modifications are usually unilateral requiring only one party to modify performance. Therefore, in order to make a modification of a contract enforceable, the modification must be based on separate consideration. At first glance, this rule may seem awkward. Why interfere with the free will of the contracting parties if they each agree to modify their original contract? However, early contract law decided that the requirement of consideration also provides a benefit to parties in making a modification. The requirement of consideration in this situation serves to ensure that the parties adequately bargain, deliberate, and consider the modification. If the parties do not incur any legal detriment in making the modification, they are less likely to think through the implications and the appropriateness of the modification. In this case, the defendants asked Levine (P) to accept less rent than was required by their original agreement. Because there was no additional consideration for this alleged modification, Levine (P) incurred no legal detriment. Levine (P), was still bound by contract to continue to lease the space to defendants and the modification did nothing to change this obligation. Therefore, the court refused to accept the defendants' argument. On the other hand, if the defendants sought the rent reduction and offered, as consideration, to renew their lease at the end of its terms, Levine's (P) obligation will have changed if he accepted the renewal. As a result, there may have been sufficient evidence for the court to consider whether the parties did agree to a modification.

THE MODIFICATION OF A CONTRACT FOR THE SALE OF GOODS DOES NOT REQUIRE CONSIDERATION TO BE ENFORCEABLE

Gross Valentino Printing Co. v. Clarke

(Printer) v. (Magazine Publisher)

120 Ill.App.3d 907, 76 Ill.Dec. 373, 458 N.E.2d 1027 (1983)

M E M O R Y G R A P H I C

Instant Facts

A magazine publisher entered into a contract with a printer to print his magazine, but the printer later increased the printing price.

Black Letter Rule

The modification of a contract for the sale of goods does not require consideration to be enforceable.

Case Vocabulary

BUSINESS COMPULSION: When a party wrongfully forces another to perform something at a time when financial restrictions limits that party's free will.
FUNGIBLE: An item that is generic, like other items in its class.
MOVANT: The person who makes a motion before the court.
REDRESS: Relief from injury or damages.

Procedural Basis: Appeal to the state appellate court of a trail court summary judgment in favor of the defendant.

Facts: In July 1979, Clarke (D), doing business as a magazine named Cinefantastique, agreed to have his magazine printed by Gross Valentino Printing Company (P) for $6,695. The parties later met to discuss the magazine's layout. According to Clarke (D), he brought the materials for printing the magazine to the Printing Company (P) on August 8, 1979. An agent of the Printing Company (P) told Clarke (D) that there were some problems with the layout, but that the layout problems could be handled "in house" with no change in price. Clarke (D) also testified that the Printing Company (P) on August 14, 1979 told him on the telephone that the printing costs were higher because the company had to "send the strippling out." Clarke (D) did not tell the Printing Company (P) that he wanted to find another printer for the job because he would not be able to meet his deadline and he was afraid that the company would not return his materials if he argued about the price. These materials were necessary for the printing of the magazine. Clarke (D) also stated that he received a letter from the Printing Company (P) showing the same work as originally agreed upon but with the price increased to $9,300. On August 30, 1979, Clarke (D) received the first 5,000 magazines from the Printing Company (P). Clarke (D) signed a purchase order showing a higher price and paid $4,650. After receiving the remaining 15,000 magazines, on October 28, 1979, Clarke (D) told the Printing Company (P) that he would not pay the price increase. The Printing Company (P) took Clarke (D) to court. Clarke (D) defended himself by arguing lack of consideration, fraudulent or innocent misrepresentation, and business compulsion. The Printing Company (P) moved for summary judgment with both sides filing their own depositions. The trial court granted summary judgment on Clarke's defenses of lack of consideration and business compulsion, and allowed Clarke (D) to amend his pleadings as to his defense of fraud. The Printing Company (P) renewed its summary judgment which the trial court granted, awarding the Printing Company (P) $5,116.20. Clarke (P) appealed.

Issue: Does a modification of a contract for the sale of goods require consideration in order to be legally enforceable?

Decision and Rationale: (Goldberg, J.) No. Since the Printing Company (P) was the movant for summary judgment, we will construe the facts most favorable to Clarke (D). The defense of lack of consideration for the modified contract will apply depending on whether this contract involved the sale of goods or the sale of services. The sales of goods are governed by the Uniform Commercial Code (UCC). Under UCC 2-209(1), the modification of a contract for the sale of goods does not require consideration. UCC 2-107 defines goods as "all things, including specially manufactured goods that are movable at the time of identification to the contract for sale." There is no case law in Illinois finding magazines to be "goods" for the purposes of the UCC. However, in Lake Wales Publishing Co., Inc. v. Florida Visitor, Inc., a court concluded that magazines were movable items and that any services provided by the printing company were directed to the production of the items. In the case at hand, we find that the primary subject of the contract was the tangible printed magazines and not printing services. Moreover, Clarke (D) admitted that he sought printers solely based on the lowest price estimate. This indicates that the printing services were "largely fungible or interchangeable" and were only incidental to the final product. Clarke's (D) cases cited to support his argument are not applicable because those cases required services of more "independent judgment, skill, and service than the contract" in this case. Therefore, the contract was governed by the UCC. As a result, the trial court was correct in striking the lack of consideration defense. Clarke (D) has also failed to allege facts to support his defense of business compulsion. Economic duress occurs when a party's free will is overcome by the other party's wrongdoing. Clarke (D) has not shown wrongdoing, how his free will was overcome or how legal redress for breach of the original contract would have been inadequate. The summary judgment in favor of the Printing Company (P) is affirmed.

Analysis:

The courts never universally accepted the pre-existing duty rule. As a result, exceptions to the rule arose. One such exception is where the parties modify a contract for the sale of goods. The rationale behind this rule is that modifications generally involve mere tweaking of the original contract because the parties encounter circumstances unforeseen by the original contract. As a result, parties should be allowed the flexibility, freedom, and utility of modifying their contracts without the hassle of making additional consideration. The Uniform Commercial Code adopted this point of view and abandoned the requirement of consideration for modifications. Therefore, in the case at hand, the key issue was whether Clarke (D) was buying a service or a "good" for purposes of the UCC. The court determined that the magazines were goods making the UCC rules applicable. It is worth noting that the case also illustrates the confusion that can arise where a contract involves an end product that requires skills and services for its production. Presumably, the outcome in this case would have been different if Clarke (P) merely contracted with the plaintiff only for composing the magazine's layout, leaving the actual printing to a third party. A better approach to take in this case would have been to differentiate the printing costs of the contract from the layout costs because Clarke (P) was clearly paying for both a service (layout design) and a good (a printed magazine). In fact, the Printing Company (P) specifically told Clarke (D) that it had to contract out to a third party to handle aspects of the layout, the sole reason for the increase in the costs. Since the increase in the costs was so clearly attributable to layout services, the court could have separated this out from the costs of actually printing the magazine. Instead, the court chose to create the legal fiction that the value of the printing services somehow outweighed the value of the layout services from Clarke's (D) point of view, thereby making the UCC applicable. In reality, the magazine was simply impossible to print without the layout services.

THE MODERN TREND IS AWAY FROM A RIGID APPLICATION OF THE PREEXISTING DUTY RULE

Angel v. Murray

(Concerned Citizens) v. (City Director of Finance)
113 R.I. 482, 322 A.2d 630 (1974)

M E M O R Y   G R A P H I C

Instant Facts

A garbageman contracted with the City for additional compensation because his route had an unexpectedly large increase in pickups.

Black Letter Rule

The preexisting duty rule does not prevent parties from modifying contracts when unexpected or unanticipated difficulties arise during the course of the performance of a contract, as long as the parties agree voluntarily.

Case Vocabulary

COERCION: Compulsion; constraint; compelling by force or threat.
EXECUTORY PROMISE: A promise that has not yet been performed by the promisor doing whatever act was promised.
PRAYER: The request contained in a bill in equity that the court will grant the process, aid, or relief which the complainant desires.
PREEXISTING DUTY RULE: A common law rule which holds that where a party does or promises to do what he or she is already legally obligated to do, there exists no sufficient consideration to support this new promise.

Procedural Basis: The defendants appeal from the trial justice's judgment in favor of the plaintiffs.

Facts: Maher (D) has provided the City with a refuse-collection service under a series of five-year contracts for almost twenty years. The latest of these contracts provided, among other things, that Maher (D) would receive $137,000 per year in return for collecting and removing all combustible and noncombustible waste materials generated within the city [who says garbageman isn't a lucrative profession?]. Three years later, Maher (D) requested an additional $10,000 per year from the city council because there had been a substantial increase in the cost of collection due to an unexpected and unanticipated increase of 400 new dwelling units. After a public meeting of the city council where Maher (D) explained in detail the reasons for his request and was questioned by members of the city council; the city council agreed to pay him an additional $10,000 for that year. Maher (D) made a similar request the next year for the same reasons, and the city council again agreed to pay an additional $10,000 for the year. Angel (P) and others brought this civil action against Murray (D), the Director of Finance of the City, and Maher (D). The trial justice found that each $10,000 payment was made in violation of law. He found that Maher (D) was not entitled to extra compensation, and entered a judgment ordering Maher (D) to repay the sum of $20,000 to the City. Maher (D) appeals.

Issue: Does the preexisting duty rule prevent parties from modifying contracts when unexpected or unanticipated difficulties arise during the course of the performance of a contract?

Decision and Rationale: (Roberts, C.J.) No. Although the preexisting duty rule has served a useful purpose insofar as it deters parties from using coercion and duress to obtain additional compensation, it has been widely criticized as a general rule of law. The modern trend appears to recognize the necessity that courts should enforce agreements modifying contracts when unexpected or unanticipated difficulties arise during the course of the performance of a contract, even though there is no consideration for the modification, as long as the parties agree voluntarily. Under the Uniform Commercial Code, section 2-209(1), which has been adopted by 49 states, an agreement modifying a contract for the sale of goods needs no consideration to be binding. Although at first blush this section appears to validate modifications obtained by coercion and duress, the comments to this section indicate that a modification under this section must meet the test of good faith imposed by the Code, and a modification obtained by extortion without a legitimate commercial reason is unenforceable. The modern trend away from a rigid application of the preexisting duty rule is reflected by section 89(a) of the American Law Institute's Restatement, Second, Law of Contracts. We believe that section 89(a) is the proper rule of law and find it applicable to the facts of this case. It not only prohibits modifications obtained by coercion, duress, or extortion but also fulfills society's expectation that agreements entered into voluntarily will be enforced by the courts. Section89(a), of course, does not compel a modification if the parties voluntarily agree and if (1) the promise modifying the original contract was made before the contract was fully performed on either side, (2) the underlying circumstances which prompted the modification were unanticipated by the parties, and (3) the modification is fair and equitable. Under the uncontradicted evidence presented in this case, we have no doubt that the City voluntarily agreed to modify the contract. We now turn our attention to the three criteria delineated above. First, the modification was made at a time when the contract had not been performed by either party. Second, although the contract provided that Maher (D) collect all refuse generated within the city, it appears this contract was premised on Maher's (D) past experience that the number of refuse-generating units would increase at a rate of 20 to 25 per year. Furthermore, the evidence is uncontradicted that the increase of 400 units went beyond any previous expectation. Clearly, the circumstances were unanticipated. Third, although the evidence does not indicate that it was a "substantial" increase, in light of this, we cannot say that the council's agreement to pay Maher (D) the $10,000 increase was not fair and equitable in the circumstances. The judgment appealed from is reversed, and the cause is remanded to the Superior Court for entry of judgment for Murray (D) and Maher (D).

Analysis:

It is generally held that a modification of a contract is itself a contract, which is unenforceable unless supported by consideration. The primary purpose of the preexisting duty rule is to prevent what has been referred to as the "hold-up game." An example of the hold-up game can be found in the area of construction contracts. Frequently, a contractor will refuse to complete work under an unprofitable contract unless he is awarded additional compensation. The courts have generally held that a subsequent agreement to award additional compensation is unenforceable if the contractor is only performing work which would have been required of him under the original contract. The courts will not enforce an agreement that has been procured by coercion or duress and will hold the parties to their original contract regardless of whether it is profitable or unprofitable. However, the courts have been reluctant to apply the preexisting duty rule when a party to a contract encounters unanticipated difficulties and the other party, not influenced by coercion or duress, voluntarily agrees to pay additional compensation for work already required to be performed under the contract. For example, the courts have found that the original contract was rescinded, abandoned, or waived.

A PROMISE MADE TO A PARTY AND RELIED ON TO THE DETRIMENT OF THAT PARTY CAN MAKE THE PROMISE ENFORCEABLE

Devecmon v. Shaw

(Nephew) v. (Uncle's Executor)
69 Md. 199, 14 A.464 (1888)

M E M O R Y G R A P H I C

Instant Facts

A nephew went to Europe after his uncle promised to reimburse all his expenses for the trip, but the uncle died before fulfilling this promise.

Black Letter Rule

A burden borne by a party based on the promise of another provides sufficient consideration to enforce that promise.

Case Vocabulary

BILL OF EXCEPTIONS: A written statement of any objections a party makes regarding trial court rulings, which establishes the record for the appellate court.
BILL OF PARTICULARS: A written statement of the cause of action against the defendant.
INDEBITATUS ASSUMPSIT: When a party in debt promises to do something in order have the debt paid off or discharged.
JUDGMENT BY DEFAULT: Where judgment is obtained against a party because the party did not appear in court to contest the action.

Procedural Basis: An appeal to the court of appeal of a trial court decision to exclude the defendant's offer of testimony.

Facts: John Semmes Devecmon (P) brought suit against the executors (D) of the deceased, John S. Comb, who was also Devecmon's uncle. Devecmon (P) lived for several years with his uncle's family and was also his clerk. The executors (D) [cried uncle] and Devecmon (P) won the judgment by default, and a jury was called on to calculate damages. Devecmon (P) offered testimony that the deceased requested that Devecmon (P) take a trip to Europe and that the deceased promised he would reimburse and repay to Devecmon (P) the entire cost of the trip. In 1878, Devecmon (P) took the trip to Europe, spending his own money, but his uncle died without reimbursing him. The court refused to allow this testimony, and Devecmon (P) appealed.

Issue: Can a promise made to a party and relied on to the detriment of that party make the promise enforceable?

Decision and Rationale: (Bryan, J.) Yes. The testimony would have shown that Devecmon (P) incurred a detriment at the request of the deceased and upon an express promise by him to reimburse Devecmon (P) for the trip. A burden undertaken at the request of another party is sufficient consideration for a promise to pay. If the law were otherwise, injury could be inflicted by inducing persons to make expenditures beyond their means. This is distinctly different from a promise to give a present or to give a gratuitous service. While Devecmon (P) spent his own money, this is irrelevant given that he was induced to spend his money in that manner, and not in any other way, based on the deceased's promise. If the promise is not carried out the expenditure will have been effected by false pretense. Devecmon (P), in this case, fulfilled his part of the contract, and nothing remained to be done except the deceased's repayment. The evidence should have been admitted. The judgment is reversed and a new trial ordered.

Analysis:

This case is a classic illustration of the doctrine of justifiable reliance. While donative promises are generally not enforceable because there is no bargained for exchange, there are limited exceptions to the rule. On of the major exceptions is where a unilateral promise affects the behavior of the person to whom the promise is made. If the promise is of the kind that changes the behavior of the promisee to the promisee's detriment, the unilateral promise becomes enforceable. However, such enforcement will only take place where the promise is of the kind that a promisee should reasonably rely on. If a homeless man promises a stranger a fortune, the stranger would be unreasonable to rely on the man's promise, thereby making it unenforceable. In the case at hand, Devecmon (P) wanted to testify that his uncle told him that, if he went to Europe, he would pay for his entire trip. In fact, the uncle may have insisted that Devecmon (P) go to Europe. In reliance of the uncle's promise, Devecmon (P) went to Europe, hoping it would fall on his uncle's pocket book and not his own. The court appropriately pointed out that if Devecmon's (P) claims were true but the uncle did not reimburse him, Devecmon's (P) expenses were made under false pretenses. The only way to avoid this injustice is to make the promise enforceable.

Feinberg v. Pfeiffer Co.

(Retired Former Employee) v. (Former Employer)
322 S.W.2d 163 (Missouri Court of Appeals, 1959).

MEMORY GRAPHIC

Instant Facts

After promising that the company would pay a retirement benefit of $200 per month for the rest of a former employee's life, and actually paying the money for several years, the company decided to cease making payments and the former employee sued.

Black Letter Rule

A promise that the maker knows is likely to be relied upon by the promisee and is so relied upon is enforceable under a theory of promissory estoppel.

Case Vocabulary

PAST CONSIDERATION: The performance of an act or services in the past: past consideration will not suffice to make a contract legally enforceable.
PROMISSORY ESTOPPEL: In contracts, a doctrine that makes an otherwise unenforceable gratuitous promise enforceable when the promisee has relied upon the promise and thereby incurred injury.

Procedural Basis: Appeal from a lower court decision finding a contract enforceable despite a lack of consideration.

Facts: Feinberg (P) began working for Pfeiffer (D) in 1910 when she was 17 years old. By 1947 she had retained the position of bookkeeper, office manager and assistant treasurer and owned 70 shares of stock in Pfeiffer (D). She periodically received dividends on the stock and often received yearly bonuses in addition to her salary for her good performance. On December 27, 1947 there was a meeting of Pfeiffer's (D) board of directors. At the meeting, the board adopted a resolution that provided that the company would increase Feinberg's (P) monthly salary to $400 and that she would be provided with retirement benefits of $200 per month for the rest of her life when she chose to retire. The resolution specified that the retirement benefits were being provided for Feinberg's (P) future security and that it was hoped that she would continue on as an employee. The resolution further acknowledged Feinberg's (P) many years of faithful service and provided that she could retire whenever she saw fit. Two board members visited Feinberg (P) at her home that day and informed her about the terms and passage of the resolution. She later testified that she had no advance knowledge that such a provision was being contemplated and that she would have continued in her employment whether or not the resolution had been adopted. Feinberg (P) did not have an employment contract and her employment was terminable at will by either herself or the company. Nevertheless, Feinberg (P) continued to work for Pfeiffer (D) for another 2 years before retiring. Pfeiffer (D) promptly began paying her $200 on the first of every month. The president of Pfeiffer died in 1949 and was replaced by his wife. His wife continued to sign the checks to Feinberg (P) each month but "fussed" about doing so. She retired in 1953 due to illness and her son-in-law took over as president. The son-in-law employed a new accounting firm, which in turn questioned the validity of the monthly payments to Feinberg (P). Upon the advice of the company attorney and the accountants, the son-in-law decided to start sending only $100 per month in April of 1956. Feinberg (P) declined to cash the check for the reduced amount and sued on the alleged contractual obligation to pay her $200 per month until her death. The trial court found in favor of Feinberg (P) and Pfeiffer (D) appealed. Pfeiffer (D) complained that the lower court had erred by admitting testimony that by the time Pfeiffer (D) stopped sending the checks, Feinberg (P) was unable to work because of a cancerous condition. The appeals court rejected the claim of error on the ground that Feinberg's (P) health was not the basis of the lower court's decision. Pfeiffer (D) also alleged various error in the trial court's findings of fact as to the sufficiency of the evidence to support the existence of a legally binding contract.

Issue: Will reliance upon an executory promise suffice to create a legally enforceable contract by means of promissory estoppel?

Decision and Rationale: (Doerner, C.) Yes. Pfeiffer (D) complains that the evidence was insufficient to find that Feinberg (P) would not have retired when she did were it not for the fact that she relied upon Pfeiffer's (D) promise to pay retirement benefits. However, there was extensive testimony from Feinberg (P) that she did in fact rely upon Pfeiffer's (D) promise to pay benefits when she made her decision to retire. She admitted that she could have worked for longer, but felt comfortable retiring when she did because of the promise to pay her $200 per month thereafter until her death. There was sufficient evidence below to support the trial court's findings of fact. We now address Pfeiffer's (D) main complaints and the crux of the issue in the instant case. Pfeiffer (D) argues that the resolution was not a legally enforceable contract because there was no consideration given. Pfeiffer (D) points out that the resolution was adopted to acknowledge Feinberg's (P) past services and was not contingent on her agreeing to stay and work in the future. We agree, and Feinberg (P) concedes, that past consideration is not sufficient to make a promise legally enforceable. If all that were present in this case was Feinberg's (P) past services, we would agree that there was no legally binding contract to pay the retirement benefits. However, Feinberg (P) contends that her change in position (retirement) and her loss of opportunity to continue in gainful employment occurred because of her reliance on Pfeiffer's (D) promise to pay her the monthly stipend. Section 90 of the Restatement of Contracts provides that "a promise which the promisor should reasonably expect to induce action or forbearance . . . on the part of the promisee and which does induce such action or forbearance is binding if injustice can be avoided only by enforcement of the promise." This doctrine is known as promissory estoppel and is commonly seen as either a substitute for consideration or a species of legal consideration. Promissory estoppel is sometimes used to enforce contracts lacking any consideration. Here in Missouri, the same result is reached without abandoning the concept of consideration. We find, under several different theories, that promissory estoppel is another species of consideration. Pfeiffer (D) argues that there was no act or forbearance induced by its promise to pay Feinberg (P) retirement benefits. We disagree. We believe that Pfeiffer's (D) promise to pay the retirement benefits induced Feinberg (P) to retire when she did in light of the fact that she testified that she was able to and would have continued to work for Pfeiffer (D) absent the promise of future retirement benefits. When promissory estoppel is used to enforce a promise, the promise is enforced only to the extent that it is necessary to prevent injustice. It is common knowledge that it is almost impossible for a woman Feinberg's (P) age to find meaningful employment. She obviously retired from Pfeiffer (D) in reliance upon its promise to pay her an annuity or pension. Affirmed.

Analysis:

Generally, in order to form a legally enforceable contract, there must be an offer, an acceptance and a validating device. As you have seen, the law of Contracts primarily recognizes consideration as the desired form of validating device. Consideration is also by far the most common validating device, but there are instances where a promise will be enforced even absent valid consideration. The instant case demonstrates a validating device that can be used to enforce contractual obligations even when the contract fails for lack of consideration. If a promisee can show detrimental reliance upon the promise, then the promise is sometimes enforceable by promissory estoppel. The theory behind promissory estoppel is that the promisor should not be allowed to get out of the promise simply because there was no consideration given when he has induced the promisee to act in reliance upon the promise. Simply put, a person shouldn't be able to back out of a promise when he knows that the promisee will act upon the certainty of the promise being fulfilled. [No reneging!] But promissory estoppel is more like an equitable remedy than a legal one. Courts use it to prevent injustice, or unjust enrichment. Accordingly, some commentators feel that promissory estoppel, or reliance, is a less desirable form of validating device than is consideration. The maxim seems to be that you must first try to establish consideration to make the promise legally enforceable to its fullest extent. Only if consideration fails would you fall back upon reliance and promissory estoppel.

Hayes v. Plantations Steel Co.

(Employee) v. (Employer)
438 A.2d 1091 (1982)

M E M O R Y   G R A P H I C

Instant Facts

A retiree gets his retirement payments cancelled after the new management of his former employer decides not to make any further payments.

Black Letter Rule

Promissory estoppel is inapplicable where the promise does not actually induce reliance.

Case Vocabulary

IMPLIED-IN-FACT CONTRACT: Where there is no express agreement between the parties, but the facts and circumstances between the parties makes it reasonable to infer the existence of a contract under law.

Procedural Basis: An appeal to the state supreme court of a trial court decision in favor of the defendant.

Facts: Edward J. Hayes (P) was an employee of Plantations Steel Company (D) from 1947 to 1972. One week before his retirement, Hayes (P) had a conversation with the son of the Steel Company's (D) co-founder, Hugo R. Mainelli. Mainelli, Jr. told Hayes (P) that the company "would take care of him" during his retirement, but no mention was made of how much Hayes (P) would receive. From 1973 until 1976, Hayes (P) received an annual sum of $5,000 from the Steel Company (D). The payments were not part of any formal pension plan that Hayes (P) was eligible for, and there was no authorization for the payments by the company's board of directors or shareholders. Mainelli, Jr. testified that his father authorized the first payment in appreciation of Hayes' (P) many years of service to the company, and it was implied that the payments would continue on an annual basis as long as Mainelli was around. Mainelli also testified that he would visit Hayes (P) each year during his retirement in which Hayes (P) would thank Mainelli for the previous check and asked how long they would continue so he could plan accordingly for his retirement. In 1976-77, the Steel Company (D) was taken over by the family of Alexander DiMartino, who was also a co-founder of the company. The new management [decided to clean house and] terminated the annual payments to Hayes (P). Hayes (P) brought suit in 1977. The trial court found in favor of Hayes (P) on the basis that an implied-in-fact contract existed and on a theory of promissory estoppel. Specifically, the trial court, without a jury, found that Mainelli, Jr.'s statement to Hayes (P) about taking care of him and the four annual payments constituted an implied-in-fact contract. In addition, the trial court found that Hayes (P) incurred detrimental reliance by voluntarily retiring in reliance upon the promise made by Mainelli. The Steel Company (D) appealed.

Issue: Can promissory estoppel be applied where the promise does not actually induce reliance?

Decision and Rationale: (Shea, J.) No. While great deference is normally given to the factual findings of the trial judge, those findings can be overturned when clearly wrong. After a careful review of the record, we conclude that the trial court erred in its factual findings. Based on the evidence, we find that Hayes (P) formed his intent to retire before Mainelli made his promise of a pension. As a result, there was no implied-in-fact contract. Implied contracts require consideration. Valid consideration must be bargained for and "must induce the return act or promise." Therefore, any alleged consideration cannot be given without reference or without response to the promise. In this case, Hayes (P) announced his retirement before Mainelli made his promise. Hayes (P) acted on his own free will to make his decision to retire. The Steel Company (D), during Hayes' (P) years of employment made no promise of a pension to encourage him to remain with the company. Hayes (P) alternatively argues a theory of promissory estoppel. For the same reason, this theory fails as well. Promissory estoppel involves a promise which the promisor should reasonably expect to induce the promisee to incur detrimental reliance and which does induce such reliance. Such a promise becomes enforceable if injustice can only be avoided by its enforcement. Here, the promise did not induce Hayes' (P) to incur detrimental reliance. Hayes (P) decided to retire without reference to Mainelli's promise. While the facts of this case are very similar to that of *Feinberg v. Pfeiffer*, in that case, the plaintiff clearly retired in reliance of the company's promise. Here, it would be unreasonable to infer such reliance given that Hayes (P) had given notice of his intention to retire some seven months in advance. Therefore, it is impossible to find that a promise made only a week before Hayes' (P) actual retirement induced him to make this decision. Moreover, each year he received his post-retirement check, Hayes (P) asked if the payments would continue. This is evidence that Hayes (P) had no certainty that the payments would continue. Reversed and remanded.

Analysis:

As pointed out by the court, this case is very similar to the prior case of *Feinberg v. Pfeiffer*. As in the prior case, the promise was of a kind that the promisor should expect the other party to rely on. The only difference between these cases is whether the promisee actually did rely on the promise. Because the doctrine of promissory estoppel does not require a bargained for exchange based on consideration, the promise must have had some effect on the promisee to justify its enforcement. This is necessary because, without any actual reliance, the promisee has suffered no detriment. If there is no detriment, the promisee has suffered no real harm, so there would be no need for the law to remedy any injustice. In a sense, the reliance serves as a substitute for the consideration. Still, courts have been reluctant to view promissory estoppel as a direct offshoot of the concept of consideration. Instead, it has developed on its own as a separate doctrine. In the case at hand, the court found that the Steel Company's (D) promise to "take care" of Hayes (P) did not cause him to suffer any detriment. He did not retire because of the promise nor did he forgo other employment because of the promise. In fact, Hayes (P) seemed to have some doubt as to whether or not he could expect the payments to continue indefinitely. Therefore, there was no detrimental reliance on the Steel Company's (D) promise.

Drennan v. Star Paving Co.

(General Contractor) v. (Paving Subcontractor)

Supreme Court of California, En Bank, 1958. 51 Cal.2d 409, 333 P.2d 757

MEMORY GRAPHIC

Instant Facts

A general contractor wants to enforce a subcontractor's bid on a construction job.

Black Letter Rule

An offer may not be freely revocable if the offeree has substantially relied on the offer.

Case Vocabulary

PROMISSORY ESTOPPEL: Justice Traynor does not identify it as such, but the rule which he cites from Section 90 of the Restatement [First] of Contracts is also known as the doctrine of promissory estoppel. As with other estoppel doctrine, the promisor is precluded from claiming that its promise is not binding if the elements apply.

Procedural Basis: Appeal from a trial court judgement for the plaintiff in a breach of contract action.

Facts: Drennan (P), a general contractor, was bidding on a construction job for the Monte Vista School. As usual, he received the bids of his subcontractors by telephone on the day before his bid was due. Star Paving Co. (Star Paving) (D) was one of those subcontractors. Its estimator called Drennan (P) and submitted a $7,131.60 bid for the paving work on the contract. This bid was included in Drennan's (P) successful bid for the job. Drennan (P) was required to guarantee his bid with a 10% bond -- over $30,000. When he stopped by Star Paving's (D) offices after his bid was accepted, its engineer told him that there had been a mistake. In fact, they refused to do the job for less than $15,000. Drennan (P) had no alternative but to find another paving company. After accepting new bids, he hired the lowest bidder at $10,948.60. He also sued Star Paving (D) for breach of contract. The trial court found that Star Paving (D) made a definite offer to do the paving work for $7,131.60. The court also found that Drennan (P) relied on this offer when he calculated his own bid and when he listed Star Paving (D) as the subcontractor. As a result, the trial court found for Drennan (P) and awarded him $3,817 in damages -- the difference between Star Paving's (D) bid and the price charged by their replacement. Star Paving (D) appeals.

Issue: Is an offer freely revocable after the offeree has relied on it?

Decision and Rationale: (Traynor) No. Star Paving (D) makes three claims in this case. The first is that their offer was freely revocable, and was in fact revoked by the time Drennan (P) communicated his acceptance. However, according to Section 90 of the Restatement [First] of Contracts, a binding agreement can be created under the following circumstances: 1) a promise is made which should reasonably be expected to induce action or forbearance of a definite and substantial character on the part of the promisee, 2) such action or forbearance is induced, and 3) injustice can be avoided only by enforcing the promise. Star Paving (D) could not justifiably revoke its offer if these elements were satisfied. Star Paving's (D) bid was reasonably expected to induce action of a definite and substantial character on the part of Drennan (P). Specifically, Star Paving (D) submitted its bid in the hopes that it would be offered the job as the low bidder. It knew that Drennan (P) would have to submit its bid along with the others for this to happen. In addition, it knew that Drennan (P) was bound by the overall bid that *he* submitted. Finally, its bid was not submitted with any language suggesting that it was freely revocable before acceptance. Despite this, there remains the question of whether consideration was required to keep Star Paving's (D) offer open. Section 45 of the Restatement [First] of Contracts notes that consideration, in the form of part performance, can bind the offeror to a unilateral contract [an offer which requests performance as acceptance]. However, Section 45 also suggests that justifiable reliance on an offer may be sufficient to bind the offeror. Implicit in this suggestion is that reliance can substitute for consideration in cases where injustice would result from a strict application of the rule. As a result, Star Paving (D) should be bound by its offer. For the reasons stated above, the judgement is affirmed.

Analysis:

This case is considered a good example of how a court can avoid unfairness to an offeree. In this case, Justice Traynor finds that the offer was accepted prior to revocation. He does this by permitting Drennan's (P) reliance on the subcontractor's bid to substitute as consideration for keeping the offer open. Normally, the bargain theory states that consideration is something of value which the offeror sought when he made the offer. However, Star Paving (D) knew full well that Drennan (P) would rely on its bid. In addition, it stood to benefit from Drennan's reliance. As a result, it would not be fair to let Star Paving revoke its offer after Drennan (P) relied to his detriment. This is the unfairness to which the court responds. Justice Traynor uses existing doctrine to circumvent the normal rule in order to achieve a desirable result.

THE LISTING OF A SUBCONTRACTOR IN THE CONTRACTOR'S PRIME BID IS NOT AN IMPLIED ACCEPTANCE OF THE SUBCONTRACTOR'S BID

Southern California Acoustics Co., Inc. v. C.V. Holder, Inc.

(Subcontractor) v. (General Contractor)

71 Cal.2d 719, 79 Cal.Rptr. 319, 456 P.2d 975 (1969)

M E M O R Y   G R A P H I C

Instant Facts

A subcontractor assumed that its bid to a contractor was accepted after reading a newspaper article about the contractor that listed the subcontractor in the contractor's prime bid.

Black Letter Rule

The listing of a subcontractor in the contractor's prime bid is not an implied acceptance of the subcontractor's bid.

Case Vocabulary

WRIT OF MANDAMUS: An order from a court of superior jurisdiction mandating that the court below perform a particular action.

Procedural Basis: An appeal to the state supreme court of a trial court decision in favor of the defendant.

Facts: On November 24, 1965, Southern California Acoustics Co., Inc. (P), a subcontractor, submitted a bid to C.V. Holder, Inc. (D1), a contractor, for the furnishing and installation of acoustic tile. Holder (D1) requested the bid from Southern (P) in order to make its own bid for a prime contract to the Los Angeles Unified School District (D2) for a public construction project. As required by state law, Holder (D1) listed Southern (P) as a subcontractor in its bid to the School District (D2). The School District (D2) on December 9, 1965 awarded the prime contract to Holder (D1) based on its bid. A local trade newspaper, which is received by subcontractors, reported that Holder was awarded the contract and also printed the name of subcontractors listed in Holder's (D1) bid, including Southern (P). Southern (P) read the report and assumed that its bid to Holder (D1) was accepted. Southern (P) refrained from bidding on other contracts in order to remain within its "bonding limits." Sometime between December 27, 1965 and January 10, 1966, Holder (D1) sought permission from School District (D2) to substitute another acoustical tile subcontractor because Holder (D1) accidentally listed Southern's (P) bid in place of the intended subcontractor. The School District (P) consented. Southern (P) sought a writ of mandamus to force the School District (D2) to revoke its consent to substitute acoustic subcontractors. The School District (D2) demurred, which the trial court sustained, and the case was dismissed. Southern (P) did not appeal, but filed the present action against Holder (D1) and the School District (D2).

Issue: Can the listing of a subcontractor in the contractor's prime bid be an implied acceptance of the subcontractor's bid?

Decision and Rationale: (Traynor, J.) No. There was no contract between the parties, because Holder (D1) did not accept Southern's (P) offer. There also was no course of dealing between the parties to which silence would constitute an acceptance of Southern's (P) offer. The listing of subcontractors in the contractor's prime bid is compelled by state law and cannot be seen as an expression of acceptance.

Analysis:

This case handles the issue of whether reliance was justified or reasonable. While a bid can become enforceable if it induces detrimental reliance, the plaintiff must have reasonably incurred any such harm. The doctrine of promissory estoppel, again, seeks to correct any possible injustice. However, no injustice can take place if the promisee incurs harm that he or she should have known better to avoid. In this case, while Southern (P) clearly relied on the newspaper article by not taking on other projects, the court found this reliance was unreasonable. There was no explicit acceptance of Southern's (P) sub-bid and no prior agreement that silence would constitute acceptance. While a listing of a subcontractor in the contractor's bid in a newspaper would normally justify reliance, in this case the publishing of the contract award was mandated by law. This was something that Southern (P) should have been aware of, thereby negating any reason to rely on it as proof that its sub-bid was accepted.

Sparks v. Gustafson

(Building Manager) v. (Estate)
750 P.2d 338 (1988)

M E M O R Y   G R A P H I C

Instant Facts

Without compensation for his services, a building manager continued to manage and maintain his friend's building after his friend's death.

Black Letter Rule

A person is unjustly enriched when he or she receives a benefit from another for services or goods for which one would normally expect to be paid.

Case Vocabulary

INEQUITABLE: Unfair.
LIEN: Where a creditor stakes a claim against the debtor's property for the payment of that debt.

Procedural Basis: Appeal to the state supreme court of a trial court decision in favor of the plaintiff.

Facts: Robert Sparks, Sr., and Ernie Gustafson (P) were personal friends and business associates for many years. In 1980, Sparks purchased a one-half interest in the Nome Center Building. Gustafson (P) managed Sparks' building free of charge. Sparks, Sr. died on March 1, 1981, but Gustafson (P) continued to manage the building by collecting rents on behalf of Sparks' Estate (D). Gustafson (P) also solicited new tenants, and sometimes paid utilities, insurance, mortgage, repairs, maintenance, and improvement costs out of his own pocket when rental income fell short. However, Gustafson (P) did not document all of his own expenditures in his monthly expense reports to the Estate (D). The building operated at a loss, and the Estate's (D) deposit of $10,000 in the Nome Center's account did not cover all of the building's expenses. In February 1982, the Estate (D) tried to sell the building to Gustafson (P), but the terms could not be agreed upon. A year later, the Estate (D) sold the building to a third party, after which Gustafson (P) stopped managing the building. On July 14, 1983, Gustafson (P) brought suit against the Estate (D), run by Sparks Sr.'s son, Robert J. Sparks, Jr. [, no doubt causing Sparks, Sr. to roll in his grave]. The suit claimed that the Estate (D) breached an oral agreement to sell the building to Gustafson (P), and the suit was later amended to include a claim for compensation for Gustafson's (P) services and expenses in managing the building on a lien theory. The Estate (D) counterclaimed for an accounting of the building's income and expenses. The trial court found no enforceable lien, but compensated Gustafson (P) $65,706.07 for his services and contributions to the building. The Estate (D) appealed.

Issue: Is a person entitled to compensation for conferring a benefit to another of a kind that one would normally expect to be paid for?

Decision and Rationale: (Matthews, J.) Yes. Unjust enrichment occurs where the defendant receives a benefit from the plaintiff and it would be inequitable for the defendant to enjoy the benefit without compensating the plaintiff for its value. A benefit is conferred if it constitutes some interest in money, land, or possessions; consists of valuable services; satisfies the debt of another; or adds to the other person's advantage in any way. Unquestionably, Gustafson (P) conferred a benefit on the Estate (D). However, even where a defendant has received a benefit, compensation is required only where it would be just or equitable given the circumstances. Therefore, compensation is not required where the benefit was given as a gratuity with no expectation of payment. A good discussion of what constitutes gratuitous intent is in *Kershaw v. Tracy Collins Bank & Trust* [where the court found that the services provided to a widow, such as driving, buying groceries, doing minor repair work, and running errands, did not require compensation because they were done in friendship and were the sort of work that would be expected from a long time friend.] In this case, Gustafson's (P) close relationship with the decedent and the fact that he never requested compensation suggest that he was acting gratuitously. However, Gustafson (P) performed services that were not of the type one would ordinarily expect to receive as a gratuity. Gustafson (P) spent approximately five hours a day conducting extensive business services for the Estate's building. These were services for which a person would normally be paid. We, therefore, agree that the Estate was unjustly enriched and agree with the trial court.

Analysis:

This case is a classic illustration of the concept of unjust enrichment. Unjust enrichment, like promissory estoppel is another form of quasi-contract. These cases do not involve any bargaining or mutual agreements. Therefore, consideration is not an issue. Instead, the issue is whether a party has unfairly derived a benefit from another. However, not all such situations require court-imposed compensation. A person who gives another an expensive item as a gift cannot later sue claiming that the recipient was unjustly enriched. This is due to the fact that the giver was

Sparks v. Gustafson (Continued)

making a gratuitous gesture which the recipient knows is a gift between friends. In the case at hand, the court focused on the issue of whether Gustafson (P) intended to make his services as building manager as a gift. However, despite the fact that there was significant evidence of a longtime friendship and that Gustafson (P) never requested compensation, the court found unjust enrichment. It did so by reasoning that Gustafson's (P) services were of the kind that would be normally paid for. This illustrates the tendency of courts to consider not just the intentions and motivations of the person conferring the benefit but also of the recipient. The court found unjust enrichment not so much because there was no evidence that Gustafson (P) was being gratuitous. The key for the court was its finding that Gustafson's services were not of the type that one would give as a gift. In a sense, this is really saying that the defendant should have known better because the defendant was clearly taking advantage of Gustafson's (P) kindness and generosity.

Mills v. Wyman

(Good Samaritan) v. (Father)
3 Pick. (20 Mass.) 207 (1825)

MEMORY GRAPHIC

Instant Facts

A father reneged on a promise to compensate a person for taking care of his dying son.

Black Letter Rule

A moral obligation is not always sufficient consideration to enforce a promise.

Case Vocabulary

ASSUMPSIT: An undertaking or promise.
FORO CONSCIENTIAE: Court of conscience.
MERCANTILE: Relating to the business of merchants.
QUID PRO QUO: Something in exchange for something.

Procedural Basis: Appeal to the state supreme court of a trial court decision in favor of the defendant.

Facts: Levi Wyman, the 25-year old son of the defendant, Wyman (D), returned from a voyage at sea, destitute and ill. Levi was taken in by Mills (P) in Hartford, Connecticut where Mills (P) took care of Levi from February 5 to February 20, 1821, when Levi died. On February 24, Wyman (D) wrote a letter to Mills (P) in which he promised to compensate Mills (P) for the expenses he incurred while taking care of his dying son. However, Wyman (D) never followed through on his promise. The court of common pleas found that there was no consideration for Wyman's (D) promise, and dismissed the action. Mills (P) appealed.

Issue: Can a moral obligation be sufficient to justify the enforcement of a promise?

Decision and Rationale: (Parker, J.) No. The rule that a promise made without any consideration cannot be enforced is universal and exceptions cannot be made in some circumstances where the failure to perform the promise may be "disgraceful." This is an unfortunate reality of any "human system of legislation." The promise made in this case was unsupported by consideration. Wyman's (D) son was no longer a member of his father's family, and Mills (P) took care of him without any influence made by his father, Wyman (D). Instead, after learning of Mills (P) kindness, Wyman (D) had a "transient feeling of gratitude" and promised to pay the expenses that Mills (P) had incurred. Cases that have enforced moral obligations involved some pre-existing obligation. These cases often involve promises to enforce debts already barred by the statute of limitations, debts incurred by minors, and debts of bankrupts. In all these cases, the promises were based on pre-existing equitable obligations that "natural justice" would require enforcement, but the legislature has deemed not worth the effort of enforcement. Taken to its fullest extent, any moral obligation could provide sufficient reason to support a promise. After all, if a man ought to do something, then why not have the law make him do it. However, the law has relegated most of these moral obligations to the "tribunal of conscience." There may be a moral obligation for an affluent son to help his destitute father or vice versa. Nevertheless, while this may serve a great interest of society, such obligations are not enforced because the "wisdom of the social law does not impose sanctions upon them." As a result, promises are only enforceable where the party making the promise benefits from it or causes detriment to the person promised. While a legal obligation is always sufficient consideration to enforce a promise, a father has no obligation to pay a debt incurred by a son who has attained manhood and independence from his father, and any promise to pay such a debt has no legally binding force. Cases concerning mercantile contracts under seal are not applicable to this case because such contracts are considerations in of themselves and are grounded in mercantile law. Judgment affirmed with costs for the defendant.

Analysis:

This case stands for the proposition that a moral obligation is not always sufficient to enforce a promise. In understanding this case, keep in mind that the term "moral obligation" is also used to refer to a pre-existing duty. If two parties enter a contract, they form a duty to follow the terms of the contract. They also create a moral duty for the parties to carry out the contract. Thus, if the contract is valid and supported by consideration, a court will enforce the "moral obligation' of the parties to follow its terms. However, not all moral obligations will be enforced by the courts. In the case at hand, there was no contract. There was no promise resulting in detrimental reliance. There was no unjust enrichment because the person who was benefited from Mills' (P) care, the son, died. The father did not benefit in a material fashion from Mills' (P) acts because his son was an adult, independent of the care of his family. However, the father obviously did benefit in a non-material sense in that his son was cared for in his dying days. Surely this had some emotional value for the father. As a result, it can be argued that the father had a moral obligation to compensate Mills (P). His promise to do so would further lend credence to the idea that Mills (P) deserved compensation. Nevertheless, this was a moral obligation that the court would not enforce. Absent any of the traditional means that would make the father's promise enforceable through the morality of contract law, the court steered away from enforcing the morality of the heart.

WHEN A MATERIAL BENEFIT IS CONFERRED TO ANOTHER WITHOUT REQUEST, THE BENEFICIARY'S SUBSEQUENT PROMISE TO PAY FOR THE BENEFIT IS SUFFICIENT CONSIDERATION

Webb v. McGowin

(Life-Saving Employee) v. (Executor of Saved Person)
(1935) 27 Ala. App. 82; 168 So. 196

MEMORY GRAPHIC

Instant Facts

Joe Webb (P) saved Greeley McGowin (D) from death or serious bodily harm during Webb's (P) course of employment, for which McGowin (D) agreed to pay Webb (P) $15 every two weeks for the remainder of Webb's (P) life.

Black Letter Rule

When a material benefit is conferred to another without request, the beneficiary's subsequent promise to pay for the benefit is sufficient consideration.

Case Vocabulary

ASSUMPSIT: In contracts this refers to oral promises made without written record as evidence of the promise.
DEMURRER: In court pleadings this is a claim that even if all of the allegations are accepted as true, the party claiming the allegations still has not shown a legal basis for recovery.

Procedural Basis: An appeal by Webb (P) from a judgment of nonsuit at trial court.

Facts: Webb's (P) work required him to clear the upper floor of a lumber mill by dropping heavy pine blocks from the upper floor of the mill to the ground below. During one such occasion, on August 3, 1925, while Webb (P) was working within the scope of his employment, Webb (P) diverted a 75-pound block, that he was clearing, from dropping on Greeley McGowin (D) below, by falling with the block to the floor below. Webb (P) was successful in preventing any injuries to McGowin (D). However, Webb (P) received serious bodily injuries, resulting in his right leg being broken, the heel of his right foot torn off and his right arm broken. He was badly crippled for life and rendered unable to do physical or mental labor. On September 1, 1925, McGowin (D) agreed to pay Webb (P) $15 every two weeks from the time he sustained his injuries to and during the remainder of Webb's life. It was agreed that McGowin (D) would pay this amount to Webb (P) for Webb's maintenance. McGowin paid the sum so agreed up until McGowin's (D) death on January 1, 1934, at which time they were discontinued. Webb (P) sued McGowin's (D) estate for the balance of the payments due.

Issue: Is there sufficient consideration where a material benefit is conferred to another without request and the beneficiary subsequently promises to pay for that benefit?

Decision and Rationale: (Bricken) Yes. Any holding that saving a man from death or grievous bodily harm is not a material benefit sufficient to uphold a subsequent promise to pay for the service, necessarily rests on the assumption that saving life and preservation of the body from harm have only sentimental value. Had McGowin (D) been accidentally poisoned and a physician, without his knowledge or request, had administered an antidote, a subsequent promise by McGowin (D) to pay the physician would have been valid. As the value of a physician's services, damages in a personal injury action, and the payment of life insurance all illustrate, life and the preservation of health have material value. Likewise McGowin's (D) promise to compensate Webb (P) for saving him from death or grievous bodily injury is valid and enforceable. It is also well settled that a moral obligation can be sufficient consideration where the promisor has received a material benefit even though there was no original duty on the promisor. While some authorities hold that a moral obligation is not sufficient consideration absent some pre-existing duty, there is a qualification where the promisor, after receiving a material benefit, makes a promise to compensate for the services received. In those cases, the subsequent promise raises the presumption that those services were originally received at the promisor's request. McGowin's (D) promise, thus, raises the presumption that Webb's (P) actions in saving McGowin (D) was done at his request. The facts also show that Webb (P), in saving McGowin (D), became crippled for life. Webb's (P) injury and McGowin's (D) benefit were sufficient consideration for the agreement to pay. The facts also show that Webb's (P) services were not gratuitous because of McGowin's (D) subsequent promise. The trial court erred in granting the demurrer, and the case is reversed and remanded.

Concurrence: (Sanford, J.) While the questions of law in this case may very well make Webb's (P) claim doubtful, I follow the principle announced by Chief Justice Marshall in *Hoffman v. Porter*, "I do not think that law ought to be separated from justice, where it is at most doubtful."

Analysis:

This case would appear to be in opposition to Mills v. Wyman, but there is an important distinction. In this case, the person who actually received the plaintiff's services was still alive. In *Mills v. Wyman*, the dying son who received the plaintiff's services did not survive, and the subsequent promise was made by the father, who really obtained no *material* benefit from the plaintiff's services. Nevertheless, the holding of this case places it in the minority because it specifically finds that consideration exists where a material benefit is conferred to another without request and the beneficiary subsequently promises to pay for that benefit. Most courts do not enforce a promise made after the promisor receives an unrequested benefit on the rationale that no consideration existed. There is merit to this argument given that such situations are not the product of a bargained for exchange in which both parties took some thought in figuring out their respective duties and obligations. In the case at hand, it hardly seems likely that Webb (P), in the split second before he acted to save McGowin (D), paused and asked McGowin (D), "Ok, here's the deal, I'll save your life and you'll pay me 30 bucks a month for the rest of my life." There was no bargaining over the value of McGowin's life (D). Yet, the court somehow justified its opinion by reasoning that McGowin's subsequent promise raises the presumption that McGowin (D) bargained for Webb's (P) help. This seems extremely artificial. A better way to handle this is suggested by the concurrence. The concurrence seems to recognize that most courts would not recognize a valid consideration under these facts, but that there should be a "just" remedy for Webb (P). This is often the subject of the law of restitution. After all, it seems intuitive that Webb (P) should receive some compensation given that he was crippled by his heroic effort. Therefore, instead of tampering with the doctrine of consideration to reach a "just" result, the court's opinion may have been more sound if it relied on the restitutionary doctrine of unjust enrichment.

Perspective
The Justice Principle

Chapter 3

Imagine that you have been asked to babysit a law school friend's two children. You arrive at the friend's house and meet a twelve-year-old girl and her six-year-old brother. Your friend has left them two packages of baseball cards, something they both really like. The kids open up the packages and find that the boy has a Ken Griffey, Jr. card in his package. The twelve-year-old girl, recognizing that the card is very valuable, offers the boy a quarter for it. The little boy, who does not recognize that the card is valuable, agrees. Once the trade is made, the girl brags to her brother that she will be able to get one hundred dollars for the card from a baseball card store. The boy then starts crying and asks you to make his sister return the card.

Putting aside the fact that both children are far too young to make enforceable contracts, what response would you give in this case? Would you hold the six year old to his bargain to teach him to be more aware of things when making deals? Would you make the twelve year old return the card to teach her that she should not take advantage of her brother? Do the circumstances of the trade favor one approach over the other? How would you explain your actions to each of them? What is the just result?

As you will see in the cases in this chapter, courts deal with similar kinds of issues all the time in contract law. A strong libertarian would argue that our capitalist society ought to favor the idea of freedom of contract. Outside of contracting for something that is clearly illegal, parties should be free to contract on whatever terms they choose and the government's responsibility should simply be to enforce those terms, regardless of whether a party makes a good or bad bargain for himself. In other words, a strong libertarian would make our six year old cry.

While in general, courts do not like to tamper with the terms of a contract, various legal doctrines and statutory approaches have developed over the years that permit courts to avoid or reform contracts under certain circumstances in order to achieve "just results" in particular cases. As a general rule, courts are less likely to step in and change the results established by a contract where they are convinced that the parties to the agreement were both well informed, well advised, and had equal bargaining power with respect to the terms of the agreement. When courts are worried that an agreement is too one-sided and is the product of a stronger party taking advantage of a weaker party for whom the particular transaction is much more important, they have applied creative legal solutions like the doctrine of unconscionability, mutual mistake, or more general principles of equity, to try to protect the weaker party. When the weaker party is a consumer or a worker battling a large business or employer, courts have been much more willing to step in and offer protection than where both parties are businesses operating in a competitive marketplace.

The cases that follow take various approaches to these issues, with considerable debate over when it is appropriate to impose a court's view of fairness over the view expressed in the parties' own written agreement.

Chapter 3

NOTE: THE PURPOSE OF THIS OUTLINE IS TO ORGANIZE THE CASES SO THAT ONE CAN QUICKLY UNDERSTAND THE RELEVANCE OF EACH CASE TO THE COURSE. NO ATTEMPT IS MADE IN THIS OVERVIEW TO ADDRESS EVERY CONCEPT THAT MUST BE STUDIED. BE SURE TO READ THE ENTIRE CASEBOOK AND/OR OTHER MATERIALS TO GAIN A FULL UNDERSTANDING OF ALL CONCEPTS.

I. The Domain of Freedom of Contract
  A. Capacity to Contract
    1. In order to be bound to a contract, a party must have legal capacity to incur at least voidable contractual duties. *Restatement 2d, Contracts § 12.*
      a. Voidable Contract: A voidable contract is an agreement which can be avoided at the exercised option of one of the parties. *Restatement 2d, Contracts § 7.*
      b. Void Contract: A void contract is a purported contract that is not legally binding on any of the parties due to the lack of an essential legal element or some other defect under contract law.
      c. A contract made by someone who is legally incompetent to contract is generally voidable at the option of that party (generally his legal guardian would make the decision) rather than void.
    2. In general, a person has full capacity to contract unless, at the time of entering into an agreement, the person is:
      a. An infant;
      b. Under legal guardianship;
      c. Mentally ill; or
      d. Intoxicated. *Restatement 2d, Contracts § 12.*
    3. Infancy: Any contract entered into by a minor is voidable at the option of the minor. *Restatement 2d, Contracts § 14.*
    4. Mental Illness
      a. The traditional standard for determining the contractual capacity of a mentally ill person was the cognitive test. Under that rule, if at the time of the transaction, the mentally ill party did not understand its nature and consequences, the transaction would be voidable by that party.
      b. The modern standard for mental capacity to contract is reflected in the *Restatement 2d, Contracts* which provides that a person incurs only voidable contractual duties by entering into a transaction if, due to mental illness, he is unable to act in a reasonable manner in relation to the transaction and the other contracting party has reason to know of his condition. *Restatement 2d, Contracts § 15; Ortelere v. Teachers' Retirement Board.*
  B. Contracts that are Unenforceable for Public Policy Reasons
    1. A contract or contractual provision will be unenforceable on grounds of public policy if legislation specifically provides that it is unenforceable. *Restatement 2d, Contracts § 178; In the Matter of Baby M.*
    2. A court can also find a contract or contractual term to be unenforceable where it concludes that enforcement is clearly outweighed by a public policy against the enforcement of such terms. *Restatement 2d, Contracts § 178.*
    3. In weighing a public policy against enforcement of a contract or a contractual term, a court generally considers:
      a. The strength of that policy as demonstrated in legislation or judicial decisions;
      b. The likelihood that a refusal to enforce the contract or contractual term will further that policy;
      c. The seriousness of any misconduct involved and the extent to which it was deliberate; and
      d. The extent of the connection between any misconduct and the contract or contractual term at issue. *Restatement 2d, Contracts § 178.*
    4. A public policy against enforcing a contract

or contractual term can be derived by a court from a legislative statement found relevant to such a policy or a perceived need to protect public welfare. *Restatement 2d, Contracts § 179; In the Matter of Baby M.*

5. A surrogacy contract has been found void and unenforceable as a violation of public policy. *In the Matter of Baby M.*

II. Mistakes: A mistake is a belief that is not in accord with the facts. *Restatement 2d, Contracts § 151.*

A. Unilateral Mistake

1. Traditionally, courts were very reluctant to relieve a party from the consequences of a contract on the basis of that party's unilateral mistake.
2. The modern approach is found in the *Restatement 2d, Contracts,* which permits a party to void a contract on the basis of unilateral mistake where:
   a. The mistake by the party was made at the time of the contract as to a basic assumption of the contract;
   b. The mistake would have a material effect on the agreed exchange of performances that is adverse to the mistaken party;
   c. Is a matter as to which the mistaken party does not bear the risk of the mistake; and either
   d. The effect of the mistake is such that enforcement of the contract would be unconscionable, or the other party had reason to know of the mistake or that party's fault caused the mistake. *Restatement 2d, Contracts § 153; Stambovsky v. Ackley.*
3. Where a condition that has been created by a seller materially impairs the value of a contract and is peculiarly within the knowledge of the seller or unlikely to be discovered by a prudent buyer exercising due care with respect to the transaction, nondisclosure by the seller constitutes a basis for rescission as a matter of equity. *Stambovsky v. Ackley.*
4. A party will bear the risk of a mistake when:
   a. The risk is allocated to him by agreement; or
   b. the party is aware, at the time the contract is made, that he has only Limited knowledge with respect to the facts to which the mistake relates but treats his limited knowledge as sufficient; *Wood v. Boynton,* or
   c. The risk is allocated to the party by a court on the ground that it is reasonable to do so under the circumstances. *Restatement 2d, Contracts § 154.*
5. Rescission of a sale is not permitted where there is conscious uncertainty by the parties as to the nature and value of the item sold. *Wood v. Boynton.*

B. Mutual Mistake

1. Under the modern approach of the *Restatement 2d, Contracts*, a party may void a contract on the grounds of mutual mistake where the first three requirements for voiding a contract on the basis of unilateral mistake are met. Thus the mistake must:
   a. Concern a basic assumption on which the contract was made;
   b. Have a material effect on the agreed exchange of performance; and
   c. Not be a risk borne by the party seeking to void the contract. *Restatement 2d, Contracts § 152.*
2. If the adversely affected party has agreed to bear the risk of the mistake, the contract will not be voidable. *Restatement 2d, Contracts § 154; Lenawee County Board of Health v. Messerly.*
3. Where a contract in whole or in part fails to express the agreement because of a mistake of both parties as to its contents or effect, a court may, at the request of a party, reform the contract to express the agreement, except to the extent that rights of third parties such as good faith purchasers for

value will be unfairly affected. *Restatement 2d, Contracts § 155.*

4. Courts are more likely to reform an agreement containing an error where the error is a clerical error, than where the error is a judgment error by a party. *Elsinore Union Elementary Sch. Dist. v. Kastorff.*

III. Unconscionability

A. Modern courts may refuse to enforce a contract or a contractual provision if, at the time the contract is made, the contract or a particular provision is "unconscionable." *Restatement 2d, Contracts § 208; Uniform Commercial Code § 2-302; Frostifresh Corp. v. Reynoso.*

B. An unconscionable contract is one that no one in their right senses and not under delusions would make, on the one hand, and which no honest and fair person would accept, on the other. *Toker v. Westerman.* There are generally thought to be two kinds of unconscionability:

1. Procedural unconscionability: the unfair surprise of a party; and
2. Substantive unconscionability: the oppression of one party by another.

C. In determining whether the terms of a contract are unconscionable, a court will employ a factual, case-specific test, looking to the prevailing business practices in the industry and at all of the circumstances existing at the time the contract was made. *Williams v. Walker-Thomas Furniture Co.; Uniform Commercial Code §§ 1-103 and 2-302.*

D. Some courts have held that a grossly excessive price renders a contract unconscionable. *Toker v. Westerman; Frostifresh Corp. v. Reynoso.* While such courts may void the contracts at issue, most will permit the seller to make a reasonable profit on any performance it has rendered under the contract. *Frostifresh Corp. v. Reynoso.*

E. Thus, a court can fully void an unconscionable contract, but could also reform it or partially enforce it in order to achieve what it perceives as a just result. *Restatement 2d, Contracts § 208; Uniform Commercial Code § 2-302.*

IV. Standard Form Contracts

A. These are pre-printed forms with blanks for parties to fill in contractual terms. They are usually drafted in advance by one party and are an effort to regularize commercial transactions by a business and reduce administrative and legal costs.

B. A standardized form contract that is offered to consumers of goods or services, without an opportunity to negotiate terms, strictly conditioned on agreement to the contract's provisions, is known as a contract of adhesion.

C. Such contracts can be very one-sided and while they are generally enforceable, courts often give great scrutiny to such contracts if they suspect that the parties did not have equal bargaining power and one party took unfair advantage of another.

D. Where the disadvantaged party is a consumer, courts are more likely to offer protection from harsh contractual terms than where the disadvantaged party is a businessman competing in the marketplace. *We Care Hair Development, Inc. v. Engen; Arnold v. United Companies Lending Corp.*

E. In general a party will be held to a contract it signs, even if it does not read the agreement. Where the advantaged party in a standardized form contract has reason to believe that the disadvantaged party would not have agreed to the contract if he had known of a particular disadvantageous term contained in the contract, however, the term will not be part of the agreement, despite the disadvantaged party's signature on the agreement. Thus, an adhesion contract will not be enforced to the extent it contains provisions that do not fall within the reasonable expectations of the adhering party. *Broemmer v. Abortion Services of Phoenix. Ltd.; Restatement 2d, Contracts § 211.*

Ortelere v. Teachers' Retirement Board

(Husband and Estate Executor) v. (City Pension Plan)

(1969) 25 N.Y.2d 196; 250 N.E.2d 460; 303 N.Y.S.2d 362

M E M O R Y   G R A P H I C

Instant Facts

A husband sued to set aside his deceased wife's retirement plan payout selection, asserting that the wife, who had suffered from involutional psychosis, had been mentally incompetent to make the payout selection.

Black Letter Rule

A person incurs only voidable contractual duties by entering into a transaction if, due to mental illness, he is unable to act in a reasonable manner in relation to the transaction and the other contracting party has reason to know of his condition.

Case Vocabulary

COGNITIVE: The mental process of understanding and reasoning.

PSYCHOSIS: A severe psychological illness in which the person suffering from the illness generally loses contact with reality.

VOIDABLE CONTRACT: A valid contract that may be canceled at the option of one or more of the contracting parties.

VOID CONTRACT: A purported contract that is not legally binding on any of the parties due to the lack of an essential legal element or some other defect under contract law.

Procedural Basis: Appeal to the New York Court of Appeals of an Appellate Division order reversing a trial court judgment that voided a contract due to mental incompetency.

Facts: Grace Ortelere ("Grace"), a New York City schoolteacher for forty years, suffered a nervous breakdown and took a leave of absence from her job. A psychiatrist diagnosed her breakdown as involutional psychosis and put her under treatment that included tranquilizer and shock therapy. Prior to her breakdown, Grace had chosen a payout option under her retirement pension plan that would have provided for her husband, Francis Ortelere ("Francis") (P), in the event of her death. After her breakdown and during her leave of absence, Grace wrote a detailed letter to the Teachers' Retirement Board ("the Board") (D), asking eight specific questions about the various retirement alternatives available to her. After receiving answers from the Board (D), Grace executed a retirement application and chose a different payout option from the one she had always had in the past, which gave her the maximum monthly retirement payout allowance possible under the pension plan, but did not provide for Francis (P) in the event of her death. The new payout option became effective the day after her application was filed. Prior to deciding to retire, Grace had been examined by the Board's (D) doctor to see if she was fit to return to work. The doctor had requested a report from Grace's psychiatrist and the Board (D) subsequently asked Grace to report to its psychiatrist for an examination. Almost immediately after changing her pension plan payout option, Grace died of an aneurysm. Francis (P) , who was the executor of Grace's estate and had left his job as an electrician to care for Grace after her breakdown, filed suit in state court to set aside Grace's application for retirement and the change in her pension payout option on the grounds that Grace was mentally incompetent to execute the application. The trial court agreed with Francis (P) that Grace had been mentally incompetent when she executed the application and found it void under the law. On appeal by the Board (D), the Appellate Division reversed, holding that, as a matter of law, sufficient proof of incompetency to void the transaction had not been shown. Francis (P) then appealed to the New York Court of Appeals.

Issue: Does a person incur only voidable contractual duties by entering into a transaction if, due to mental illness, he is unable to act in a reasonable manner in relation to the transaction and the other contracting party has reason to know of his condition?

Decision and Rationale: (Breitel, J.) Yes. Traditionally, contractual mental capacity has been measured by a cognitive test. Under this standard, the issue is whether the mind was so affected as to render the person signing the contract totally incompetent to understand the nature and consequences of the transaction. The contracting party also had to be able to make a rational judgment concerning the particular transaction. These standards were developed when psychiatric knowledge was quite primitive. They fail to account for a person who due to mental illness is unable to control his conduct even though his cognitive ability seems unimpaired. When these standards were developed, it was thought that all mental faculties were simultaneously affected by mental illness. This is no longer the prevailing psychiatric view. Since the cognitive rules are, for the most part, too restrictive and rest on a false factual basis, they must be re-examined. Section 15(1)(b) of the *Restatement 2d, Contracts* states the modern rule on competency to contract, providing that a person incurs only voidable contractual duties by entering into a transaction if, due to mental illness, he is unable to act in a reasonable manner in relation to the transaction and the other party has reason to know of his condition. We adopt this rule. Here, Grace's psychiatrist testified that her involutional psychosis rendered her incapable of making a voluntary rational decision. The Board (D) was or should have been fully aware of Grace's condition, knowing of her leave of absence for medical reasons and having requested that she see their psychiatrist prior to any reinstatement. The announced goal of the Board's (D) retirement plan is the protection of its members and those in whom its members have an interest. It is not a sound system that would permit 40 years of contribution and participation to be nullified by a one-instant act committed by a person known to be mentally ill. Since we are announcing a change from the traditional rules regarding competency to contract and the testimony below attempted to fit the traditional rules, we order a new trial under these new standards. Reversed.

Dissent: (Jasen, J.) I cannot agree that the traditional rules governing competency to contract are too restrictive and rest on a false basis. It is common knowledge that the present state of psychiatric knowledge is inadequate to provide a fixed rule for each and every type of mental disorder. Thus, the generally accepted rules that have evolved to determine mental capacity are general enough in application to cover all types of mental disorders and are phrased in a way that can be understood and practically applied by laymen on juries. The rule that a party who was capable of understanding the nature and consequences of the act or transaction he challenges cannot void his contract represents a balance struck between policies to protect the security of transactions between individuals on the one hand, and protection of the mentally ill on the other hand. The traditional test harmonizes the competing policy considerations with layman experience to achieve the fairest result in the greatest number of cases. I fear that the majority's changes will prove unworkable in practice and make many contracts vulnerable to frivolous psychological attacks. The reasonable expectations of those who innocently deal with persons who appear rational and who understand what they are doing should be protected. In the present case, the evidence conclusively shows that Grace understood her selection at the time she filed her retirement application. She wrote a detailed letter to the Board (D) asking eight very specific questions about the options available to her. These explicit and extremely relevant questions reveal a mind fully in command of the important features of the retirement plan and demonstrate Grace's full capacity to understand and decide whether to change her payout option. As I read the record, the evidence shows that Grace's selection was based on a need for a higher income to support herself and her husband, who had left his job to care for her. The payout was to be their only retirement income. It was an economic necessity for her to choose a higher payment during her lifetime in return for giving up a continuation of payments to her husband in the event of her death. Our cases hold that, in the absence of convincing evidence that the incompetent would have made a different selection, it is presumed that he would have chosen the largest option yielding the largest return in his lifetime. I would affirm.

Analysis:

As the Court of Appeals explains here, the traditional standard for determining the contractual capacity of a mentally ill person is the cognitive test. Under that rule, if at the time of the transaction, the mentally ill party did not understand its nature and consequences, the transaction would be voidable by that party. The court adopts the modern standard of the *Restatement 2d, Contracts* which applies a broader test of competency, not limited to cognitive ability. Under that test, even if a party understands the nature and consequences of his actions, he may void the contract if his illness compels him to act in an irrational manner with respect to the transaction and the other contracting party knows or has reason to know of this condition. Note that this modern standard applies the objective theory of contracts in that it only binds the non-mentally ill party to the contract if he should have reasonably known from all the facts and circumstances that the other party was mentally ill. Here, the Board (D) was on notice that Grace had psychological problems. The dissent's concern that the majority's change in the standard will greatly increase the number of attacks on contracts for psychological reasons seems overblown given the adoption of this objective standard. Most states still apply the traditional standard for determining mental incapacity to contract. In some states, the contracts of the mentally disabled are automatically void, as opposed to being merely voidable. Thus, if one party to the contract is found to have been mentally incompetent, the contract cannot be enforced even against the competent party. Here, as in most states today, the court holds that a finding of mental incapacity makes the contract merely voidable. Thus, if the contract were beneficial to the mentally incompetent party, he would have the option of requiring performance.

NEW JERSEY SUPREME COURT VOIDS SURROGACY CONTRACT AS VIOLATION OF PUBLIC POLICY

In the Matter of Baby M

(Child Custody Dispute)
(1988) 109 N.J. 396; 537 A.2d.1227

M E M O R Y   G R A P H I C

Instant Facts

The father of a baby sued the baby's natural mother, who had contracted to turn over the baby to him and terminate her parental rights after the baby was born in return for $10,000, seeking judicial enforcement of the contract.

Black Letter Rule

A surrogacy contract is void and unenforceable as a violation of public policy.

Case Vocabulary

BEST INTERESTS OF THE CHILD: Traditional standard by which family law courts determine the custody of a child, looking to what is determined to be "best" for that child.
PENDENTE LITE: Pending the outcome of the litigation.
PRIVATE PLACEMENT ADOPTION: A parent putting a child up for adoption directly, rather than through an adoption agency.

Procedural Basis: Direct grant of certification by the New Jersey Supreme Court on an appeal of a Superior Court order enforcing a surrogacy contract.

Facts: William Stern ("William") (P) and his wife, Elizabeth, were unable to have children and went to the Infertility Center of New York ("ICNY") which arranged a surrogacy contract for them with Mary Beth Whitehead ("Mary Beth") (D). Under the contract, Mary Beth (D) agreed to become pregnant through artificial insemination of William's (P) sperm, to carry the child to term, deliver it to William (P) and Elizabeth, and then do whatever was necessary to terminate her maternal rights so that Elizabeth could adopt the child. In return, William (P) was to pay Mary Beth $10,000, upon delivery to him of the child. In a separate contract, William (P) agreed to pay ICNY $7,500. Mary Beth (D) was artificially inseminated with William's (P) sperm, became pregnant, and delivered a daughter. Despite telling William (P) and Elizabeth at the hospital that she did not know if she could give up the child, Mary Beth (D) did turn over the child to them and they named the child Melissa ("Baby M"). The next day, Mary Beth (D) went to William (P) and Elizabeth's home and told them that she could not live without the child. She said that if they let her have the child for a week, she would return her to them. Wanting to prevent Mary Beth (D) from her threat to commit suicide, William (P) and Elizabeth gave her the baby. Subsequently, when Mary Beth (D) refused to return the child, William filed a complaint in New Jersey Superior Court seeking enforcement of the surrogacy contract. Mary Beth (D) then fled to Florida with the baby. Eventually, William (P) found them and obtained a Florida court order requiring Mary Beth (D) to turn over Baby M. The Florida police enforced the order and Baby M was returned to William (P) and Elizabeth in New Jersey. The New Jersey Superior Court gave temporary *pendente lite* custody of Baby M to William (P), with limited visitation rights to Mary Beth (D). Following a trial, the court held that the surrogacy contract was valid; ordered that Mary Beth's (D) parental rights be terminated and that sole custody be granted to William (P); and entered an order allowing the adoption by Elizabeth. Mary Beth (D) then appealed directly to the New Jersey Supreme Court, which granted certification.

Issue: Is a surrogacy contract void and unenforceable as a violation of public policy?

Decision and Rationale: (Wilentz, C.J.) Yes. We invalidate the surrogacy contract here because it conflicts with the law and public policy of this State. The use of money to achieve a private placement adoption is illegal and perhaps criminal under New Jersey statutes. We have no doubt whatsoever that the money was paid here to obtain an adoption and not, as William (P) argues, for Mary Beth's (D) personal services. In addition to the inducement of money, there is the coercion of contract: the natural mother's irrevocable agreement, prior to birth, even prior to conception, to surrender the child to the adoptive couple. Under New Jersey law, such an agreement is totally unenforceable in private placement adoptions where the formal agreement can occur only after birth, and then only after the mother has been offered counseling. Equally invalid is the related agreement by the natural mother to cooperate with proceedings to terminate her parental rights, as well as her contractual concession that the child's best interests would be served by giving custody to the natural father and his wife. All of this is agreed to by the natural mother before she has even conceived, and in some cases, before she has the slightest idea of what the natural father and adoptive mother are like. Under the contract the natural mother is irrevocably committed before she knows the strength of her bond with the child. She never makes a totally voluntary, informed decision. Clearly, any decision prior to the baby's birth is uninformed and any decision after that, compelled by pre-existing contractual commitment, the threat of lawsuit, and the inducement of a $10,000 payment, is less than totally voluntary. Her interests are of little concern to those who controlled this transaction. The contract's premise, that the natural parents can decide in advance of birth which one is to have custody of the child, bears no relationship to the settled law that the child's best interests shall determine custody. The contract totally disregards the best interests of the child. There is not the slightest suggestion that any inquiry will be made at any time to determine the fitness of William (P) and Elizabeth as custodial parents, of Elizabeth as an adoptive parent, their superiority to Mary Beth (D), or the effect on the child of not living with her natural mother. In the scheme here, a middleman, propelled by profit, promotes the sale. Whatever idealism may have motivated any of the participants, the profit motive predominates and ultimately governs the transaction. This is the sale of a child, or at the very least, the sale of a mother's right to her child, the only mitigating factor being that one of the purchasers is the father. Almost every evil that prompted our prohibition on the payment of money in connection with adoptions exists here. William (P) argues that Mary Beth (D) agreed to the surrogacy arrangement, supposedly fully understanding the consequences. Putting aside the issue of how compelling her need for the money may have been and how significant her understanding of the consequences, we suggest that her consent is irrelevant. There are, in a civilized society, some things that money cannot buy. In America, we decided long ago that merely because conduct purchased by money was "voluntary" did not meant that it was good or beyond regulation and prohibition. Employers can no longer purchase the agreement of children to perform oppressive labor or of workers to subject themselves to unsafe or unhealthy working conditions. Thus, there are values that society deems more important than granting to wealth whatever it can buy. We note that we find no offense to our present laws where a woman voluntarily and without payment agrees to act as a surrogate mother, provided that she is not subject to a binding agreement to surrender her child. Our holding today also does not prevent the Legislature from altering the current statutes, within constitutional limits, to permit surrogacy contracts. Under current law, however, the surrogacy contract here is illegal and void. Accordingly, we void both the termination of Mary Beth's (D) parental rights and the adoption by Elizabeth. With no contract to decide the issue, we decide the custody question under a best-interests-of-the-child standard, giving equal weight to the claims of each natural parent as required under New Jersey statute. Independent of the trial court's order, we find that Baby M's best interests call for custody by William (P) and Elizabeth. We remand to the trial court for a consideration of visitation rights for Mary Beth (D). Affirmed in part, reversed in part, and remanded.

Analysis:

The Court here finds that a surrogacy contract, in which a woman agrees, prior to the conception and birth of her baby and in return for money, to turn over the baby to another party following birth and do whatever she can to terminate her parental rights in favor of that party violates public policy. Section 178 of the *Restatement 2d, Contracts* provides that a promise is unenforceable on grounds of public policy if legislation provides that it is unenforceable or the interest in its enforcement is clearly outweighed in the circumstances by a public policy against the enforcement of such terms. The comment to § 178 indicates that courts that void a contractual term or promise for violating public policy generally reach that conclusion either from their own perception of the need to protect some aspect of the public welfare or from legislation that is relevant to that policy even though it may say nothing explicit about whether a term may or may not be enforced. Unless the term clearly and explicitly contradicts a particular law, a court must balance the traditional freedom of parties to enter into agreements against the factors it views as justification for not enforcing the parties' expectations. Here, the court finds several justifications for not enforcing the parties' contractual terms. Looking to a state law that prohibited the use of money to obtain a private placement adoption, the court concludes that the surrogacy contract at issue here falls under that prohibition, rejecting William's (P) argument that the contract was not for the sale of the baby, but merely for Mary Beth's (D) "services." The court also concludes that the contract violates established legislative policies such as determining custody according to the child's best interests and requiring counseling and fully informed consent before permitting the termination of parental rights. The critical point here is that freedom of contract is not unlimited in modern society, even where the parties have equal bargaining power and full information about the circumstances of their bargain. Courts may step in and override the desires of the individual parties in the interest of enforcing societal standards that are viewed as more important.

Stambovsky v. Ackley

(House Buyer) v. (House Seller)
(1991) 169 A.D.2d; 572 N.Y.S.2d 672

M E M O R Y G R A P H I C

Instant Facts

After learning that the house he had just contracted to buy was reputed to be haunted, the buyer filed suit to rescind the contract.

Black Letter Rule

Where a condition that has been created by a seller materially impairs the value of a contract and is peculiarly within the knowledge of the seller or unlikely to be discovered by a prudent buyer exercising due care with respect to the transaction, nondisclosure by the seller constitutes a basis for rescission as a matter of equity.

Case Vocabulary

CAVEAT EMPTOR: Let the buyer beware. A legal standard under which the buyer of an item is obligated to examine the item himself, with no recourse against the seller if he judges wrongly about the item's quality or value.

EQUITY: A system of jurisprudence that operates alongside the common law, under which the object is to reach a just and fair result between the parties to a dispute, which may or may not be the same result that would be obtained under the rules of the common law. Historically, where a party was dissatisfied with a result under common law, the party could seek redress in a separate court of equity. In most states today, courts of equity and courts of law have been merged, permitting a court of law to review equitable claims.

ESTOPPED: Being precluded by one's own conduct from claiming a right to the detriment of another party who relied on that conduct.

RESCISSION: The cancellation of a contract, where the parties to the contract are put back into the positions they occupied prior to entering into their agreement.

Procedural Basis: Appeal of a trial court order granting a motion to dismiss a complaint for rescission of a contract.

Facts: Stambovsky (P), who was seeking to move from New York City to Nyack, New York, contracted to purchase Ackley's (D) house in Nyack. After signing the contract, Stambovsky (P), learned that Ackley's (D) home was widely reputed to be possessed by ghosts which Ackley (D) and her family had reported seeing on many occasions over the past nine years. Ackley (D) had reported seeing the ghosts in her home in both *Readers' Digest* and local newspapers several years before the contract was signed. On learning of the house's reputation, Stambovsky (P) filed suit in state court, seeking rescission of the sale contract. Following a motion by Ackley (D), the trial court dismissed the complaint, holding that Stambovsky (P) had no remedy at law because New York law imposed no duty on the seller to disclose any information regarding the property sold. Stambovsky (P) then appealed.

Issue: Can nondisclosure of a condition that was created by a seller, that materially impairs the value of a contract, and is peculiarly within the seller's knowledge or unlikely to be discovered by a prudent buyer exercising due care with respect to the transaction, constitute a basis for rescission of the contract as a matter of equity?

Decision and Rationale: (Rubin, J.) Yes. The unusual facts of this case clearly warrant a grant of equitable relief to Stambovsky (P), who as a New York City resident, cannot be expected to have any familiarity with the folklore of Nyack. Not being a "local," Stambovsky (P) could not readily learn that the home he had contracted to buy is haunted. Whether the ghosts seen by Ackley (D) are real or in her mind, having reported their presence in *Readers' Digest* and the local press, she is estopped to deny their existence and, as a matter of law, the house is haunted. It was Ackley's (D) promotional efforts in publicizing her encounters with these spirits which fostered the home's reputation in the community. The impact of the reputation thus created goes to the very essence of the parties' bargain, impairing both the value of the property as well as its resale potential. New York real estate law follows the doctrine of caveat emptor (buyer beware), imposing no duty to disclose information concerning the premises unless there is a confidential or fiduciary relationship between the parties or some conduct by the seller which constitutes "active concealment." Normally, some affirmative misrepresentation or partial disclosure is required to impose on a seller a duty to communicate undisclosed conditions affecting the property. The rule differs, however, at law and in equity. While the law courts would permit no recovery of damages against a seller because of concealment of certain facts, if the buyer refuses to complete the contract because of the concealment of a material fact by the seller, equity would refuse to force the buyer to do so, because equity only compels the specific enforcement of a contract that is fair and open and with regard to which all material matters known to each party have been communicated to the other. Where fairness and common sense dictate that an exception should be created, the evolution of the law should not be stifled by rigid application of a legal maxim. The doctrine of caveat emptor requires a buyer to act prudently to assess the fitness and value of his purchase and bars the buyer who fails to exercise due care from seeking the equitable remedy of rescission. Here, even the most careful inspection of the premises and search of the available public records regarding title to the property would not have revealed the presence of ghosts or the house's reputation for having ghosts. There is no sound reason to deny Stambovsky (P) relief for failing to discover a state of affairs that even the most prudent of buyers would not be expected to contemplate. Where a condition that has been created by the seller materially impairs the value of the contract and is peculiarly within the knowledge of the seller or unlikely to be discovered by a prudent buyer, exercising due care with respect to the transaction, nondisclosure constitutes a basis for rescission as a matter of equity. Any other outcome puts on the buyer not merely the duty to exercise care in his purchase, but the duty to be all-knowing about any fact that may affect the bargain. No practical purpose is served by imposing such a burden. Instead, it encourages predatory business practices and offends the principle that equity will suffer no wrong to be without a remedy. Here, Ackley (D) deliberately fostered the public belief that her home was possessed by ghosts. Having undertaken to inform the public at large, to whom she has no legal relationship, she owes no less a duty to her buyer. Where, as here, a seller not only takes unfair advantage of a buyer's ignorance, but has created and perpetuated a condition about which the buyer is unlikely to even inquire, enforcement of the contract is offensive to the court's sense of equity. While I agree with the trial court that the seller was under no duty to disclose the house's reputation and that a claim for fraudulent misrepresentation would fail, I am moved by the "spirit" of equity to allow the buyer to seek rescission of the contract and recovery of his down payment. Stambovsky's (P) complaint for rescission should be reinstated. Reversed.

Dissent: (Smith, J.) It is settled law in New York that the seller of real property is under no duty to speak when the parties deal at arm's length. The mere silence of the seller, without some act or conduct which deceived the buyer, does not amount to concealment that is actionable as fraud. Under the applicable doctrine of caveat emptor, the buyer has a duty to satisfy himself as to the quality of his bargain. Here, the parties were represented by counsel and dealt at arm's length. There was no confidential or fiduciary relationship between the parties that imposed a duty to disclose and there is no allegation that the seller here did anything to thwart the buyer's efforts to fulfill his responsibilities fixed by the doctrine of caveat emptor. If the longstanding doctrine of caveat emptor is to be discarded, it should be for a reason more substantive than a ghost. I would affirm the trial court's dismissal of the complaint.

Analysis:

The court here concludes that Stambovsky's (P) complaint, contrary to the decision of the trial court, was sufficient to state a cause of action for rescission of the contract for the sale of the house by Ackley (D). The court acknowledges that New York law has traditionally adhered to the doctrine of caveat emptor, imposing no general duty on the seller to disclose anything about the property. The court turns to principles of equity, however, and suggests that fairness should override the usual rule because no reasonable buyer would legitimately inquire into whether the house being sold was haunted. In the court's view, this condition is not something that would be found by a reasonable inspection, unlike termites or environmental waste. Is it so unreasonable to think, however, that before spending a large sum of money on a house, an out-of-town buyer would speak to neighbors or at least ask the seller about the house's reputation in the community? In the court's view, the buyer here acted reasonably and the seller's hands were not clean, having given rise to the reputation for ghosts on the property by publishing accounts of having seen ghosts in *Readers' Digest* and local newspapers. The court says that fairness would require Ackley (D) to make the same report she made to the newspapers to any prospective buyer.

WISCONSIN SUPREME COURT FINDS NO MISTAKE JUSTIFYING RESCISSION OF A SALE WHERE THE PARTIES KNEW THEY WERE UNCERTAIN AS TO THE NATURE AND VALUE OF THE ITEM SOLD

Wood v. Boynton

(Diamond Owner) v. (Jeweler)
(1885) 64 Wis. 265; 25 N.W. 42

M E M O R Y G R A P H I C

Instant Facts

After learning that the stone she had sold to a jeweler for one dollar was really an uncut diamond worth $700, the seller filed suit seeking rescission of the sale.

Black Letter Rule

Rescission of a sale is not permitted where there is conscious uncertainty by the parties as to the nature and value of the item sold.

Case Vocabulary

TITLE: The right to ownership of particular property.

Procedural Basis: Appeal of a directed verdict denying an action to recover possession of personal property.

Facts: Wood (P) owned a small stone. She did not know that it was an uncut diamond that was very valuable. Wood (P) went to Boynton's (D) jewelry store on another matter and happened to show Boynton (D) the stone, telling him that she had found it and had been told that it was a topaz. She asked Boynton (D) if he knew what the stone was. Boynton (D), who did not know that the stone was actually an uncut diamond, said that he thought it might be a topaz and offered Wood (D) one dollar (remember it is 1885!) for it. Wood (P) refused the offer. Later on, needing money, she returned to the store and sold the stone to Boynton (D) for one dollar. Subsequently, Boynton (D) learned that the stone was actually an uncut diamond worth $700. When Wood (P) heard of this fact, she went to Boynton's (D) store and presented $1.10, demanding the stone's return. Boynton (D) refused and Wood (P) filed suit to recover possession of the stone. Following a trial, the trial judge directed the jury to find a verdict in favor of Boynton (D). Wood (D) then appealed to the Wisconsin Supreme Court.

Issue: Is rescission of a sale permitted where there was conscious uncertainty by the parties as to the nature and value of the item sold?

Decision and Rationale: (Taylor, J.) No. The only reasons we know of for rescinding a sale and revesting title in the seller so that he may maintain an action at law for recovery of possession against the buyer are: (1) that the buyer was guilty of fraud in getting the seller to sell to him; and (2) that there was a mistake in fact, made by the seller, in delivering an item which was not the item that was to be sold. In reality, this is not technically a rescission of the sale since the item delivered was not the item sold, and no title ever passed to the seller by such delivery. Here, there is no evidence that Wood (P) was induced to make the sale by any fraud or unfair dealing by Boynton (D). Both were entirely ignorant at the time of the sale of the character of the stone or its real value. Boynton (D) was not an expert in uncut diamonds and had made no careful examination of the stone. Wood (P) had the stone in her possession for a long time and had made some previous inquiry about its nature and qualities. If she chose to sell it without further investigation as to its intrinsic value to a person who was guilty of no fraud or unfairness which caused her to sell for so small a sum, she cannot repudiate the sale because it is later determined that she made a bad bargain. There is no mistake as to the identity of the item sold. It was produced by Wood (P) and shown to Boynton (D) before the sale was made and the thing sold was delivered to the buyer when the purchase price was paid. Wood (P) argues that, because it turned out that the stone was much more valuable than the parties thought at the time of the sale, that fact alone was evidence of fraud by the buyer requiring rescission of the sale. Whether inadequacy of price is to be received as evidence of fraud, even in a suit in equity to avoid a sale, depends on the facts known to the parties at the time of sale. Here, the value of the stone was open to the investigation of both parties, neither knowing its intrinsic value, and both thought the price paid was adequate. This action was brought at law and we need not consider whether the sale should be avoided in equity. We can find nothing, however, in the evidence that suggests that Boynton (D) had any real knowledge of the stone's value or that he believed it was a diamond. Thus, it cannot be said that here was a suppression of information by Boynton (D) that might justify voiding the sale in equity. However unfortunate Wood (P) may have been in selling this valuable stone for a nominal sum, she has failed to make out a case of either fraud or mistake that will entitle her to rescission of the sale in an action at law. Affirmed.

Analysis:

The court holds here that there was no mutual mistake by the parties justifying rescission of the sale contract. The modern approach of the *Restatement 2d, Contracts* regarding rescission for mutual mistake permits rescission where the parties were mistaken as to a "basic assumption" on which they based their bargain. As this court rightly points out, there was no mistake of fact in this case. Both parties went into the transaction consciously uncertain of the nature and quality of the item being bought and sold. Had they both really assumed the stone was a topaz and then learned subsequently that it was a diamond, the result might be different, at least under the standard of the *Restatement 2d, Contracts*. In that case, there really would have been a "mistake," rather than simply uncertainty by the parties. Here, though, the evidence showed that neither party thought they knew with certainty what was being traded. Thus, each party made a conscious decision to assume the risk of a bad bargain.

CONTRACT BASED ON MUTUAL MISTAKE IS VOIDABLE UNLESS ADVERSELY AFFECTED PARTY ASSUMES RISK OF MISTAKE

Lenawee County Board of Health v. Messerly

(County) v. (Seller)
417 Mich. 17, 331 N.W.2d 203 (1982)

MEMORY GRAPHIC

Instant Facts

The Messerlys (P) sold property containing an apartment building to the Pickleses (D). It was then discovered that there was a leaking septic tank on the property.

Black Letter Rule

A contract based on a mutual mistake is voidable unless the adversely affected party agrees to bear the risk of the mistake.

Case Vocabulary

RESCISSION: Any of several means of ending a contract, such as by mutual agreement, by exercising an option in the contract allowing the party to do so, or as an equitable remedy when the contract was based on fraud, mistake, or similar problems.

Procedural Basis: Appeal of action to rescind contract.

Facts: In 1971, the Messerlys (P) acquired one acre plus 600 square feet of land. On the 600 square feet was a three-unit apartment building. The prior owner of the apartment building had installed a septic tank without a permit and in violation of the applicable health code. The Messerlys (P) sold the apartment building to the Barneses. When the Barneses defaulted on their contract, the Pickleses (D) expressed an interest in purchasing the building. The Pickleses (D) did not like the terms of the Barnes-Messerly contract and wanted to deal directly with the Messerlys (P). So the Barneses executed a quit-claim deed conveying their interest in the property back to the Messerlys (P). In 1977, the Pickleses (D) executed a contract with the Messerlys (P) that included an "as is" clause stating that the Pickleses (D) had inspected the property and agreed to accept it in its present condition. A few days later, the Pickleses (D) discovered raw sewage seeping out of the ground. The Lenawee County Board of Health (the "County") (P) condemned the property and sued the Messerlys (P) and the Pickleses (D). The County (P) sought an injunction proscribing human habitation of the premises until it was brought up to code. After the injunction was granted, the County (P) withdrew from the lawsuit. When the Pickleses (D) failed to make payments on the contract, the Messerlys (P) filed a cross-complaint against them for foreclosure, sale of the property, and a deficiency judgment. The Pickleses (D) counterclaimed against the Messerlys (P) and the Barneses for rescission based on misrepresentation and fraud. The trial court held for the Messerlys (P) on their foreclosure action and held that the Pickleses (D) had no cause of action against the Barneses or the Messerlys (P). The trial court based its decision on its finding that the Messerlys (P) and the Barneses did not know about the sanitation problem and that the Pickleses (D) bought the property "as is." The Court of Appeals affirmed the holding for the Barneses, but held that the Pickleses (D) and the Messerlys (P) based their contract on a mutual mistake that went to a basic element of the contract and made the contract void.

Issue: Is a contract based on a mutual mistake voidable if the adversely affected party agrees to bear the risk of the mistake?

Decision and Rationale: (Ryan, J.) No. A mistake is a belief that is not in accord with the facts. The belief must be about a fact in existence at the time the contract is executed. It may not be a prediction about a future occurrence. Here, the parties were mistaken about the property's income-producing capacity. The Messerlys (P) claim the defect in the sewage system arose after the contract was executed, whereas the Pickleses (D) claim the defect existed previously, but was only discovered after. We conclude that the septic system was defective before the parties executed the contract. We now determine the legal significance of the mistake. The Messerlys (P) claim the mistake relates only to the quality or value of the property, and that such a mistake is collateral to the contract and does not justify rescission. The Pickleses (D) argue that the parties were mistaken about the very nature of the consideration, making rescission appropriate. These distinctions do not provide a satisfactory analysis. A mistake may relate to a fact which directly affects value, but may also materially affect the essence of the consideration. Here, the fact that the property was uninhabitable affected the property's value and it affected the essence of the consideration. Like the barren cow in *Sherwood v. Walker* [mutual mistake regarding character of consideration makes contract voidable], here the income-generating rental property did not exist. We think the legal effect of a mistake should be analyzed on a case-by-case basis to determine whether the mistake relates to a basic assumption upon which the contract is based and materially affects the parties' agreed performance. Here, the Pickleses (D) and the Messerlys (P) believed the contract involved income-generating property. This mistake is about a basic assumption that materially

affects the parties' agreed performance. However, a court need not grant rescission in every such case. Where both parties are equally innocent, we must determine which party should bear the risk of loss resulting from the mistake. Equity suggests that here the Pickleses (D) should bear the loss. We look first at whether the parties agreed between themselves who should bear the risk of loss. Here, the "as is" clause in the contract indicates that the parties considered that the Pickleses (D) should bear the risk regarding the "present condition" of the property. If an "as is" clause is to have any meaning at all, it must refer to defects which were unknown at the time the contract was executed. Reversed.

Analysis:

Here the court adopts the approach to mutual mistake found in the Restatement (Second) of Contracts §152 and holds that rescission should be granted only when a mistake relates to a basic assumption of the parties upon which the contract is made, and which materially affects the agreed performance of the parties. Section 152 further provides that a contract based on a legally significant mistake is voidable by the adversely-affected party unless the adversely-affected party bears the risk of the mistake. In this case, by agreeing to the "as is" clause, the Pickleses (D) bore the risk of the mistake. If a seller is adversely affected by a mutual mistake, an "as is" clause does not affect the voidability of the contract because the clause does not pass the risk of loss onto the seller. A party may also be deemed to assume the risk of loss when the party is uncertain or consciously ignorant of a vital fact. For example, a man finds a stone that appears to be a gem and takes it to a jeweler to be appraised. The jeweler honestly states that he does not know whether the stone is valuable and offers $1 for it. The man agrees to sell it. The stone turns out to be an uncut diamond worth $10000. The sale is not voidable because the parties were uncertain about the nature of the stone, but they were not mistaken about it.

Elsinore Union Elementary School District v. Kastorff

(School District) v. (Construction Contractor)

Supreme Court of California, 1960. 54 Cal.2d 380, 6 Cal. Rptr. 1, 353 P.2d 713

M E M O R Y   G R A P H I C

Instant Facts

A general contractor made an error in a bid for a job and tried to get released from his bid.

Black Letter Rule

A contractor's error in calculating a bid can be grounds for rescission.

Case Vocabulary

GENERAL CONTRACTOR: A person responsible for assembling and overseeing the subcontractors necessary to the completion of a construction project. They will frequently do some of the construction work themselves, and are responsible for bidding on jobs and keeping track of the expenses associated with all of the work. When bidding on jobs with public entities, their bids are generally binding.

UNCONSCIONABILITY: A doctrine which strikes terms out of contracts or voids whole contracts. In order for a party to succeed under this doctrine, they must show that there was a procedural defect in the contract formation process, or that the contract is substantially unfair.

Procedural Basis: Appeal from a trial court judgement for the plaintiff in a breach of contract action.

Facts: Kastorff (D), a general contractor, intended to bid on a construction job for Elsinore Union Elementary School District (the School District) (P). However, he submitted his bid with an error which lowered his price somewhere between $6500 and $9285. His total bid was $89,994. The competing bids were opened at the School District (P) and Kastorff's (D) bid was found to be $11,306 lower than the next lowest bid. As a result, the superintendent and the school board members asked Kastorff (D) if he was sure that his figures were correct. He checked with his assistant and told them that his bid was correct. The school board subsequently voted to award Kastorff (D) the contract. This was on August 12th, 1952. The next day, Kastorff (D) double-checked his worksheets and discovered his mistake. He met with the architects who were overseeing the project, explained his mistake and asked to be released from his bid. The architects communicated all of this to the superintendent. On August 15th, the school board received a letter from Kastorff (D) again requesting that he be released from his bid due to the error. The school board met and voted to refuse his request. On August 28th, they notified Kastorff (D) in writing that he was awarded the contract. When they sent him the contract itself, he returned it and again explained his error and asked that they reconsider their refusal to release him from his bid. The School District (P) subsequently accepted bids from other contractors and hired the lowest bidder. They sued Kastorff (D) for breach of contract and asked for $12,906 in damages -- the difference between his bid and the bid they ultimately accepted. The trial court found for the School District (P). Kastorff (D) appeals.

Issue: Is a contractor bound by a bid which contains an error of which both parties are aware?

Decision and Rationale: (Schauer) No. Kastorff (D) argues that, as in *M.F. Kemper Const. Co. v. City of Los Angeles* [California Supreme Court states the circumstances under which a contractor's bid may be rescinded], a contractor is entitled to rescind his bid when he has made a clerical error in its computation. This is true if the requirements set forth in *Kemper* are met. First, it should be noted that a contractor's bid gives the soliciting party an irrevocable option to bind the contractor to a construction agreement. This is a contract right which is subject to the requirements for rescission if the contractor wants to be released from the bid. In order for rescission to be granted, the contractor must show 1) that the soliciting entity knows or has reason to know that there is a mistake in the bid, 2) that the mistake was material and did not result from the neglect of a legal duty, 3) that enforcement of the contract would be unconscionable, 4) that the soliciting entity can be returned to the position they were in prior to contracting, 5) that the contractor promptly notified the soliciting entity of the mistake, and 6) the contractor restores or offers to restore to the soliciting entity everything of value they have received under the contract. Of these six requirements, the second and third are the most pivotal in this case. With regard to the second requirement, the School District (P) argued that the amount of the error was immaterial. However, this court has permitted rescission in similar circumstances when the percentage error was far smaller. In addition, Kastorff's (D) mistake, and his failure to recognize it when the board asked him to check his figures, does not rise to the level of neglect of a legal duty. With regard to the third requirement, it can only be said that if the School District (P) had committed an error which would deny them a significant portion of their construction, but force them to pay for it, they would be here demanding rescission rather than Kastorff (D). Likewise, it would be inequitable to force Kastorff (D) to suffer under the bargain which the School District (P) would like to impose. Reversed.

Analysis:

This case may seem confusing because of the sequence of events and the number of requirements for rescission. The facts, as always, should be analyzed carefully and chronologically. The status of the parties should be considered at each juncture in order to determine what their obligations are to each other. With regard to the action for rescission, you will find that courts will generally grant relief if both parties are aware of the mistake and neither party has relied on the contract. More generally, the seemingly complicated requirements for rescission are frequently interpreted in favor of an equitable outcome on a case by case basis. Consider also the similarities between this case and *Lucy v. Zehmer* [Supreme Court of Virginia upholds a contract of sale for real estate even though the seller was joking]. It was noted that *Lucy v. Zehmer* would probably be decided differently today because both parties were aware that the seller was joking, albeit not until after the contract was signed and delivered. Courts will not be solicitous when one party holds the last clear chance to avoid damages due to a misunderstanding but fails to exercise their power to let the other party out of the contract.

Williams v. Walker-Thomas Furniture Co.

(Welfare Customer) v. (Furniture Store)
350 F.2d 445, 18 A.L.R.3d 1297 (1965)

MEMORY GRAPHIC

Instant Facts

Williams bought furniture and a stereo on credit from Walker-Thomas while on welfare, and Walker-Thomas repossessed the items when Williams defaulted.

Black Letter Rule

A contract is unenforceable if its terms, when considered in light of the circumstances existing when the contract was made, are so extreme as to appear unconscionable according to prevailing mores and business practices.

Case Vocabulary

LOAN SHARK: One who lends money to others at extremely high rates of interest, often threatening violence against the borrower if he or she defaults.
PRO RATA: At a proportional rate.
REPLEVIN: An action to recover taken property, and not the value of the property.

Procedural Basis: Appeal from judgment in action for replevin.

Facts: Walker-Thomas Furniture Company (Walker-Thomas) (D) runs a retail furniture store. From 1957 to 1962, Williams (P) and others (P) bought several household items from Walker-Thomas (D). Payments for these items were to be made through installment plans. The terms of each purchase were contained in a printed form contract which stated the value of the purchased item and the amount of monthly rent payment to be made by the customer. The contract also provided that Walker-Thomas (D) would remain the owner of the purchased item until all monthly payments were made. At that point, the customer could take title to the goods. In the event of a default in the payment of any monthly installment, Walker-Thomas (D) could repossess the item. Moreover, under the contract, any payments made would be credited pro rata on all outstanding balances. In other words, if a customer had bought more than one item on installments, his or her payments would be credited to all the debts for all the different items. This overall balance would then exist until all balances due were paid in full. On April 17, 1962, Williams (P) bought a stereo set for $514.95. By that point, Williams had an outstanding balance of about $164 for previously purchased goods. Her (P) new balance thus increased to $679. Williams (P) was receiving a $218 stipend from the government every month. Walker-Thomas (D) was aware of Williams' (P) financial status when selling the stereo to her (P), and Williams' (P) social worker's name was even written on the back of the contract. Williams (P) eventually defaulted on her (P) payments shortly thereafter, and Walker-Thomas (D) sought to replevy all the items she (P) purchased after December 1957. The Court of General Sessions granted judgment for Walker-Thomas (D). The District of Columbia Court of Appeals affirmed, and leave to appeal was granted.

Issue: Can a contract which appears unconscionable at the time it is made be enforceable?

Decision and Rationale: (Wright) No. A contract is unenforceable if its terms, when considered in light of the circumstances existing when the contract was made, are so extreme as to appear unconscionable according to prevailing mores and business practices. Congress should consider enacting corrective legislation to protect the public from such exploitative contracts as were used by Walker-Thomas (D) in this case. In fact, Congress has recently enacted the Uniform Commercial Code, which specifically provides that the court may refuse to enforce a contract which it finds to be unconscionable at the time it was made. This court now holds in accordance with this position. Unconscionability has generally been considered as including the absence of meaningful choice for one party combined with contract terms which are unreasonably favorable to the other party. Whether a party has a meaningful choice may depend on several factors, including the manner in which the contract was entered, or the disparity of bargaining power. Granted, a party that signs a contract without full knowledge of its terms may often be assumed to have entered a one-sided bargain. It is unlikely, though, that a party with little bargaining power or choice when entering such a contract could give his or her consent to all the terms of the contract. In determining the reasonableness or fairness of a contract, the primary concern must be with the terms, considered in light of the circumstances existing when the contract was made. This test cannot be mechanically applied. Case remanded to trial court for further proceedings.

Dissent: (Danaher) There must be thousands upon thousands of this kind of transaction occurring everyday. Because the law has long allowed parties such latitude in making contracts, any approach to this problem should be a cautious one. Here, Williams (P) apparently knew precisely where she (P) stood in this contract. The District of Columbia Court of Appeals was correct in its disposition of the issues.

Analysis:

Another method of apportionment used with installment plans of this kind is to do so in relation to the original debt for each item. As it turned out, Williams (P) had bought about sixteen items from Walker-Thomas (D) between 1957 and 1962. She owed only 25 cents on the first item, though, 3 cents on the second item, and similarly trivial amounts on the other items, except for the stereo. Thus, if Walker-Thomas (D) had applied Williams' (P) payments in the way suggested above, she (P) would have paid in full for about a dozen of the sixteen items she (P) had bought. Because such payment plans can potentially vary to detrimental results for a buyer, the manner of apportioning payments has been widely prescribed by various statutes. A broad consumer-protection rule of the Federal Trade Commission, however, has addressed this problem. If this rule were applied in this case, it would have limited Walker-Thomas (D) to reserving an interest in any items it (D) sold so that only the unpaid price of the item or items subject to that transaction would be secured. In other words, the stereo could only serve as collateral for the outstanding balance on the stereo alone. This kind of regulation would seem to offer far more protection to Williams (P) than the original plan.

Toker v. Westerman

(Assignee of Appliance Dealer) v. (Refrigerator-Freezer Buyer)

(1970) 113 N.J. Super. 452; 274 A.2d 78

MEMORY GRAPHIC

Instant Facts

An appliance dealer brought suit to enforce a sales contract against a customer who asserted that the contract price was unconscionable and could not be enforced.

Black Letter Rule

An unconscionable contract is one that no one in their right senses and not under delusions would make, on the one hand, and which no honest and fair person would accept, on the other.

Case Vocabulary

ASSIGNOR: A person or entity that transfers rights or property to another.

INSTALLMENT CONTRACT: An agreement under which performance and/or payment are made periodically.

UNCONSCIONABLE CONTRACT: Contractual provisions benefitting one party that are so one-sided as to unfairly surprise or oppress the other party.

Procedural Basis: District court action to enforce an installment contract for the sale of goods.

Facts: A door-to-door salesman for People's Foods of New Jersey ("People's Foods") sold a refrigerator-freezer to Westerman (D) under an installment contract which called for 36 monthly payments of $34.16, totaling $1,229.76, which included sales tax, life insurance, and a time-price differential. After paying $655.85 over a period of time, Westerman (D) refused to pay the balance of $573.89, claiming that the unit sold was so over-priced that the sales contract was unconscionable and unenforceable in New Jersey, which had adopted the Uniform Commercial Code ("UCC"). Some time after the contract had been signed, People's Foods assigned its contractual rights to Toker (P). Toker (P) filed suit in New Jersey district court to enforce the contract against Westerman (D). At trial, Westerman (D) presented an appliance dealer who had inspected the refrigerator-freezer at issue. The dealer testified that the unit was not frost-free, had no special features, and only 18 cubic feet of capacity. He said it was known in the trade as a "stripped unit" and estimated the reasonable retail price at the time of the sale as between $350 and $400, stating that the most expensive refrigerator on the market of comparable size would have sold for $500.

Issue: Is a contract with a total sale price that is 2.5 times the reasonable retail price for comparable goods unconscionable within the meaning of the UCC?

Decision and Rationale: (McKenzie, J.) Yes. The issue here is whether the sale price in this case was "unconscionable." The UCC does not define the term "unconscionable." Elsewhere an unconscionable contract has been defined as one that no one in their right senses and not under delusions would make, on the one hand, and which no honest and fair person would accept, on the other. While a court should not allow the unconscionability provision of the UCC Code to be used as a manipulative tool to let a buyer avoid the consequences of a bargain he later finds to be unfavorable, here, the court finds shocking and therefore unconscionable the sale of goods for approximately 2.5 times their reasonable value. It is particularly shocking where, as here, the sale was made by a door-to-door salesman for a dealer, who therefore would have less overhead expense than a dealer maintaining a store or showroom. In addition, it appears that Westerman (D) was forced to seek welfare assistance during the course of making the payments on the refrigerator. While there are no other cases in New Jersey on this precise issue, it appears that those few states that have considered the issue, have uniformly held that the purchase price alone may be found to be unconscionable. While courts continue to recognize that persons should not be unnecessarily restricted in their freedom to contract, there is an increasing willingness to invalidate unconscionable contractual provisions which clearly tend to injure the public in some way. In this case, the court finds that in receiving $655.85, Toker (P) and his assignor have received a reasonable sum from Westerman (D). The payment of the balance of the purchase price will not be enforced. Judgment for Westerman (D).

Analysis:

Section 2-302 (1) of the Uniform Commercial Code ("UCC") provides that if a court, as a matter of law finds a contract or any clause of a contract to have been "unconscionable" at the time it was made, the court may refuse to enforce the contract, may enforce the contract without the unconscionable clause, or limit the application of the unconscionable clause to avoid any unconscionable result. As the court here notes, the UCC does not define unconscionability. Comments to the UCC suggest that there can be two kinds of unconscionability: (1) procedural unconscionability, which essentially amounts to the unfair surprise of a party; and (2) substantive unconscionability, which is the oppression of one party by another. Here, the court seems to focus on substantive unconscionability, finding the contract unconscionable on the grounds that the grossly excessive purchase price shocks its conscience and offends basic notions of fairness. At the same time, though, the court notes that Westerman (D) was so poor that he had to go on welfare after the sale, which at least hints at greatly unequal bargaining power, a kind of procedural unconscionability. Unlike other cases in the unconscionability area, the court here makes no specific finding of actual misconduct in the bargaining process, simply holding that the excessive price was oppressive, by itself. Assuming that Westerman (D) was fully aware of the terms of the contract and freely consented to the transaction, classical contract law (economic libertarianism) would hold him to his bargain, even if it was a bad bargain. Applying the modern approach of the UCC, the court here reformulates the bargain to achieve what it views as a fair result for both parties.

Frostifresh Corp. v. Reynoso

(Appliance Company) v. (Refrigerator-Freezer Buyer)

(1966) 52 Misc.2d 26; 274 N.Y.S.2d 757

MEMORY GRAPHIC

Instant Facts

An appliance company brought suit to enforce an installment sales contract against a couple who had not paid for a refrigerator-freezer they had bought under the contract.

Black Letter Rule

Under § 2-302 of the Uniform Commercial Code, courts have the power to modify the general rule that parties may make whatever contracts they please so long as there is no fraud or illegality, in order to prevent oppression or unfair surprise by contracts or terms they find to be unconscionable.

Case Vocabulary

OVERHEAD: Administrative expenses of a business, including salaries, office expenses, sales commissions, and other indirect costs.

Procedural Basis: District court action to enforce an installment contract for the sale of goods.

Facts: A Spanish-speaking door-to-door salesman for Frostifresh Corp. ("Frostifresh") (P) sold a refrigerator-freezer to the Reynosos (D), a husband and wife who only spoke Spanish. During the sales negotiation, Mr. Reynoso (D) told the salesman that he was about to leave his job and could not afford to buy the appliance. The salesman told the Reynosos (D) that the appliance would end up costing them nothing because they would get $25.00 commissions on all the sales that he would make to their neighbors and friends. The salesman then gave the Reynosos (D) a retail installment contract, entirely in English, which he neither translated nor explained to them. The contract contained a sales price of $900, plus a credit charge of $245.88, for a total price for the appliance of $1,145.88. The Reynosos (D) made only one payment of $32 on the appliance. Subsequently, Frostifresh (P) filed suit seeking $1,364.10, consisting of the total contract price, plus attorney fees and a late charge. At trial, Frostifresh (P) admitted that its cost for the appliance was $348.

Issue: Does § 2-302 of the Uniform Commercial Code give courts the power to modify the general rule that parties may make whatever contracts they please so long as there is no fraud or illegality, in order to prevent oppression or unfair surprise by contracts or terms they find to be unconscionable?

Decision and Rationale: (Donovan, J.) Yes. The court finds that the sale of the appliance at the price and terms indicated in this contract is shocking to the conscience. The service charge, which almost equals Frostifresh's (P) cost for the appliance, by itself shows the oppression that was practiced on the Reynosos (D). The Reynosos (D) were handicapped by a lack of knowledge, both as to the commercial situation and the nature and terms of the contract, which was submitted in a language that was foreign to them. Normally, parties are free to make whatever contracts they please, so long as there is no fraud or illegality. No defense of fraud was pleaded here, and no such defense is available. It is the apparent intent of § 2-302 of the Uniform Commercial Code ("UCC"), however, to modify the general rule, by giving courts the power to police explicitly against contracts or clauses they find to be unconscionable. The principle is one of the prevention of oppression and unfair surprise. The comment to § 2-302 cites a case in which a farmer refused to deliver carrots at the contract price of $23 to $33 a ton, since the market price had since increased to $90 a ton. In that case, the court found the contract "too hard a bargain and too one-sided an agreement to" be enforced by "a court of conscience." Here, I find that this contract also was "too hard a bargain" and the conscience of this court will not permit its enforcement as written. Accordingly, Frostifresh (P) will not be allowed to recover the price set forth in the contract. However, since the Reynosos (D) still have the refrigerator, they must reimburse Frostifresh (P) for its cost for the appliance, $348, minus the $32 they already paid toward the appliance. No allowance is permitted for any of Frostifresh's (P) other overhead costs, such as salesmen commissions, legal fees, or service charges.

Analysis:

This was one of the first cases to explore the reach of § 2-302 of the UCC. The court here finds both procedural unconscionability and substantive unconscionability reasons for refusing to enforce the contract. The court emphasizes the fact that the Reynosos (D) were poor and spoke only Spanish and that the salesman never translated the contract they signed. In addition, Frostifresh's (P) salesman employed misleading sales tactics. This suggests unfair surprise to the Reynosos (D) or procedural unconscionability. The Court also emphasizes the huge difference in the cost of the appliance to Frostifresh (P), $368, and the total contract price the Reynosos (D) were charged, $1,145.88. In the court's view, this disparity was too shocking and oppressive to be enforced. This is substantive unconscionability. Since the Reynosos (D) retained the appliance, however, the court's answer here was to reform the contract, requiring the Reynosos (D) to pay only the cost of the appliance to Frostifresh (P) with no profit for Frostifresh (P) and no reasonable allocation of overhead expenses. On appeal, Frostifresh (P) was granted a reasonable profit and reasonable overhead expenses by the appellate court.

Frostifresh Corp. v. Reynoso

(Appliance Company) v. (Refrigerator-Freezer Buyer)
(1967) 54 Misc.2d 119; 281 N.Y.S.2d 964

M E M O R Y   G R A P H I C

Instant Facts

An appliance company appealed a trial court judgment that refused to enforce an installment sales contract against a consumer as unconscionable and ordered the consumer to merely pay the cost to the appliance company of the product sold, with no allowance for profit.

Black Letter Rule

Although a party may not be entitled to the full benefit of a contract that has been found unconscionable, the party should be permitted to make a reasonable profit on any performance it has rendered under the contract.

Case Vocabulary

FINANCE CHARGE: Interest on an amount borrowed or owed over time.

Procedural Basis: Appellate court review of a district court judgment refusing to enforce an installment contract for the sale of goods.

Facts: A Spanish-speaking door-to-door salesman for Frostifresh Corp. ("Frostifresh") (P) sold a refrigerator-freezer to the Reynosos (D), a husband and wife who only spoke Spanish. During the sales negotiation, Mr. Reynoso (D) told the salesman that he was about to leave his job and could not afford to buy the appliance. The salesman told the Reynosos (D) that the appliance would end up costing them nothing because they would get $25.00 commissions on all the sales that he would make to their neighbors and friends. The salesman then gave the Reynosos (D) a retail installment contract, entirely in English, which he neither translated nor explained to them. The contract contained a sales price of $900, plus a credit charge of $245.88, for a total price for the appliance of $1,145.88. The Reynosos (D) made only one payment of $32 on the appliance. Subsequently, Frostifresh (P) filed suit seeking $1,364.10, consisting of the total contract price, plus attorney fees and a late charge. At trial, Frostifresh (P) admitted that its cost for the appliance was $348. The trial court held that the contract was unconscionable and therefore unenforceable. Since the Reynosos (D) retained the appliance, however, the trial court ordered them to pay Frostifresh (P) $316, the cost of the appliance to Frostifresh (P), $348, minus the $32 the Reynosos (D) had already paid. The trial court specifically denied Frostifresh (P) any reimbursement for its overhead expense, including sales commissions, legal fees, and service charges. Frostifresh (P) appealed.

Issue: Should a party be permitted to make a reasonable profit on any performance it has rendered under an unconscionable contract?

Decision and Rationale: (Per Curiam) Yes. While the evidence justifies finding the contract unconscionable under § 2-302 of the Uniform Commercial Code ("UCC"), we unanimously agree that Frostifresh (P) should recover its net cost for the appliance, plus a reasonable profit, as well as necessary trucking and service charges, and reasonable finance charges. We remand for a new trial solely to assess proper damages. Reversed.

Analysis:

Section 2-302(1) of the UCC provides that where a court has found a contract or a provision of a contract to be unconscionable, the court may refuse to enforce the contract, may enforce the contract without the unconscionable clause, or may limit the application of the unconscionable clause to avoid any unconscionable result. The trial court had limited Frostifresh (P) to its cost for the refrigerator-freezer, reforming the unconscionable contract to set what it viewed as a reasonable price under the circumstances. The appellate court here agrees that the contract was unconscionable, but holds that a reasonable price would permit recovery of a reasonable profit, any necessary expenses like delivery and service charges, and a reasonable finance charge. Neither court was completely willing to absolve the Reynosos (D) of all responsibility under the contract, but the courts appear to differ as to the purpose of the remedy they impose. The trial court's remedy essentially penalized Frostifresh (P) for trying to get away with a 325% mark-up. The appellate court, while clearly feeling sympathy for the Reynosos' (D) situation, took the approach of § 208(g) of the *Restatement 2d, Contracts,* which says that the policy behind the unconscionability doctrine is not penal. Under the *Restatement* approach, unless the parties can be restored to their pre-contract positions, the offending party in an unconscionable contract will ordinarily be awarded at least the reasonable value of the performance rendered.

We Care Hair Development, Inc. v. Engen

(Franchisor) v. (Franchisee)
(1999) 180 F.3d 838

M E M O R Y   G R A P H I C

Instant Facts

A franchisor filed suit in federal court pursuant to the Federal Arbitration Act to enjoin a state court lawsuit by franchisees who had signed a franchise agreement with a provision requiring arbitration of any dispute arising from or relating to the franchise agreement.

Black Letter Rule

Where there has been fair advance disclosure of the effect of a contractual provision between a franchisor and a franchisee that requires arbitration of disputes under the contract for the franchisee, but leaves the franchisor an option to litigate disputes, the provision will not be deemed so one-sided as to be unconscionable and unenforceable against the franchisee.

Case Vocabulary

ARBITRATION: A dispute resolution mechanism that takes place outside of the formal judicial system in which a neutral third party agreed to by the disputing parties hears a dispute and renders a decision. Generally, the procedures are informal and the arbitrator's decision is binding on the parties.

ARBITRATION CLAUSE: A provision in a contract requiring the parties to resolve a dispute through arbitration rather than through litigation.

FRANCHISEE: A person or entity that is granted a license or legal right to conduct a particular business under detailed operational methods established and regulated by a person or entity known as the franchisor.

FRANCHISOR: A person or entity that grants a license or legal right to conduct a particular business, according to detailed standards and methods it establishes, to persons or entities known as franchisees.

OFFERING CIRCULAR: A statement required by law to be distributed to prospective franchisees by a franchisor, disclosing the terms and risks involved in accepting a franchise.

Procedural Basis: Appellate review by the U.S. Court of Appeals for the Seventh Circuit of a U.S. District Court order enjoining state court litigation and compelling arbitration of the state law disputes.

Facts: We Care Hair Development, Inc. ("We Care Hair") (P) was a subsidiary of Doctor's Associates, Inc., a corporation that was the franchisor of several different national business franchises, including Subway sandwich shops, Cajun Joe's Fried Chicken, and We Care Hair (P). Engen (D) and other franchisees of We Care Hair (P) brought a class action lawsuit against We Care Hair (P) in Illinois state court, alleging breach of fiduciary duty, fraud, and other state law claims arising out of the franchise agreements they had signed with We Care Hair (P). Each of the franchise agreements with We Care Hair (P) contained a clause requiring arbitration of all disputes arising out of or relating to the franchise agreements. Additionally, all franchisees of We Care Hair (P) were required to sublease their franchise premises from a leasing company owned by We Care Hair (P). Under the subleases, arbitration was not required and the leasing company could file an eviction lawsuit against a franchisee for any breach of the sublease. The subleases contained cross-default provisions which made every breach of the franchise agreement an automatic breach of the sublease. Before any franchise agreement or sublease was signed, We Care Hair (P) gave all prospective franchisees a uniform offering circular that specifically disclosed that the franchise agreement's arbitration provisions did not apply to the sublease and that, despite the arbitration clause in the franchise agreement, the leasing company could terminate the sublease and evict a franchisee for any breach of the sublease, including a breach of the franchise agreement. The circular also noted that We Care Hair (P) could terminate a sublease without also terminating a franchise agreement, which would render the franchise agreement worthless to the franchisee. After Engen (D) and the other franchisees filed their state class actions, We Care Hair (P) filed suit in federal district court asserting that, under the Federal Arbitration Act ("FAA"), Engen (D) and the other franchisees should be enjoined from proceeding with their lawsuits and compelled to arbitrate their claims pursuant to the franchise agreements they had signed. The district court agreed with We Care Hair (P), enjoining the class actions and ordering arbitration. Engen (D) and the other franchisees appealed, arguing the arbitration clause in the franchise agreement, when combined with the cross-default provision in the sublease, was unconscionable and against public policy.

Issue: In the absence of unfair surprise, will a contractual provision between a franchisor and a franchisee that requires arbitration of disputes under the contract for the franchisee, but leaves the franchisor an option to litigate disputes, be deemed so one-sided as to be unconscionable and unenforceable against the franchisee?

Decision and Rationale: (Wood, J.) No. Under the FAA, arbitration clauses are valid and enforceable except on such grounds as may exist at law or in equity for the revocation of any contract. State contract defenses may be applied to invalidate arbitration clauses if those defenses apply to contracts generally. Here, Illinois law applies. Engen (D) and the other franchisees argue that the arbitration clause in the franchise agreement, when combined with the cross-default provision of the sublease, is unconscionable because it forces franchisees to arbitrate their claims, but lets the franchisor litigate its claims through eviction actions filed by its leasing company. To decide if a contractual provision should be disregarded as unconscionable, Illinois courts look to the circumstances existing at the time of the contract's formation, including the relative bargaining positions of the parties and whether the provision's operation would result in unfair surprise. A contract is unconscionable when, viewed as a whole, it is oppressive or totally one-sided. Here, the arbitration clause did not unfairly

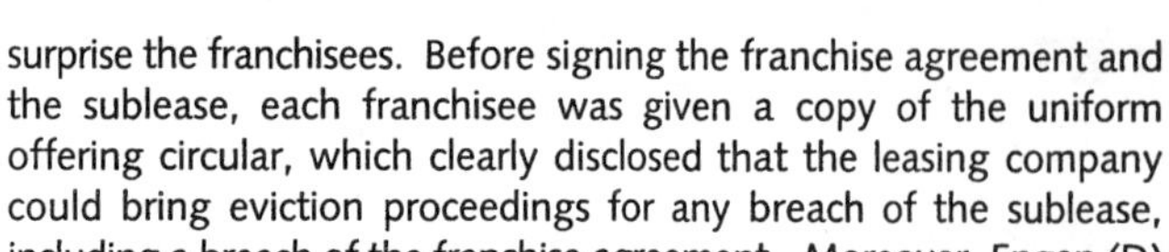

surprise the franchisees. Before signing the franchise agreement and the sublease, each franchisee was given a copy of the uniform offering circular, which clearly disclosed that the leasing company could bring eviction proceedings for any breach of the sublease, including a breach of the franchise agreement. Moreover, Engen (D) and the other franchisees were not vulnerable consumers or helpless workers, but business people who bought franchises. We cannot find that they were forced to swallow distasteful terms. The arbitration clause here was not unconscionable. Affirmed.

Analysis:

The court here gives two reasons for upholding the franchise agreement's requirement that the franchisees must arbitrate all claims arising from or relating to the franchise agreement as not unconscionable. First, it notes that the franchisees each received a uniform offering circular before they signed any agreements with the franchisor, which specifically disclosed the fact that while the franchisees would have to arbitrate all disputes, the franchisor would have the ability to cause its leasing company to file an eviction lawsuit against the franchisee for any breach of the franchise agreement and would not necessarily have to bring its claims to an arbitrator. Since these facts were clearly disclosed in the offering circular, the court says there was no unfair surprise to the franchisees which should result in a finding of unconscionability. Second, the court suggests that, the franchisees, as business persons, were not as vulnerable as consumers or workers might be in contracting with the franchisor and do not need the same heightened level of protection that consumers or workers would receive from a court scrutinizing their bargains. Franchisees, however, while business persons, do not always have equal bargaining power with their franchisor. Franchisors gain considerable cost savings by having standard form franchise agreements and regularized policies for all franchisees. Often, the franchisee is in a take-it-or-leave-it position with respect to signing a franchise agreement presented by the franchisor. They either accept whatever terms have been proposed by the franchisor or lose the ability to obtain a franchise. Under such circumstances, a court might be justified in finding flagrantly oppressive terms of a franchise agreement to be unconscionable, regardless of disclosure by the offending party.

ARIZONA SUPREME COURT REFUSES TO ENFORCE AN ARBITRATION AGREEMENT AGAINST A YOUNG, POOR AND NOT-WELL-EDUCATED WOMAN WHO SIGNED UNDER STRESS

Broemmer v. Abortion Services of Phoenix, Ltd.

(Patient) v. (Medical Practice)
(1992) 173 Ariz. 148; 840 P.2d 1013

M E M O R Y   G R A P H I C

Instant Facts

A woman who had been injured by a doctor during a medical procedure brought a malpractice suit for damages in state court, despite having signed a standardized form contract presented to her by the doctor agreeing to arbitrate any disputes related to the medical procedure.

Black Letter Rule

An adhesion contract will not be enforced to the extent it contains provisions that do not fall within the reasonable expectations of the adhering party.

Case Vocabulary

ADHESION CONTRACT: A standardized form contract that is offered to consumers of goods or services without an opportunity to negotiate terms with the receipt of the desired good or service strictly conditioned on agreement to the contract's provisions.
BINDING ARBITRATION: A dispute resolution mechanism in which parties agree to have their case heard and decided by a neutral third party whose decision the parties must accept, subject to whatever appeal rights, if any, may be provided by their agreement.
WAIVER: The intentional and voluntary giving up of a known right or privilege.

Procedural Basis: Appeal to the Arizona Supreme Court of a decision of the Arizona Court of Appeals affirming a trial court grant of summary judgment.

Facts: Melinda Kay Broemmer ("Broemmer") (P), an unmarried, 21-year-old woman, was 16-17 weeks pregnant. She had no medical benefits, was earning less than $100 a week, and only a high school education. The baby's father insisted Broemmer (P) have an abortion. Her parents advised against it. Broemmer (P) was in a state of considerable confusion and emotional and physical turmoil. Finally, her mother helped her arrange an appointment with Abortion Services of Phoenix, Ltd. ("ASP") (D). When she arrived at ASP's (D) clinic, she was asked to complete three forms: a two-page consent-to-operate form, a questionnaire asking for a complete medical history, and an "Agreement to Arbitrate." The agreement to arbitrate provided that any dispute arising between the parties as a result of the fees and/or services provided by ASP (D) would be settled by binding arbitration, conducted by an arbitrator appointed by the American Arbitration Association ("AAA") who was required to be a licensed medical doctor specializing in obstetrics/gynecology. Broemmer (P) completed all three forms in less than five minutes and returned them to the front desk. ASP (D) staff made no attempt to explain the agreement to arbitrate to Broemmer (P) before or after she signed and did not provide her with copies of any of the forms. Broemmer (P) was told to return the next day, at which time ASP's (D) doctor performed the abortion. As a result of the procedure, Broemmer (P) suffered a punctured uterus that required medical treatment. Approximately 1 ½ years later, Broemmer (P) filed a malpractice complaint against ASP (D) and its doctor in Arizona court. Broemmer (P) did not recall having signed the agreement to arbitrate. ASP (D) moved to dismiss the case, arguing that the trial court lacked subject matter jurisdiction because arbitration was required. The trial court treated the motion as one for summary judgment, which it granted to ASP (D). On appeal, the Arizona Court of Appeals held the arbitration agreement was a contract of adhesion, it was enforceable because it did not fall outside Broemmer's (P) reasonable expectations and was not unconscionable. Broemmer (P) then appealed to the Arizona Supreme Court, which granted review of her petition.

Issue: Is an agreement to arbitrate all claims beyond the reasonable expectations of the adhering party to an adhesion contract, such that it should be deemed unenforceable against that party?

Decision and Rationale: (Moeller, J.) Yes. We hold that, under the undisputed facts in this case, the agreement to arbitrate is not enforceable against Broemmer (P). When agreements to arbitrate are freely and fairly entered, they will be welcomed and enforced. They are not, however, exempted from the usual rules of contract law. Arizona statute authorizes written agreements to arbitrate and provides that they are valid and enforceable, except on such grounds as exist at law or in equity for the revocation of any contract. Thus the validity of the arbitration agreement is determined by general principles of contract law. Under those principles, this was an adhesion contract. Such contracts are typically a standardized form offered to consumers of goods and services on essentially a take-it-or-leave-it basis, without giving the consumer a realistic opportunity to bargain. Generally, the consumer cannot obtain the desired product or service except by agreeing to the form contract. Bargaining position and leverage let one party select and control the risks assumed under the contract. Here, the printed form signed by Broemmer (P) is a standardized contract, offered on a take-it-or-leave-it basis. In addition to removing from the courts any potential dispute concerning fees or services, ASP (D), the drafter, inserted additional terms potentially advantageous to itself, requiring that any arbitrator appointed by the AAA be a licensed medical doctor specializing in obstetrics/gynecology. The contract was not negotiated, but was instead prepared by ASP (D) and presented to Broemmer (P) as a condition of treatment. ASP's (D) staff neither explained its terms nor indicated that Broemmer (P) could refuse to sign the form. They simply told her that she had to complete the three forms. An adhesion contract, however, is fully enforceable, unless certain other factors operate to render it unenforceable. The comment to § 211 of the *Restatement 2d, Contracts* [provision of the *Restatement* dealing with the enforceability of standardized contracts] explains that although customers typically adhere to standardized agreements and are bound by them without even appearing to know the standard terms in detail, they are not bound to unknown terms which are beyond the range of reasonable expectation. Thus, the issue here is whether it was beyond Broemmer's (P) reasonable expectations to expect to arbitrate her medical malpractice claims, which included waiving her right to a jury trial, as part of the completion of the three forms under the facts and circumstances of this case. Clearly, there was no explicit waiver of the fundamental right to a jury trial or any evidence that such rights were knowingly, voluntarily, and intelligently waived. The only evidence presented compels a finding that waiver of such fundamental rights was beyond Broemmer's (P) reasonable expectations. Moreover, ASP's (D) failure to explain to Broemmer (P) that the agreement required all potential disputes, including malpractice disputes, to be heard only by an arbitrator who was a licensed obstetrician/gynecologist, requires us to view the "bargaining" process with suspicion. It would be unreasonable to enforce such a critical term against Broemmer (P) when it was not a negotiated term and ASP (D) failed to explain it to her or call her attention to it. Broemmer (P) was under a great deal of emotional stress, had only a high school education, was inexperienced in commercial matters, and is still not sure what arbitration is. We find the arbitration provision unenforceable. Reversed.

Dissent: (Martone, J.) The court's conclusion that the agreement to arbitrate was outside of Broemmer's (P) reasonable expectations is without basis in law or fact. I fear that today's decision reflects a preference for litigation over alternative dispute resolution that I think is improper under our law. The court ignores several undisputed facts. At the top of the agreement to arbitrate, it states in bold capital letters "PLEASE READ THIS CONTRACT CAREFULLY AS IT EFFECTS [sic] YOUR LEGAL RIGHTS." Right below that phrase in all capital letters are the words " AGREEMENT TO ARBITRATE." The agreement recited that the parties agreed it to be in their respective best interests to settle any disputes as quickly and economically as possible and to that end, the parties agreed to settle any disputes over services by arbitration in accordance with the rules of the AAA through an arbitrator appointed by the AAA who would be a licensed medical doctor specializing in obstetrics/gynecology. Broemmer (P), an adult, signed the document. The court seizes on the doctrine of reasonable expectations to revoke this contract. There is nothing in the record, however, to justify a finding that an agreement to arbitrate a malpractice claim was not within the reasonable expectations of the parties. On this record, the exact opposite is likely to be true. For all we know, both sides might wish to avoid litigation like the plague and seek a more harmonious resolution to disputes. Nor is there anything in the record to suggest that arbitration is bad. Where is the harm? An arbitration provision does no more than specify a forum for settlement of disputes. There can be many benefits over litigation. Arbitration may be faster and less expensive. The simplified procedures and relaxed rules of evidence in arbitration may aid an injured plaintiff in presenting his case. Plaintiffs with less serious injuries, who cannot afford high litigation expenses, will benefit greatly from the simplicity and economy of arbitration. Arbitration could resolve many minor malpractice claims that might not otherwise ever be heard due to economic reasons. The court wrongly attempts to apply § 211 of the *Restatement 2d, Contracts* as a basis for its decision that the arbitration agreement was beyond Broemmer's (P) reasonable expectations. Under § 211, standardized agreements are enforceable, except where a party has reason to believe that the other party would not agree if he knew that the writing contained a particular term. Such belief may be shown by the prior negotiations of the parties or inferred from the circumstances, as where the term is bizarre or oppressive. The inference is reinforced if the adhering party never had a chance to read the term, or if it is illegible or otherwise hidden from view. Here, there are no facts to support any of these factors. There were no prior negotiations that were contrary to arbitration. An agreement to arbitrate is hardly bizarre or oppressive. It is a preferred method of alternative dispute resolution that our legislature has expressly acknowledged by statute. Broemmer (P) had a chance to read the agreement, which was legible and in bold capital letters. Thus, the reasonable expectations standard of the *Restatement 2d, Contracts* does not support the court's conclusion. Moreover, the introductory note to chapter 8 of the *Restatement 2d, Contracts* specifically approves of agreements to arbitrate future disputes as serving the public interest by saving court time and specifically provides that the rules of the *Restatement* do not preclude their enforcement. All that could explain the court's decision here is a preference for litigation over arbitration. The court expresses sympathy for Broemmer (P) as though arbitration were harmful to her interests. Arizona public policy, however, has long supported arbitration as good not evil. I would affirm.

Analysis:

The majority's recitation of the facts here stresses that Broemmer (P) was in a confused and emotional state when she signed the agreement, had limited education, was poor, and was desperate. The majority suggests that arbitration is less advantageous than litigation to a patient like Broemmer (P), and suggests that it was beyond her reasonable expectations that, by signing the agreement to arbitrate, she would be waiving all right to litigate any malpractice by ASP (D). By stressing that this was an adhesion contract that was not really the result of traditional bargaining between the parties, the court feels justified in overlooking the parties' "agreement." Perhaps if the contract had more clearly spelled out that Broemmer (P) was agreeing to waive her right to malpractice litigation, the issue would have been harder for the majority. The dissent highlights the fact that Broemmer (P), an adult, read and signed the agreement, which very clearly (in bold, capital letters) indicated that she was agreeing to arbitrate any claims related to fees or services. In its view, a reasonable adult should have recognized that by signing such an agreement she would be waiving a right to litigate malpractice claims. While the dissent correctly recognizes that arbitration, in and of itself, is not necessarily a bad thing for a plaintiff, it does not pay enough attention to the unequal bargaining power at play here and the desperate circumstance under which Broemmer (P) came to ASP (D) seeking medical services.

WEST VIRGINIA SUPREME COURT FINDS AGREEMENT REQUIRING A BORROWER TO ARBITRATE, BUT PERMITTING A LENDER TO LITIGATE, TO BE UNCONSCIONABLE

Arnold v. United Companies Lending Corp.

(Mortgagor) v. (Mortgagee)
(1998) 204 W.Va. 229; 511 S.E.2d 854

M E M O R Y   G R A P H I C

Instant Facts

An elderly couple sought a declaratory judgment that a contract they had signed with a lender that required them to arbitrate any claims they had against the lender but permitted the lender to litigate collection of its debt or foreclosure proceedings in court to be void as unconscionable.

Black Letter Rule

Under certain circumstances, gross inadequacy in bargaining power, together with contractual terms that are unreasonably favorable to the stronger party, and a lack of meaningful alternatives for the weaker party will indicate that such terms are unconscionable and therefore void.

Case Vocabulary

MORTGAGE BROKER: A person or entity who arranges loans for borrowers with lenders in return for a fee.

Procedural Basis: West Virginia Supreme Court review of certified questions from a state circuit court regarding a declaratory judgment action to declare an agreement unenforceable.

Facts: Michael Searls ("Searls") (D1), a mortgage broker arranged a $19,300 mortgage loan from United Companies Lending Corp. ("United') (D2) for Orville and Maxine Arnold ("the Arnolds") (P), an elderly couple each with less than a ninth grade education. At the loan closing, the Arnolds (P) were presented with more than 25 documents to sign. Among these documents was a two-page form labeled "Acknowledgment and Agreement to Mediate or Arbitrate," which stated that all legal controversies relating to the loan, including the validity and construction of the arbitration agreement were to be resolved solely by arbitration. The agreement, however, expressly did not apply to United's (D2) right to pursue collection of the debt or foreclosure of the Arnolds' (P) mortgaged property in court, upon default by the Arnolds (P). United (D2) was represented by counsel at the closing, but the Arnolds (P) were not. Within less than one year of the closing, the Arnolds (P) fully paid off their loan. In a dispute about the loan that is not clear in the record, however, the Arnolds (P) subsequently filed a declaratory judgment action in West Virginia state court against Searls (D1) and United (D2) seeking a court order declaring the arbitration agreement void and unenforceable. United (D2) moved to dismiss the action on the basis of the arbitration agreement. The Arnolds (P) moved for summary judgment. The trial court certified the issue of the validity of the arbitration agreement to the West Virginia Supreme Court.

Issue: Under certain circumstances, can gross inadequacy in bargaining power, together with contractual terms that are unreasonably favorable to the stronger party, and a lack of meaningful alternatives for the weaker party, render such contractual terms unconscionable and therefore void?

Decision and Rationale: (McCuskey, J.) Yes. The Arnolds (P) argue that the arbitration agreement is void as unconscionable, invoking the West Virginia Consumer Credit and Protection Act, which was specifically designed to eradicate unconscionability in consumer transactions. The Arnolds (P) point to the unfairness resulting from the terms of the agreement in this case that bind the consumer to relinquish his right to a day in court and virtually all substantive rights, while the lender retains the right to a judicial forum for purposes of collection and foreclosure. The principle of unconscionability is one of the prevention of oppression and unfair surprise and not the disturbance of reasonable allocation of risks or reasonable advantage because of superior bargaining power or position. The test is whether, given the background and setting of the particular contract, the contract or clauses are so one sided as to be unconscionable under the circumstances existing at the time the conduct occurs or is threatened at the time of the making of the contract. The particular facts of each case are critical. A contract may be unconscionable in some circumstances, but not in others. Gross inadequacy in bargaining power, together with terms unreasonably favorable to the stronger party, may confirm indications that the transaction involved elements of deception or compulsion or may show that the weaker party had no meaningful, real alternative, or did not in fact assent to the unfair terms. A determination of unconscionability must focus on the relative positions of the parties, the adequacy of the bargaining position, the meaningful alternatives available to the plaintiff, and the existence of unfair terms in the contract. Applying these rules here, we conclude that the arbitration agreement between the Arnolds (P) and United (D2) is void for unconscionability as a matter of law. This kind of contract has aptly been characterized as a contract between the rabbits and the foxes. The relative positions of the parties, a national corporate lender on one side and elderly, unsophisticated consumers on the other, were grossly unequal. In addition, Searls (D1), the loan broker, made no other option

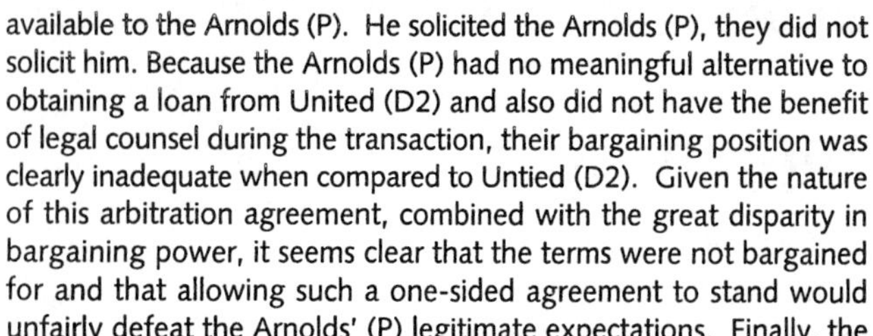

available to the Arnolds (P). He solicited the Arnolds (P), they did not solicit him. Because the Arnolds (P) had no meaningful alternative to obtaining a loan from United (D2) and also did not have the benefit of legal counsel during the transaction, their bargaining position was clearly inadequate when compared to Untied (D2). Given the nature of this arbitration agreement, combined with the great disparity in bargaining power, it seems clear that the terms were not bargained for and that allowing such a one-sided agreement to stand would unfairly defeat the Arnolds' (P) legitimate expectations. Finally, the terms of the agreement are unreasonably favorable to United (D2). United (D2) could act in a way that might seriously damage the Arnolds (P) and they would only be able to submit the matter to binding arbitration. United (D2), however, would have its access to the courts preserved in every conceivable situation for which it might want to secure judicial relief against the Arnolds (P). This disparity is inherently inequitable and unconscionable because in a way it nullifies all the other provisions of the contract.

Analysis:

The court views this transaction as a contract between rabbits and foxes and refuses to enforce an agreement to arbitrate which it finds was one-sided and essentially forced on the Arnolds (P) and was not the result of a true "bargain" between the parties. Compare the result here with the result in *We Care Hair Development, Inc. v. Engen,* earlier in this chapter. In *We Care Hair*, the Seventh Circuit Court of Appeals refused to find that a franchise agreement that permitted a franchisor to litigate, while requiring a franchisee to arbitrate its claims was unconscionable. It found that the franchisor had fully disclosed the disparity in an offering document that was given to prospective franchisees before they signed their franchise agreements. United (D2) gave no similar kind of disclosure to the Arnolds (P) in this case. Moreover, in *We Care Hair*, the franchisees were sophisticated business persons with legal counsel. Here, the Arnolds (P) were elderly consumers with very little education, no legal representation, and were relying to a large extent on their mortgage broker. While a strong argument could be made that the franchisees were in a weak bargaining position just like the Arnolds (P) were, courts are generally much more willing to step in to protect consumers than to protect business persons competing in the marketplace.

Perspective
The Compensation Principle

Chapter 4

The goal of contract law is to provide a remedial mechanism aimed at enforcing contractual obligations incurred voluntarily. The law accomplishes this goal by requiring that a party in breach of contract pay damages to the nonbreaching party. The fundamental purpose of damages is to compensate the nonbreaching party's loss resulting from the broken promise. Although easy to understand from a conceptual point of view, the compensation goal often proves difficult to apply in "real life."

This chapter addresses two issues with regard to the law of contractual remedies. The first answers the question: What does it mean to *compensate* the nonbreaching party? The answer depends on the contractual theory upon which the plaintiff has brought his claim and the interest he seeks to protect. In most cases, the law seeks to place the nonbreaching party in the position he would have occupied had the contract been performed – i.e., protect the parties' expectation interest. In other cases however, reliance damages are the proper remedy. Reliance damages seek to place the nonbreaching party in the position it occupied just prior to the contract. A third remedy applied by courts is restitution, the goal of which is the place the breaching party in the position he occupied before the contract arose. In other words, restitution seeks to disgorge the breaching party of any benefits received as a result of the contractual or quasi-contractual relationship. It is important to note that these remedies are not mutually exclusive and all may apply in any one case.

This chapter also addresses a second, often more complicated issue, which is very much related to the first. Once it has been determined which remedy will apply, it becomes incumbent upon the plaintiff to prove (and the court to determine) the extent of the his loss. For example, suppose that a manufacturer enters into written agreement to sell 10,000 custom made widgets at a price of $1 each. If the buyer breaches the agreement by refusing to take possession and pay the purchase price, the manufacturer is entitled to recover his expectation damages. The manufacturer's expectation may be measured in one of two ways: (1) He may be entitled to recover the difference between the contract price and the market price at the time of breach; or (2) if that remedy proves inadequate, he may recover lost profits. The latter remedy then brings up the question of how to measure profits: Are gross profits to be used? Or do profits refer to net profit? Suppose that before trial the manufacturer winds up finding another buyer who takes the custom widgets at a price of 75¢ each. Is the buyer then entitled to a credit for the sale which resulted from his breach? Or would the manufacturer have made that sale regardless? Regardless of the outcome, the point of the hypothetical sale is to illustrate how these measurement issues can become numerically, economically and conceptually complicated, depending on the applicable facts. This chapter shows how courts deal with many of these issues.

Chapter Overview Outline
The Compensation Principle

Chapter 4

NOTE: THE PURPOSE OF THIS OUTLINE IS TO ORGANIZE THE CASES SO THAT ONE CAN QUICKLY UNDERSTAND THE RELEVANCE OF EACH CASE TO THE COURSE. NO ATTEMPT IS MADE IN THIS OVERVIEW TO ADDRESS EVERY CONCEPT THAT MUST BE STUDIED. BE SURE TO READ THE ENTIRE CASEBOOK AND/OR OTHER MATERIALS TO GAIN A FULL UNDERSTANDING OF ALL CONCEPTS.

I. Compensation or Punishment?
   A. The purpose of awarding contract damages is to compensate the injured party, not to punish the party in breach. *Restatement (Second) of Contracts §355.*
      1. Consequently, as a general matter, a plaintiff suing for breach of contract is not entitled to punitive damages. *White v. Benkowski.*
      2. The judicial policy disfavoring punitive damages in the case of a breach of contract also leads courts to refuse to enforce contractual provisions which provide that a breaching party must pay a predetermined amount of damages, regardless of the amount of damage actually done. *City of Rye v. Public Serv. Mut. Ins. Co.*
         a. Damages which are predetermined by contract are referred to as "liquidated" damages and are enforceable only if the actual amount of damage is difficult to ascertain with precision and the predetermined amount bears a reasonable relationship to the damage actually suffered. *City of Rye v. Public Serv. Mut. Ins. Co.*
   B. Note on the Efficient Breach Hypothesis
      1. The efficient breach theory is an economic theory which holds that contractual breaches should not be punished because they may be economically efficient, meaning that at least one party is better off, and no party is worse off as a result of the breach.
      2. For example, suppose that Farmer contracts to sell to Buyer 10 tons of wheat at $10,000 per ton (or whatever wholesale wheat is worth). Buyer, relying on the contract, contracts to sell the same wheat at $11,000 per ton.
         a. If Farmer is thereafter offered $12,000 a ton for the same wheat he agreed to sell to Buyer, it would be "efficient" for him to break the contract with Buyer and sell at the higher price.
         b. Selling at the higher price allows Farmer to cover Buyer's $10,000 profit lost as a result of the breach and realize for himself an extra $10,000 total profit.

II. Expectation Remedies
   A. The purpose of expectation remedies is to place the nonbreaching party in the position he would have occupied had there been no breach by the other party. Expectation damages have two components.
      1. The first component are the losses sustained in reliance on the contract.
         a. An example of these losses would be the value of auto parts purchased by a mechanic hired to fix a car.
      2. The second component is the nonbreaching party's opportunity cost, i.e. the gain prevented.
         a. The measure of the gain forgone is usually the profit the nonbreaching party would have realized had there been no breach.
         b. An example of an opportunity cost is the amount a mechanic could have made by agreeing to fix another car.
   B. Specific Performance
      1. Specific performance is an equitable remedy whereby courts, rather than requiring the payment of money damages, order the breaching party to complete the terms of the contract.
      2. Specific performance is a remedy available only in a few circumstances, most notably in contracts for the sale of real property.

a. Specific performance is unavailable for contracts for the sale of personal property, unless the property has some unique quality or value. *McCallister v. Patton*.

b. Specific performance is almost never available to remedy the breach of a contract for personal services. *London Bucket Co. v. Stewart.*

C. General Damages

1. General damages, as opposed to special or consequential damages, are those which are the normal consequence of any particular breach.

a. Turning again to the example of the mechanic who has suffered a breach, the general damages include the cost of any parts and materials purchased in reliance on the contract and the profit the mechanic was to make on the contract.

2. The measure of general damages depends heavily on the type of contract and identity of the breaching party.

a. Upon breach by the buyer, the seller of goods is normally entitled to the difference between the market price and unpaid contract price. *U.C.C. §2-708(1).*

(1) However, in cases where the contract price and the market price are the same, the seller is entitled to his lost profit, if the seller has an unlimited supply of the goods which make up the subject matter of the contract and those goods are of standard price. *Neri v. Retail Marine Corp.*

b. Upon breach by the seller, the buyer's damages are usually measured by the difference between the market price and the contract price. *U.C.C. §2-713(1).*

(1) The buyer is also allowed to "cover" – purchase substitute goods within a reasonable time – and recover from the breaching seller the difference between the contract price and the cover price. *Fertico Belgium S.A. v. Phosphate Chemicals Export Ass'n.*

(2) The measure of a seller's profit is the difference between the cost of the goods and the contract price – the gross margin – without any provision for overhead or fixed costs. *Vitex Manufacturing Corp. v. Caribtex Corp.*

c. Upon breach by the recipient, a provider of services is entitled to the whole of the contract price, less any monies realized for services rendered as a result of the breach. *Parker v. Twentieth Century-Fox Film.*

d. Upon breach by the provider of services, the recipient is entitled to the cost of performance, unless the economic loss resulting from the breach is dramatically lower than the cost of performance. *Peevyhouse v. Garland Coal & Mining Co.*

(1) In *Peevyhouse*, a landowner leased his farm to a mining company on the condition that company make any necessary restorative or remedial work prior to the end of the lease. When the mining company refused to complete the restoration, the court did not order the company to pay the landowner the cost of performing the work because the damage done to the land lessened its economic value by only a fraction of the cost of performance.

D. Limitation on Damages

1. Special or consequential damages are those which result from losses which are peculiar to the transaction or the nonbreaching party.

a. For example, if a dry cleaner contracts for the repair of its machines and the repairman fails to perform the work, the dry cleaner may suffer a loss of customers (and profits) due to its inability to service them on time.

2. To recover as consequential damages the loss of profits resulting from the breach of a contract, the nonbreaching party need prove the likelihood and extent of those

profits only with reasonable probability, not absolute certainty. *Locke v. United States*.

a. A newly formed business or venture with no track-record of profits bears such a high burden of proof with regard to lost profits that it severely limits the ability of new businesses or ventures to obtain consequential damages relating to profits. *Kenford Co., Inc. v. County of Erie*.

3. A plaintiff may recover only those consequential damages which were reasonably foreseeable to the defendant at the time the parties entered into the contract. *Hadley v. Baxendale*.

a. For example, suppose a bar takes its television in for repair so that the television is available for patrons to watch the Super Bowl the following week. The repair shop is unaware of the purpose of the repair. If the repair shop fails to fix the television on time, it cannot be held liable for the losses resulting from the bar's lack of patronage on the date of the Super Bowl because lost profits are not likely a foreseeable consequence of the failure to fix a television.

III. Reliance Remedies

A. Reliance remedies are intended to compensate the plaintiff for the detriment suffered in reliance on the contract. *Sullivan v. O'Connor*.

B. A party suing for breach of contract is entitled to recover those expenses incurred by relying on the performance of the contract, even if the expenses were incurred prior to the contract. *Security Stove & Mfg. Co. v. American Ry. Express Co.*

1. In *Security Stove*, the court allowed the plaintiff company to recover expenses incurred in reserving a spot at a trade show when the defendant company failed to timely transport the goods to be displayed at the show.

C. Lost Profits and Reliance

1. Some courts take the view that lost profits are protected by an expectation interest, and, therefore, are not recoverable when the plaintiff's claim is based on reliance, promissory estoppel or some similar theory. *Goodman v. Dicker*.

2. On the other hand, other courts take the opposite view, holding that lost profits may be protected by the reliance interest if the plaintiff gave up some profit making opportunity in reliance on the contract. *Walters v. Marathon Oil Co.*.

IV. Restitution

A. The purpose behind restitution is to place the party in breach in the position he occupied prior to the contract.

1. Thus, restitution focuses on the benefits conferred on the breaching party, rather than the detriment suffered by the non-breaching party.

B. Restitution is a quasi-contractual remedy which may be wholly separate from any underlying contract. *Oliver v. Campbell*.

1. Restitution is the remedy most often sought for part-performance because it allows the plaintiff to recover an amount based on the benefit conferred rather than the actual contract price. *United States v. Algernon*.

White v. Benkowski

(Married Couple Whose Water Was Supplied By Neighbors' Well) v. (Neighbors With Well)

37 Wis.2d 285, 155 N.W.2d 74 (1967)

M E M O R Y G R A P H I C

Instant Facts

A married couple who had contracted with their neighbors to purchase their supply of water from the neighbors' well filed a suit seeking punitive damages when the neighbors breached the contract by willfully shutting off the water supply from time to time in order to encourage water conservation.

Black Letter Rule

Punitive damages are not recoverable for breach of contract.

Case Vocabulary

COMPENSATORY DAMAGES: Damages intended to compensate a person for losses actually sustained.

NOMINAL DAMAGES: An small amount of damages, the purpose of which is to acknowledge the occurrence of a breach of contract which resulted in a negligible loss.

PECUNIARY DAMAGES: Money damages.

Procedural Basis: Appeal to the Supreme Court of Wisconsin to review the judgment of the trial court reducing a jury's compensatory award from $10 to $1 and granting a motion to strike the award of punitive damages.

Facts: Seeking a source of running water for their home, Virgil and Gwynneth White (the Whites) (P) entered into a written contract with Paul and Ruth Benkowski (the Benkowskis) (D) whereby the Benkowskis (D) promised to supply water from their well to the Whites' (P) home for a period of ten years, or until such earlier date as the Whites (P) could obtain water from the municipality or build their own well. In consideration for the supply of water, the Whites (P) agreed to pay $3 per month and one-half the cost of any future repairs or maintenance the well would require. On several days in 1964 the Benkowskis willfully shut-off the water supply to the Whites' (P) home. The Benkowskis (D) claimed the water was shut-off to allow sand to settle or to remind the Whites (P) that their water use was excessive. Claiming they were seriously inconvenienced by the lack of water and seeking compensatory and punitive damages for "a deliberate violation of the contract," the Whites (P) sued the Benkowskis (D) for breach of contract. When the jury was charged with a special verdict they were asked: (1) whether the Benkowskis (D) maliciously or wantonly shut-off the water supply for harassment purposes, and if so (2) what compensatory and punitive damages they were awarding the Whites (P). The jury rendered a verdict for the Whites (P), awarding them compensatory damages of $10 and punitive damages of $2,000. In addition to reducing the compensatory damages to $1, the court granted the Benkowskis' (D) motion to strike the punitive damages question and answer. The Whites (P) appealed.

Issue: Are punitive damages available for a breach of contract?

Decision and Rationale: (Wilkie, J.) No. Punitive damages are not recoverable for breach of contract. In this, and other, jurisdictions the large weight of authority recognizes the principle that a breach of contract does not lead to the award of punitive damages. In this state, punitive damages arising solely from a breach of contract are available only with respect to the breach of a promise to marry. It is true that a breach of contract may also be a tort which gives rise to punitive damages, but the Whites (P) neither pled nor proved a tort in this case. We also find that the court erred in reducing the award of compensatory damages from $10 to one dollar. When a plaintiff fails to prove actual damages, he is entitled to nominal damages. The jury's award of $10 signifies that they were not awarding nominal damages. Although Whites (P) did not prove they suffered any pecuniary damages and the jury was instructed as such, Mrs. White (D) did testify that she suffered some inconvenience. The jury was well within it province to award reasonable compensatory damages based solely on the inconvenience to Mrs. White (D). Thus, the reduction by the court was in error. Reversed in part and affirmed in part.

Analysis:

The editors have included this case in the book in order to illustrate the general and widely accepted principle that the purpose of contract law is to compensate aggrieved parties for actual harm sustained and not to deter any kind of conduct. Accordingly, punitive damages are available only in select categories of contract cases. The most common of these is where the breach of contract was accompanied by a tort. For example, where an appliance repairman negligently services a refrigerator which subsequently explodes and injures the homeowner or his family. Although the relationship between the repairman and the homeowner was contractual in nature, the repairman's negligence gave rise to a tort based on an implied duty to provide reasonable and non-injurious repair service. This case also brings up the issue of nominal damages. Nominal damages are trivial damages awarded when the plaintiff has proved the defendant breached his contractual obligation, but the plaintiff fails to show that he was injured in any measurable way. Nominal damages rarely amount to more than one dollar.

CONTRACTING PARTIES MAY PROVIDE FOR A PREDETERMINED AMOUNT OF DAMAGES IN CASE OF A BREACH ONLY IF THE AMOUNT IS REASONABLY RELATED TO THE HARM DONE

City of Rye v. Public Serv. Mut. Ins. Co.

(Municipal Owner of Construction Contract) v. (Surety on Construction Contract)
34 N.Y.2d 470, 358 N.Y.S.2d 391, 315 N.E.2d 458 (1974)

M E M O R Y   G R A P H I C

Instant Facts

Although it failed to prove the extent of its pecuniary loss, a city sought to recover the face amount of a surety bond when developers failed to finish construction on six buildings within a period of time required by a municipal contract for certificates of occupancy.

Black Letter Rule

A provision fixing the amount of damages in advance of any breach will be upheld where the amount of the damages are difficult to ascertain, but not if the amount fixed is grossly disproportionate to the anticipated probable harm.

Case Vocabulary

LIQUIDATED DAMAGES: An agreed upon amount of damages to be paid by a party in breach of contract.
SURETY BOND: A bond in which one party assumed responsibility to pay for the consequences of another's failure to perform his contractual obligation.

Procedural Basis: Appeal to the New York Court of Appeals to review the judgment of the Appellate Division, which affirmed the trial court's decision to deny the plaintiff's motion for summary judgment.

Facts: In order to obtain certificates of occupancy for luxury co-operative apartment buildings, a group of developers ("Developers") (D) were required to post a bond with the City of Rye (the City) (P) to ensure timely completion of the six buildings. The letter agreement with the City (P) required the Developers (D) to pay $200 per day, up to the face amount of the bond, for each day after the deadline that the buildings remained unfinished. When more than 500 days passed without completion by the deadline, the City (P) sought to recover the entire amount of the bond. Prior to trial, the City (P) moved for summary judgment, but the motion was denied by the trial court, which was affirmed on appeal.

Issue: May a contract provide for an amount of damages in advance of a breach?

Decision and Rationale: (Breitel, C.J.) Yes. A provision fixing the amount of damages in advance of any breach will be upheld where the amount of the damages are difficult to ascertain, but not if the amount fixed is grossly disproportionate to the anticipated probable harm. Damages provided in advance of any breach are referred to as liquidated damages. Where a municipality is not given statutory authority to exact a penalty from developers, the rule stated above regarding liquidated damages must apply. Although the City (P) has made arguments as to the increased expense in inspectorial services and a decrease in tax revenue, those types of losses are not contained in the record regarding summary judgment. Furthermore, there is nothing to show that the sum of $200 per day or the face amount of the bond bore any reasonable relationship to the harm suffered by the City (P). A municipality's extraction of penal bonds in exchange for permits to developers has a potential for abuse. When such bonds may be authorized is a subject better left to legislators. Affirmed.

Analysis:

The rule regarding liquidated damages seems to many an inexplicable departure from the policy favoring freedom of contract. As a general matter courts exhibit a reluctance to allow parties to establish the remedy which will be provided in case of a breach. Notwithstanding their general reluctance to enforce contractual provisions providing for a predetermined amount of damages, courts will give such provisions effect under limited circumstances. When faced with the issue of enforcing a liquidated damages provision courts will require that the damages be difficult to quantify with any reasonable precision. An example might be where the breach of a contract leads to the damage of an intangible asset like goodwill. Paradoxically, the requirement that damages be difficult to ascertain before a liquidated damages provision will be enforced is accompanied by a requirement that the fixed amount of damaged bear a reasonable relation to the amount of harm actually suffered. However, notice that, in most jurisdictions, the amount of liquidated damages must bear a relationship to the reasonably predictable amount of damages, and not those damages actually suffered as a result of the breach. In other words, the reasonableness of the amount of the liquidated damages is to be determined at the time of contracting, not trial.

McCallister v. Patton

(Car Buyer) v. (Car Dealer)

214 Ark. 293, 215 S.W.2d 701 (1948)

M E M O R Y G R A P H I C

Instant Facts

After a car dealer refused to comply with the provisions of a purchase contract, a customer sought to have a court order the dealer to sell him the automobile described in the contract for sale.

Black Letter Rule

The mere scarcity of a good does not give it such a special, peculiar or unique quality that courts will order the specific performance of a contract for its sale.

Case Vocabulary

CHATTEL: Personal property; property which is not real estate.

PERSONALTY: Personal property; property which is not real estate.

SPECIFIC PERFORMANCE: An equitable remedy whereby one party is ordered to complete performance of a contract, rather than being ordered to pay money damages.

Procedural Basis: Appeal to the Arkansas Supreme Court to review the judgment of the court of chancery, which sustained the defendant's demurrer and dismissed the complaint when the plaintiff refused to amend it.

Facts: A. J. McCallister (P) entered into a contract with R.H. Patton (D) for the purchase of a new Ford automobile. The contract provided that Patton (D), a Ford dealer, was to fill McCallister's (D) contract for a new Ford in the order it was received, 37th in this case. When Patton (D) failed to sell McCallister (D) a vehicle after having received over 37 vehicles, McCallister (P) filed suit in the court of chancery, seeking specific performance of the sales contract.

Issue: May a contract for the sale of a new automobile be specifically enforced solely on account of a scarcity in the number of such automobiles available?

Decision and Rationale: (Millwee, J.) No. The mere scarcity of a good does not give it such a special, peculiar or unique quality that courts will order the specific performance of a contract for its sale. The general rule applied by most courts is that specific performance of a contract for the sale of personal property will not be granted if an action at law affords an adequate remedy. However, one of the exceptions to this rule is where the chattel forming the basis of the contract has a peculiar, unique or sentimental value to the buyer not measurable in money damages. Few cases have granted specific performance in the context of the sale of a new car. As other courts have stated, cars simply are not in the category of a unique chattel, despite the difficulty in obtaining them under certain economic conditions. McCallister (P) has made no allegation that the car ordered has any special or peculiar qualities not commonly possessed by others of the same make so as to make it practically impossible to replace it in the market. Thus, McCallister's (P) inconvenience can be compensated by money damages. Specific performance was properly denied. Affirmed.

Analysis:

The *sine qua non* of specific performance is the ineffectiveness of a remedy at law, i.e., inadequacy of money damages. If requested, specific performance will almost always be granted when a seller breaches a contract for the sale of land. The rationale for making specific performance the baseline remedy with respect real estate contracts is based on the assumption that each parcel of real property is unique in some way. However, specific performance is rarely granted when a contract for the sale of personalty is breached. The principal exception is mentioned in this case. It is only where the personal property has some unique character that specific performance will be ordered. The court refused to associate scarcity of a good with uniqueness of a good. This rationale makes sense because all resources are scarce to some degree or another. Consequently, if scarcity were coterminous with uniqueness, the availability of specific performance would depend solely on the demand for any product at any particular point in time. Thus, courts require more than scarcity. The usual types of contracts for the sale chattels that qualify for specific enforcement are those for heirlooms, art or some other article which is near impossible to obtain in the market.

SPECIFIC PERFORMANCE GENERALLY WILL NOT BE ORDERED FOR BREACHES OF BUILDING CONSTRUCTION CONTRACTS BECAUSE IN SUCH CASES DAMAGES ARE ORDINARILY AN ADEQUATE REMEDY

London Bucket Co. v. Stewart

(Contractor) v. (Not Stated)
(1951) 314 Ky. 832, 237 S.W.2d 509

M E M O R Y G R A P H I C

Instant Facts

A suit was filed against a contractor when the contractor failed to perform the services that he contracted to perform.

Black Letter Rule

A court will not order specific performance unless the ordinary common law remedy of damages for a breach of contract is an inadequate and incomplete remedy for injuries arising from the failure to carry out the terms of the contract.

Case Vocabulary

SPECIFIC PERFORMANCE: A contract-law remedy which requires complete performance or fulfillment of a party's contractual obligations; specific performance is generally ordered only when monetary damages are an inadequate remedy.

Procedural Basis: Appeal to the Court of Appeals of Kentucky of a lower court judgement ordering specific performance of a contract to furnish and install a heating system for a large motel.

Facts: London Bucket Co. (D) made a contract with Stewart (P) under which it promised to furnish and install a heating system for a large motel. London Bucket began performance of the job, but failed to finish. Further, the work that it did do was of inferior quality. When London Bucket (D) claimed to be finished, Stewart (P) filed suit against them, seeking specific performance. The trial court ordered specific performance, and London Bucket (D) appealed.

Issue: When a building contractor fails to fully perform the work that he has contracted to do, is a court required to order specific performance and force the contractor to go back and do the job right?

Decision and Rationale: (Stanley, Commissioner) No. A court will not order specific performance unless the ordinary common law remedy of damages for a breach of contract is an inadequate and incomplete remedy for injuries arising from the failure to carry out the terms of the contract. In this case, the lower court ordered the contractor to go back, correct defective work, and complete its job. It is the general rule that contracts for building construction will not be specifically enforced because ordinarily damages are an adequate remedy and, in part, because of the incapacity of the court to superintend the performance. Even though it may be difficult to prove damages, specific performance should not have been decreed in this case. Reversed.

Analysis:

London Bucket sets forth the general rule with respect to the imposition of specific performance—an order requiring completion of a party's contractual obligations—as a remedy for a breach of contract: a court generally will not order specific performance as a remedy for a breach of contract unless the ordinary common law remedy of monetary damages is shown to be inadequate. (A remedy is inadequate when it can be shown that irreparable injury will result if specific performance is not compelled.) To put it another way, specific performance is an inappropriate remedy when an award of monetary damages adequately remedies the harm caused by the breach of contract. The reason for this rule, as the Court of Appeals of Kentucky states, is that specific performance is a more difficult remedy to enforce. Assuming compliance with the court's order, with an award of money damages, the breaching party simply pays money to the other and all is done. With specific performance, however, there must be a continued supervision of the breaching party, which in some cases may go on for years. As such, there exists a rebuttable presumption that monetary damages are adequate and that specific performance is an inappropriate remedy because that is simply an easier and more efficient remedy to apply in most cases. It should be noted that, as the court states, specific performance is generally not an appropriate remedy in construction contract breach cases. This is not to say, however, that specific performance is never appropriate in such cases.

Neri v. Retail Marine Corp.

(Boat Buyer) v. (Boat Seller)
30 N.Y.2d 393, 334 N.Y.S.2d 165, 285 N.E.2d 311 (1972)

MEMORY GRAPHIC

Instant Facts

Neri (P) contracted with Retail Marine to buy a boat, but after the boat had already been ordered and delivered, Neri (P) changed his mind and wanted his deposit back.

Black Letter Rule

A retail dealer may recover loss of profits and incidental damages upon the buyer's repudiation of a contract governed by the Uniform Commercial Code.

Case Vocabulary

COUNTERCLAIM: A claim presented by a defendant in opposition to or deduction from the claim of the plaintiff.
OFFSET: A claim that serves to counterbalance or to compensate for another claim.
RESCINDING: The canceling of a contract.
RESTITUTION: An equitable remedy under which a person is restored to his original position prior to the loss or injury, or is placed in the position he would have been in had the breach not occurred.
SPECIAL TERM: The branch of the court which is held by a single judge for hearing and deciding motions and equitable causes.

Procedural Basis: Appeal from the Appellate Division's affirmance of the trial court's judgment in favor of the plaintiff.

Facts: Neri (P) contracted with Retail Marine (D) to purchase a new boat for $12,587.40. Neri (P) initially made a deposit of $40, which he thereafter increased to $4,250 in consideration of Retail Marine's (D) agreement to arrange with the manufacturer for immediate delivery on the basis of a "firm sale," instead of the four to six week delivery originally specified [just gotta have it now!]. Six days after the date of the contract, Neri's (P) lawyer sent a letter to Retail Marine (D) rescinding the sales contract because Neri (P) was to undergo surgery and hospitalization and would therefore be unable to make any payments [bad timing!]. The boat had already been ordered from the manufacturer and was delivered to Retail Marine (D) at or before the time the letter was received. Retail Marine refused to refund Neri's (P) deposit, and this action to recover it was commenced. Retail Marine (D) counterclaimed, alleging Neri's (P) breach of the contract and Retail Marine's (D) resultant damages of $4,250. Upon motion, Retail Marine (D) had summary judgment on the issue of liability, and the Special Term directed an assessment of damages, upon which it would be determined whether Neri (P) was entitled to the return of any portion of the down payment. Upon trial, it was shown that the boat ordered and received by Retail Marine (D) in accordance with Neri's (P) contract was sold four months later to another buyer for the same price as that negotiated with Neri (P). Neri (P) argues that Retail Marine's (D) loss on the sale was recouped, while Retail Marine (D) argues that but for Neri's (P) default, it would have sold two boats and have earned two profits instead of one [seems logical]. Retail Marine (D) proved that its profit on the sale would have been $2,579, and that during the time the boat remained unsold incidental expenses aggregating $674 were incurred. Additionally, Retail Marine (D) sought to recover $1,250 in attorney's fees. The trial court awarded Retail Marine $500 upon its counterclaim, and directed that Neri (P) recover the remainder of the deposit, amounting to $3,750. The Appellate Division affirmed, and this appeal followed.

Issue: May a retail dealer recover loss of profits and incidental damages upon the buyer's repudiation of a contract governed by the Uniform Commercial Code?

Decision and Rationale: (Gibson, J.) Yes. The issue is governed in the first instance by section 2-718 of the U.C.C. which provides, among other things, that the buyer, despite his breach, may have restitution of the amount by which his payment exceeds: (a) reasonable liquidated damages stipulated by the contract or (b) absent such stipulation, 20% of the value of the buyer's total performance or $500, whichever is smaller. Sections 2-718, however, establishes an alternative right of offset in favor of the seller to the extent that the seller establishes a right to recover damages under the provisions of this Article "other than subsection (1)." Among the provisions of "this Article other than subsection (1)" are those to be found in section 2-708, which the courts below did not apply. Subsection (1) of that section provides that the measure of damages for non-acceptance or repudiation by the buyer is the difference between the market price at the time and place for tender and the unpaid contract price together with any incidental damages provided in this Article, but less expenses saved in consequence of the buyer's breach. However, this provision is made expressly subject to subsection (2), which provides that if the measure of damages provided in subsection (1) is inadequate to put the seller in as good a position as performance would have done then the measure of damages is the profit (including reasonable overhead) which the seller would have made from full performance by the buyer, together with any incidental damages provided in this Article, due allowance for costs reasonably incurred and due credit for payments or proceeds of resale. It is evident, first, that this retail seller is entitled to its profit and, second, that the reference in subsection (2) to "due credit for payments or proceeds of resale" is inapplicable to this retail sales contract. The buyer's breach in this case, depleted the dealer's sales to the extent of one, and the measure of damages should be the dealer's profit on one sale. Section 2-708 recognizes this, and it rejects the rule developed under the Uniform Sales Act by many courts that the profit cannot be recovered in this case. The record which in this case establishes Retail Marine's (D) entitlement to damages in the amount of its prospective profit, at the same time confirms Retail Marine's (D) right to any incidental damages. From the language employed, it is too clear to require discussion that the seller's right to recover loss of profits is not exclusive and that he may recoup his incidental expenses as well. The trial court's denial of incidental damages of $674 was erroneous, however it correctly denied Retail Marine's (D) claim for recovery of attorney's fees incurred by it in this action. Attorney's fees incurred in an action such as this are not in the nature of the protective expenses contemplated by the statute. It follows that Neri (P) is entitled to restitution of the sum of $4,250 paid by them on account of the contract price less an offset to Retail Marine (D) in the amount of $3,253 on account of its lost profit of $2,579 and its incidental damages of $674. The order of the Appellate Division should be modified, with costs in all courts, in accordance with this opinion and, as so modified, affirmed.

Analysis:

Prior to the code, the New York cases applied the "profit" test, contract price less cost of manufacture, only in cases where the seller was a manufacturer or an agent for a manufacturer. Its extension to retail sales was designed to eliminate the unfair and economically wasteful results arising under the older law when fixed price articles were involved. This section permits the recovery of lost profits in all appropriate cases, which would include all standard priced goods. Additionally, in all cases the seller may recover incidental damages. Neri's (P) right to restitution was established at Special Term upon the motion for summary judgment, as was Retail Marine's (D) right to proper offsets, in each case pursuant to section 2-718. The only question before this Court, following the assessment of damages at Special Term, is that as to the proper measure of damage to be applied. The conclusion is clear from the record that the measure of damages provided in subsection (1) is inadequate to put the seller in as good a position as performance would have done and hence, that the seller is entitled to "its profit (including reasonable overhead) together with any incidental damages, and due allowance for costs reasonably incurred." The Court had a relatively simple decision once the applicable statute and measure of damages was identified.

Fertico Belgium S.A. v. Phosphate Chemicals Export Ass'n

(Fertilizer Buyer/Dealer) v. (Breaching Seller)

70 N.Y.2d 76, 517 N.Y.S.2d 465, 510 N.E.2d 334 (1987)

M E M O R Y   G R A P H I C

Instant Facts

A buyer/dealer of fertilizer sought to recover from a seller the difference between the contract price and the price the buyer had to pay to make up for the seller's breach upon late delivery, even though the buyer eventually accepted the late arriving goods, and sold them at a profit to a third party.

Black Letter Rule

Under the Uniform Commercial Code, a buyer-trader who accepts nonconforming goods from the seller is entitled to damages from the seller equal to the increased cost of cover plus consequential and incidental damages, and the seller is not entitled to an offset when the buyer-trader sells the nonconforming goods at a profit.

Case Vocabulary

COVER: When a buyer purchases substitute goods to make up for a seller's breach.

LETTER OF CREDIT: A document which requires the issuer (usually a bank) to pay a contract price upon presentation of documents acknowledging delivery or shipment of goods.

NONCONFORMING GOODS: Goods which fail to comply with the terms of a contract for sale.

Procedural Basis: Appeal to the Court of Appeals of New York to review the decision of the Appellate Division, which vacated a jury's award of $1.07 in damages resulting from a sellers breach of an international sales contract.

Facts: Fertico Belgium S.A. (Fertico) (P) contracted with frm Phosphate Chemicals Export Ass'n (Phoschem) (D) to purchase 15,000 tons of fertilizer, which Fertico (P) planned to sell to the country of Iraq. Phoschem (D) agreed to deliver the fertilizer no later than November 20, so that the Fertico (P)-Iraq contract could be consummated. Nevertheless, shortly before delivery was due, Phoschem (D) advised Fertico (P) that the fertilizer would not arrive until early December. When Fertico (P) learned of late delivery date, it decided to purchase the same fertilizer at market prices so that it would not have to breach its contract with the Iraqi government. The price paid by Fertico (P) to cover for Phoschem's (D) breach was $700,000 more than Phoschem's (D) sale's price. Fertico (P) also agreed with the Iraqi government to incur greater delivery charges so that it could postpone its own delivery. When Phoschem's delivery arrived almost one-month late, Fertico (P) was forced to accept the late arriving fertilizer because Phoschem (D) had already presented Fertico's (P) letter of credit and received payment. Finding itself with 15,000 tons of fertilizer it did not require, Fertico (P) went on the market and sold the late-arriving fertilizer to Janssens at a $454,000 profit. Fertico (P) then filed suit against Phoschem (D) seeking to recover the difference between the sales contract and the cover contract, or $700,000, plus consequential damages from having to incur delivery expenses. Phoschem (P) defended on the ground that it was entitled to offset Fertico's (P) profit realized from the sale to Janssens and that the increased costs of delivery to the Iraqi government were not consequential damages.

Issue: Is a buyer who accepts nonconforming goods entitled to seek from the seller the increased cost of cover, without any offset as a result of a profit made on the sale of the nonconforming goods?

Decision and Rationale: (Bellacosa, J.) Yes. The Appellate Division erred in offsetting the profit realized by Fertico (P) on its sale to Janssens. Even though the fertilizer sold in the sale to Janssens was that shipped by Phoschem (D), the sale was not a result of Phoschem's (D) breach because Fertico (P), as a buyer/trader, would have pursued such commercial transactions. Had Phoschem (D) fully performed, Fertico (P) would have had the benefit of both the contract with Iraq and the sale to Janssens. Thus, Phoschem (D) is not entitled to an offset from the profit realized by Fertico (P). This decision does not fit squarely within the remedies envisioned by the Uniform Commercial Code (UCC) because Fertico (P) was forced to take the unusual step of covering and accepting non-conforming goods. Therefore, the UCC does not provide an adequate remedy. The decision of the Appellate Court should be modified to reinstate the jury award.

Dissent: (Titone, J) The majority has erroneously concluded that an aggrieved buyer may retain both cover damages and the profit from the resale of conforming goods. This result is not consistent with the UCC. The UCC assumes that an aggrieved buyer who has purchased substitute goods and sued for "cover" damages has rejected the nonconforming goods. Allowing the buyer to sue for cover damages and retain the benefit of the transaction is a windfall. The UCC makes this clear. Section 2-712(1) defines cover as a purchase of goods "in substitution for those due from the seller" and authorizes an aggrieved buyer to resort to cover only "after a breach within §2-712(1)," which specifically states that cover under §2-711 is available when the seller fails to make delivery or the buyer rightfully rejects or revokes acceptance. Accordingly, the cover remedy is available only when a buyer neither has the goods or cannot use them due to a defect. The rule in *Neri v. Retail Marine Corp.* [buyer who rescinds on the purchase of a boat is not credited with the sale of the boat to another customer] is inapplicable because here we have an aggrieved buyer, not a seller. The UCC does not contain a provision which allows a buyer to recover profits from lost sales, the reason being that a buyer cannot have an unlimited supply of goods at his disposal and he must resort to market prices.

Analysis:

The majority in this case unwisely attempts to apply the rule adopted in *Neri* to a case where the seller is the party in breach. In *Neri* the court refused to permit a breaching buyer to be credited with a subsequent sale of the goods the breaching buyer was scheduled to purchase. The reason given in *Neri* was that, had the buyer not breached, the seller would have the benefit of two sales. However, that rule is applicable only when the seller has an unlimited supply of fungible goods. For example, a car dealer has a virtually unlimited supply of vehicles with a standard price. The problem with applying that rule in this case is that Fertico (P) was subject to the market. It had to purchase fertilizer from somewhere to sell to Janssens. The majority is simply incorrect when it states that, absent the breach, Fertico (P) would have had the benefit of both the contract with Iraq and the sale to Janssens. As you will see in the cases that follow, Fertico (P) did what it was legally obligated to do, and that is to take reasonable steps to mitigate its damages flowing from the late delivery.

Vitex Manufacturing Corp. v. Caribtex Corp.

(Wool Processor) v. (Wool Seller)
377 F.2d 795 (1967)

MEMORY GRAPHIC

Instant Facts

Caribtex breached a contract to supply Vitex with woolen material, and Vitex sued to recover for its lost profits.

Black Letter Rule

When overhead expenses are not affected by the performance of a particular contract, such expenses should not constitute a performance cost to be deducted when computing lost profits.

Case Vocabulary

DUTY-FREE: Term to describe goods which are free from customs payments when imported into a country.

TARIFFS: A list of articles which outlines the rates of duties, or taxes, that are to be imposed upon goods imported into a country.

Procedural Basis: Appeal from judgment in action for breach of contract and award for loss of profits.

Facts: At the time of this dispute, the importation of foreign wool products into the United States was met with high tariff barriers. These high tariffs would be avoided under statute if such wool products were imported into the Virgin Islands and processed in some way that their finished value exceeded their importation value by 50%. The Virgin Islands Legislature imposed quotas to limit the output of businesses engaged in such wool processing. Vitex Manufacturing Company, Ltd. (Vitex) (P) chemically shower-proofed imported cloth so that it could be imported duty-free into the United States. To this end, Vitex (P) operated a processing plant in the Virgin Islands, but had closed it when there was a lack of customers. Caribtex Corporation (D) imported cloth into the islands, secured its processing, and exported it to the United States. In the fall of 1963, the two companies (P and D) entered into a contract in which Vitex (P) agreed to process 125,000 yards of Caribtex's (D's) material at a price of 25 or 26 cents per yard. Vitex (P) re-opened its Virgin Islands plant, recalled its employees, and ordered the necessary chemicals so it (P) could comply with the contract. Caribtex (D) did not deliver the material, however, because it (D) feared the wool would not be entitled to duty-free treatment by customs officials. Vitex (P) sued to recover its (P's) lost profits resulting from Caribtex's (D's) breach. The trial court found that Vitex's (P's) gross profits for processing the woolen material would have been $31,250 and that its (P's) costs would have been $10,136. Thus, Vitex's (P's) damages for loss of profits were set at $21,114. Caribtex (D) appealed, claiming in part that the trial court erred in disregarding Vitex's (P's) overhead expenses, including those continuous expenses of the business like employee salaries, purchasing chemicals, etc., in determining lost profits.

Issue: Should constant overhead expenses be deducted from gross proceeds when computing lost profits?

Decision and Rationale: (Staley) No. Despite the presence of contrary authority, as a general rule, it would be better that overhead be treated as a part of gross profits and be recoverable as damages. Overhead should not be considered as part of the seller's costs. When overhead expenses are not affected by the performance of a particular contract, such expenses should not constitute a performance cost to be deducted when computing lost profits. In other words, because overhead is fixed and nonperformance of the contract would produce no overhead cost savings, no deduction from profits should result. Here, Vitex (P) had closed its plant when business activity had temporarily slowed down. If Vitex (P) had entered no other contracts for the rest of the year, Vitex's (P's) profits would have been determined by deducting its production costs and overhead from gross profits resulting from previous transactions. When Vitex (P) contracted to process Caribtex's (D's) wool, the only new costs that Vitex (P) would incur would be those of reopening its (P's) plant and the direct costs of processing, such as labor, chemicals, and the like. Overhead costs would have been constant, regardless of whether Vitex (P) contracted with Caribtex (D) or Vitex (P) actually processed Caribtex's (D's) wool. Because overhead remained constant and was totally unaffected by the Caribtex (D) contract, it would be improper to consider it as a cost of Vitex's (P's) performance and deduct it from the gross proceeds of the Caribtex (D) contract. Caribtex (D) may argue that this position is incorrect, as overhead is as much a cost of production as other expenses. Granted, successful businessmen do set prices at a level high enough to recoup all expenses, including overhead, and reap profits. Still, this does not automatically mean that fixed overhead costs, even when allocated in part to each transaction, should be considered a cost factor when computing lost profits on individual transactions. While overhead is paid for by the proceeds of the business, such costs generally do not bear a direct relationship to individual transactions to be considered a cost in determining lost profits. Moreover, with fewer transactions, overhead is spread out to a far lesser degree; these overhead costs would then lead to a loss of profitability for each existing transaction. This loss should thus be considered a compensable item of damage. The UCC provides that, if the difference between the contract price and market price is insufficient to put a seller in as good a position as if the contract had been fully performed, a different measure of damages should be used. The measure of damages should then be the profit, *including reasonable overhead* which the seller would have received from the buyer. Judgment of district court affirmed.

Analysis:

UCC 2-708(2) states that the measure of damages is "the *profit (including overhead)* which the seller would have made from full performance by the buyer." (Emphasis added.) In the case of *Universal Power Sys. v. Godfather's Pizza*, 818 F.2d 667 (8th Cir. 1987), the Eighth Circuit gave a ruling similar to that of the Third Circuit in *Vitex*, holding that the measure of damages under § 2-708(2) should be read as not subtracting fixed costs from calculating profit. Instead, only variable overhead costs, such as those for electrical power or heat that can be turned off once a breach occurs, etc., were to be considered in such calculations. Thus, when overhead costs are variable, they should be included in the general formula for measuring damages, which finds damages equal to the loss in value plus any other loss, minus any *cost avoided* and loss avoided as a result of the breach. Clearly, as the amount lost due to this kind of overhead can be adjusted, it should be included in this formula. When the overhead is indeed a fixed cost, as was the case here, it makes no sense to include the overhead in the formula. This is because such costs like insurance premiums, property taxes, and the like cannot be avoided simply by having one party breach the contract.

UPON BREACH BY THE RECIPIENT, A PROVIDER OF SERVICES IS ENTITLED TO THE WHOLE OF THE CONTRACT PRICE LESS ANY MONIES RECEIVED FROM SERVICES AS A RESULT OF THE BREACH

Parker v. Twentieth Century-Fox Film Corp.

(Actress) v. (Film Studio)
3 Cal.3d 176, 474 P.2d 689 (1970)

MEMORY GRAPHIC

Instant Facts

Parker contracted to act in a musical in California, but Fox abandoned the musical and offered her a role in a western in Australia.

Black Letter Rule

A wrongfully discharged employee's rejection of or failure to seek other available employment of a different or inferior kind cannot be used by the employer as a means of mitigating damages.

Procedural Basis: Appeal from summary judgment in breach of contract action for damages.

Facts: Mrs. Parker (P), known professionally as Shirley MacLaine, was [and still is, "Mrs. Winterbourne" notwithstanding] a prominent film actress. Under a contract with Twentieth Century-Fox Film Corporation (Fox) (D), dated August 6, 1965, Parker (P) was to play the female lead in Fox's (D's) proposed production of a film entitled "Bloomer Girl." Fox (D) agreed to pay Parker (P) a total of $750,000 over a period of 14 weeks, beginning May 23, 1966. This contract also provided Parker (P) with certain rights of approval regarding the choice of director and content of the screenplay. Before May 1966, however, Fox (D) decided not to produce the film. In a letter dated April 4, 1966, Fox (D) notified Parker (P) of this decision, and with the express purpose "to avoid any damage to you," offered Parker (P) the leading female role in another film, tentatively entitled "Big Country, Big Man." ("Big Country") The monetary compensation for this new role was to be identical to the amount offered previously. "Big Country," however, was a dramatic "western" movie, while "Bloomer Girl" was to have been a musical production. Also, "Big Country" was to be filmed in Australia, while "Bloomer Girl" had been set for production in California. Moreover, Parker (P) was not given director and screenplay approval by the "Big Country" contract. Parker (P) was given a week to accept this second contract. She (P) did not accept Fox's (D's) offer, and then filed suit seeking recovery of the agreed guaranteed compensation. She (P) set forth a cause of action under the contract itself, and another for damages from the breach of the contract. Fox (D) admitted the existence and validity of the contract, and that it (D) had breached and repudiated the contract. Fox (D) denied, however, that Parker (P) was entitled to any money under the contract or as a result of the breach. Fox (D) claimed, as an affirmative defense, that Parker (P) deliberately failed to mitigate her (P's) damages by unreasonably refusing to accept the role in "Big Country." Parker (P) moved for and was granted summary judgment, with an award of $750,000 plus interest. Fox (D) appealed.

Issue: Should a wrongfully discharged employee's rejection of an offer of different and inferior employment by his or her employer be considered when measuring damages for the employer's breach?

Decision and Rationale: (Burke) No. A wrongfully discharged employee's rejection of or failure to seek other available employment of a different or inferior kind cannot be used by the employer as a means of mitigating damages. Generally, a wrongfully discharged employee is entitled to recover the amount of salary he or she was promised. This amount is to be reduced by the amount that the employer affirmatively proves the employee has earned or could have earned with reasonable effort since being discharged. The employer must show, however, that any job opportunities that the employee rejected were comparable, or substantially similar, to the original job that the employee had agreed to perform. Here, Fox (D) has raised no issue as to the reasonableness of Parker's (P's) efforts to gain other employment. The only issue is whether her (P's) refusal of the "Big Country" role may be used to mitigate her (P's) damages. It is clear that Parker's (P's) refusal to accept the latter role offered by Fox (D) should not be applied in mitigation of damages. This is because the "Big Country" lead was different from and inferior to the role offered for "Bloomer Girl." The female lead as a dramatic actress in a western style motion picture cannot be considered substantially similar to a female lead in a song-and-dance production. In addition, no expertise is required to see that the "Big Country" offer, which proposed to eliminate or impair Parker's (P's) director and screenplay approval rights under the "Bloomer Girl" contract, was an offer of inferior employment. Parker's (P's) rejection of the role in "Big Country" should not be a means of mitigating damages. Judgment affirmed.

Dissent: (Sullivan) Only in California is there a rule that an employee is only required to accept employment that is "substantially similar." There is no historical or theoretical justification for adopting a standard regarding employment of a "different or inferior kind." It has never been the law that the mere existence of differences between two jobs in the same field is sufficient to excuse an employee from accepting an alternative offer of employment in order to mitigate his or her own damages. All the majority has done is attempt to prove their proposition that the two roles offered by Fox (D) were different by repeating the idea that they were different. The relevant question is not whether one offer of employment is different from the other, but whether there are enough differences in the kind of employment, or whether one offer is truly inferior to the other. These questions are part of the ultimate issue, which is whether or not the employee in question has acted reasonably. Summary judgment should be withheld.

Analysis:

The question of what is an appropriate substitute offer of employment will depend greatly on the facts and circumstances of each case. These can include the work the injured party is to perform, the time and place at which the performance is to be rendered, and the compensation to be given for the work. The cases where latter offers of employment have not been found to be appropriate have tended to involve very vivid situations. The Eighth Circuit in *Jackson v. Wheatley School Dist.*, 464 F.2d 411 (8th Cir.1972), held that a job which would require a teacher to live apart from her husband was not an appropriate substitute for a job in the same school where the husband also worked as a teacher. In addition, the court in *State ex rel. Freeman v. Sierra County Bd. of Educ.*, 49 N.M. 54, 157 P.2d 234 (1945), found that a principal and teacher in a school could not be required to accept a job as fourth-grade teacher in the same school.

UPON BREACH BY A PROVIDER OF SERVICES, THE RECIPIENT IS ENTITLED TO RECOVER THE COST OF PERFORMANCE, UNLESS SUCH PERFORMANCE IS ECONOMICALLY WASTEFUL

Peevyhouse v. Garland Coal & Mining Co.

(Owner/Lessor) v. (Lessee Mining Company)
382 P.2d 109 (Okla. 1962)

MEMORY GRAPHIC

Instant Facts

A farm owner who leased his land to a mining company sought to recover from the company the cost of repairing the damage to his land caused by the mining when, in breach of their lease, the company refused to do so.

Black Letter Rule

Where the provision breached is incidental to the main purpose of the contract and where the cost of performance greatly exceeds the resulting economic benefit to the plaintiff, the plaintiff may recover damages equal only to the economic loss and is not entitled to the cost of performance.

Procedural Basis: Appeal to the Supreme Court of Oklahoma to review the judgment of the trial court entered after a jury awarded $5,000 in damages to the plaintiff.

Facts: Willie and Lucille Peevyhouse (the Peevyhouses) (P) leased their farm to the Garland Coal and Mining Company (Garland) (D) for the latter to mine coal for five years. The lease contained one clause which required that, upon expiration of the lease, Garland (D) perform any needed restorative and remedial work to the farmland. The cost of this work, which Garland (D) refused to perform at the end of the lease, amounted to $29,000. However, the damage to the Peevyhouses' (P) farm resulted in a diminution of its value of only several hundred dollars. At trial Garland (D) introduced evidence as to the diminution in value of the Peevyhouses' (P) land. After receiving instruction that they had to find for the Peevyhouses (P) and could decide the measure of damages based on the cost of performance or any other evidence, the jury returned a verdict for $5,000.

Issue: Is a plaintiff entitled to damages equal to the cost of performance if such measure of damages greatly exceeds the actual economic harm suffered?

Decision and Rationale: (Jackson, J.) No. Where the provision breached is incidental to the main purpose of the contract and where the cost of performance greatly exceeds the resulting economic benefit to the plaintiff, the plaintiff may recover damages equal only to the economic loss and is not entitled to the cost of performance. Only one case has been brought to our attention where the cost of performance rule has not been followed despite it greatly exceeding the diminution in value resulting from the breach. The reason that the cost of performance is not used in situations where it is economically wasteful to do so is that it is highly unlikely that the ordinary property owner would agree to pay $29,000 for improvements that would increase the value of his property only $300. It is well agreed upon that the cost of performance is unavailable where it is economically wasteful. Therefore, we find that that the judgment entered was excessive. The judgment of the trial court should be modified and reduced to $300 and affirmed.

Dissent: (Irwin, J.) Its is unfair to allow Garland (D), which has already received its full benefits under the contract, to claim that the measure of damages should be the economic harm. If the measure of damages applied by the majority is the be applied in any case, consideration should also be given to the benefits received or contracted for by the party asserting application of the rule. Here, Garland (D) gained the right to mine on the Peevyhouses' (P) farm partly in exchange for an agreement to perform repairs. Thus, at the time of contracting Garland (D) must have thought it economically advantageous to agree to the repairs. This notwithstanding, the diminution in value measure has been wrongly applied in this case. The majority has essentially rewritten the parties' contract for them. Garland (D) has made no attempt to perform and its breach is in bad faith.

Supplemental Opinion on Rehearing: (Jackson, J.) In a Petition for Rehearing, the Peevyhouses (P) claim that the trial court improperly excluded evidence that the damage done to the land affected the portion of the property not leased to Garland (D). However, the record shows that there was no objection as to the court's exclusion. The record also shows that, in their motion for a new trial, the Peevyhouses (P) did not complain that they were being prevented from offering evidence as to the diminution in value of their property. In fact, they complained admitting any evidence as to that point. Thus, it appears that the Peevyhouses (P) argued their case upon the assumption that the "cost of performance" theory would be the sole measure of damages. They did so, however, with notice that the defendant would introduce evidence as to the diminution in value. At no time did they ask permission to amend the petition to describe the whole of their lands. Petition denied.

Analysis:

This case serves as an illustration of the rule that the cost of performance is not the proper measure of damages where it is economically wasteful. However, as the dissent points out, the majority applies the rule to the wrong set of facts. In those cases where, on the basis of wastefulness, the cost of performance is eschewed in favor of the diminution in value, the defendants' breach is usually inadvertent or negligent. What happened in this case was that Garland (D) did not realize the total benefits it expected when it leased the land from the Peevyhouses (P). In order to blunt its disappointment with the outcome of the mining operation Garland (D) willfully breached its contractual obligation. By allowing Garland (D) to resort to the diminution in value measure the majority sanctions this willful breach.

A PLAINTIFF IS REQUIRED TO PROVE THE LIKELIHOOD AND EXTENT OF DAMAGES WITH REASONABLE PROBABILITY, NOT EXACT PRECISION

Locke v. United States

(Typewriter Repairman) v. (Government)
151 Ct.Cl. 262, 283 F.2d 521 (1960)

MEMORY GRAPHIC

Instant Facts

A repairman sought to sue the federal government for breach of contract after he was wrongfully excluded from a schedule of repairmen government agencies could turn to for typewriter servicing.

Black Letter Rule

A plaintiff seeking lost profits from a breach of contract will not be precluded from recovery if he can establish the amount of those profits with reasonable probability.

Case Vocabulary

COURT OF CLAIMS: A federal court with jurisdiction over cases against the United States.
GENERAL SERVICES ADMINISTRATION: A central management agency that sets Federal policy in such areas as Federal procurement, real property management, and information resources management.

Procedural Basis: Appeal to the Court of Claims to review a decision of the Board of Review, General Services Administration.

Facts: Harvey Ward Locke (P) owned a typewriter repair company which was awarded a General Services Administration (GSA) Federal Supply Schedule Contract. The contract gave Locke's (P) company the right to be listed in an approved schedule of repair services. Although federal agencies were not required to use any one particular service, they were required to select one of the scheduled companies. Five months prior to the date on which the contract was to end, the Government's (D) contracting officer terminated the contract for default and removed Locke's (P) name from the schedule. Locke (P) then filed an appeal with the Board of Review, General Services Administration. The Board found that the government had wrongfully terminated the contract, but denied Locke's (P) claim for lost profits. Locke (P) appealed the Board's decision to the United States Court of Claims. The Government (D) defended on the ground that, since no agency was required to use Locke's (P) services, he could not establish any loss of profits.

Issue: Must a plaintiff seeking lost profits from a breach of contract establish his loss with exact precision?

Decision and Rationale: (Jones, C.J.) No. A plaintiff seeking lost profits from a breach of contract need only establish the amount and likelihood of those profits with reasonable probability. The facts of this case show that Locke (P) received a substantial portion of his business from similar government contracts. It therefore appears that being listed on the schedule created a reasonable probability that business would be obtained. Although the Government (D) was not required to use any outside repair service, there was evidence establishing that the Government (D) did indeed require such services and that other contractors in Locke's (P) position filled those requirements. The fact that the precise amount of the loss is difficult to ascertain will not alone preclude recovery. Here, Locke (P) had a chance at obtaining at-least one-fourth of the total typewriter-repair business let by the Government (D). That probability may form the basis of the measure of damages.

Analysis:

The nature of some contracts is such that at least one of the parties' expectations is determined by future profits. The fact that these profits are to be realized in the future makes them difficult to establish with certainty. Accordingly, courts have developed a rule that a plaintiff may recover the loss of *expected* profits. However, the plaintiff must meet two different evidentiary requirements. First, the plaintiff must establish with reasonable certainty that some profits were reasonably likely to result from the contract. The plaintiff must then go on to establish the extent of those profits with similar probability.

A BUSINESS WITH NO RECORD OF PROFITS BEARS A HIGHER STANDARD OF PROOF WHEN CLAIMING DAMAGES FOR LOST PROFITS

Kenford Co. v. Erie County

(Stadium Operators) v. (County)

67 N.Y.2d 257, 502 N.Y.S.2d 131, 493 N.E.2d 234 (1986)

M E M O R Y G R A P H I C

Instant Facts

A stadium builder sued the county for breach of contract in failing to execute an agreement to build and operate a stadium for 20 years.

Black Letter Rule

Loss of future profits as damages for breach of contract must be reasonably certain and directly traceable to the breach in order to be recoverable.

Case Vocabulary

PER CURIAM: Literally, "by the Court"; An opinion which is credited to the Court as a whole, instead of one particular author.

SET ASIDE THE VERDICT: To vacate or cancel the judgment of the court.

Procedural Basis: Appeal from the Appellate Division's reversal of the decision of the trial court which awarded damages to the plaintiff.

Facts: Erie County (D) entered into a contract with Kenford (P) and DSI (P) for the construction and operation of a domed stadium facility. The contract provided that the construction of the facility by the County (D) would commence with a year of the contract date and that a mutually acceptable 40-year lease between the County (D) and DSI (P) for the operation of the facility would be negotiated by the parties and agreed upon within three months of the receipt by the County (D) of preliminary plans, drawings and cost estimates. It was further provided that in the event a lease could not be agreed upon within the three months, a separate management contract between the County (D) and DSI (P) would be executed providing for the operation of the stadium facility by DSI (P) for a period of twenty years. The parties never agreed upon the terms of the lease, nor did construction of the stadium ever begin. A breach of the contract thus occurred and this action was commenced by Kenford (P) and DSI (P). Prolonged pretrial and preliminary proceedings transpired throughout the next ten years, culminating with the entry of summary judgment against the County (D) on the issue of liability and directed a trial limited to the issue of damages. The ensuing trial ended with a multimillion dollar jury verdict in favor of the plaintiffs. [Not so bad for no work at all!] The County (D) appealed, and the Appellate Court reversed portions of the judgment awarding damages for loss of profits and for certain out-of-pocket expenses incurred, and directed a new trial upon other issues.

Issue: May a plaintiff in a breach of contract action recover loss of prospective profits for a contemplated 20-year future business operation?

Decision and Rationale: (Per Curiam) No. On appeal to this Court, we are concerned only with that portion of the verdict which awarded DSI (P) money damages for loss of prospective profits during the 20-year period of the proposed management contract. That portion of the verdict was set aside by the Appellate Division and the cause of action dismissed. The court concluded that the use of expert opinion to present statistical projections of future business operations involved the use of too many variables to provide a rational basis upon which lost profits could be calculated and, therefore, such projections were insufficient as a matter of law to support an award of lost profits. We agree with this ultimate conclusion, but upon different grounds. Loss of future profits as damages for breach of contract have been permitted in New York under long-established and precise rules of law. First, it must be demonstrated with certainty that such damages have been caused by the breach and, second, the alleged loss must be capable of proof with reasonable certainty. In other words, the damages may not be merely speculative, possible or imaginary, but must be reasonably certain and directly traceable to the breach, not remote or the result of other intervening causes. In addition, there must be a showing that the particular damages were fairly within the contemplation of the parties to the contract at the time it was made. If it is a new business seeking to recover for loss of future profits, a stricter standard is imposed for the obvious reason that there does not exist a reasonable basis of experience upon which to estimate lost profits with the requisite degree of reasonable certainty. Despite the massive quantity of expert proof submitted by DSI (P), the ultimate conclusions are still projections, and as employed in the present day commercial world, subject to adjustment and modification. We of course recognize that any projection cannot be made absolute, nor is there any such requirement, but it is axiomatic that the degree of certainty is dependent upon known or unknown factors which form the basis of the ultimate conclusion. Quite simply, the multitude of assumptions required to establish projections of profitability over the life of this contract require speculation and conjecture, making it beyond the capability of even the most sophisticated procedures to satisfy the legal requirements of proof with reasonable certainty. Accordingly, that portion of the order of the Appellate Division being appealed from should be affirmed.

Analysis:

It is difficult to conclude what additional relevant proof could have been submitted by DSI (P) in support of its attempt to establish, with reasonable certainty, loss of prospective profits. Nevertheless, the Court deemed its proof insufficient to meet the required standard set forth. Initially, the proof does not satisfy the requirement that liability for loss of profits over a 20-year period was in the contemplation of the parties at the time of the execution of the basic contract or at the time of its breach. Indeed, the provisions in the contract providing remedy for a default do not suggest or provide for such a heavy responsibility on the part of the County (D). In the absence of any provision for such an eventuality, the common sense rule to apply is to consider what the parties would have concluded had they considered the subject. The evidence here fails to demonstrate to the Court that liability for loss of profits over the length of the contract would have been in the contemplation of the parties at the relevant times. The economic facts of life, the whim of the general public and the fickle nature of popular support for professional athletic endeavors must be given great weight in attempting to ascertain damages 20 years in the future. New York has long recognized the inherent uncertainties of predicting profits in the entertainment field in general and, in this case, it was dealing in large part with a new facility furnishing entertainment for the public. Accordingly, the Court acted correctly in disallowing the recovery for loss of future, speculative at best, profits.

A PLAINTIFF MAY RECOVER CONSEQUENTIAL DAMAGES ONLY IF SUCH DAMAGES WERE REASONABLY FORESEEABLE AT THE TIME OF CONTRACTING

Hadley v. Baxendale

(Mill Operator) v. (Carrier Service)
9 Exch. 341 (1854)

MEMORY GRAPHIC

Instant Facts

Hadley (P) used Baxendale's (D) carrier service to transport a broken shaft, but the transport was delayed through neglect, resulting in lost profits to Hadley's (P) business.

Black Letter Rule

Where two parties have made a contract which one of them has broken, the damages which the other party ought to receive in respect of such breach of contract should be such as may fairly and reasonably be considered either arising naturally from such breach itself, or such as may reasonably be supposed to have been in the contemplation of both parties as the probable result of the breach.

Case Vocabulary

RULE NISI: Indicates that the rule is to stand as operative and valid *unless* the party affected by it can show cause against it.

Procedural Basis: Appeal from the jury's award of damages to the plaintiff.

Facts: Hadley (P) operated an extensive milling business. The crank shaft which operates the mill broke and, as a result, all work was stopped. Hadley (P) was required to send the shaft as a pattern for a new one to another city. An employee took the shaft to Baxendale (P), who was a well-known carrier, to transport the shaft. Hadley (P) paid for the transport, and offered an additional sum to speed up the delivery. The delivery of the shaft was delayed through neglect, and as a result the mill was shut down for several days after it would otherwise have been [should have used Federal Express!]. The mill thus lost profits it would otherwise have received, and Hadley (P) filed suit to recover these damages. Baxendale (D) objected on the ground that these damages were too remote, and that the carrier company was not liable with respect to them. The jury found in favor of Hadley (P) and awarded £50 in damages.

Issue: Should the defendant be liable for the plaintiff's loss of profits due to the defendant's breach when the plaintiff has not communicated his special needs to the defendant?

Decision and Rationale: (Alderson, B.) No. Where two parties have made a contract which one of them has broken, the damages which the other party ought to receive in respect of such breach of contract should be such as may fairly and reasonably be considered either arising naturally from such breach itself, or such as may reasonably be supposed to have been in the contemplation of both parties as the probable result of the breach. If the special circumstances under which the contract had actually been made were communicated By Hadley (P) to Baxendale (D), and thus were known to both parties, the damages resulting from the breach of contract, which they would reasonably contemplate, would be the amount of injury which would ordinarily follow from a breach of contract under the circumstances. On the other hand, if these special circumstances were wholly unknown to the party breaking the contract, he, at the most, could only be supposed to have had in his contemplation the amount of injury which would arise generally from such a breach. Here, it is true that the broken shaft was the cause of a complete mill shutdown, but it seems that ordinarily, in the great multitude of millers sending off broken shafts, a broken shaft would not signify such a shutdown to the carrier. These special circumstances were never communicated to the carrier (D). It follows, therefore, that the loss of profits here cannot reasonably be considered such a consequence of the breach of contract as could have been fairly and reasonably contemplated by both the parties when they made this contract. The judge, therefore, should have told the jury that, upon the facts before them, they ought not to take the loss of profits into consideration at all in estimating the damages. There must therefore be a new trial in this case.

Analysis:

The Court in this case laid down two important rules which still govern today. First, the aggrieved party may recover those damages as may fairly and reasonably be considered arising naturally, according to the usual course of things, from such breach of contract itself. Today, such damages are frequently referred to as general damages. Second, recovery is allowed for damages such as may reasonably be supposed to have been in the contemplation of both parties, at the time they made the contract, as the probable result of the breach of it. These less obvious kinds of damages are deemed to be contemplated if the promisor knows or has reason to know the special circumstances which will give rise to such damages. These damages are frequently known as special or consequential damages. Presumably, had Hadley (P) specifically told Baxendale (D) that the shaft had to be delivered by a certain time or the mill could not open, and if Baxendale (D) agreed to delivery on time knowing the consequences if he failed to do so, Baxendale (D) might be held responsible for the full cost to Hadley (P) in not being able to open the mill on time.

Security Stove & Mfg. Co. v. American Rys. Express Co.

(Furnace Manufacturer) v. (Railroad)

(1932) 227 Mo.App. 175; 51 S.W.2d 572

MEMORY GRAPHIC

Instant Facts

A manufacturer of a furnace sued to recover its expenses for arranging a display of the furnace at a convention when the railroad that had promised to ship the furnace to the site of the convention in time to be displayed, failed to deliver the furnace on time.

Black Letter Rule

In some instances, a injured party may recover expenses incurred in relying on performance of a contract, even if the expenses were incurred prior to contracting.

Case Vocabulary

COMMON CARRIER: A public carrier required by law to ship freight or transport passengers without a right of refusal so long as an approved charge is paid by the entity or person purchasing its services.

LOST PROFITS: This is the amount of money a party would have made had a contract been performed. In general damages for lost profits are not awarded where a party cannot show with reasonable certainty the amount of profit it would have made had the other party performed its contractual duties as anticipated.

RELIANCE DAMAGES: Damages awarded to the non-breaching party to a contract to reimburse that party for its out-of-pocket costs spent in the expectation that the breaching party would perform its contractual duties.

Procedural Basis: Appeal from a state trial court's judgment of damages for breach of contract.

Facts: Security Stove & Mfg. Co. ("Stove") (P) designed and built a special furnace equipped with a combination oil and gas burner that it wanted to show to a potential customer at a gas association convention in Atlantic City. Stove (P) booked space to display the furnace at the convention, but by did not have enough time to ship the furnace from its factory in Missouri to Atlantic City by regular freight train in order to make the convention. Stove (P) contacted American Rys. Express Co. ("Railways") (D), told them of the need to get the furnace to Atlantic City very quickly for the convention and on Railways' (D) promise to ship the furnace by express train in time to be displayed at the convention, engaged Railways (D) to do so. Stove's (D) president and a workman went to Atlantic City and found that only twenty of twenty-one packages making up the parts needed to assemble the furnace had been delivered. The missing package, containing the gas manifold, which controlled the flow of gas to the burner, was the most important part of the convention exhibit and a similar part could not be obtained in Atlantic City. Stove (P) reported the missing package and Railways (D) found it in St. Louis, but could not ship it in time for the furnace to be displayed at the convention. Stove's (P) president was unable to show the furnace to the customer and returned home to Missouri. Stove (P) filed suit against Railways (D) in Missouri state court for breach of contract, seeking damages in the amount of all of the expenses it had incurred for setting up the convention exhibit. The damages claimed included shipping charges for the furnace, rail fares for the train tickets for Stove's (P) president and the workman, the cost of their hotel room in Atlantic City, money to reimburse Stove (P) for its president's time and its workman's wages, and the amount spent for the convention booth rental. The trial court found in favor of Stove (P), granting the full amount of claimed damages, plus interest. Railways (D) appealed, arguing that it was improper to grant damages that would put Stove (P) back in the position it would have been if it had never entered into the contract. Instead, Railways (D) argued, Stove (P) was limited to recovering only what it would have had in the event the contract had not been broken.

Issue: If damages for lost profits from a breach of contract are too speculative to be determined with any certainty, can the non-breaching party to the contract recover its out-of-pocket expenses spent in reliance on the breaching party's promise to perform?

Decision and Rationale: (Bland, J.) Yes. We think it was proper to allow Stove's (P) expenses as its damages for Railways' (D) breach of contract. The general rule where there is a breach of contract is that the party suffering the loss can recover only that which he would have had if the contract had not been broken. This is merely the general rule, however, and in some instances, the injured party may recover expenses incurred in relying upon the contract, even though such expenses would have been incurred had the contract not been breached. In this case, Stove (P) is not seeking to recover damages for lost profits because of Railways' (D) failure to ship the furnace in time for the Atlantic City convention. There were no profits contemplated. The furnace was simply to be shown at the convention and shipped back to Missouri. Other than the expenses at issue, any money loss was too speculative for Stove (P) to obtain damages. Thus, unless Stove (P) is permitted to recover the expenses that went into the attempt to display the furnace at the convention, it will be deprived of any substantial compensation for its loss. The law does not contemplate any such injustice. It ought to allow as damages the loss in the amount of the expenses to which a non-breaching party spent in reliance on the breaching party's promise to perform the contract. While it is true that Stove (P) had incurred some of these expenses before entering into its contract with Railways (D), in that it had already rented space at the convention for its display, nevertheless, Stove (P) arranged for the exhibit knowing that it could call on Railways (D), a common carrier, to perform its common law duty to accept and transport the shipment with reasonable dispatch. Affirmed.

Analysis:

In contract law, courts attempt to put the non-breaching party to a contract that has been breached in the position it would have been in if the breaching party had properly performed under the contract. In general, this means that the non-breaching party is entitled to both the out-of-pocket costs it has incurred in anticipation of the contract being performed and the profit it would have made had the contract been fully performed. Sometimes, as in this case, it is too difficult to determine if any profit would have been made by the non-breaching party if the contract had been performed. Although lost profits are too speculative to be recovered, courts, as here, still permit reimbursement for the amounts spent in reliance that the breaching party would perform. Courts generally will reduce the amount of such recovery, however, to the extent the breaching party can show that the non-breaching party would have actually lost money, rather than made a profit, had the contract been fully performed. Note that most courts will not permit pre-contractual expenses to be recovered as an element of reliance damages. Here, however, the court finds that certain pre-contractual expenses, such as the amount spent for the rental of the convention booth in Atlantic City, which would have been rented even if the contract was never entered into with Railways (D), were recoverable. The court appears to base the permitted recovery on the fact that, if Railways (D) had not agreed to ship the furnace, it would have been subject to potential tort liability as a common carrier for failing to accept a reasonable offer to purchase its services.

A PLAINTIFF WHOSE CLAIM IS BASED ON A THEORY OF RELIANCE MAY RECOVER ONLY THOSE DAMAGES SUFFERED AS A RESULT OF THE RELIANCE

Goodman v. Dicker

(Franchise Appplicant) v. (Distributor)
83 U.S.App. D.C. 353, 169 F.2d 684 (1948)

MEMORY GRAPHIC

Instant Facts

After having his application for a dealer franchise rejected, an applicant sought to recover lost profits and capital outlays relating to labor and advance orders from the defendant distributor, who encouraged the expenditures with representations that the franchise would be granted.

Black Letter Rule

Lost profits are not recoverable in an action based on a theory of justified reliance.

Procedural Basis: Appeal to the District of Columbia Circuit Court of Appeals to review the judgment of the district court, which awarded the plaintiff $1,150 for capital outlays and $350 for lost profits.

Facts: Dicker (D), a distributor for the Emerson Radio and Phonograph Corporation, encouraged Goodman (P) to apply for a dealer franchise to sell Emerson's products. After Dicker (D) told Goodman (P) that the application had been accepted and that the franchise would be granted, Goodman (P) spent $1,500 in hiring salesmen and soliciting orders. When his application was denied, Goodman (P) filed suit against Dicker (D) for the $1,500 in cash outlays and $350 in lost profits. The district court found for Goodman (P) and awarded him $1,800.

Issue: May a plaintiff whose claim relies on the theory of reliance recover damages for lost profits?

Decision and Rationale: (Proctor, A.J.) No. Lost profits are not recoverable in an action based on a theory of justified reliance. The theory of promissory estoppel is well settled to allow a plaintiff who has relied to his detriment to recover for losses resulting from that reliance. However, the true measure of damage in this case is the loss of expenditures made in reliance on the assurances of Dicker. Lost profits were wrongly awarded. The judgment is modified and affirmed as such.

Analysis:

The editors have included this case in the text to illustrate that, in most cases, courts resort to a remedy that corresponds to the contractual interests which support the plaintiff's claim. For example, a claim based on unjust enrichment will lead to the award of restitution, while a claim based on justified reliance will lead to an award for damages incurred in reliance. Accordingly, the court did not award lost profits in this case because such damages are based on an expectation interest, which usually is not protected in a case based in the theory of promissory estoppel. However, as the following case will illustrate, courts do not always require such symmetry between the theory of the claim and the remedy awarded.

Walters v. Marathon Oil Co.

(Service Station Owner) v. (Petroleum Distributor)
642 F.2d 1098 (7th Cir. 1981)

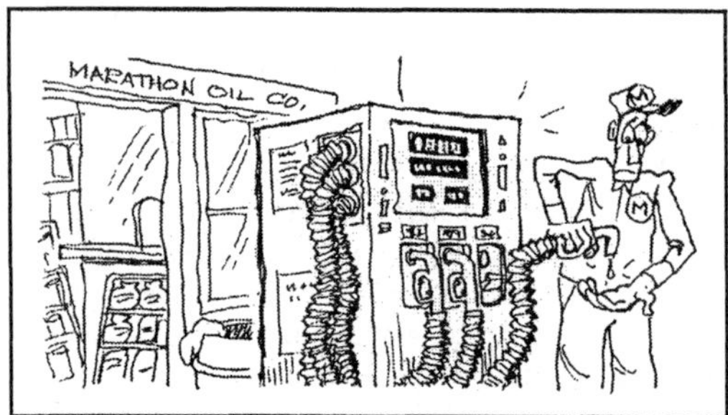

M E M O R Y G R A P H I C

Instant Facts

A man who was induced into purchasing and improving a service station filed suit against the petroleum distributor which failed to review the dealer application despite making assurances that the application would be approved and the station would receive a supply of gasoline.

Black Letter Rule

A plaintiff suing on a theory of promissory estoppel may recover profits lost as a result of his reliance.

Procedural Basis: Appeal to the Seventh Circuit Court of Appeals to review the decision of the district court awarding lost profits in a case based on promissory estoppel.

Facts: Dennis Walters (P) contacted the Marathon Oil Co. (D) about the possibility of opening a foodstore and service station on a vacant station site. Walters (P) purchased the site and made improvements thereon as he continued to negotiate with Marathon (D) representatives. The paper work proceeded normally and Marathon (D) received a three-party agreement signed by Walters (P) and the company which had previously supplied gasoline to that station. However, as a result of uncertainty in oil supplies due to the Iranian revolution, Marathon (D) placed a moratorium on new applications and refused to sign the agreement. Walters (P) sued Marathon (D) on a theory of promissory estoppel and was awarded damages relating to the costs of improving the station. The district court found for Walters (P) and awarded damages for profits lost. Marathon (D) appealed.

Issue: May a plaintiff suing on a theory of promissory estoppel recover profits lost as a result of his reliance?

Decision and Rationale: (Spears, D.J.) Yes. A plaintiff suing on a theory of promissory estoppel may recover profits lost as a result of his reliance. It is reasonable to assume that in investing time and money into the purchase and improvement of the station, Walters (P) was forced to forgo other profit making opportunities. Furthermore, the record is replete with evidence establishing Walters' anticipated profits at $22,000. Thus, it is clear that Walters (P) suffered a loss of profits as a result of his reliance upon the promise made by Marathon (D). This loss was ascertained with reasonable certainty. Promissiory estoppel is an equitable matter, and as such, a court sitting in equity posses discretion in how it awards damages so as to complete justice. Therefore, the district court committed no reversible error in awarding damages for loss of profits. Affirmed.

Analysis:

This case stands in somewhat stark contrast to *Goodman v. Dicker*, which held that lost profits are not recoverable in a case based on promissory estoppel. Although the courts reach opposite conclusions as to the availability of lost profits in a case based on promissory estoppel, it cannot be said that either case was "wrongly" decided. The Restatement (Second) of Contracts §90, which illustrates the theory of promissory estoppel, does not expressly limit recovery to damages spent in reliance. Indeed, the court in this case accurately notes that as an equitable matter, recovery under a theory of promissory estoppel should be malleable so as to allow equity to be done. In this case, lost profits may have been more appropriate than in *Goodman* because the capital expended was likely significant and represented sunk costs which could not likely be recovered quickly.

SUPREME COURT OF MASSACHUSETTS ENFORCES A DOCTOR'S PROMISE REGARDING A SUCCESSFUL NOSE JOB

Sullivan v. O'Connor

(Patient) v. (Plastic Surgeon)

Supreme Judicial Court of Massachusetts, 1973. 363 Mass. 579, 296 N.E.2d 183

M E M O R Y G R A P H I C

Instant Facts

Plastic surgeon disfigures patient in the course of performing a nose job.

Black Letter Rule

Clear proof of a doctor's promise of specific medical results may give rise to an enforceable contract.

Case Vocabulary

BILL OF EXCEPTIONS: Formal written statement of the objections by a party during trial to the trial judge's decisions, rulings or instructions.
CASE AT BAR: Case before the court.
CHARLATAN: A quack or fraud; one who makes a noisy, showy pretense to knowledge or ability.
COUNT: (n.) One of the plaintiff's causes of action.
EXCEPT: (v.) To leave out of an account or consideration; to object.
EXPECTANCY: That which is expected or hoped for, sometimes conditioned on or dependent on an expected event.
NONSUITED: A case that has a judgment given against it because plaintiff is unable to prove his case (involuntary nonsuit) or refuses or neglects to proceed to trial (voluntary nonsuit).
SEDULOUS: Diligent in application or pursuit.
SPECIAL QUESTION: A point in dispute which is submitted for the decision of a jury.
STATUS QUO ANTE: The state of things before.

Procedural Basis: Appeal from a jury verdict for the plaintiff in a breach of contract action.

Facts: Sullivan (P), a professional entertainer, went to O'Connor (D) to have plastic surgery performed on her nose. O'Connor (D) promised to do the surgery. He also promised that it would make Sullivan (P) more beautiful and would enhance her appearance. In fact, the surgery was a disaster. O'Connor (D) told her the nose job would only require two operations, but it required three. He told her she would be more beautiful, but instead, she was left with an asymmetrical nose which was flat and broad in some places and bulbous in others [aren't all noses?]. Her appearance could not be improved by further surgery. Sullivan (P) subsequently sued O'Connor (D) for malpractice]. She also sued for breach of contract based on O'Connor's (D) representations prior to the surgery. It seems that O'Connor (D) never took this claim seriously since it appeared to be without precedent in Massachusetts. The jury ruled in Sullivan's (P) favor on the breach of contract issue and O'Connor (D) appeals this verdict.

Issue: Can an agreement between a doctor and a patient for a specified medical result be enforced?

Decision and Rationale: (Kaplan) Yes. Courts have occasionally enforced agreements between doctors and patients. However, they generally enforce these agreements reluctantly and with certain considerations in mind. Medical practice is inherently uncertain. The physical needs and reactions to treatment vary from patient to patient. Doctors cannot be held liable for every optimistic opinion of a patient's condition [not a problem for Dr. Kevorkian]. Unfortunately, patients are likely to interpret these opinions as promises, especially when things do not work out as planned. In addition, patients must be protected from unscrupulous doctors who fraudulently promise miraculous results. The difficulty lies in the grey area between optimistic opinions and unfounded promises. It is necessary to balance the protection which individual doctors require against the need to protect the integrity of the medical profession. As a result, courts have required clear proof before considering a breach of contract action in a doctor/patient relationship. In this case, there was no error in permitting the breach of contract claim to go forward. Judgement Affirmed.

Analysis:

Justice Kaplan lays out the competing goals at stake when enforcing a contract between a doctor and a patient. He also implicitly concedes the determination of whether a contract existed in this case as a matter of fact for the trial court. In other words, he deals exclusively with the question of whether an enforceable contract *can* exist between a doctor and a patient. In this regard, Justice Kaplan appears to support an inquiry into the patient's subjective interpretation of a doctor's opinion in order to determine if a promise has been made. This is not necessarily at odds with the objective intent theory. Consider that courts will frequently assume that parties to business contracts have a working knowledge of the terms and conditions which are generally associated with their business. In this case, the court is simply charging doctors with the knowledge that their objectively harmless opinions may have a significant impact on a distraught or confused patient. This seems reasonable since doctors are sought out precisely because they take control of situations which are beyond the abilities of their patients to handle. Another possible approach to this problem is used in Michigan, where agreements regarding the success of medical treatment are now statutorily void unless signed and in writing.

RESTITUTION IS A QUASI-CONTRACTUAL REMEDY, THE AMOUNT OF WHICH MAY BE WHOLLY SEPARATE FROM ANY UNDERLYING CONTRACT

Oliver v. Campbell

(Decedent's Attorney) v. (Decedent's Administratrix)
43 Cal.2d 298, 273 P.2d 15 (1954)

M E M O R Y G R A P H I C

Instant Facts

An attorney filed suit against the estate of one of his former clients to recover an amount he deemed was the reasonable value of services rendered in a divorce proceeding.

Black Letter Rule

A party who has been injured by the breach of an express contract may elect to pursue a variety of remedies, including restitution and damages.

Procedural Basis: Appeal to the Supreme Court of California to review the judgment of the trial court, which found for the defendant in an action for restitution.

Facts: In 1949, Oliver (P) began to represent Roy Campbell (D) in a divorce proceeding. The representation agreement stated that Oliver (P) was to receive a "total fee" of $750 plus $100 in costs and expenses. Oliver (P) represented Campbell (D) for nearly six months and conducted the divorce trial, which lasted for 29 days. After the trial ended and the court indicated it would grant a divorce to Campbell's (D) wife, Oliver (P) was terminated and Campbell (D) substituted himself as counsel. At that point, Oliver (P) stated that he was holding Campbell (D) liable for the full value of the services rendered. A few days thereafter, the findings of the trial court in the divorce action were filed. After Campbell (D) died, Oliver (P) filed suit against the estate to recover $9,550, or the reasonable value of legal services rendered by Oliver (P) in the divorce proceeding minus $450 paid to Oliver (P) by Campbell (D). The administratrix of Campbell's (D) estate denied the claim and defended on the ground that all of the services rendered by Oliver (P) were pursuant to an express written contract for $750. The trial court found for the estate on the grounds that the suit was not on the express contract and that no restitution could be had for a services rendered pursuant to an express contract.

Issue: May a party make a claim for restitution as a result of another's breach of an express contract?

Decision and Rationale: (Carter, J.) Yes. A party who has been injured by the breach of an express contract may elect to pursue a variety of remedies, including restitution and damages. Thus, Oliver (P) could have sued "on the contract" and made a claim for the total sum stated therein. Oliver also had the option of treating the contract cancelled and filing suit for the value of services rendered, even if such value far exceeded the face amount of the contract. In order to pursue this latter course, the aggrieved party must notify the party in breach that he is treating the contract as cancelled, which Oliver (P) did in this case. The lone problem with Oliver's (P) case, however, is that restitution may not be had where the party making the claim has rendered full performance under an express contract and the only part of the agreed exchange yet to be performed is the payment of money; but full performance does note prevent the recovery of any party of the consideration due. Accordingly, the trial court erred in refusing to order Campbell's estate to pay Oliver $350, the balance due on the contract. Reversed.

Analysis:

This case provides a good overview on the remedy of restitution and how it differs from an award of damages. Restitution has been termed a "quasi-contractual" remedy, meaning that it is not based on the amount stated in any express contract, but rather on the value of benefits conferred on one party. This subtle difference provides the reason that Oliver (P) chose to file a claim based on restitution and not one on the contract. Had Oliver (P) filed suit for breach of contract, his recovery would be limited to only $350, the unpaid amount of the contract price. In contrast, under a quasi-contractual theory, Oliver (P) could recover the fair value of his services, which he estimated was $10,000. However, Oliver's (P) claim was unsuccessful because the had fully rendered performance and all that was left for Campbell (D) to do was to pay. The reason for this limitation on the right to sue for restitution should be obvious. If a party could always file suit for the fair value of services rendered without regard to the contract price, a party whose performance turned out to be more expensive than was thought at the time of contract could makeup for his disappointment by filing suit for restitution.

THE MEASURE OF RESTITUTION IN THE FORM OF *QUANTUM MERUIT* RECOVERY IS THE REASONABLE VALUE OF THE PERFORMANCE RENDERED, AND CANNOT BE DIMINISHED BY ANY LOSS THAT WOULD HAVE RESULTED FROM COMPLETE PERFORMANCE

United States v. Algernon Blair, Inc.

(Owner of Naval Hospital) v. (Construction Company)

479 F.2d 638 (4th Cir.) (1973)

M E M O R Y G R A P H I C

Instant Facts

When Blair refused to pay crane rental costs, Coastal Steel terminated its performance and sued to recover for labor and equipment it had already furnished.

Black Letter Rule

The measure of recovery for quantum meruit is the reasonable value of the performance, and recovery is undiminished by any loss which would have been incurred by complete performance.

Case Vocabulary

SURETY: A person or entity who is held liable for the payment of a debt or performance of an obligation by another person or entity.

Procedural Basis: Appeal from award of damages in action for breach of contract.

Facts: Algernon Blair, Inc. (Blair) (D) entered a contract with the United States (U.S.) (P) for the construction of a naval hospital. Blair (D) then contracted with Coastal Steel Erectors, Inc. (Coastal) (P) to conduct steel erection operations and supply equipment as part of Blair's (D's) contract with the U.S. (P). Coastal (P) began performing its obligations and supplied its own cranes for handling and placing the required steel. Blair (D) claimed that the cost of crane rental was not its (D's) responsibility under its (D's) subcontract with Coastal (P), and refused to pay those costs. Because of this refusal to pay, Coastal (P) terminated its performance. This occurred after Coastal (P) had completed roughly 28 percent of its subcontract. Blair (D) went ahead and completed its contract with the U.S. (P) with a new subcontractor. Coastal (P) sued in the name of the United States (P) under the Miller Act to recover damages for labor and equipment already furnished. The district court found that Blair (D) was required under the subcontract to pay for crane use. Also, the refusal to pay was a material breach and justified Coastal's (P's) termination of performance. This finding is not questioned on appeal, but the court also found that Coastal (P) , less what it (P) was already paid, was owed roughly $37,000. Moreover, the court found that Coastal (P) would have actually lost $37,000 (as compared to making $37,000) if performance was completed. The court thus denied recovery to Coastal (P), finding that any amount due would have to be reduced by any loss that would have resulted from complete performance of the contract.

Issue: Should a subcontractor who justifiably ceases work after the main contractor breaches the contract be entitled to restitution based on the value of the services already rendered?

Decision and Rationale: (Craven) Yes. The measure of recovery for quantum meruit is the reasonable value of the performance, and recovery is undiminished by any loss which would have been incurred by complete performance. In *United States for Use of Susi Contracting Co. v. Zara Contracting Co.*, 146 F.2d 606 (2d.Cir.1944), the Second Circuit faced a similar situation involving a prime contractor who had unjustifiably breached a subcontract after partial performance by a subcontractor. There, the court stated that the subcontractor could choose not to file suit based on the contract, and instead could make a claim for the reasonable value of his or her performance. Here, Coastal (P) paid for the costs of labor and equipment that Blair (D) has used. Blair (D) then breached the subcontract and retained the benefits of this labor and equipment without having fully paid for them. Based on these facts, it is clear that Coastal (P) is entitled to restitution in quantum meruit. As Fuller & Perdue wrote in their piece on The Reliance Interest in Contract Damages, 46 Yale L.J. 52, 56 (1936), "if A not only causes B to lose one unit but appropriates that unit to himself, the resulting discrepancy between A and B is not one unit but two." Quantum meruit allows a promisee to recover the value of services he or she gave to the promisor. This recovery is possible regardless of whether the promisee would have lost money on the contract and been unable to recover in a suit on the contract. The standard measuring the reasonable value of the services rendered is the amount for which such services could have been purchased from one in the plaintiff's position at the time and place the services were rendered. The district court must determine the reasonable value of the labor and equipment that Coastal (P) provided for Blair (D). This amount should then be awarded to Coastal (P), minus any payment Blair (D) may have already made under the contract. Decision reversed and remanded with instructions.

Analysis:

Many courts have made similar rulings on questions of this nature. In addition to the Fourth Circuit here, the Second Circuit in *Scaduto v. Orlando*, 381 F.2d 587 (2d Cir. 1967), and in the aforementioned *Zara Contracting* case, ruled that the subcontractor should recover the "actual value of labor and materials" from the contractor in the event of the contractor's breach. Generally, the courts that follow this reasoning must face the minor problem of measuring the benefit received by the breaching party. This difficulty is greatly eased by relying on the reasonable value of the services rendered, as trying to measure the benefit based on the other party's expectation interest will be far more difficult. Indeed, the use of the reasonable value standard is favorable, for even if the party in breach abandons the contractual enterprise entirely, any performance taken by the nonbreaching party will be, presumably, for the benefit of the party in breach. This was certainly the case here, as the steel erection and crane usage provided by Coastal (P) certainly helped Blair's (D's) construction work.

Perspective
The Autonomy Principle Again

Chapter 5

In contracts, what's written on the page isn't necessarily all that's expected of the signer. It doesn't necessarily even mean what it says. A few weeks ago, you studied what is needed to make a contract binding. At that time, you studied the "autonomy principle," which says that the contract should mean whatever the parties agreed to. This chapter stands this principle on its ear.

This chapter is about "interpreting" contracts, which means predicting how a judge will enforce them if they are challenged in court. Thus, interpretation isn't really about what the *parties* intended it to mean, but what a judge thinks it *should* mean. If you're planning to draft contracts, most of your billable hours will be spent considering how your words will be interpreted, and misinterpreted. If you understand the rules of interpretation, you will understand the full implications of what you are writing, and avoid unexpected consequences and litigation.

Interpreting contracts involves several discrete steps. First, you will learn to identify and separate any contract's exact "express" terms, which tell you what each party explicitly agreed to do. This sounds easy, but can get complicated when the contract has gone through several revisions, and someone claims a term got left out of the final draft. Next, you will learn what an express term *means*, which often goes beyond the literal language to carry additional responsibilities. But that's not the end of the analysis. Next, you will find that, in addition to the contract's express terms and those added to reflect the parties actual, unwritten intent, the law also "implies" (forces) certain consequences onto express terms, whether the parties want it or not, and has a set of default rules to fill in contractual "gaps" and safeguard the parties' unwritten expectations. Finally, you will learn when a term is a "condition," which may excuse the parties from ever being bound by the contract.

Chapter Overview Outline
The Autonomy Principle Again

Chapter 5

NOTE: THE PURPOSE OF THIS OUTLINE IS TO ORGANIZE THE CASES SO THAT ONE CAN QUICKLY UNDERSTAND THE RELEVANCE OF EACH CASE TO THE COURSE. NO ATTEMPT IS MADE IN THIS OVERVIEW TO ADDRESS EVERY CONCEPT THAT MUST BE STUDIED. BE SURE TO READ THE ENTIRE CASEBOOK AND/OR OTHER MATERIALS TO GAIN A FULL UNDERSTANDING OF ALL CONCEPTS.

I. Identifying Contracts' Express Terms
  A. "Parol Evidence Rule" Limits Contracts to Express Terms
    1. Once the parties draft a contract which they *intend* to be complete and final, its written terms cannot be changed through "parol evidence" of their prior promises or actual intentions, except to prevent fraud or mistake.
    2. Whether a contract was "intended" as final is determined by examining its express language to see if it purports to be complete, and is not vague.
    3. Writing Supersedes Promises: If the parties' agreement includes both oral promises and a written contract, then the writing supersedes the oral promise if reasonable parties in similar circumstances would normally have included any such promises into a final contract.
    4. The contract is deemed to supersede the verbal promise if both relate to the same subject matter, and are so interrelated that both would normally be executed in the same contract.
      a. Thus, if the written contract mentions a subject, then whatever it says on the subject is presumed to be the parties' entire agreement about that subject. This is a question of law. *Gianni v. R. Russel & Co., Inc.* [soda shop owner cannot claim landlord promised him exclusivity, in spite of lease agreement].
      b. *See also UCC § 2-202; Restatement (Second) of Contracts § 209-17.*
  B. Collateral Agreements Admissible
    1. Courts interpreting a disputed contract may consider evidence of "collateral" (side) agreements, if they are of the sort which would naturally be made separately from the disputed contract. *Masterson v. Sine* [married couple buys in-laws' ranch, but refuses to honor the buy-back option].
    2. "Collateral" Defined: Courts generally deem a contract as "collateral" if:
      a. Its form shows it is a collateral agreement, and
      b. It does not contradict the written contract's express or implied terms, and
      c. It is of a type that parties would not ordinarily embody in the written contract. *Moore v. Pennsylvania Castle Energy Co.* [landowner cannot sue the gas company mining her land based on unrecorded promise to limit drilling to specified sites].
    3. Courts may deem an agreement "collateral" if reasonable persons would (i.e., customarily do) draft agreements of that type separately from the main agreement in question. *Lee v. Joseph E. Seagram & Sons, Inc.* [oral promise to employ corporation owner's sons was collateral to agreement to sell the corporation].
  C. Merger Clauses
    1. Contracts often include a "merger clause" (a.k.a. "integration clause") stating it is the complete and final contract, and supersedes all prior agreements.
    2. Including such an integration clause creates a strong presumption that parol evidence is inadmissible, though this is rebuttable.
    3. Some courts may void merger clauses, especially when they are form/adhesion contracts forced on unsophisticated parties, and violate reasonable expectations.

II. Interpreting Contract Terms
  A. Some courts interpret contracts according to their express terms. Others are more willing to modify express terms if there is proof the parties actually intended, or agreed to, something other than what they wrote.
  B. Ambiguity
    1. Contracts which are "ambiguous" (imprecise)

are problematic when challenged in court, because judges often lack evidence of what the parties actually said or intended. Imprecise drafting creates several risks:

a. The parties may actually have agreed to different things.

b. Parties may be unsure what the contract means, and later forget what they agreed to.

c. Even honest disputes may lead to costly litigation.

d. Dishonest parties may convince a judge to give an interpretation which was never agreed to in fact.

2. Parol Evidence Admissible To Clarify Ambiguity

a. When a contractual term is found "ambiguous," courts admit parol evidence to "interpret" (clarify) its meaning. *Dennison v. Harden* [orchard buyer, who contacted for "peach trees," cannot complain when they proved to be worthless scrub "peach trees" instead of marketable ones].

b. Courts cite the general principle that parol evidence is still inadmissible to change a partially-integrated contract's terms or add terms to a fully-integrated contract.

(1) But in practice, "interpreting" contractual "ambiguities" often alters the contract's express terms.

3. "Ambiguity" Defined: But courts vary in when they will find a term ambiguous.

a. Narrow Definition: Some courts hold a contractual word is ambiguous only if it has *no* meaning ascertainable from the contract itself (e.g., "Seller will deliver the *stuff* to Buyer."). *Dennison* ["peach trees" is unambiguous, and includes unsaleable scrub "peach trees"].

b. Broad Definition

(1) Other courts -- possibly the minority -- consider the parties' actual intent more than the contract's literal wording.

(2) Typically, such courts may find ambiguity if a term has two possible meanings, or if there is strong evidence the parties actually intended something other than what they wrote. *Pacific Gas & Electric Co. v. G. W. Thomas Drayage & Rigging Co.* [after repairmen damage turbine, court deciding whether indemnity clause covers self-inflicted damage should consider extrinsic evidence of the parties' actual intent].

C. Contractual "Interpretation": "Interpreting" a contract refers, technically, to defining terms' *meaning*, according to either the plain language or the parties' subjective intent. *See Restatement (Second) of Contracts § 200, Com. C.*

1. Categories of Imprecision: Interpretation disputes occur when contractual language is imprecise, for several analytical reasons:

a. "Vagueness" happens when a term overlaps into other words, making people disagree on its limits (e.g., "within a reasonable time" can mean a range of dates).

b. "Term ambiguity" happens (technically) when a word has multiple possible meanings (e.g., "dollar" can refer to American dollars, Bahamiam dollars, etc.). But many judges say "ambiguity" to mean *any* imprecision.

c. "Sentence ambiguity" occurs when the individual words are clear, but the sentence structure makes it unclear which word is referred to (e.g., "When I hold this nail and nod my head, hit *it* with the hammer.").

2. Lawyers' Role

a. Lawyers drafting contracts must choose how detailed to make them.

b. Cursory contracts create the risk of mistake, confusion, litigation, and bad faith challenges.

c. Overly-detailed contracts add transaction costs, needlessly. No contract can be completely specific; it would be nearly endless.

3. Judges' Role: Judges usually say they are effectuating the parties' "intent." But this can have different meanings.

a. "Intent" can mean the speaker's/drafter's intent. But the counterparty may have interpreted his words as meaning something else, and that counterparty's expectation is no less important than the drafter's.

b. Or, it can mean the counterparty's understanding; same issue.

c. Or, it can mean what a reasonable person would understand the words to mean, presumably at execution.

D. Principles of Interpretation

1. Interpretations Cannot Contradict Text

a. An integrated contract's ambiguities may be clarified through parol evidence, but such evidence must be reasonably consistent with the contractual language.

b. In other words, parties cannot claim contractual terms were intended to mean the opposite of their common meaning. *Brinderson-Newburg Joint Venture v. Pacific Erectors, Inc.* [subcontractor who contracted to "erect complete" a gas pipe cannot claim it agreed to build only the supports].

2. *UCC* Approach: Under the *UCC*, contracts are interpreted according to the parties' actual bargain, so that express contractual terms may be modified by parties' prior dealings and "trade usage," unless these are irreconcilable with the contract's language. *See Nanakuli Paving and Rock Co. v. Shell Oil Co., Inc.* [asphalt contract implies price protection where such protection was standard and expected]. But note that courts vary in their willingness to reconcile incompatible terms.

3. Extrinsic Evidence Required

a. Parties urging an uncommon interpretation of contractual language usually must present objective, extrinsic evidence supporting that interpretation. *Frigaliment Importing Co. v. B.N.S. International Sales Corp.* ["What is chicken?"]

b. Extrinsic evidence can come from, e.g., dictionaries, trade usage within the industry, usage by government agencies or industry associations, and common usage of the words.

4. Canons

a. Judges may resort to "canons of construction," a set of doctrines used to resolve ambiguities in a pre-set way. These cannons are written in the (non-binding) *Restatement (Second) of Contracts* and sometimes in case law.

b. But since canons are often contradictory, it is still possible for judges to decide cases based on private whims, then justify their choices publicly by citing whichever canon concurs.

5. Course of Dealing: If a contractual term has multiple meanings, but both parties acted in ways that suggest they understood it similarly, this is proof of their subjective intent, and (possibly) the term's objective meaning. *Frigaliment Importing Co. v. B.N.S. International Sales Corp.* [chicken importer which accepted older birds as "chicken" cannot later claim it contracted to buy only young birds].

6. Trade "Usages"

a. If a commercial practice is so common in a place, vocation, or trade that contractual parties reasonably expect it will be observed in their transaction, then parties are bound by it to the extent they actually knew/should have known about it, unless the contract's language flatly contradicts it. *UCC § 1-205(2)*.

b. Parties are bound by the usages of the places where they do business, even if they are not in that line of business. Whether a practice is widespread and regular enough to be a "usage" is a question of fact. *See Nanakuli Paving and Rock Co. v. Shell Oil Co., Inc.* [asphalt supplier must offer paver price protection as part of their contract, because it is universal in that state's paving industry].

7. Dealings with Others Relevant: Under the *UCC*, courts hold that one party's dealings *with other contractual partners* is equivalent to a "course of dealing," even though it doesn't qualify literally as a "course of dealings" between *the litigants*. *Corenswet, Inc. v. Amana Refrigeration, Inc.* [distributor whose contract allowed cancellation "for any reason" could place *limited* reliance on

manufacturer's policy of continuing others distributors' agreements indefinitely].

8. "Good Faith" Obligation Varies
   a. The *UCC* states "every [*UCC*] contract ... imposes an obligation of good faith in its performance." *UCC § 1-203*.
   b. This cannot be disclaimed by agreement. *UCC § 1-102*.
   c. Some courts extend this rule to curb opportunism and protect parties' reasonable expectations. Other courts decline. *See, e.g., Corenswet* ["good faith" obligation cannot override express terms].
9. Unconscionable Terms Void
   a. Under the *UCC*, contractual terms which courts deem "unconscionable" are void.
   b. "Unconscionability" is usually defined as using superior bargaining power to obtain a contract whose terms are one-sided. *See, e.g., Corenswet* [right to end distributorship agreement without cause is not unconscionable].
   c. Generally, judges are reluctant to find terms unconscionable.

III. Terms' Implications
  A. In addition to contract's express terms and those added to reflect the parties actual, unwritten bargain, the law also "implies" (forces) certain legal requirements into certain contractual terms. The purpose is the following:
    1. When the parties both assumed certain terms but did not write them because they seemed obvious, to protect parties' subjective intent
    2. When the parties did not contemplate a scenario which occurred, to protect their reasonable expectations
    3. To further public policy by preventing injustice.
  B. Unexpected Events: If a contract fails to provide for an event, then judges may "imply" terms which effectuate the parties' clear intent, if such implications do not contradict express terms. *Spaulding v. Morse* [divorced father, who contracted to pay son's support and education through college, is excused when son is drafted].
  C. Exclusivity Implies Best Efforts
    1. If a contract makes one party the other's *exclusive* agent, the agent is implicitly obligated to use "best efforts" in fulfilling his contractual duties. *UCC § 2-306*; *Wood v. Lucy, Lady Duff-Gordon* [fashion designer's exclusive distributor is implicitly obligated to use best efforts to sell her products].
    2. But even a duty to use "best efforts" does not require the agent to incur large losses to perform the contract. *Bloor v. Falstaff Brewing Corp.* [struggling liquor distributor violated "best efforts" by advancing its own interests over supplier's, even more than was necessary to stay solvent].
  D. Autonomy Unaffected
    1. It may seem that judges' power to imply terms which the parties never actually discussed subverts their autonomy (i.e., freedom of contract).
    2. But in practice, judges tend to imply fairly reasonable terms, so the parties are rarely saddled with wholly-unexpected obligations.
  E. Discretion Implies Good Faith
    1. Contracting parties often want to retain some flexibility for unforeseen occurrences.
    2. They may do this by leaving a choice to a party's discretion (e.g., "best efforts," "within a reasonable time," "at the seller's best business judgment").
    3. If a contract expressly gives parties discretion, then implicitly, that discretion must be exercised in good faith. *UCC*; *Restatement (Second) of Contracts § 205*.
    4. "Good Faith" Defined: Courts differ in defining good faith.
      a. Most hold that, if the contract gives a party the right to do something for a certain agreed-upon reason, then that party has very broad discretion in deciding whether or not to act *for that reason*, but cannot act on the basis of *another* reason, which was not agreed upon as a permissible basis.
        (1) See, for example, *Greer Properties, Inc. v. LaSalle National Bank* [when land sale contract allowed sellers to terminate

if pollution cleanup costs made sale impracticable in their "best business judgment," they cannot terminate just to shop for better price].

b. Good Faith Defined By Custom

(1) If a business practice is accepted over time, by the industry and/or the parties, then it is likely to be found to be in "good faith." *Eastern Air Lines, Inc. v. Gulf Oil Corp.* [airline's common practice of refueling planes at stops where fuel is cheaper does not violate its requirements contract].

(2) Other business practices are seen as too opportunistic, and forbidden.

(3) For example, buyers under a requirements contract cannot intentionally increase their need or demand supplies for arbitrage. *Orange and Rockland Utilities, Inc. v. Amerada Hess Corp.* [when oil prices soar, requirements buyer demands more oil for resale].

F. "Lawful Performance Doctrine"

1. If a contract is subject to legal regulations, the parties must obey the law.
2. A few courts hold that this effectively implies additional terms into the contract.
   a. For example, a state housing code may imply into a lease a warranty of habitability.
   b. Thus, in such jurisdictions, if a party violates a statute while performing the contract, this violation may also constitute breach. *Citizens for Preservation of Waterman Lake v. Davis* [recognizing lawful performance doctrine, but declining to apply it to enable town and citizens to sue polluting contractor].

IV. Promises and Conditions

A. Triggering Event

1. A contractual "promise" obligates the promisor to perform what he promised.
   a. For example, "I will shovel your already-snowy sidewalk for payment."
2. But a "condition" only obligates the promisor to perform when (and if) a certain event triggers the promise.
   a. For example, "*If it snows, then* I will shovel your sidewalk for payment."
3. If the triggering event never happens, the promisor need not perform the condition.
   a. If a promise is also a condition, it is called a "promissory condition."

B. Conditions Precedent

1. A "condition precedent" is a circumstance which *must exist* before the contract becomes binding on the parties. (E.g., "*If it snows* ... ")
   a. Thus, if the condition precedent "fails" (never happens), then the contract is unenforceable (e.g., If it doesn't snow, I'm not obligated to shovel, and you're not obligated to pay). *Luttinger v. Rosen* [homebuyers may recover deposit after failing to obtain a mortgage, because the mortgage was a condition precedent].
2. Sometimes, the contract is unclear whether a contractual term is a condition precedent, or just an assumption.
   a. For example, if a subcontract says the subcontractor will be paid after the general contractor receives full payment from the builder, this could mean either
      (1) Generally, the subcontractor is to be paid later than the general contractor, or
      (2) Payment to the general contractor is a condition precedent, so that if the general contractor is not paid, it need not pay the subcontractor.
   b. Such ambiguities are a question of law. *Peacock Construction Co., Inc. v. Modern Air Conditioning, Inc.* [subcontractors' right to payment after general contractor receives "full payment" is *not* a condition precedent, unless stated explicitly].

C. Conditions May Be Voidable: Courts may modify or void contractual conditions for equitable reasons.

1. Waiver by Conduct: If one party's conduct indicates that he is not requiring literal performance, then he cannot start demanding literal performance without giving notice and a reasonable time to comply. *Burger King*

Corp. v. Family Dining, Inc. [franchisor, which ignored franchise's lateness in building new restaurants for 5 years, cannot then declare the contract terminated].

2. Disproportionate Forfeiture
   a. "A condition may be excused without other reason if its requirement [(i)] will involve extreme ["disproportionate"] forfeiture or penalty, and [(ii)] [it] ... forms no essential part of the exchange for the promisor's performance." *Restatement of Contracts § 302*; *Restatement (Second) of Contracts § 229.*
   b. Whether a forfeiture is "disproportionate" weighs the breacher's fault against the potential penalty.

D. Conditions Within Parties' Control
1. Sometimes, a condition which may void the contract is within the control of one party.
   a. This creates "moral hazard" (bad incentives), since that party can trigger the condition intentionally, thus releasing itself from all contractual obligations.
2. Good Faith Implied: Courts prevent such moral hazard by implying a duty of good faith on controlling parties. *Fry v. George Elkins Co.* [homebuyer who agreed to buy, conditional on getting a mortgage, breached by not seeking the mortgage diligently].
   a. Some courts decide "good faith" by subjective standards, especially when the contract specifically makes a condition subject to one party's "fancy, taste, or judgment" or "satisfaction."
   b. For example, "The portraitist will be paid only if the patron is satisfied.
      (1) In this case, a party may trigger the condition unreasonably (e.g., reject an objectively-adequate portrait), as long as he does so because he is *genuinely* dissatisfied.
      (2) See, e.g., *Pannone v. Grandmaison* [radiation-phobic homebuyer may refuse to buy house which has minimal radiation].
   c. Other courts evaluate "good faith" by objective standards, especially when the contract calls for an evaluation of "commercial value or quality, operative fitness, or mechanical utility." *See, e.g., Fry* [homebuyer who needed mortgage was unreasonable in snubbing the only likely lender].
3. Non-Interference Implied
   a. Each party is implicitly obligated not to impede *unreasonably* the other's performance.
   b. Thus, if a party prevents the other's performance by violating the contract's express/implied terms or breaking other laws, then the other party is discharged, and may sue for breach.
   c. But if a party makes the counterparty's performance merely more difficult (but not impossible or impracticable), this does not discharge the counterparty, unless the "prevention" is wrongful or unforeseeable. *Godburn v. Meserve* [live-in housekeepers who contracted to care for nag are not discharged because her nagging became unbearable].

Gianni v. R. Russel & Co., Inc.

(Commercial Tenant) v. (Landlord)
281 Pa. 320, 126 A. 791 (1924)

M E M O R Y G R A P H I C

Instant Facts

A candy stand owner, facing competition from a nearby soda shop, claims the landlord orally promised him the exclusive right to sell soda.

Black Letter Rule

Once the parties draft a complete, final written contract, its written terms cannot be changed through parol evidence of the parties' prior promises, except to prevent fraud or mistake.

Case Vocabulary

"ENTIRE" CONTRACT: Contract intended by the parties to include all terms of their final agreement. An "entire" contract cannot be modified by parol evidence. A.k.a. "[fully] integrated contract."
MERGE: In contract law, when contractual parties reduce their agreement to a final, complete written contract, any prior promises they made are deemed "merged" into (superseded by) the written contract.
PAROL EVIDENCE RULE: Doctrine that, once an agreement is written out as a final complete contract, its terms cannot be modified by presenting evidence of parties' promises which were not included in the contract.

Procedural Basis: In contract suit, appeal from judgment for plaintiff.

Facts: Merchant Gianni (P) leased a candy stand inside an office building owned by landlord R. Russel & Co., Inc. ("Landlord") (D). The lease provides Gianni (P) can "use the premises only for the sale of fruit, candy, soda water," etc., and cannot sell tobacco. Later, Landlord (D) leased an adjoining stand to a drugstore, which sold soda and reduced Gianni's (P) profits. Gianni (P) sued Landlord (D) for breach, contending Landlord (D) agreed orally to give Gianni (P) exclusive rights to sell soda. The lease lacks such provisions. Gianni (P) claimed Landlord (D) made this promise orally, 2 days before signing the lease, in exchange for a higher rent and promise not to sell tobacco. As evidence, Gianni (P) produced a witness who testified Landlord's (D) agent told Gianni (P), days before execution, that he would have exclusivity. Landlord (D) contends it never promised exclusivity, and that testimony about such promises violates the parol evidence rule. After trial, the court held for Gianni (P). Landlord (D) appeals.

Issue: Can a final, complete written contract be modified to reflect the parties' earlier promises?

Decision and Rationale: (Schaffer) No. Once the parties draft a complete, final written contract, its written terms cannot be changed through parol evidence of the parties' prior promises, except to prevent fraud or mistake. When parties deliberately write out their agreements, then the writing is binding (to the exclusion of parol evidence), absent fraud or mistake. All preliminary statements are merged into the subsequent written contract, whose terms cannot be changed through parol evidence, except to prevent fraud, accident, or mistake. To exclude parol evidence, the contract must have been intended as the complete statement of the parties' agreement; intent is determined by examining the contract's language to see if it purports to be complete, and is not vague. If the parties' agreement includes both oral promises and a written contract, then the writing supersedes the oral promise if reasonable parties in similar circumstances would normally include the promise into the contract. Put another way, the contract is deemed to supersede the verbal promise if both relate to the same subject matter, and are so interrelated that both would normally be executed in the same contract. If the written contract mentions a subject, then whatever it says on the subject is presumed to be the parties' entire agreement about that subject. This is a question of law, to be determined by the court. Holding otherwise would violate written contracts' integrity. Here, we find the alleged promise of exclusivity would naturally be written into the final contract, because it is extremely pertinent. Thus, any parol evidence about Landlord's (D) oral promises of exclusivity is inadmissible. Reversed.

Analysis:

Gianni basically reiterates the importance of the parol evidence rule: once an agreement is reduced to a written contract which appears intended as final and complete, its written terms are the only express terms which have legal effect. (Though the court may *impute* certain terms into the contract, as illustrated later.) The justification of the parol evidence rule is that it preserves written contracts' "integrity," thus allowing courts and parties to rely on the written word. More importantly, this bright-line rule saves courts from having to make decisions about what the final agreement was; such decisions are tricky because often there is no evidence other than one party's word against the other's. Also, the parol evidence rule forces parties to finalize their negotiations by making sure the written contract represents their final understanding of the terms. However, the parol evidence rule is applied inconsistently, since courts have considerable leeway to find that a contract they dislike is actually incomplete, and thus not the "entire" agreement.

Masterson v. Sine

(In-Laws) v. (Ranch Owners)

Supreme Court of California, 1968. 68 Cal.2d 222, 436 P.2d 561

M E M O R Y   G R A P H I C

Instant Facts

A married couple takes possession of their in-laws' ranch, but refuses to honor their in-laws' option to buy it back.

Black Letter Rule

A court, when considering a disputed contract, may consider evidence of a collateral agreement if it is of a sort that would naturally be made separately from the disputed contract.

Procedural Basis: Appeal from a trial court judgment in favor of the plaintiff in an action for declaratory relief.

Facts: The Mastersons (P) owned a piece of property as tenants in common [the actual plaintiffs in this case were Mrs. Masterson and her husband's trustee in bankruptcy]. They transferred this property to Mr. Masterson's (P) sister and her husband, Lu Sine (D). The Mastersons (P) retained an option in the grant deed to buy back the land within ten years. If they exercised the option, the Mastersons (P) were obligated to pay an amount equal to "the same consideration as paid heretofore," plus the depreciation value of any improvements that the Sines (D) made to the property after two and a half years. These confusing payment terms were part of the subsequent litigation between the parties. The litigation was sparked by the Masterson's (P) desire to repurchase the property. At the time, Mr. Masterson (P) was bankrupt. His trustee in bankruptcy and Mrs. Masterson (P) brought an action for declaratory relief. They sought an interpretation of the agreement which would secure their right to exercise the repurchase option. During the trial, the court admitted extrinsic evidence which resolved the confusing payment terms. The court found that the parties intended "the same consideration as paid heretofore" to equal $50,000. In addition, the parties intended the depreciation value of any improvements to be measured by United States income tax regulations. The Sines (D), however, wanted to present extrinsic evidence that the option provision was nonassignable because it was intended to keep the property in the family. As a result, the Sines (D) argued that the option could not be exercised by Masterson's (P) trustee in bankruptcy. The trial court rejected this evidence as a violation of the parol evidence rule and found for the Mastersons (P). The Sines (D) appeal. Rather than dispute the exclusion of their own evidence, they claim that the trial court erred in admitting extrinsic evidence to clarify the option payment terms.

Issue: Can extrinsic evidence be used to clarify the terms of an agreement which would otherwise remain too uncertain to be enforceable?

Decision and Rationale: (Traynor) Yes. The trial court was justified in admitting extrinsic evidence in order to further the goals of the parties by clarifying the terms of their agreement. The trial court erred, however, in refusing to admit any evidence regarding the Mastersons' (P) right to assign the option. The crucial question in this case is whether the agreement between the Mastersons (P) and the Sines (D) was an integration. By this, we mean a contract which the parties intended to be their final and exclusive agreement. There are two ways to determine whether a contract is an integration. First, a court can rely on the language of the contract itself. Frequently, a contract will contain language which identifies it as an integration. If so, the parol evidence rule precludes the consideration of evidence which would alter the contract's terms. Without this language, a court can either find that the contract is not an integration, or it can look at the circumstances surrounding the transaction to make its determination. However, even if the contract states that it is an integration, it may be necessary to look at other agreements between the parties in order to decide whether they fall within its scope or whether they are separate agreements. This is particularly necessary when a contract is silent on a point which is disputed by the parties. As a result, it has proven impossible to rely solely on the language of the contract in order to determine its status. This does not obviate the need for the parol evidence rule, however. Several policies have been advanced for the preservation of the rule. First, the written word may be inherently more reliable than a party's memory of contract negotiations. Second, courts are afraid that witnesses will be encouraged to manufacture contract terms which are favorable to the respective parties. Finally, courts fear that juries may be overly sympathetic to parties who seek the introduction of parol evidence, since they are usually the underdogs in the dispute. All of these policies reflect a desire to ensure the credibility of evidence in contract disputes. The Restatement and the Uniform Commercial Code take two different approaches to this evidence. The Restatement admits evidence of collateral agreements only if the parties would naturally have made them as separate agreements from the contract in question. The UCC excludes this evidence only if the parties would certainly have made the agreements part of the contract. In this case, the contract does not state that it is an integration. It is also silent on the question of assignability. However, a deed, by its very nature, is unlikely to embody all of the rights and obligations of the parties. The Mastersons (P) may have included the option provision to put potential buyers on notice of their reserved rights. There is no evidence to suggest that the parties understood the danger of not including the entire agreement in the deed. As a result, the Restatement and the UCC tests are both satisfied. The assignment provision would naturally be agreed to in a separate document, calling for its admission under the Restatement. Similarly, under the UCC, it cannot be said that the parties would certainly have included the assignment provision in the grant deed since it was not the proper document in which to place such a provision. The Mastersons (P), on the other hand, claim that option provisions are presumptively assignable regardless of the language of the contract. This does not prevent the court from considering parol evidence which might defeat this presumption, however. As a result, the trial court erred in excluding evidence on the assignment provision and its judgment must be reversed.

Dissent: (Burke) I dispute the majority's findings on virtually every issue in this case. First, the majority violates the spirit of the parol evidence rule by permitting evidence of a collateral agreement to obliterate an existing written agreement. This compromises the reliability of many transactions, including conveyances and debtor/creditor relationships. The central problem with the majority's approach is its failure to acknowledge the strength of option agreements in general, and the nature of the option in this case, in particular. Options are, by nature, assignable property rights. The only way to limit an option is by specific language in the agreement. If this rule were otherwise, a party to a contract could always find a way out of an unfavorable option by fabricating an agreement which limited its effect. In this case, the Mastersons' (P) creditor is deprived of a valid property right as a result of this approach. The majority invites this result by characterizing the parol evidence rule as a rule of credibility. The parol evidence rule is specifically designed to exclude *any* extrinsic evidence of a contract's terms, not just evidence which might be unreliable. This is because extrinsic evidence is presumed to be unreliable. In addition, the majority favors the Restatement's approach to the parol evidence rule. California courts must now determine whether an agreement would naturally be arrived at separately from the disputed contract. Courts might easily disagree as to whether an agreement was naturally separate or not, however. Finally, the majority relies on the fact that the agreement is a deed in order to determine that the absence of the assignment provision is to be expected. This is absurd. If the option itself is contained in the deed, why would the parties have shrunk from including one more line, limiting the option's assignability. For all of these reasons, I would affirm the judgment of the trial court.

Analysis:

Once again, you are treated to an exhaustive analysis of the parol evidence rule. More importantly, the majority and the dissent present quite different approaches to the rule. Justice Traynor is willing to look at all aspects of the parties' transaction in order to determine whether the parol evidence rule applies. Justice Burke is clearly uncomfortable with this approach. He is more likely to favor the "four corners" approach to contract interpretation. This approach limits the courts attention to the language of the contract. However, Justice Burke loses sight of the fact that deeds and contracts are not equivalent documents. Indeed, he berates the majority for resting its interpretation on this distinction. However, a deed is not a contract of sale. Parties do not usually put the details of a real estate transaction in the deed. In this case, the Mastersons (P) were obviously concerned with securing their right to repurchase the property against prospective buyers. They might have put this provision in the deed in order to avoid fighting a future purchaser for the return of the property after it was already sold. Once they added the provision, however, they invited the difficulties which arose in this case -- namely, that any caveats which might limit their repurchase option would normally be in the contract of sale, another legally enforceable document. Think of the deed as a declaration of rights and the contract of sale as an agreement regarding those rights. The majority relies on this distinction, above all others, as the key to its analysis.

Moore v. Pennsylvania Castle Energy Co.

(Landowner) v. (Land User's Assignee)
89 F.3d 791 (11 Cir. 1996)

M E M O R Y G R A P H I C

Instant Facts

A landowner sued the gas company which mined her land, contending its predecessor promised orally to limit its drilling to specified sites.

Black Letter Rule

"Integrated" contracts' terms cannot be modified with parol evidence, but "collateral" agreements are enforceable separately.

Case Vocabulary

APPURTENANT: Related to [land].
DIVERSITY [CASE/JURISDICTION]: Grounds for bringing a claim in federal court, rather than a state court, applicable when the plaintiffs and defendants are residents of different states.
EASEMENT: Right to use another's land, or travel through it without liability for trespass.
INTEGRATED CONTRACT: A.k.a. "Fully-integrated contract." Contract intended by the parties to contain all the terms of their agreement. In practice, such contracts often say they are the complete and final version. By law, if a contract is "integrated," its terms supersede all prior agreements and representations, which become inadmissible under the parol evidence rule.
REMITTUR: Judge's reduction of a jury award.
SEVERANCE DEED: Apparently, a "deed" (land-related contract) allowing a party to remove land-related goods (e.g., minerals, crops).

Procedural Basis: In suit for contract breach and trespass, appeal from verdict for plaintiff.

Facts: Ms. Moore (P) owned land containing methane gas. Moore (P) sold subsurface mineral rights to miner TRW, through a severance deed. The deed contained a "surface access and surface damage agreement," which compensated Moore (P) for land damage caused by drilling. This clause provided TRW would pay Moore $10K for a "perpetual easement" allowing it to dig 6 gas wells. Under the deed, 2 wells' locations were fixed, and 4 were subject to later negotiation. Moore (P) claims TRW agreed orally to drill only at 6 fixed sites indicated on a map, and to not drill in a certain area ("Field"). Moore (P) negotiated for 3 hours before signing, and demanded to change the deed from a fixed fee to an open one. However, the final written agreement does not limit TRW to 6 wells, or ban drilling in Field; instead, it says, "TRW has the final decision for location" for the 4 wells, and does not refer to any map. Moore (P) claims TRW also assured her, at execution, that it would drill only on mapped sites. Later, TRW assigned its lease to Pennsylvania Castle Energy Co. ("Penn Castle") (D). TRW asked to drill additional wells, but Moore (P) refused. Nevertheless, Penn Castle (D) drilled an extra well, in the middle of Field. Moore (P) sued Penn Castle (D) in state court, claiming breach and trespass. Penn Castle (D) removed to federal court based on diversity jurisdiction. At trial, the court held for Moore (P), admitting evidence of the oral promises and map. The jury found for Moore (P). Penn Castle (D) moved for judgment as a matter of law, contending the map and negotiations were inadmissible parol evidence. The district court denied the motion. Penn Castle (D) appeals.

Issue: Can a court hearing a contract suit consider parol evidence of oral promises which do not appear in the contract?

Decision and Rationale: (Anderson) No. "Integrated" contracts' terms cannot be modified with parol evidence, but "collateral" agreements are enforceable separately. Under Alabama law, once contractual parties reduce their agreement to writing, then all prior promises are merged into the written contract. Parol evidence is inadmissible to vary a complete and unambiguous written contract's express terms. This parol evidence rule applies only when the contract is written, and is intended by the parties to represent their entire agreement. To determine the parties' intent, we examine both the contract itself, the parties' conduct, and surrounding circumstances. Alabama caselaw holds a collateral agreement is admissible if (i) its form shows it is a collateral agreement, (ii) it does not contradict the written contract's express or implied terms, and (iii) it is of a type that parties would not ordinarily embody in the written contract. [Here, we find the contract unambiguous.] Also, we find the written agreement was intended to be a complete integration, so that any oral agreement between Moore (P) and TRW is merged into it, as a matter of law. This is because the written agreement is a formal document purporting to embody the entire agreement. Moore's (P) negotiations showed she viewed it as such, and had the opportunity to require TRW put its promises into writing. Also, the agreement covers the same subject as the written contract. Finally, TRW's alleged promise never to drill over 6 wells is not collateral to the written agreement, whose purpose was to define the parties' duties with respect to mining on Moore's (P) land. Since this parol evidence is inadmissible, Moore's (P) contract claim fails as a matter of law. Reversed.

Analysis:

Moore continues to restate the majority "parol evidence rule," but adds some doctrinal details, especially regarding the "collateral agreement" exception. *Moore* stresses that the rule excludes parol evidence only when the written contract is intended as "fully-integrated" -- i.e., when it (i) is intended by the parties to be, and (ii) actually appears to be, a (iii) final draft (iv) which includes all terms relating to the subject. Even if the contract is finalized thus, there is still a loophole in the form of the "collateral document" doctrine, which enforces "separate" contracts related tangentially to the final contract. However, once a contract is finalized, it becomes more difficult to argue that a related writing is "collateral" rather than "merged" (subsumed). The test to distinguish "collateral" contracts is the "reasonable person" test; if the judge decides that reasonable people would write out the disputed term as a "side" agreement separate from the main contract, then it may be deemed "collateral." But this is a tougher hurdle for plaintiffs to overcome, as shown in *Moore*.

Lee v. Joseph E. Seagram & Sons, Inc.

(Business' Seller) v. (Business' Buyer)
(2nd Cir. 1977) 552 F.2d 447

MEMORY GRAPHIC

Instant Facts

A liquor wholesaler sold his business on condition the buyer relocate him and his sons to another dealership, but the relocation term was omitted from the final contract.

Black Letter Rule

An oral promise is enforceable as a "collateral agreement" if reasonable persons would not ordinarily include promises of that type into a written contract of that type.

Case Vocabulary

INTEGRATED CONTRACT: a.k.a. "Fully-integrated contract." Contract intended by the parties to contain all the terms of their agreement. By law, if a contract is "integrated," its terms supersede all prior agreements and representations, which become inadmissible under the parol evidence rule.

INTEGRATION CLAUSE: Contractual term included in an "integrated contract," which states that this contract is the final version, and represents every term which the parties agreed to. By law, if a contract contains an integration clause, this creates a strong presumption that it is complete and final.

Procedural Basis: In contract action, appeal from verdict for plaintiffs.

Facts: Liquor dealer Harold Lee and his sons ("the Lees") (P) owned 50% of liquor wholesaler Capitol City Liquor Company, Inc. ("Capitol City"). Capitol City sold boozes produced by distiller Joseph E. Seagram & Sons, Inc. ("Seagram") (D), among others, and Harold Lee (P) had a good 36-year relationship with Seagram's (D) managers. The Lees (P) wanted to sell Capitol City to Seagram (D), apparently to move to another city. The Lees (P) approached Seagram's (D) VP Yogman, a friend of Harold Lee (P), and offered to sell Capitol City, conditioned on Seagram's (D) agreement to relocate the Lees (P) to a new distributorship in another city. Yogman agreed. Later, Seagram's (D) representative Barth negotiated the sale, and obtained a contract to purchase the assets of Capitol City. *The contract did not include any promise to relocate*. The contract also did not include an integration clause. Later, Seagram (D) refused to relocate the Lees (P). The Lees (P) sued Seagram (D) for breach of oral contract. Seagram (D) defended, contending the promise to relocate was invalid under the parol evidence rule. The Lees (P) rebutted, contending it was enforceable as a "collateral agreement." At trial, Seagram (D) moved to dismiss. The District Court denied the motion and admitted parol evidence, finding the contract was ambiguous on whether it was intended to integrate the parties' *entire* agreement. Seagram (D) offered no evidence on this issue. Later, the judge instructed that the jury could find the parties' agreement included a promise to relocate. The jury returned a verdict for the Lees (P). Seagram (D) appeals.

Issue: May a court hearing a contract dispute admit parol evidence of an oral promise made contemporaneously with a written contract?

Decision and Rationale: (Gurfein) Yes. An oral promise is enforceable as a "collateral agreement" if reasonable persons would not ordinarily include promises of that type into a written contract of that type. Preliminarily, we must accept the jury's finding that Seagram (D) promised to relocate the Lees (P). The governing law is New York's, which follows general common law. If a contract is not intended as completely integrated, the parol evidence rule does not apply. Intent is determined objectively, considering the contract's scope, the oral promise's content, and the transaction's type. Certain oral collateral agreements are admissible even if made contemporaneously and related to the same subject, if they are (i) separate, (ii) independent, and (iii) complete contracts. Agreements are "separate" and "independent" if they are of a type which parties would not be expected to include in the writing. Here, we find Seagram's (D) promise to relocate the Lees (P) was not a term expectable to be integrated into a written contract for the sale of a corporation's assets. This is because a corporate asset-sale agreement does not normally include employment/consulting agreements for shareholders, who are not necessarily parties to the sale. Also, since Harold Lee (P) was a long-standing friend of Seagram's (D) Yogman, it is reasonable a handshake deal between them would suffice. Also, the actual transaction was executed by Seagram's (D) Barth, who may not have realized the 2 transactions were integrated. Finally, the contract does not contain the customary integration clause. Nor does it contradict or vary the asset sale's terms. Thus, the promise to relocate was not integrated, and introducing it as parole evidence was proper. Affirmed.

Analysis:

Lee represents the majority common law rule regarding collateral agreements. It expands (very) slightly on the prior cases' recitation of the "collateral agreement" rule, again emphasizing that parties' *intent* to make a contract "integrated" or "collateral" is determined objectively, under the "reasonable person" standard. *Lee* illustrates that determining an oral agreement as "collateral" often involves categorizing both the oral agreement and the related written contract as a transaction "type," then asking whether agreements of those 2 types are customarily drafted separately. Also, this case illustrates that, if a contract contains an integration clause, this creates a strong presumption that it is complete and final, though the presumption is rebuttable. Thus, if you as a lawyer want to bar parol evidence, make sure your final contract includes an integration clause.

Dennison v. Harden

(Land Buyer) v. (Land Seller)

(Wash. 1947) 29 Wash.2d 243, 186 P.2d 908

M E M O R Y G R A P H I C

Instant Facts

When a landowner sells land containing peach trees whose quality turns out to be less than promised orally, the buyer sues for breach of warranty.

Black Letter Rule

In Washington, parol evidence is admissible to clarify contractual ambiguities, but not to admit evidence of contemporaneous collateral agreements to modify contractual terms.

Case Vocabulary

EXECUTORY CONTRACT: Contract which is to be performed later. Here, this apparently means buyer Dennison (P) prepaid for the land, and took possession later.

WARRANTY: Contractual term whereby a party "warrants" (represents) a certain fact is true. Typically, a seller warrants his goods are of a certain quality. Usually, if the warranted fact proves false, the buyer is entitled to rescind the contract or collect compensation.

Procedural Basis: In contract action seeking damages, appeal from dismissal.

Facts: Land-buyer Dennison (P) entered an executory contract to buy land from Harden (D). During preliminary negotiations, Harden (D) said the land included a commercial orchard containing 276 peach trees, of commercial grade, and displayed documents from a tree-nursery certifying their breed. The final contract stated, "Purchase price to include property and fruit trees, all tools, ..., etc., fruit trees, ... and crops in ground." Later, Dennison (P) found the trees were worthless "scrub" varieties. Dennison (P) sued Harden (D) for breach of express warranty. At trial, the court admitted parol evidence of Harden's (D) representations. Harden (D) did not object. Later, the judge recanted, because he decided the evidence was barred by the parol evidence rule. Thus, the judge ordered the evidence stricken, and dismissed Dennison's (P) claim. Dennison (P) appeals, contending the evidence was admissible because (i) Harden (D) did not object to admitting it; (ii) it falls under an exception admitting parol evidence to explain ambiguities, and (iii) it qualifies under an exception admitting parol evidence of contemporaneous collateral agreements, granted as inducement to enter the main contract, to show the parties' intent regarding the main contract.

Issue: Is parol evidence admissable if there is no objection to its introduction?

Decision and Rationale: (Hill) Yes. In Washington, parol evidence is admissible to clarify contractual ambiguities, but not to admit evidence of contemporaneous collateral agreements to modify contractual terms. First, evidence barred by the parol evidence rule does not become admissible if a party fails to object to it, because the parol evidence rule is a substantive law rather than evidentiary rule. Second, if the contract is ambiguous, parol evidence is admissible to explain ambiguities. But here, we find no ambiguity, since the meaning of "fruit trees" and "crops in ground" is neither mysterious nor confusing. Dennison (P) knew he was getting fruit trees, and got them. The only word which may be ambiguous is "etc.," but Dennison (P) does not challenge it as unclear. Third, some jurisdictions admit evidence of contemporaneous, collateral agreements which were entered as an inducement to enter the written contract, even absent fraud, accident, or mistake. But this is the minority rule, and is not the law here in Washington. Affirmed.

Analysis:

Apparently, the casebook author included *Dennison* to illustrate the problem of contractual ambiguity. *Dennison* recognizes a contract's terms may be "ambiguous," in which case parol evidence is admissible to clarify their meaning. Courts vary in their definition of "ambiguity." Some courts, like *Dennison*, adopt a narrow definition, apparently holding a word is ambiguous only if it has *no* meaning ascertainable from the contract itself (e.g., "Seller will deliver the *stuff* to Buyer."). The next case, *Pacific Gas & Electric*, illustrates other courts' use of a broader definition. *Dennison*'s narrow reading is unfair to Dennison (P). The evidence suggests Harden (D) defrauded him by implying the peach trees were of commercial grade, while knowing they were not, and knowing Dennison (P) expected them to be. Thus, while the judge is literally correct that Dennison (P) got "fruit trees," there is a vast difference between getting trees which produce saleable peaches, and those that don't.

CALIFORNIA SUPREME COURT ADMITS EXTRINSIC EVIDENCE TO SETTLE A DISPUTE OVER A CONTRACT TERM

Pacific Gas & Electric Co. v. G.W. Thomas Drayage & Rigging Co.

(Turbine Owner) v. (Turbine Repairmen)

Supreme Court of California, 1968. 69 Cal.2d 33, 69 Cal.Rptr. 561, 442 P.2d 641

M E M O R Y   G R A P H I C

Instant Facts

The parties to a turbine repair contract dispute the interpretation of an indemnification clause in the agreement.

Black Letter Rule

Extrinsic evidence of a party's intent is admissible to assist in the interpretation of a disputed contract term.

Facts: G.W. Thomas Drayage & Rigging Co. (Thomas) (D) agreed to replace the cover on Pacific Gas & Electric Co.'s (PG&E) (P) steam turbine. The agreement required Thomas (D) to indemnify PG&E (P) against any property damage resulting from Thomas's (D) work. To that end, Thomas (D) was obligated to purchase an insurance policy with more than $50,000 liability coverage for property damage. PG&E (P) was to be listed as an additional insured. In addition, PG&E (P) was supposed to be specifically covered for damage to its property. Thomas (D) subsequently damaged PG&E's (P) engine in the course of its work. PG&E (P) then sued Thomas (D), requesting the cost of repairs under the indemnification clause. Thomas (D) argued that the indemnification clause only covered damage to property owned by third parties. The trial court rejected its proof on this issue, however. The judge acknowledged that the indemnification clause was of a sort which normally covered only the property of third parties. Nonetheless, he decided that the plain language of the contract indemnified against damage to PG&E's (P) property as well. The trial court then found in favor of PG&E (P). Thomas (D) appeals.

Issue: Is a court required to admit extrinsic evidence which may assist in the interpretation of a disputed contract term?

Decision and Rationale: (Traynor) Yes. It is not appropriate for a judge to presume that his interpretation of particular contract language is so secure that it could not be swayed by relevant evidence to the contrary. The judge's own linguistic ability is not infallible, nor is the language in the contract likely to be free from any ambiguities. We understand that many judges rely on particular language to give rise to certain contractual obligations. However, California courts should not rely on the magical incantation of special phrases in order to create and destroy contract rights. Contractual obligations are created by the intent of the parties. If a court can determine this intent from the language of the contract, then it need not admit any further evidence. However, language is seldom so clear as to warrant this approach. Ordinarily, the court must admit any evidence which is "relevant to prove a meaning to which the language of the instrument is reasonably susceptible." This rule does not compromise the parol evidence rule, which still precludes the consideration of evidence which would add to or vary the terms of a contract. Instead, the rule protects the parties' intent by using the circumstances surrounding the transaction as a guide to the meaning of their contract. The judge must at least take a preliminary look at the parties' evidence in order to determine if it should be admitted. He should endeavor to place himself in the circumstances in which the parties found themselves at the time of contracting. The judge can do this through the consideration of evidence regarding the contract's object, nature and subject matter, among other things. If the court cannot settle on a single interpretation of the contract's language at this point, then extrinsic evidence should be admissible to further its interpretation. In this case, the trial court erred in two ways. First, the court refused to consider extrinsic evidence which was relevant to the determination of whether the indemnification clause covered PG&E's (P) property. Second, the court failed to admit this evidence even though the indemnification clause was equivocal on this point. As a result, the trial court's judgment must be reversed.

Analysis:

Welcome to Chief Justice Traynor's neighborhood. Earlier in this chapter, you read *Masterson v. Sine* [a court may consider evidence of a collateral agreement if it is of a sort that would naturally be made separately from the disputed contract]. You now have an idea of how Chief Justice Traynor feels about the introduction of extrinsic evidence to assist courts in contract interpretation. His views are controversial to say the least. Some commentators [and dissenting justices] feel that his approach subverts the parol evidence rule to the point where there is little left to enforce. He does walk a fine line between admitting evidence of subjective intent and permitting that intent to govern and change the contract in a way that violates the parol evidence rule. He defends this approach as a means of protecting the intent of the parties. There is some validity in this defense. Contracts are supposed to reflect the common intent of the parties. When the language of the contract itself fails to make this intent clear, a court must have resort to evidence of the parties' intent in order to preserve the enforceability of the contract. As you saw in *Oswald v. Allen* [a contract should be voided if the parties each held different understandings of an ambiguous term] there is a point at which this evidence fails to yield a consensus and the contract is unenforceable. Chief Justice Traynor tries to avoid this result rather than surrender to it without a fight.

Brinderson-Newburg Joint Venture v. Pacific Erectors, Inc.

(General Contractor) v. (Subcontractor)
(9th Cir. 1992) 971 F.2d 272, cert. denied 507 U.S. 914, 113 S.Ct. 1267, 122 L.Ed.2d 663

M E M O R Y   G R A P H I C

Instant Facts

After a subcontractor contracted to "erect complete" a gas pipe, it claimed the general contractor said it need build only the pipe's steel supports.

Black Letter Rule

An integrated contract's ambiguities may be clarified through parol evidence, but such evidence must be reasonably consistent with the contractual language.

Case Vocabulary

DIRECTED VERDICT: "Verdict" rendered by a *judge* acting as *fact-finder* in a *jury trial*, when the judge decides the evidence is so overwhelming that no jury could reasonably find otherwise. Equivalent to summary judgment.

GENERAL CONTRACTOR: Contractual party who undertakes to do something directly for a client. Usually found in the construction industry, where a general contractor receives a contract to build something, does part of the work itself, then contracts with smaller "subcontractors" (specialists) to build certain specialty components.

JNOV (JUDGMENT *NON OBSTANTE VEREDICTO*): (Judgment "notwithstanding the verdict.") Judge's reversal of a jury finding, granted if the judge decides the verdict is unjustifiable.

PERFORMANCE BOND: Bond (money deposit) given to insure a contractual party fulfills its contractual duties. Typically, general contractors demand subcontractors obtain a performance bond from a financial institution before starting work. If the subcontractor defaults, the bond money enables the general contractor to hire substitutes to finish the job by the deadline.

Procedural Basis: In contract action, appeal from judgment for defendant.

Facts: General contractor Brinderson-Newburg Joint Venture (Brinderson) (P) was awarded a Navy contract to build a coal-burning power plant. Brinderson (P) negotiated with subcontractor Pacific Erectors, Inc. (Pacific) (D) to build one component, a Flue Gas System (FGS) to control pollution. Pacific (D) offered to erect the FGS' support steel (a.k.a. the "pick and sets"). Brinderson (P) wanted Pacific (D) to erect both the support steel and other large steel components. They negotiated. After the second meeting, Brinderson (P) sent Pacific (D) a draft, which required Pacific (D) to "*erect complete* ... including [certain other components], Steel Gratings and appurtenances to *make a complete installation*." Pacific (D) considered the draft. Later, at the final negotiation, Pacific (D) asked to change this provision. Brinderson (P) claims it refused, and Pacific (D) agreed. Pacific (D) claims Brinderson (P) relented, but told it no change was necessary, because the language required only pick and sets, and limited Pacific's (D) duties to the type of work it customarily performs (i.e., only support steel). Pacific (D) signed the contract, whose language copied the draft's, and included a complete-integration clause. Later, the parties disputed whether Pacific (D) was obligated to erect the other components. Brinderson (P) sued. At trial, the district court allowed the jury to consider parol evidence that Brinderson (P) assured Pacific (D) the contractual language referred only to structural steel supports. After trial, the jury found for Pacific (D). Brinderson (P) moved for JNOV or directed verdict, but was denied. Brinderson (P) appeals.

Issue: Can a contractual party introduce parol evidence suggesting the final contract contradicted the parties' actual agreement?

Decision and Rationale: (Wiggins) No. An integrated contract's ambiguities may be clarified through parol evidence, but such evidence must be reasonably consistent with the contractual language. Under California law, a contractual ambiguity may be clarified through parol evidence if (i) the evidence does not add new terms to a contract intended as fully-integrated, and (ii) the ambiguous term is reasonably susceptible of the meaning offered by the party. Generally, parol evidence is inadmissible to add terms to fully-integrated contracts. One broad exception is that parol evidence may be introduced to show express terms' meaning, because no contract should be interpreted with a meaning neither party intended. *Pacific Gas & Electric v. G.W. Thomas Drayage & Rigging Co.* But the parol evidence must only clarify an integrated contract's terms, not reverse them. Holding otherwise would eviscerate the parol evidence rule, because any party would be able to change contractual terms by claiming it intended something else. The issue of whether a proffered meaning is reasonable is a question of law, reviewable de novo. Here, the contract was fully-integrated, on its face. We find the contract's language -- "erect complete" and "make a complete installation" -- cannot be interpreted to release Pacific (D) from the additional work, as a matter of law. This is because, first, when the contract requires Pacific (D) to perform "the work includ[ing] ... Any ... labor ... reasonably inferred by the plans ... *or* customarily furnished by a subcontractor performing work in this line," this does not limit Pacific (D) to perform *only* work it does customarily. Second, adopting Pacific's (D) explanation would violate the interpretive canon, "Since an agreement is interpreted as a whole, it is assumed ... no part ... is superfluous," *Restatement (Second) of Contracts § 203(a) cmt. b.* This is because allowing Pacific (D) to perform part of the work voids the obligation to "erect complete," and the detailed description of the additional steelwork. Third, Pacific's (D) interpretation violates the canon, "where there is an inconsistency between general provisions and specific provisions, ordinarily the specific ... qualify the meaning of the general." *Restatement (Second) of Contracts § 236(c).* This is because it contradicts the more specific mandate to "erect complete." Finally, it violates the canon, "where [individualized] written provisions are inconsistent with [boilerplate] printed provisions, [an interpretation which effectuates the individualized provisions is preferable]." *Restatement (Second) of Contracts § 236(c)*. Pacific's (D) interpretation is strained. Pacific's (D) argument basically contends its construction is reasonable because Brinderson (P) promised this interpretation, but that is irrelevant, because any such promises were merged into the fully-integrated contract. Reversed.

Analysis:

Brinderson represents the more literal version of the parol evidence rule, which looks first at the contract to see if its wording is intrinsically ambiguous. Its opinion discounts the parties' intent, saying essentially that, if Pacific (D) had intended something else, it should have written the contract to say what it meant. Thus, it is consistent with the doctrine behind *Masterson v. Sine* and *Pacific Gas and Electric*, but not with *G.W. Thomas*. Again, the policy underlying the parol evidence rule is certainty; courts do not want to disturb explicit contracts based on one party's unprovable claim that the agreement was for something different. *Brinderson* also introduces the "canons of construction," which are a set of doctrines used to resolve ambiguities in a pre-set way. These cannons are codified in the *Restatement (Second) of Contracts*, but as such they are persuasive rather than binding. Commentators note that the canons are often contradictory, so it is possible for judges to decide cases based on their own private whims, then justify their choice publicly by citing an convenient canon. Just like precedent.

Frigaliment Importing Co. v. B.N.S. International Sales Corp.

(Chicken Importer) v. (Chicken Exporter)

United States District Court, S.D.N.Y., 1960. 190 F.Supp. 116

MEMORY GRAPHIC

Instant Facts

An importer and an exporter dispute the meaning of the word "chicken" in their supply contract.

Black Letter Rule

The subjective interpretation of a contract term must be coupled with objective evidence supporting that interpretation.

Case Vocabulary

CHICKEN: Any sort of poultry type thingy which can be broiled, fried, stewed, pressed, marinated, grilled, poached, blackened, shredded, boiled, braised, or rotisseried; alternatively, a person who is afraid to do a particular act.]

Procedural Basis: District court judgment on a breach of warranty action.

Facts: B.N.S. International Sales Corp. (B.N.S.) (D) is an exporting firm based in New York. Frigaliment Importing Co. (Frigaliment) (P) is a Swiss import firm represented by its agent, Mr. Stovicek. B.N.S. (D) had two contracts to supply Frigaliment (P) with frozen chickens. The first contract called for 25,000 lbs. of 1½-2 lbs. chickens at $36.50 per 100 lbs. It also listed 75,000 lbs. of 2½-3 lbs. chickens at $33.00 per 100 lbs. The second contract called for different quantities of each weight and listed the 1½-2 lbs. chickens at $37.00 per 100 lbs. The two contracts had delivery dates of May 2nd, 1957 and May 30th, 1957 respectively. The problem arose when the first delivery arrived. Frigaliment (P) was expecting the 2½-3 lbs. chickens to be broiler/fryers. As it turns out, B.N.S (D) shipped 2½-3 lbs. *stewing* chickens which are older than broiler/fryers. Frigaliment (D) complained about the mix-up but accepted the second shipment. This shipment also contained stewing chickens instead of broiler/fryers. They then sued B.N.S. (D) for breach of warranty, claiming that B.N.S. (D) delivered goods which did not correspond to the description in the contract.

Issue: Can a court resolve a dispute based on differing interpretations of contract vocabulary?

Decision and Rationale: (Friendly) Yes. The parties urge different interpretations of the word "chicken" [you mean, um, apart from the obvious?]. In order to resolve this dispute, the court will look at the contract itself, the actual and trade usage of the word, and the behavior of the parties. In this case, the contract provides some guidance. Frigaliment (P) claims that since 1½-2 lbs. chickens are necessarily young chickens, the 2½-3 lbs. chickens should have been young as well. This argument begs the question since it has been established that the 2½-3 lbs. chickens come in two types. B.N.S. (D), on the other hand, argues that the contract incorporated the Department of Agriculture's regulations because Frigaliment (P) requested "US Fresh Frozen Chicken, Grade A, Government Inspected." The USDA regulations refer to "chickens" as broilers, fryers, and stewing chickens (also known as fowl). As a result, the regulations favor B.N.S.'s (D) interpretation of the contract, permitting the shipment of any type of chicken. Indeed, Stovicek's first communication with B.N.S. (D) also referred, generically, to chickens. Finally, at least one food industry witness for B.N.S. (D) relies on the Department of Agriculture's guidelines in his work. These circumstances, together, suggest that the USDA guidelines were intended to govern the contract definition of "chicken." In actual usage, the parties repeatedly used the word chicken during their negotiations. Frigaliment (D) claims that this was because most of the negotiations were in German and they wanted to avoid any confusion between the German word for chicken, "huhn," and the English word "chicken." They thought that "chicken" meant "young chicken" and avoided using the word "huhn" because it included both broilers and stewing chickens. However, when B.N.S. (D) asked Stovicek to be more specific, he told them that any type of chicken would do. The trade usage of the word "chicken" is also at issue in this case. Frigaliment (P) contends that "chicken" means "young chicken" in the poultry trade. Since B.N.S. (D) is new to the poultry trade, they are not charged with this knowledge unless Frigaliment (P) can demonstrate that the definition is so prevalent as to create a "violent" presumption that B.N.S. was aware of it. Frigaliment (P) failed to demonstrate this level of use in the industry. Their own witnesses frequently confirm the types of chicken in their business transactions by asking whether the parties are talking about broilers or stewing chickens. Other Frigaliment (P) witnesses were more certain that "chicken" refers to "young chickens" in the trade, but they were countered by witnesses for B.N.S. (D) which support the contrary conclusion. As noted above, some of B.N.S.'s (D)

Frigaliment Importing Co. v. B.N.S. International Sales Corp.
(Continued)

witnesses rely on the USDA regulations which categorize many types of poultry under the word "chicken." The conduct of the parties further supports our conclusion in favor of B.N.S. (D). First, the market rate for broilers was higher than the rate that B.N.S. (D) was charging Frigaliment (P) for the 2½-3 lbs. chickens. The market rate for stewing chickens was lower. The only way for B.N.S. (D) to make a profit on this transaction was to supply Frigaliment (P) with stewing chickens. B.N.S (D) claims that Frigaliment (P) should have known this and we agree. In addition, Frigaliment (P) accepted the second shipment of chickens even though B.N.S. (D) did not acknowledge their complaint about the first shipment. While they might have a claim for damages due to a nonconforming shipment of chickens, their behavior supports the conclusion that the contract called for the shipment of *any* type of chicken. Taking into account all of the arguments above, one thing is clear. Frigaliment (P) harbored a subjective belief that the contract called for the shipment of 2½-3 lbs broiler/fryers but failed to demonstrate an objective meaning of the word "chicken" which supports their interpretation. B.N.S. (D), on the other hand, demonstrated a subjective belief that is consistent with a number of objective circumstances that favor their definition. As a result, the term "chicken" in the contract will be interpreted broadly. Frigaliment's (P) claim is dismissed.

Analysis:

If you are not in the habit of reading the original opinions in your casebook, you are missing out. Judge Friendly's opinion is well known for a variety of reasons, not the least of which is his comprehensive approach to contract interpretation. He uses every trick in the book to resolve a seemingly easy question of interpretation which becomes more complicated at every turn. Much of the opinion implicitly relies on objective intent. In other words, the court asks how a reasonable person would interpret the language and behavior of the parties. This approach should be familiar since it also used in determining the existence of a contract. Judge Friendly also relies on trade usage to determine the definition of "chicken." Even this approach is fraught with complications, however, since B.N.S. (D) was new to the poultry industry. Finally, Judge Friendly interprets certain ambiguities in the parties' communications against Frigaliment (P). This is a less common device which is used to allocate the burdens of poor contract drafting. In this case, Stovicek's first cablegram referred ambiguously to "chickens." You will see in the text that an ambiguous word has more than one meaning, as it does in this case. If nothing else, Judge Friendly's analysis should give you some idea of the sheer variety of ways that a simple contract term can be interpreted. It should also give you an idea of just how difficult the analysis can be when two parties approach a contract from different cultural, professional, and linguistic backgrounds.

Nanakuli Paving and Rock Co. v. Shell Oil Co., Inc.

(Asphalt Buyer) v. (Asphalt Seller)

(9th Cir. 1981) 664 F.2d 772

M E M O R Y G R A P H I C

Instant Facts

A paving company claims its contract with an asphalt supplier was intended to include price protection because it is customary.

Black Letter Rule

Under the *UCC*, contracts for the sale of goods are interpreted according to the parties' actual bargain, so that express contractual terms may be modified by parties' prior dealings and trade usage, unless the two are irreconcilable.

Case Vocabulary

COURSE OF PERFORMANCE: The parties' actual actions in performing *this* contract. *Compare* "prior dealings."

CUSTOM: At common law, a practice which was implied into contracts because it was "universal" and longstanding. Custom is now superseded by the less restrictive "usage," which gives the same effect to practices which are newer and regional.

F.O.B.: ("Free on board.") Commercial idiom, meaning the seller of goods must deliver them to a fixed pick-up point, and remains responsible for them in transit.

PRIOR DEALINGS: (A.k.a. "course of dealings.") The parties' manner of performing *previous* contracts or transactions.

[TRADE] USAGE: An industry practice which is so widely-accepted (in a certain industry and/or region) that merchants expect it to be implied in their contracts. Under the *UCC*, "usages" are legally binding.

Procedural Basis: In contract action seeking damages, appeal from verdict for plaintiff.

Facts: Hawaiian paving giant Nanakuli Paving and Rock Co. (Nanakuli) (P) bought asphalt from supplier Shell Oil Co., Inc. (Shell) (D) under long-term supply contracts. Under the contracts' literal language, Nanakuli's (P) price was "Shell's Posted Price at the time of delivery." Customarily, Hawaiian pavers' asphalt suppliers always gave them "price protection," meaning that if they had ordered asphalt already, the supplier would not increase its price after the order and before delivery. This is because in Hawaii, most paving is done for the government, which accepts the paver's quoted price as binding, and will not pay any more later due to increased asphalt costs. (Pavers bid on government contracts in reliance on current asphalt prices, and cannot pass along costs increases.) Shell (D) offered Nanakuli (P) price protection under the contract from 1969 to 1974, but then refused. This is because, in 1974, (i) the partial oil embargo raised the price of (raw material) petroleum, and (more importantly) (ii) Shell's (D) management was replaced by people unfamiliar with its prior dealings and Hawaii's paving market. When Shell's (D) new managers refused to continue offering Nanakuli (P) price protection, Nanakuli (P) sued in state court for breach. After trial, the jury found for Nanakuli (P). Shell (D) appealed to the district court. After trial, the district judge set aside the verdict, and granted Shell's (D) motion for judgment n.o.v., apparently deciding no jury could reasonably find that the contract obligated Shell (D) to offer price protection. Nanakuli (P) appeals.

Issue: Can a contract's express terms be modified by evidence of industry custom?

Decision and Rationale: (Hoffman) Yes. Under the *Uniform Commercial Code*, contracts for the sale of goods are interpreted according to the parties' actual bargain, so that express contractual terms may be modified by parties' prior dealings and trade usage, unless the two are irreconcilable. Under the *Uniform Commercial Code* (adopted in Hawaii) an "agreement" goes beyond the written words, and means "the bargain of the parties in fact as found in their language *or by implication from other circumstances including course of dealing or usage of trade or course of performance." UCC 1-201(3)*. Parties' actual course of dealings is more important than trade usages, because they are specific to those parties. *UCC § 1-205(4)*. Evidence of performance, usages, and prior dealings is always admissible (even for integrated contracts) unless they cannot reasonably be construed as reconcilable with the contract's express terms. *UCC 1-205(4)*. The *UCC* defines "usage of trade" as "any practice or method of dealing having such regularity of observance in a place, vocation or trade as to justify an expectation that it will be observed with respect to the transaction in question." *UCC § 1-205(2)*. If a practice qualifies as a trade usage, parties are bound by it to the extent they actually knew about it, or should have known, even though it is not stated in the contract. Thus, practices qualify as "usages" if they have "such regularity of observance ... as to justify an expectation that it will be observed." *UCC § 1-205(2)*. (Old common law required they be "universal" or "immemorial," but this is not necessary under the *UCC*.) Parties are bound by the usages of the places where they do business, even if they are not in that line of business, or are not headquartered there. Whether a practice is widespread and regular enough to be a "usage" is a question of fact. Also, the *Code* suggests parties' prior course of dealing has binding effects, similar to "usage." The *Code*'s policy is to "permit the continued expansion of commercial practices through custom, usage and agreement of the parties," *UCC § 1-102(2)(b)*, rather than maintaining inflexible, narrow interpretational rules. The jury verdict's validity depends on 4 legal questions, including (i) whether price protection was so widespread in the Hawaii paving market that it became "trade usage" binding on Shell (D), and (ii) whether the express contractual term of Shell's (D) posted price is reasonably consistent with the prevailing trade usage and Shell's (D) "course of performance." [The other questions are omitted.] First, Nanakuli (P) proved that, in Hawaii's paving market, price protection was universal and long-standing, making it a binding "usage." Second, Nanakuli (P) proved Shell's (D) prior performance unambiguously indicated it understood its obligation to price-protect, and previously offered price protection. We find price protection is not inconsistent with the contract's express terms. [How?!] Thus, the jury's verdict was not unreasonable, and should not have been reversed. Reversed.

Analysis:

Nanakuli introduces the *UCC* approach to contract interpretation. The *UCC* generally effectuates the parties' *actual agreement* rather than the contract's express language. Thus, its philosophy is in line with *Frigaliment* [chicken importer which accepted older birds as "chicken" cannot later claim it contracted to buy only young birds] and *Pacific Gas & Electric* [after repairmen damage turbine, court deciding whether indemnity clause covers self-inflicted damage should consider extrinsic evidence of the parties' actual intent], but opposed to the literalism of *Gianni* [soda shop owner cannot claim landlord promised him exclusivity, since lease had no such term]. Of course, the *UCC* approach is the law governing very many contracts. However, its approach is at odds with the parol evidence rule, which remains the law (in various degrees). Thus, courts must try to reconcile these 2 interpretive philosophies, often with strained interpretations. Here, the court basically subsumes the parol evidence rule as much as possible, by accepting even the most strained constructions as consistent with the express terms. A more honest approach would be to admit that the parol evidence rule is relevant only where third parties relied on the writing, or where the court believes one party is lying about what the bargain actually was. Thus, the best solution would be to start by effectuating the parties' actual intent, but to require a higher standard of proof for parties urging unusual constructions of contractual language.

Corenswet, Inc. v. Amana Refrigeration, Inc.

(Distributor) v. (Manufacturer)

(5th Cir. 1979) 594 F.2d 129

MEMORY GRAPHIC

Instant Facts

When a distributorship was canceled, it claimed the bad faith cancellation was forbidden by the contract and *UCC*.

Black Letter Rule

Under the *UCC*, contracts' express terms cannot be overridden by parties' past dealings or the general duty of "good faith."

Case Vocabulary

LETTER OF CREDIT: Bank's promise to guarantee (pay) the debts of a client if it defaults on paying creditors. Here, Amana (D) demanded Corenswet (P) get such a guarantee from its bank.

PROMISSORY ESTOPPEL: Doctrine holding that, where a contractual party makes a promise which is not legally binding, and thus makes the other party lose a legal right by relying on that promise reasonably, the promisor becomes bound by his promise.

SECURITY INTEREST: Creditor's contractual right to seize a debtor's enumerated property if the debtor defaults on payments.

TEMPORARY RESTRAINING ORDER: Court order temporarily preventing a litigant from taking actions which might harm the other party's interests irreparably, pending the outcome of litigation.

UNCONSCIONABILITY: A contract is "unconscionable," and thus void, if a judge decides its terms are grossly unfair to one party, usually because the other party had vastly superior bargaining power. The standard for finding a term unconscionable is very high, though it differs among courts.

WORKING CAPITAL: Company's assets which may be sold quickly for cash, to pay short-term debts. Working capital includes cash, receivables (payments owed to it), and inventory. Here, Amana (D) demanded, among other things, that Corenswet's (P) corporate parent give Corenswet (P) more cash.

Procedural Basis: In contract action seeking injunction and damages, appeal from judgment for plaintiff and injunction.

Facts: Appliance wholesaler Corenswet, Inc. (Corenswet) (P) contracted to be exclusive distributor of Amana Refrigeration, Inc.'s (Amana) (D) appliances. The distributorship agreement allowed either to cancel anytime, "with or without cause," on 10 days' notice. Corenswet (P) believed the distributorship would last as long as it performed satisfactorily, based on Amana's (D) treatment of other distributors. Gradually, Corenswet (P) invested $1.5 million to market Amana's (D) goods, and increased sales greatly. But 7 years later, Amana (D) told Corenswet (P) it would cancel the distributorship unless Corenswet (P) gave it a security interest in its inventory of Amana (D) appliances. Corenswet (P) gave the security interest, but Amana (D) canceled anyway, apparently because Amana's (D) president hated Corenswet's (P) president, and/or wanted to give the distributorship to a rival. Corenswet (P) sued Amana (D) in state court for breach, contending the contract and *UCC* forbade terminations which were arbitrary or in bad faith. The state court issued a temporary restraining order preventing termination. Amana (D) removed to federal court, on diversity jurisdiction. The district court also held for Corenswet (P), finding the termination arbitrary, and holding it violated the contract, because the contract's termination language "for any reason" requires some reason which is not arbitrary. Amana (D) appeals, contending even arbitrary or bad faith termination is permitted by the contract and *UCC*.

Issue: If a distributorship contract allows termination "for any reason," may parties terminate opportunistically, without cause?

Decision and Rationale: (Wisdom) Yes. Under the *UCC*, contracts' express terms cannot be overridden by parties' past dealings or the general duty of "good faith." This contract is construed under Iowa law. Also, courts often evaluate distributorship and franchise agreements under the *UCC*, even though they are not "sale of goods" contracts. Under the *UCC*, analysis begins with the contract's express terms. *UCC §§ 1-205; 2-208(2)*. Here, the contract said Amana (D) could terminate "at any time and for any reason." This means, in common understanding, for any action it deems sufficient, without requiring cause. This meaning is supported by the dictionary definition. Even if Amana (D) needed "some reason," it would be enough that it wanted to give the distributorship to another. Next, there is no evidence the parties understood the phrase otherwise. That Corenswet's (P) officials believed Amana (D) would not terminate arbitrarily, based on its treatment of other distributors, does not bind Amana (D). Third, parties' prior courses of commercial conduct may override express terms. Courts interpreting such conflicts must construe the terms and dealing/usage as consistent, whenever reasonably possible. While Corenswet (P) has no past dealings with Amana (D), we hold Amana's (D) historic treatment of other distributors has the effect of prior dealings. But here, the contract's express terms give Amana (D) the right to terminate arbitrarily, which is irreconcilable with Corenswet's (P) interpretation. Contractually-reserved powers are not lost through disuse, except where the disuse rises to the level of promissory estoppel. Alternately, we consider whether arbitrary termination contravenes the *UCC*'s general obligation of good faith dealing. The *UCC* states "every [*UCC*] contract ... imposes an obligation of good faith in its performance." *UCC § 1-203*. This obligation cannot be disclaimed by agreement. *UCC § 1-102*. Some commentators note that this good faith obligation may be applied to curb arbitrary termination of distributorships and franchises, to protect reasonable expectations. But we hold the *UCC*'s good faith obligation cannot override contracts' express terms. We believe applying the "good faith" test to terminations yields erratic results, because any termination without cause can be characterized as "bad faith," but public

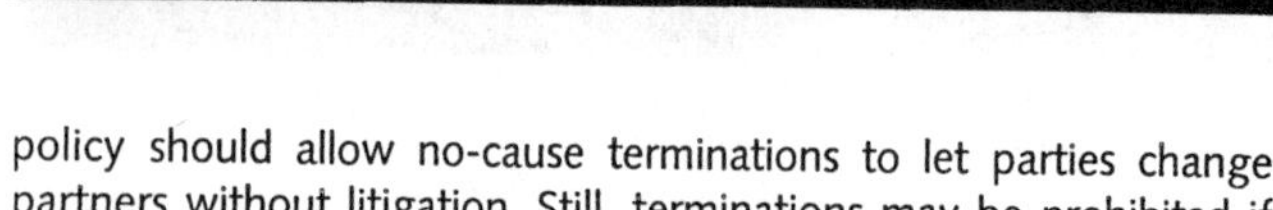

policy should allow no-cause terminations to let parties change partners without litigation. Still, terminations may be prohibited if they rise to the level of unconscionability, under *UCC 2-302.* Unconscionability is the use of superior bargaining power to secure grossly unfair advantages. Here, the contractual clause is not unconscionable. Reversed.

Analysis:

Corenswet applies the *UCC* approach to contract interpretation, like *Nanakuli*, but demonstrates a stricter emphasis on the contractual language even within the *UCC*'s framework. *Corenswet* basically says that, while the *UCC* urges courts to reconcile express terms with parol evidence of the actual bargain, there is no way to reconcile explicit "no-cause" cancellation with "for cause" termination. (Compare *Nanakuli*, which was willing to find a contract to buy at the "Posted Price at ... delivery" was compatible with price protection, by fiat.) The *Corenswet* court has the better argument in rejecting Corenswet's (P) claim. Corenswet (P) basically contends that *it believed* Amana (D) would continue the distributorship arrangement indefinitely, because Corenswet (P) knew Amana (D) did so with other distributors. But this does not mean that *Amana* (D) agreed to this. Thus, enforcing Corenswet's (P) unilateral expectation would subvert Amana's (D) intent to Corenswet's (P), forcing Amana (D) into a "bargain" it never accepted. Put another way, Nanakuli's reliance on the widespread inclusion of price protection was more reasonable than Corenswet's (P) reliance on Amana's (D) past conduct. Also, *Corenswet* introduces the *UCC* doctrines of "good faith" and "unconscionability," and demonstrates how some courts stretch the "good faith" concept to prohibit opportunistic behavior, especially in franchise/distributorship agreements where the agent expects the arrangement will last long enough to recoup his investment and turn a profit. But note that *Corenswet*'s application is not necessarily the majority rule; courts are divided.

IF CONTRACTUAL PARTIES FAILED TO PROVIDE FOR AN EVENT, THEN JUDGES MAY "IMPLY" TERMS WHICH EFFECTUATE THEIR ORIGINAL AIM

Spaulding v. Morse

(Son's Trustee) v. (Father)
(Mass. 1947) 322 Mass. 149, 76 N.E.2d 137

MEMORY GRAPHIC

Instant Facts

A divorced father agrees to pay his son's support and education, but contends his duty is suspended while the son is drafted.

Black Letter Rule

If a contract fails to provide for an event, then judges may "imply" terms which effectuate the parties' clear intent, if such implications do not contradict express terms.

Case Vocabulary

MAINTENANCE: Technically, "maintenance" is support money paid to an ex-spouse for the spouse's own expenses, not for the child's. Here, the court means "child support," which is money paid by a divorced non-custodial parent for a child's upkeep.

TRUSTEE: Representative who administers a trust (fund) for the benefit of the beneficiary, usually a minor child who cannot handle his own money. Here, the parents agreed to provide for Son (P) by setting up a trust (fund) for him; the beneficiary would ensure the money went towards his maintenance and education.

Procedural Basis: In contract action seeking damages, appeal from judgment for plaintiff.

Facts: After the divorce of Ruth Morse (Ruth) and George Morse (George) (D), the divorce court granted custody of son Richard (Son) (P) to Ruth, and decreed George (D) must pay child support. Ruth and George (D) signed a trust agreement providing support for Son (P). Under the agreement, Ruth would retain custody of Son (P) , and " [George (D)] ... will pay to the trustee ...[,] in trust for [Son (P),] $1,200 per year ... until the entrance of [Son (P)] into some college ... beyond ... high school ..., and thereupon, instead ... he ... will pay ... $2,200 per year for a period of said higher education but not more than four years. The ... trustee shall turn over said ... payments to ... [Ruth] ..., to be applied ... toward the maintenance and education of [Son (P)], so long as she shall maintain and educate [him]." But Son (P) graduated during World War II, and was immediately drafted. So, George (D) refused to pay anything for the time Son (P) was in the army, reasoning that during that time, Son's (P) maintenance was being provided by the army. Son's (P) trustee Spaulding (P) sued George (D), demanding continued maintenance while Son (P) served. At trial, the parties stipulated the facts, and submitted the question of whether George (D) "is excused from performance under the agreement while [Son (P)] is in the armed services." After hearing, the state court held for Son (D), ordering George (D) to continue paying $100/month while Son (P) served, and $2,200/year if and when Son (P) began college. George (D) appeals, contending the agreement's intent was to maintain Son (P) through college, but not while his maintenance was provided by other sources.

Issue: May a court imply terms of a contract to account for circumstances never contemplated by the parties?

Decision and Rationale: (Dolan) Yes. If a contract fails to provide for an event, then judges may "imply" terms which effectuate the parties' clear intent, if such implications do not contradict express terms. Every written instrument is to be construed to effectuate the parties' main desired end, considering the parties' circumstances and knowledge at the time of execution. The instrument's words are to be illumined by all attendant factors, unless they are repugnant to (i.e., contradict) the instrument's other terms or violate other legal rules. If the instrument, as a whole, produces sufficient conviction the parties desired fixedly a particular result but did not write it, then courts may imply such terms. But courts should not use conjecture to insert terms which are not clearly intended. Here, we find it is manifest the agreement's main purpose is to provide for Son's (P) maintenance and education. The instrument specifically provided all payments should be applied for Son's (P) "maintenance and education and benefit." Son's (P) education was interrupted by the draft, but since then, his maintenance was provided by the government, and he was not in Ruth's custody or studying in any college. Thus, neither of the main objects for which George (D) bound himself to provide existed when Son (P) was drafted. In these circumstances, we find the proper construction is that George (D) is not required to pay while Son (P) served. Reversed.

Analysis:

Spaulding is the first text case illustrating "implied" terms rather than "interpretations" of contractual words. The facts show why it is useful to allow judges to imply terms. Sometimes, after parties draft a contract, something happens which neither party could foresee or think to plan for in the contract. When this happens, judges "imply" terms they believe the parties *would have included, had they anticipated the event*. This is done by examining the contract's purposes, and deciding how the parties would have handled the event, while maintaining that main purpose. Note the court is *not* suggesting the Morses actually intended or agreed that, if war broke out and their son was drafted, then payments would be suspended while he served; clearly, neither parent foresaw this. What the implied term here is saying is that, if the parties' aim was to provide for Son (P), then if they had foreseen the draft, they probably would have agreed to this.

Wood v. Lucy, Lady Duff-Gordon

(Distributor) v. (Fashion Designer)
228 N.Y. 88, 118 N.E. 214 (1917)

M E M O R Y   G R A P H I C

Instant Facts

A famous fashion designer attempts to invalidate an exclusive-dealing arrangement by arguing that the supplier never made any promise to market her goods.

Black Letter Rule

Exclusive dealing arrangements impose an obligation by the seller to use his best efforts to distribute and market goods.

Case Vocabulary

EXCLUSIVE DEALING ARRANGEMENT: An agreement whereby a distributor expressly or implicitly contracts to supply all of a seller's goods, using the distributor's best efforts.

Procedural Basis: Appeal from order reversing denial of demurrer to complaint for breach of contract.

Facts: Lucy, Lady Duff-Gordon (D) was a famous fashion designer. In order to profit from her fame, Lucy (D) employed Wood (P). Wood (P) was granted the exclusive right to endorse products using Lucy's (D) famous name for one year. In return, Wood (P) agreed to split the profits with Lucy (D). Wood (P) sued for breach of contract after he discovered that Lucy (D) had endorsed products without his knowledge and without splitting the profits. Lucy (D) demurred on the ground that a valid contract never existed between the parties. In granting the demurrer and dismissing the complaint, the Appellate division found that the contract lacked mutuality, as Wood (P) never promised to do anything. Wood (P) appeals.

Issue: May a court imply a promise to make reasonable efforts in an exclusive-dealing arrangement?

Decision and Rationale: (Cardozo, J.) Yes. A court may imply a promise to make reasonable efforts in an exclusive-dealing arrangement. Indeed, Wood (P) never expressly promised to use reasonable efforts to endorse Lucy's (D) products or to market her designs. However, such a promise may be fairly implied by the court. Lucy (D) gave an exclusive privilege to Wood (P), and his acceptance of the exclusive agency was an assumption of its duties. To hold otherwise would be to undermine the purpose of the agreement. Lucy's (D) sole compensation for the grant of exclusive agency was to receive one-half of all profits. He agreed to account monthly for all moneys received, and to take out the necessary patents, copyrights, and trademarks. Unless Wood (P) gave some reasonable effort, Lucy (D) could never get anything. In line with the intention of the parties, we determine that Wood (P) made an implied promise, and thus that the contract was not lacking in mutuality of obligation. Reversed.

Analysis:

One of the fundamental bases of contract law is that the parties should be free to establish the terms of the contract. Ordinarily a court should not interfere and create implied promises or duties. For this reason, the holding of the Court of Appeals of New York in this opinion is open to some criticism. Obligations should be created voluntarily by contracting parties, not imposed by courts. Wood (P) never promised to make any efforts whatsoever in marketing Lucy's (D) designs and endorsing products under her name. Ironically, however, Wood (P) is saved by the court imposing a reasonable-efforts duty on him! Without the court's imposition, no valid contract would have existed, and Lucy (D) could have endorsed any product without his knowledge or consent. An illusory promise is an expression cloaked in promissory terms, but which, on closer examination, reveals that the promisor is not committed to any act or forbearance. One of the methods of circumventing the illusory promise problem is interpolating into an agreement that otherwise seems illusory the requirement of good faith or reasonableness. The method of this case is to find a promise by inferences drawn from the facts. Under some circumstances the promise inferred is called an implied promise and in others it is referred to as a constructive promise. The UCC adopts the reasoning of *Wood v. Lucy, Lady Duff-Gordon*; indeed, the UCC goes even further. It provides in §2-306(2), (and the 1997 revision draft, §2-304, is substantially the same): "A lawful agreement by either the seller or the buyer for exclusive dealing in the kind of goods concerned imposes unless otherwise agreed an obligation by the seller to use best efforts to supply the goods and by the buyer to use best efforts to promote their sale." Of course the Code provision has reference only to exclusive dealings in "goods." Thus, it would not be applicable to an agreement such as was involved in the *Wood* case, but the UCC adopts and extends its rationale by imposing the obligation of best efforts as a matter of legislative fiat rather than as a matter of interpretation. The road opened by *Wood v. Lucy* has been much traveled. It is now common for courts to find a means of implying promises to give effect to the intent of the parties.

COURT OF APPEALS PERMITS A FACT-SPECIFIC INQUIRY TO DETERMINE A PARTY'S OBLIGATIONS UNDER A "BEST EFFORTS" CLAUSE

Bloor v. Falstaff Brewing Corp.

(Reorganization Trustee) v. (Brewery)

United States Court of Appeals, Second Circuit, 1979, 601 F.2d 609

M E M O R Y   G R A P H I C

Instant Facts

A brewery fails to use best effort to continue the sales of an acquired label.

Black Letter Rule

A contract clause requiring best efforts to ensure profits does not require the promisor to spend itself into bankruptcy in the course of performance.

Case Vocabulary

REORGANIZATION TRUSTEE: A reorganization trustee holds title to and is responsible for protecting the fiduciary interests of a corporation which is undergoing bankruptcy, merger, or a variety of other possible organizational or financial changes.

Procedural Basis: Appeal by both parties from a district court judgment for the plaintiff in a breach of contract action.

Facts: Falstaff Brewing Corporation (Falstaff) (D) bought the rights to produce and market beer which formerly produced by P. Ballantine & Sons (Ballantine). The contract required Falstaff (D) to use best efforts to promote Ballantine's labels and to maintain a high volume of sales. In addition, Falstaff (D) was supposed to pay Ballantine $.50 per barrel in royalties for six years. If Falstaff (D) ever substantially discontinued the sale of Ballantine beer, it would trigger an onerous liquidated damages clause. The Ballantine label had been in trouble for years before Falstaff (D) stepped in. Ballantine had already been taken over once and had failed to turn a profit. Falstaff (D) continued the effort, but Ballantine performed more poorly than any of Falstaff's (D) other beers. In fact, Falstaff (D) was approaching the point where it would be unable to meet their payroll or other credit obligations. A change in Falstaff's (D) corporate control, however, resulted in a healthy infusion of cash and a subsequent reduction in its effort to market Ballantine beer. It reduced the advertising budget for Ballantine from $1,000,000 to $115,000 and closed or restructured the distribution centers which handled Ballantine beer. This caused a drop in Ballantine sales which was, again, far worse than that suffered by Falstaff's (D) other brands. Ballantine's reorganization trustee, Bloor (P), ultimately sued Falstaff (D) for breach of contract, making two claims. First, Bloor (P) claimed that Falstaff (D) failed to use best efforts to maintain Ballantine's sales. As a result, Bloor (P) claimed that Falstaff (D) also triggered the liquidated damages clause by substantially discontinuing the distribution of Ballantine beer. The district court found for Bloor (P) on the first claim and for Falstaff (D) on the second claim. Both parties appeal this result. Falstaff's (D) arguments are the focus of the decision.

Issue: Does a best efforts clause require the promisor to satisfy its contractual obligations at any expense?

Decision and Rationale: (Friendly) No. Falstaff (D) argues that the district court held it to a "best efforts" standard which required it to continue marketing Ballantine beer regardless of the consequences. This is not true. The district court did cite to a case which required performance even to the point of financial difficulty or economic hardship. Falstaff (D) cites an alternative case, *Feld v. Henry S. Levy & Sons, Inc.* [performance is not required to result in bankruptcy] which held that a party would be excused from performance if its losses were more than trivial. The dispute over precedent is unnecessary, however, because the district court did not apply the rule it cited. Instead, the court examined the evidence to determine whether Falstaff (D) used its best efforts to "promote and maintain a high volume of sales" for Ballantine. This evidence did not favor Falstaff (D). In fact, it was not until *after* Falstaff (D) returned from the brink of insolvency that its controlling shareholder, Kalmanovitz, announced a policy which abandoned any efforts to resuscitate Ballantine. Falstaff (D) closed key Ballantine distributorships and, at times, placed Ballantine's distribution in the hands of its competitors. It also rejected other offers to distribute Ballantine, focused attention on their own beers -- which were free of the $.50 per barrel royalty -- and adopted a general policy favoring profit over volume. In essence, it violated its duty of good faith by preferring its own interests to Ballantine's, well beyond the point necessary to preserve its survival. The only excusable act which Falstaff (D) committed was spending more to advertise its beers than Ballantine's in regions which were traditionally Falstaff (D) territory. Otherwise, it demonstrated a lack of attention to Ballantine which was not consistent with its duty to maintain a high volume of sales. This duty was linked to the royalty payments, which were such an inextricable part of the purchase price for Ballantine that they were protected by a liquidated damages clause. As a result, the district court correctly found for

Bloor (P) and calculated Ballantine's damages against the sales of comparable northeast beers. The judgment of the district court is affirmed [including the rejection of Bloor's (P) liquidated damages claim -- presumably to avoid giving Bloor (P) double damages for the same breach].

Analysis:

Judge Friendly's opinion follows a familiar theme in contract law which requires a case-by-case analysis under certain circumstances. However, he never really announces a rule of law which governs this case. Instead, he relies on the findings of the district court, implicitly endorsing a factual inquiry rather than a bright line rule. Judge Friendly may have followed this approach because, as he notes, the specific language in the contract called for a *high* volume of sales. In other words, the contract itself set a standard for Falstaff's (D) best efforts. The contract also contained a notable synergy between the purchase price for Ballantine and the best efforts clause. In essence, Falstaff (D) ignored an implied obligation to supply Ballantine with royalties which were an intended part of Ballantine's consideration for the right to promote its beers. It not only breached its duty, but circumvented the intent of the agreement and gained a windfall in the process. On a separate note, the casebook version of this opinion places the burden of proof on Falstaff (D) to show that there was nothing it could have done to avert Ballantine's difficulties. Judge Friendly does not say so, but the disposition of the case presumes that Falstaff (D) failed to meet this burden.

Greer Properties, Inc. v. LaSalle National Bank

(Land Buyer) v. (Landowners' Title Holder)
(7th Cir. 1989) 874 F.2d 457

MEMORY GRAPHIC

Instant Facts

A land sale contract allowed the sellers to terminate if pollution cleanup costs made the sale impracticable, in their "best business judgment." When the sellers canceled and sold to another for more, the buyer sued, claiming "bad faith" termination.

Black Letter Rule

If a contract expressly gives parties discretion, that discretion must implicitly be exercised in good faith.

Procedural Basis: In real estate contract action seeking specific performance, appeal from summary judgment for defendants.

Facts: Several real estate Sellers (D) bought commercial land, failed to develop it, and decided to sell it. Sellers (D) negotiated first with potential buyer G.D. Searle Co. (Searle). Sellers (D) agreed to sell to Searle, under a contract permitting Searle to terminate if the property was contaminated. Searle commissioned a soil study, which found contamination whose cleanup was estimated to cost $500K. Searle demanded Sellers (D) reduce their price. When Sellers (D) refused, Searle terminated. So, Sellers (D) began negotiations with bidder Greer Properties, Inc. (Greer) (P). Sellers (D) contracted to sell to Greer (P) for $1.25M. Under the contract, Sellers (D) had to decontaminate at their own expense, but could terminate the contract if clean-up became "economically impracticable." The contract's language said: "Seller is ... having a [Soils Study] conducted.... Seller further agrees to take all action recommended by the Soils Study and the Illinois Environmental Protection Agency to bring the soil into compliance with all ... laws ...; *provided*, however, that *if the cost of such clean-up work will, in Seller's best business judgment, be economically impracticable, then Seller, at its option, may terminate* this Contract." Sellers (D) told Greer (P) the soil was contaminated, but did not tell the estimated cleanup costs, possibly because Sellers (D) though Searle's estimate was inflated. Sellers (D) told Greer (P) cleanup would cost $60K - $100K. But later, their soil study estimated the cost at $100K - $200K. Sellers (D) *may* have informed Greer (P) this cost made the contract impracticable, but did not formally announce they intended to terminate. Sellers (D) reopened negotiations with Searle, which offered $1.455M. Afterwards, their soil study revised the clean-up costs to $190K - $240K. Then, Sellers (D) notified Greer (P) they would terminate, but told Greer (P) it could still buy for an extra $250K. Greer (P) refused. Sellers (D) terminated. [And for the record, their clean-up cost $251,825.] Greer (P) sued Sellers (D) in district court, seeking specific performance and damages, on the grounds Sellers (D) terminated their contract in bad faith (i.e., to shop around). Sellers (D) answered and counterclaimed, seeking declaratory judgment that their termination was proper. At trial, Sellers (D) moved for summary judgment. The judge granted summary judgment for Sellers (D), finding the contract's term "best business judgment" gave them broad discretion to terminate, and that they had decided to terminate the contract with Greer (P) before re-approaching Searle. Greer (P) appeals.

Issue: If a contract allows a party to terminate if his "best business judgment" is that performance would be impracticable, then if the party terminates, is he free from liability, as a matter of law?

Decision and Rationale: (Wood) No. If a contract expressly gives parties discretion, that discretion must implicitly be exercised in good faith. Summary judgment is proper if "the pleadings and [evidence] on file, together with the affidavits, ... show there is no genuine issue as to any material fact ...." *Fed. R. Civ. P. 56(c)*. Here, the contractual language allowing one party to exercise "best business judgment" gives broad discretion, but this discretion is implicitly limited by good faith. Under Illinois law [and the *UCC*, were it applicable to land sales], "every contract implies good faith and fair dealing between the parties." This implied obligation of good faith and fair dealing in the performance of contracts limits parties' contractual discretion. Under Illinois caselaw, "a party vested with contractual discretion must exercise his discretion reasonably and ... not ... arbitrarily or capriciously." If parties exercise discretion in bad faith, they breach, and courts must grant relief. Here, Sellers (D) had the right to terminate if they judged, in good faith, that the cleanup costs' increase made the transaction impracticable. But if Sellers (D) terminated their contract with Greer (P) just to seek a better price from Searle, this would be bad faith, because Sellers (D) had given up their opportunity to shop around by contracting with Greer (P). The district court's finding that Sellers (D) terminated in good faith, as a matter of law; is incorrect, since material questions of fact remain about Sellers' (D) motives for terminating. Reversed and remanded.

Analysis:

Greer Properties illustrates the majority position, and the *UCC*'s, in holding that, if the contract gives a party the right to cancel for a stated/agreed reason, then that party has very broad discretion to cancel for that reason, but cannot cancel for *another* reason, which was not agreed upon as a permissible basis for termination. Here, Sellers (D) could cancel if, in their discretion, environmental cleanup costs made the sale impracticable. Thus, if their cancellation was honestly motivated by increased costs, then presumably they may cancel, even if reasonable people would say the increase does not justify termination. But if their cancellation was motivated by other reasons, unrelated to environmental liability, then it is impermissible, and constituted actionable bad faith. This limit of discretion is just a category of the "good faith" obligation imposed on all *UCC* contracts, and many other contracts governed by state laws.

Eastern Air Lines, Inc. v. Gulf Oil Corporation

(Airline) v. (Fuel Supplier)

United States District Court, Southern District of Florida, 1975, 415 F.Supp. 429

M E M O R Y   G R A P H I C

Instant Facts

An airline and its fuel supplier dispute the price terms of their jet fuel contract.

Black Letter Rule

UCC § 2-306 asks the parties to output and requirements contracts to conduct their business in good faith and according to commercial standards of fair dealing so that their output or requirements will be reasonably foreseeable.

Case Vocabulary

FREIGHTING: The practice of buying extra fuel at an airport where the price is low to avoid needing fuel at a stop where the price is higher.

GOOD FAITH: Good faith is a phrase which can have a variety of meanings depending upon the legal context in which it used. Many areas of the law rely on a definition of good faith which is unique to that practice area. The UCC's definition governs commercial transactions. The UCC, however, defines good faith differently from one article to the next. Article 1 posits a subjective definition of good faith as "honesty in fact in the conduct or transaction concerned." Article 2 requires honesty in fact as well as the objective observance of "reasonable commercial standards of fair dealing in the trade."

Procedural Basis: Judgment of the district court in a breach of contract action, following the entry of a preliminary injunction against the defendant.

Facts: Gulf Oil Corporation (Gulf) (D) had a contract to supply Eastern Air Lines, Inc. (Eastern) (P) with jet fuel. The contract required Eastern (P) to pay for fuel based on a calculation which was linked to the fluctuating crude oil market. The market price for crude oil was posted by the big oil companies in a periodical called Platts Oilgram Service. Platts failed to publish all of the prices, however. There were actually two market prices for oil which resulted from a two-tiered pricing scheme put in place by the Government. The scheme was intended to encourage the increased production of oil by deregulating the price of "new" oil. New oil was any quantity of oil produced over the existing capacity of a well. Any oil produced at or below the existing capacity was deemed "old" oil and still subjected to price controls. In any event, Platts only published the price of old oil in its periodical. This might not have mattered if the 1970s Arab oil embargo had not driven up the price of new domestic oil. Platts' failure to publish the price of new oil resulted in a dispute between Eastern (P) and Gulf (D) over the price that Eastern (P) was required to pay for its jet fuel. Gulf (D) threatened to cut off Eastern's (P) fuel supply unless it paid a price which reflected the increased price of new oil. Eastern (P) then sued Gulf (D) for breach of contract, requesting an injunction against its threatened action. The district court entered a preliminary injunction which preserved the status quo until a full hearing could be had. Among other things, the district court determined that the contract between the parties was a valid requirements contract. Gulf (D) claims that Eastern (P) violated the contract, however, by manipulating its requirements in order to take advantage of Gulf's (D) lowest prices. Gulf (D) claims that Eastern (P) engages in "fuel freighting" [the practice of buying extra fuel at airports where the price is low to avoid needing fuel at a stop where the price is higher].

Issue: Can a party violate a requirements contract by failing to adhere to its terms in good faith?

Decision and Rationale: (King) Yes. According to UCC § 2-306, a party to a requirements contract must "conduct his business in good faith and according to commercial standards of fair dealing in the trade" so that his output or requirements are reasonably foreseeable. Eastern (P) and Gulf (D) have supply contracts which extend back over thirty years. During this time, Eastern's (P) fuel requirements have continually changed with the vagaries of the airline industry. As a result, Eastern (P) has occasionally requested large amounts of fuel at particular Gulf (D) stations. The parties have always been aware of this problem and, indeed, it has played a part in their contract negotiations. We can conclude from these facts that fuel freighting is simply a part of the airline business. In addition, it has long been a part of the dealings between the parties. There is no evidence that Eastern (P) is abusing the privilege to raise and lower its requirements as needed. It is still constrained by its established routes to buy fuel when and where they need it. This case would be different if Eastern (P) was asking for unreasonable amounts of fuel, or requesting no fuel at all. This is not the case, however. Gulf (D) is complaining of a practice that is common in the industry and between the parties. With this in mind, it cannot be said that Eastern (P) acted in bad faith. [For this reason and others, the court granted Eastern's (P) request for a permanent injunction, requiring Gulf (D) to continue supplying fuel at the posted rates.]

Analysis:

The requirement of good faith in commercial dealings may seem a bit malleable. That is as it should be. The Uniform Commercial Code attempts, through gap-filling and other provisions, to preserve an already dynamic and specialized system of commercial transactions. The drafters recognized that many long term transactions develop lives of their own which take, as their sustenance, the knowledge that the parties have of each other and their industry. The implied duty of good faith is designed to respect the relationship of the parties without defining the actual requirements of good faith in every case. As a result, the question of good faith is necessarily a factual one which can only be answered on a case by case basis. However, as with all rules, its refinement through case law can provide some guidance for the parties to future transactions. In this way, the rule provides general guidance for every commercial transaction and specific guidance under previously judicially recognized circumstances.

Orange and Rockland Utilities, Inc. v. Amerada Hess Corp.

(Oil Consumer) v. (Oil Producer)

(N.Y. App. Div. 1977) 59 A.D.2d 110, 397 N.Y.S.2d 814

MEMORY GRAPHIC

Instant Facts

After an oil company contracted to supply a utility's oil requirements, the price soared, and the utility demanded huge amounts.

Black Letter Rule

Requirements contracts are subject to the *UCC*'s "good faith" obligations, so that buyers may exceed their estimated requirements but cannot intentionally increase their need or demand supplies for resale.

Case Vocabulary

REQUIREMENTS CONTRACT: Contract where a materials supplier contracts to supply as much raw materials as the buyer requests over time.

Procedural Basis: In contract action seeking damages, appeal from dismissal.

Facts: Oil supplier Amerada Hess Corp. (Hess) (D) contracted to supply the oil requirements of electric company Orange and Rockland Utilities, Inc. (O & R) (P) in 1969. [At that time, the *UCC* was not yet enacted, so it doesn't apply.] The contract set a fixed price per barrel through 1974, when the price would be renegotiated. The contract estimated O & R's (P) projected requirements, though it specified those estimates were not binding. After 5 months, oil prices skyrocketed. During this time, O & R (P) increased its requirements 63% over its estimates. Hess (D), after performing for several months, refused to deliver more than 10% above the estimates, accusing O & R (P) of selling the oil to other regional utilities for profit. O & R (P) protested, contending its increased requirements was caused by its inability to use alternative fuels (natural gas), and increased demand for electricity. Further negotiations failed. O & R (P) was forced to buy extra fuel at (high) market prices. Later, O & R (P) sued Hess (D) in state court for breach, demanding expectation damages. Hess (D) answered, contending O & R (P) should recover nothing because (i) its requirements were in bad faith, since it had sold electricity made from the oil to other utilities, and (ii) its demands were "unreasonably disproportionate" to its estimates. [Apparently, New York caselaw suggested that, if demands were more than double the estimate, this was void as unreasonable.] After trial, the state judge held for Hess (D), finding O & R (P) acted in bad faith by selling electricity to other New York utilities for profits, and deliberately avoiding using gas in favor of cheaper oil. The judge did not reach the issue of whether O & R's (P) demands were an impermissible increase over its estimates. O & R (P) appeals, contending (i) there is insufficient evidence of its bad faith, and (ii) requirements which double the estimated needs are not necessarily invalid as a matter of law.

Issue: If a buyer under a requirements contract increases demand by 63% over estimates for resale, is this "bad faith" which excuses the seller?

Decision and Rationale: (Margett) Yes. Requirements contracts are subject to the *UCC*'s "good faith" obligations, so that buyers may exceed their estimated requirements but cannot intentionally increase their need or demand supplies for resale. There is ample pre-*UCC* caselaw on "good faith." First, it is settled that buyers in rising markets cannot use fixed-price requirements contracts to speculate (i.e., to resell). Nor can buyers change conditions unilaterally and arbitrarily to take advantage of market trends, at sellers' expense (e.g., stop using replacement goods to increase demand). Here, there is ample evidence O & R (P) did both, which constituted bad faith. O & R's (P) lateral sales increased sixfold, presumably because it used up oil bought from Hess (D) to generate electricity, then resold it to other New York utilities. This is unfair to Hess (D), because it could not have foreseen this increase. It is equivalent to making other utilities silent partners to the contract. Thus, Hess's (D) refusal to supply extra oil was justified. [Second, the *UCC* forbids demands which are "unreasonably disproportionate" to estimates. *UCC § 2-306(1)*. We decline to hold that demands amounting to double the estimate are always "disproportionate," as a matter of law. But we find O & R's (P) demands were disproportionate.] Affirmed.

Analysis:

Orange & Rockland states the *UCC* (and majority) position on what constitutes "good faith" in requirements contracts. Again, the *UCC* implies into all contracts a "good faith" obligation. This case demonstrates some opportunistic behaviors which most courts would characterize as "bad faith." One such misdeed is increasing the demand for supplies when their market price increases, in order to resell them. This case states the justification for banning this: buyers could demand a virtually unlimited amount for purposes of arbitrage, forcing the seller to produce much more than was foreseeable, and eventually causing the seller to suffer large losses. But the last case, *Eastern Air Lines*, the court approved the questionable practice of "fuel freighting," which can also be called opportunistic. Thus, there is often no principled distinction between practices which courts will reject, and those which are accepted in the industry.

Citizens for Preservation of Waterman Lake v. Davis

(Environmental Group and Town) v. (Town's Landfill Contractor)
(R.I. 1980) 420 A.2d 53

M E M O R Y   G R A P H I C

Instant Facts

When a commercial dump contractor hired by a town violated its ordinances on landfills and pollution, the town and environmental activists claimed standing to sue.

Black Letter Rule

If a contract's subject is regulated by statute, then the statutory requirements are implied as terms of the contract.

Case Vocabulary

EQUITY: Courts' power to grant remedies other than monetary damages, especially injunction (court order forbidding harmful acts) and specific performance (court order requiring breaching parties to fulfill contractual duties). Today, any court can award both money damages and equitable remedies.
INTERVENTION: Right of persons who are interested in a pending lawsuit's outcome to be added as either plaintiffs or defendants, and thus allowed to participate.
PREROGATIVE WRIT: A.k.a. "Extraordinary writ." A writ (court order enjoining an action, in the name of law enforcement authorities) which is granted at the court's discretion.
PRIVATE RIGHT OF ACTION: Right of a person to sue when a statutory violation affects him.
STANDING: Common law doctrine whereby a person cannot sue unless he personally has been injured, and has a personal stake in the lawsuit's outcome.

Procedural Basis: In contract and nuisance action seeking injunction and damages, appeal from dismissal of plaintiffs' complaint.

Facts: The town of Glocester (Town) (P) contracted with businessman Davis (D), allowing him to use its land as a commercial dump. But Davis (D) illegally dumped in wetlands on the land, in violation of the *Fresh Water Wetlands Act* (*Wetlands Act*). Also, Davis accepted garbage from other towns, which violated Town's (P) ordinances. Environmental activists, including Citizens for Preservation of Waterman Lake (Citizens Group) (P) sued Davis (D) for violating *Wetlands Act* and illegally importing non-local garbage, demanding damages and an injunction or declaration declaring the contract invalid. Also, Town (P) intervened as plaintiff, suing Davis (D) for breach, violating local ordinances, and pollution, and seeking similar injunctions. [Basically, the plaintiffs' contended that Davis' (D) violation of *Wetlands Act* gave them a private right of action.] At trial, the Rhode Island Superior Court justice held for Davis (D), holding (i) Citizens Group (P) and Town (P) lacked standing to enforce *Wetlands Act*, and (ii) Town (P) cannot enforce its ordinances through courts' equitable powers. Citizens Group (P) and Town (P) appeal.

Issue: If a contractual party violates statutes while performing the contract, may the counterparty and third parties sue?

Decision and Rationale: (Bevilacqua) Yes. [Maybe.] If a contract's subject is regulated by statute, then the statutory requirements are implied as terms of the contract. First, the trial justice did not err in finding Citizens Group (P) and Town (P) lacked standing to sue under *Wetlands Act*. It is settled that, when a statute's language is clear and unambiguous, it must be applied literally, and may not be construed or extended. Here, *Wetlands Act* expressly vests all enforcement powers in the Director of the Department of Natural Resources, who designates wetlands, reviews applications to alter them, and has the right to remedy violations through equity or prerogative writ. Nothing in *Wetlands Act* indicates any intent, express or implicit, to create a remedy for a private citizen or town to enforce it. Thus, we hold no one but the Director may initiate proceedings under *Wetlands Act*. Next, we hold Town (P) cannot treat *Wetlands Act*'s requirements as terms of its contract with Davis (D). It is well-settled that existing laws are an implied term in every contract. However, this principle is not applicable to the case before us. Also, if a contract is ambiguous, then existing law may be used as an extrinsic aid to discern the parties' intent. But Davis' (D) contract is unambiguous. If a statute expressly creates a specific obligation between the contracting parties, then the statute is deemed to be incorporated into the contract. But this is not the case here. Third, we hold Town (P) cannot enforce violations of its garbage ordinances through suits in equity. Previously, we held that towns cannot resort to state courts' equitable powers for every violation of local ordinances, absent a cause of action at common law or a specific grant of authority. Rather, the town must resort to the applicable ordinance's penal sanctions. Here, Town's (P) rights under its ordinances is limited strictly to filing a criminal action against Davis (D) in federal court, and we will not permit Town (P) to enhance its rights through the contract. Affirmed.

Analysis:

Citizens is included to state the "lawful performance doctrine." This common law doctrine -- which is still the *minority* rule -- states that, if the contract is regulated by law, the governing law is implied into the contract. Thus, if 1 party violates the law, this will likely breach the contract as well. In effect, this doctrine comes close to granting contractual parties a private right of action to sue counterparties for violating statutes, as long as the violation is material to the contract. But this effect contradicts constitutional "standing" doctrine; modern Supreme Court decisions tend to restrict the number of people who can sue for statutory violations. Thus, courts are wary to avoid overextending the lawful performance doctrine, which has the potential to conflict with Supreme Court precedent. Unfortunately, *Citizens* makes little attempt to explain why the doctrine is inapplicable here. Apparently, the court finds that Davis' (D) contract unambiguously permitted use of the entire dump. But, it is not clear that this explains why the statutes were not interpreted as being a part of the contract.

CONNECTICUT SUPREME COURT EXPLAINS THE CONSEQUENCES OF A FAILED CONTRACT CONDITION

Luttinger v. Rosen

(Prospective Purchasers) v. (Landowner)

Supreme Court of Connecticut, 1972. 164 Conn. 45, 316 A.2d 757

M E M O R Y   G R A P H I C

Instant Facts

The prospective buyers of a piece of real estate try to get their deposit back after failing to get a mortgage.

Black Letter Rule

The failure of a condition precedent renders a contract unenforceable.

Case Vocabulary

CONDITION PRECEDENT: A condition precedent is a circumstance which must exist before the parties to a contract will be bound. Similarly, a condition *subsequent* voids an already binding contract depending upon circumstances not existing at the time of contracting.

Procedural Basis: Appeal from a trial court judgment for the plaintiffs in a breach of contract action.

Facts: The Luttingers (P) contracted to purchase an $85,000 property owned by Rosen (D). They also paid him an $8500 deposit on the property. In addition, the purchase contract was subject to a condition that the Luttingers (P) obtain a mortgage from a bank or lending institution for $45,000. The mortgage would have to be for a term of at least twenty years and financed at no more than 8½ percent. The Luttingers (P), in turn, agreed to use due diligence to acquire the mortgage. The parties also agreed that the Luttingers' deposit would be refunded if they could not satisfy the mortgage condition. Unfortunately, the Luttingers (P) were unable to get a mortgage for less than 8¾ percent. Their lawyer knew the rates being offered by the various local banks and applied to the one bank that he knew might make the loan. Rosen (D) offered to finance the extra ¼ percent in order to meet the contract condition, but he refused to return the Luttingers' (P) deposit. The Luttingers (P) declined his offer and sued him for breach of contract. Rosen (D) claimed that the Luttingers (P) failed to use due diligence in obtaining a mortgage because they did not apply to other lenders. The trial court ruled for the Luttingers (P). Rosen (D) appeals.

Issue: Is it necessary for a party to follow every possible course of action in order to satisfy a contract condition requiring due diligence?

Decision and Rationale: (Loiselle) No. Rosen (D) claims that the Luttingers did not try hard enough to get a qualifying mortgage. However, it is not necessary to perform futile acts in order to satisfy a condition requiring due diligence. In this case, the Luttingers' (P) lawyer knew that no other lending institution would make the loan that they needed. It would have been pointless to apply to those banks under the circumstances. Rosen (D) also claims that the mortgage condition was satisfied, obviating the need to return the Luttingers' (P) deposit, because he offered to make the additional loan necessary to bring the mortgage down to 8½ percent. However, the condition states that the loan must come from a bank or another lending institution. The Luttingers (P) were under no obligation to accept Rosen's (D) offer. As a result, the condition failed and the Luttingers were entitled to the return of their deposit. Affirmed.

Analysis:

The mortgage condition in the Luttingers' (P) contract is referred to as a "condition precedent." The court defines a condition precedent as a fact or event which must exist or take place before there is a right to performance. In other words, the parties agree to a set of circumstances which must exist before they will be bound by their contract. This case deals with an agreement requiring the Luttingers' due diligence in trying to satisfy the contract conditions. This is very much like the agreements to negotiate in good faith which you saw in Chapter 2. The agreement only binds the Luttingers to their precontractual behavior. However, as this case demonstrates, if the Luttingers failed to exercise due diligence, they might have forfeited their deposit. As a result, the failure of a condition should not be viewed as a benign deal-breaker. It can have a significant impact on the parties to an agreement. In addition, future cases will demonstrate that conditions come in a variety of shapes and sizes, each having their own unique impact on an agreement. Most important to remember is that conditions are not promises. As a result, they cannot be breached. If a condition is not satisfied, it "fails." If a condition fails, there is no contract between the parties. These points will be relevant to all of the cases in this section.

Peacock Construction Co. v. Modern Air Conditioning, Inc. [and Overly Manufacturing]

(General Contractor) v. (Subcontractors)

Supreme Court of Florida, 1977. 353 So.2d 840

MEMORY GRAPHIC

Instant Facts

A general contractor did not make final payments to two of his subcontractors after he failed to receive payment from the owner of the project.

Black Letter Rule

A contract condition may be interpreted as a question of law when the circumstances are so common that the parties' intent can be gleaned from their relationship.

Case Vocabulary

QUESTION OF FACT: Questions of fact are classically the province of the jury. They involve the interpretation of evidence against everyday experience. This is particularly well-suited to the role of the jury as members the general community.

QUESTION OF LAW: Questions of law are the province of the judge. The judge rules on the interpretation and application of legal rules and may, if necessary, determine the outcome of a case as a matter of law.

Procedural Basis: Two cases, both joined on appeal by the state supreme court after successful motions for summary judgment by the plaintiffs in breach of contract actions which were affirmed by the court of appeals.

Facts: Modern Air Conditioning, Inc. (Modern Air) (P) and Overly Manufacturing (Overly) (P) were hired by Peacock Construction Co. (Peacock) (D) as subcontractors on a condominium construction project for which Peacock (D) was the general contractor. Modern Air (P) was hired to install the heating and air conditioning. Overly (P) was hired to install a rooftop swimming pool. Both of their contracts indicated that final payment would arrive within thirty days of the completion of their work. The payment clause concluded with the phrase, "written acceptance by the Architect and full payment therefor by the Owner." This clause provides the central controversy for the actions for breach of contract which both subcontractors brought after the Peacock (D) failed to pay them. Peacock (D) claimed that he never received full payment from the Owner. He argues that the payment clause is a condition precedent to his obligation to pay the subcontractors -- a condition which failed. In each case, the trial court granted the subcontractors' motions for summary judgment. Peacock (D) appealed both judgments. The judgments were affirmed by the court of appeal. Peacock (D) now appeals to this court.

Issue: Is it appropriate for a court to grant summary judgment, ruling as a matter of law on an ambiguous condition to a contract?

Decision and Rationale: (Boyd) Yes. The trial court's grant of summary judgment implies that the payment clause was not a condition on Peacock's (P) obligation to pay his subcontractors. Similarly, the court of appeals follows the majority rule which interprets provisions like the one at issue here as "absolute promises to pay." Consequently, the owner's payment to the general contractor merely sets a reasonable time limit on the general contractor's payment to the subcontractors. Both of these opinions conflict with Florida precedent which calls for an interpretation consistent with the intent of the parties to the contract. This is potentially a factual determination which would be inappropriate for a grant of summary judgment. Peacock (P) argues that, at best, the trial court must hear evidence before granting a directed verdict on the issue. However, this outcome is not required. The general rule is that the interpretation of a document is a question of law rather than a question of fact. It is quite possible for the court to determine the parties' intent from the language of the contract. This is particularly so when the relationship between the parties, like the one between general contractors and subcontractors, is so common that their intent rarely varies from transaction to transaction. In most cases, the subcontractor would not willingly assume the risk of the owner's nonpayment. This is a burden that the general contractor must bear unless the risk is unambiguously shifted in the agreement with the subcontractor. As a result, the trial court and the court of appeals ruled correctly in this matter. To the extent that Florida precedent is at odds with this outcome it is overruled.

Analysis:

Justice Boyd's approach to this case should seem familiar. The canon of contract interpretation is brought to bear on one more element of contracts: the condition. As in the cases dealing with the construction bidding process, the courts have found ways of dealing with certain familiar business transactions. Judges can apply a single rule which is based on the most common dealings between parties. As Justice Boyd notes, the parties can always contract around the application of this rule but they must do so unambiguously. This protects subcontractors who are the most likely parties to suffer from a misapplication of the rule. In the bidding cases, it seemed as if the subcontractors were being short-changed because the general contractors were not obligated to hire them even if they used their bids. Here, Justice Boyd recognizes that it may seem as if general contractors are unfairly bearing all of the risk of non-payment. However, in both cases the court understood that an equitable allocation of risk between the parties demanded the particular outcome.

Burger King Corp. v. Family Dining, Inc.

(Franchisor) v. (Franchise)

(3d Cir. 1977) 426 F.Supp. 485, *affirmed mem.* 566 F.2d 1168

MEMORY GRAPHIC

Instant Facts

When an exclusive franchise builds new restaurants slower than it promised, the home office waives the delays, then abruptly declares the franchise terminated.

Black Letter Rule

Courts may modify or void contractual conditions for equitable reasons.

Case Vocabulary

CONDITION: Contractual term which activates the contract (or a single contractual provision) only if and when a certain event occurs. (E.g., "If it snows, then shovel my walkway for $20.") If the triggering event never happens, the party need not perform the contract/provision.

CONDITION PRECEDENT: Even which, if it *fails* to occur, voids a contract.

CONDITION SUBSEQUENT: A contractually-specified event which, if it happens *after* the parties start performance, excuses them from finishing. (E.g., "If it snows, and the Sanitation Dept. cleans my walkway, then you are excused.")

CONDITIONAL PROMISE: A "promise" which is also a condition.

PROMISE: A contractual term which binds the promisor immediately and unconditionally. (E.g., "I'll shovel your walkway for $20.") *cf.*. condition.

Procedural Basis: In trademark action seeking declaration, motion to dismiss.

Facts: Franchiser Burger King Corp. (Burger King) (P) contracted with franchisee Family Dining, Inc. (Family Dining) (D) to build Burger King brand restaurants in Pennsylvania. Family Dining's (D) founder Carl Ferris was a close friend of Burger King's (P) president James McLamore. Under the parties' Territorial Agreement, Burger King (P) would grant Family Dining (D) an exclusive franchise in Pennsylvania's counties of Buck and Montgomery for 90 years, if Family Dining (D) built restaurants in the area at one per year for 10 years, then continued to operate the 10 restaurants for the remaining 80 years. The Agreement provided, "If a the end of [any year], there are less than the ... requisite number of [restaurants operating or under construction] in the "exclusive territory" ... this agreement shall terminate and be of no further ... effect." Thereafter, [Burger King (P)] may operate or license others [to operate] ... restaurants anywhere within the exclusive territory ...." Family Dining experienced delays in opening the restaurants 4 and 5. Burger King (P) and Family Dining (D) signed a modification to the Agreement, whereby Burger King (P) waived Family Dining's (D) failure, without consideration. Simultaneously, McLamore told Ferris his growth rate was satisfactory, even though it lagged behind the contract. By now, Burger King (P) had become a corporate bureaucracy, and Ferris/Family Dining (D) was forced to deal with its executives rather than McLamore. Again, Family Dining (D) was late in building the 6th restaurants, partly because Burger King's (P) executives delayed approving its site for no good reason, and partly because of zoning laws. But Burger King (P) granted Family Dining (D) an extension. Then, Burger King's (P) executives decided the exclusive territory could support more franchises. Later, Burger King (P) demoted McLamore, making Arthur Rosewall CEO. Family Dining (D) began developing restaurants 9-12 simultaneously, but could not make restaurant 9 operational by the deadline. McLamore suggested Burger King (P) grant Family Dining (D) an extension. But Family Dining (D) experienced more delays in building restaurant 9. Burger King's (P) documents administrator sent Family Dining (D) a warning it was in default, though this letter did not say Burger King (P) was terminating. For 6 months, Burger King (P) failed to communicate with Family Dining (D), as various Burger King (P) executives were assigned to deal with the problem. Finally, the Burger King (P) executive who was placed in charge of the account abruptly informed Family Dining (D) that it was in default, and that Burger King (P) considered the Agreement terminated. Negotiations failed. Family Dining (D) told Burger King (P) that it would open its 9th restaurant, but Burger King (P) insisted Family Dining (D) sign a separate franchise agreement for it. Family Dining (D) refused and opened the restaurant. Burger King (P) sued to enjoin Family Dining (D) from using Burger King's (P) trademarks at restaurant 9 (i.e., it basically argued Family Dining's (D) franchise license was no longer valid for subsequent restaurants). During trial, the district court granted Burger King (P) a temporary restraining order. Burger King (P) and Family Dining (D) settled on an agreement letting Family Dining (D) operate restaurant 9. But Burger King (P) amended its complaint, seeking a declaration the Agreement was invalid, because Family Dining (D) defaulted on its literal terms. Family Dining (D) moved for involuntary dismissal, contending that voiding the Agreement would cause inequitable forfeiture of its exclusivity rights, especially after Burger King (P) repeatedly waived its deadlines.

Issue: May a court void a condition on equitable grounds?

Decision and Rationale: (Hannum) Yes. Courts may modify or void contractual conditions for equitable reasons. If a contractual term raises no duty in and of itself, but rather modifies or limits the promisee's right to enforce the promise, then the term is considered a condition. Whether a term constitutes a condition or a promise depends on the parties' intent, which is ascertained by considering the language's reasonable construction and the circumstances. Here, we find Agreement's development rate was a condition subsequent rather than a promise, because Agreement's promised exclusivity did not obligate Family Dining (D) to do anything, but was given to induce Family Dining (D) to develop its territory. [Rather circular, no?] Ordinarily, parties are entitled to have their conditional promises enforced literally, unless their conduct makes enforcement unjust. E.g., if one party's conduct indicates that literal performance is not required, then he cannot begin demanding literal performance without giving notice and a reasonable time to comply. Here, Burger King (P) waived exact compliance with its development schedule, and never communicated its changed attitude to Family Dining (D). Under the circumstances, Burger King (P) was unreasonable in declaring the Agreement terminated without giving Family Dining (D) enough time to comply, so Burger King (P) cannot enforce the Agreement strictly. Further, equitable principles are applicable. Under the *Restatement of Contracts § 302*, "A condition may be excused without other reason if its requirement [(i)] will involve extreme forfeiture or penalty, and [(ii)] [it] ... forms no essential part of the exchange for the promisor's performance." Such equitable principles are applicable to suits seeking declaratory relief if the declaration would amount to forfeiture. Here, we find that declaring the contract terminated would forfeit Family Dining's (D) right to exclusivity. This forfeiture would be extreme, because Family Dining (D) assumed risk and expended effort in developing its franchise to retain exclusivity. Agreement's development rate was not essential to Burger King (P), which indicated Family Dining's (D) growth rate was satisfactory. It is interesting that Burger King (P) never expressed dissatisfaction until Rosewall replaced McLamore and discovered the territory could accommodate more restaurants. Family Dining's (D) slower growth was justified, and caused no loss to Burger King (P), so forcing it to lose exclusivity would be punitive. Thus, Burger King (P) is not entitled to a declaration that Agreement is terminated. Dismissed.

Analysis:

Burger King illustrates some of the ways courts can circumvent contractual conditions they find inequitable. First, since courts may "interpret" a condition-like term as something other than a condition, they can excuse parties who fail to comply. This tactic was also used in *Peacock Construction* [subcontractors' right to payment after general contractor receives "full payment" is *not* a condition precedent, unless stated explicitly]. *Burger King* adds the additional equitable defenses of waiver and forfeiture. The latter is now called "disproportionate forfeiture," as re-codified by *Restatement (Second) of Contracts § 229*. This "disproportionate forfeiture" basically potentially gives judges blanket power to disregard contracts' express conditions, if they can find the condition was not critical to the bargain.

CONDITIONS WITHIN A PARTY'S CONTROL OBLIGATE THE PARTY TO TRY IN GOOD FAITH TO FULFILL THEM

Fry v. George Elkins Co.

(Homebuyer) v. (Real Estate Broker)
(2d Cir. 1958) 162 Cal.App.2d 256, 327 P.2d 905

M E M O R Y   G R A P H I C

Instant Facts

A homebuyer agreed to buy conditional on obtaining a mortgage, but then made minimal efforts to get the mortgage.

Black Letter Rule

If a condition is within one party's control, that party must use good faith efforts to fulfill the condition.

Case Vocabulary

ESCROW [ACCOUNT]: Funds set aside in a bank account, to be released only when a contractual party performs his obligations and becomes entitled to the money.

MORTGAGE: Loan given on real estate/buildings, using the property as collateral.

PREPAYMENT "PRIVILEGE"/PENALTY: In a loan, a penalty the borrower must pay to the lender if the borrower repays a long-term loan long before it is due (thus depriving the lender of its expected interest). Here, Western Mortgage's terms were that if Fry (P) repaid the 20-year loan within 3 years, he would have to pay an additional 2% of the loan amount.

Procedural Basis: In contract action, plaintiff's appeal from partial judgment for plaintiff.

Facts: Homebuyer Fry (P) offered to buy the house of the Millers (D), through their real estate broker George Elkins Co. (Elkins) (D). Fry's (P) written offer provided, "This offer is ... conditioned upon the buyer obtaining a $20,000.00 loan at 5% for 20 years." Fry (P) was told that he could obtain such a loan from current mortgageholder Western Mortgage Co., but that ordinary banks would not lend on such terms. Fry (P) paid the Millers (D) a deposit of $4,250. The Millers (D) accepted. Under the Millers' (D) brokerage contract, if Fry (P) defaulted, they had to pay broker Elkins (D) half the deposit. Fry (P) never contacted Western Mortgage for a loan. Instead, Fry (P) requested a loan from 2 banks, but was rejected. Elkins (D) repeatedly urged Fry (P) to apply to Western Mortgage, but he refused, claiming he did not want to pay Western Mortgage's 2% prepayment penalty. Also, Fry (P) indicated he had changed his mind about buying the house. (Western Mortgage later testified that, had Fry (P) applied, he would have been approved on those terms.) Thus, Fry (P) forfeited the deposit. Fry (P) sued the Millers (D) and Elkins (D) to recover it. At trial, the judge found for Fry (P), but reduced his award by the Millers' (D) incidental costs (hiring an attorney to close the deal quickly) and consequential damages (Elkins' (D) commission and added consideration paid to an alternate buyer), awarding only $937.50. Fry (P) appeals the amount, contending (i) the judge erred in finding he did not make good faith efforts to refinance, (ii) he was not obligated to accept Western Mortgage's refinancing because it contained a prepayment penalty, (iii) he performed all express contractual provisions, and (iv) the Millers (D) should not have paid Elkins (D) a commission.

Issue: If a contract is predicated on a condition within one party's control, must that party attempt to fulfill that condition?

Decision and Rationale: (Fox) Yes. If a condition is within one party's control, that party must use good faith efforts to fulfill the condition. First, the court below did not err in finding Fry (P) failed to make good faith efforts to refinance. Fry's (P) failed applications to 2 banks are irrelevant. Different types of financial institutions' lending policies vary greatly, as is common knowledge. That a bank will not lend on certain terms does not mean that other lending institutions will not make such a loan. Here, Fry (P) was told that Western Mortgage would lend while banks wouldn't, so he should not have contented himself with applying to banks. Further, there was evidence Fry (P) lost interest in buying the property. Thus, there is sufficient evidence to infer Fry (P) did not in good faith try to refinance. Second, Fry (P) was not entitled to reject Western Mortgage's loan offer on the grounds it contained a prepayment penalty, because the contract dd not restrict Fry (P) to seeking only penalty-free loans. Third, Fry's (P) contention that he performed all the express contractual terms is irrelevant, because implicit in the contract was the obligation that Fry (P) seek the loan in good faith, since it was essential to the deal's consummation. Thus, there was enough evidence to find Fry (P) breached this implied term by not trying to refinance. Fourth, Fry's (P) claim that the Millers (D) should not have paid Elkins (D) is invalid, since they were obligated to do so under their contract once Fry (P) defaulted. Affirmed.

Analysis:

A quick note for understanding the case's business aspects: the reason that Western Mortgage would give Fry (P) the loan where other banks would not is that it (i) it specialized in mortgages, so presumably was more willing to grant them than general-business banks, and (ii) it had already lent money to the Millers (D) using the house as collateral, so it had already assessed the house's value and decided it was a worthwhile credit risk. *Fry* merely illustrates the universal principle that, if a condition (whose failure may void the contract) is within the control of one party, that party has an implied duty of good faith to try to make the condition happen. The reason is clear: if a party can void the contract by not trying, then he has a "moral hazard" (bad incentive) to evade an unwanted contract just by failing to seek the condition. In effect, this makes his side of the bargain illusory, since he has an effective option to void the contract. Courts prevent such opportunism by implying a duty of good faith. Note that the *Fry* court suggests the test of whether a party's efforts constituted "good faith" is *objective*; while Fry may have applied to other banks, the court condemns his choice as unreasonable, since it is "common knowledge" (i.e., reasonable people would know) such applications were doomed.

Pannone v. Grandmaison

(House Buyer) v. (House Seller)
(Ct. Super. Ct. 1990) 1990 WL 265273

MEMORY GRAPHIC

Instant Facts

A radiation-phobic homebuyer contracted to buy subject to his approval of a radiation inspection, then refused when the inspection revealed minimal radiation.

Black Letter Rule

Contracts which are conditional on one party's satisfaction may be terminated if the party is genuinely displeased in good faith, even if his displeasure is objectively unreasonable.

Procedural Basis: Contract action, seeking specific performance (return of deposit) and damages.

Fact s: The Pannones (P) contracted to buy a house from the Grandmaisons (D). The contract contained a contingency clause, providing, "Offer is contingent upon [Pannone's (P)] approval of the result of a ... radon gas inspection." [Radon is radioactive gas.] The radon inspection revealed minimal radiation, which was probably standard throughout Connecticut, and which could not be reduced. Based on this, Joseph Pannone (P) terminated. This is partly because Mr. Pannone (P) had been exposed to radiation during Korean War service, and was paranoid about irradiation, despite being in good health. Alternately, it may have been caused by several disputes between the Pannones (P) and Grandmaisons (D). The Pannones (P) sue the Grandmaisons (D), demanding return of their deposit, and other damages.

Issue: If a contract is conditional on a party's approval, may he withhold approval unreasonably?

Decision and Rationale: (McWeeny) Yes. Contracts which are conditional on one party's satisfaction may be terminated if the party is genuinely displeased in good faith, even if his displeasure is objectively unreasonable. This result is mandated by our case law, and by the *Restatement (Second) of Contracts'* implied duty of good faith and fair dealing. Here, the contract was contingent on "Purchaser's approval." Under the implied duty of good faith, purchaser Pannone (P) was obligated to exercise this discretion honestly. But he was not obligated to exercise it reasonably. Here, we find Mr. Pannone's (P) termination was objectively unreasonable, but was due to honest concern. This finding is reinforced by the evidence Pannone (P) did not buy another home instead, and did not use the termination to extract a better price from Grandmaison (D). That Pannone (P) previously argued with the Grandmaison (D) appears to be proof of his difficult nature, but not any desire to evade the contract. Thus, the Pannones (P) are entitled to recover their deposit, but have not presented evidence justifying other damages. Judgment for plaintiff.

Analysis:

Pannone shows how some types of conditions within a party's control are deemed satisfied in "good faith" if the party makes efforts which are honest *but unreasonable*. *Cf. Fry* [homebuyer's rejection of most likely mortgage and attempt to get loan from less-likely sources was not a good faith effort because it was (objectively) unreasonable]. The different result is based not on any difference of common law, but based primarily on the *type* of condition. If a condition requires "satisfaction" about a factor which is generally evaluated objectively, or which rarely triggers personal feelings, then courts are likely to require *objective* satisfaction. Typically, this is true when the contract calls for an evaluation of "commercial value or quality, operative fitness, or mechanical utility." But if the condition calls for one party's "fancy, taste, or judgement" or "satisfaction" about a factor on which people may reasonably differ, then "satisfaction" is evaluated subjectively, meaning parties may claim dissatisfaction honestly but unreasonably. Generally, if the contract uses the word "satisfaction," this suggests subjective satisfaction. But courts interpreting contracts have discretion to interpret it as (objective) "commercial" satisfaction, especially if the litigants' dissatisfaction seems pretextual.

Godburn v. Meserve

(Caretakers) v. (Patient)

(Conn. 1944) 132 Conn. 723, 37 A.2d 235

MEMORY GRAPHIC

Instant Facts

Live-in housekeepers contracted to care for a hag for life in exchange for her house, but later left because of her nagging, and demanded damages.

Black Letter Rule

If a contractual party makes the counterparty's performance more difficult (but not impossible or impracticable), this does not discharge the counterparty, unless the "prevention" is wrongful or unforeseeable.

Case Vocabulary

DECEDENT: A dead person.

DISCHARGE: When a party is "discharged" from performing under the contract, it need not finish performing its duties, but is entitled to the contractual benefits, as if it had finished performance. Usually, a party is discharged when circumstances make finishing impossible or pointless.

EXECUTOR: Representative who manages the "estate" (property) of decedents.

QUANTUM MERUIT: ("As much as is deserved.") "Quasi-contractual" damages, awarded to a party who performed part of his contractual duties, but didn't finish. Generally, the amount of such damages is the reasonable value of the work completed.

SET ASIDE [A VERDICT]: Cancel, annul or revoke [a verdict] at the instance of a party unjustly or irregularly affected by it.

Procedural Basis: In contract action seeking expectation damages or *quantum meruit*, appeal from verdict for plaintiff.

Facts: The Godburns (P) were acquaintances, and later tenants, of Ms. Wells (D), aged 76. They contracted to live with Wells (D) and care for her for the rest of her life, in exchange for reduced rent and Wells' (D) promise to will her house to them. Accordingly, the Godburns (P) moved in with Wells (D), who willed her house. The Godburns (P) cared for Wells (D) for 2 years without incident. Then, over the next 3 years, Wells (D) became increasingly irritating, complaining about the Godburns' (P) family guests, cooking, water use, etc. The Godburns (P) suggested they renegotiate the contract, paying more rent but requiring Wells (D) to do her own cooking and laundry. Wells (D) refused. Finally, the Godburns (P) moved out. Wells (D) revoked her will, and died a year later. [So close ....] The Godburns (P) sued Wells' (D) executor Meserve (D) for breach, or for *quantum meruit*. At trial, the jury returned a verdict for the Godburns (P), implicitly finding Wells (D) breached the contract. Wells' (D) executor moved to set aside the verdict, but was denied. Wells' (D) estate appeals, contending the trial court erred in not setting aside the judgment (i.e., contending Wells' (D) nagging did not amount to breach).

Issue: If a party which controls a contractual condition makes the other party's performance more difficult, does this amount to a breach?

Decision and Rationale: (Brown) No. If a contractual party makes the counterparty's performance more difficult (but not impossible or impracticable), this does not discharge the counterparty, unless the "prevention" is wrongful or unforeseeable. Case law holds that, if the counterparty was prevented from completing the contract, then it may sue the party for breach. But for the party's conduct to rise to the level of "prevention," it must be wrongful, or in excess of his legal rights. If a party makes a contract obligating the counterparty to do something, it is implied the party cannot hinder or obstruct the counterparty's performance. But if the hindrance is an action which the party is permitted to take, under the contract's express or implied terms, then it is permissible without breaching the contract. *Restatement of Contracts* § 295. That such permitted conduct renders the counterparty's performance merely unpleasant or inconvenient does not discharge performance. Conduct is "wrongful," or violative of the contract's obligations, if it is not *fairly* within the parties' contemplation at formation [i.e., if it is objectively unreasonable or unforeseeable]. Here, we find Wells' (D) behavior was expectable. The Godburns (P) knew Wells' (D) character as her acquaintance for several years, then as her tenants for 3½ years. It is common knowledge that old people become more stubborn and eccentric as they become more feeble [especially if appointed to the bench], so the Godburns (P) should have expected Wells (D) to be a [pain in the @$$], increasingly. The Godburns (P) voluntarily chose to leave, since Wells (D) did not evict them. Wells' (D) stubbornness was within her legal rights. Thus, Wells' (D) motion to set aside the verdict should have been granted. Reversed and remanded for retrial.

Analysis:

This case illustrates another universally-implied contractual term: each party is implicitly held under a duty not to impede *unreasonably* the other's performance of his contractual duties. This is the rule under the *Restatement (Second) of Contracts*, and appears to be the rule everywhere. The reason is obvious; if a party is allowed to frustrate the other, then that party effectively has the option of voiding the contract anytime, making his obligations illusory. However, this is not to say parties cannot act against their counterparty's interests *at all*, only that they cannot do so unreasonably. Courts vary in how much interference they will tolerate as reasonable. Obviously, any frustration which violates the contract's express terms, its implied terms, or other laws is unreasonable. But frustrating the parties' expectation may not be. Here, the *Godburn* court suggests reasonability must be judged objectively, because it says the Godburns (P) *should have been aware* that oldsters like Wells (D) age like vinegar, become more bitter and unpalatable with each passing year. But other courts may consider the parties' subjective expectations; even here, the court notes the Godburns (P) actually knew Wells (D) was a nightmare to live with.

Perspective
The Security Principle

Chapter 6

One of the main contractual interests protected by the law of contract damages is a party's interest in present and future performance, or in other words, a party's expectation interest. Often, parties to a contract will have contractual interests that conflict with one another, and courts may be called upon to balance each interest, in order to determine which is more deserving of legal protection. This chapter focuses on balancing and "securing" each party's expectation interest in performance under a contract, in recognition that this interest can be harmed even before performance is due under a contract.

Under the law, every contract imposes an obligation on each party not to impair the other party's interest both in receiving performance as promised, and in a continuing sense of reliance and security that the promised performance will occur when due. Accordingly, the law enforces this obligation by providing a number of enforcement rights and powers.

In situations where performances are to be rendered by each party in a simultaneous exchange, it is a condition of each party's duty to render performance, that the other party either render performance, or offer to render performance with a present ability to do so. Thus for example, if we agree to an exchange in which I promise to give you one dollar for your newspaper, and I hold the dollar out and offer to give it to you, my offer will obligate you to give me the newspaper in exchange for the dollar.

A party's expectation interest in future performance, and his or her interest in a continuing sense of security, is generally protected by the law of breach by anticipatory repudiation. This law allows the injured party to a contract for future performance, to bring an action for breach of contract even before the day actual performance is to commence. More specifically, when a party renunciates or repudiates a contract requiring future performance through some act or definite statement, the other party may bring an action for damages resulting from a breach of contract immediately, rather than on the day performance is due. This right, of course, may be qualified by the interest of the party in breach and is subject to important exceptions. For instance, if it appears that the injured party would not have been able to perform his return promise on the day specified, the repudiating party's duty to pay damages for total breach would be discharged. Furthermore, a repudiating party has the right to retract his or her repudiation, and reinstate both party's obligations under the contract, up until the time actual performance is due, as long as the other party has not materially changed his or her position, or notified the repudiating party that the repudiation is considered final.

In some situations where one party breaches, the injured party may be given the right of cancellation, which ends the contract and discharges the remaining obligations of either party, in addition to compensatory damages. However, before a party is given this right, a breach must be deemed "material." Although, determining "materiality" seems to be of unquantifiable significance, the relevant criteria to be used is currently unsettled. Under the Restatement (Second), it is important to consider, among other things, the extent to which the injured party will be deprived of the expected benefit, the extent to which the breaching party will be injured, and the likelihood that the breaching party will cure his or her failure. Others argue that because "material breach" is a remedial concept, its definition should turn on whether a cancellation would be justified. Nevertheless, when a breach or omission is not material, or both trivial and innocent, an injured party will not be given the right to cancel. Instead, courts may generally allow the breaching party to cure within a reasonable time, or in situations where the breaching party has substantially performed, a court may order mere payment for the resulting damage.

In the final section of this chapter, you will see that the enforcement rights and powers provided to

Perspective (Continued)
The Security Principle

contracting parties under the law and generally mentioned above, may be varied or supplemented by mutual agreement. However, as you will also see, courts can decline to honor these supplemented rights, where enforcement would conflict with a party's obligation to act in good faith, or if enforcement would be violative of public policy. As you probably know, every contract imposes an obligation of good faith and fair dealing in its performance and enforcement. While bad faith in contract performance generally constitutes a breach, bad faith in contract enforcement precludes a party from enforcing particular rights or powers provided in a contract. Moreover, just as an entire contract may be held invalid as contrary to public policy, specific provisions of a contract can be held unenforceable on similar grounds.

Chapter Overview Outline
The Security Principle

Chapter 6

NOTE: THE PURPOSE OF THIS OUTLINE IS TO ORGANIZE THE CASES SO THAT ONE CAN QUICKLY UNDERSTAND THE RELEVANCE OF EACH CASE TO THE COURSE. NO ATTEMPT IS MADE IN THIS OVERVIEW TO ADDRESS EVERY CONCEPT THAT MUST BE STUDIED. BE SURE TO READ THE ENTIRE CASEBOOK AND/OR OTHER MATERIALS TO GAIN A FULL UNDERSTANDING OF ALL CONCEPTS.

I. Introduction
  A. Although the law generally protects the expectation, reliance, or restitution interests of each party to a contract, often the contractual interest of each party will conflict.
  B. In such cases, courts may be called upon to balance each interest, in order to determine which is more deserving of legal protection, or in other words, to determine which interest should be a "contractual right."

II. Interests of the Parties Injured or Impaired by a Breach
  A. The "security principle" applies to the concept that each party to a contract has an expectation interest in both present and future performance. It implies that a contract obligates each party not to impair the other party's interest in receiving performance as promised. *U.C.C. § 2-609 (1), Restatement (Second) § 2-609.*
  B. Where performances to be rendered, "under an exchange of promises are due simultaneously, it is a condition of each party's duties to render such performance, that the other party either render or, with manifested present ability to do so, offer performance of his part of the simultaneous exchange." *Restatement (Second) of Contracts § 238.*
    1. Accordingly, where the promises between two parties constitute mutual conditions to be performed simultaneously, the first party's offer to perform when having the present ability to do so, will make the second party's performance a condition precedent to the first party's actual performance. *Kingston v. Preston.*
  C. A party's expectation interest in future performance may generally be protected by the law of breach by anticipatory repudiation and related doctrines, depending upon the circumstances and interests of the breaching party.
    1. An affirmative statement of renunciation by a party to a contract for future services, may give rise to an immediate cause of action for breach of contract damages prior to the agreed date of actual performance. *Hochster v. De La Tour.*
      a. The statement must be reasonably interpreted to convey an unwillingness or inability to perform in order to constitute a breach. Statements of passing intention or a "mere expression of doubt as to [the] willingness or ability to perform is not enough to constitute a repudiation." *Restatement (Second) of Contracts § 250.*
      b. Anticipatory repudiation can only be demonstrated by an absolute and unequivocal refusal to perform or a distinct and positive statement of an inability to do so. *McCloskey & Co. v. Minweld Steel Co.*
    2. The repudiating party's duty to pay damages for total breach will be discharged if it appears that after the breach, the injured party would not have been able to perform his or her return promise, or if it appears that after the breach, the duty repudiated would have been discharged by impracticability or frustration before any non-performance. *Restatement (Second) of Contracts § 254.*
    3. A repudiation may be nullified by a retraction, if the injured party is notified of the retraction before he or she materially changes his or her position in reliance on the repudiation or indicates to the other party that he or she considers the repudiation to be final. *Restatement (Second) of Contracts § 256.*
      a. Although generally a party may withdraw its repudiation if the other party has not yet relied on it, the other party has the power to finalize the repudiation. Thus, a party cannot freely retract its repudiation of a contract once the other party had filed suit or given a limited time to retract. *United States v. Seacoast Gas Co.*
      b. A retraction includes any method which clearly indicates that the repudiating party intends to perform, and reinstates the repudiating party's rights under the contract with some allowance for injuries sustained by the other party because of the repudiation.

U.C.C. § 2-611.

D. When reasonable grounds for insecurity concerning either party's performance arises, the other party may demand adequate assurance of due performance, and may, if reasonable, suspend any performance "for which he has not already received the agreed" exchange. *U.C.C. § 2-609, Restatement (Second) of Contracts § 251.*
   1. A demand for adequate assurance of performance must be predicated on objective and reasonable grounds for insecurity. *Pittsburgh-Des Moines Steel Co. v. Brookhaven Manor Water Co.*

E. When a party repudiates a contract for future performance and thereby substantially impairs the value of the contract to the other, the injured party may await performance by the repudiating party for a commercially reasonable time, or resort to any remedy for breach. *U.C.C. § 2-610.*
   1. Damages for non-delivery or repudiation by the seller, are measured according to the difference between the market price *at a commercially reasonable time after the buyer learned of the breach*, and the contract price together with any incidental and consequential damages. *Cosden Oil & Chemical Co. v. Karl O. Helm Aktiengesellschaft.*

F. Where a party breaches a contract for services before its completion, the breaching party may recover the reasonable value of services actually rendered in a quantum meruit action, when an obligation to pay can be implied by the conduct of the parties and/or when the other party has been unjustly enriched. *Britton v. Turner.*

III. Cancellation in Response to Breach

A. In situations where a party materially breaches, or in other words does not substantially perform, the right of "cancellation," which ends the contract and discharges the remaining obligations of either party, may be available to the injured party in addition to compensatory damages.
   1. However, the criteria for determining the materiality of a breach is currently unsettled.

B. In order to discharge a duty or obligation under a contract, full performance is required. Any nonperformance whether material or immaterial will be considered a breach. *Restatement (Second) Contracts § 235.*

C. However, when an omission is both trivial and innocent, courts may order mere payment for the resulting damages, and not consider the omission a breach.
   1. In determining whether an omission is either important or trivial, it is necessary to weigh the purpose to be served, the desire to be gratified, the excuse for derivation, and the cruelty of enforced adherence. *Jacob & Youngs v. Kent.*
   2. When a contractual obligation is substantially though not fully performed, when the omission made in the attempted fulfillment of the contract is both trivial and innocent, and when the cost of fixing that omission would be great, a court may order as damages payment of the difference in value between the fulfillment of the contract as completed and the fulfillment as contemplated under the contract instead of the cost of fixing the omission. *Jacob & Youngs v. Kent.*
   3. Were a party who fails to complete work under a construction contract has substantially performed, the party's recovery will be reduced by the diminished value of the project (the market value of the completed project minus the value of the structure as it stands), or the cost of completion of the unfinished work. *Plante v. Jacobs.*

D. A party may discontinue performance on a contract which has been materially breached by the other party. *Walker & Co. v. Harrison.* In determining whether a failure to perform is material, a court should consider:
   1. The extent to which the injured party will be deprived of his or her reasonably expected benefit;
   2. The extent to which the party failing to perform will suffer forfeiture;
   3. The likelihood that the party failing to perform will cure his failure; and
   4. The extent to which the behavior of the party failing to perform comports with standards of good faith and fair dealing. *Restatement (Second) of Contracts § 241.*

E. The main reason for the difficultly in determining a criteria for "material breach" has been the failure to recognize that "material breach" is a remedial concept. Since classifying a breach as material gives the nonbreaching party the power to cancel, the definition of material breach should turn on whether the cancellation is justified. *Eric*

G. Andersen, A New Look at Material Breach in the Law of Contracts.

1. Accordingly, some courts have found that a seller may justifiably cancel a contract for the delivery and payment of goods in installments, only when a buyer's failure to pay for one of the installments constitutes a material breach, by making it financially impossible or unreasonably burdensome for the seller to continue, or by creating a reasonable apprehension with respect to payments for future installments. *Plotnick v. Pennsylvania Smelting & Refining Co.*

F. A party who materially breaches a contract may not respond to the non-breacher's cessation of performance by repudiating the contract. *H & G Construction Co. v. Harris.*

1. A breach by non-performance followed by a repudiation, will generally give rise to a claim for damages for total breach. *Restatement (Second) of Contracts § 243.*

G. When performances to be exchanged under a contract can be apportioned into corresponding pairs of part performances, so that the parts of each pair are properly regarded as equivalents, a party's performance of his or her part will have the same effect on the other's duties to render performance of his part as it would if only that pair of performances had been promised. *Restatement (Second) of Contracts § 240.*

1. If a contract is severable, as opposed to entire (i.e. when only one payment is made upon completion of performance), then payment may be requested for the measure of performance which was completed. *Gill v. Johnstown Lumber Co.*

H. If goods or the tender of delivery under a sales contract, fails in any respect to conform to the contract, the buyer may reject the goods, accept the goods, or accept the goods in part. *U.C.C. § 2-601.*

1. Where any tender or delivery by the seller is rejected because of nonconformity, the seller may cure within the contract time if performance is not yet due. However, if the time for performance has already expired, the seller may have a further reasonable time to cure if he or she had reasonable grounds to believe that the original tender would've been acceptable with or without money allowance. *U.C.C. § 2-508.*

2. Accordingly, a buyer may reject the tender or delivery of goods that do not conform to what was contracted for, but may only cancel if the seller fails to cure the defective goods within a reasonable period of time. *Ramirez v. Autosport.*

IV. Agreed Enforcement Terms

A. The enforcement rights and powers provided to contracting parties under the law, may be varied or supplemented by mutual agreement for the purposes of further protecting a party's interests in future performance.

B. However, court's may decline to honor such enforcement rights or powers when, under the circumstances, enforcement would conflict with a party's obligation to act in good faith.

1. Every contract imposes an obligation of good faith and fair dealing in its performance and enforcement, which requires each party to act honestly, faithfully, and consistently with the justified expectations of the other party. *Restatement (Second) of Contracts § 205, U.C.C. §2-103.*

2. While bad faith in contract performance will constitute a breach, bad faith in the enforcement of contract provisions will preclude a party for exercising that enforcement right or power. *Baker v. Ratzlaff.*

C. Contract provisions that allow a party to accelerate payment or performance obligations "at will", "when he deems himself insecure," or in words of similar import, will enable acceleration only if the party believes in good faith, that the prospect of payment or performance is impaired. *U.C.C. § 1-208.*

1. Although the main concern of § 1-208 is with acceleration provisions that contain "at will" or similar language, it is not applicable only to those situations. A party must have a good faith belief that the prospect of future payments or performance will be impaired, even under "default" acceleration provisions that allow acceleration upon the occurrence of specified event. *Brown v. Avemco Investment Corp.*

D. Provisions of a contract may be disregarded or rendered unenforceable if they are found violative of public policy. *Burne v. Franklin Life.*

A PROMISE TO GIVE SECURITY FOR MONTHLY PAYMENTS FOUND A CONDITION PRECEDENT TO A PROMISE TO CONVEY AN INTEREST IN A BUSINESS

Kingston v. Preston

(Apprentice) v. (Business Owner)
Court of King's Bench, 99 Eng.Rep. 606 (1773)

M E M O R Y G R A P H I C

Instant Facts

The owner of a silk business is discharged from his contractual duty to convey his interest in the business to his apprentice, after the apprentice is found not to have fulfilled his promise to give good security, for monthly payments which were to be given to the owner.

Black Letter Rule

Where the promises between two parties constitute mutual conditions to be performed simultaneously, the first party's offer to perform when having the present ability to do so, will render the second party's performance a condition precedent to the first party's actual performance.

Case Vocabulary

CONDITION PRECEDENT: A promise or obligation that must be performed or fulfilled before another promise or obligation can be performed or fulfilled.
COVENANT: A promise to perform one or more specified acts.

Procedural Basis: Judgment by the Court of Kings Bench in favor of the defendant in an action for breach of contract.

Facts: Preston (D) operated a silk business and planned to retire within the next 15 months. Kingston (P) joined Preston's (D) business as an apprentice, and contracted with Preston (D) to continue the business with another person who would be chosen by Preston (D). For Preston's (D) interest in the business, Kingston (P) promised to pay $250 per month, and agreed to give Preston (D) sufficient security for these payments. Preston (D) was to approve of the security before transferring the business. Preston (D) later refused to surrender the business as promised, on the grounds that Kingston (P) failed to provide sufficient security. Although Kingston (P) admitted that the personal security given was worth nothing, Kingston (P) sued Preston (D) contending that because the covenants were mutual and independent, breaching his covenant did not bar an action for Preston's (D) breach of the covenant he had bound himself to perform. Accordingly, Kingston (P) further argued that Preston (P) had the right to maintain a separate action for Kingston's (P) breach. Preston (D), on the other hand, argued that the covenants were dependent by their nature, that the security to be given for the money was manifestly the chief object of the transaction, and that it would be highly unreasonable to construe the agreement so as to oblige the defendant to give up a beneficial business and valuable stock, and to trust the plaintiff's personal security for the performance of his part.

Issue: When the promises between two parties are determined to constitute mutual conditions, may a party in breach of his or her promise recover damages caused by the other party's breach?

Decision and Rationale: (Lord Mansfield) No. There are three kinds of covenants or promises. The first are "mutual and independent," and allow either party to recover damages for the other party's breach, even if the complaining party is alleged to have breached his covenants. In the second kind, "conditions and dependents," performance of one depends on the prior performance of another. Here, the other party is not liable for a breach of his promise until the prior condition is performed. The third types of covenants consist of "mutual conditions," that require simultaneous performance. In these, although it is not readily apparent which party is obliged to do the first act, the party who was ready and offered to perform his part may maintain an action against a party who neglected or refused to perform his part. The dependence or independence of covenants is to be determined according to the evident sense and meaning of the parties. In other words, the determination depends on the order of time in which the intent of the transaction requires their performance. In the instant case, the essence of the agreement was that Preston (D) would not trust the personal security given by Kingston (P), but instead required good security for the payment of money before he delivered his interest in the business. Thus, this security must necessarily be a condition precedent to Preston's (D) performance, and Preston (D) is therefore not liable for the non-performance of his promise.

Analysis:

The purpose of this case is to introduce you to the security principle and the laws that protect each party's expectation interest in the present performance of the other under a contract, by laying the foundation of common law concepts. Here, Kingston (P) promised to pay Preston (D) $250 per month while continuing Preston's (D) silk business. However, in addition to the promise to pay $250 per month, Preston (D) required that Kingston (P) give security, to ensure that the payments would be made. It is evident from these facts that these promises were conditioned on each other, or as the court states, "mutual conditions," since both parties were obligated to perform their duties under their contract, at the same time. In such cases, if one party actually performs, that performance fully discharges that party of his obligations under the contract, and is considered the occurrence of a condition of the other party's performance. However, as this case illustrates, actual performance is not necessary in order for it be considered that a condition to the other party's performance took place. A party's offer to perform with the present ability to do so, is enough to constitute the occurrence of a condition to the other party's performance. This makes the other party's performance a condition precedent to the first party's actual performance.

Hochster v. De La Tour

(Courier) v. (Employer)

Court of Queen's Bench, 2 E. & B. 678, 118 Eng.Rep. 922 (1853).

MEMORY GRAPHIC

Instant Facts

A courier hired to perform services during a three months tour of Europe, beginning on June 1st, sues his employer for breach of contract in May, shortly after the employer informs the courier that the contract has been rescinded.

Black Letter Rule

An affirmative statement of renunciation by a party to a contract for future services, may give rise to an immediate cause of action for breach of contract damages prior to the agreed date of actual performance.

Case Vocabulary

RENUNCIATION: Voluntary affirmative acts or statements that indicate a parties unwillingness to perform future duties under a contract, and give rise to an immediate claim of damages for a full breach of contract.

Procedural Basis: Appeal to the Court of Queen's Bench of a judgment in favor of the plaintiff for a breach of contract

Facts: In April, 1852, Hochster (P), a courier, contracted to tour with De La Tour (D) in Europe for three months beginning on June 1st. On May 11, De La Tour (D) informed Hochster (P) that his services were no longer needed and refused to make any compensation. On May 22nd, Hochster (P) commenced an action against De La Tour (D), and soon after, contracted with Lord Ashburton on terms equal to that of the contract with De a Tour (D), but starting on July 4th. De La Tour (D) contended that there could be no breach of its contract with Hochster (P) before June 1st. The jury found for Hochster (P) and De La Tour (D) appeals.

Issue: Is a contracting party's statement of an unwillingness to perform as promised in the contract, sufficient to constitute renunciation?

Decision and Rationale: (Campbell, J.) Yes. An affirmative statement of renunciation by a party to a contract for future services, will give rise to an immediate cause of action for breach of contract damages prior to the agreed date of actual performance. De La Tour (D) contends that if Hochster (P) was not content with dissolving the contract and abandoning all remedy upon it, then he was bound to remain ready and willing to perform until the day of actual employment. De La Tour (D) further contends that there could be no breach of the agreement before the date of actual employment that would give a right of action. However, it cannot be laid down as a universal rule that, where by agreement an act is to be done on a future day, no action can be brought for a breach of that agreement until the day for doing that act has arrived. If a man contracts to execute a lease on a future day for a specified term, and before that day executes a lease to another for the same term, he may be immediately sued for breaking the contract. Accordingly, if a man contracts to sell and deliver goods on a future day, and before that day sells and delivers the goods to another, he is immediately liable to an action brought by the originally contracted buyer. Although it can be argued that such an action may be brought because the defendant has made it impossible for him to perform his obligations, this may not always be the case since prior to the day of commencement, a surrender of the lease may be obtained, or the defendant might have repurchased the goods, making it possible for him to sell and deliver them to the original buyer. Another reason could be that the contracting parties have formed a relationship before the future day, and have impliedly promised that neither will do anything to the prejudice of the other, inconsistent with that relationship. The declaration here states a great deal more than a passing intention on the part of De La Tour (D) which he may repent of, and could only be proved by evidence that he had utterly renounced the contract, or done some act which rendered it impossible for him to perform it. If Hochster (P) were to have no remedy for breach unless he treated the contract as in force until June 1st, it follows that until then he could not enter into new employment that would interfere with his promise to begin work on that day, and that he must be properly equipped to fulfill his duties as a courier. However, it is more rational and of more benefit to both parties that after the renunciation of the agreement by De La Tour (D), Hochster (P) should be at liberty to consider himself absolved from his future obligation, retaining the right to sue for any damages he has suffered from the breach. This allows Hochster (P) to mitigate the damages he would otherwise be entitled to for a breach of contract. It seems odd that De La Tour (D), after renouncing the contract, should be permitted to object that faith was given to his assertion, and that he was not given the opportunity to change his mind. Suppose that De La Tour (D), at the time of his renunciation, had embarked on a voyage for Australia, so as to render it physically impossible for him to employ Hochster (P) as a courier from June through August. According to previous decisions, an action might have been brought before June 1st. However, renunciation may be determined by other facts which would equally have rendered the defendant's performance of the contract impossible. The party who renounces a contract which had entered into deliberately, cannot justly complain if he is immediately sued for compensatory damages by the party he has injured. Furthermore, it seems reasonable to allow the injured party to either sue immediately, or wait till the time when the act was to be done, still holding it as prospectively binding for the exercise of this option. Although an argument against an action before June 1s could stem from the difficulty of calculating the damages, this argument is equally strong against an action before September 1st when the three months would expire. Either way, the jury would be justified in looking to all that happened, or was likely to happen, and to increase or mitigate the loss of Hochster (P) down to the day of trial when assessing damages. We find the declaration in this case sufficient, and give judgment for the Hochster (P).

Analysis:

Like the previous case, this case serves as an introduction to the security principle. However, unlike the previous case, the expectation interes of a party in future performance is illustrated here. More specifically, this case deals with the law of breach by anticipatory repudiation, which protects the expectation interests of parties to a contract for future performances. This court realizes that a party's expectation interest can be harmed before the date of actual performance, and rationalizes the need for an immediate remedy through what is implied by the security principle. In other words, that contracting parties have formed a relationship even before the future day, and are obligated to refrain from act that will prejudice the other in ways inconsistent with that relationship. Indeed, this obligation not to impair the other party's expectation o receiving due performance, has been codified in the *Uniform Commercial Code § 2-609(1)*, and is quoted in the comments of the *Restatemen (Second) of Contracts § 251*. Thus, acts by a party to a contract that make it impossible for him or her to perform on the specified date, wil give rise to an immediate action for a full breach of contract. As stated in this opinion, renunciation or repudiation may be determined by facts other than say, physical voluntary acts, that may render a party's breach inevitable. Accordingly, statements indicating an intention to breach can be sufficient to constitute a renunciation of contractual obligations. However, a declaration of renunciation must, like De La Tour's (D), be more than just "a passing intention," in order to constitute a breach. As stated in the comments under *§ 250* of the *Restatement*, "mere expression of doubt as to [the] willingness or ability to perform is not enough to constitute a repudiation." The statement must be reasonabl interpreted to convey an unwillingness or inability to perform.

United States v. Seacoast Gas Co.

(The Government) v. (Utility Company)

United States Court of Appeals, Fifth Circuit, 1953. 204 F.2d 709. Certiorari denied 346 U.S. 866 (1953)

M E M O R Y G R A P H I C

Instant Facts

A utility company repudiates its agreement with the government and then tries to retract its repudiation.

Black Letter Rule

A party cannot freely retract its repudiation of a contract once the other party has filed suit or given it a limited time to retract.

Case Vocabulary

LOCUS POENITENTIAE: Literally, a place for repentance. The phrase signifies an opportunity to change one's mind, such as that granted by the United States (P) to Seacoast (D).

Procedural Basis: Appeal from a district court judgement in favor of the defendant in a breach of contract action.

Facts: Seacoast Gas Co. (Seacoast) (D) had a year long contract to provide gas to a federal housing project. Seacoast (D) repudiated the contract several months into performance, blaming its anticipated cancellation on the United States' (P) breach of contract. It gave the United States (P) a month's notice before the threatened cancellation. The United States (P), in turn, notified Seacoast (P) that it was going to solicit bids from other gas companies. It ultimately received a low bid from the Trion Company. At this point, it gave Seacoast (D) three days to retract its repudiation. If not, the United States (P) would hold it (and its surety) liable for breach of contract. Seacoast (D) did not respond in time and, as a result, the United State's (P) hired the Trion Company in its place. As it happens, Trion and Seacoast (D) had the same president, Zell. He notified the Public Housing Authority that Seacoast (D) was retracting its repudiation. This was not until three days after Trion was hired and two days before Seacoast (D) planned on cancelling its service as threatened. Despite the fact that the United States (P) and Trion had not yet signed their contract, it refused Seacoast's (D) retraction. The United States (P) also sued Seacoast (D) for breach of contract. Seacoast (D) argued that its repudiation was healed before the United States (P) relied on it to its detriment. The district court agreed and found in its favor. The United States (P) appeals, arguing that Seacoast's (D) retraction was too late.

Issue: Can a party retract an anticipatory repudiation if the other party has not changed position in reliance on the repudiation?

Decision and Rationale: (Hutcheson) Yes. A party may withdraw its repudiation if the other party has not yet relied on it. However, the other party has the power to finalize the repudiation at will. It may either bring suit for breach of contract, or may notify the guilty party that its repudiation will be final if a retraction is not received within a specified time. Seacoast (D) argues that the United States (P) did not rely on its repudiation because it was retracted before the new utility contract was signed. This is beside the point. The United States had already warned Seacoast (D) that it was soliciting bids and gave it three days to retract its repudiation. At this point, the *locus poenitentiae* for a retraction was reduced from one month, as originally threatened by Seacoast (D), to three days as announced by the United States (P). This conclusion seems particularly compelling since Seacoast (D) and Trion's mutual president, Zell, was involved in this dispute at all times. The United States (P) repeatedly asked him for a retraction and he repeatedly refused. Zell did not attempt to rectify the situation until just before Trion and the United States (P) were ready to sign their contract. In fact, the signing was delayed because Trion was late in filing its bond. This behavior, coupled with the United States' (P) limitation on the acceptable time for a retraction, justifies our decision. The judgment of the trial court will be reversed and remanded for a judgment in favor of the United States (P).

Analysis:

The court lists at least two ways that Seacoast's (D) repudiation might become final. First, the United States (P) might file suit. Second, it might rely on Seacoast's (D) repudiation but give it a chance to retract. However, it was not required to do so in order to preserve Seacoast's (D) liability. If the United States (P) had materially changed position in reliance on the repudiation, it would have become final regardless of whether it notified Seacoast (D). A third option, not mentioned in the case, would be for the United States to ignore the repudiation and hope that Seacoast (D) performed when the time arrived. This is obviously the least desirable option since the United States (P) would be leaving itself open to an eventual breach. In any event, the circumstances of the parties' dispute will help determine the appropriate response to an anticipatory breach of contract. In this case, for instance, the United States (P) was certainly hoping to avoid the uncertainty of a new bidding process and the unpredictability of a new utility provider by giving Seacoast (D) a chance to retract.

A PARTY'S REASONABLE GROUNDS FOR INSECURITY AS TO WHETHER THE OTHER PARTY WILL PERFORM WILL ENABLE THE FIRST PARTY TO DEMAND AN ADEQUATE ASSURANCE OF PERFORMANCE.

Pittsburgh-Des Moines Steel Co. v. Brookhaven Manor Water Co.

(Water Tank Fabricator) v. (Water Tank Buyer)

United States Court of Appeals, 7th Circuit, 532 F.2d 572 (1976).

M E M O R Y   G R A P H I C

Instant Facts

After a water tank fabricator/seller became nervous about the financial ability of its buyer to complete the sale, it demanded that the buyer comply with conditions that were not contracted for before it would deliver the tank.

Black Letter Rule

A demand for adequate assurance of performance must be predicated on objective and reasonable grounds for insecurity.

Case Vocabulary

ADEQUATE ASSURANCE OF PERFORMANCE: A protective doctrine that enables a party who has reasonable grounds for insecurity regarding the other party's future performance to demand that the other party assure its willingness and ability to perform.

MERGER: In this instance, the combination or fusion of the pre-contractual negotiations with the written contract so that the written contract represents the entire contractual agreement and understanding between the parties.

Procedural Basis: Appeal of a judgment notwithstanding the verdict in favor of the buyer (defendant).

Facts: Pittsburgh-Des Moines Steel Company (PDM) (P) contracted with Brookhaven Manor Water Company (Brookhaven) (D) to construct a one-million-gallon water tank for $175,000. After negotiations about the payment terms, PDM (P) agreed to accept payment of 100% of the purchase price within 30 days after the tank had been delivered, tested and accepted. The contract was signed on November 26, 1968. Sometime during the following month, a PDM (P) manager talked to a representative of the company who had contracted with Brookhaven (D) to build the foundation for the tank and learned that Brookhaven (D) had obtained a loan from Diversified Finance Corporation to finance the tank. In fact, Brookhaven (D) had not yet obtained the loan but was negotiating to do so. On January 3, 1969, PDM's (P) credit manager wrote to Diversified and requested a letter assuring that the $175,000 payment for the tank was available and would be held in escrow until the tank's completion. The contract between PDM (P) and Brookhaven (D) contained no provision for escrow financing. Diversified did not provide the requested assurance and PDM's (P) credit manager then wrote to Betke, Brookhaven's (D) president, demanding that he personally guarantee the payment of $175,000 for the tank. In addition, the letter again demanded that once Brookhaven (D) obtained a loan, PDM (P) would require that the funds be held in escrow. The letter intimated that as soon as the personal guarantee was made, PDM (P) would resume the manufacture of the tank. The foundation for the tank was built, but the tank was never installed. Betke sent PDM's (P) Comptroller a copy of his financial statements but did not send a personal guarantee. PDM (P) took no further steps towards its performance. On April 29, 1969, at a meeting between Brookhaven (D) and PDM (P), PDM's (P) sales manager told Betke that he could finish the tank and install it within a matter of weeks, but Betke told him that he wouldn't need the tank until the following year. Further efforts to implement the contract broke down. Brookhaven (D) had the foundation installed but never installed the tank. Instead, it located another piece of property and developed additional wells to provide an adequate water supply. The foundation had cost it about $18,895 and the removal of the foundation was estimated at an additional $7,000. PDM (P) brought suit against Brookhaven (D) alleging that Brookhaven (D) repudiated the contract on April 29 when Betke informed PDM's (P) sales manager that he did not need the tank. Brookhaven (D) counterclaimed for breach of contract. The trial court entered a judgment notwithstanding the verdict in favor of Brookhaven (D) on its counterclaim and PDM (P) appealed.

Issue: Does a party have to have objectively reasonable grounds for insecurity before it can demand an adequate assurance of performance?

Decision and Rationale: (Pell, Cir. J.) Yes. Under the terms of the contract, into which all prior negotiations had merged, Brookhaven's (D) obligation to pay the $175,000 was not due until 30 days after the installation, testing and acceptance of the tank. Nevertheless, within a month after contracting, PDM (P) was requesting a prospective lender to hold the funds due it in escrow, despite the fact that the contract did not provide for such an arrangement. At that point, months before the time for payment was due, PDM (P) had no reasonable grounds for insecurity to justify its demand for escrowing the funds. In fact, Brookhaven (D) was not even obligated at that time to have a ready financial source for the funds. The contract was also silent as to any right of PDM (P) to insist upon a personal guarantee by Betke. Although it is common for a corporate officer to provide such a guarantee in circumstances where a seller is unsure of the company's financial abilities, there was nothing in the contract that

Pittsburgh-Des Moines Steel Co. v. Brookhaven Manor Water Co. (Continued)

justified PDM's (P) request. If it had wanted such a guarantee, a provision for one should have been contracted for. Article 2 Section 2-609 of the UCC enables a party who has reasonable grounds for insecurity to request an adequate assurance of performance from the other party. But there must first be reasonable grounds for insecurity in order to justify such a request. We do not find that PDM (P) had such reasonable grounds for insecurity as was necessary to demand adequate assurance of performance. An additional problem is that PDM (P), by its letters to Diversified and to Betke, demanded more than it was entitled to demand under the contract. The funds in question were not to be available until after the installation of the tank. The record is silent as to any reasonable ground for insecurity on PDM's (P) part. PDM's (P) credit manager intimated in the letters that it was requesting such items as a matter of good business. But something more than a subjective questioning or belief is necessary to demonstrate reasonable grounds for insecurity. All that PDM (P) knew was that Brookhaven (D) had not yet acquired the necessary funds to pay for the tank. That should not have been problematic because Brookhaven (D) was not contractually required to have such funds until 30 days *after* the completion of the project. PDM's (P) credit manager testified that he was unaware of any change in Brookhaven's (D) financial condition. Additionally, it appears that PDM (P) offered to finance Brookhaven (D) itself at an interest rate of 9 & 1/2%--an offer that Brookhaven (D) declined. If PDM (P) was not worried about Brookhaven's (D) ability to repay the loan according to a promissory note, it is curious why it would be nervous about Brookhaven's (D) ability to pay on the underlying contract. Section 2-609 is a protective device available when reasonable grounds for insecurity arise—it is not a license to rewrite a contract or to ask for more than that to which a party is entitled under the circumstances. In this case, we cannot find that PDM (P) had the reasonable grounds for insecurity that would act as a predicate to a demand for adequate assurance of performance. As such, its conduct was itself a breach of the contract. Brookhaven's (D) request to delay the contract for a year clearly came after PDM's (P) repudiation of the contract. As such, the trial court properly entered judgment notwithstanding the verdict for Brookhaven (D). Affirmed.

Concurrence: (Cummings, Cir. J.) While I agree with the result in this case, I do not agree with the reasoning behind it. I believe that, in the circumstances, a prudent businessman in PDM's (P) situation would have reasonable grounds for uncertainty after learning that Brookhaven (D) failed to acquire a loan to pay for the tank. However, I think PDM (P) overstepped itself by requesting the kinds of assurances that it did. PDM's (P) conduct crossed the line between requesting adequate assurances and rewriting the contract. The district court could have properly concluded that PDM (P) made more than a commercially reasonable demand for adequate assurances and that its conduct itself constituted a breach of the original contract.

Analysis:

This case is illustrative of one of the remedies available to a party when it becomes apparent that the other party might not be able to perform, but has not yet anticipatorily repudiated the contract. The first party is kind of in limbo at this point. The other party may not have made the all-important *unequivocal and absolute* manifestation of an unwillingness or inability to perform that would constitute an anticipatory repudiation, but the circumstances might be enough to make the first party pretty nervous! If the first party simply assumes that the other has anticipatorily repudiated, he runs the risk of being liable for breach himself if it later turns out that the other has not repudiated. So what is the poor uncertain first party to do when faced with such circumstances? Well, both the UCC and the common law allow a party who has become uncertain of the other's performance to demand an adequate assurance of performance. But, as can be seen in the instant case, the UCC requires that a party have objectively reasonable grounds for insecurity before it makes such a demand upon the other party. In the event that reasonable grounds for insecurity exist, the UCC allows a party to make a demand for adequate assurances and to suspend its own performance until such assurances are forthcoming. This is apparently what PDM (P) was trying to do in the instant case. PDM's (P) problem is that it jumped the gun. The code does not allow a party to demand adequate assurances absent a reasonable ground for insecurity. PDM (P) didn't have such grounds in the instant case. As a result, PDM's demand for assurances to which it was not entitled absent reasonable grounds for insecurity amounted to a breach of contract. That is simply because a party is not entitled to demand more than was contractually agreed to from the other party and then threaten not to perform unless its demands are met. To allow such conduct would mean that a party could unilaterally change the terms of a contract—which we all know [or at least, should know by now!] isn't the case.

AN INJURED BUYER IS HELD TO HAVE A RIGHT TO AWAIT PERFORMANCE BY A REPUDIATING SELLER FOR A COMMERCIALLY REASONABLE TIME

Cosden Oil & Chemical Co. v. Karl O. Helm Aktiengesellschaft

(Petroleum Seller) v. (Petroleum Buyer)

United States Court of Appeals, Fifth Circuit, 736 F.2d 1064 (1984).

MEMORY GRAPHIC

Instant Facts

After a petroleum seller contracts to deliver four orders of polystyrene, then repudiates three orders due to problems with its production plant, the seller sues the buyer for a failure to pay for successfully delivered polystyrene, and the buyer counterclaims for the seller's failure to deliver the contracted amount of polystyrene.

Black Letter Rule

Damages for non-delivery or repudiation by the seller, are measured according to the difference between the market price at a commercially reasonable time after the buyer learned of the breach, and the contract price together with any incidental and consequential damages.

Case Vocabulary

COVER: Actions undertaken by an injured party (purchase of substitute goods) to reasonably mitigate or minimize damages resulting from a breach of contract.

"LEARNED OF BREACH": A commercially reasonable time after one party to a contract becomes aware of the other party's repudiation.

Procedural Basis: Appeal to the United States Court of Appeals of the district court's award of damages for the anticipatory repudiation by the seller (plaintiff).

Facts: Karl O. Helm Aktiengesellschaft [gesundheit] (Helm Hamburg) (D), an international trading company based in Hamburg, West Germany, decided to purchase a large amount of polystyrene, a petroleum derivative, in anticipation of a tightening in the world petrochemical supply due to the political turmoil in Iran, a major petroleum producer. Helm Hamburg (D) ordered Helm Houston, a wholly-owned subsidiary, to initiate negotiations with Cosden Oil & Chemical Company (Cosden) (P), a Texas based producer of polystyrene. Helm Hamburg (D) and Cosden (P) agreed to the purchase and sale of 1,250 metric tons of high impact polystyrene at $.2825 per pound and 250 metric tons of general purpose polystyrene at $.265 per pound. On January 18, 1979, the general manager of Helm Houston met with the national sales coordinator of Cosden (P) in Dallas leaving behind confirmation 04 containing the terms for high impact and 05 containing the terms for general purpose. Both confirmations stated the price quantity, delivery, and payment terms. The polystyrene was to be delivered in January and February in one or more lots. Confirmation 04 also specified that Helm Hamburg (D) had an option for an additional 1,000 metric tons of high impact, and 05 expressed a similar option for 500 metric tons of general purpose. Both options were to be declared at the latest, by January 31, and were to be delivered in February and March. On January 22, Helm Hamburg (D) called for the first shipment of high impact to be delivered at a New Jersey port. Then on January 23, Helm Hamburg (D) telexed Cosden (P), exercising his options on both purchase orders, and designated these orders as 06 for high impact and 07 for general purpose. Helm Hamburg (D) then sent purchase confirmations 06 and 07 which Cosden (P) received on January 29, the same day Helm Houston received confirmations 04 and 05. On January 26, Cosden (P) shipped 90,000 pounds of high impact polystyrene to Helm Hamburg (D), and sent an invoice for that quantity to Helm Houston on January 31. In late January, polystyrene prices began to rise, and Cosden (P) began experiencing problems at two of its plants. Cosden's (P) Illinois plant, which was to supply the high impact polystyrene, was normally supplied with styrene monomer, the main ingredient of polystyrene, by barges that traveled up the Illinois Rivers to a canal that lead to the plant. However, due an extremely cold winter, the Illinois River and the canal froze suspending barge travel for a few weeks. In Cosden's (P) New Jersey plant, which was to supply the general purpose polystyrene, a new reactor used in polystyrene manufacturing needed to be sent back to its manufacturer to repair for several weeks. In late January Cosden (P) notified Helm Hamburg (D) that delivery under 04 might be delayed, and on February 6, Cosden (P) informed Helm Houston that it was canceling order 05, 06, and 07 because two plants were down. After Cosden (P) confirmed the cancellation in a letter dated February 8, received by Helm Houston on February 12, a member of Helm Hamburg's executive board sent an internal memo to Helm Houston outlining a strategy by which Helm Hamburg (D) would offset amounts owning under 04 after its reception, against Helm Hamburg's (D) damages for nondelivery of the balance of polystyrene. Helm Houston was also instructed to urge Cosden (P) to immediately deliver several hundred tons of high impact to meet the February shipping. In mid February, Cosden (P) shipped 1,260,000 pounds of high impact under 04. The shipment invoice specified that Helm Hamburg(D) owed $355,950, due by mid March. Helm Hamburg (D) then requested that Cosden (P) deliver the rest of order 04 for shipment on a vessel departing March 16. On March 15, due to production problems, Cosden (P) offered to sell 1,00 metric tons of styrene monomer at $.41 per pound. Helm Hamburg (D) refused the offer, insisted on delivery by March 31 at the latest, and Cosden (P) cancelled the balance of orde

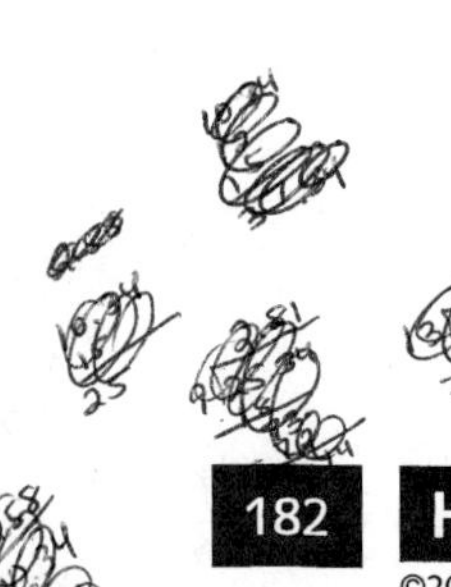

04 around the end of March. Cosden (P) sued Helm Hamburg (D) for Helm Hamburg's (D) failure to pay for delivered polystyrene, and Helm Hamburg (D) counterclaimed for Cosden's (P) failure to deliver polystyrene as agreed. The jury found that Cosden (P) had agreed to sell polystyrene to Helm Hamburg (D) under all four orders, that Cosden (P) anticipatorily repudiated orders 05, 06, and 07, and that Cosden (P) cancelled order 04 before Helm Hamburg's (D) failure to pay for the second 04 delivery constituted repudiation. The per pound market prices under each order were fixes at three different times: 1) When Helm Hamburg (D) learned of the cancellation, 2) at a commercially reasonable time thereafter, and 3) at the time for delivery. The district court, viewing the four orders as representing one agreement, determined that Helm Hamburg (D) was entitled to recover $628,676 in damages representing the difference between the contract price and the market price at a commercially reasonable time after Cosden (P) repudiated its polystyrene delivery obligations, and that Cosden (P) was entitled to an offset of $355,950 against those damages for the delivered polystyrene. Both Cosden (P) and Helm Hamburg (D) appeal contesting the time at which damages for the anticipatory repudiation of orders 05, 06, and 07, were measured. Order 04 was determined not to be anticipatorily repudiated since Helm Hamburg (D) learned of Cosden's (P) intent to make no more deliveries under 04 at the same time as the last date of performance.

Issue: When calculating damages caused by the seller's repudiation, is market price determined at a commercially reasonable time after the buyer learns of the repudiation?

Decision and Rationale: (Reavley, J.) Yes. Cosden (P) argues that damages should be measured when Helm Hamburg (D) learned of the repudiation, while Helm Hamburg (D) contends that the market price of the last day for delivery is proper for calculating damages. Under the Uniform Commercial Code (the Code), § 2-713 damages for repudiation by the seller are measured according to the difference between the market price at the time when the buyer learned of the breach, and the contract price together with any incidental and consequential damages. This total is reduced by expenses saved as a result of the breach. The time the buyer "learned of the breach," has been interpreted to mean: 1) when the buyer learns of the repudiation, 2) when the buyer learns of the repudiation plus a commercially reasonable time, or 3) when performance is due under he contract. Where a seller repudiates and buyer does not cover, the Code § 2-610 allows the aggrieved party to await performance for a commercially reasonable time before resorting to his remedies of cover or damages. However, if the buyer awaits performance beyond a commercially reasonable time, the buyer may not recover resulting damages that should have been avoided. Interpreting the "learned of breach" language to mean the time when the seller first communicates his anticipatory repudiation, would undercut the time given to the buyer under the Code to await performance. Furthermore, a buyer's option to wait interacts with a seller's opportunity to retract his repudiation under § 2-611 of the Code. If we were confronted with this issue during a rising market, measuring the market price at the time of a seller's repudiation would give the seller the ability to fix his or her liability for damages and may induce the seller to repudiate. On the other hand, measuring a buyer's damage at the time of performance will tend to dissuade the buyer from mitigating damages, in hopes that the market price will continue to rise. By allowing a commercially reasonable time, a buyer has the opportunity to investigate his cover possibilities in a rising market, free from the fear of being relegated to a market-contract damage remedy measured at the time of repudiation if he is unsuccessful. The Code § 2-712, clearly provides the buyer with the option to cover or choose damages for non-delivery. If this section of the Code is not intended to limit the time necessary for a buyer to investigate existing cover possibilities, it would be anomalous to fix the buyer's damages, should he choose damages, at a time before the investigation and before the buyer elects his remedy. Furthermore, under the Code, when a buyer chooses to seek damages, the market is measured at the time he could have covered when it is a reasonable time after repudiation. We realize that our interpretation fails to explain the language of this section of the Code in relation to aggrieved buyers. However, this section has limited applicability, since cases that come to trial before the time of performance are rare. Furthermore, the Code's method of determining market price or damages was not intended to exclude other reasonable methods. In light of the Code's persistent theme of commercial reasonableness, the prominence of cover as a remedy, and the time given to an aggrieved buyer to await performance and investigate cover before selecting his remedy, we hold that damages for non-delivery or repudiation by the seller, are measured according to the difference between the market price at a commercially reasonable time after the buyer learned of the breach, and the contract price together with any incidental and consequential damages. Affirmed.

Analysis:

This case offers a straightforward, well written explanation of the interplay between a number of U.C.C. provisions. Generally under § 2-610, when either party repudiates a contract with respect to a performance not yet due, the injured party has the option of either awaiting performance for a commercially reasonable time or resorting to any remedy for breach. Under § 2-611, the repudiating party may retract his repudiation up until the next performance is due, unless the aggrieved party has materially changed his or her position, or has otherwise indicated that he or she has considered the repudiation final. Here, by interpreting the Code's "learned of breach" language to mean a commercially reasonable time after actual notification, the court does a good job of protecting both the buyer's and the seller's protected interest under the contract. The court's interpretation allows a breaching party some time to exercise his or her rights to retract its repudiation, and minimizes their liability for damages that could have been reasonably avoided. Furthermore, the court's interpretation gives an injured party the incentive and opportunity to fulfill his or her obligation to mitigate damages. All in all, this decision seemed equitable in light of the fact that Cosden's (P) breach, while a breach nonetheless, was not intentional or undertaken for the purposes of gaining a commercial advantage in a rising market.

A LABORER IS ALLOWED TO RECOVER FOR PARTIAL PERFORMANCE, DESPITE VOLUNTARILY BREACHING HIS LABOR CONTRACT BEFORE ITS COMPLETION

Britton v. Turner

(Laborer) v. (Employer)

Superior Court of Judicature of the State of New Hampshire, 6 N.H. 481 (1834).

MEMORY GRAPHIC

Instant Facts

After completing nine and a half months of a one-year labor contract, a breaching laborer sues his employer in equity to recover a reasonable sum for services actually performed, despite voluntarily failing to complete the entire contract.

Black Letter Rule

A breaching party may recover the reasonable value of services actually rendered under quantum meruit, when an obligation to pay can be implied from the conduct of the parties, and/or when the other party has been unjustly enriched.

Case Vocabulary

IMPLIED-IN-FACT CONTRACT: A contract established pursuant to the conduct of the parties involved, rather than by their language.

QUANTUM MERIUT: Latin for as much as he or she deserves. It was originally a count in an assumpsit action brought in order to recover the reasonable value of services rendered pursuant to an implied-in-fact employment contract, and is mainly used today to provide restitution for another party's unjust enrichment.

Procedural Basis: Action for quantum meruit brought in the Superior Court of Judicature of the State of New Hampshire by the breaching party to a labor contract to recover for partial performance.

Facts: Britton (P) contracted with Turner (D) to labor for one year in exchange for $120.00. After performing for nine and a half months, Britton (P) voluntarily ceased performance. Turner (D) refused to pay Britton (P) for the services rendered and Britton (P) sues in quantum meruit.

Issue: Can a breaching party recover for services rendered to another under a contract despite having failed to complete all of the services contracted for in breach?

Decision and Rationale: (Parker, J.) Yes. It is considered a settled rule of law, that a contract for labor to be performed at a specified price must be fully performed in order to recover any part of the compensation. Thus, when the laborer voluntarily fails to fulfill his obligation to fully perform, the laborer may not recover anything for what has actually been performed. It is obvious that such a rule is unjust. When a party who contracts to perform specified labor breaks his or her contract without attempting to perform, he or she can only be made liable to pay for the damage which the other party has sustained because of the breach. While on the other hand, a party who has nearly completed the required performance under the contract before abandoning any further attempts, is subjected to a loss for labor which has been completed, even if the other party has had the full benefit of all that has been done and has perhaps sustained no loss. In this situation, a party who attempts to perform can be placed in a worse position than a party who completely disregards the contract, and the other party may receive more by a breach of contract than the injury which he or she has sustained. In the instant case, if Britton (P) had never performed under the contract, his liability for damages would likely not exceed some small expense for procuring another laborer. However, by having performed for a substantial portion of the time required under the contract, the value of which was determined to be $95.00 by the jury, Britton (P) may in fact receive nearly five sixths of the value of a whole year's labor should he be successful. The party who contracts for labor for a certain period of time, does so with full knowledge that he or she must be accepting performance from day to day, and with knowledge that the other may eventually fail to complete the entire term. Thus, where a party actually derives a benefit and advantage over and above the resulting damage, the labor actually done and the value received furnish new consideration, and the law thereupon raises a promise to pay to the extent of the reasonable worth of such success. Of course where a laborer fails to perform in entirety, the employer is entitled to reject what has been done and refuse to receive any benefit from the partial performance. In such a case, the employer has received nothing, is not bound to pay for his or her express promise to pay upon reception of the whole, and the law cannot and ought not raise an implied promise to pay. The rule is the same whether the value was received and accepted by the assent of the party prior to or subsequent to the breach. If the party receives the benefit under such circumstances as to preclude him from later rejecting it, it has still been received by his assent. Reasoning that the performance of the whole labor is a condition precedent, that there can be no apportionment, or that because an express contract exists, no other can be implied, is not applicable to this species of contract. Where a beneficial service has been actually performed, the general understanding of the community is that the hired laborer shall be entitled to compensation for the partial performance, and that such contracts must be presumed to be made with reference to that understanding unless otherwise stipulated in the contract. However, the contract price for the service should not be exceeded. If the employer actually receives a benefit over and above the damages he sustains by

the failure to complete performance, he should pay the reasonable worth of what has thus been done for his or her benefit. Thus, the benefit and advantage that the party takes by the labor, is the amount of value which he receives after deducting the amount of damages. Accordingly, a plaintiff may not recover where damages are equal to or greater than the amount of the labor performed. This rule leaves no temptation to the employer to drive the laborer from his services near the close of his term, nor to the laborer to desert his services before the stipulated time without sufficient reason. Furthermore, it will, in most instances, settle the whole controversy in one action, preventing a multiplicity of suits. We hold that a breaching party may recover for the benefits conferred to the other party by services actually rendered, despite failing to fulfill his or her contractual obligation to fully perform. In the instant case, Britton (P) is entitled to judgment on the verdict. Turner (D) has defended solely on the grounds of breach, has not offered any evidence to show that he was injured by such breach, and has not asked for a deduction to be made upon that account. The jury was therefore correct in allowing Britton (P) pro rata compensation for the time he labored.

Analysis:

The action brought by Britton (P) in the instant case was for a contract "implied in fact," rather than an "express contract." While an "express contract" is established pursuant to the language of the parties, an "implied-in-fact" contract is created by the conduct of the parties. Originally, the action of assumpsit was proper for breach of either an express contract or one implied in fact. For breach of an employment contract, "quantum meruit" was the proper count for recovery. Such actions were generally brought in situations where a promise to pay could be implied from the conduct of the parties, or in situations where there was no agreement, but the promise to pay was implied in law in order to avoid unjust enrichment. Today, quantum meruit is mainly used as an equitable remedy to provide restitution for the unjust enrichment of another. Here, the court explicitly stated that a contract for labor must be fully performed in order to recover any part of the compensation. Accordingly, since Britton (P) had no remedy based on an express contract, he sought compensation for the services he already rendered to Turner (D) in quantum meruit. Based on the facts given in the instant case, it is obvious that Turner (D) would be unjustly enriched if he were allowed to keep the benefits he derived from Britton's (P) completed services. For that reason, the court assumed that Turner (D) had in fact been accepting Britton's (P) performance from day to day, and implied a promise to pay. It is important to remember, however, that this promise may not have been implied by the court, had there been some specific provision in the contract expressing a contrary intention.

Jacob & Youngs v. Kent

(Home Builder) v. (Home Owner)

(1921) 230 N.Y. 239, 129 N.E. 889, 23 A.L.R. 1429

M E M O R Y   G R A P H I C

Instant Facts

A homeowner sued the builder of his home when it was discovered that the builder used a different brand of pipe from that called for in the contract.

Black Letter Rule

When a contractual obligation is substantially though not fully performed, the omission made in the attempted fulfillment of the contract is trivial, and the cost of fixing that omission would be great, a court may order as damages payment of the difference in value between the fulfillment of the contract as completed and the fulfillment as contemplated under the contract instead of the cost of fixing the omission.

Case Vocabulary

DOCTRINE OF SUBSTANTIAL PERFORMANCE: A doctrine of equity under which a good-faith attempt to fulfill one's contractual obligations that results in substantial completion of the purpose of the contract will be held to be a completion of the contract even though all of the terms of the original agreement were not fully met.

Procedural Basis: Appeal to the Court of Appeals of New York (the State's highest court) of an appellate court reversal of a trial court decision granting a directed verdict in favor of a homeowner who refused to pay the builders of his home.

Facts: Jacob & Youngs (P) built a home for Kent (D) at a cost of approximately $77,000. After the home was completed, but before Jacob & Youngs (P) was paid in full, it was discovered that in building the home a subcontractor used a galvanized wrought-iron pipe made by a company named Cohoes. The pipe used was the same type of pipe called for in the contract, except the contract specified that Reading brand pipe would be used. When the mistake was discovered, Kent (D) refused to pay $3,483.46 due to Jacob & Youngs (P) and demanded that it do whatever was necessary to install Reading pipe in the home (i.e., redo a substantial amount of work at a substantial cost). Jacob & Youngs (P) filed suit seeking payment of the $3,483.46. At trial, Jacob & Youngs (P) attempted to bring forth evidence that Cohoes pipe and Reading pipe are identical except for the name stamped on the pipe, but the trial judge excluded the evidence. A directed verdict was then entered in favor of Kent (D), and Jacob & Youngs (P) appealed.

Issue: When an omission made in the fulfillment of a contract is trivial, and the cost of fixing that omission would be great, may a court order as damages payment of the difference in value of the ultimate performance resulting from the omission instead of payment of the cost of fixing the omission?

Decision and Rationale: (Cardozo, J.) Yes. The omission of the prescribed brand of pipe was neither fraudulent nor wilful; it was the result of oversight and inattention. We think that if the evidence of similarity of the brands had been admitted, it would have shown that the defect was insignificant in relation to the cost and work that would be required to remedy it. Courts have never said that one who makes a contract fulfills his obligations thereunder by less than full performance. However, an omission both trivial and innocent may sometimes be atoned for by mere payment of the resulting damage, and will not always be considered a breach of contract. Where the line is to be drawn between what omissions are important and which are trivial depends on the circumstances of the case. Substitution of equivalents may not have the same significance in fields of art on the one side and those of mere utility on the other. Nowhere will change be tolerated, however, if it is so dominant or persuasive as in any real or substantial measure to frustrate the purpose of the contract. There is no general license to install whatever, in the builder's judgment, may be regarded as "just as good." In determining what remedy to apply, we must weigh the purpose to be served, the desire to be gratified, the excuse for derivation, and the cruelty of enforced adherence. Only then can we tell whether literal fulfillment is to be implied by law as a condition. In this case, we think the measure of the allowance is not the cost of replacement, which would be great, but the difference in value, which would be nominal. It is true that in most cases the cost of replacement is the proper measure of damages, but when the cost of replacement is grossly and unfairly out of proportion to the good to be attained, the proper measure is the difference in value. The reversal of the trial court's decision is affirmed.

Concurrence and Dissent: (Mclaughlin, J.) Jacob and Youngs' (P) failure to perform was either intentional or due to gross neglect, which in either case amounts to the same thing. Furthermore, Jacob & Youngs (P) did not present any evidence with respect to the cost of compliance where compliance was possible. Although Jacob & Youngs (P) agreed that the pipe should be that of Reading Manufacturing Company, only about two-fifths of it was of that kind. If more were used, the burden of proving that fact was upon Jacob & Youngs (P). Had Jacob & Youngs (P) complied with the terms of the contract except as to minor omissions due to inadvertence, then they might be allowed to recover the contract price, less the amount necessary to fully compensate Kent (D) for resulting damages. Here, however, Jacob & Youngs (P) installed between 2,00 and 2,500 feet of pipe, only 1,000 feet of which complied with the contract. No explanation was given for why a different pipe was used, nor was any effort made to show what it would cost to remove the other manufacturer's pipe and install the correct one. Kent (D) had the right, before making payments, to get what he contracted for, and it is no excuse to either say that the pipe is of equivalent quality or that the difference in the value of the pipes is either nominal or nothing. What Kent's (D) reasons were for requiring the Reading brand pipe is of no importance. He was entitled to it nevertheless. Therefore, the rule of substantial performance, with damages for unsubstantial omissions, has no application, and the trial court was correct in directing a verdict for Kent (D).

Analysis:

The case of *Jacob & Youngs v. Kent* addresses a basic principle of contract law known as the doctrine of substantial performance. In brief, substantial performance is an exception to the general rule requiring that all parties to a contract fully perform their obligations under the contract. Under the doctrine of substantial performance, a failure to complete exactly the required performance of a contract will not be deemed a breach of contract, but simply incomplete performance for which at least some of the promised consideration must be given. In cases in which money is to be exchanged in return for the performance of services, one who substantially performs a contract but does not do so completely will still be paid under the contract, just not as much if the failure to perform fully results in a difference in value between the completed performance and the contemplated performance. For the doctrine of substantial performance to apply, a default cannot be willful, nor can the resulting defects be so significant as to deprive the services of their value. In this case, the home builders failed to fully perform their obligations under the contract because they did not use the specified brand of pipe. However, because the omission was trivial, it was not purposely made, the defect did not deprive the home of any significant value, and to order a redoing of the pipes would be disproportionate to the value achieved thereby, the doctrine of substantial performance applied.

Plante v. Jacobs

(General Contractor) v. (Homeowners)
Supreme Court of Wisconsin, 1960. 10 Wis.2d 567, 103 N.W.2d 296

MEMORY GRAPHIC

Instant Facts

Homeowners refuse to make their final payment to the contractor who built their house.

Black Letter Rule

Substantial performance on construction contracts may be less than perfect, but recovery will be reduced by the diminished value of the project or the cost of completion of the unfinished work.

Case Vocabulary

COST OF COMPLETION: A measure of damages, frequently present in construction cases, which compensates the injured party for the cost of repairing or completing defective or unfinished work. This measure of damages will be granted unless it is grossly disproportionate to the value which is produced by the work. If it is grossly disproportionate, damages will be measured by the diminution in value.

DIMINUTION IN VALUE: As it sounds, the diminution in market value of a construction project is one possible measure of damages resulting from defective or incomplete performance by the builder. The court determines the market value of the project as completed per the contract and subtracts the value of the structure as it stands.

Procedural Basis: Appeal from a trial court judgement for the plaintiff in a suit to establish a lien on the defendant's property.

Facts: Plante (P) a contractor, agreed to build a house for the Jacobs (D) for $26,765. After $20,000 worth of work was paid for, the parties had a falling out which resulted in Plante (P) walking off of the job. He had not completed the house. In fact, there was at least $1601.95 worth of work to be completed. Despite this, he sued to establish a lien on the Jacobs' (D) property in order to recover the remainder of the construction price. He admits that he is not entitled to compensation for the uncompleted work. The Jacobs' (D) complain that, among other defects, Plante (P) misplaced the wall between their living room and kitchen by a foot. As a result, they claim that he is not entitled to compensation because he has not substantially performed the contract. It would cost roughly $4000 to tear down and rebuild the wall. However, the placement of the wall has no effect on the market value of the house. The trial court found for Plante (P). The Jacobs (D) appeal.

Issue: Can performance be considered substantial despite mistakes which will be costly to correct?

Decision and Rationale: (Hallows) Yes. The first question is whether substantial performance has been tendered. This cannot be answered according to precise formulae, especially with regard to construction contracts. In other cases, substantial performance was denied because performance was useless to the other party or a total failure with regard to the object of the contract. In construction cases, the rule is that something less than perfection will count as substantial performance unless the parties indicate otherwise in the contract. In this case, Plante (P) was not given any blueprints for the house. He built it based on standard floor plans, resolving problems by practical experience. Given the circumstances surrounding construction, and notwithstanding the Jacobs' (D) unhappiness with the job, the trial court did not err in finding substantial performance. However, this is not the end of our inquiry. The house was still left uncompleted. The next question which must be answered is how to measure the damages owed to Plante (P). Normally, he would receive the full contract price, minus the damages caused by incomplete performance. The damages caused by incomplete performance should be determined by comparing the diminution in value of the house, against the cost of completing the work. When the cost of completion is prohibitive, the diminution in value should be applied. The trial court parsed out the defects, applying the diminished-value rule to some defects, and the cost of completion rule to others. While the trial court applied cost of completion to some defects which this court may not have, we cannot say that their judgement was so erroneous as to require reversal. In particular, the trial court measured the misplaced wall by the diminished-value rule. This was appropriate. The Jacobs (P) never made it clear that the wall was being built in the wrong place. In addition, replacing the wall would require substantial demolition of the existing structure. This would be economically wasteful and unreasonable. Since the trial court did not err in its measure of damages, the judgement will be affirmed.

Analysis:

Recall the case of *Jacob & Youngs v. Kent* [substantial performance on a construction job not defeated by a trivial difference in plumbing brands]. Justice Hallows' approach in this case is not wholly different from Justice Cardozo's approach in *Jacob & Youngs*. Both justices realize that a mathematical approach is unsuited to determining substantial performance in construction cases. The work is simply too complicated and unpredictable to give rise to exact measurements regarding performance. On the other hand, Justice Hallows has broader concerns in the apportionment of damages than are evident in *Jacob & Youngs*. While both courts desired an equitable result, Justice Hallows is more explicitly concerned with efficiency than fairness. In fact, the diminished-value rule is a rule of efficiency. It is wasteful, albeit also unfair, to force parties to pay for defects which would be costly to repair, but have little impact on the value of the house.

Walker & Co. v. Harrison

(Sign Company) v. (Dry Cleaner)

Supreme Court of Michigan, 1957. 347 Mich. 630, 81 N.W.2d 352

MEMORY GRAPHIC

Instant Facts

A dry cleaner stops making rental payments on his neon sign when the sign company refuses to clean it according to routine maintenance.

Black Letter Rule

A party may discontinue performance on a contract which has been materially breached by the other party.

Case Vocabulary

MATERIAL BREACH: If one party to a contract materially (or substantially, or totally) breaches the contract, the other party may be excused from performance. In this event, the non-breaching party may still sue on the contract to recover damages due to lack of performance. In order to determine whether a breach is material, a court is likely to consider the elements outlined by Justice Smith, above.

Procedural Basis: Appeal from a trial court judgement for the plaintiff in an action for assumpsit.

Facts: Walker & Co. (Walker) (P) agreed to provide Harrison (D) with a neon sign for his dry cleaning business. Walker (P) rented the sign to Harrison (D) subject to a number of terms contained in the lease. These included a rental price of $148.50 per month, a term of 36 months, and a maintenance clause which required Walker (P) to clean and repaint the sign whenever necessary to keep it in "first class advertising condition." The sign was installed in July. Soon after, it began to fall into disrepair. Someone had thrown a tomato at it, and it was also covered with graffiti, cobwebs, and rust. Harrison (D) complained again and again but Walker (P) never serviced the sign. Consequently, Harrison (D) only made one rental payment. Finally, in October, Harrison (D) sent Walker (P) a telegram, renouncing their contract and any further obligations to pay rent for the sign. Walker (P) responded with a letter, drawing Harrison's (D) attention to a Breach of Agreement clause in the contract. This clause stated that, in the event of the lessee's failure to pay rent, Walker (P) could remove the sign and demand the remainder of the rental payments. Harrison (D) never responded, so Walker (P) sued in assumpsit for the entire balance due under the contract, $5197.5. Harrison (D) claimed that Walker (P) had already materially breached their agreement by the time he stopped paying rent. He claims that his repudiation was justifiable under the circumstances. Nonetheless, the trial court found for Walker (P). Harrison (D) appeals.

Issue: Can a party cease performance on a contract once the other party has materially breached the agreement?

Decision and Rationale: (Smith) Yes. A material breach by one party entitles the other party to discontinue performance on the contract. However, a party who responds to a material breach in this manner does so at his own peril. It is difficult to determine the point at which a breach becomes material. The Restatement [First] of Contracts provides some criteria which are helpful to this end. A court engaged in this analysis should examine the extent to which the non-breaching party will obtain the substantial benefit from the contract which they reasonably anticipated, the extent to which damages can adequately compensate the non-breacher, the extent to which the breacher has performed or prepared to perform, the hardship on the breacher of terminating the contract; the willful, negligent, or innocent behavior of the breacher; and the likelihood that the breacher will complete performance. Taking these elements together, it is clear that Walker (P) did not materially breach their obligations under the lease. First, Harrison (D) is unclear on the number of times he actually complained to Walker (P). In addition, it appears that some of the problems with the sign, notably the cobwebs and rust, were easily within Harrison's (D) reach. He could have taken care of those problems himself. The rust, itself, could not have been very severe since the sign had only recently been installed. Finally, Walker (P) repaired the sign within a week of Harrison's (D) telegram. Given Harrison's (D) complaint, which can be reduced to a stain from a thrown tomato, it cannot fairly be said that Walker (P) was guilty of a material breach in not repairing the sign sooner. The trial court did not err in its analysis. As a result, their judgment will be affirmed.

Analysis:

As George tells Lennie in *Of Mice and Men*, "I tole you, and tole you, and tole you." Many of our earlier cases raised the prospect of a party mistaking a breach of a contract for a *material* breach which relieves them of their obligations. It is perhaps the most popularly misunderstood element of contracts law. Many people think that any deviation from the terms of an agreement gives them the right to stop paying the landlord, the plumber, or any other party with whom they have a disagreement. Since this is not the case, it is one of the most dangerous misconceptions hovering in the popular imagination. If you take anything from the study of contracts, it must be the concept of material breach. While this case makes it clear that a material breach is difficult to quantify, it is always necessary to analyze a breach according to the criteria which the court outlines. At the very least, this analysis will provide some indication of the breach's magnitude and suggest an outcome in one party's favor.

UNDER AN INSTALLMENT CONTRACT, A FAILURE TO PAY FOR ONE INSTALLMENT IS HELD A NON-MATERIAL BREACH, IN LIGHT OF THE JUSTIFICATIONS FOR THE NON-BREACHING PARTY'S CANCELLATION

Plotnick v. Pennsylvania Smelting & Refining Co.

(Lead Dealer) v. (Lead Buyer)

United States Court of Appeals, Third Circuit, 194 F.2d 859 (1952).

M E M O R Y   G R A P H I C

Instant Facts

A seller of battery lead, after entering into a series of agreements to sell and deliver a specified amount of lead to a buyer in installments by December, sues the buyer for failing to pay on the third installment, which was delivered three months past the December deadline, and the buyer counterclaims for the seller's failure to deliver the balance of lead due under the contract.

Black Letter Rule

A seller may justifiably refuse to proceed under a contract for the delivery and payment of goods in installments, when a buyer's failure to pay for one of the installments constitutes a material breach, by making it financially impossible or unreasonably burdensome for the seller to continue, or by creating a reasonable apprehension with respect to payments for future installments.

Case Vocabulary

SIGHT DRAFT: A written order directing another person to pay a third person (e.g. a check), upon the holder's demand or upon a proper specified showing.

Procedural Basis: Appeal to the United States Court of Appeals, of a judgment by the district court awarding damages for a buyer's failure to pay for a delivered installment, and for a seller's failure to deliver remaining installments.

Facts: Plotnick (P), a Canadian dealer of battery lead, entered into a series of agreements with Pennsylvania Smelting & Refining Co. (Pennsylvania Smelting) (D), between June and October of 1947. Under these contracts, Plotnick (P) made a number of lead shipments to Pennsylvania Smelting (D) in Philadelphia. Plotnick (P) often complained, with justification, that payments were overly delayed. On the other hand, several shipments were not made at the times required by the contract. Nevertheless, by the end of March 1948, all contracts other than the one in suit had been fully performed by both parties. The contract in suit was executed on October 23, 1947, and called for deliveries totaling 200 tons of battery lead before December 25, 1947. The agreed price was 8.1 cents per pound or more if quality warranted it. Sixty-three percent of this price was to be paid shortly after each shipment was delivered, and the balance within four weeks after that delivery. The earliest shipment involved in this suit, the third under the contract, was a carload received on March 23, 1948, which followed a March 12 conference by the parties. At that time, about 290,000 pounds of lead were still to be delivered under the contract despite being well past the agreed upon deadline. After the conference, one carload of 43,000 pounds was delivered, but not paid for. It is not disputed that Plotnick (P) is entitled to the price of this shipment. On April 27, Pennsylvania Smelting (D) informed Plotnick (P) that he would buy in the open market and charge them any cost in excess of 8.1 cents per pound, unless they delivered the balance of the lead within thirty days. On April 10, Plotnick (P) replied refusing to ship unless the third carload was paid for. On May 12, Pennsylvania Smelting (D) threatened to sue unless the undelivered lead was promptly shipped, and promised to pay 75 percent of this shipment along with the full price of the third shipment already received. On May 22, Plotnick (P) replied that the contract was regarded as cancelled, but that it was willing to deliver at the originally agreed price if the overdue payment was tendered with a letter of credit established to cover the price of the lead not yet shipped. On May 25, Pennsylvania Smelting (D) replied that it was withholding the price of the third carload as a set-off due to Plotnick's (P) failure to deliver, and that it would place the overdue payment in escrow and accept the remaining lead if shipped. A sight draft was attached to this reply for the full invoice price of each car. On May 27, Plotnick (P) reiterated its position and on June 2, notified Pennsylvania Smelting (D) that the Canadian government had imposed export control on lead. Plotnick (P) sued to recover the price of the third carload, and Pennsylvania Smelting (D) counterclaimed for damages caused by the failure to deliver the balance of lead. The district court first found that between October 1947 and May 1948, the market price of battery lead increased from 8.1 cents to 11½ cents per pound. It then allowed recovery on both the claim and the counterclaim, concluding that while Pennsylvania Smelting's (d) failure to make a down payment for the third carload constituted a breach, the breach was not material enough to justify Plotnick's (P) refusal to ship the balance due under the contract within the meaning of section 45 of The Sales Act. Plotnick (P) appeals.

Issue: May a seller justifiably refuse to proceed under a contract for the delivery and payment of goods in installments, when a buyer's failure to pay for one of the installments constitutes a material breach?

Decision and Rationale: (Hastie, J.) Yes. Section 45 of the Sales Act provides, that in a contract to sell goods to be delivered and paid for in installments, where the buyer neglects or refuses to pay for one or more installments, the terms of the contract and the circumstances of each case determine whether the breach of contract is so material that it justifies the injured party's refusal to proceed, or whether the breach is severable, giving rise to a claim for compensation but not to a right to treat the whole contract broken. In determining the legal effect of non-payment in a particular case, the commercial sense of the statute yields two guiding considerations. First, non-payment for a delivered shipment may render it impossible or overly burdensome from a financial point of view for the seller to supply future installments. Second, non-payment may create such a reasonable apprehension in the seller's mind with respect to future installments, that the seller should not be required to take the risk involved in continuing deliveries. Thus, a seller may justifiably refuse to proceed under a contract for the delivery and payment of goods in installments, when a buyer's failure to pay for one of the installments constitutes a material breach, by making it financially impossible or unreasonably burdensome for the seller to continue, or by creating a reasonable apprehension with respect to payments for future installments. In the instant case, Plotnick (P) admits that he had sufficient lead on hand to fully perform the contract, and there is no evidence that the delay in payment for one carload made it difficult to provide additional lead. Moreover, the district had found that Plotnick's (P) fear that Pennsylvania Smelting (D) would not pay for the balance of battery lead due, was without foundation and unreasonable under the circumstances. The uncontroverted findings are that no impairment of Pennsylvania Smelting's (D) credit had been shown, and that Pennsylvania Smelting (D) urgently needed the undelivered lead because of the rising market. In fact, as early as March 1, before the delivery of the third carload, Pennsylvania Smelting (D) had complained quite urgently of the non-delivery of the entire balance overdue since December. Thereafter, when Plotnick (P) delivered only about one-seventh of what was due, Pennsylvania Smelting (P) insisted that it was withholding payment because of the delay in delivery of the overdue balance. Most importantly, evidence shows that Plotnick (P) had the privilege of shipping on sight draft but elected not to do so. Under these circumstances, it is incredible that Plotnick (P) would refuse to honor sight drafts for the contract price, and the district court was justified in concluding that Plotnick (P) had no valid reason to be fearful that payment would not be forthcoming upon full delivery. One other relevant fact is that Plotnick (P) was using his stock of lead in a rising market for sales to other purchasers, instead of for the full performance of this contract. Without a doubt, Plotnick's (P) desire to avoid a bad bargain, rather than apprehension, caused him to renounce the agreement and charge Pennsylvania Smelting (D) with repudiation. Thus, Plotnick (P) has failed to establish justification for recession under Section 45 of the Sales Act and the district court's judgment on the counterclaim was proper. Affirmed.

Analysis:

As you have already seen, the criteria for determining the materiality of a breach is unsettled. Therefore, as previously stated, it is necessary to analyze a breach according to the criteria which the court outlines, since this criteria will almost certainly vary from jurisdiction to jurisdiction, depending upon the circumstances of each case. In a UC Davis law review article written by Professor Eric G. Andersen, it is argued that a general failure to recognize "material breach" as a remedial concept is responsible for the difficulties in determining a criteria. He contends that since classifying a breach as "material" enables a party to cancel a contract, the definition of "material breach" should necessarily turn upon whether the cancellation is justified, or whether a party should be entitled to end the contract in response to a breach in light of the relevant facts. The court in the instant case does exactly that. In construing Pennsylvania Smelting's (D) non-payment as a non-material breach, the court focused on whether Plotnick (P) was justified in canceling the contract. Plotnick (P) had continually provided delayed deliveries, used their supplies to make deliveries under other, more profitable contracts, and most importantly, was not prevented from fulfilling his duties under the contract, nor had any reason to be apprehensive because of Pennsylvania's Smelting's (D) failure to pay. Thus, in light of these facts, the court refused to give Plotnick (P) the right of cancellation for a material breach, in accordance with the recognition that "material breach" is a remedial concept.

COURT OF APPEALS DISTINGUISHES BETWEEN ANTICIPATORY REPUDIATION AND STATEMENTS EXPRESSING DOUBT ABOUT PERFORMANCE

McCloskey & Co. v. Minweld Steel Co.

(General Contractor) v. (Subcontractor)

United States Court of Appeals, Third Circuit, 1955. 220 F.2d 101

Instant Facts

A subcontractor is accused of repudiating a contract despite their difficulty in getting supplies due to market and governmental forces beyond their control.

Black Letter Rule

Anticipatory repudiation can only be demonstrated by an absolute and unequivocal refusal to perform or a distinct and positive statement of an inability to do so.

Case Vocabulary

TOTAL BREACH: This is a phrase which is used interchangeably with the terms "substantial breach" or "material breach" and which carries the same connotation of a breach serious enough to result in legal liability and to release the other party from their obligations.

Procedural Basis: Appeal from a district court judgement for the defendant in a breach of contract action.

Facts: McCloskey & Co. (McCloskey) (P), a contractor, hired Minweld Steel Co. (Minweld) (D) as the steel subcontractor on a construction job. Minweld (D) agreed to supply and erect all of the structural steel for two buildings on which McCloskey (P) was working. The parties' contract stated that Minweld (D) could be terminated if they failed to supply enough materials for the job. Minweld (D) agreed to provide samples, drawings, and work schedules when they received the contract drawings or at McCloskey's (P) request. They further acknowledged that the delivery and installation of the steel was of the essence. The trouble began when McCloskey (P) sent the contract drawings to Minweld (D) in May of 1950. McCloskey (P) wanted to know how long it would take them to supply and erect the steel. Minweld (D) sent him a letter stating that the work would take until November 15th. As early as July, however, McCloskey (P) threatened to fire Minweld (D) if they did not assure him that they would have the necessary materials within thirty days. Minweld (D), unfortunately, was having problems buying steel. None of the major steel companies could fill their orders. In addition, the President of the United States further constricted the domestic steel market due to the outbreak of the Korean War in June. Minweld (D) informed McCloskey (P) of these problems and requested their help in lobbying the General State Authority for the necessary steel. McCloskey (P) took this as a repudiation of Minweld's (D) ability to perform their obligations and sued them for breach of contract. The district court found for Minweld (D). McCloskey (P) appeals.

Issue: Can a party be guilty of anticipatory repudiation for announcing difficulties which might preclude them from performing on the contract?

Decision and Rationale: (McLaughlin) No. This case is in federal court by way of diversity jurisdiction. Pennsylvania state law applies since the contract was executed there. In that regard, in order for a repudiation to rise to the level of breach of contract, there must be an "absolute and unequivocal refusal to perform or a distinct and positive statement of an inability to do so." Even if a party does nothing in preparation for performance which is due at a later date, it is not tantamount to a repudiation of the contract. In this case, Minweld (D) simply explained the difficulties that they were having. At no time did they refuse to perform the contract or suggest that performance would be impossible for them. They justifiably looked to McCloskey for help and were denied. In fact, McCloskey (P) was able to procure the necessary steel from two different manufacturers in order to have the work completed. One of their suppliers, Bethlehem Steel, was actually in competition with Minweld (D) for the original contract and refused to supply Minweld (D) with steel when they requested it. Nonetheless, McCloskey (P) argues that Minweld (D) specifically repudiated the deadline that McCloskey (P) announced in his July letter. Suffice it to say that Minweld (D) no more repudiated that deadline than they did the entire contract. In any event, there is nothing in the contract which entitles McCloskey (P) to set a deadline for Minweld's (D) assurance of completion. As a result, Minweld's (D) letter does not constitute an anticipatory repudiation of their contract with McCloskey (P). The judgement of the district court will be upheld.

Analysis:

Pennsylvania's law regarding anticipatory repudiation is typical of most states. Generally, repudiation cannot be assumed from comments which merely place the party's performance in doubt. In fact, the repudiation must be so far-reaching as to offer the injured party a remedy for a total breach of contract. This rule makes sense if you consider the consequences of a more liberal approach. In the above case, for instance, the court was well aware that Minweld (D) sought McCloskey's (P) help in completing the contract and that McCloskey (P) refused. Instead, McCloskey (P) took the first sign of trouble as an excuse to discontinue his own performance. This approach does not advance the goal of securing transactions in a competitive marketplace. On the contrary, it would unleash the worst behavior of the parties, each seeking to cut and run whenever a contract became the least bit burdensome or unprofitable. You should be aware that the Restatement (Second) of Contracts § 251 now permits a party to an agreement to demand assurances of performance from the other party. If the other party does not respond within a reasonable time, the failure may constitute a repudiation of the contract. In this case, the new rule could easily have worked to Minweld's (D) disadvantage.

K & G Construction Co. v. Harris

(General Contractor) v. (Subcontractor)

Court of Appeals of Maryland, 223 Md. 305, 164 A.2d 451 (1960).

MEMORY GRAPHIC

Instant Facts

A general contractor ceased making installment payments to a subcontractor after the subcontractor accidentally damaged part of a building on the project and refused to pay for repairs.

Black Letter Rule

A failure of one party's performance that amounts to a material breach of the agreement will excuse the other party's nonperformance.

Case Vocabulary

MUTUALLY DEPENDENT PROMISES: Promises in a contract that the parties intend to be conditioned each upon the performance of the other.

TIME IS OF THE ESSENCE: A common clause in contracts used to demonstrate the necessity of the promises contained therein being performed by a specific time or without undue delay.

Procedural Basis: Appeal from a trial court verdict in favor of the defendant subcontractor in a breach of contract action.

Facts: K&G Construction Company (K&G) (P) was a general contractor on a construction project. K&G (P) subcontracted the excavating and earth-moving portion of the project to Harris and Brooks (Harris) (D). The contract called for Harris (D) to do the necessary work without delay, time being of the essence, at the bidding of K&G (P) as the general contractor, and in a workmanlike manner. Harris (D) was to obtain adequate liability insurance against property damage and provide K&G (P) with the certificates necessary to prove that such insurance had been obtained. The contract also provided that K&G (P) would make monthly installment payments to Harris (D). Harris (D) was to submit an invoice on the 25th of each month for the work done that month. K&G (P) was then supposed to pay Harris (D) by the 10th of the following month. On August 9, during the course of the project, a bulldozer operator working for Harris (D) accidentally drove his machine into the wall of a house and caused $3,400 in damage. Harris (D) submitted a claim to its insurance provider but the insurance company denied liability. Afterward, Harris (D) refused to pay for the damage, claiming that it was not liable for the damage. Up until that point, K&G (P) had been satisfied with the quality of Harris' (D) work. K&G (P) refused to make the installment payment due Harris (D) on August 10 for $1,484.50 because of the damage to the wall of the building. Harris (D) continued to work until September 12, after which date it refused to work anymore until K&G (P) paid the installments it had withheld. K&G (P) requested Harris (D) to continue working, but Harris (D) refused. K&G (P) filed suit against Harris (D) to recover the cost of repairing the damage to the house wall and to recover $450 in damages representing the cost above the contract price that K&G (P) had to pay to get the excavating work done by a substitute subcontractor. Harris (D) filed a counterclaim seeking payment for the work completed and lost profits. Each party claimed that the other had repudiated the contract. A jury found in favor of K&G (P) on the liability claim for damage to the wall and awarded the full $3,400 cost of repair. The other issues were tried before the court without a jury and the trial court found in favor of Harris (D). K&G (P) appealed.

Issue: Will a material breach of an agreement by one party excuse the other party's duty to perform?

Decision and Rationale: (Brune, C.J.) Yes. The question in this case must be what the rights and liabilities of the parties were under the provisions of the contract providing all work be done in a workmanlike manner with time of the essence. Harris (D) contends that K&G's (P) failure to make the installment payment on August 10 constituted a material breach and excused Harris (D) from further performance. We do not agree. More persuasive is K&G's (P) argument that it was Harris (D) that materially breached the contract on August 9 by failing to perform its work in the workmanlike manner required under the contract. It was Harris (D), and not K&G (P) who first breached the contract. As a result, Harris (D) had no right to cease performance on September 12, and doing so constituted yet another breach, which made it liable to K&G (P) for further damages. K&G (P) had a right to refuse to make the installment payment due on August 10. It is clear from the contract language that the promises to perform were mutually dependent, with Harris's (D) performance (the work) to precede K&G's (P) performance (payment). Thus, K&G's (P) duty to pay was conditioned upon Harris's (D) having performed the work in a workmanlike manner and submitting an invoice therefor. Harris (D) did not so perform and that fact constituted a material breach of its obligations. Such a breach excused K&G (P) from its duty to render payment. Alternatively, Harris's (D) later refusal to continue work was itself a wrongful repudiation and was unexcused. K&G (P) had the option to treat the

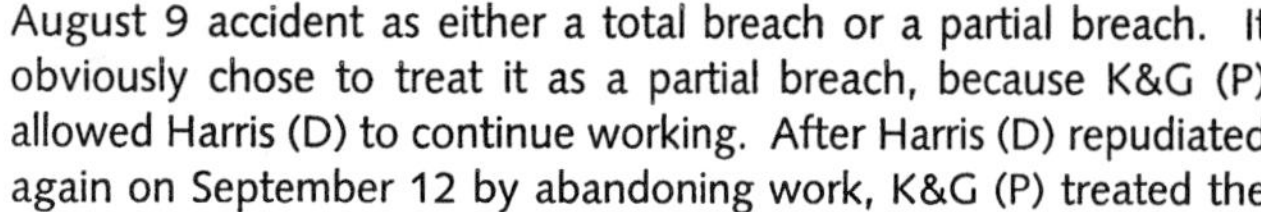

August 9 accident as either a total breach or a partial breach. It obviously chose to treat it as a partial breach, because K&G (P) allowed Harris (D) to continue working. After Harris (D) repudiated again on September 12 by abandoning work, K&G (P) treated the second repudiation as a total breach and was therefore justified in seeking damages. K&G (P) should recover $450 representing the increased cost to it to find a replacement subcontractor to do the work Harris (D) was obligated by contract to do. Reversed.

Analysis:

This is yet another example of a party mistakenly believing that the other has breached the contract and subsequently breaching it himself by ceasing performance. As if you haven't heard it enough—be extremely careful about counseling a client about the propriety of ceasing performance under a contract. When contract performances are conditioned upon each other and one party fails to substantially perform, the other party is excused from performance. The failure to substantially perform is a material breach of the contract. Any material breach of a contract will excuse performance by the non-breaching party. That's the general rule. The problem is, it is not always easy to determine what kinds of activities constitute a material breach. Your client may believe that the other party has materially breached and so might feel justified in ceasing performance. You might agree. But if the two of you are wrong—your client could himself be liable for breaching the contract and you could have opened yourself up to a malpractice suit. [A very ugly situation!]

Gill v. Johnstown Lumber Co.

(Lumber Driver) v. (Lumber Mill)
Supreme Court of Pennsylvania, 1892. 151 Pa. 534, 25 A. 120

M E M O R Y G R A P H I C

Instant Facts

A lumber driver requests full payment for his work, despite losing a percentage of his client's logs.

Black Letter Rule

If a contract is severable, as opposed to entire, then payment may be requested for the measure of performance which was completed.

Case Vocabulary

ASSUMPSIT: An action for the recovery of damages due to a breach of contract.
ENTIRE: A contract is "entire" when a single payment is promised for the performance of all of its terms.
SEVERABLE: A contract is "severable" when payment is divided among the terms of the contract. In that event, a party can recover payment for part performance. This rule is subject to the limitations which are discussed above.
VENIRE FACIAS DE NOVO: An order for a new jury. This order may be given after some irregularity or impropriety in the original jury's conduct or verdict. A court ordering a new jury is, in essence, ordering a new trial.

Procedural Basis: Appeal from a trial court directed verdict for the defendant in a breach of contract action.

Facts: Gill (P), a lumber driver, had an agreement with Johnstown Lumber Co. (Johnstown) (D) to deliver a load of logs and cross-ties to a variety of locations, including Johnstown's (D) mill. The delivery was to be made by river from certain specified points of departure to specified locations. In addition, Johnstown (D) promised to pay Gill (P) rates which varied according to the types of logs and the delivery destinations. Unfortunately, a flood hit while Gill (P) was delivering the logs and he permitted a large percentage of them to float past Johnstown's (D) mill. Undaunted, he sued Johnstown (D) in assumpsit for the money he was owed under the contract. The trial court directed a verdict for Johnstown (D), holding that the contract was entire -- in other words, not subject to a disaggregation of obligations and payment that would permit partial recovery. Gill (P) appeals.

Issue: Can a contract which is "entire" give rise to a recovery for a party tendering incomplete performance?

Decision and Rationale: (Heydrick) No. However, the contract in this case is not entire. A contract is entire if only one payment is made for the completion of performance. It does not matter whether a single act is promised, or if several distinct acts make up the completed performance. On the other hand, a contract is severable if it divides payment up among several distinct acts which constitute performance. The contract is also severable if it does not specify how payment is to be made for these distinct acts. In this case, Gill (P) had a variety of responsibilities. He had to deliver logs made of different woods to different locations. He also had to deliver cross-ties to varying locations. The contract specifically apportioned payment among the types of wood, cross-ties, and shipping locations. As a result, the agreement is severable, not entire. Accordingly, Gill (P) is entitled to payment for the work completed. He is not, however, entitled to payment for the logs which were lost. Johnstown (D) promised to pay for all of the lumber which was delivered. They should not have to pay for lumber which was not delivered. However, since Gill (P) is otherwise entitled to compensation, the judgement of the trial court is reversed and a *venire facias de novo* is ordered.

Analysis:

A contract which is severable is also called "divisible." A court's interpretation of a contract as divisible is much like the determination of substantial performance in that there is no set rule determining the outcome. According to the Restatement, courts should determine whether the elements of performance can be paired up with a promise of payment. For instance, in the above case, Johnstown (D) promised to pay $1 per thousand feet of oak logs delivered. Gill (P) promised to deliver the logs for that amount. It is easy to see this pair of promises functioning as an individual mini-agreement within the contract. In addition, the court must determine whether it is appropriate to treat the pair of promises as "agreed equivalents." This means that the promises which were exchanged are worth the same to the parties regardless of the rest of the contract. If Johnstown's (D) oak logs, for instance, were worthless to them if the pine logs were not delivered, then it seems unfair to make them pay for the delivery of the oak logs. This item is not severable because Johnstown's (D) promise to pay for the delivery is now worth more to Gill (P) than his promise to deliver the remaining logs -- they are no longer agreed equivalents. This is simply another way of saying that the parties are not getting what they bargained for. This is clearly a consequence which, like other issues of fairness, preoccupies courts in their decision-making.

PURCHASERS ARE ALLOWED TO RESCIND THEIR PURCHASE AGREEMENT FOR A NEW VAN, AFTER THE AUTODEALER FAILS TO CURE DEFECTS IN THE VAN UPON DELIVERY

Ramirez v. Autosport

(Van Buyer) v. (Defective Van Seller)
Supreme Court of New Jersey, 88 N.J. 277, 440 A.2d 1345 (1982).

M E M O R Y   G R A P H I C

Instant Facts

Would-be purchasers of a mobile home institute an action against an auto dealership seeking a rescission of the purchase agreement and restitution, due to the auto dealership's failure to cure defects in the mobile home after two rejections by the purchasers.

Black Letter Rule

A buyer may reject the tender or delivery of goods that do not conform to what was contracted for, but may only cancel if the seller fails to cure the defective goods within a reasonable period of time.

Case Vocabulary

CANCELLATION: The termination of a contract that discharges the remaining obligations of either party, the right to which arises only after a seller fails to cure imperfect tender or delivery within a reasonable time after rejection by the buyer in a contract for the sale of goods.
CURE: The act of remedying goods that do not conform to a contract, either by removing defects from the rejected goods or by substitution of acceptable goods.
REJECTION: The right to refuse the tender or delivery of goods for any nonconformity to the contract.

Procedural Basis: Appeal to the Supreme Court of New Jersey, of a decision by the court of appeals, affirming the trial court's judgment in favor of the plaintiff in an action for restitution and rescission of a purchase agreement for a van.

Facts: On July 20, 1978, following a mobile home show and after visiting Autosport's (D) showroom, Mr. and Mrs. Ramirez (the Ramirezes) (P) and Donald Graff (Graff), an Autosport (D) salesman, agreed to the sale of a new camper and the trade-in of the Ramirezes' (P) van. Both parties signed a contract reflecting a $14,100 purchase price for the new van with a $4,700 trade-in allowance, which the Ramirezes (P) left with Autosport (D). The net price of the new camper was about $9,902. On August 3, after giving Autosport (D) two weeks to prepare the new van, the Ramirezes (P) returned with their checks. Upon inspection of the van, several defects were disclosed, including scratched paint, missing electric and sewer hookups, and uninstalled hubcaps. Another Autosport (D) salesman advised the Ramirezes (P) not to accept the camper because it was not ready. Afterwards, the Ramirezes (P) called several times, and each time Graff told them that the van was not ready. Finally, on August 14, the Ramirezes (P) went to Autosport (D) to accept delivery after being notified by Graff that the van was ready. However, when they arrived, workers were still touching up the outside paint and the dining area cushions were soaking wet. Mr. Leis, Autosport's (D) manager, suggested that the van be taken and that Autosport (D) would replace the cushions later. The Ramirezes (P) counter-offered to accept the van if they could withhold $2,000, but Leis agreed to no more than $250. The Ramirezes (P) refused and Leis agreed to replace the cushions and to tell them when the van was ready. On August 15, unbeknownst to the Ramirezes (P), title of the van was transferred to them. The Ramirezes (P) continually called Graff, and were finally informed that the van was ready on September 1. The Ramirezes (P) went to the showroom and after being asked to wait by Graff and subsequently waiting for one and a half hours, the Ramirezes (P) left in disgust. They returned on October 5th with an attorney friend in order to discuss whether they should proceed with the deal or whether Autosport (D) should return Ramirezes' trade-in. While the Ramirezes (P) claimed that they rejected the new van and requested the return of their trade-in, Mr. Lustig, Autosport's (D) owner, believed that the deal could be salvaged if the parties could agree on the dollar amount of a credit for the Ramirezes (P). Later in October, Autosport (D) sold the trade-in to a third party for $4,995. Autosport (D) claimed that the trade-in had a book value of $3,200 and that it had spent $1,159.62 on repairs, resulting in a profit of $600-$700. On November 20, the Ramirezes (P) sued Autosport (D) seeking, among other things, rescission of the contract, and Autosport (D) counterclaimed for breach of contract. The trial court found that the Ramirezes (P) rightfully rejected the van and awarded them the fair market value of their trade-in van. The Appellate Division affirmed. Autosport (P) appeals to the Supreme Court of New Jersey.

Issue: May a buyer reject the tender or delivery of goods that do not conform to what was contracted for?

Decision and Rationale: (Pollock, J.) Yes. Originally, sellers were required to deliver goods that complied exactly with the agreement, or in other words, the seller was under a duty to make a "perfect tender." Leaving no room for the doctrine of substantial performance in commercial contracts, the harshness of this rule lead courts to seek to ameliorate its effects and to bring the law of sales in closer harmony with the law of contracts, which allows rescission only in cases of material breach. To the extent a buyer can reject goods for any nonconformity, the Uniform Commercial Code (U.C.C.) retains the perfect tender rule, but mitigates the harshness of the rule through its provisions for revocation of acceptance and cure. Under the U.C.C., the rights of each party vary depending on when the rejection occurs. While the buyer may reject goods for any nonconformity before acceptance, the rejection does not necessarily discharge the contract because of a seller's right to cure. Within the time set for performance in the contract, the seller's right to cure is unconditional. If a rejection occurs after the time set for performance, the seller has a further reasonable time to cure, as determined by the surrounding circumstances, if he or she believed that goods would be acceptable. Surrounding circumstances include the change in the buyer's position, the amount of inconvenience to the buyer, the length of time needed for correction, and the seller's ability to salvage the goods by resale to others. After acceptance, a buyer may only revoke if the nonconformity substantially impairs the value of goods to him. We conclude that while the perfect tender rule is preserved to the extent of permitting a buyer to reject goods for any defects, that rejection will not terminate the contract in light of the seller's right to cure. However, we must still determine the remedy available to a buyer who rejects goods with insubstantial defects, when the seller fails to cure within a reasonable time. Under the UCC, a buyer who rightfully rejects has the right to cancel with respect to the goods involved. Although neither "rejection" nor "revocation of acceptance," are defined in the U.C.C., rejection includes both the buyer's refusal to accept or keep delivered goods, and his notification to the seller that he will not keep them. Revocation of acceptance, while similar to rejection, occurs after the buyer's acceptance of the goods, and is intended to provide the same relief as rescission of a contract for the sale of goods. Thus, subject to a seller's right to cure, a buyer who rightfully rejects goods, just like a person who revokes his acceptance, may cancel the contract. In the instant case, the Ramirezes (P) sought not only rescission of the contract, but also restoration to their pre-contractual position, which incorporates the equitable doctrine of restitution. General contract law permits rescission only for "material breaches", which is termed "substantial impairment" under the UCC. Although the UCC permits cancellation by rejection for minor defects, it only permits revocation for substantial impairments. Once a buyer accepts goods, he or she has the burden of proving any defect. However, where goods are rejected for not conforming to the contract, the burden is on the seller to prove correction. The UCC recognizes that the purchase of goods is no longer a simple transaction, and that buyers no longer expect a "perfect tender," but rather expect that defective goods will either be repaired or replaced by the seller. Accordingly, the UCC permits a seller to cure imperfect tenders, and shifts the balance in favor of the buyer, who may elect to cancel or seek damages when a seller fails to cure the defects. In this case, although the trial court did not determine whether Autosport (D) cured the defects within a reasonable time, we find that Autosport (D) did not effect a cure, as the van was not ready for delivery during August, nor had Autosport (D) demonstrated that the van conformed to the contract on September 1st. Therefore, the trial court properly concluded that the Ramirezes (P) were entitled to rescind the contract. Since the trade-in was sold to an innocent third party, the trial court determined that the Ramirezes (P) were entitled to its fair market value, which the court set at the contract price of $4,700. Under the UCC, a buyer who rightfully rejects good and cancels the contract, may recover so much of the purchase price as has been paid. The term "pay" is not defined, does not require payment in cash, and therefore includes the common method of partial payment for automobiles by "trade-in." When concerned with used automobiles, the trade-in market is an acceptable, and perhaps most appropriate market in which to measure damages, because the parties had contracted in this market. In other circumstances, other means of calculating damages may be appropriate. We have defined fair market value as the price at which the property would be exchanged between a willing buyer and a willing seller, who both have reasonable knowledge of relevant facts. Though the value of the trade-in as set forth in the sales contract was not the only possible standard, it is an appropriate measure of the fair market value. Affirmed.

Analysis:

This case provides a detailed explanation of how the U.C.C. protects the interest of both parties to a contract, and generally reiterates the policies illustrated in the previous cases, but this time with respect to a contract for the sale of goods. Specifically, similar to the rule that non-performance, whether material or immaterial, will be considered a breach, under § 2-601 of the U.C.C, a buyer has the right to reject the tender of goods that do not "perfectly" conform to the contract. However, under § 2-508, when a seller's tender or delivery before the time for performance is due, is rejected as less than perfect, the seller is given time to cure any defects. Furthermore, even if the delivery or rejection was made subsequent to the time performance is due, a seller may still have a reasonable time to cure, as long the seller had reasonable grounds to believe that his or her tender would have been acceptable. Therefore, a buyer's right of cancellation will only rise when the seller fails to cure within a reasonable time, just like a party's right to rescind a contract only arises when the breach is material. As you have certainly noticed, the provisions of the Restatement (Second) of Contract and the provisions of the U.C.C., parallel each other in most respects. All in all, as the court explicitly states, this case provides an example of how the law of sales is harmonized with the law of contracts.

A FARMER IS HELD TO BE "ENFORCING" A CONTRACT BY EXERCISING HIS OPTION TO TERMINATE

Baker v. Ratzlaff

(Popcorn Distributor) v. (Popcorn Harvester)

Court of Appeals of Kansas, 1 Kan.App.2d 285, 564 P.2d 153 (1977).

M E M O R Y G R A P H I C

Instant Facts

A popcorn harvester is found to have breached his obligation of good faith in exercising his options under a sales contract with a popcorn distributor, by enforcing a termination clause after the distributor failed to pay for delivered popcorn, despite the harvester's failure to request or demand payment.

Black Letter Rule

Parties to a contract are obligated to deal fairly and in good faith with each other when enforcing provisions of the contract.

Case Vocabulary

BAD FAITH: Conduct which violates the relevant community standards of fairness, decency, or reasonableness.

GOOD FAITH AND FAIR DEALING: An obligation imposed in every contract, which requires each party to act honestly, fairly, and consistently with the justified expectations of the other party.

Procedural Basis: Both parties appeal to the Court of Appeals of Kansas, a judgment by the trial court awarding plaintiff damages for defendant's breach of his obligation of good faith and fair dealing in enforcing a contract.

Facts: In 1973, Ratzlaff (D), a farmer, agreed to raise 380 acres of popcorn and deliver it to Baker's (P) plant in Texas. In exchange, Baker (P) a buyer and distributor of popcorn, agreed to provide seed popcorn and to purchase the popcorn from Ratzlaff (D) at a price of $4.75 per hundredweight. Baker (P) was to order delivery of one-third of the crop by March 30, 1974, another one-third by June 30, and the balance by September 30. Among other provisions, paragraph 12 of the contract provided that Baker (P) would pay for the corn, storage fees, "in and out charges, transportation charges, and the accrued interest on each bushel of corn as delivered." In addition, paragraph 13 provided that if Baker (P), "for any reason, fails neglects, or refuses to pay [Ratzlaff (D)]...at the time of delivery," then Baker (P) would release the remaining popcorn in Ratzlaff's (D) possession so that Ratzlaff (D) could retain or dispose of it as he wishes. Upon Baker's (P) request, Ratzlaff (D) and his employee delivered one truckload of popcorn on February 2, and another on February 4, to Baker's (P) plant. Both times, Baker's (P) plant manager, Martin, gave Ratzlaff (D) a weight ticket, but payment for the popcorn was neither asked for nor given. During the week of February 4, Martin telephoned Ratzlaff (D) to enquire about further deliveries, and Ratzlaff (D) later informed Martin and Baker (P) that he was having equipment problems and that his employee was ill. Again, no discussion of payment occurred. On February 11, Ratzlaff (D) sent a written notice of termination of the contract claiming that Baker (P) had breached by failing to pay upon delivery. The next day, after receiving the notice, Baker (P) sent the payment for the two loads already delivered. Ratzlaff (D), however, had already entered into a contract with a third party for the sale of the balance of the popcorn at $8.00 per hundredweight, which was later performed by Ratzlaff's (D) delivery of 1,600,000 pounds of popcorn. Martin testified that, as a usual practice, copies of the weight tickets were sent to Baker's (P) business office in Garden City, Kansas, where checks were written and mailed. However, Martin could not recall when he had sent the weight tickets for Ratzlaff's (D) two deliveries. Ratzlaff (D) testified that at the time he contracted with the third party, popcorn was selling for $8.00, the commodity market price was between $7.00 and $7.25, and that after the 1974 harvest, popcorn was selling for around $14.00. Baker (P) testified that he had to pay $10.30 for some replacement popcorn. Among other things, the trial court found that Ratzlaff (D) knew or should have known that Baker's (P) business office was in Garden City, that in the normal course of events, payment would be made from that office, and that because the office is on a direct route from Baker's (P) plant to Ratzlaff's (D) farm, nothing prevented him from stopping off to obtain payment. Moreover, evidence disclosed that any request for payment would have been handled promptly since Baker (P) had ample funds, and that the only reason payment was not made was due to Ratzlaff's (D) failure to request it. The trial court also found that the price of popcorn had risen sharply, making it more profitable for Ratzlaff (D) to find some way to get out of the contract. The trial court awarded Baker (P) $52,000 in damages, representing the value of 1,600,000 pounds at $3.25 per hundredweight, the difference between the contract price of $4.75 and an $8.00 price. Both parties appeal. Ratzlaff (D) contends that the trial court erred in its finding that he breached the contract, and Baker (P) contests the amount awarded to him.

Issue: Does a party have an unrestricted right to exercise the enforcement provisions provided in a contract?

Decision and Rationale: (Rees, J.) No. Parties to a contract are obligated to deal fairly and in good faith with each other when enforcing provisions of the contract. The trial concluded that Ratzlaff (D) had breached his duty of good faith and fair dealing with Baker (P) by declaring a termination of the contract upon a technical pretense. The trial court further concluded that interpreting the contract to require immediate payment upon delivery, without a request or demand, would result in an unconscionable and unenforceable contract. Ratzlaff (D) maintains that he was not under a good faith obligation because termination is not "performance" or "enforcement" of a contract, and that nevertheless termination was made in good faith. However, the termination clause in paragraph 13 does not permit termination at will, but only upon a failure to pay upon delivery. This right to terminate and retain or dispose of the balance of the popcorn is inseparable from the "enforcement" of substantive provisions of the contract, and therefore may not exempt from an obligation of good faith. Furthermore, Ratzlaff's (D) failure to demand payment after delivery of either of the two loads, his failure to demand payment during the subsequent telephone conversations with Baker (P) and Martin, and his hasty resale of the popcorn to another for a higher price, provided substantial competent evidence to support the trial court's finding that Ratzlaff (D) had breached his obligation of good faith. Affirmed.

Analysis:

This case provides an introduction to the section on agreed enforcement terms. It illustrates that the enforcement rights, powers, and contractual remedies provided by law, and explained in the previous sections, are not exclusive. Parties to a contract have the option of restricting or expanding these rights by mutual agreement. However, as you can see from the instant case, courts will refrain from allowing a party to exercise his or her rights under a contract, when such actions conflict with a party's obligation to act in good faith. The U.C.C. § 1-203, provides further protection of the contractual interest of each party, by imposing an obligation of good faith in the performance or enforcement of every contract. Between merchants, good faith is defined as "honesty in fact and the observance of reasonable commercial standards of fair dealing in trade." Accordingly, a party's performance under a contract that is deemed to be in "bad faith," for violating community standards of reasonableness or fairness, will constitute a breach of contract. Furthermore, as in this case, acts of bad faith when enforcing the provisions of a contract will disable a party's ability to exercise these enforcements rights or powers.

JURY INSTRUCTIONS ALLOWING THE AUTOMATIC ENFORCEMENT OF AN ACCELERATION CLAUSE WITHOUT THE REQUIREMENT OF GOOD FAITH ARE HELD ERRONEOUS

Brown v. AVEMCO Investment Corp.

(Plane Owners) v. (Plane Mortgagers)

United States Court of Appeals, Ninth Circuit, 603 F.2d 1367 (1979).

M E M O R Y G R A P H I C

Instant Facts

Mortgagees of an airplane institute an action for conversion against the mortgager, after mortgager exercises its option to accelerate payments for breach of contract's "no-lease-without-consent" provision, repossesses the airplane, and sells it.

Black Letter Rule

When exercising an option to accelerate payments for a breach under an acceleration provision, a creditor must have a good faith belief that the prospect of future payments or its security interest has been impaired.

Case Vocabulary

ACCELERATION CLAUSE: A contract provision that allows a party to accelerate payment or performance obligations upon the occurrence of a specified event, such as a breach by the other party.

Procedural Basis: Appeal to United States Court of Appeals, of judgment by the trial court in a diversity action for conversion of an airplane, i favor of the defendants.

Facts: On September 22, 1972 Robert Herriford (Robert) borrowed $6,50 from AVEMCO Investment Corporation (AVEMCO) (D) and executed promissory note for $9,607.92 which included interest and credit for insurance Robert secured the note by an agreement granting AVEMCO (D) a securit interest in an airplane. The security agreement contained an acceleration claus that generally provided that any principal sum unpaid, including any accrue interest, would become due and payable immediately at the option of AVEMCC (D), if Robert defaulted in any of the payments, if the plane were sold, leasec transferred, mortgaged, or otherwise encumbered without AVEMCO's (D consent, or if for any reason AVEMCO (D) deemed itself insecure. On July 4 1973, Robert entered into a lease and option agreement with the three plaintiff whereby the plaintiffs would pay hourly rentals and contribute equally towards th payment of Robert's debt. Upon completion of the plane's mortgage payments the plaintiff's would have the option to purchase one-fourth ownership of th plane. Plaintiffs became co-insured with Robert, and copies of this policy wer sent to AVEMCO (D). On July 9, 1975, after two years of continual payment, th plaintiffs advised AVEMCO (D) that they had exercised their option with Robert and tendered the $4,3859.93 still owed by Robert. AVEMCO (D) refused thi offer and informed Robert that they were accelerating the payments because hi failure to comply with the note and security agreement, which was due an payable before July 28. According to AVEMCO (D) the entire balance total $5,078.97, after adding an additional amount to reimburse AVEMCO (D) of it purchase of "Vendor's Single Interest Insurance." One of the plaintiff subsequently informed AVEMCO (D) that that its rejection of the tender was no accepted, and that the money to satisfy the debt would be available to AVEMCC (D) at the First Security Bank of Bozeman, Montana, upon presentation of satisfaction of the mortgage. Around July 30, 1975, AVEMCO's (D) agent use a passkey to start the plane and flew to Seattle. AVEMCO (D) then informe Robert of the repossession, and demanded that payment be made by August 10 1975, or the plane would be sold with the proceeds to be applied to sale expense and Roberts' account. On August 15, 1975, the plaintiffs filed an action fo conversion, and AVEMCO (D) counterclaimed charging interference with contrac rights. On August 25, 1975, the plane was sold for $7,000 and a bill of sale fo the plane was subsequently filed with the Federal Aviation Agency on Septembe 22, 1975. The jury returned a verdict in favor of AVEMCO (D) on both the clain and counter-claim, but no damages were assessed. Both AVEMCO's (D subsequent motion for judgment notwithstanding the verdict and the plaintiff' subsequent motion for a new trial were denied, and the plaintiffs appeal.

Issue: Must a creditor have a good faith belief that the prospect of futur payments or its security interest will be impaired by a breach, before exercising it option to accelerate payments under a contract?

Decision and Rationale: (Ferguson, J.) Yes. When exercising an option to accelerate payments for a breach under an acceleration provision, creditor must have a good faith belief that the prospect of future payments or it security interest has been impaired. AVEMCO's (D) complete disregard of th plaintiff's offer, even if the offer may not have met the legal requirements of valid tender, and their eagerness to accelerate payment, repossess the plane an sell it, should have prompted an examination of fairness. This duty is impose both in equity and under the Uniform Commercial Code (UCC), and the plaintiff sought its protection by proposing to instruct the jury that acceleration could on be done if AVEMCO (D) believed in good faith that its security interest was impaired by the breach of the security agreement. However, the trial court erroneously rejected this, and instead instructed the jury that there could be an automatic enforcement of the acceleration clause as long as the technical breach of a "lease without consent" was found. Acceleration clauses are designed to protect the creditor from actions by the debtor which jeopardize the creditor's security, and are not to be used offensively for say, commercial advantage. It is a matter of equity, and Texas courts have long required, that these clauses be reasonable in light of the facts. Similarly, the UCC imposes an obligation of good faith in the performance or enforcement of every contract or duty within the code under section 1-203. Furthermore, under section 1-208, the UCC imposes the good faith obligation to options to accelerate, by requiring that the accelerating party believe in good faith that the prospect of payment is impaired. Although the fifth circuit has applied Texas' version of section 1-208, to accelerations based on clauses that authorize acceleration when a creditor "deems himself insecure," a more difficult question is whether the statute applies to "default" accelerations as well. While the security agreement here contained both types of clauses, AVEMCO's (D) asserted basis for the acceleration is breach of the consent-for-lease provision. Although this question has not yet been answered by the Texas courts, the Utah Supreme Court has applied § 1-208 to accelerations authorized by an agreement which did not include any "deem itself insecure" language, recognizing that acceleration is a harsh remedy which should only be used if some reasonable justification exists. According to its language, § 1-208 applies when a party in interest may accelerate payment "at will" or "when he deems himself insecure." Because the agreement here provided that AVEMCO (D) may, at its option, accelerate payments upon a lease-without-consent, arguably § 1-208 applies. However, arguably an option to accelerate when the debtor leases without consent is different than one based on feelings of insecurity, since feelings of insecurity are subject to the whim and caprice of the creditor. The greatest concern of the drafters of § 1-208 was with possible abuse due to the uncontrolled will of the creditor. Accordingly, some may contend that § 1-208 only applies to "insecurity" clauses. While this type of clause may be the primary focus of § 1-208, we do not believe it is the only one. Abuse is also possible with options to accelerate based on a lease, which can be used as a sword for commercial gain rather than as a shield against security impairment. Section 1-208 provides protection from such abuse. The facts presented in the case at bar sufficiently suggest the possibility that AVEMCO (D) accelerated out of an inequitable desire to take advantage of a technical default. Indeed, acceleration based on a lease executed two years earlier is subject to significant suspicion. Furthermore, there was no suggestion that the prospect of payment was impaired. We find that the trial court's error in refusing to give instructions on acceleration which incorporated the UCC and equitable principles, prejudiced the plaintiffs. Reversed and remanded.

Analysis:

Like the previous case, the court here recognizes that each party has an obligation to act in good faith when enforcing a contract. However, this case deals specifically with the enforcement of acceleration provisions. These provisions deserve special attention because of its increasing use in, among other things, contracts for a sale on credit and security transactions. Accordingly, contractual provisions that allow a party to accelerate payments or performance, are explicitly dealt with under § 1-208 of the U.C.C. That section provides that "acceleration clauses," which allow a party to accelerate payment under an "at will" or similar provision, will enable a party to undertake such action only if he or she has a good faith belief that the prospect of payment or performance will be impaired. Importantly, this section should not be understood as applying only to "at will" or "deem himself insecure" type language. Under the U.C.C., any acceleration option must be exercised in the good faith belief that the prospect of payment or performance is impaired. Thus, in recognizing that even "default" acceleration provisions may be used contrary to the intent of the U.C.C., this court correctly imposed an obligation of good faith upon AVEMCO (D).

A NINETY-DAY ACCIDENTAL DEATH BENEFIT PROVISION OF AN INSURANCE POLICY IS HELD UNENFORCEABLE AS UNJUSTIFIED AND VIOLATIVE OF PUBLIC POLICY

Burne v. Franklin Life Insurance Co.

(Accident Victim) v. (Insurance Company)

Supreme Court of Pennsylvania, 451 Pa. 218, 301 A.2d 799 (1973).

MEMORY GRAPHIC

Instant Facts

The widow of an accident victim who died four and a half years after the accident, sues the life insurance company that issued the victim's insurance policy, which contained a double indemnity provision in cases of accidental death, after the insurance company refused to pay the accidental death benefits based on a provision requiring that death occur no more than 90 days after the accident.

Black Letter Rule

Provisions of a contract may be disregarded if found violative of public policy.

Case Vocabulary

PUBLIC POLICY: A standard of conduct or principles that are regarded as fundamental or of significant importance to society.

Procedural Basis: Appeal to the Supreme Court of Pennsylvania of an order by the Court of Common Pleas, granting defendant's motion for summary judgment in action for breach of an insurance contract.

Facts: In 1949, Franklin Life Insurance Co. (Franklin Life) (D), issued a life insurance policy to Bartholomew Burne in the face amount of $15,000, which contained a double indemnity proviso for an additional $15,000 for death resulting from purely accidental means. However, according to the policy, the accidental death benefits would only be payable if death occurred within ninety days from the date of the accident. The beneficiary of this policy was Mr. Burne's wife, Mrs Burne (P). On January 30, 1959, Mr. Burne was struck by an automobile while crossing the street. Immediate and extensive brain surgery was required, and for four and one-half years, vast sums of money were expended by Mrs. Burne (P) merely to keep Mr. Burne medically alive. However, from the moment of accident until his death, Mr. Burne remained in a vegetative state. Although Franklin Life (D) conceded that the injuries sustained were the direct and sole cause of Mr Burne's death, they only paid the face amount of the policy, and refused to pay the accidental death benefits pursuant to the policy's ninety-day exception. Mrs Burne (P) brought an action in assumpsit to recover the accidental death benefits under the policy, and the trial court granted Franklin Life's (D) motion for summary judgment based on the policy's ninety-day exception. Mrs. Burne (P) appeals.

Issue: Are provisions of a contract enforceable when they violate public policy?

Decision and Rationale: (Roberts, J.) No. Provisions of a contract may be disregarded if found violative of public policy. Here, strong public policy reasons militate against the enforceability of the ninety-day provision. Since the provision's origin, three decades of progress in the field of medicine have past. Physicians have since become startlingly adept at delaying death for indeterminate periods, and posses the awesome responsibility of sometimes deciding whether and what measures should be used to prolong an individual's life. The legal and ethical issues of this are extremely complex. The result reached by the trial court presents a gruesome paradox. While it would permit double indemnity recovery for accident victims that die instantly or within ninety days, it denies such recovery for the deaths of accident victims who endure the agony of prolonged illness and require greater expense in order to sustain life even ephemerally. This offends the basic concepts and fundamental objectives of life insurance and is contrary to public policy. The mental anguish that accompany these tragic occurrences should not be aggravated by concerns of whether the moment of death will permit defeat of the double indemnity claim. More importantly, decisions with respect to an accident victim's medical treatment, should be unhampered by considerations of financial penalties for successful care. These factors would be effectively removed by rejecting the arbitrary ninety-day provision. Furthermore, aside from public policy considerations, the ninety-day provision possesses no persuasive decisional support. The leading case construing this provision, *Sidebothom v. Metropolitan Life Insurance Co.*, is thirty years old, and in that case the insured suffered injuries from two different exposures to carbon monoxide, and from a fall from a hospital bed. This and other similar cases, found that the underlying purpose of the provision was to govern situations where there existed some possible uncertainty over whether the injuries sustained in accident would actually result in death. Ninety days was the arbitrary period advanced by the carrier within which to ascertain whether death will in fact result from the accident. *Sidebothom* is distinguishable from the instant case, and its interpretation of the ninety-day limitation, is based on considerations which have no pragmatic applicability to the factual situation here. In *Sidebothom*, the injury was not the type that could b regarded as fatal with any degree of certainty, and because injuries were sustained both before and after the ninety-day period, there existed a distinct problem with causation. In the instant case, it was immediately clear that Mr. Burne would die as a result of the accident, and there was no causation problem since Franklin Life (D) conceded that the sole cause of death were the injuries sustained in the accident. Lastly, it is a well settled rule of law that provisions of an insurance policy should be disregarded when it cannot be reasonably applied to a particular factual situation. We may not assume that purely arbitrary conditions involving forfeiture, are introduced by insurance companies merely as a trap to the insured or a means of escape for the company in case of loss. Therefore, where the reasons justifying the condition do not present itself in the particular factual situation, the condition drops out. Accordingly, here, we cannot assume that the ninety-day provision was merely a trap or a means of escape, and therefore may not apply this provision to cases where the record clearly establishes that no dispute exists as to the cause of death. Reversed.

Concurrence and Dissent: (Pomeroy, J.) Traditionally, courts construing contracts arguably violative of public policy, began by determining the intent of the parties, and only reached the question of public policy if necessary. The majority here, however, invalidates the ninety-day provision on public policy grounds first, and only then advances to "well settled" principles of law. Courts should be careful not to defeat the intention of the parties by applying terms and conditions of the contract, to situations that the parties could not have intended them to apply. There is no doubt that both Mr. Burne and Franklin Life (D) intended that the additional recovery for accidental death, be precluded should death occur more than ninety days after the accident. Therefore, the case does not present the problem of interpreting the intention of the parties. Furthermore, the majority's public policy argument suffers from ambiguity. Either the reader is to understand that all ninety-day provisions in accidental death benefit endorsements are invalid, or only where there is no possible uncertainty as to causation when the insured dies after ninety days. The "gruesome paradox" the majority believes would exist by enforcing the 90-day provision, in no way depends on a distinction between those that die after 90 days with possible uncertainty as to causation, and those that do not. Neither do considerations of financial penalties in determining appropriate medical treatment, depend on whether or not the insured in fact died outside the 90-day period and without uncertainty as to causation. It is obvious that the majority is determining the validity of a contract by means of hindsight, and has failed to observe the fundamental principle that judicial function should be limited to examining the circumstances known to the parties at the time of contracting. We must allow parties to make contracts which are reasonable in light of the circumstances known to them at the time of contracting. Therefore, absent some violation of some external rule limiting freedom of contract, a court should not redraft contracts which were reasonable at the time they were entered into.

Analysis:

This case provides a final illustration of situations in which a court may decline to enable a party to enforce rights under an agreed enforcement term. Just as contracts as a whole, may be found invalid as contrary to public policy, specific provisions of a contract may be rendered unenforceable when violative of relevant community standards. Here, the court gave numerous justifications for finding a violation of public policy. Included was the fact that Franklin Life (D) had in fact benefitted from not having to pay any of the money for an additional number of years. However, in light of the court's discussion of the "well settled" principles of law with respect to these ninety-day provisions, it is questionable whether a finding of a violation of public policy was essential to the court's conclusion. If in fact the court's statement of the law is correct, it would seem that public policy concerns were already considered prior to this case, and the law adapted accordingly. But in any event, this case seems to generally conform to the previous cases in this section. Just as the obligation of a good faith belief in a loss of security is imposed on the enforcement of acceleration clauses, this case can be construed as requiring a good faith belief in the uncertainty of causation. In both instances, the courts interpreted the contracts in ways that would protect the reasonable expectation interests of each party, by assuming that the parties did not expect the provisions involved to be used for purposes other than what they were intended to secure.

Perspective
The Boundaries of Autonomy

Chapter 7

A long-standing principle in American jurisprudence is that individuals enjoy the freedom to contract. If two individuals agree to take on certain obligations in exchange for some form of consideration from the other, the law upholds their agreement. Traditional contract law has thus developed in such a way as to always protect an individual's freedom to contract.

In some situations, however, the freedom to contract must give way to other considerations. For instance, the law does not allow individuals to agree to do something illegal. The law also does not allow the parties to act in contravention of public policy. An individual's freedom to contract is also qualified, not by what the law will not allow them to do, but by what the law presumes they have done even if they have not actually done so. In this regard, modern contract law sets forth a set of default rules that will aid the parties in the event circumstances change in such a way as to render their initial agreement ineffective. Modern contract law also implies terms into an agreement in order to govern the conduct of the parties as they perform their mutual obligations. In some cases, the law allows a court to modify the parties' agreement in order to give effect to their original intent.

Among the default rules courts may apply are the doctrine of impossibility, impracticability and frustration of purpose. Generally speaking, courts will not require a party to perform when that performance is rendered impossible because of an unforeseen event. In other words, even though the parties did not specifically agree that performance would not be required if something occurred or failed to occur, the court puts itself in the parties' shoes and says, had they realized this would or would not occur, they would not have required performance. Even when performance is not impossible, *per se*, but is merely impracticable, courts will still excuse a party's performance. However, a court will not excuse performance when a risk that party assumed materializes. Recognizing that parties still must have the freedom to contract, courts will hold a party to its bargain if, as part of that bargain, the party assumed a certain risk. Finally, even if performance is possible and practical, courts will nevertheless excuse a party's duty to perform if the underlying purpose of the agreement has been frustrated by unforeseen events.

In addition to applying default rules to situations where changed circumstances have affected a party's performance, courts also imply a duty of good faith and fair dealing into each and every agreement. Under this duty, a party must perform its obligations in good faith; that is, a party must not take any actions that will interfere with the other party's rights. However, this duty cannot be used to expand a party's obligations or to force a party to accept a material change in terms. This duty of good faith helps to characterize the relationships between contracting parties and governs their actions when performing their contractual obligations. Should a breach of that duty occur, however, courts are split on whether an aggrieved party can bring a claim merely for breach of contract or whether they can bring a claim in tort. Allowing the tort claim has significant advantages in terms of the remedies that are available, most notably, the availability of punitive damages. Some courts believe, however, that contract law is adequate to protect the aggrieved party and that the law of torts should not recognize a claim for breach of an implied contractual duty of good faith and fair dealing.

In unique situations, some courts, using their equitable powers, have gone so far as to modify a parties' agreement in order to give effect to the underlying purpose of the parties' agreement. Those who favor individual autonomy over all else have difficulty with this type of court interference with contractual relations because it feels like the court is simply rewriting the contract. Regardless, it is clear that the courts must play a role in interpreting contracts, especially in cases where circumstances have changed in ways the parties never anticipated. Whether the courts look at it from the application of default rules, by implying a duty of good faith into the agreement, by looking to see if there has been an allocation of risk, through the eyes of contract, tort or equity, the underlying idea for all courts is an individual's freedom to contract and the limits that are or should be placed on that freedom.

Chapter 7

NOTE: THE PURPOSE OF THIS OUTLINE IS TO ORGANIZE THE CASES SO THAT ONE CAN QUICKLY UNDERSTAND THE RELEVANCE OF EACH CASE TO THE COURSE. NO ATTEMPT IS MADE IN THIS OVERVIEW TO ADDRESS EVERY CONCEPT THAT MUST BE STUDIED. BE SURE TO READ THE ENTIRE CASEBOOK AND/OR OTHER MATERIALS TO GAIN A FULL UNDERSTANDING OF ALL CONCEPTS.

I. The autonomy of parties to a contract plays a key role in how the courts interpret those contracts and the law applied in such cases.
   A. That autonomy is not limitless, however, but is instead qualified in two important ways.
      1. First, the law, rather than the parties' autonomy, is the ultimate source of any agreement's binding power.
         a. Thus the law may limit the parties' ability to contract in certain ways according to the needs of the public, such as by prohibiting parties from agreeing to do an illegal act.
         b. The law may also imply certain terms into an agreement on the basis that the public policy in support of such terms outweighs the parties' freedom to contract.
      2. Second, the law must supply terms that the parties failed to include with regard to a change in circumstances.
         a. This area of contract law requires a court to determine what the parties would have agreed to had they foreseen the change in circumstances, since the parties failed to include an agreement on such a change in circumstances in their agreement.
         b. This approach is not without controversy, however.
            (1) For those who believe a contract should be construed narrowly, such that if it is not within the four corners of the document the contract has no authority over it, this means of implying a term into the contract to fill the gap flies in the face of the parties' freedom to contract.
            (2) More often, however, most believe, as does the law, that the parties' agreement should not lose its authority simply because a change of circumstances has occurred that the parties have not foreseen.
   B. By limiting contracting parties' autonomy, the law thus gives the courts the authority to determine what the parties intended when circumstances have gone beyond what the parties anticipated. There are three ways in which courts have attempted to do this.
      1. First, courts have turned to a set of default rules that are used to decide when and if an unforeseen change in circumstances will relieve a party of their duty to perform.
      2. Second, courts have turned to implied terms, such as the duty of good faith and fair dealing, to judge a party's conduct in carrying out performance of the contractual obligations and whether that conduct should result in liability for acting in bad faith.
      3. Finally, courts have split over whether to allow a party that is subjected to a breach of the duty of good faith to recover in tort or in contract.

II. Often, a party to a contract finds itself in the unique situation of not being able to perform or not being able to perform in a commercially reasonable manner because of an event that neither party anticipated. In these situations, a party can seek relief from performance in court.
   A. Generally, when performance depends upon the continued existence of a specific person or thing, the courts will imply a condition that the impossibility of performance due to the perishing of that person or thing without the fault of either party excuses the duty to perform. This is known as the doctrine of impossibility. *Taylor v. Caldwell.*
      1. Thus, if a party promises to pay rent for a concert hall and the concert hall burns

down, the duty to pay is excused because the hall no longer exists. *Taylor.*

2. Similarly, if an author dies before completing a work he has contracted to complete, his estate will be excused from performing under the agreement. *Taylor.*
3. Or if a farmer agrees to sell onions to a store but the onions perish due to a storm before they are delivered, the parties' performance under the agreement will be excused because it has become impossible to perform.

B. Even when performance is possible, but the purpose of the agreement has been frustrated by an unforeseen event, courts will still excuse performance. This is known as the frustration of purpose doctrine. *Krell v. Henry.*

1. The key to excusing performance because of a frustration of purpose is that the non-occurrence of the event that was supposed to occur was a basic assumption of the parties' agreement. *Krell.*
2. Additionally, the event must not have arisen because of the party seeking to be excused, and the party seeking to be excused must not have taken on a greater obligation than the law imposes. *Krell.*
3. Thus, if Ed rents an apartment balcony to view a parade, but the parade is canceled, Ed will be excused from having to pay for the apartment balcony, even though performance is still technically possible. *Krell.*
4. The Uniform Commercial Code has not yet adopted the frustration of purpose doctrine, however.

C. Performance will not be excused in all circumstances, however, even where there is a change in circumstances.

1. If the parties have allocated a risk that an event will occur to one party, and the event occurs, the courts will not excuse performance simply because that party no longer wishes to assume the risk. In this way, the autonomy of the parties is preserved.
2. Thus, when parties enter into a fixed-price contract, thereby assuming the risk of market fluctuations, the subsequent rise or fall in the market will not excuse a party's performance. *Northern Indiana Public Service Co. v. Carbon County Coal Co.*
   a. This is true even when the parties have included a force majeure clause, which states that in the event of circumstances beyond the parties' control, performance is excused. *Northern Indiana Public Service Co.*
3. Moreover, a court will not alter an agreement to ship goods at a set price simply because the party has incurred costs greater than expected due to a change in circumstances that was foreseeable and built into the quoted price. *Transatlantic Financing Corp. v. United States.*

D. To recover in such a case, the party seeking to be excused must show that performance is commercially impracticable.

1. This requires a showing that (1) some unexpected event occurred, (2) the risk of the unexpected event was not allocated to either party, and (3) the event must have rendered performance commercially impractical. *Transatlantic Financing Corp.*
2. This is the approach taken by the UCC in § 2-615.
3. The key to commercial impracticability is that the event was unforeseeable. If the event was foreseen, it is more likely that the parties allocated that risk to one party or the other in their agreement.
4. Further, a party seeking to be excused from performing on the basis of commercial impracticability must show more than a mere loss of profits. *Eastern Air Lines, Inc. v. Gulf Oil Corp.*
   a. Rather, they must show real hardship. *Eastern Air Lines*, UCC § 2-615.

E. A party may also be excused from performing where there arises a reasonable expectation that the other party will not require strict compliance with the contractual obligations. *Burger King Corp. v. Family Dining, Inc.*

1. Such an expectation can arise from the

parties' course of dealing. *Burger King Corp.*

III. Along the same lines, courts are often called upon to adjust the parties' contractual obligations based upon a change in the parties' relationship.
   A. Thus, as we have seen, if a party indicates through dealings with the other party that they will not require strict compliance, strict compliance will be excused and only substantial compliance required. *Burger King Corp.*
   B. Other means of altering the parties' contract based on changes in their relationship include the doctrines of waiver, estoppel and election.
   C. Some scholars, however, believe a different approach is required in situations where the parties' relationship has changed over time.
      1. Professor Ian MacNeil, for example, has proposed using something he calls "relational contract law." *Contracts: Adjustment of Long-Term Economic Relations under Classical, Neoclassical, and Relational Contract Law.*
         a. Professor MacNeil posits that under traditional contract law, the key is to adhere to the discreteness and "presentiation" of the parties' agreement.
            (1) By "discreteness" Professor MacNeil is referring to a way of understanding the contract and its performance in isolation form the broader relationship of the parties and the expectations that their relationship may generate.
            (2) By "presentiation" Professor MacNeil is referring to the habit of viewing performance as it was supposedly understood at the time the contract was formed.
         b. Under Professor MacNeil's relational contract law, however, the broader circumstances surrounding the parties' agreement is looked at.
            (1) Thus, under relational contract law, the role of consent is downplayed to the point where it is equal or subordinate to the relationship in terms of determining legal rights and duties.
      2. Professor Richard E. Speidel has posited a different theory based upon Professor MacNeil's relational contract law that is easier to understand and to apply. *The New Spirit of Contract* (1982) and *Court-Imposed Price Adjustments Under Long-Term Supply Contracts* (1981).
         a. Under Professor Speidel's approach, the disadvantaged party is to propose a modification of the agreement that would be enforceable if accepted by the advantaged party.
            (1) In proposing the modification, the disadvantaged party should follow the criteria set forth in Restatement (Second) of Contracts § 89.
         b. Next, Professor Speidel would require that the disadvantaged party make it clear that it did not assume the risk of the unanticipated event.
      3. In considering either approach, however, the focus is on the relationship of the parties.
         a. Often the most important relationship for terms of interpreting the parties' agreement is the long-term business relationship where it can be assumed that the parties impliedly agreed to the default rules regarding excuse of performance and other implied conditions and obligations in order to preserve their long-standing relationship.
   D. Although courts have not given much weight to either Professor MacNeil or Professor Speidel, they often look to the relationship of the parties in determining what the underlying purpose of the agreement is and how to interpret the agreement in order to give effect to that purpose. *Burger King Corp. v. Family Dining, Inc.*
   E. One way the courts have approached difficult questions regarding a party's obligations in light of the parties' relationship is to imply a duty of good faith and fair dealing into every contract. *Bak-A-Lum Corp. of America v. Alcoa Bldg. Prods., Inc.*

Chapter Overview Outline The Boundaries of Autonomy

1. Generally speaking, the duty of good faith and fair dealing requires a party to perform its contractual obligations without interfering with the other party's rights.
2. It does not require a party to accept a change in the material terms of the agreement, however. *Badgett v. Security State Bank* (1991)
   a. Although courts differ on this issue, it is generally held that the duty of good faith cannot be expanded to include obligations that are not set forth in the parties' agreement. *Badgett* (1991).
   b. Further, it cannot be used to force a party to assume new obligations or modify the existing ones. *Badgett* (1991)
   c. Some courts, however, have held that the parties' course of dealing can alter their obligations if a reasonable expectation arises on the other party's part that the party will act a certain way despite the contractual obligations. *Badgett* (1990).

F. In some cases, courts have even gone so far as to provide an obligation in order to give effect to the parties' expressed intent when changed circumstances render the original agreement ineffective. *J.J. Brooksbank Co. v. Budget Rent-A-Car Corp.*
   1. This is in effect the reverse application of the frustration of purpose doctrine in that the court implies a new term into the agreement, effectively modifying it, in order to preserve the purpose of the agreement. *J.J. Brooksbank Co.*
   2. In some respects this is an equitable adjustment of the parties' agreement.
      a. Equity developed as a means of correcting the inefficiencies of law, since it is impossible to make a universal statement about all things.
      b. As Aristotle expounded, when a case arises that is not covered by the universal rules, it is necessary for the court to put himself in the shoes of the legislator and ask what would have been done had this problem been envisioned.
      c. The same is true in contract situations where the parties failed to foresee a given event that now has occurred: the court must put itself in the parties' shoes to determine what they would have agreed to had they foreseen the event.
      d. Equitable adjustment is sought only in those cases where a party wishes to change his/her obligations under the existing agreement, rather than when the party wants to be excused from performance.
         (1) In this respect, equity is often seen as doing the fair or just thing.
      e. Interestingly, the problems of trying to do equity while adhering to the rule of law do not exist when a case is brought to mediation or arbitration.

IV. In some cases, a party in a contractual relationship is forced to bring a claim in court to remedy an injustice that they have suffered at the hands of the other party.
   A. While the usual claim is for breach of contract, there are cases where a party to a contract brings a claim for a breach of a duty that is not a specific contractual obligation, such as a claim for breach of the implied duty of good faith and fair dealing.
   B. These sorts of claims, however, raised an issue regarding whether such a claim sounds in contract or tort.
   C. Professor Grant Gilmore, in his book *The Death of Contracts*, theorized that such claims were dissolving the line between contracts and torts, creating a new area of law he called "Contorts."
      1. While it is generally recognized that a breach of contract is not a tort, all realize that there are situations where the same act may constitute both a breach of contract *and* a tort.
      2. Consider, for example, a medical malpractice case where the surgeon may perform negligently while performing a surgery he is obligated to do under a contract for ser-

vices.

3. Even in these situations, however, a plaintiff must choose a remedy, either contractual or tort, so as to avoid a double recovery.
   a. Contractual damages include general damages, those flowing naturally from the breach, and consequential damages, those that are reasonably foreseeable at the time the contract is formed.
   b. Tort damages, on the other hand, are much more liberal insofar as a tort claimant can recover actual damages, emotional loss and punitive damages.

D. A majority of courts have recently recognized that a claim for the breach of the implied duty of good faith and fair dealing, at least in the insurance context, is a tort claim. *Gruenberg v. Aetna Insurance Co.*
1. For those courts that recognize a tort claim for breach of the implied duty of good faith and fair dealing, they do so based on public policy rather than set legal rules. *Gruenberg.*
2. These courts reason that since every contract includes an implied duty of good faith and fair dealing that is independent of any contractual obligation, the breach of that duty sounds in tort rather than contract. *Gruenberg.*
   a. In this regard, it is irrelevant for purposes of a breach of the implied duty of good faith whether the other party is in breach of his contractual obligations. *Gruenberg.*
3. The tort jurisdictions also reason that contract law does not provide an adequate remedy for a breach of the duty of good faith. *Gruenberg.*

E. A minority of courts have refused to allow an insured to bring a tort claim for breach of the implied duty of good faith and fair dealing.
1. The minority position is that it is unnecessary to provide a tort claim simply to assure that the insurer does not take advantage of the insured. *Beck v. Farmers Insurance Exchange.*
2. The minority further believes that the majority position is strained and flies in the face of traditional contract law. *Beck.*
   a. The minority is of the opinion that traditional contract law provides an adequate remedy. *Beck.*
      (1) For these courts, traditional contract law does not require the remedy to be limited to the policy limits, since those limits only apply to payment of benefits by the insurer, not payments for the insurer's breach. *Beck.*
      (2) Further, these courts point out that in certain circumstances, emotional distress damages can be awarded even under traditional contract law. *Beck.*
3. Although these courts recognize a tort claim in third party situations, where a third party sues the insurer for breach, they see the relationship between an insurer and its insured as not necessitating a tort approach. *Beck.*

F. Regardless of whether the breach of implied duty of good faith and fair dealing is a contract claim or a tort claim, all jurisdictions agree that the duty requires an insurer to act in a certain manner. *Beck.*
1. An insurer must therefore fairly evaluate a claim and thereafter act promptly and reasonably to bargain and settle that claim. *Beck.*
2. The insurer is also required to deal with laymen as laymen and to refrain from taking actions that will deprive the insured of its rights under the policy. *Beck.*

LANDMARK CASE USES AN IMPLIED CONDITION TO APPLY THE IMPOSSIBILITY DOCTRINE TO THE DESTRUCTION OF THE SUBJECT MATTER OF A CONTRACT

Taylor v. Caldwell

(Concert Performer) v. (Music Hall Owner)

3 Best & S. 826 (1863)

MEMORY GRAPHIC

Instant Facts

Caldwell (D) agreed to let Taylor (P) use his music hall to give concerts, but before the first concert date a fire destroyed the hall, and Taylor (P) sued Caldwell (D) for damages.

Black Letter Rule

When performance depends upon the continued existence of a specific person or thing, the contract includes an implied condition that the impossibility of performance due to the perishing of that person or thing without the fault of either party excuses the duty to perform.

Case Vocabulary

CONDITION: A contract term which requires the occurrence of an event or the existence of a particular state of things in order for performance to become or remain due.

CONTINGENCY: An event which may or may not occur.

IMPOSSIBILITY: A doctrine under which a court may excuse a party from his duty to perform where that performance has become impossible without his fault, such as by the perishing of something or someone necessary for performance or by a change that makes the contract illegal.

POSITIVE CONTRACT: An absolute contract with no additional qualifications, conditions, exceptions or restrictions.

RULE ABSOLUTE: A final order, as opposed to an order to show cause why the relief requested should not be granted.

Procedural Basis: Breach of contract action for damages.

Facts: Caldwell (D) entered into a contract with Taylor (P) by which Caldwell (D) agreed to let Taylor (P) use The Surrey Gardens and Music Hall on four specific dates to give concerts for £100 per day. After the parties entered into this contract, but before the first concert date, and without the fault of either party, a fire completely destroyed the Hall and Taylor (P) was unable to give concerts on the agreed dates. Taylor (P) brought this action to recover his advertising and preparation expenses. The existence of the Hall and Gardens in a state fit for a concert was essential for the fulfillment of the contract because the concerts which the parties contemplated could not otherwise occur. However, Taylor (P) and Caldwell (D) did not consciously consider the destruction of the Hall when they entered into their agreement, and did not expressly provide for it in their contract.

Issue: When performance depends upon the continued existence of a specific thing, does the impossibility of performance due to the destruction of that thing without the fault of either party excuse the duty to perform?

Decision and Rationale: (Blackburn) Yes. Because the parties did not expressly provide for this type of disaster in their contract, we must apply the general rules of law to resolve this issue. As a general rule, when a party contracts to do a thing which is not unlawful, he must either perform or pay damages for not performing, even if unforeseen circumstances make that performance unexpectedly burdensome or even impossible. However, this rule only applies when the contract is positive and absolute, and not subject to any express or implied condition. Where the parties must have known when they entered into the contract that it could not be performed unless some particular thing continued to exist at the time of performance, and thus contemplated that continuing existence as the foundation of the performance, then, absent an express or implied warranty that the thing shall exist, the court must construe the contract as subject to an implied condition that the parties shall be excused if, before breach, destruction of that thing makes performance impossible. Such a construction tends to fulfill the intent of the parties, since men would generally state such a condition if the matter occurred to them. Contracts which require a person to personally perform some promise, such as a promise to marry, do not generally contain an express exception for the death of that person. By the terms of such contracts, if the person dies before performing his promise, he breaches the contract. However, it has long been the rule that when performance is personal, executors are not liable. Thus, if an author dies before completing a work he has contracted to compose, his executors are discharged from the contract because the performance was personal and the death made it impossible. Similarly, a painter who becomes blind before completing a painting he has contracted to provide may be excused from further performance. The basis for such excuses is that the continued life of the author and the eyesight of the painter are implied conditions of their duty to perform. Further, the person who is necessary for performance need not be the contractor himself. For example, if an apprentice dies before completing the term of his contract, a third party who has guaranteed his promise will not be liable for his performance. It is also not necessary that the implied condition be the continued life of a human being. Where a party sells specific chattels and promises to deliver them on a future date, and before the delivery date the chattels perish without his fault, his nonperformance is excused because delivery of those chattels has become impossible. Similarly, in contracts for the loan of chattels or bailments, if, through no fault of the borrower or bailee, it becomes impossible for him to perform his promise to return the thing lent or bailed, this impossibility excuses his failure to perform. Thus, the principle is that when performance of a contractual promise depends upon the continued existence of a specific person or thing, that contract includes an implied condition that the impossibility of performance arising from the perishing of that person or thing excuses the duty to perform. Although the promises in these examples do not ıclude any express stipulation that the destruction of the person or ning shall excuse the duty to perform, this excuse is implied by law ecause the nature of the contract indicates that the parties ontracted on the basis of the continued existence of the person or hing. In this case, considering the whole contract, we find that the arties contracted on the basis of the continued existence of the Hall at the time the concerts were to be given because its existence was essential to giving the concerts. Because the Hall ceased to exist without the fault of either party, both parties are excused, Taylor (P) from his promise to pay for the use of the Hall and Gardens, and Caldwell (D) from his promise to provide them for Taylor's (P) use. Rule absolute.

Analysis:

This landmark case gave rise to the modern doctrine of impossibility. The traditional common law rule was "pacta sunt servanda," agreements nust be kept. Courts would not usually require specific performance of a promise, but, as the court explained in *Taylor*, they would require a arty to pay damages for not performing even if unforeseen circumstances had made performance "unexpectedly burdensome or even npossible." The rationale behind this rule was that parties to a contract should protect themselves against different contingencies by negotiating ppropriate contractual provisions. In certain cases courts did excuse performance which had become literally impossible, such as where erformance of personal services became impossible due to the person's death or unavoidable illness. Similarly, courts would excuse erformance which had become illegal, and therefore legally impossible, due to a supervening change in the law. With *Taylor* courts began ɔ expand their application of the impossibility doctrine by expressing it in terms of implied conditions. In *Taylor* the court found an implied ondition based on the tacit assumption between the parties that Caldwell's (D) music hall would continue to exist. The failure of this condition, ne unexpected destruction of the hall, excused both parties from their duties under the contract. The court did not find it necessary that this nplied condition be based on a conscious assumption of the parties. Rather, just as we unconsciously assume that the floor will be there to neet us when we walk down a familiar hallway while looking out the window, the court found that the parties unconsciously assumed that there vould be no fire and that the building would continue to exist, and that these assumptions, though unstated in the contract, were nonetheless he foundation of the agreement. *Taylor* thus demonstrates that even performance of a seemingly absolute promise may be excusable if a court nds that the parties did not intend to require performance if some contingency made it impossible. Several policy reasons support the doctrine f impossibility. One is that contract liability stems from consent. Where the parties consent to a certain allocation of risks, but some event ccurs which they did not contemplate and which drastically shifts the nature of those risks, they may not have consented to an allocation of he risks as they exist after the circumstances changed. As under the doctrine of mutual mistake, discussed in the previous chapter, courts look or an unexpected, unbargained-for gain by one party and unexpected, unbargained-for loss by the other. Another policy reason is fairness. ust as the law may deem it unconscionably harsh to take advantage of a mistake as to existing facts, it may also deem it unconscionable to take dvantage of a mistake as to future events. Courts have also used several conceptual models to analyze impossibility cases. Like *Taylor*, earlier ourts spoke in terms of the existence of an implied term. Similarly, other courts looked to the "contemplation of the parties" and would etermine whether they could infer from the facts that the parties did not intend to require performance if an unexpected event radically hanged the nature of that performance. Critics argue that the theory of implied terms does not really represent the truth because the parties, ad they considered certain contingencies, would likely have different views about how to handle them. Some scholars have suggested that ather than implying a condition to adjust to the parties intent, courts might impose a constructive condition to clarify what intent they find easonable or advisable, and to steer future contracts in that direction. Indeed some later cases, such as *Transatlantic Financing Corp. v. United tates* [constructive condition approach to impossibility], discussed later in this chapter, rejected the approaches of implied terms and the parties' ontemplation and instead imposed a constructive condition in the interests of justice. The newest rationale for impossibility cases is that the ontract simply does not cover the situation that arose, and that the court is therefore free to fill the gap and supply a term that will do justice. oday, the Uniform Commercial Code (UCC) and the Restatement generally follow the common law. Under *UCC § 2-615* [commercial npracticability], unless a seller assumes a greater obligation, his non-delivery is not a breach of contract where a basic assumption on which he contract was made is that a particular contingency would not occur, but that contingency does occur and renders performance impracticable. n UCC terms, Caldwell's (D) performance was excused because he did not expressly assume the risk of the destruction of the music hall, erformance was not only impracticable but impossible, and the continued existence of the music hall was a basic assumption on which the ontract was made. Similarly, under the *Restatement (Second) of Contracts § 261* [supervening impracticability], if a party's performance has ecome impracticable without his fault due to an event which occurred after he entered into the contract, and a basic assumption on which the arties entered into the contract was that such an event would not occur, then the party's performance is discharged unless the contract or the ircumstances indicate otherwise. As in *Taylor*, § 261 explains that even where a party undertakes a duty in a contract with no qualifying anguage, a court can still excuse him from performing that duty if some unexpected supervening event makes the performance impracticable. oth § 2-615 of the UCC and § 261 of the Restatement address two types of assumption of risk. Both sections require that the nonoccurrence f the supervening event was a basic assumption on which both parties entered into the contract. This "basic assumption" element addresses he assumption of risk which the law implies, constructs, supplies, or otherwise imposes upon the parties in the interests of justice. In addition, oth sections include an element that addresses the assumption of risk a party undertakes more directly. Section 2-615 states that the excuse pplies unless the party has assumed a greater obligation, and § 261 states that the excuse applies unless the contract or circumstances indicate hat it does not. Thus, a party may expressly agree to perform even if performance becomes impracticable, and may then be liable for damages ven if he cannot perform. Even if a party does not expressly agree to assume such a risk, a court may find that the circumstances indicate that e did so. The court might consider such circumstances as the party's ability to insert a term in the contract that shifts the risk of impracticability o the other party, which in turn might depend on the extent to which the contract terms were standardized or supplied by the other party or vere the usual practice of the trade. The court might also consider whether the party is generally expected to insure himself against such a risk; vhether the contingency which developed is one which the parties could reasonably be thought to have foreseen as a real possibility which could ffect performance; and whether it was one of the risks which they allocated implicitly by failing to provide for it explicitly.

A COURT CAN EXCUSE PERFORMANCE WHEN THE PURPOSE HAS BEEN FRUSTRATED EVEN IF PERFORMANCE IS STILL POSSIBLE

Krell v. Henry

(Hotel Owner) v. (Hotel Renter)
(1903) 2 K.B. 740

M E M O R Y   G R A P H I C

Instant Facts

Krell (P) rented a room in his hotel to Henry (D) and both believed that the room would be used to watch the King's coronation.

Black Letter Rule

Even though performance is possible, a court can still excuse a party's duty to perform if an event that both parties considered the foundation of the contract ceases to exist.

Case Vocabulary

AFFIDAVIT: A written statement.
DISCHARGE: To "discharge" performance means basically the same thing as to "excuse" performance.
LICENSE: Permission to use something that belongs to another for a limited purpose or time.

Procedural Basis: Appeal from judgment for a breach of contract.

Facts: Krell (P) advertised that his hotel would rent rooms to see the King's coronation. Henry (D) saw this written announcement and paid Krell (P) a deposit in advance for those days when the King would have his coronation ceremony. Unfortunately for both, the King got really sick and the ceremonies were canceled. Krell demanded the balance of the hotel rent, but Henry refusted to pay. Krell then filed this action for breach of contract.

Issue: Even though performance is still possible, can a court excuse a party's duty to perform if an event the parties considered the foundation of the contract ceases to exist?

Decision and Rationale: (Williams) Yes. Even though performance is still possible, a party's duty to perform is excused if an event that both parties considered the foundation of the contract does not occur on the basis of frustration of purpose. Here, performance was clearly still possible. Nothing in the written contract stated that the room was rented to view the coronation. Thus, Henry (D) could still use the room even though the coronation didn't occur. But the purpose of renting the room was frustrated because the coronation was canceled. Moreover, both Krell (P) and Henry (D) had assumed that the coronation was the foundation of the contract. Without the coronation, there was no purpose for Henry (D) to have rented the room, and as evidenced by his (P) announcement of the event, Krell (P) knew it. In other words, what occurred here was more like a license whereby Krell (P) agreed to let Henry (D) use his hotel room solely for the purpose of viewing the King's coronation ceremony. That ceremony never taking place due to circumstances beyond the parties' control, there becomes no need for the license. Thus, the basis for the contract no longer exists thereby requiring performance to be excused. Appeal dismissed.

Analysis:

The Uniform Commercial Code hasn't explicitly recognized the doctrine of frustration. However, most American courts, like the English court in Krell, have adopted the doctrine of frustration. The first and second Restatements have also adopted it. The Restatement lists four requirements needed to show frustration of purpose: 1) The event must have substantially frustrated the party's main purpose; 2) the nonoccurrence of the event must have been a basic assumption of the contract; 3) the frustration must not have occurred by the party seeking to be excused; and 4) the party seeking excuse must not have assumed a greater obligation than the law imposed. Notice that the four requirements in the Restatement are very similar to its requirements for the impracticability of performance. In fact, only the first requirement is different from the requirements for impracticability. Notice also how similar the frustration excuse discussed in this case is to the doctrine of impossibility discussed in *Taylor v. Caldwell* [renter's duty to pay for use of concert hall excused after hall burned down because contract, which depended on continued existence of specific thing included an implied condition that impossibility of performance due to the perishing of that thing without the fault of either party excuses the duty to perform]. In both cases, the duty to perform was excused because something the parties took the existence of for granted suddenly ceased to exist. In *Taylor*, the concert hall burned down; here, the coronation ceremony was canceled. In both instances, the parties failed to account for such an occurrence. Viewed in this light, it becomes easy to see how the frustration excuse is really an extension of the doctrine of impossibility: both are default rules applied by a court in an attempt to give effect to the parties' original intent by determining to whom, implicitly, did the parties allocate the risk. The allocation of risk is not always implicit, however. As will be seen in *Northern Indiana Public Service Co. v. Carbon County Coal Co.*, the case that follows in this chapter, sometimes the parties specifically allocate the risks to one party in their contract. In such a case the court's role is to interpret the agreement rather than to apply the default rules. The unique aspect of frustration, however, is that performance is still possible but the duty to perform is nonetheless excused because the reason the parties contracted has suddenly ceased to exist. This unique situation where performance is excused is important to keep in mind when looking at factual scenarios because even if performance is possible, thus ruling out the doctrine of impossibility, a party's duty to perform may still be excused if the underlying purpose of the agreement has been frustrated. [Law professors love this stuff!] Thus, as broad as the doctrine of impossibility is since it encompasses impracticability as well as impossibility, when frustration of purpose is thrown in, excuse abounds.

Northern Indiana Public Service Co. v. Carbon County Coal Co.

lectric Company) v. (Owner of Coal Mine)

986) 799 F.2d 265

EMORY GRAPHIC

Instant Facts

Northern Indiana Public Service Company (P) IPSCO) entered into a fixed-price contract with arbon (D) that did not allow it to renegotiate its terms.

Black Letter Rule

Even though there is a force majeure clause (a ause which lists certain events that are beyond the ntrol of the parties and thus excuses performance), a rty has assumed the risks for market fluctuations if at party has agreed to a fixed-priced contract.

Case Vocabulary

.EVATION CLAUSE: This allows a party to raise the ntract price from time to time according to provisions the contract.

ORCE MAJEURE CLAUSE: A clause which lists certain ents that are beyond the control of the parties and us excuse performance.

EQUIREMENT CONTRACT: A type of contract where ller agrees to furnish everything that buyer needs and here buyer agrees to buy exclusively all of his goods om the particular seller.

Procedural Basis: Appeal from judgment on an action for court declaration excusing performance.

Facts: NIPSCO (P) is an electric company. It (P) contracted with Carbon (D) to buy Carbon's (D) coal which would be used to run NIPSCO's (P) electric plant. The contract stated that NIPSCO (P) would buy 1.5 million tons every 20 years. The contract wasn't a requirements contract (a type of contract where seller agrees to furnish everything that buyer needs and where buyer agrees to buy exclusively all of his goods from the particular seller), and so NIPSCO (P) was bound to buy all 1.5 million tons no matter how much it actually needed. Moreover, the contract didn't allow NIPSCO (P) to renegotiate the terms. The contract also contained an "elevation clause" (this allows a party to raise the contract price from time to time according to provisions of the contract) such that Carbon (D) could raise the price. Finally, the contract contained a force majeure clause which excused NIPSCO from accepting and paying for Carbon's (D) coal for "any cause beyond [its] reasonable control....which wholly or partly prevented...the utilizing...of the coal." NIPSCO (P) entered into the agreement in order to secure itself an inexpensive source of electricity for its plant, believing that the price of electricity would soar while the price of coal would not. As it turned out, NIPSCO (P) was able to purchase electricity at much lower rates than it cost to purchase coal and generate its own electricity. To make matters worse, about five years after NIPSCO (P) and Carbon (D) entered into the contract, a state commission regulating NIPSCO (P) issued an order preventing NIPSCO (P) from shifting its (P) costs to its (P) customers. Believing the increased cost of the coal, which it could not pass on to its customers, made it prohibitive to continue purchasing coal under the contract NIPSCO (P) invoked the force majeure clause and brought a declaratory judgment action seeking to be excused from performance.

Issue: Even though there is a force majeure clause, has a party assumed the risks for market fluctuations if that party has agreed to a fixed-priced contract?

Decision and Rationale: (Posner) Yes. Even though there is a force majeure clause, a party has assumed the risks of market fluctuations if that party has agreed to a fixed-priced contract. Here, there was a force majeure clause excusing performance if there are certain supervening events. But the clause was never triggered. NIPSCO (P) claims that it was triggered because the state commission's orders prevented NIPSCO (P) from shifting the costs to its (P) consumers. But obviously, this doesn't prevent NIPSCO (P) from actually performing its duties -- accepting the coal and paying for it. Moreover, NIPSCO (P) had explicitly assumed the risks for market fluctuations by signing a fixed-priced contract. NIPSCO (P) gambled that the fuel costs would rise over the life of the contract. If the gamble paid off, NIPSCO (P) would save money through this fixed-priced contract. If the gamble didn't pay off, NIPSCO (P) agreed to live with the consequences. Thus, NIPSCO (P) is bound to perform its duties because NIPSCO (P) explicitly agreed to assume the risks of market fluctuations and because the force majeure clause was never triggered. NIPSCO (P) also argues that the trial court erred in not submitting its defenses of impracticability and frustration of purpose to the jury. The trial court ruled that Indiana law does not allow a buyer to claim impracticability and further ruled that Indiana law does not recognize the frustration defense. These defenses arose over time as courts began to realize that even when a force majeure clause is used, the parties cannot possibly anticipate every contingency or risk that could arise, raising the need for the courts to interpolate terms the parties would have agreed to had they foreseen a given risk. To aid in this interpolation, the doctrines of impracticability/ impossibility and frustration of purpose were judicially created. The question in an impracticability case, unlike an impossibility one, is not whether the promisor could nperform but rather whether performance should be excused because had the parties foreseen the risk, they would have allocated it to the promisee. UCC

Northern Indiana Public Service Co. v. Carbon County Coal Co.
(Continued)

§2-615 takes this approach. Under § 2-615, however, it is the seller who may seek to be excused; there is no suggestion that a buyer may seek the same recourse. Rarely, if ever, will it be impossible for a buyer to perform. However, where some unforeseen change in circumstances occurs that renders the buyer's performance useless, the frustration of purpose doctrine kicks in, as it did in *Krell v. Henry* [lessee excused from paying for room he rented to view coronation ceremony because ceremony was unexpectedly canceled due to King's illness]. Both defenses, however, are doctrines meant to shift risk to the party better able to bear it. Here, however, the parties clearly allocated the risk of increased costs to NIPSCO (P). Such is the underlying purpose of a fixed-price contract like the one the parties here entered into. Therefore, we need not decide whether Indian law recognizes the frustration defense or whether a buyer may clai the benefit of § 2-615 [although this would make an interestin subject to debate with your friends!], as these defenses are nc implicated here. Such defenses have no place in a case like this whe the parties have explicitly allocated the risk involved. Finally, it mak no difference that a government action is involved. In this industr the parties must have known that price fluctuations and resultin costs are often the result of government action and accounted for th in affixing a price. In this case, NIPSCO (P) gambled and lost, bu having so gambled, it cannot now seek to be saved by this cour Judgment affirmed.

Analysis:

In the previous cases in this chapter, we saw courts struggling to determine to whom the parties would have allocated a given risk had the foreseen it. In *Taylor v. Caldwell* [lessee of concert hall excused from paying rent when hall burned down], the Court applied the doctrine impossibility in reaching its conclusion that the parties would have allocated the risk of the hall burning down to the owner of the hall rath than to the lessee. In *Krell*, the Court applied the frustration defense in concluding that the parties impliedly allocated the risk of the coronatic ceremonies being canceled to the owner rather than the lessee. In this case, NIPSCO (P) argued that its performance should be excused eith because of the force majeure clause or because its performance had become impossible or the purpose of the agreement had become frustrate. The Court here quickly dismissed the force majeure argument, however, finding that the clause was never triggered since it was still possib for NIPSCO (P) to use the coal. The Court also rejects NIPSCO's (P) argument that its performance is impractical or frustrated. The reasor Both impracticability and frustration are default rules that have no application in a case where the parties have allocated the risk at issue, as w done here. In this case, the parties specifically allocated the risk of increased costs to NIPSCO (P) by entering into a fixed-price contract. In oth words, by entering into a fixed-price contract, the parties not only foresaw that the price may change, but allocated the risk of such a chang to NIPSCO (P). As such, there is no need to apply the default rules. Further, it becomes irrelevant whether Indiana law recognizes frustratic or allows a buyer to claim impracticability. The key here is to recognize that the parties have specifically allocated the risk at issue and tha having done so, the default rules will not be applied to alter their allocation. Further, take note that it was the nature of the agreement, ar not a specific clause, that allocated this particular risk. Do not just assume that if a force majeure clause does not apply, the parties' agreeme does not allocate a given risk. Rather, look to the contract as a whole before turning to the default rules. More importantly, keep in mind th a court will not alter a parties' agreement if it is clear that they have allocated the risk at issue in that agreement. As a sidenote, this opinic also gives a brief summary of how the default rules developed and illustrates the difference between impracticability [performance is excuse because it has become impractical or impossible due to an unforeseen change in circumstances] and frustration [performance is excused becau the purpose of the agreement has been frustrated by an unforeseen change in circumstances]. Interestingly, the Court also notes th impracticability usually applies to sellers and frustration to buyers. Notice also how the Court refers to both doctrines as a means of allocatir risk. Thus, in any situation, the question is who should bear the risk, although the Court assumes that the parties, given the chance, would ha agreed to allocate the risk to the party better able to bear it. Regardless, keep these allocation of risk issues in mind as you finish the remainir cases in this chapter.

A COURT WILL NOT GRANT ADDITIONAL EXPENSES OVER AND ABOVE WHAT WAS AGREED TO UNDER A THEORY OF QUANTUM MERUIT

Transatlantic Financing Corporation v. United States

(Ship Operator) v. (Cargo Owner)
(1966) 363 F.2d 312

M E M O R Y   G R A P H I C

Instant Facts

Transatlantic (P) contracted with the United States (D) to deliver cargo to Iran, but contrary to usual practice, it sailed around the Cape of Good Hope instead of the Suez Canal.

Black Letter Rule

A court won't grant a party additional costs other than that agreed in the contract on a theory of quantum meruit (under this equitable doctrine, the court will imply a promise to pay for labor and goods if a party stands to unjustly enrich himself on the labor and goods of another) unless the party can show that its contract performance was impractical.

Case Vocabulary

LIBEL: In admiralty law, this used to be the equivalent of a complaint.
QUANTUM MERUIT: Under this equitable doctrine, the court will imply a promise to pay for labor and goods if a party stands to unjustly enrich himself on the labor and goods of another.

Facts: Transatlantic (P) contracted with the United States (D) to deliver cargo to Iran. Both parties intended that Transatlantic (P) would go through the Suez Canal. Because of military unrest, however, this wasn't an option. So Transatlantic (P) sailed around the much longer route of the Cape of Good Hope. The United States (D) never promised Transatlantic (P) that it (D) would reimburse Transatlantic (P) for the extra costs of going around the Cape. Transatlantic (P) safely delivered the cargo to Iran. The United States (D) paid Transatlantic (P) the contract price. Transatlantic (P) then demanded that the United States (D) reimburse Transatlantic (P) for the extra costs of having to go around the Cape. The United States (D) refused, and this action followed.

Issue: Will a court grant a party additional costs other than that agreed in the contract if the party relies on a theory of quantum meruit and the party cannot show that its contract performance was impractical?

Decision and Rationale: (Wright) No. A court won't grant a party additional costs other than that agreed in the contract under quantum meruit when the party cannot show that its contract performance was impractical. Here, Transatlantic (P) relied on a theory of quantum meruit in order to collect the additional cost of going around the Cape. Was Transatlantic (P) able to show that its contract performance was impracticable? To be impracticable, all three of the following conditions must be met: 1) something unexpected must have occurred; 2) the risk of the unexpected occurrence must not have been allocated either by agreement or by custom; and 3) occurrence of the unexpected event must have rendered performance commercially impracticable. Here, the first requirement was met when the Suez was blocked off because of political unrest. The second requirement wasn't met. Transatlantic (P) assumed the risk. Transatlantic (P) like most commercial shippers knew that the Suez could become a dangerous place. It (P) nonetheless entered the contract. The third requirement wasn't met either. Transatlantic's (P) performance wasn't commercially impractical. Transatlantic (P) was financially and physically able to sail around the Cape without problems. This is a generally used alternative course on which ships rely if the Suez is blocked. Granted, Transatlantic (P) incurred extra expenses of $43,972 beyond the contract price. Still, to show impracticability, there must be a greater difference between the contract price and the actual costs incurred to perform the duties. Thus, Transatlantic (P) wasn't faced with impracticability, and accordingly, it (P) can't receive through the theory of quantum meruit any additional costs incurred outside of the contract price.

Analysis:

An important aspect of Transatlantic focuses on the issue of foreseeability. Citing the UCC §2-615, the court stated that foreseeability alone doesn't necessarily mean that a party has assumed the risks. However, it is one factor that the court will consider in deciding whether there was legal impossibility. Consider the Restatement (Second), Introductory Note to Chapter 11: "The fact that the event was unforeseeable is significant as suggesting that its nonoccurrence was a basic assumption. However, the fact that it was foreseeable, or even foreseen, does not, of itself, argue for a contrary conclusion, since the parties may not have thought it sufficiently important a risk to have made it a subject of their bargaining." Another important aspect here is the underlying notion that a court will not alter the parties' agreement if the parties have allocated the risk at issue. As was the case in *Northern Indiana Public Service Co. v. Carbon County Coal Co.* [fixed-price contract necessarily allocates risk of price fluctuations], the parties here have expressly allocated the risk of extra expenses. It was common knowledge at the time that the Suez Canal may be blocked and if so, that the Cape of Good Hope route would be used instead. It can be assumed the parties incorporated this contingency into its contract negotiations and in arriving at a price. Further, the fact that performance cost more than was bargained for does not justify a court stepping in and changing the terms of the parties' agreement by using alternative theories, such as quantum meruit. Like the default rules of impossibility or frustration, quantum meruit provides a basis for recovery in the absence of agreement. Here, there was an agreement. It is for this reason that the Court turned to the impossibility and impracticability doctrines to determine if performance under the agreement was excused, thus giving rise to a claim for relief under quantum meruit. Keep in mind that if proceeding on a theory of quantum meruit, the expenses for the entire trip should have been sought, and not just those in excess of the agreement. Either there is a contract, in which case quantum meruit is not allowed, or there isn't, in which case quantum meruit is allowed but the contract price is not. The overall reasoning leading up to the Court's conclusion follows the same steps we have seen thus far, but the Court does provide an interesting and helpful rule: "A thing is impossible if it is impractical and a thing it impractical when it can only be done at an excessive and unreasonable cost."

THOSE WHO ASSERT THE DEFENSE OF COMMERCIAL IMPRACTICALITY BEAR THE BURDEN OF SHOWING THAT THE CIRCUMSTANCES ARE UNJUST AND UNFORESEEABLE

Eastern Air Lines, Inc. v. Gulf Oil Corporation

(Airline) v. (Fuel Supplier)

United States District Court, Southern District of Florida, 1975, 415 F.Supp. 429

M E M O R Y   G R A P H I C

Instant Facts

In the midst of an oil embargo, Gulf Oil attempts to get out of its requirements contract with Eastern Air claiming the increased cost of oil made performance impracticable.

Black Letter Rule

The party seeking to establish commercial impracticality bears the burden to show that the events causing impracticality were not foreseeable and that the cost increase complained of was unjust.

Case Vocabulary

U.C.C. § 2–615 (in pertinent part): "Except so far as a seller may have assumed a greater obligation . . . . (a) Delay in delivery or non-delivery in whole or in part by a seller . . . is not a breach of his duty under a contract for sale if performance as agreed has become impracticable by the occurrence of a contingency the non-occurrence of which was a basic assumption on which the contract was made . . . ."

Procedural Basis: Judgment of district court in breach of contract action, following entry of a preliminary injunction against defendant.

Facts: Please see facts as summarized on page 161 of this book.

Issue: May a seller be excused from supplying goods under a requirements contract when the cost of raw materials to the seller dramatically increases to the point where the seller claims the contract is no longer profitable?

Decision and Rationale: (King) No. To excuse a seller from performing a contract because costs have unforeseeably increased, the unforeseen costs "must be more than merely onerous or expensive. It must be positively unjust to hold the parties bound." A mere showing of unprofitability, without more, will not excuse the performance of a contract. Gulf contends that the escalator indicator did not work as intended by the parties because of the advent of the two-tier pricing of government controls. It also argues that crude oil prices increased substantially without a similar rise in the pricing indicator. But, the language of the contract is clear and unambiguous. It is clear that the parties intended to be bound by the specified entries in *Platt's* which has been published at all times material here, and which is still published. With regard to Gulf's contention that the contract has become "commercially impracticable" within the meaning of U.C.C. § 2–615 because of the increase of market price of foreign crude oil, the court finds that the tendered defense has not been proved. On this record the court cannot determine how much it costs Gulf to produce a gallon of jet fuel for sale to Eastern, whether Gulf loses money or makes a profit on its sale of jet fuel to Eastern, either now or at the inception of the contract, or at any time in between. The party undertaking the burden of establishing "commercial impracticability" by reason of allegedly increased raw material costs undertakes the obligation of showing the extent to which he has suffered, or will suffer, losses in performing his contract. The record here does not substantiate Gulf's contention on this fundamental issue. Gulf transfers oil from one subsidiary to another. Each of the various subsidiaries charges the buyer subsidiary different prices. As a result, Gulf is able to shift the tax consequences of the profits it earns from one subsidiary to another. But because of the use of such accounting practices, it impossible to determine Gulf's actual costs for fuel sold to Eastern. This is especially true in light of the fact that Gulf earned substantial profits during the periods in question. Under no theory of law can it be held that Gulf is guaranteed preservation of its intra-company profits. The burden is upon Gulf to show what its real costs are, not its "costs" inflated by its internal profits at various levels of the manufacturing process. But, even if Gulf had established great hardship under U.C.C. § 2–615, which it has not, Gulf would not prevail because the events associated with the so-called energy crisis were reasonably foreseeable at the time the contract was executed. If a contingency is foreseeable, it and its consequences are taken outside the scope of U.C.C. § 2–615 because the party disadvantaged by fruition of the contingency might have protected himself in his contract. The record is replete with evidence of the volatile situation in the Middle East, and Gulf assumed the risk that the OPEC nations would do exactly what they have done. With respect to Gulf's argument that "two-tier" was not "foreseeable," the record shows that domestic crude oil prices were controlled at all material times, that Gulf foresaw that they might be de-controlled, and that Gulf was constantly urging the Government that they should be de-controlled.

Analysis:

A mere increase in the expense of performing does not give rise to a defense of impossibility. Consider an official comment to the UCC which states that "increased cost alone does not excuse performance unless the rise in cost is due to some unforseen contingency which *alters the essential nature of performance.*" It goes on to say that "a severe shortage of raw materials or of supplies due to a contingency such as war, embargo, local crop failure, unforseen shutdown of major sources of supply or the like, which causes a marked increase in cost is within the contemplation of this section." On the surface, it seems that Gulf's position fell squarely within the contemplation of the UCC and it was entitled to the defense. Ultimately, however, Gulf lost because of a failure of proof; it could not prove its increased cost to supply Eastern. Moreover, due to its own efforts to alter price controls, the court decided that the risk of a change in such controls was foreseeable by Gulf and, accordingly, should have been addressed in the contract. The law was on Gulf's side; the facts were not.

STRICT PERFORMANCE OF A CONDITION SUBSEQUENT MAY BE EXCUSED IF THE CONDITION IS NOT AN ESSENTIAL ELEMENT OF A CONTRACT

Burger King Corp. v. Family Dining, Inc.

(Franchise) v. (Franchisee)
566 F.2d 1168 (3d Cir. 1977)

M E M O R Y G R A P H I C

Instant Facts

Burger King (P) sought to terminate an exclusivity agreement with a franchisee claiming that the franchisee had failed to comply with a condition subsequent when it failed to develop Burger King restaurants exactly on schedule.

Black Letter Rule

Substantial compliance with a condition subsequent may entitle a party to enforce a conditional promise made under a contract so long as strict compliance of the condition was not an essential element of the contract.

Case Vocabulary

CONDITION SUBSEQUENT: A contractual term which does not impose a duty on a party but which, if performed, allows the party to enforce a promise made by the other party to the contract.

Procedural Basis: Trial Court's order on franchisee's motion to dismiss franchise's suit for declaratory relief from exclusivity agreement.

Facts: Burger King (P) and the Family Dining Corporation (Family) (D) entered into a contract which provided that if, over a period of ten years, Family (D) opened ten Burger King restaurants in two Pennsylvania Counties at a rate of one per year, Burger King (P) would give Family (D) exclusive rights to franchise Burger King restaurants in the two counties for the next eighty years. Burger King (P) intended the promise of exclusivity to induce Family (D) to aggressively establish Burger King restaurants in the two county area and, in fact, over the following years Family (D) did open restaurants at a rate of approximately one per year. While circumstances sometimes prevented Family (D) from opening restaurants on schedule, Burger King (P) expressed satisfaction that Family (D) was in substantial compliance with the franchise agreement and routinely excused the delays in development. At the end of the ten-year period, Family (D) had opened eight Burger King restaurants. When Family (D) informed Burger King (P) that it intended to open its ninth restaurant, Burger King (P) informed Family (D) that, because it had not satisfied the terms of the franchise agreement, it did not have the franchise rights required to open the restaurant. Family (D) opened the Burger King restaurant anyway and Burger King (P) filed suit seeking to enjoin Family (D) from using the Burger King (P) trademark. Family (D) filed a motion to dismiss Burger King's (P) suit.

Issue: Must a party strictly satisfy a condition subsequent before the party will be entitled to enforce another party's promise under a contract?

Decision and Rationale: (Hanum, J.) No. Whether a party must strictly satisfy a condition subsequent before it may enforce another party's obligation under a contract depends largely on whether strict performance of the condition subsequent was an *essential* element of the contract. The first issue for the court to decide in this case, however, is whether the development rate, which called for Family (D) to open Burger King (P) restaurants at a rate of one per year, was a promise or a condition subsequent. A promise is something that imposes a duty on a contracting party, a condition subsequent, on the other hand, is a condition which, depending on whether or not it is met, will modify or limit a party's ability to enforce a promise. Simply put, this court must decide whether Family (D) had a duty to open restaurants at the prescribed rate of development or whether the development rate and the attendant promise of exclusivity was merely an inducement for Family (D) to develop the territory quickly and aggressively. If Family (D) had a duty to open ten restaurants in ten years, it is clearly in breach of its agreement and Burger King (P) does not need to honor the exclusivity agreement. If, on the other hand, Family (D) merely failed to meet the literal requirements of a condition subsequent, Burger King (P) may still have to grant exclusivity. Whether words constitute a condition or a promise is largely a matter of the intention of the parties and may be ascertained from a reasonable construction of the language used, considered in light of the surrounding circumstances. On the facts presented, it seems clear that the true purpose of the exclusivity agreement was to create an inducement to Family (D) to develop the two-county area. Family (D) did not have a duty to develop Burger King restaurants at the prescribed rate; the development rate was merely a condition subsequent which Family (D) had to fulfill in order to enforce Burger King's (P) promise of exclusivity. Having found that the development rate was a condition subsequent, the court must then answer the second question of whether Burger King (P) has the right to have the condition protecting its promise strictly enforced. While a party does ordinarily have the right to strictly enforce a condition subsequent before it will be obligated to perform on its promise, The Restatement of Contracts §302 provides that a condition may be excused if its existence or occurrence is not an essential part of the contract. In this case, the circumstances and prior dealings of the parties indicate that the development rate was not considered by either to be an essential part of the contract. Burger King (P) on several occasions excused delays by Family (D) in opening restaurants and seemed to be satisfied with Family's (D) performance. The purpose of the development rate agreement was to see that Family (D) actively developed the franchise territory and this Family (D) did: Family (D) has developed at least ten restaurants as originally contemplated in the agreement. Because Burger King (P) got the benefit of its bargain and Family's (D) delay did not in any way materially affect the agreement, we find that Burger King (P) must now grant Family (D) exclusive territorial franchise rights as originally contemplated. To deprive Family (D) of exclusive territorial rights would constitute a forfeiture without any commensurate breach since Family's (D) failure to strictly comply with the development rate caused Burger King (P) no serious injury. Accordingly, this court finds that Burger King (P) is not entitled to a declaration that the exclusivity agreement is terminated and Family's (D) motion for dismissal is therefore granted.

Analysis:

The court here relied on principles of equity as well as contract to deny Burger King's (P) motion to terminate the exclusivity agreement. While the court recognized that Family (D) did not strictly comply with the conditions of the exclusivity agreement, it also seemed to recognize that this failure in no way harmed Burger King (P) or served to deprive it of the benefit of its bargain. Burger King (P) entered the agreement with Family (D) with the goal of having the two county area developed in an efficient and timely manner. Specifically, Burger King (P) wanted there to be ten Burger King restaurants in the area within ten years. As an inducement meant to encourage Family (D) to meet this goal, Burger King (P) promised Family (D) exclusive franchise rights to the territory if it complied and built the restaurants on schedule. Essentially, the court stated, the development rate agreement was not a foundation of the contract, it was simply a condition subsequent which, if met, would give Family (D) the right to enforce Burger King's (P) promise of exclusivity. Though at times a party to a contract is entitled to have the terms of a condition subsequent strictly enforced before it will have to meet the obligations of its promise, this is not always the case. Whether the terms of a condition subsequent must be strictly met is largely dependent on the intention of the parties as evidence of the language used in the contract and by the actions of the parties themselves. In this case, the court noted that Burger King (P) had excused strict compliance with the development rate condition on several occasions and, in fact, Burger King (P) seemed perfectly happy with Family's (D) performance under the agreement. It was not until Burger King (P) had a change in management and subsequently realized that it could develop the two-county area much more densely than previously believed that it chose to make an issue of strict compliance with the development rate. The court rightly rejected Burger King's (P) cynical ploy. After all, the court reasoned, Family (D) had assumed considerable risk and expense in constructing the restaurants and, since at the time the court heard the case there were ten Burger King restaurants in place, Burger King (P) had gotten exactly what it had bargained for. Consequently, the court held that Family (D) had the right to enforce Burger King's (P) promise of exclusivity; in effect, the court was not about to let Burger King out of its obligation on the basis of a technicality. The lesson of this case seems to be that, if a party considers strict compliance with a condition subsequent to be an essential element of a contract, the party should insist on strict compliance. A party may not repeatedly excuse another party's non-compliance and then hope to use the non-compliance as a basis for excusing its own performance. It is this excuse which is relevant to our studies in this chapter. Up until now, we have looked at cases where a sudden unforeseen change in circumstances led the court to either excuse performance under the doctrines of impossibility, impracticability or frustration of purpose, or have seen cases where the court refused to alter a parties' agreement because they had allocated the risk that arose to one party. In this case, however, we see a party seeking to be excused from performing its end of the bargain based on the language of the agreement and the other party's failure to comply. How is this relevant to our inquiry? Well, first, it is a case in which one party seeks to be excused from performance. Second, and more importantly, it is an example, like the previous two cases *Northern Indiana Public Service Co. v. Carbon County Coal Co.* [fixed-price contract necessarily allocates risk of price fluctuations], *Transatlantic Financing Corp. v. United States* [cannot recover expenses over contract price under quantum meruit unless performance otherwise excused] and *Eastern Air Lines, Inc. v. Gulf Oil Corp.* [parties took possibility of price increase into consideration when entering agreement and cannot now seek to change allocation of that risk now that it has arisen], where a court refused to change the parties' agreement at one parties' insistence. While the underlying reasoning here is more in line with equitable principles and not the default rules, it is still a case where the court is asked to consider excusing a party's performance.

Bak-A-Lum Corp. of America v. Alcoa Bldg. Products, Inc.

(Exclusive Distributor) v. (Manufacturer)

Supreme Court of New Jersey, 1976, 69 N.J. 123, 351 A.2d 349

M E M O R Y G R A P H I C

Instant Facts

An aluminum siding manufacturer cancelled its distributor's exclusive contract without notice.

Black Letter Rule

Every contract is subject to an implied covenant of good faith and fair dealing.

Case Vocabulary

CROSS APPEAL: An appeal brought by the respondent to an existing appeal. In this case, Alcoa (D) was required to answer BAL's (P) appeal, but raised an issue of its own on appeal. Although omitted from the casebook, Alcoa's (D) appeal claimed that its behavior was not actionable.

Procedural Basis: Appeal and cross appeal from a trial court judgement for the plaintiff in a breach of contract action.

Facts: Bak-A-Lum Corp. of America (BAL) (P) had a verbal agreement with Alcoa Bldg. Products, Inc. (Alcoa) (D) to be the exclusive distributor for Alcoa's (D) aluminum siding and other goods in Northern New Jersey. BAL (P) agreed to use its best efforts to market Alcoa's (D) products and, indeed, Alcoa (D) was satisfied with its performance. Nonetheless, Alcoa (D) hired four new distributors in Northern New Jersey, effectively terminating BAL's (P) exclusive contract. In fact, Alcoa (D) was planning on hiring the new distributors at a time when BAL (P) was expanding its warehouse in order to handle Alcoa's (D) business. Alcoa (D) continued to encourage the expansion while it concealed its other plans. BAL subsequently sued for breach of contract. The trial court found for BAL (P). The court determined that the parties' agreement was terminable only after a reasonable period of time and with reasonable notice. The judge further determined that while Alcoa (D) met the first requirement, they had failed the second by not giving BAL (P) reasonable notice of the termination. The court figured reasonable notice at a period of seven months. As a result, the court granted BAL (P) damages in the amount of $5000 for every month where notice was lacking. This, despite the fact that BAL (P) had proven its damages at $10,000 a month. BAL (P) appeals the court's damage determination. Alcoa (D) cross-appeals from the court's judgement.

Issue: Can a court imply a reasonable termination clause in a contract for exclusive dealing?

Decision and Rationale: (Conford) Yes. The trial court correctly interpreted the contract to require a reasonable period of notice before termination. However, the court calculated that period at seven months, an assessment with which we disagree. The trial court offered a detailed description of Alcoa's (D) bad behavior during the final stages of its relationship with BAL (P). First, Alcoa (D) made a deliberate decision to conceal its plans from BAL (P) because it was afraid that BAL (P) would shirk its responsibilities during the termination period. They even went so far as encourage BAL's (P) purchase of $150,000 worth of merchandise in the same month that it cancelled the distributorship. Finally, they inexplicably encouraged BAL (P) to lease expanded warehouse space in order to store its products. Ordinarily, Alcoa (D) might not have had an obligation to notify BAL (P) before it terminated the agreement. However, its behavior was so reprehensible as to violate a covenant which is part of every contract -- the duty of good faith and fair dealing. The trial court should have taken this breach into consideration when it figured the appropriate notice period. In addition, the trial court should have considered the impact of BAL's (P) new warehouse lease on the amount of notice it would need in the event of a termination. BAL (P) argues that it should be compensated for the remaining 4½ years of the new lease. We are not willing to go this far, considering its ability to use the warehouse for other purposes consistent with its duty to mitigate damages. We do, however, hold that a reasonable period of notice for termination would be 20 months. This period takes into account all of the circumstances of this case. In addition, we modify the trial court's damage award to meet BAL's (P) unchallenged claim for damages in the amount of $10,000 per month. The trial court's judgement is modified in accordance with this opinion and is otherwise affirmed in opposition to Alcoa's (D) cross appeal.

Analysis:

Judge Conford announces an implied duty which is broader and more common than any you have seen thus far. By the same token, the implied duty of good faith and fair dealing is probably the least burdensome duty that a court could imply. Like many of the opinions in this chapter, Judge Conford's decision assumes that the parties entered into a contract in order to satisfy a mutual goal. In addition, he recognizes that every contract gives rise to a duty to avoid behavior which subverts the rights of the other party. Judge Conford then tries to arrive at a decision which satisfies both of these premises. In a similar vein, we once considered whether the parties would have agreed to the current conditions of its relationship when they originally negotiated their contract. In this case, the question is whether BAL (P) would have agreed to a clause permitting Alcoa (D) to cancel the contract without notice. While BAL (P) might have consented to this provision, it certainly would have asked for more compensation in the process. You can see from this approach that Judge Conford reached a reasonable conclusion. Alcoa (D) should not be permitted to take advantage of circumstances which were not contemplated at the time of contracting, but which would have altered the parties' relationship if they had been the subject of proper negotiations. In other words, because the parties did not foresee termination of their exclusivity agreement, the court was forced to determine what they would have agreed to had they foreseen such a result. As with all of the other cases in this chapter, the court is faced with a difficult decision. In essence, it must put itself in the shoes of the parties and decide what they themselves did not decide. Notice that here, however, it is not a default rule, *per se*, that leads the court to its ultimate conclusion that reasonable notice was a term of the contract. Rather, it was the duty of good faith and fair dealing, which is an implied term in every contract. As stated in the opinion: "in every contract there is an implied covenant that neither party [will] do anything [that] will have the effect of destroying or injuring the right of the other party to receive the fruits of the contract". Thus, it is an implied term that essentially holds each side to their bargain and gives the court leeway to find an equitable solution. Unlike the cases we previously saw where courts are unwilling to alter a parties' agreement, here we see a situation where alterations are required in order to give effect to the parties' agreement. In other words, while parties may agree to allocate risk a certain way, as in *Northern Indiana Public Service Co.*, or set definite terms before a promise will become binding, as in *Burger King*, their freedom to contract is not without limit.

THE DUTY OF GOOD FAITH INHERENT IN EVERY CONTRACT APPLIES ONLY TO EXISTING OBLIGATIONS UNDER A CONTRACT; THE DUTY DOES NOT REQUIRE A PARTY TO DO MORE THAN AGREED TO UNDER A CONTRACT

Badgett v. Security State Bank

(Dairy Farmers) v. (Bank)

807 P.2d 356 (Supreme Court of Washington, 1991)

M E M O R Y   G R A P H I C

Instant Facts

Dairy farmers brought an action against the bank claiming that the bank had breached its duty of good faith when it refused to renegotiate the terms of a loan agreement.

Black Letter Rule

The Duty of Good Faith requires only that parties to a contract carry out their existing obligations under a contract in good faith, it cannot be used to require that parties undertake new or additional obligations.

Case Vocabulary

COLLATERAL: Property, real or personal, pledged as security for a debt.

SECURITY AGREEMENT: Agreement by debtor to pledge collateral to be used to pay off debt in the event of default.

Procedural Basis: Appeal to Washington Supreme Court following Court of Appeal's decision to reverse trial court's grant of summary judgment in favor of the bank.

Facts: Raymond and Audrey Badgett (P) (Badgetts) borrowed approximately $1,500,000 from Security State Bank (D) (Security) in order to support their dairy farm. The Badgetts (P) had borrowed money from Security (D) on other occasions and the bank had in the past worked with them to restructure their loans. When the Badgetts (P) decided to get out of the dairy farm business, they approached Security (D) with a settlement proposal which would have settled their loan. Under the settlement proposal, the Badgetts (P) would participate in the government's DTP program (Dairy Termination Program) whereby the government would pay them to cease dairy farming. The Badgetts (P) planned to submit a bid to the DTP program which, if accepted, would have resulted in a $1,200,000 payment form the government. The Badgetts (P) proposed that Security (D) accept the $1,200,000 as satisfaction of their debt. Security (D) rejected the Badgett's (P) proposal and, as a result, the Badgetts (P) submitted a higher bid to the DTP program which the government rejected. Soon after the rejection of the DTP bid, the Badgetts (P) ceased making loan payments to Security (D) and Security (D) began to auction off the Badgetts (P) collateral. The Badgetts (P) sued Security (D) claiming that, by refusing to negotiate a settlement amount, Security (D) had effectively refused them permission to participate in the DTP program. Security (D) filed a counterclaim against the Badgetts (P) for payment of the loan amount. The trial court dismissed the Badgett's (P) claim holding that Security (D) had no duty to negotiate the loan amount and granted Security (D) summary judgment on its counterclaim. The Court of Appeals reversed the trial court's holding that the parties' course of dealing had created a good faith obligation on the part of Security (D) to consider the Badgett's (P) settlement proposal. Security (D) then appealed to the Washington Supreme Court.

Issue: Does the duty of good faith implied in every contract require a party to accept a material change in the terms of a contract?

Decision and Rationale: (Durham, J.) No. The Badgetts (P) contend that the duty of good faith implied in every contract required Security (D) to at least attempt to renegotiate the terms of the loan agreement. We disagree. The duty of good faith does not obligate a party to accept a material change in the terms of its contract. Rather, the duty of good faith requires only that the parties perform in good faith the obligations imposed by their agreement. The Badgetts (P) are in effect urging this court to expand the existing duty of good faith to create an obligation that Security (D) did not agree to, namely, the duty to negotiate a restructuring of the loan. We refuse to apply the duty of good faith to create any new obligations on the part of Security (D). The loan agreement does not contain language pertaining to the restructuring of the loan and the agreement clearly states that the written agreement is the "entire agreement." This court will not now use the duty of good faith to rewrite the agreement. We further find that Security (D) did not breach its duty when it refused to restructure the loan: as a matter of law, there cannot be a breach of the duty of good faith when a party simply stands on its right to require performance of a contract according to its terms. Because it is clear that Security (D) had no good faith obligation to negotiate for the restructure of the agreement, we do not need to address the Badgett's (P) contention that their prior course of dealing with Security (D) required Security (D) to renegotiate the contract. While a prior course of dealing may be used to interpret the existing terms of a contract, it in no way creates new or additional obligations. In sum, we hold that the implied duty of good faith implied in every contract did not give rise to a duty on the part of

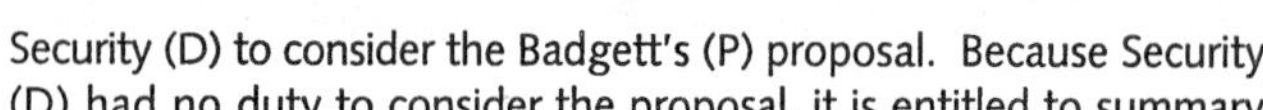

Security (D) to consider the Badgett's (P) proposal. Because Security (D) had no duty to consider the proposal, it is entitled to summary judgment as a matter of law. Accordingly, we reverse the Court of Appeals and reinstate the trial court's grant of summary judgment.

Analysis:

This opinion attempts to define the parameters of the covenant of good faith and fair dealing that was discussed in the previous case, *Bak-A-Lum Corp. v. Alcoa Bldg. Prods., Inc.* [duty of good faith required reasonable notice before termination of agreement.] Here, the court confirms that parties have a great deal of freedom and latitude when negotiating for the terms and conditions of a contract despite the implied covenant. The agreement between the Badgetts (P) and Security (D) did not contemplate any duty to renegotiate or restructure the loan and specifically stated that the written agreement constituted the entire agreement. The Badgetts (P), in effect, urged the court to apply the duty of good faith inherent in every contract to rewrite the loan agreement. The court refused to be persuaded by the Badgett's (P) argument. The duty of good faith, the court pointed out, does apply to every contract but the duty only operates to obligate the parties to cooperate with each other so that each may obtain the full benefit of the bargain agreed to. The duty of good faith may not be used to change the terms of the bargain itself. In short, the court upheld the principle that parties should be free to negotiate for the terms and conditions of a contract that they choose. A court will not later come in and apply the duty of good faith to rewrite a freely bargained for contract. If the Badgetts (P) had wanted Security (D) to have the obligation to renegotiate the terms of the loan agreement at a later date, they should have negotiated that term before they agreed to the loan. They could not use the duty of good faith to impose upon Security (D) an obligation it had never agreed to undertake. Notice how the result here is in stark contrast to that in *Bak-A-Lum Corp.*, where the Court essentially used the covenant of good faith and fair dealing to imply a reasonable notice term into the parties' agreement. It is doubtful that this Court would have reached the same conclusion. However, consider that it may be that unlike here, the reasonable notice term was not material to the agreement. Also, consider that the course of dealing between the parties here as opposed to *Bak-A-Lum Corp.* does not cry out for equity to favor one side over the other. Additionally, since the Court in this case is ultimately persuaded that the covenant not be used to imply an obligation that did not arise from terms the parties already agreed to, it may be that unlike this case, *Bak-A-Lum Corp.* involved a situation where the reasonable notice obligation could be said to have arisen out of the parties' termination provision in the existing contract. While this Court seems to skirt the course of dealing argument by not reaching it, it is certainly arguable that the history of the parties in this case was not so egregious as it was in *Bak-A-Lum Corp.*. The ultimate explanation, however, more likely lies in the amorphous nature of the implied covenant of good faith and fair dealing. While it meant implying a term into the parties' agreement that they had not bargained for in *Bak-A-Lum Corp.*, it meant sticking to the strict terms of the parties' agreement in this case. Obviously, the covenant of good faith and fair dealing can be manipulated by the courts to fit whatever equitable result the court wishes to reach. [Which unfortunately does not make it easy to apply if you are not a court!] The important thing to keep in mind, however, is that there are limits to what the implied covenant of good faith and fair dealing can do and in general, it cannot be used to imply a new material term into the parties' agreement, especially in a situation such as this which could have been foreseen by the parties. Also, notice how the Court here disagrees with the Court of Appeals' conclusion that the course of dealing here imposed a duty on the bank to renegotiate in good faith. As you will see in the next case, which is the Court of Appeal's opinion, the Court of Appeals ruled that in some situations, such as the one here, a party's duty of good faith could be expanded to include obligations not set forth in the parties' contract. The Supreme Court here flatly disagreed, holding that as a matter of law, the duty of good faith could not expand a party's obligations and thus concluding that the parties' course of dealing is irrelevant. Do you agree? For a more thorough discussion of the reasons for or against allowing course of dealing to expand the duty of good faith, see the next case.

Badgett v. Security State Bank

(Borrower) v. (Lender)
786 P.2d 302 (Wash. Ct. App. 1990)

M E M O R Y G R A P H I C

Instant Facts

Dairy farmers brought an action against the bank claiming that the bank had breached its duty of good faith when it refused to renegotiate the terms of their loan, despite having done so in the past.

Black Letter Rule

A party's duty of good faith can be expanded by the actions of a contracting party that give rise to a reasonable expectation on the part of the other party.

Case Vocabulary

COURSE OF DEALING: Conduct of the parties in performing their agreement and in their business relationship in general.

Procedural Basis: Appeal of the Trial Court's order granting the bank's motion for summary judgment.

Facts: Same as previous case, *Badgett v. Security State Bank* [Dairy farmers borrowed $1.5 million to run dairy farm and then, after deciding to get out of the dairy business for the second time, sought to have loan renegotiated as bank had done the first time they quit the dairy business.]

Issue: May a party's conduct give rise to an obligation not otherwise part of the agreement?

Decision and Rationale: (Petrich) Yes. The implied duty of good faith and fair dealing is the single most important concept underlying the entire Uniform Commercial Code. While this duty does not require a party to accept a material change in the terms of its agreement, the scope of that duty may be expanded by the party's conduct if such conduct gives rise to a reasonable expectation on the other party's part. Such expectations can arise from the parties course of dealing, among other things. Here, the evidence showed that Security State Bank (D) anticipated changes in the Badgett's (P) situation, as well as in those of its other agricultural customers, and routinely restructured and renegotiated agricultural loans like the one the Badgett's (P) had because of a change in circumstances. In fact, Security State Bank (D) had done this over the course of its six-year relationship with the Badgett's (P). The latest agreement itself even referenced the possibility of an amendment because of changed circumstances. This was enough to support a reasonable inference that the parties' course of dealing had created a good faith obligation on the part of Security State Bank (D) to at least consider renegotiating the Badgett's (P) loan. Whether the parties' course of dealing actually created such an obligation and whether, if so, good faith was present are questions of fact a jury should have been allowed to consider. As such, the Trial Court's grant of summary judgment in light of these factual issues was improper. Reversed.

Analysis:

Here we see the Court of Appeals opinion that was reversed by the Supreme Court in the case we just read, *Badgett v. Security State Bank* [duty of good faith does not obligate party to do any more than it already agreed to do]. Unlike the previous opinion where the Supreme Court concluded that the duty of good faith could never be expanded by the parties' course of dealing, the Court of Appeals concluded that in some situations, like the one here, a party's conduct that gives rise to a reasonable expectation on the other party's party that the party will take a certain action like they have in the past. Here, the Court of Appeals was of the opinion that all of Security State Bank's (D) prior dealings with the Badgett's (P) could have given the Badgett's (P) a reasonable expectation that the bank (D) would continue to treat them the same way thus giving rise to a good faith obligation on the bank's (D) part to at least consider renegotiating their loan, as it had before. The Supreme Court, however, disagreed concluding that as a matter of law, the parties' course of dealing is irrelevant since the duty of good faith could never expand a party's obligations under the agreement. In the Supreme Court's view, a party is not bound to do more than it agreed to do in the contract. However, in limiting the implied duty of good faith and fair dealing in this way, the Supreme Court seemed to overlook the importance the duty of good faith plays in commercial dealings. Consider, for example, that most parties assume they will be treated fairly and that those with whom they have business relationships will act in good faith. The Court of Appeals' opinion incorporated that basic assumption into the duty of good faith by allowing the duty to include reasonable expectations created by one party's actions. Under the Supreme Court's opinion, however, the duty of good faith is limited such that a party is only obligated to act in good faith in carrying out its express obligations under the agreement. Does this do justice to the underlying purpose of the implied duty of good faith and fair dealing? In some ways, yes. If the duty of good faith is subject to ever-expansion based on the parties' dealings, how would a party know whether their actions are subjecting them to potential liability for a breach of the duty of good faith in actions that they are not obligated to take? Moreover, notice how difficult it would be to fashion a remedy for a breach of an obligation the parties did not initially agree would be undertaken. In this case, for example, what remedy would the Badgett's (P) be entitled to if the Court of Appeals' opinion had been affirmed? What would cure the defect here in the bank's (D) failure to consider renegotiating? Could the bank (D) be ordered to consider renegotiating the loan? Would such an order be effective? As you can see, there are numerous problems with an amorphous duty of good faith that are not present if the duty is limited solely to obligations a party has specifically agreed to undertake. While this may seem like a case where the duty of good faith is implicated, keep in mind that, as in typical commercial transactions, the law still holds true to that age-old ideal: caveat emptor!

J.J. Brooksbank Co. v. Budget Rent-A-Car Corp.

(Licensee) v. (Licensor)
337 N.W.2d 372 (Minn. 1983)

MEMORY GRAPHIC

Instant Facts

Licensor sought to excuse its performance under a 1962 agreement that required it to transfer reservations to licensee free of charge because of changed circumstances, that being licensor's updated technology.

Black Letter Rule

For a party's performance to be excused due to changed circumstances, there must be an event that was not expected to occur and whose nonoccurrence was a basic assumption of the contract.

Case Vocabulary

DECLARATORY JUDGMENT: A ruling by the court setting forth the way things are under the law.
FRANCHISE: A form of license agreement that allows one business to operate under the name and model of another.
LICENSEE: The party that is given permission to use something that belongs to another by agreement.
LICENSOR: The party that grants another permission to use something.
PRACTICAL CONSTRUCTION OF A CONTRACT: Uses the parties' conduct during the course of performance that may support inferences as to the meaning of language used in the contract as well as intentions with regard to gaps or omissions.

Procedural Basis: Appeal from the order of the Trial Court after a bench trial.

Facts: In 1960, J.J. Brooksbank Co. (P) ("Brooksbank") entered into a franchise agreement with Budget Rent-A-Car Corp. (D) ("Budget"). Under the agreement, Brooksbank (P) was allowed to operate Budget Rent-A-Car center, using Budget's name and receiving the perks that come along with operating a nationally known business. After the franchise agreement, the parties entered into a licensing agreement in 1962 whereby Brooksbank (P) received a better deal on franchise fees, per car service charges and reservation costs than those offered to franchisees that came after Brooksbank (P). Under the parties licensing agreement, Budget (D) was to spend a minimum of 50% of the per car service charge paid by all licensees on advertising, maintain reservation offices in New York City, Los Angeles and Chicago, and forward to Brooksbank (P) all applicable reservations made at Budget's (D) reservation offices in the selected cities to Brooksbank (P). Brooksbank (P), in return, was to take and transmit all reservations it received that were applicable to other licensees free of charge. The obligations were to continue during the existence of the franchise agreement, which was automatically renewable every five years. During the 1960s, Budget (D) operated a two-tier reservation system that was dependent on its licensees taking and transmitting reservations to other licensees as well as Budget (D) forwarding reservations taken at its national offices in Los Angeles, New York City and Chicago. As business grew, however, Budget (D) began to centralize its operations in Chicago and increased the number of licensees to over 350 from the previous 15 to 20 it had in the early 1960s. During this time period, Brooksbank (P) received approximately one-third of its reservations from Budget's (D) reservation offices in New York City, Los Angeles and Chicago. Eventually, as the business and the number of licensees continued to grow, problems began to arise. Licensees would fail to transmit reservations or would transmit incomplete information. Some counter personnel at certain licensees were rude and would simply not take reservations for other areas during busy times. In response to these problems, Budget (D) considered developing a centralized computer reservation system featuring a single 800 number for taking and transmitting reservations. To pay for the upgraded system, however, Budget (D) would need to pass the cost along to its licensees. In general, this did not present a problem as Budget (D) was already charging many of its licensees for reservations received from the main offices. However, Brooksbank (P), pursuant to its license agreement, continued to insist that it should receive the reservations Budget (D) took at the three main offices free of charge. In June 1970, Budget (D) implemented the centralized computer reservation system. To settle the dispute with Brooksbank (P), Budget (D) proposed an agreement, which Brooksbank (P) accepted, which would require Brooksbank (P) to pay the franchise fees and costs for receiving the reservations but would compensate Brooksbank (P) in advertising approximately one-third of its costs relating to computerized reservations. Brooksbank (P) specifically reserved its rights under the prior 1962 agreement, however. When the supplemental agreement expired in 1974, Budget (D) refused to extend any further credit and demanded that Brooksbank (P) pay its share of the reservation costs. Brooksbank (P) then brought this action seeking a declaratory judgment that it was entitled to receive reservations from the three main offices free of charge. At trial, Brooksbank (P) argued that the 1962 agreement mandated that it receive all of its reservations from the main offices free of charge, or, at the very least, that it should receive at least one-third of its reservations free of charge. Budget (D), on the other hand, argued that the free reservations applied only to the two-tier reservation system and not the new centralized computer reservations system. The Trial Court concluded that the central computerized reservation system was not covered by the parties 1962 agreement and that the technology giving rise to the new system was not

foreseeable in 1962. Nonetheless, it concluded that Budget (D), as an incentive to Brooksbank (P) to become a licensee, intended to give Brooksbank (P) free reservations from the offices in New York City, Los Angeles and Chicago. Based on this intention, the Trial Court concluded that Brooksbank (P) was entitled to receive a 10% reduction in its computerized reservation costs in lieu of its contractual rights. The Trial Court arrived at the 10% figure based upon equitable considerations. Both parties appeal.

Issue: May a party be excused from performing when an event whose nonoccurrence was not a basic assumption of the contract occurs?

Decision and Rationale: (Peterson) No. From our own review of the 1962 agreement and the practical construction given it by the parties, we conclude that Brooksbank (P) is entitled to a one-third reduction in its reservation costs. Beginning with the language of the agreement itself, which is a standard licensing form agreement prepared by Budget (D), it is clear that the 1962 agreement contemplated a two-tier reservation system as it existed at that time. Our job thus becomes one of interpreting the omissions in the agreement, which, as Judge Learned Hand eloquently stated, involves an "imaginative projection of the expressed purpose upon situations arising later, for which the parties did not provide and which they did not have in mind". Thus, where the parties' intent is discernible, even if difficult to ascertain, it must be followed. Keeping these principals in mind, the 1962 agreement, interpreted under the conditions that exist today, supports a one-third reduction in reservation costs for Brooksbank (P). This one-third reduction reflects the bargain the parties reached in 1962, when, in return for Brooksbank's (P) participation, Budget (D) agreed to give it free reservations from the areas where it already had offices: New York City, Los Angeles and Chicago. The evidence shows that under this arrangement, Brooksbank (P) had received one-third of its reservations from this area. For all other reservations from other areas, Brooksbank (P) paid the costs for reservations, as did all subsequent licensees. Preserving this one-third of Brooksbank's (P) reservations as free of charge thus preserves the parties' bargain. Having so concluded, we reject Brooksbank's (P) argument that it is entitled to all of its reservations free of charge. This would defeat the purpose of the original agreement, not continue it. We also reject Budget's (D) contention that Brooksbank (P) should not receive any reservations free of charge simply because Budget (D) changed the way in which it takes reservations. To do so ignores the plain meaning of the parties' agreement, and especially ignores the language that the agreement "continues during the existence of the [franchise] agreement" and flies in the face of the implied duty of good faith and fair dealing. In light of this language and the implied duty, we believe the contract obligates Budget (D) to cooperate with Brooksbank (P) regarding the allocation of costs associated with reservations. Thus, even though the parties may not have anticipated technological changes, they are still bound by the bargain reached in 1962. To preserve that bargain, Budget (D) must remain bound to provide a portion of reservations free of charge, as it originally agreed. The fact that the reservation system has now changed did not change the intent of the parties in dividing up reservation costs based upon geographic location. We further reject Budget's (D) argument that it should be excused from performing because of impracticability or frustration of purpose. Both of these doctrines require that an event occur whose nonoccurrence was a basic assumption of the contract. Here, the reservation system remaining the same was not a basic assumption of the contract. Having concluded that Brooksbank (P) is not entitled to all of its reservations free of charge and that Budget (D) is not excused from its performance, we must now examine whether the 10% reduction granted by the Trial Court was supported by the evidence. We find that it was not. The Trial Court arrived at the 10% figure based solely on equitable principles, but it did not consider the actual effect of the parties' bargain nor did it strive to achieve a result here that is the same as the parties' original agreement. Though the Trial Court was correct in recognizing that Brooksbank (P) was entitled to some sort of a reduction in its reservation costs, the evidence does not support its deduction. Historically, Brooksbank received one-third of its reservations from the offices in New York City, Los Angeles and Chicago. Brooksbank (P) paid for all other reservations it received from other licensees. Thus, requiring Brooksbank (P) to pay for all other reservations it receives except the one-third it receives from these areas preserves the parties' original agreement. Therefore, the Trial Court's judgment is Modified and, as modified, Affirmed.

Dissent: (Simonett) It makes no difference whether or not the parties assumed the reservation system would not change. It is clear that the parties did not foresee a change in the system and that, the change having occurred, the manner of dividing up costs for reservations as set forth in the 1962 agreement is no longer possible. No rules of contract construction allow us to nevertheless attempt to enforce the agreement in an equivalent fashion as the majority has done. All we know from applying the rules of construction is that the parties do not agree on what they would have agreed to had they foreseen such a change. Thus, we are not being asked to interpret an agreement but rather to arbitrate a dispute. Where, as here, the contract offers no help in resolving the dispute, equitable principles may be used to reach a resolution. This is what the Trial Court did in this case, albeit without explanation. Clearly a reduction in reservation costs is required to preserve the parties' bargain, but in what amount should be determined after looking at the equities of the entire relationship. I would thus reverse and remand with instructions that the Trial Court consider all of the equities to reach a reasonable reduction amount and set out its reasons in detail.

Analysis:

Here we see another case where one party seeks to be excused from performing its obligations under an agreement because of changed circumstances. Like *Taylor*, *Krell*, *Northern Indiana Public Service Co.*, *Transatlantic Financing Corp.* and *Eastern Airlines*, all of which preceded this case, the Court must struggle with what the parties would have done had they foreseen the change in circumstances. Unlike all of the other cases, however, the Court here seems to have taken the most liberty and actually rewrote the parties agreement in order to achieve a result it believed preserved the parties' bargain. But notice that the parties never said Brooksbank (P) would get one-third of its reservations free of charge, but rather said it would receive reservations from three specific cities free of charge. Even though Brooksbank (P) may have historically received one-third of its reservations from these cities, this does not mean the parties intended that it continue to always receive one-third of its reservations free. Didn't the change in reservations systems prevent the parties from determining what reservations came from those three cities and what came from elsewhere? Clearly under the new reservation system it appears that Budget (D) cannot allocate costs of reservations as it had when the parties entered into their agreement. Shouldn't this mean continued performance is impracticable, if not impossible? The Court here seems to conclude that since the underlying purpose of the agreement can still be maintained by allowing a one-third reduction in costs that the reduction should be read as part of the contract. They thus seem to apply a reverse frustration of purpose test. Notice also that there is an element of the duty of good faith present here. Like the good faith cases we read previously, *Burger King*, *Bak-A-Lum Corp.* and *Badgett*, the Court states that Budget (D) had a duty to work with Brooksbank (P) to continue its agreement despite the change in reservation systems. The Court thus seems to be of the opinion, as was the Court of Appeals in *Badgett*, that the duty of good faith required more than merely sticking to its obligations as strictly stated in the agreement. Both the majority and the dissent agree that the change in reservation systems was not foreseeable, and neither the majority nor the assent give that unforeseeability any weight in determining whether to excuse Budget's (D) performance. In fact, the dissent only differs in the amount of the reduction. On the one hand, the dissent argues that the majority had no basis for awarding Brooksbank (P) a one-third deduction but then goes on to say that some sort of reduction is called for based on a review of all of the equities. Doesn't this contradict itself? In the same breath, the dissent criticizes the majority for modifying the parties' agreement by awarding Brooksbank (P) a reduction but then says it would also award some sort of a reduction. The difference may be in the reasoning behind the reduction. The majority grandfathers its reduction into the contract and its interpretation thereof; the dissent, on the other hand, gives up on the contract and simply imposes a reduction as a matter of equity. But should the courts be involved in arbitrating disputes where no rule of law applies? If there is no basis upon which to grant a reduction in the contract, shouldn't Budget (D) win? Obviously neither the majority nor the dissent believed so, which raises interesting questions about the role of a court in filling in the blanks in a parties' agreement, whether those are blanks as to material terms as you have already seen in other chapters, or blanks resulting from the failure of the parties to foresee certain changes. This question of what role the courts should play is an underlying theme in this and several other chapters – keep it in mind.

Gruenberg v. Aetna Insurance Co.

(Insured) v. (Insurer)
510 P.2d 1032 (Cal. 1973)

MEMORY GRAPHIC

Instant Facts

Insured sued his insurance company for failing to consider his claim for fire loss solely because he refused to attend an examination under oath while he was on trial for arson.

Black Letter Rule

An insurer has a duty to deal in good faith with its insured and, if that duty is breached, the insured can bring a tort action against the insurer because the duty does not arise out of the contract.

Case Vocabulary

ARSON: A crime charging that one intentionally set fire to a structure with the intent to destroy.
CONSEQUENTIAL DAMAGES: Those damages that were reasonably within the contemplation of or reasonably foreseeable by the parties at the time the contract was made.
GENERAL DAMAGES: Those damages that flow naturally from the breach of a contractual obligation.
IMPLIED COVENANT: A promise implied as a matter of law.
PRELIMINARY HEARING: A court proceeding at which the court is to determine whether there is sufficient evidence to support a finding of probable cause that the defendant committed the crime with which he is charged.

Procedural Basis: Appeal from the Trial Court's order of dismissal of the complaint.

Facts: Mr. Gruenberg (P) owned a cocktail lounge and restaurant in Los Angeles known as the Brass Rail. The Brass Rail was insured by Aetna Insurance Co. (D) ("Aetna") against fire loss of up to $35,000. In the early hours of November 9, 1969, a fire occurred at the Brass Rail. Mr. Gruenberg (P) arrived on scene and immediately argued with a member of the arson detail of the Los Angeles Fire Department. Mr. Gruenberg (P) was subsequently arrested. Immediately upon learning of the charges, Aetna (D) hired a claims firm to handle Mr. Gruenberg's (P) fire loss claim. A claims adjuster from that firm went to the scene to investigate and told an arson investigator that Mr. Gruenberg (P) had excessive fire coverage. Shortly thereafter, Mr. Gruenberg (P) was charged with arson and defrauding an insurance company. A preliminary hearing was then set for January 12, 1970. Aetna (D) also hired counsel to represent it. On November 25, 1969, one of Aetna's (D) attorneys demanded in writing that Mr. Gruenberg (P) submit to an examination under oath. Mr. Gruenberg's (P) attorney refused the request, explaining that until his criminal proceedings were concluded, he had advised Mr. Gruenberg [wisely!] not to make any statements. Mr. Gruenberg (P), through counsel, requested that Aetna (D) waive the examination requirement until the criminal charges were resolved. Aetna (D) refused and, on December 16, 1969, denied Mr. Gruenberg's (P) claim due solely to his failure to submit to an examination. At the preliminary hearing on January 12, 1970, the charges against Mr. Gruenberg (P) were dismissed for lack of probable cause. On January 26, 1970, Mr. Gruenberg (P) offered to submit to the examination. Aetna (D) again declined, standing on its previous denial. Mr. Gruenberg (P) then brought this action alleging that as a result of Aetna's (D) actions, both on its own and through and in concert with its agents and attorneys, he had suffered severe economic and noneconomic damages. Mr. Gruenberg (P) thus asserted various tort claims against Aetna (D) based on bad faith and outrageous conduct. Aetna (D) moved to dismiss for failure to state a claim, and the Trial Court granted the motion. This appeal followed.

Issue: May an insured bring a tort claim against his insurer for breach of the implied duty of good faith and fair dealing?

Decision and Rationale: (Sullivan) Yes. Mr. Gruenberg (P) argues that his complaint alleges sufficient facts to state a claim against Aetna (D) for breach of the implied duty of good faith and fair dealing. This duty, which sounds in both contract and tort, is imposed as a matter of law because every contract, including insurance policies, contains an implied covenant that neither party will do anything to injure the other party's rights under the agreement. Thus, liability is imposed on an insurer not for bad faith breach of the contract itself but for breach of this implied covenant. Here, we are faced with the duty of an insurer to act in good faith with respect to its own insured. In this case, that duty required Aetna (D) to not unreasonably withhold payments due under the policy. It is important to note that this duty does not arise out of the obligations in the contract *per se*. Rather, it arises out of the insurer's obligation to deal fairly and in good faith with its insured. In a case like this, where an insurer refuses, without proper cause, to pay a claim, such refusal may give rise to a cause of action in tort for breach of the implied covenant of good faith and fair dealing. In this case, Mr. Gruenberg (P) alleges that Aetna (D) willfully and maliciously entered into a scheme to deprive him of his benefits under his policy, that it encouraged criminal charges against him and, in knowing he would not appear for an examination during the pendency of such charges, used his failure to appear as a pretense for denying coverage. Viewing these allegations in a light most favorable to Mr. Gruenberg (P), while his complaint is not a model pleading, it does allege sufficient facts to state a claim against Aetna (D) for breach of the duty of good faith and fair dealing. The same is not true as to the other defendants, however. Mr.

Gruenberg (P) has also asserted claims against the claims firm that handled his claim for Aetna (D), the claims adjuster and Aetna's (D) attorneys. These parties, however, were all acting as agents of Aetna (D) and thus cannot be held personally liable for a breach of Aetna's (D) duty. Further, insofar as these individuals were acting on behalf of a corporation, their actions are privileged. Aetna (D) argues, however, that Mr. Gruenberg (P) was required by the parties' agreement to appear for an examination as a condition precedent to receiving benefits and that his failure to appear is a bar to his recovery of benefits. Mr. Gruenberg (P), on the other hand, argues that his failure to appear is of no consequence to his receiving benefits. Both parties, however, have missed the point. Both parties assume that Mr. Gruenberg's (P) contractual duty is a dependent condition to Aetna's (D) duty of good faith and fair dealing. This is not true, however. It is irrelevant for purposes of Aetna's (D) duty of good faith whether or not Mr. Gruenberg (P) is in compliance with his contractual obligations. The key issue is not whether Mr. Gruenberg's (P) obligation is precedent or subsequent to Aetna's (D) obligation. Rather, the key issue is whether Aetna's (D) duty of good faith is absolute or conditional. Here, as we have said, Aetna (D) has a duty of good faith and fair dealing that arises out of its contractual relationship with Mr. Gruenberg (P). This duty required Aetna (D) to refrain from doing anything that would injure Mr. Gruenberg's (P) rights under the policy. Even assuming Mr. Gruenberg's (P) failure to appear is a breach of the parties' agreement, this does not excuse Aetna's (D) duty of good faith, which is implied by law. Aetna's (D) duty of good faith and fair dealing is unconditional and independent of Mr. Gruenberg's (P) contractual obligations. We therefore conclude that an insurer's duty of good faith and fair dealing is absolute and that nonperformance by one party of his contractual duties does not excuse the other party from their implied duty of good faith so long as the contract between them is in effect. Reversed in Part and Remanded.

Analysis:

With this opinion we are switching gears from the "please excuse my performance" cases back to the good faith cases. However, unlike the good faith cases we have seen thus far, such as *Bak-A-Lum Corp.* and *Badgett*, this case puts us on a new path towards whether a breach of the duty of good faith is a contract claim or a tort claim. At first blush, one may wonder why the distinction is important. The answer is the remedy. If the claim sounds in contract, a plaintiff is limited to contract damages, both general and consequential. If the claim sounds in tort, however, a whole slew of remedies open up, including the possibility of noneconomic damages [pain and suffering, emotional distress] and exemplary damages [punitive damages]. It is often the damages issue that drives the debate about whether a breach of the implied duty of good faith and fair dealing is a contract or a tort claim. In this case, the Court does not spend much time on whether the claim is a contract claim or a tort claim. Rather, the Court seems to say that because the duty sounds both in contract and tort, the breach of the duty can be the basis of a tort claim even though it arises out of a contractual relationship. It does so as a matter of policy. Such a claim has become known as a "contort", which is reflective of the integral nature of the claim to both contracts and torts. [And you thought torts would never find their way into your other classes!] It is important here to recognize that there are problems with anchoring a breach of the duty of good faith and fair dealing in either contract or tort. On the one hand, the duty does not exist independent of the contract, since if there is no contract there can be no duty. Moreover, if one follows the rationale of the Washington Supreme Court in *Badgett* that the duty of good faith cannot be used to expand one's obligations under the contract, it becomes difficult to separate out a breach of the duty of good faith from a breach of the contract. Notice how the Court of Appeals approach in *Badgett*, however, insofar as it opens the door to expanding a party's obligations under the duty of good faith would allow for much stricter penalties, including the possibility of exemplary damages, if the duty, vague as it may be, is breached. The problems make it seem as if the breach of the duty of good faith should be a contract claim, not a tort claim. But consider that in such a case we have a duty that is breached resulting in damages, which is the classic tort claim, and not a breach of a contractual obligation, which is the basis of a contract claim. Thus the issue is revealed: can a classic tort claim where there is a breach of a duty implied at law be limited to a contract claim simply because the duty arises from a contractual relationship? In some states, including Colorado, courts have attempted to reconcile the difference by allowing the breach of a duty of good faith to be a tort claim but only if the duty is independent from the contract. That is, that the party's duty of good faith cannot require it to do something it is obligated to do under the contract. This way, there cannot be a double recovery for a breach of contract, as some worry can occur if the breach of the duty of good faith is a tort claim. Not all jurisdictions recognize the breach of the implied duty of good faith as a tort claim. As you will see in the next case, *Beck v. Farmers Insurance Exchange*, Utah is one of these few jurisdictions. For those jurisdictions that do not allow a tort claim for a breach of the duty of good faith the key is that the duty of good faith requires only that the insurer act fairly in handling, settling and paying the claim: obligations they have under the contract itself. Since there is no difference between what the policy requires of the insurer and what the duty of good faith has been held to require, the claim must be one for breach of an implied contractual obligation, not merely a duty implied at law. Notice that the contract approach as taken in *Beck*, however, does not allow a court any leeway in remedying situations where there may be a clear case of bad faith if it does not relate to a specific obligation in the contract, as a court could under the tort approach. The discretion or leeway comes in the definition of the duty, which, if it is implied at law can be expanded as necessary, but if implied by the contract, can only be expanded by the express provisions in the agreement. There are a couple of other points to keep in mind here. First, there is a difference between a bad faith breach of contract, which often arises in insurance cases, and a breach of the duty of good faith. In a bad faith breach of contract case, the plaintiff is claiming the insurer intentionally and willfully breached a specific obligation of the contract, as opposed to its implied duty to handle a claim fairly. Second, Aetna (D) was not the only defendant in this case. Mr. Gruenberg (P) also brought suit against Aetna's (D) agents that also worked on Mr. Gruenberg's (P) claim. The Court tosses the claims against these other defendants because all of their actions were taken within the scope of their agency. Although this is not an area of law with which you are familiar yet, notice that since the other defendants were all acting on Aetna's (D) behalf, only Aetna (D) can be held responsible.

Beck v. Farmers Insurance Exchange

(Insured) v. (Insurer)
701 P.2d 795 (Utah 1985)

MEMORY GRAPHIC

Instant Facts

Insured injured in an accident with an uninsured motorist sued his insurance company for failing to investigate, bargain or settle his claim with good faith.

Black Letter Rule

In a first-party relationship between an insured and an insurer, the duties and obligations are contractual not fiduciary and a breach of such duties gives rise to a contract claim not a tort claim.

Case Vocabulary

CONSEQUENTIAL DAMAGES: Those damages that were reasonably within the contemplation of or reasonably foreseeable by the parties at the time the contract was made.
GENERAL DAMAGES: Those damages that flow naturally from the breach of a contractual obligation.
NO-FAULT BENEFITS: Insurance benefits that cover an insured's medical costs and lost wages suffered as a result of an automobile accident regardless of who was at fault for the accident.
SUMMARY JUDGMENT: A ruling by the court that there are no genuine issues of material fact and that, based on the undisputed facts, one party is entitled to judgment as a matter of law.
UNINSURED MOTORIST BENEFITS: Benefits payable to an insured to cover losses sustained, other than those covered by no-fault benefits, as a result of an automobile accident caused by an uninsured motorist who otherwise would be liable for such losses.

Procedural Basis: Appeal from Trial Court's order granting summary judgment to Farmers (D).

Facts: On January 16, 1982, Mr. Beck (P) injured his knee in a hit-and-run accident, when he was struck by a car owned by Ann Kirkland. Mr. Kirkland's car had been stolen, however, and so her insurance company denied Mr. Beck's (P) claim. Thereafter, Mr. Beck (P) filed a claim with his own insurance carrier, Farmers Insurance Exchange (D) ("Farmers") for no-fault and uninsured motorist benefits. Mr. Beck's (P) no-fault claim had been filed while his claim against Ms. Kirkland's insurance company was pending. During that time, Farmers (D) paid Mr. Beck (P) $5,000 in no-fault benefits (the policy limit) and an additional $1,299.43 for lost wages. Mr. Beck's (P) claim for uninsured motorist benefits, filed after Ms. Kirkland's insurance company denied coverage, sought payment of the entire $20,000 policy limit. Farmers (D) rejected the claim without explanation on July 1, 1982. This action followed. In this action, Mr. Beck (P) alleges three causes of action: (1) breach of contract for Farmer's (D) failure to pay uninsured motorist benefits, for which Mr. Beck (P) sought general damages, (2) breach of the implied duty of good faith and fair dealing for Farmer's (D) failure to investigate, bargain or settle Mr. Beck's (P) claim for uninsured motorist benefits, for which Mr. Beck (P) sought compensatory damages, and (3) intentionally causing emotional distress, for which Mr. Beck (P) sought punitive damages. After filing the action, Mr. Beck (P) again offered to settle his claim for $20,000. Farmers (D) again rejected the claim. Farmers (D) subsequently flied an answer and moved to strike Mr. Beck's (P) claim for punitive damages. The Trial Court granted that motion and then bifurcated Mr. Beck's (P) remaining claims. Thereafter, the parties agreed to settle only Mr. Beck's (P) breach of contract claim for failure to pay uninsured motorist benefits for $15,000. Mr. Beck (P) expressly reserved his remaining claim for breach of the implied duty of good faith. Following the partial settlement, Farmers (D) moved to dismiss Mr. Beck's (P) remaining claim on two grounds. First, Farmers (D) argued that, based on our prior case law, it had no duty to bargain with or settle Mr. Beck's (P) claim. Second, Farmers (D) argued that even if it had such a duty, the facts did not establish a breach of the same. In response, Mr. Beck (P) submitted affidavits setting forth his offers to settle and the rejection of the same without explanation or counteroffer, and a statement from a former claims adjuster with 19 years experience that a reasonable and prudent insurance company would have valued the claim between $30,000 and $40,000 and attempted to settle the claim within weeks. According to the former claims adjuster, who is now a paralegal, the only reason to delay settling the claim is to put the insured in financial need and stress so as to get the insured to settle for less. Mr. Beck (P) also submitted an affidavit that the only reason he accepted the $15,000 settlement was because he was in financial need due to the ten months the case had been pending. The Trial Court granted Farmers (D) summary judgment without explanation. This appeal followed.

Issue: May an insured bring a tort claim against his insurer for breach of the implied duty of good faith and fair dealing?

Decision and Rationale: (Zimmerman) No. Mr. Beck (P) has asked this Court to overrule its prior case, *Lyon v. Hartford Accident and Indemnity Co.* [no tort action for breach of implied duty of good faith], in order to permit him to sue an insurer for bad faith refusal to bargain or settle. Mr. Beck (P) points out that many states now allow such a tort claim. Assuming we decide to accept Mr. Beck's (P) invitation, he argues that his affidavits were sufficient to create a factual dispute and thus defeat summary judgment. Farmers (D) does not argue, as it did to the Trial Court, that it has no duty to bargain or settle. Rather, Farmers (D) now argues that it cannot be held liable for bad faith solely on its refusal to bargain or settle. It is Farmer's (D) position that there must be evidence of actual bad faith apart from the bare refusal. While we decline to overrule our decision in *Lyon*, we recognize that our decision in *Lyon* left an insured without a remedy if an insurer refuses to bargain or settle in good faith. This lack of remedy puts an insured at an extreme disadvantage, heightening the disadvantage the insured is in to begin with given the emotional, physical and often financial difficulties that follow an accident such as Mr. Beck's (P). Moreover, failure to accept a settlement offer can lead to catastrophic consequences for an insured in this situation, leading an insurer more likely to give in to the temptation to delay a settlement of a claim in order to pressure an insured into settling for less. In light of these considerations, we agree that some sort of remedy should be available to an insured that is taken advantage of. We do not believe, however, that allowing a tort claim in these circumstances is the answer. Instead, we find that an insurer's good faith duty to bargain or settle a claim under an insurance contract is only one aspect of the duty of good faith and fair dealing implied in all such contracts and that a violation of that duty gives rise to a claim for breach of contract. Insofar as *Lyon* indicates that no cause of action exists for breach of the duty of good faith, it is overruled. Further, we are not persuaded by Farmers (D) that more than a mere refusal to bargain or settle is required to prove a case of breach of the duty of good faith. We thus hold that the refusal to bargain or settle, in and of itself, may, in the right circumstances, be sufficient. We realize that in so holding we are going against the majority of states that allow an insured to bring a tort claim for an insurer's breach of the duty of good faith. The first to take this approach was California, which, in *Gruenberg* [insured may bring tort claim against insurer for breach of duty of good faith], adopted the tort approach as a matter of public policy. California, and the majority of states that have followed in its footsteps, apparently believe contractual damages provide an inadequate remedy for an insurer's breach of the duty of good faith and, in adopting the tort approach, have seen fit to expand the potential remedies for a plaintiff such as Mr. Beck (P). According to the majority, if the claim were merely left to contract law, the insurer could not be held liable for more than the maximum amount of the policy, which provides the insurer no incentive to act promptly and faithfully in bargaining or settling an insured's claim. In our opinion, however, those courts that have adopted the tort approach have done so without a sound theoretical foundation and have opened the door for distortion of well-settled principles of contract law. We believe insurer's can be given an incentive to act in good faith and promptly settle claims filed by their insured through contract law without resorting to the tort approach. The weakness of the tort approach is easy to see. Like the Court in *Gruenberg*, the majority of courts have held that an insurer has a duty to deal with its insured in good faith and that if an insurer breaches that duty, the insured can bring an action in tort because the duty is imposed by law and is nonconsensual and thus not contractual. Although we ourselves have taken this approach in third party cases where a third party sues an insurer for breach of the duty of good faith, we do not believe the same approach is justified in first party situations. The distinction is found in the basis of the relationship. In the third party context, the insurer must act zealously to protect the interests of its insured and its own. In the first party situation, however, the insured becomes an adversary of the insurer and so the role the insurer plays is different. Stated another way, in a third party case, the contract between the insurer and the insured puts the insurer in a fiduciary relationship with the insured in terms of handling third party claims on behalf of the insured. This fiduciary relationship does not exist when the insured itself is making the claim, however, since the insured is now adequately capable of protecting his own interests. We thus hold that in a first party situation, such as this, the duties and obligations of the parties are contractual, not fiduciary, and the breach of any of these duties, including the implied duty of good faith and fair dealing, gives rise to a breach of contract claim, not a tort claim. Although we do not adopt the tort approach, we nevertheless turn to the tort cases to determine the extent of an insurer's duty to act in good faith. Having reviewed those cases, we find that the duty of good faith requires an insurer, at the very least, to fairly evaluate the claim, and thereafter act promptly and reasonably in rejecting or settling the claim. The duty of good faith also requires the insurer to deal with laymen as laymen and not as experts and to refrain from taking actions that will inure the insured's ability to obtain benefits. We also note that in adopting the contract approach we are not unmindful of the purpose for adopting the tort approach: to provide a remedy in excess of the policy limits. We believe, however, that there is no reason to limit the recovery of damages for an insurer's failure to bargain or settle in good faith to the policy limits. No rule of interpretation or other principle of contract law requires such a narrow reading of an insurance contract. The contract here contains limits as to the amount the insurer will pay our in benefits, but it in no way defines the amount the insurer will pay if it is found in breach of its obligations. Damages for breach of contract include both general damages and consequential damages, and consequential damages may reach beyond the terms of the contract. Thus, in an action for breach of the duty of good faith, a broad range of damages is recoverable, especially in an insurance case such as this. Although other courts following the approach we adopt today have not allowed damages for emotional distress, we find no reason to preclude such damages in an unusual case that warrants them. Of course, to be recoverable, such damages must have been foreseeable and the foreseeability of such damages will always hinge upon the nature and language of the contract and the reasonable expectations of the parties. Having laid out the principles of law that apply to this type of case, we turn now to the merits of Mr. Beck's (P) appeal. The affidavits Mr. Beck (P) submitted indicate that Farmers (D) rejected his settlement offer on two occasions, both without further explanation and without a counteroffer. Under these circumstances, when resolving all doubts in Mr. Beck's (P) favor, we cannot say that a jury could not find that Farmers (D) breached its duty of good faith in failing to settle Mr. Beck's (P) claim or to investigate the matter further. Reversed and Remanded.

Analysis:

This case represents the minority view, while the case we just saw, *Gruenberg*, represents the majority. Unlike the *Gruenberg* opinion, however, the Court here goes to great lengths to detail the issues on both sides of the coin and its reasons for taking the minority approach. In essence, the Court here does not buy into the reason for adopting the tort approach because it sees no reason to limit an insured to recovering only policy limits and also believes an award of emotional distress damages is possible. The Court thus criticizes the majority of courts that have taken the tort approach, noting that these courts have distorted contract law in allowing a tort claim in a contract situation. But hasn't the Court also

distorted contract law by allowing recovery of damages in excess of the contract and for emotional distress? Another reason the Court here declines the tort approach is because it believes the insured is not in a fiduciary relationship with the insurer when it makes a first party claim as it is when a third party makes a claim. Is this true? Isn't an insured still in a disadvantaged position when dealing with its insurer, as the Court here recognized in deciding that some type of remedy is necessary? The Court seems to contradict itself. Moreover, notice that the Court, while refusing to adopt the tort approach, looks to the tort cases to determine the extent of the duty of good faith, and does so right after opining that the tort cases have had difficulty in determining what degree of bad faith is required to sustain a claim. If the duty is the same whether the claim sounds in contract or tort, and damages in excess of the policy limits and emotional distress damages are available in both cases, isn't the difference simply a matter of whether or not punitive damages are awarded? Regardless of which side you come down on, the important thing here is to be able to distinguish between the two approaches and to identify the arguments both for and against the tort approach. It is also interesting to note that the Utah Court here has given itself some room to maneuver should it decide to change the course of action it has taken in this opinion. In concluding that a breach of the duties and obligations an insurer has with its own insured gives rise only to a breach of contract action, the Court states that a breach "without more" is a contract claim and not a tort. This opens the door, however, for the Court to say that in a situation where there is a breach and something more that a tort claim exists. This puts this case more in line with those courts that allow a bad faith breach of contract claim, which is a tort, for cases where there is a bad faith breach of an obligation on the part of an insurer. At the same time, however, by limiting whether emotional distress damages are available to the language in the contract and the parties' reasonable expectations, the Court has left it up to insurers themselves to redraft their insurance agreements to make it clear that emotional distress damages are not available. [Freedom of contract at its best?] Finally, notice that both this and *Gruenberg* involved insurance companies. Should a breach of the duty of good faith, which is incorporated into every kind of contract, give rise to a tort claim in other contexts? Some courts have taken that approach, much to the dismay of the Utah Supreme Court. Does it make sense to extend the tort of breach of the duty of good faith to all areas or should it be limited to the insurance context? If the duty is implied in all kinds of contracts, why not extend the tort claim to all breaches of that duty? These are the issues with which you should be familiar when discussing this line of cases. [Law professors love this sort of thing!] In the end, however, note that both the majority and minority positions allow some sort of claim, whether in tort or contract, for damages in excess of the policy limits when an insurer breaches its duty of good faith and fair dealing when dealing with its insured.

Perspective
Third Party Rights

Chapter 8

This chapter covers three main topics: third party beneficiaries, assignment, and delegation.

A word of caution—as the casebook author notes, "the materials will challenge your skill at legal analysis." Put another way, the chapter is *really difficult*!

However, it is more easily understood by putting pen to paper and drawing diagrams. When you read the briefs, you can follow along on the diagram, and it becomes much easier to understand.

You have learned by now that parties to a contract may enforce their rights under the contract. But what about third parties who are not parties to the contract? Well, they sometimes have rights too, and can enforce a contract. It depends upon how they are classified—creditor beneficiary, donee or intended beneficiary, or incidental beneficiary. There are also different tests used to determine their status.

When a party to whom a contractual duty is owed wishes to transfer that right to performance to a third person, the law concerning assignment of rights comes into play. You will learn how and when those rights may be assigned.

Finally, when a party who owes a duty of performance under a contract wishes to delegate that duty to a third party, the law concerning delegation applies. Some duties can be delegated, while others cannot. You will learn how to distinguish between the two.

Chapter 8

NOTE: THE PURPOSE OF THIS OUTLINE IS TO ORGANIZE THE CASES SO THAT ONE CAN QUICKLY UNDERSTAND THE RELEVANCE OF EACH CASE TO THE COURSE. NO ATTEMPT IS MADE IN THIS OVERVIEW TO ADDRESS EVERY CONCEPT THAT MUST BE STUDIED. BE SURE TO READ THE ENTIRE CASEBOOK AND/OR OTHER MATERIALS TO GAIN A FULL UNDERSTANDING OF ALL CONCEPTS.

I. Third Party Beneficiaries
  A. Historical Development.
    1. A third party, not in privity of contract, may nevertheless sue the promisor to enforce the contract between the promisor and the promisee, where the promisor promises to pay the promisee's debt owed to the third party but fails to do so. *Lawrence v. Fox.*
    2. A third party donee beneficiary may bring an action against the promisor on the contract between the promisor and promisee intended for the benefit of the third party. *Seaver v. Ransom.*
  B. The First Restatement of Contracts defines three types of third party beneficiaries:
    1. *Donee beneficiary*: Where the purpose of obtaining the promise is to make a gift to the beneficiary or to confer upon the beneficiary a right against the promisor to some performance not due from the promisee to the beneficiary.
    2. *Creditor beneficiary:* Where the purpose of obtaining the promise is to satisfy an actual or supposed or asserted duty of the promisee to the beneficiary.
    3. *Incidental beneficiary*: One who benefits from the contract, but is not a donee or creditor beneficiary.
  C. "Intent to Benefit" and "Direct Benefit" Tests.
    1. In determining the existence of a third party donee beneficiary, an "intent to benefit" test is used to inquire whether the contracting parties intended that a third person should receive a benefit. *Bain v. Gillispie.*
    2. "Direct benefit" test is used to determine third party intended beneficiary status. It requires that the parties intend that the promisor assume a direct obligation to the intended beneficiary at the time they enter into the contract. *Lonsdale v. Chesterfield.*
  D. The Second Restatement of Contracts.
    1. The Restatement [Second] of Contracts substitutes the term "intended" beneficiary for both "creditor" and "donee" beneficiary. This new classification eliminates the subclass of "donee beneficiary."
    2. The "intent to benefit" test is used to determine whether a third party is an intended beneficiary.
  E. Surety Bond Cases.
    1. A surety's performance bond, intended for the exclusive use and benefit of the obligee, affords no contractual rights to third party subcontractors or suppliers who are left unpaid by a defaulting principal. *The Cretex Companies, Inc. v. Construction Leaders, Inc.*
  F. Public Contracts.
    1. The mere fact that a Government program for social betterment confers benefits upon individuals who are not required to render contractual consideration in return does not necessarily imply that the benefits are intended as gifts thereby making the individuals donee third party beneficiaries. *Martinez v. Socoma Companies, Inc.*
  G. Promisor's Defenses Against Third Party Beneficiary (*XL Disposal Corp. v. John Sexton Contractors Co.*)
    1. Whether a promisor may assert a defense against a third party beneficiary that the promisee might have asserted against the beneficiary depends upon the nature of the obligation undertaken.
    2. If the promisor agrees to discharge the promisee's liability to the third party, then it may assert the promisee's defenses, but if the promisor only agrees to pay a certain

sum of money to the third party, the promisor may not assert the promisee's defenses.

H. Vesting of Third Party's Rights.
   1. If a third party beneficiary's rights have vested, the promisor and promisee may not rescind those rights.
   2. If an agreement by a promisor and promisee and benefiting a third party does not contain an express reservation to alter, amend, or rescind, then the parties to the contract cannot rescind the contract without the third party beneficiary's consent after he has accepted, adopted or relied upon the contract. *United States v. Wood.*

II. Assignment and Delegation
   A. Assignment - Where one who has the right to receive performance under a contract transfers that contract right to a third person.
   B. Delegation - Where one who has the obligation to perform under a contract delegates to another person the duty to render the performance owed to a third person.
      1. Mere words promising a gratuitous assignment of indebtedness due do not alone create an enforceable assignment. *Adams v. Merced Stone Co.*
         a. A verbal gift is not valid, unless the means of obtaining possession and control of the thing are given.
         b. Where a donor makes a verbal gift of a chose of action, which he knows the donee has within his power to secure the possession and control of the thing given, the delivery or transmission from the donor to the donee of the means of obtaining possession and control of the subject of the gift is still necessary.
      2. A subrogee of an assignment contract has the same rights and limitations against the obligor as does the assignee, and the obligor may raise the defense of set-off against the subrogee of an assignee which could have been raised against the assignor. *Ertel v. Radio Corp. of America.*
      3. An obligor cannot delegate duties to another where performance is personal to the obligor. *Crane Ice Cream Co. v. Terminal Freezing & Heating Co.*
      4. Where a person contracts with another to do work or perform service, and it can be inferred that the person employed has been selected with reference to his individual skill, competency, or other personal qualification, those duties cannot be delegated to a third person. *The British Waggon Co. and the Parkgate Waggon Co. v. Lea & Co.*
         a. Thus, if the performance of the original obligor is required, or the obligor's personal supervision, then the duties under the contract are not delegable. Personal performance will be implied as a term of the contract if the unique skills of the obligor are the essence of the contract.
      5. Assignment of an exclusive distributorship contract, which delegates duty of performance, requires the obligee's consent. *Sally Beauty Co., Inc. v. Nexxus Prods. Co., Inc.*

-awrence v. Fox

3rd Party Beneficiary) v. (Promisor)

1859) 20 N.Y. 268

ᴍ E M O R Y G R A P H I C

Instant Facts

Lawrence (P), a third party beneficiary of a :ontract between Fox (D) and Holly, sued Fox (D), the ›romisor for a debt owed by Holly to Lawrence (P).

Black Letter Rule

Where a promisor enters into a contract with a promisee and agrees to pay the promisee's debt owed to a third party creditor, but fails to so do, the third party creditor may sue the promisor to enforce the agreement.

Case Vocabulary

ASSUMPSIT: A promise, either express or implied, by one person to pay, or doing something for, another, and which can be an enforceable cause of action.
BILL OF EXCHANGE: A written order by a drawer directing the drawee or payor to pay money on demand or at a set time to a third party payee, or to the bearer; also referred to as *draft*, and a check is an example.
CESTUI QUE TRUST: A beneficiary of a trust.
CONSIDERATION: A thing of value or a benefit received by a promisor from a promisee, and necessary for an enforceable contract.
EXECUTOR: The person named in a will to carry out the testator's intentions.
JUDGMENT: The final determination by the court with respect to the parties' rights and obligations.
NONSUIT: Where a defendant makes a motion before the court at trial asserting that the case should be dismissed because the plaintiff has not offered sufficient evidence to prove the case.
PRIVITY: A relationship between two parties concerning a contract or other transaction, whereby each has a legally recognized interest in the matter.
TRUSTEE: The person who administers a trust.

Procedural Basis: Appeal following jury trial in action by third party beneficiary for breach of contract seeking money damages.

Facts: Holly owed Lawrence (P) $300 for money borrowed. At the request of Fox (D), Holly loaned and advanced Fox (D) $300. In consideration thereof, Fox (D) promised Holly that he would pay Lawrence (P) the money the next day. [Why did he bother borrowing the money if he had to pay it back the next day?] Lawrence (P) was not paid and he sued (D) Fox (D) for the $300. Fox (D) moved for nonsuit upon the grounds that (1) Holly was not indebted to Lawrence (P), (2) the contract between Lawrence (P) and Fox (D) was void for lack of consideration, and, (3) there was no privity between Lawrence (P) and Fox (D). The court denied the motion for nonsuit. The matter was submitted to the jury and they found in favor of Lawrence (P). Upon entry of the judgment, Fox (D) appealed.

Issue: Where a promisor enters into a contract with a promisee and agrees to pay the promisee's debt owed to a third party creditor, but fails to so do, may the third party creditor sue the promisor to enforce the agreement?

Decision and Rationale: (Gray) Yes. Where a promisor enters into a contract with a promisee and agrees to pay the promisee's debt owed to a third party creditor but fails to so do, the third party creditor may sue the promisor to enforce the agreement. We begin by addressing the [unmeritorious] contentions raised by Fox (D) on appeal. With respect to Fox's (D) contention that the contract was void for want of consideration, the highest court of this state long ago put to rest such objection. The promise by Fox (D) to Holly, although made for the benefit of Lawrence (P), could inure to his benefit. With respect to the lack of privity contention, the state's highest court has stated in *Schemerhorn v. Vanderheyden*, "That where one person makes a promise to another for the benefit of a third person, that third person may maintain an action upon it." Fox (D), upon ample consideration received $300 from Holly, and promised Holly to pay his debt to Lawrence (P); the consideration received and the promise to Holly made it as plainly his duty to pay Lawrence (P) as if the money had been remitted to him for that purpose, and as well implied a promise to do so as if he had been made a trustee of property to be converted into cash with which to pay. With respect to lack of indebtedness by Holly to Lawrence (P), Holly's purpose in loaning Fox (D) money was to have Lawrence (P) paid. The judgment should be affirmed.

Dissent: (Comstock) Lawrence (P) had nothing to do with the promise on which the action is brought. It was not made to him, nor did the consideration proceed from him. In general, there must be privity of contract. The party who sues upon a promise must be the promisee, or he must have some legal interest in the undertaking. In this case, it is plain that Holly, who loaned the money to Fox (D), and to whom the promise was made, could at any time have claimed that it should be performed to himself personally. If he requested payment to him and received it, Fox's (D) obligation to pay Lawrence (P) would have ceased to exist. Fox (D) borrowed the money of Holly and received it as his own. Lawrence (P) had no right in the fund. The promise to repay the money created an obligation in favor of the lender to whom it was made and not in favor of any one else. The judgment should be reversed.

Analysis:

This is considered a landmark case concerning the right of a third party beneficiary to sue to enforce the terms of a contract between a promisor and a promisee. There was no privity of contract between Lawrence (P) and Fox (D). However, Lawrence (P) was the third party beneficiary of the contract between Holly—the promisee—and Fox (D)—the promisor because Holly obtained the promise of Fox (D) to pay Holly's debt to Lawrence (P) if Holly loaned him $300 dollars. It was clear that Lawrence (P) was a *creditor beneficiary* of the contract between Holly and Fox (D). Under the First Restatement of Contracts, there were two types of third party beneficiaries—creditor beneficiaries and donee beneficiaries. Those that have no enforceable rights are called incidental beneficiaries. Holly's purpose in obtaining Fox's (D) promise to pay off the debt owed to Lawrence (P) was to discharge Holly's debt to Lawrence (P). This makes Lawrence (P) a creditor beneficiary. Had Holly purpose been merely to confer a gift upon Lawrence (P), then Lawrence (P) would have been a *donee beneficiary*. The dissenting justice believe that privity of contract should exist, and that had Holly changed his mind and paid Lawrence (P) directly, Lawrence (P) would no longer hav the right to sue Fox (D). When Fox (D) did not pay Lawrence (P), he choose to sue Fox (D). Note that he could have also sued Holly for th money owed him, and Holly could have then sued Fox (D).

Seaver v. Ransom

(The Niece) v. (Judge Beman's Executor)
Court of Appeals of New York, 1918 224 N.Y. 233, 120 N.E. 639, 2 A.L.R. 11 87

M E M O R Y   G R A P H I C

Instant Facts

Judge Beman fails to fulfill his wife's deathbed wish, as he promised, giving the house or an equivalent amount to their niece, Marion Seaver.

Black Letter Rule

Any third party beneficiary donee has the right to bring an action on a contract made specifically for his/her benefit.

Case Vocabulary

AVOUCH: To guarantee
BEQUEATH: Usually the giving of personal property by will rather than real property
COLLATERALS: Relatives not directly related for purposes of inheritance, such as cousins.
EQUITY: Fairness
EXECUTOR: Someone who is appointed to act in the place of the deceased in order to carry out their wishes as expressed in their will.
INTESTATE: Dying without leaving a will
LEGACY: Refers to a general legacy, providing a gift of personal property or money by means of a will.
PECUNIARY: Concerning money or its equivalent.
RESIDUARY LEGATEE: a person who gets whatever is left over after the specific gifts have been given.
TESTAMENTARY: Refers to any sort of document which fails to take effect until after the death of the individual who is making it.
TESTATOR: Anyone who leaves a will and is now dead.
TESTATRIX: A dead woman who has left a will.

Procedural Basis: Appeal from the affirming judgment of the appellate court for plaintiff for recovery of damages.

Facts: Shortly before her death, Mrs. Beman requested that her husband, Judge Beman, make out her will. In the will she left $1000 to Seaver (P), the use of the house to her husband for life and small amounts to various relatives and the ASPCA. Mrs. Beman then decided to change the will and give the house to her niece, Seaver (P), and leave the rest of the will unchanged. Mrs. Beman didn't believe she would live long enough for her husband to draw and execute a new document. But her husband, Judge Beman, swore an oath to leave Seaver (P) a sufficient amount in his own will to make up the difference. However, when Judge Beman died, his will made no provision for Seaver (P) as promised, and Seaver (P) brought suit. Ransom (D) is one of the executors of Judge Beman's estate.

Issue: Whether a third party beneficiary, who is neither a creditor nor a member of the immediate family, may maintain an action for damages without privity?

Decision and Rationale: (Pound) Yes. The trial court found for Seaver (P), based on the theory that Mrs. Beman was fraudulently induced to execute the will by her husband. But Seaver's (P) action is maintainable on grounds defined in Lawrence v. Fox [supra] "... the right of the beneficiary to sue on a contract made expressly for his benefit...." Such a right is "just and practical" since it allows the party who is benefiting from the contract to enforce it against the party who is in breach. The right of a third party to enforce a contract, to which he/she is the intended beneficiary, has been upheld in various situations. This case presents a category of beneficiary that is yet to present itself. The Bemans were childless and Seaver (P) was, virtually, the daughter they never had. The contract between Judge and Mrs. Beman was for the sole benefit of Seaver (P) and she is the only person "substantially damaged by its breach." The fact that Seaver was not a member of the immediate family in no way should prevent her from seeking recovery. The personal relationship between the Bemans and Seaver (P) is certainly worthy of consideration. It defines the moral obligation that the law seeks in establishing the intentions of the parties in a contract. An arbitrary line of demarcation between members of a family, based merely on marital status and lineage, fails to account for relationships that develop over a period of time, without a traditional legal status. The fact that Judge Beman, intentionally or unintentionally, failed to redraw the will as promised, does not change the promise or the intent Mrs. Beman had to give the house to Seaver (P), as a third party beneficiary. Seaver (P) was the intended beneficiary donee of the contract between the Bemans and is, therefore, entitled to recover damages. The judgment, with costs, is affirmed.

Analysis:

Writing for the lower court Kellogg, P.J. wrote, "The doctrine of *Lawrence v. Fox* is progressive not retrograde. The course of the late decisions is to enlarge, not limit, the effect of that case." The New York court truly takes this language to heart in reaching its decision in *Seaver*. Although the case involved a family member, it is clear that a familial tie is no longer necessary. The court recognizes the legal rights of a third party beneficiary donee in order to enforce the intent behind a contract. The court completely abandons any prior legal pretense that prevents the intent of a contracting party to give a benefit to whomever he/she pleases, as an intended recipient donee. Furthermore, the court forcefully concludes that the intended donee has the legal right to enforce such contracts without the need to demonstrate justifiable reliance on the promise. An intended beneficiary, according to *Seaver*, has greater legal authority than the common law legal authority once granted children and spouses. Such is the power of a valid contract.

Bain v. Gillispie

(Referee) v. (Sports Memorabilia Store Operators)
(1984) 357 N.W.2d 47

MEMORY GRAPHIC

Instant Facts

Gillispies (D & alleged 3rd party bene)—sports memorabilia sellers—sued referee Bain (P), claiming that they were third party donee beneficiaries of Bain's employment contract with the Big Ten Athletic Conference.

Black Letter Rule

In determining the existence of a third party donee beneficiary, an "intent to benefit" test is used to inquire whether the contracting parties intended that a third person should receive a benefit.

Case Vocabulary

AMICUS CURIAE: A "friend of the court" brief, submitted by interested non-parties.
APPELLEE: Party who is responding to an appeal, rather than initiating it.
COUNTERCLAIM: Pleading, like a complaint, by defendant against plaintiff or others.
DEPOSITION: Pre-trial discovery method whereby person is questioned, under oath and in the presence of a court reporter, by attorneys for the parties to the action.
EXEMPLARY DAMAGES: Damages awarded to injured party to punish the defendant for acting in a malicious, oppressive, or fraudulent manner so as to make an example of the defendant.
INJUNCTIVE RELIEF: Seeking a court order for an injunction to command an act or to prohibit or restrain an act.
MOTION FOR SUMMARY JUDGMENT: A legal motion requesting the judge to enter judgment, before trial, on the grounds that the action has no merit or there is no defense to the action.
PUNITIVE DAMAGES: Damages awarded to injured party to punish the defendant for acting in a malicious, oppressive, or fraudulent manner.

Procedural Basis: Appeal from dismissal of counterclaim after granting of motion for summary judgment in action seeking damages for sports referee malpractice.

Facts: Bain (P), a college basketball referee, called a foul on a University of Iowa player, which resulted in free throws that caused a last-minute victory by the opposing team—Purdue University. Some fans claimed that the foul was clearly in error and blamed Bain (P) for their team's loss. Mr. and Mrs. Gillispie (D & alleged 3rd party bene) operate a novelty store specializing in University of Iowa sports memorabilia, but have no association with the University of Iowa or its sports program. A few days after the game, the Gillispies (D & alleged 3rd party bene) marketed T-shirts bearing a reference to Bain (P) by showing a man with a rope around his neck with the caption "Jim Bain Fan Club." Bain (P) [not the least bit happy with the T-shirts] sued Gillispies (D & alleged 3rd party bene) for injunctive relief and damages. The Gillispies (D & alleged 3rd party bene) counterclaimed against Bain (P) alleging that his officiating the game was below the standard of competence required of a professional referee, thereby constituting malpractice and entitling them to damages for loss of earnings and business advantage, emotional distress and anxiety, loss of good will, and expectancy of profits plus exemplary damages. They contend that because Iowa's loss of the game to Purdue eliminated Iowa from the championship of the Big Ten Basketball Conference, this destroyed a potential market for their memorabilia touting Iowa as a Big Ten champion. The trial court [believing Gillispies' (D & alleged 3rd party bene) did not have a leg to stand on] dismissed their counterclaim following the granting of summary judgment. Gillispies (D & alleged 3rd party bene) appeal contending that (1) their damages were a reasonably foreseeable consequence of Bain's (P) acts as a referee, or (2) that Gillispies (D & alleged 3rd party bene) are beneficiaries of an employment contract between Bain (P) and the Big Ten Athletic Conference.

Issue: May an "intent to benefit" test be used to determine whether one is a third party donee beneficiary?

Decision and Rationale: (Snell) Yes. With respect to the malpractice claim, which is based upon negligence, there must first be a duty owed. We conclude [without wasting much time on the subject] that the trial court properly granted summary judgment in that it is beyond credulity that Bain (P), while refereeing a game, must make his calls at all times perceiving that a wrong call will injure Gillispies' (D & alleged 3rd party bene) business or one similarly situated and subject him to liability. With respect to whether Gillispies (D & alleged 3rd party bene) were beneficiaries under Bain's (P) contract with the Big 10, they must be direct beneficiaries in order to maintain an action, and not merely incidental beneficiaries. A direct beneficiary is either a donee beneficiary or a creditor beneficiary. A donee beneficiary is defined as where the purpose of the promisee in obtaining the promise is to make a gift to the beneficiary or to confer upon him a right against the promisor to some performance neither due nor supposed or asserted to be due from the promisee to the beneficiary. A creditor beneficiary is defined as where the purpose of obtaining the promise is to satisfy an actual or supposed or asserted duty of the promisee to the beneficiary. Gillispies (D & alleged 3rd party bene) do not contend that they are creditor beneficiaries of anyone. The real test is said to be whether the contracting parties intended that a third person should receive a benefit which might be enforced in the courts. It is clear that the purpose of any promise which Bain (P) might have made was not to confer a gift on Gillispies (D & alleged 3rd party bene). Likewise, the Big 10 did not owe any duty to the Gillispies (D & alleged 3rd party bene) such that they would have been creditor beneficiaries. If a contract did exist between Bain (P) and the Big 10, Gillispies can be considered nothing more than incidental beneficiaries [without any enforceable rights] and as such are unable to maintain a cause of action. Affirmed.

Analysis:

This case examines the "intent to benefit" test. Under the First Restatement of Contracts, a third party beneficiary was determined based upon three categories—creditor, donee, and incidental beneficiaries. The court in this case states that the "real test is ... whether the contracting parties intended that a third person should receive a benefit which might be enforced in the courts." Thus, the court considered the intent of both the promisee and promisor. The courts will presume that parties contract for their own benefit and not for the benefit of a third party, unless they expressly have an intent to benefit the third party. There was no equivocation by the court—any promise that Bain (P) might have made was *not* to confer a gift on the Gillispies (D & alleged 3rd party bene). Note how the law on contracts and torts overlap in this case. The Gillispies (D & alleged 3rd party bene) unsuccessfully sought tort recovery based upon the negligence of Bain (P), i.e., referee malpractice. The Gillispies (D & alleged 3rd party bene) were equally unsuccessful in asserting rights under contract law by claiming to be third party beneficiaries of an employment contract between Bain (P) and the Big Ten Athletic Conference. The court was mindful—rightfully so—of the "uncharted morass a court would find itself in if it were to hold that an athletic official subjects himself to liability every time he might make a questionable call."

"DIRECT BENEFIT TEST" USED TO DETERMINE THIRD PARTY INTENDED BENEFICIARY STATUS

Lonsdale v. Chesterfield

(Purchasers and 3rd Party Beneficiaries) v. (Developer)
(1983) 99 Wash.2d 353, 662 P.2d 385

M E M O R Y   G R A P H I C

Instant Facts

Lonsdale (P & 3rd party bene) sued to enforce agreement between Chesterfield (D1) and Sansaria (D2) whereby Sansaria (D2) assumed obligation to install water system.

Black Letter Rule

The creation of a third-party beneficiary contract requires that the parties intend that the promisor assume a direct obligation to the intended beneficiary at the time they enter into the contract.

Case Vocabulary

ASSIGNEES: Those who receive property rights or powers from another, called the assignor, under the terms of assignment.
CLASS ACTION: A lawsuit brought by a group of people that have the same or similar characteristics and have a common legal position against the opposing side.
DECLARATORY JUDGMENT ACTION: Action to have court declare judgment concerning one's rights, such as under a contract or to specific property.
MOTION TO DISMISS: Challenging the right of the court to entertain the matter before it on various legal theories.
MOTION TO VACATE: To undo or void some act, record or judgment.
RESCISSION: A remedy whereby a contract will be undone for proper legal reasons, such as a material breach.

Procedural Basis: Appeal to state Supreme Court from dismissal of class action lawsuit for rescission and damages following motion to dismiss at close of plaintiff's case.

Facts: Chesterfield Land, Inc. (Chesterfield) (D1)—which had platted a portion of a development known as Sansaria on land along the Oregon coast—sold 81 lots to various purchasers by real estate contracts. In each contract, Chesterfield (D1) agreed to install a water system for the use of the plat. In turn, each purchaser agreed to pay a portion of the cost of installation and to use the water system. Chesterfield (D1) later sold and assigned its vendor interest in the real estate contracts to Lonsdale (P & 3rd party bene) and others, thereby giving them a deed to the land to secure payment from the purchasers of the outstanding balance on each real estate contract. Thereafter, the remaining undeveloped portion of the land was sold to Sansaria, Inc. (Sansaria) (D2), which assumed Chesterfield's (D1) obligation to install a water system for the entire development. Neither Chesterfield (D1) nor Sansaria (D2) installed the system. As a result, many of the purchasers of the land defaulted. Lonsdale (P & 3rd party bene) sued Chesterfield (D1) for failure to install the water system and also sued Sansaria (D2) claiming to be third party beneficiaries of the contract between Chesterfield (D1) and Sansaria (D2). The trial court dismissed Lonsdale's (P & 3rd party bene) lawsuit, holding that Chesterfield's (D1) obligation to supply water did not run to Lonsdale (P & 3rd party bene) and thus Lonsdale and the others (P & 3rd party bene) were not third party beneficiaries. The court of appeals [after various legal maneuverings] decided the merits of the case and held that Chesterfield's (D1) obligation did run to Lonsdale (P & 3rd party bene) and thus Lonsdale and the others (P & 3rd party bene) were third party beneficiaries of the contract between Chesterfield (D1) and Sansaria (D2). [More appeals and legal maneuverings occurred.] On appeal again after remand, the court of appeals held that Lonsdale and the others (P & 3rd party bene) were not third party beneficiaries. Eventually the state Supreme Court granted review to determine [that very thorny issue of] whether Lonsdale and the others (P & 3rd party bene) were third party beneficiaries of Sansaria's (D2) promise [that means it's the promisor] to Chesterfield (D1) [the promisee] to install the water system. [Unless you're really smart, it would behoove you to draw a diagram of the parties and contracts involved!]

Issue: Can a party's third party beneficiary status be determined based upon whether the parties to the contract intended that the promisor assume a direct obligation to the third party beneficiary?

Decision and Rationale: (Williams) Yes. In determining whether Lonsdale and the others (P & 3rd party bene) are third party beneficiaries of the contract between Sansaria (D2) and Chesterfield (D1), it depends upon whether the parties to the contract intended that Sansaria (D2) assume a direct obligation to Lonsdale and the others (P & 3rd party bene). As we observed in *Burke & Thomas, Inc. v. International Organization of Masters*, the creation of a third-party beneficiary contract requires that the parties intend that the promisor assume a direct obligation to the intended beneficiary at the time they enter into the contract. We held in *Vikingstad v. Baggott* that if the "terms of the contract necessarily require the promisor to confer a benefit upon a third person, then the contract, and hence the parties thereto, contemplate a benefit to the third person. The 'intent' ... is not a desire or purpose to confer a particular benefit upon him, nor a desire to advance his interests, but an intent that the promisor shall assume a direct obligation to him." Thus, so long as the contract necessarily and directly benefits the third person, it is immaterial that this protection was afforded, not as an end in itself, but for the sole purpose of securing to the promisee some consequent benefit or immunity. The motive, purpose, or desire of the parties is a quite different thing from their intention. In the parties' contract, Sansaria (D2) ssumed Chesterfield's (D1) obligation to construct a water system for e entire development. The fact that neither Sansaria (D2) nor hesterfield (D1) subjectively intended to benefit Lonsdale and the thers (P & 3rd party bene) is not determinative. Despite other motives y Sansaria (D2) and Chesterfield (D1), the contract required Sansaria)2) to confer a benefit upon Lonsdale (P & 3rd party bene). Under the terms of the contract, Sansaria (D2) could not fully perform its promise to install the water system without directly benefiting Lonsdale and the others (P & 3rd party bene) as deeded owners of the lots. [They'd sure have a hard time selling the lots without a water system.] Thus, they were third party beneficiaries of the performance due under the contract. Reverse and remand to the trial court.

Analysis:

ecall in the previous case, *Bain v. Gillispie* [sports memorabilia sellers not third party beneficiaries of referee's employment contract], the court pplied an "intent to benefit" test and inquired whether the contracting parties intended that a third person should receive a benefit. In this ase, the court applies a "direct benefit test" and concludes that the promisor's performance—Sansaria's (D2) promise to install the water ystem—ran directly to the third party beneficiary—Lonsdale (P & 3rd party bene)—because Sansaria (D2) could not fully perform its promise ithout directly benefiting Lonsdale and the others (P & 3rd party bene). The court also examined exactly what is meant by "intent" when etermining if the parties intended that the promisor assume a direct obligation to the intended beneficiary. The motive, purpose, or desire of e parties is not material, so long as the contract necessarily and directly benefits the third person. Thus, the court correctly chose not to place eight on the parties' underlying motives for entering into the contract.

The Cretex Companies, Inc. v. Construction Leaders, Inc.

(Unpaid Materialmen) v. (Defaulting General Contractor)
(1984) 342 N.W.2d 135

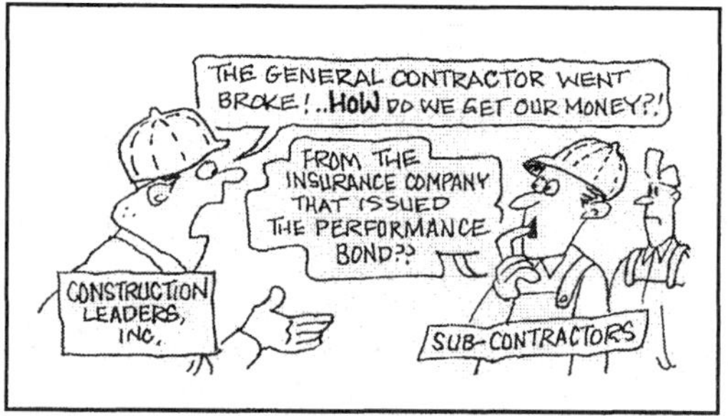

M E M O R Y   G R A P H I C

Instant Facts

Sub-contractors, The Cretex Companies (P), sued surety company claiming that they were third party beneficiaries of the performance bonds between the surety and the general contractor, Construction Leaders (D1).

Black Letter Rule

A surety's performance bond, intended for the exclusive use and benefit of the obligee, affords no contractual rights to third party subcontractors or suppliers who are left unpaid by a defaulting principal.

Case Vocabulary

MECHANIC'S LIEN: A lien filed to assure payment for labor or materials supplied for working on real or personal property.
OBLIGEE: The recipient of that promised.
PAYMENT BOND: Where a surety issues a bond to ensure payment to a subcontractor or materialman in the event that general contractor defaults.
PERFORMANCE BOND: Where a surety issues a bond to ensure performance of a contract.
PRINCIPAL: The one who is the highest ranking.
SURETY: One who agrees to pay money or perform an obligation if another person who is obligated to pay or perform fails to do so.

Procedural Basis: Appeal from granting of summary judgment ir action to collect on performance bond.

Facts: Northland Mortgage Co. owned certain real property and hirec Construction Leaders, Inc. (Construction contractor) (D1) as its general contracto to do the utilities construction for certain development projects. Travelor Indemnity Company (Indemnity Co.) (D2) wrote a total of five performance bond for the construction projects. Indemnity Co. (D2) was the surety, Constructior contractor (D1) was the principal, and Northland Mortgage was the obligee During the course of the project, Construction contractor (D1) defaulted anc became insolvent. Indemnity Co. (D2) hired another contractor to complete the work but some suppliers and subcontractors of Construction contractor (D1) including The Cretex Companies, Inc. (The Cretex) (P) were left unpaid. Althougl The Cretex (P) could have filed mechanic's liens against Northland Mortgage, they failed to do so. [Big mistake—they're kicking themselves now!] The Cretex (P) sued Indemnity Co. (D2) to collect on the performance bonds, and also sued [fo whatever it was worth] Construction contractor (D1) for breach of thei subcontracts. [Recall the saying, you can't get blood from a turnip.] The trial cour granted summary judgment in favor of The Cretex (P) against both Indemnity Co (D2) and Construction contractor (D1). Indemnity Co. (D2) appealed and assertec that The Cretex (P) were not third party intended beneficiaries under the performance bonds.

Issue: Are third party subcontractors or suppliers who are left unpaid by a defaulting principal afforded any contractual rights under the surety's performance bond intended for the exclusive use and benefit of the obligee?

Decision and Rationale: (Simonett) No. The constructior contracts between Northland Mortgage and Construction contractor (D1) calls for a performance bond rather than a payment bond. The contracts provide that the performance bond shall guarantee the contractors performance as required by the contract, satisfaction of all lien rights of sub-contractors and materials suppliers. The purpose of the performance bond is to ensure that the principal or his surety will perform the contract for an agreed price. Because performance of the work alone is not sufficient to protect the owner-obligee, the surety also agrees to indemnify the owner-obligee for any loss from liens filed against the property by reason of the contractor-principal's default in payment of his materialmen. Thus, Indemnity Co. (D2) claims that its bonds were intended for the exclusive use and benefit of its obligee, Northland Mortgage, and afford no contractual rights to third party subcontractors or suppliers. It further claims that if the owner and general contractor had wished to protect third party materialmen, they could have purchased an additional "labor and material payment bond," which expressly provides for the surety to pay the claims of third party subcontractors and materialmen if the general contractor fails to do so. The Cretex (P) assert, however, that the performance bond was also a payment bond intended for the benefit of third persons who are not parties to the surety's contract. It is undisputed that the underlying construction contracts are incorporated by reference into the bonds. The contract provides in part, "the Contractor shall provide and pay for all materials, labor, ... and other facilities necessary for the execution and completion of the work." Other portions provide that if the contractor fails to pay subcontractors or materialmen, the owner may terminate the contract or withhold payments. From this, The Cretex (P) argue that the bond is conditioned on full and faithful performance of the construction contract by the principal-general contractor; performance of the contract by the contractor includes payment by the contractor of the claims of his subcontractors and materialmen; therefore, the surety has agreed that if the contractor does not pay his suppliers, the surety will do it for him; thus making the suppliers third party beneficiaries of the bond. [Ge it?] The trial court [apparently did and] accepted this argument. We reject The Cretex' (P) argument that the "duty owed" test—that the promisor's performance under the contract must discharge a duty otherwise owed the third party by the promisee—is met in this case where payment of their claims by the surety would discharge a duty owed them by Northland Mortgage as owner of the project improved at their expense. Thus, if they are to recover on the bonds, they must do so under the "intent to benefit" test. Contrary to Indemnity Co.'s (D2) argument, only one test need be met, and not both. The Second edition of the Restatement of Contracts substitutes the term "intended" beneficiary for both "creditor" and "donee" beneficiary. This new classification eliminates the subclass of "donee beneficiary." We hereby adopt the intended beneficiary approach outlined in the Restatement (Second) of Contracts. Although only one test need be satisfied, we conclude that the requisite intent to make subcontractors and materialmen third party beneficiaries of Indemnity Co.'s (D1) bonds is not shown and that The Cretex (P) are at best, incidental third party beneficiaries. The performance bond read alone evidences intent to protect and benefit only the owner-obligee. The Cretex (P) argue that if the construction contract is read as part of the bond, a further intent to confer a benefit on them appears, notwithstanding that the construction contract expressly states that the general contractor need only furnish a performance bond. We do not agree. The issue is whether the benefit was intended by the contracting parties. The fair import of the surety contract is that the contracting parties intended the surety's performance to be rendered to Northland Mortgage, the owner-obligee, not to the materialmen. The bond provides that if the contractor-principal defaults, the surety is obligated to complete the project. If there are any liens filed, the surety is obligated to satisfy them, and the lienholders, would be third party intended beneficiaries of the bond. If there are any unpaid materialmen who have failed to file lines, the surety need only pay these claims to the extent necessary to save the owner-obligee harmless from loss by reason of the contractor-principal's failure so to do. There would seem to be no reason for the contracting parties to intend to confer a benefit on materialmen who can protect their own interests by filing liens against the property. If unpaid materialmen wanted to be protected their recourse was to file a lien on the owner's property, whereupon the owner would have the surety bond for protections. We therefore hold that The Cretex (P) are not third party intended beneficiaries of Indemnity Co.'s (D2) bonds covering performance of this private construction project. Reversed.

Dissent: (Yetka) The performance bond obligates Indemnity Co. (D2) to faithfully perform the contract. It incorporates portions of the general contract, which provides that the "Contractor shall provide any pay for all materials, labor, water, tools, ... and other facilities necessary for the execution and completion of the work." Under this language, the contract is not "performed" until all materials provided thereunder are paid for. I would affirm the trial court.

Analysis:

First, the Restatement (Second) of Contracts is applied in this case to determine if The Cretex (P) are intended beneficiaries of the performance bond. The primary issue is whether The Cretex (P) can satisfy the "intent to benefit" test, which the Restatement (Second) adopted. Second, the subject of surety bonds is explored in detail, with the court analyzing the various types of bonds that are commonly used, thereby ultimately reaching the parties' intent. The Cretex (P) argued that the performance bond should also be considered a payment bond. The reason this argument was made is that payment bonds are the most likely to create a third party beneficiary situation. If the contractor fails to pay those named in the bond, such as sub-contractors and materialmen, the surety company will pay them. The court rejected The Cretex's (P) argument, and found that only a performance bond existed. The performance bond assures performance should the contractor not perform. Clearly, the subcontractors are not third party beneficiaries of this bond. Thus, the argument is made that because the underlying contract has been incorporated into the bond, the language of the contract establishes the parties' intent that the sub-contractors should be paid in the event of the contractor's default. The court ultimately faulted The Cretex (P) for not filing mechanic's liens. It is interesting to note that the reason given for not filing the mechanic's liens was that they erroneously believed the project involved public, as opposed to private land. If public land was involved, no mechanic's liens could have been filed. This mistaken belief did not dissuade the court from ruling that there was no intent by the contracting parties to confer a benefit on The Cretex (P). Finally, the dissenting justice relied upon the language of the underlying contract to assert that the contract could not be "performed" until all materials thereunder are paid for.

LOCAL UNEMPLOYED INDIVIDUALS HELD TO BE ONLY INCIDENTAL BENEFICIARIES UNDER PUBLIC CONTRACT BECAUSE THEY WERE ONLY THE MEANS TO THE SOCIAL END

Martinez v. Socoma Companies, Inc.

(Unemployed Residents) v. (Promisor of Public Contracts)
(1974) 11 Cal.3d 394, 113 Cal.Rptr. 585, 521 P.2d 841

MEMORY GRAPHIC

Instant Facts

Unemployed residents of community sued promisor under public contract with government as third party beneficiaries.

Black Letter Rule

The mere fact that a Government program for social betterment confers benefits upon individuals who are not required to render contractual consideration in return does not necessarily imply that the benefits are intended as gifts thereby making the individuals donee third party beneficiaries.

Case Vocabulary

DEMURRER: A challenge to the legal sufficiency of the pleading, such as a complaint.
LIQUIDATED DAMAGES: Where the parties to a contract agree to a fixed amount of damages to be recovered should one party breach the contract, regardless of the actual damages incurred due to the breach.
STANDING TO SUE: Having a right to bring a legal proceeding.
WITHOUT LEAVE TO AMEND: When ruling upon a demurrer, the court refuses to give permission to the party to modify, change, or add facts or legal theories to a complaint, resulting in dismissal of the action.

Procedural Basis: Appeal to state Supreme Court from dismissals after demurrers were sustained without leave to amend in actions for damages for breach of contract.

Facts: Martinez (P) brought a class action lawsuit on behalf of over 2,000 East Los Angeles residents—certified as disadvantaged unemployed—against Socoma Companies Inc. (D) and others for defendants' failure to perform contracts with the United States government. Under a federal program designed to furnish disadvantaged persons with training and employment opportunities, the government entered into contracts with Socoma (D) and others whereby funds would be provided in consideration of Socoma (D) and others agreeing, among other things, to train and employ a specified number of the qualified East Los Angeles residents. Although the government paid money to Socoma (D) and others, it is alleged that they failed to perform and provide the required number of jobs. The complaint alleges that the express purpose of the government in entering into the contracts was to benefit the certified disadvantaged hard-core unemployed residents of East Los Angeles for whom Socoma (D) and others promised to provide training and jobs. Martinez (P) and the other members of the class alleged that they are third party beneficiaries of the contracts and are entitled to damages for Socoma's (D) breach. [In other words, they want their paychecks!] The trial court dismissed the actions after Socoma's (D) general demurrer was sustained without leave to amend. Martinez (P) and the other plaintiffs appeal contending that the contracts' intent is to confer a gift, thereby making them third party donee beneficiaries of the contract.

Issue: Does the mere fact that a Government program for social betterment confers benefits upon individuals who are not required to render contractual consideration in return necessarily imply that the benefits are intended as gifts thereby making the individuals donee third party beneficiaries?

Decision and Rationale: (Wright) No. We conclude that the contracts do not state that either the government or Socoma (D) is to be liable to persons such as Martinez (P) for Socoma's (D) nonperformance. The benefits to be derived from Socoma's (D) performance were clearly intended not as gifts from the government to such persons but as a means of executing the public purposes stated in the contracts and in the underlying legislations. Martinez (P) and the other plaintiffs were only incidental beneficiaries and have no right of recovery. Martinez (P) and the other class members contend they are third party beneficiaries under California Civil Code section 1559, which provides that "a contract, made expressly for the benefit of a third person, may be enforced by him at any time before the parties thereto rescind it." This section excludes those who are only incidentally or remotely benefited by it. California decisions follow American law that classifies persons having enforceable rights under contracts to which they are not parties as either creditor or donee beneficiaries. Since the government (the promisee) at no time bore any legal duty toward Martinez (P) or the other class members to provide the benefits set forth in the contracts, they are not creditor beneficiaries. Nor can Martinez (P) and the other class members be considered donee beneficiaries since, as discussed below, no intention to make a gift can be imputed to the government as promisee. Unquestionably, Martinez (P) and the other residents were among those whom the government intended to benefit through the performance of the contracts by Socoma (D) and the others. [Hold on—this does not mean that Martinez (P) and the other unemployed are going to prevail.] However, the fact that a government program for social betterment confers benefits upon individuals who are not required to render contractual consideration in return does not necessarily imply that the benefits are intended as gifts. The benefits of such programs are provided not simply as gifts to the recipients but as a *means* of accomplishing a larger public purpose. The furtherance of the public purpose is in the nature of consideration to the government, displacing any governmental intent to furnish the benefits as gifts. The Restatement of Contracts covers contractual promises of the government to render services to members of the public. It provides, "A promisor bound to the United States or to a State or municipality by contract to do an act or render a service to some or all of the members of the public, is subject to no duty under the contract to such members of the public, is subject to no duty under the contract to such members to give compensation for the injurious consequences of performing or attempting to perform it, or of failing to do so, unless, ... an intention is manifested in the contract, as interpreted in the light of the circumstances surrounding its formation, that the promisor shall compensate members of the public for such injurious consequences." The present contracts manifest no intent that Socoma (D) and the others pay damages to compensate Martinez (P) and the members of the class, or other members of the public for their nonperformance. To the contrary, the contracts' provisions for retaining the government's control over determination of contractual disputes and for limiting defendants' financial risks indicate a governmental purpose to exclude the direct rights against Socoma (D) and the others claimed here. The provisions in the contracts regarding resolving disputes and providing liquidated damages indicates an absence of any contractual intent to impose liability directly in favor of Martinez (P) and the class. Thus, the contracts were designed not to benefit individuals as such but to utilize the training and employment of disadvantaged persons as a means of improving the East Los Angeles neighborhood. Thus, Martinez (P) and the class have no standing as third party beneficiaries to recover the damages sought in the complaint. Affirmed.

Dissent: (Burke) The certified hard-core unemployed of East Los Angeles were the express, not incidental, beneficiaries of the contracts, and thus have standing to sue. The intent of the contracts is expressed in their preambles, i.e., "to help find jobs and provide training for thousands of the Nation's hardcore unemployed, or underemployed, by ... providing training and work opportunities for such seriously disadvantaged persons." Thus, the contracting parties clearly state as one of their purposes their intent to find jobs for the hard-core unemployed.

Analysis:

Third party beneficiary enforcement of public contracts is the subject of this case. The state statute and decisional law acknowledge the classifications of creditor and donee beneficiaries. The main issue concerns whether Martinez (P) and other unemployed residents of East Los Angels are third party donee beneficiaries of the government's contract with Socoma (D) and the others. The court was required to analyze the contract to determine if there was an intent by the government to make a gift to Martinez (P) and the other class members. The court concluded that the benefits of the federal program did not just confer a gift upon the recipient residents, but that they were a *means* of accomplishing a larger public purpose—improving the neighborhood, establishing permanent industries with long term employment opportunities, opportunities for managerial level employment and business ownership, all of which would benefit the local economy and the government itself through reduction of law enforcement and welfare costs. The dissenting justice concluded the opposite—that the unemployed residents were the express beneficiaries of the contracts, because the purpose of the program benefited both the residents and the communities. It appears that the dissent asserts a more persuasive argument that the unemployed were express beneficiaries. But, generally, contracts that are intended to benefit the public in general are held to be not the type of contract enforceable by alleged third party beneficiaries.

COURT PROHIBITS A PROMISOR FROM ASSERTING AGAINST A THIRD PARTY BENEFICIARY THOSE DEFENSES THAT THE PROMISEE HAD AGAINST THE BENEFICIARY

XL Disposal Corp. v. John Sexton Contractors Co.

(Seller of Facility) v. (Buyer & Third Party Beneficiary)
(1995) 168 Ill.2d 355, 659 N.E.2d 1312, 213 Ill. Dec. 665

M E M O R Y   G R A P H I C

Instant Facts

Sexton purchased a facility from XL and agreed to pay attorney Blair for past services, but filed counterclaim against Blair and attempted to assert defenses XL had against Blair.

Black Letter Rule

Whether a promisor may assert a defense against a third party beneficiary that the promisee might have asserted against the beneficiary depends upon the nature of the obligation undertaken; if the promisor agrees to discharge the promisee's liabilty to the third party, then it may assert the promisee's defenses, but if the promisor only agrees to pay a certain sum of money to the third party, the promisor may not assert the promisee's defenses.

Case Vocabulary

AFFIRMATIVE DEFENSE: Facts that constitute a defense even if the allegations in the complaint are true.
DECLARATORY RELIEF: Action merely to have court declare one's rights, such as under a contract or to specific property.
PAROL EVIDENCE RULE: Prior oral or written agreements cannot be used to change or modify the terms of a written agreement, unless mistake or fraud exists.

Procedural Basis: Appeal to state Supreme Court for review of court of appeal's reversal of dismissal of counterclaim and reversal of grant of summary judgment in actions for declaratory relief and recovery of money paid.

Facts: XL Disposal Corporation (XL) (P) operated two facilities. It entered into an agreement with its attorney Blair (Cross-D), memorialized by a typewritten letter, to pay Blair (Cross-D) a certain amount each month for past services until such time as XL (P) ceased operating two of its facilities. Thereafter, John Sexton Contractors Co. (Sexton) (D and Cross-P), the buyer, bought the assets of one of XL's (P) facilities. As part of the consideration for the assets of the business, Sexton (D & Cross-P) agreed to pay attorney Blair (Cross-D), for his past services rendered for the seller XL (P), but based upon a modified monthly amount, and until such time as Sexton (D & Cross-P) ceased to operate the facility. Sexton's (D & Cross-P) promise to pay attorney Blair (Cross-D) was set out in an addendum to the letter stating XL's (P) previous agreement to pay Blair (Cross-D), and was incorporated by reference into the typewritten contract setting forth the terms of the asset sale. Blair (Cross-D) was not a party to the addendum. Sexton (D & Cross-P) stopped paying Blair (Cross-D) [based upon excessive attorney's fees] and XL (P) sued Sexton (D & Cross-P) seeking a declaration that the asset sale contract obligated Sexton (D & Cross-P) to pay Blair (Cross-D). Sexton (D & Cross-P) filed a counterclaim against Blair (Cross-D) seeking declaratory relief and recovery of the money it had paid Blair (Cross-D). Arguing, among other things, that Sexton (D & Cross-P) had no standing to challenge XL's (P) original promise to pay him, Blair (Cross-D) moved to dismiss the counterclaim against him. XL (P) moved for summary judgment on its complaint against Sexton (D & Cross-P). The trial court granted Blair's (Cross-D) motion to dismiss and awarded XL (P) summary judgment. Sexton (D & Cross-P) appealed and the appellate court ruled in his favor, holding that he had standing to challenge XL's (P) agreement to pay Blair (Cross-D). Thereafter, Blair (Cross-D) appealed concerning the viability of Sexton's (D & Cross-P) counterclaim.

Issue: If the promisor only agrees to pay a certain sum of money to the third party, may the promisor assert against the intended third party beneficiary defenses that the promisee might have against the third party?

Decision and Rationale: (Freeman) No. Sexton (D & Cross-P) contends that it stepped into XL's (P) shoes and assumed a direct contractual obligation to Blair (Cross-D). [As will be discussed later, it actually only stepped into one shoe.] Therefore, it claims that it can challenge the legality of XL's (P) agreement to pay Blair (Cross-D) as one for excessive legal fees, though it was not a party to the agreement. Blair (Cross-D) contends that Sexton's (D & Cross-P) obligation is distinct from his previous agreement with XL (P)—in that the promise to pay Blair (Cross-D) was but a component of its contract payment to XL (P) for the payment of the facility assets—and it makes no difference that the form of the monthly payments were directed to him. This State follows the "intent to benefit" test, which avoids the distinction between "donee" and "creditor" beneficiaries. The asset sale contract and the addendum it incorporates as a term plainly show Blair (Cross-D) to be an intended—as opposed to an incidental—third party beneficiary of the asset sale contract. That makes Sexton (D & Cross-P) the promisor with respect to Blair (Cross-D) and XL (P) the promisee. We must determine wither Sexton (D & Cross-P) as the promisor may assert against Blair (Cross-D), as the third party beneficiary, defenses which XL (P), the promisee, might have against Blair (Cross-D). The seminal decision is *Rouse v. United States* wherein the court concluded that under the facts of that case the promisor could not assert a defense against the third party beneficiary that the promisee might have asserted. The court said that whether a promisor could assert a defense against a third party beneficiary that the promisee might have asserted against the beneficiary depended upon the nature of the obligation undertaken. If a promisor agrees to discharge whatever liability the promisee is under to the third party, then the promisor must be allowed to step into the promisee's shoes to show that the promisee was under no enforceable liability. But if the promisor only agrees to pay a certain sum of money to the third party, it is immaterial whether the sum is actually owed by the promisee. In that situation, the promisor has no basis to assert a defense that the promisee might have enjoyed. Was Sexton's (D & Cross-P) obligation one to pay Blair (Cross-D) regardless of whether XL (P) actually owed anything to him or was Sexton's (D & Cross-P) obligation one to discharge a liability running between XL (P) and Blair (Cross-D)? A closer look at the nature of XL's (P) promise to Blair shows that it did not represent liability Sexton (D & Cross-P) could assume. The promise to pay Blair (Cross-D) for past legal services could hardly be said to be based upon a liquidated debt for the actual value of services rendered. The amounts owed to Blair (Cross-D) were determined only in connection with the operation of the facilities. If XL (P) had closed one of its facilities the day after the agreement with Blair (Cross-D) took effect, its liability to Blair (Cross-D) would have been completely discharged. Sexton's (D & Cross-P) promise to pay Blair (Cross-D) was its own, separate promise to Blair (Cross-D). Since Sexton's (D & Cross-P) payment to Blair (Cross-D) were roughly half of the XL (P) promised amount—presumably because only one facility was purchased—Sexton (D & Cross-P) could argue that it stepped into one of XL's (P) shoes. However, no authority has been found stating that the assumption of only part of a promisee's liability to a third party entitles a promisor to avail himself of the promisee's defenses. Thus, we conclude that Sexton (D & Cross-P) promised no more than to pay Blair (Cross-D) the monthly sums independent of whether XL (P) truly owed Blair (Cross-D) anything. Sexton (D & Cross-P) therefore cannot assert defenses that XL (P), as promisee, might have asserted based on its relationship with Blair (Cross-D). With respect to Sexton's (D & Cross-P) own defenses as the promisor against Blair (Cross-D) the third party beneficiary, the defenses do not go to the validity of the asset sale contract. What Sexton (D & Cross-P) has attempted to do is to assert defenses to its obligation to pay Blair (Cross-D) based upon some other direct contractual relationship with Blair (Cross-D). Thus, the allegations of Sexton's (D & Cross-P) counterclaim that its payments to Blair (Cross-D) were excessive legal fees or constituted a perpetual contract were also properly dismissed. We reverse the appellate court and affirm the judgment of the circuit court dismissing Sexton's (D & Cross-P) amended counterclaim against Blair (Cross-D).

Analysis:

This case examines the circumstances under which a promisor may assert against a third party beneficiary a defense that the promisee has against the beneficiary. The case is complicated because the promisor Sexton (D & Cross-P) attempted to sue the third party beneficiary Blair (Cross-D) based upon the affirmative defenses Sexton (D & Cross-P) asserted against XL (P). Note that the case of *Rouse v. United States* cited by the court sets forth the applicable law concerning when a promisor may use the defenses that the promisee might have had against the third party beneficiary. If the contract is interpreted so that the promisor agreed to pay whatever the promisee owed, then the promisor may assert the promisee's defenses against the beneficiary. However, if the promisor promises to pay irrespective of the promisee's liability to the beneficiary, the promisor may not assert the defense against the beneficiary. In this case, the Court interpreted the parties' contract to mean that XL (P) agreed to pay Blair (Cross-D) regardless of whether XL (P) actually owed anything to him, because the amounts owed Blair (Cross-D) were determined, not based upon a liquidated debt, but in connection with the length of time the facilities were operated. Note that often times, where the promise is to pay a specific debt, it is held that the promise is to pay irrespective of the promisee's defense.

United States v. Wood

(3rd Party Beneficiary IRS) v. (Promisor Ex-Wife)
(1989) 877 F.2d 453

M E M O R Y   G R A P H I C

Instant Facts

IRS, as third party beneficiary of a husband/wife property settlement agreement, sued Ms. Wood (D) to collect money to pay ex-husband's tax liens from sale of family home.

Black Letter Rule

If an agreement by a promisor and promisee and benefiting a third party does not contain an express reservation to alter, amend, or rescind, then the parties to the contract cannot rescind the contract without the third party beneficiary's consent after he has accepted, adopted or relied upon the contract.

Case Vocabulary

INTER ALIA: Latin for among other things.
NOTICE OF LEVY: A formal notice advising that one's property has been legally seized for purposes of sale or satisfaction of debt owed.
QUITCLAIM: Usually referring to a quitclaim deed, which conveys real property but without warranty of title and without covenants.

Procedural Basis: Appeal from granting of summary judgment in action by third party beneficiary to enforce terms of contract.

Facts: Mr. Wood and his soon to be ex-wife Ms. Woods (D) executed a property settlement agreement wherein it required Mr. Wood to convey the marital residence to Ms. Wood (D), who promised to sell the property and pay Mr. Wood's taxes from the proceeds. Shortly after the execution of the agreement, Mr. Wood informed the IRS of the terms of the property settlement agreement, and it [being very trusting] accepted Mr. Wood's representation regarding Ms. Wood's (D) obligation under the Agreement. The bank holding the mortgage to the Woods' property obtained a judgment ordering the sale of the residence in order to satisfy the mortgage obligations. On the same date, Mr. Wood conveyed the residence to Ms. Wood (D). The residence was sold at auction and because the sale price was less than two-thirds of the appraised value, the sale created a right of redemption under state law. The Woods thereafter executed an Addendum to the property settlement agreement, which provided that Mr. Wood would quitclaim his right of redemption under the judicial sale and waive his interest in any proceeds realized from the sale. Following the execution of this Addendum, Ms. Wood (D), having exercised the right of redemption, contracted to sell the residence. The Government (P) served Ms. Wood (D) with a notice of levy on all property and rights thereto which belonged to her husband and in her possession and demanded payment of his tax liabilities. It thereafter filed suit against the Woods. The district court held that the Government (P) was a direct creditor beneficiary of the property settlement agreement and ordered judgment against Ms. Wood (D). She appealed claiming the lower court erred in finding the Government (P) to be an intended third party beneficiary because the agreement does not expressly indicate that it was intended to benefit the Government (P), and in fact, the express purpose was not to benefit it. Moreover, relying upon the Addendum to the agreement, Ms. Wood (D) also contended that the agreement did not obligate her as a promisor to Mr. Wood's tax liability.

Issue: Can a third party beneficiary contract be rescinded at any time by the promisor?

Decision and Rationale: (Jones) No. Under the law of this State, all that is necessary for an enforceable contract for the benefit of a third party is that there be consideration for the agreement flowing to the promisor and that the promisee intends to extract a promise directly benefiting the third party. Under the Agreement, Ms. Wood (D) promised to distribute the sales proceeds of the resident in payment of a federal tax lien against Mr. Wood's assets. In consideration for this promise, Mr. Wood conveyed the residence and other land to Ms. Wood (D). The relevant intent of the promisee—Ms. Wood (D)—is reflected by the terms of the Agreement, which provided that "the parties agree that the property shall be sold ... and the net proceeds thereof shall be distributed as received as follows ... a federal tax lien existing against the assets." Mr. Wood's intent to exact Ms. Wood's (D) promise for the direct benefit of the Government (P) is evidenced by his prompt notification to the IRS of the terms of the Agreement. Given this evidence, we find that the Government (P) was a creditor beneficiary under the Agreement and was entitled to enforce Ms. Wood's (D) promise to pay the tax liability. [Having lost on that ground, Ms. Wood (D) tries a different ground.] With respect to the issue of rescission of the agreement, the law of this State pursuant to *Rhodes v. Rhodes* provides that when the right to alter, amend or rescind the contract is specifically provided or reserved therein, it may be rescinded without liability to a third party beneficiary. Should an agreement not contain an express reservation, then the parties to the contract cannot rescind the contract without the third party's consent after he has accepted, adopted or relied upon the contract. Ms. Wood (D) argues that, despite *Rhodes*, the case of a creditor beneficiary, a contract for the benefit of the reditor can be rescinded anytime before the creditor changes his osition in reliance on the contract. According to Ms. Wood (D), the ddendum rescinded her obligation to satisfy the tax liens because it vas executed before the Government (P) changed its position in eliance upon the Agreement. On the contrary, we find that the iovernment (P) changed its position in reliance upon Mr. Wood's tatements to it and the reliance occurred prior to the attempted escission. With both a donee or creditor beneficiary, the power to escind a contract for the benefit of a third person terminates upon the third party's acceptance. Finally, with respect to the argument that the Restatement (First) of Contracts should apply so that the creditor's reliance is necessary to negate the power of the promisee to rescind the promise, rather the Second Restatement, which states that creditors' rights vest upon their learning of the contract and assenting to it, we hold that the Restatement (Second) represents the majority view, and should be applied. Thus, there was no rescission of the Government's (P) right to receive the benefit promised it under the Agreement. [Moral of the story—two things are certain, paying the IRS and death.] Judgment affirmed.

Analysis:

his case concerns when the rights of a creditor beneficiary vest. If a contract exists between a promisor and a promisee for the benefit of a third arty, the promisor and the promisee may not rescind the beneficiary's rights by a subsequent agreement if the rights have vested before the ubsequent agreement was made. The issue becomes when do those rights vest. The court quickly disposed of the issue of whether the parties ntended to enter into an agreement benefiting the third party Government (P), finding that such intent existed. Although Ms. Wood (D) argued gainst such intent, the court correctly interpreted the agreement, examined the conduct of the parties, and found in favor of such intent to enefit the Government (P). The next issue considered whether a rescission of the Agreement occurred, and to decide this question, the court iad to determine whether the Government's (P) rights, as a third party beneficiary, had vested. The court concluded that the Government (P) iad changed its position in reliance upon the property settlement agreement before the subsequent Addendum was entered into. Finally, note hat the court discusses the differing views among the original Restatement Contracts and the Restatement (Second). The primary difference etween the two is that the original Restatement differentiates between donee and creditor beneficiaries—with vesting of the donee's rights ipon the making of a contract and vesting of the creditor's rights upon material change in position in reliance on the contract—and under the Restatement (Second) the rights of either a donee or creditor beneficiary vest upon learning of the contract and assenting to it.

A GRATUITOUS ASSIGNMENT OF INDEBTEDNESS DUE IS NOT VALID, UNLESS THE MEANS OF OBTAINING POSSESSION AND CONTROL OF THE *THING* ARE GIVEN

Adams v. Merced Stone Co.

(Representative of Gratuitous Assignor) v. (Debtor)
(1917) 176 Cal. 415, 178 P. 498

M E M O R Y   G R A P H I C

Instant Facts

Alleged donee of verbal gift of right to indebtedness asserted that because he had the means of obtaining the possession and control of the indebtedness it was a valid assignment.

Black Letter Rule

A verbal gift is not valid, unless the means of obtaining possession and control of the thing are given; thus, where a donor makes a verbal gift of a chose of action, which he knows the donee has within his power to secure the possession and control of the thing given, the delivery or transmission from the donor to the donee of the means of obtaining possession and control of the subject of the gift is still necessary.

Case Vocabulary

CHOSE IN ACTION: Also referred to as a *thing in action*, where one may bring an action for personal rights, such as an action of debt, for which physical possession cannot be had.

INFORMATION AND BELIEF: Generally used in a pleading such as a complaint where the declarant asserts what he believes to be true based upon other than firsthand information.

Procedural Basis: Appeal from judgment following trial in action seeking to collect indebtedness due creditor.

Facts: On behalf of Thomas Prather (Thomas), deceased, Adams (P) sued Merced Stone Co. (Merced) (D) for its alleged indebtedness to Thomas. Merced (D) denied that it was indebted to Thomas, and alleged that prior to his death, Thomas made a gift of said indebtedness to his brother Samuel Prather (Samuel) and that therefore Samuel was the owner of said indebtedness. Samuel was the president, general manager, and board member of Merced (D), a corporation. [Thus, Merced (D) owed the money to its own president Samuel.] At the time of the alleged assignment from Thomas to Samuel, Thomas knew that Samuel had full and exclusive charge and control of Merced's (D) books of account, and knew that he had the means of obtaining possession and control of the said indebtedness so given to him. The trial court found that prior to his death, Thomas made a gift to his brother Samuel of all of the indebtedness due from Merced (D) to Thomas, being the indebtedness sued for by Adams (P). At trial, Samuel testified that in talking business matters, Thomas told him, "Now, in reference to the account of Thomas Prather in the Merced Stone Company, I want to give you that account, all that is due me from that account. ... I give the keys to my office, the combination of my safe and keys to my desk, and with these I give you all accounts, books, ... everything that belongs to me in that office. It is yours." The court concluded that Thomas gave to Samuel the means of obtaining the possession and control of the indebtedness. Adams (P) contends that the transaction did not constitute a valid gift of indebtedness. No change was made upon the books of Merced (D) regarding the indebtedness up to the time of trial, and when the action was begun Merced's (D) account books showed it indebted to Thomas. [If Samuel were smart, he would have at least changed those books!] Adams (P) [presumably believing he was acting in the best interests of the decedent Thomas] appealed from the judgment in favor of Merced (D).

Issue: Where a donor makes a verbal gift of a chose of action, which he knows the donee has within his power to secure the possession and control of the thing given, is delivery or transmission from the donor to the donee of the means of obtaining possession and control of the subject of the gift necessary?

Decision and Rationale: (Shaw) Yes. This case depends on the meaning and effect of California Civil Code section 1147, which provides, "A verbal gift is not valid, unless the means of obtaining possession and control of the thing are given, nor, if it is capable of delivery, unless there is an actual or symbolical delivery of the thing to the donee." Merced (D) contends that this section is complied with in every case of a gift of a chose of action where, at the time the donor makes such gift, he knows that the donee has it within his power to secure the possession and control of the thing given, and that in such a case no delivery or transmission from the donor to the donee of the means of obtaining possession and control of the subject of the gift is necessary. We do not agree. In order to comply with this section, the "means" must be "given," and the effect is that such means must be given by the donor to the donee. In the case of a chose in action not evidenced by a written instrument, the only means of obtaining control that is recognized by the authorities is an assignment in writing, or some equivalent thereof. Although Samuel was possessed of the physical power and the official authority, by reason of his relation to Merced (D), to make the necessary changes on its books to show that the indebtedness was due to him and not to Thomas, this power did not emanate from Thomas. Samuel possessed it before the asserted gift as well as after. The law intends something more than a mere power to make physical entries in the books of the debtor. The authority to make the change, or cause it to be made, must be vested in the debtor by reason of some act or direction of the creditor. If verbal gifts could be made in such loose manner,

it would open the door [or floodgates] to innumerable frauds and perjuries. Something more than mere physical power is necessary; something more than the previous possession of the property or of the means of obtaining it; something emanating from the donor which operates to give to the donee the means of obtaining such possession and control. The conclusion of the trial court that Thomas transferred the debt to Samuel by way of a verbal gift is not supported by the evidence. Reversed.

Analysis:

Thomas was a gratuitous assignor, Samuel claimed he was the assignee [but the court of appeal didn't buy it] and Merced (D) was the debtor. The corporation, Merced (D), asserted as a defense to the suit by Adams (P)—on behalf of the deceased Thomas—that Thomas had verbally made a gift of the indebtedness due him to Samuel. If this position had been affirmed, Adams (P) would have lost because Merced (D) was no longer indebted to Thomas, rather it was indebted to its own President, Samuel. Thomas asserted that the "means of obtaining possession and control of the thing" requirement of the Civil Code was met because he had exclusive control of Merced's (D) books of account, including the physical power and official authority to show that the indebtedness was due to him and not to Thomas. The court held that this was not sufficient because this power did not emanate from Thomas, the assignor/donor. Thus, we learn from this case that (1) mere words promising a gratuitous assignment do not alone create an enforceable assignment and, (2) a verbal gift of a chose of action is not assignable unless there is something emanating from the assignor/donor, which operates to give to the assignee/donee the means of obtaining such possession and control.

SUBROGEE OF ASSIGNMENT CONTRACT HAS SAME RIGHTS AND LIMITATIONS AGAINST OBLIGOR AS DOES THE ASSIGNEE

Ertel v. Radio Corp. of America

(Guarantor/Subrogee) v. (Account Debtor)
(1974) 261 Ind. 573, 307 N.E.2d 471

M E M O R Y   G R A P H I C

Instant Facts

Ertel (P) filed a third party complaint against obligor/account debtor RCA (D) for wrongful payments and was subrogated to the assignee's rights against RCA (D).

Black Letter Rule

An obligor may raise the defense of set-off against a subrogee of an assignee which could have been raised against the assignor.

Case Vocabulary

ASSIGNOR: Under an assignment contract, the party who transfers its rights or powers to another, called the assignee.
GUARANTOR: A person who makes a promise of payment, or performance of an obligation, under a guaranty agreement.
SET-OFF: A counter-demand by the debtor defendant against the plaintiff arising out of an independent transaction, which results in a subtraction from the amount of the debt owed.
SUBROGATED: Derived from the doctrine of subrogation where one person is substituted in place of another with respect to rights or a claim.
SUBROGEE: One who steps into the shoes of another thereby having the same rights, duties, claims, and limitations.
SURETY: One who agrees to pay money or perform an obligation if another person who is obligated to pay or perform fails to do so.
THIRD PARTY COMPLAINT: A complaint filed by the defendant against one who is not currently a party to the lawsuit, alleging that the third-party is liable for the damages suffered by the plaintiff.

Procedural Basis: Appeal to State Supreme Court from the reversal of summary judgment in an action for wrongful payments following notice of assignment.

Facts: [Warning – the facts are extremely complicated, so start making a diagram of who's who and the claims and defenses being asserted!] *The Original Lawsuit.* A lawsuit was filed by Economy Finance Corp. (Economy) against its debtor, Delta Engineering Corp. (Delta) for amounts due under a loan and security agreement covering revolving inventory and accounts receivable. Also named as defendants in the lawsuit as personal guarantors for the payment by Delta were its president and general manager, Dugan, and its secretary-treasurer, Ertel (P) [you'll understand why Ertel is labeled as a plaintiff shortly]. Delta defaulted on the note, Dugan could not be found, and [unlucky] Ertel (P) faced the liability as a defendant. *The Third Party Lawsuit.* In response to the original complaint, Ertel (P) filed a third party complaint against Radio Corporation of America (RCA) (D) for wrongful payment. The basis of this claim arises from the following alleged facts. (1) RCA (D) was a customer and account debtor of Delta. (2) Delta, in order to secure its loans from Economy, assigned its accounts receivable, including its accounts with RCA (D) to Economy. (3) RCA (D) was allegedly given notice of this assignment, which would in turn require it to make all payments to Economy for any machinery it purchased from Delta, but RCA (D) instead made all payments directly to Delta rather than to Economy. (4) RCA wrongfully paid these accounts receivable to Delta and allegedly remained liable to Economy. [That ends the summary of what the third party lawsuit is about.] Ertel (P), as the guarantor defendant in the original lawsuit, paid Economy for Delta's debt. As a result of this payment to Economy, Ertel (P) claims to be the subrogee of Economy vis-à-vis RCA (D). Account debtor RCA (D), in its answer to the third party lawsuit, asserted that even if it were liable to Economy (the assignee) for the payments wrongfully made to Delta (the assignor), it had a right of set-off against Economy (the assignee), and because Ertel (P) was a subrogee of Economy, Ertel (P) was also subject to its right of set-off. The trial court found against Ertel (P) as a defendant in the original lawsuit, and also found against Ertel (P) in his third party lawsuit. The court of appeals reversed the summary judgment against Ertel (P) in his third party lawsuit, holding that he should be subrogated to Economy's rights as assignee of the accounts receivable from RCA (D) and that the assignee-Economy (thus, Ertel (P) as subrogee) would take free of certain set-off rights claimed by account debtor RCA (D) against its account-creditor Delta. The matter was appealed to the State Supreme Court.

Issue: May an obligor raise the defense of set-off against a subrogee of an assignee which could have been raised against the assignor?

Decision and Rationale: (Hunter) Yes. The first issue is whether assignee Economy has a claim against account debtor RCA for wrongful payments made to Delta, the assignor of the accounts receivables. Under section 9-318(3) of the Commercial Code, the account debtor, upon receipt of notice of an assignment, has a duty to pay the assignee and not the assignor. Payment to the assignor, after notification of assignment, does not relieve the account debtor of his obligation to pay the assignee unless the assignee consents to such a collection process. The account debtor's failure to pay the assignee after receiving due notification gives rise to an assignee's claim for wrongful payment. The facts of this case establish that RCA (D) received adequate notification of the assignment. Economy mailed the notice by certified mail, an authorized RCA (D) dock employee signed for it, but the notice was never received by the accounting department. Nevertheless, this is sufficient receipt of notification, and thus because RCA (D) was notified of the assignment, Economy has a claim for wrongful payment. The second issue in this case is whether Ertel (P), as guarantor of the note between Delta and Economy, is subrogated to Economy's rights against RCA (D). We agree with the court of appeals that Ertel (P) became subrogated to the rights of Economy upon payment of the debt owing from Delta to Economy. The general rule is that a surety, upon satisfaction of debt, is subrogated to all the rights that the creditor had against the principal debtor prior to satisfaction of the debt. Additionally, the surety is subrogated to the interests which the creditor has in security for the principal's performance. Thus, Ertel (P), as subrogee of Economy, has a right to the accounts pledged by Delta as security for the initial obligation, including the RCA accounts. The third and final issue in the case is whether RCA (D) has rights of set-off against Economy, and therefore, against Ertel (P). The assignment agreement between Delta and Economy covered Delta's present and future receivables. The accounts receivable in question are from the contracts between Delta for the sale of machinery to RCA (D). RCA (D) claims to have a set-off right against Delta for Delta's incomplete performance of the last contract and that, *ergo*, Ertel (P), as subrogee of Economy also takes subject to those rights. The court of appeals was incorrect in holding that RCA (D) had no set-off rights because the sales transaction between it and Delta occurred after notice of the assignment was given, and that this somehow made it a "separate transaction." The Commercial Code distinguishes between contract-related and unrelated defenses and claims. Defenses and claims "arising" from the contract can be asserted against the assignee whether they arise before or after notification. Any other defense or claim is available against the assignee only if it accrues before notification. The official comment to the Code is consistent. It states, "When the account debtor's defenses on an assigned account, ... or a contract right arise from the contract between him and the assignor it makes no difference whether the breach giving rise to the defense occurs before or after the account debtor is notified of the assignment. Thus, in this case, the fact that RCA's claim arose after Economy gave notice of assignment is irrelevant. Ertel (P), as subrogee of Economy, succeeds to the rights of Economy vis-à-vis RCA (D). Ertel (P) becomes subrogated to Economy's interest in the RCA (D) accounts. However, the rights acquired are no greater or better than those which the person for whom he is substituted had at the time of the payment which effected the subrogation. Therefore, Ertel (P) has succeeded to the rights of Economy, subject to the RCA set-off claim. Transfer granted and cause remanded.

Analysis:

In analyzing the status of the parties, RCA (D) is the obligor and Delta is the obligee-assignor. RCA (D) had a contract to purchase machinery from Delta, and was thus its account debtor. Delta, as assignor, assigned its accounts receivables, which included the RCA (D) accounts, to its own creditor, Economy, the assignee, as security for its loan from Economy. Because Ertel (P), as a guarantor of Delta's debt to Economy, paid Economy, he was entitled to subrogate to the rights [or step into the shoes] of Economy. As a result, Ertel (P) had the right to sue RCA (D) for wrongful payment. In other words, even though RCA (D) wrongfully paid assignor-Delta instead of assignee-Economy, RCA (D) was still liable to Economy. Since Ertel (P) was a subrogee of Economy, he could sue RCA (D) for the payments due under the Delta/RCA machinery contracts. However, as a subrogee, Ertel (P) did not acquire any greater rights than those held by Economy and, of importance in this case, he takes those rights subject to any set-off claims that may be raised by the obligor/account-debtor, i.e., RCA (D). Since RCA (D) contended that the machines it purchased from Delta were incomplete, it asserted that the amount it owed should be set-off because of having to complete the machines itself.

OBLIGOR CANNOT DELEGATE DUTIES TO ANOTHER WHERE PERFORMANCE IS PERSONAL TO THE OBLIGOR

Crane Ice Cream Co. v. Terminal Freezing & Heating Co.

(Assignee Purchaser) v. (Ice Deliverer)
(1925) 147 Md. 588, 128 A. 280

M E M O R Y   G R A P H I C

Instant Facts

Crane (P), an assignee purchaser of ice cream manufacturing business, sued to enforce performance of the contract between assignor and Terminal (D) for delivery of ice.

Black Letter Rule

Assignment of rights and delegation of duties under a contract, where the personal qualification and action of the assignor with respect to both the benefits and burdens of the contract were essential inducements in its formation, and which repudiates future liability of the assignor, is not an enforceable assignment.

Case Vocabulary

DELEGATION OF DUTIES: Where one party to a contract assigns the duties to be performed thereunder to a third party.
EXECUTORY BILATERAL CONTRACT: A contract in which each party is obligated to perform, but where neither has yet so performed.
INTER VIVOS: Latin for, "between the living", and referring to conveyance during life, and not by will.

Procedural Basis: Appeal from judgment following sustaining of demurrer in action for breach of contract to recover damages.

Facts: Mr. Frederick, an ice cream manufacturer, entered into a contract for the delivery of ice by Terminal Freezing & Heating Co. (Terminal) (D). The contract between Terminal (D) and Frederick required Terminal (D) to sell and deliver to Frederick such quantities of ice as he might use to the extent of 250 tons per week, for the price of $3.25 a ton of 2,000 pounds on the loading platform of Frederick. Terminal (D) was to be paid every Tuesday during the contract for all ice purchased by Frederick during the preceding week, and Frederick was not to buy ice from any other source, except in excess of the weekly maximum of 250 tons. Before the expiration of the contract, Frederick [cooling of the ice cream business] assigned the executory bilateral contract to Crane Ice Cream Co. (Crane) (P), a large ice cream business operating in two different states. The assignment of the contract was part of a transaction between Frederick and Crane (P), whereby Crane (P) as purchaser acquired Fredericks' entire ice cream business. Terminal (D) refused to deliver ice to Crane (P) and notified Frederick that the contract was at an end. Crane (P) brought an action on the contract against Terminal (D) to recover damages for breach. Terminal's (D) demurrer was sustained and judgment entered against Crane (P). An appeal followed.

Issue: Is there an enforceable assignment of rights and delegation of duties under a contract, where the personal qualification and action of the assignor with respect to both the benefits and burdens of the contract were essential inducements in its formation, and which repudiates future liability of the assignor?

Decision and Rationale: (Parke) No. We must determine whether the attempted assignment of rights, or the attempted delegation of duties, must fail because the rights or duties are of too personal a character. In so doing, we must examine the nature of the contract and the express or presumed intention of the parties. The contract was made by a corporation with an individual, Mr. Frederick, with whom the corporation had dealt for 3 years before it executed a renewal contract for a second like period. The character, credit, and resources of Frederick had been tried and tested by Terminal (D) before it renewed the contract. Not only had his ability to pay as agreed been established, but also his fidelity to his obligation not to buy or accept ice from another source had been ascertained. [In other words, the ice cream maker was loyal to the icemaker.] From the time of the weekly delivery of ice to the date of the payment therefore, the title to the ice was in the purchaser, and the seller had no security for its payment, except for the integrity and solvency of Frederick. The performance of the nonassigning party to the contract was to precede the payments by the assignor Frederick. The conclusion is inevitable that the inducement for Terminal (D) to enter into the original contract and into the renewal was Terminal's (D) reliance upon its knowledge of an average quantity of ice consumed, and to be needed, in the usual course of Frederick's business, its confidence in the stability of his business, and his continuing financial responsibility. After Frederick went out of business and turned everything over to Crane (P), it became the business of a stranger, whose skill, competency, and requirements of ice were altogether different from those of Frederick. While a party to a contract may assign all his beneficial rights, except where a personal relation is involved, his liability under the contract is not assignable inter vivos, because one who is bound to any performance or who owes money cannot cast off his own liability and substitute another's liability. One cannot assign his liabilities under a contract, but one who is bound to bear the liability may delegate the performance of his obligation to another, if the liability be of such a nature that its performance by another will be substantially the same thing as performance by the promisor himself. In such circumstances, the performance of the third party is the act of the promisor, who remains liable under the contract if the performance is not fulfilled. In this case, there was an attempt to transfer the rights and to delegate the duties of the assignor under an executory bilateral contract where the personal qualification and action of the assignor were essential inducements in the formation of the contract, and that the assignment was a repudiation of any future liability of the assignor. Judgment affirmed.

Analysis:

Frederick, the assignor, attempted to assign and delegate the entire contract—liabilities and duties—to Crane (P). When Terminal (D) refused to deliver ice, Crane (P) sued. Terminal (D) successfully defended however by arguing that the contract was not assignable. The court relied upon the fact that there was an existing relationship between Terminal (D) and Frederick whereby the former knew the amount of ice that usually would be required, trusted him, knew that he paid his accounts, and knew he did not buy ice from others. Thus, the inducement for Terminal (D) to re-enter into a contract with Frederick was based upon the trust and confidence it placed in Frederick. Where such a situation exits, the duties under the contract are non-delegable. However, note that Crane (P) operated a large business in two different states. At first blush, one would question why Terminal (D) could not feel confident that Crane (P) too would honor the terms of the contract as compared with an individual such as Frederick. However, it was the size and vastness of Crane's (P) operation that caused the court to rule as it did. The court commented that Crane (P) could wholly supply the needed ice from its own manufactory thereby resulting in not purchasing any ice from Terminal (D). If that occurred, Terminal (D) would be deprived of the benefit of the contract.

The British Waggon Co. and the Parkgate Waggon Co. v. Lea & Co.

(Waggon Repairers) v. (Waggon Renting Co.)
(1880) 5 Q.B.D. 149

M E M O R Y   G R A P H I C

Instant Facts

Lea &Co. (D), renter of wagons, sought to end contract for repair after Parkgate Waggon (P) delegated the duty of repair to The British Waggon Co. (P).

Black Letter Rule

Where a person contracts with another to do work or perform service, and it can be inferred that the person employed has been selected with reference to his individual skill, competency, or other personal qualification, those duties cannot be delegated to a third person.

Case Vocabulary

INDENTURE: A formal written agreement among parties with different interests, traditionally having distinguishing edging to prevent forgery.
QUI FACIT PER ALIUM FACIT PER SE: He who acts through another acts himself.
WINDING UP: The act of settling the accounts and selling the assets prior to the dissolution of a corporation of partnership.

Procedural Basis: Trial before the Court of Queen's Bench in which judgment was entered for breach of contract.

Facts: The British Waggon Co. and the Parkgate Waggon Co. (P) brought action against Lea & Co. (D) to recover rent for the hire of railway waggons [known as wagons in America]. Parkgate Waggon Co. (P) entered into two written agreements with Lea & Co. (D) for the hire of waggons for use by Lea & Co. (D) in its coal business for a term of seven years. The agreements expressly provided that Parkgate Waggon Co. (P) would keep the waggons in good repair and working order. Thereafter, a voluntary winding up of the Parkgate Waggon Co. (P) occurred under the supervision of the court. Subsequently, the Parkgate Waggon Co. (P) assigned and transferred to the British Co. (P), all sums of money due or to become due, which included the contracts with Lea & Co. (D). The British Co. (P) agreed to perform under the terms of the contracts. As a result, the British Co. (P) took over from the Parkgate Co. (P) the repairing stations used for the repair of the waggons let to Lea & Co. (D), and was ready and will to execute all necessary repairs to the waggons. Lea & Co. (D) contended however that the contract was at an end because the Parkgate Waggon Co. (P) had, by assigning the contracts, incapacitated itself from fulfilling the obligation to keep the waggons in repair and had no right to substitute a third party to do the work. [Lea & Co. (D) may have won if it had explained why it felt only Parkgate (P) should have been able to repair the wagons.]

Issue: Where a person contracts with another to do work or perform service, and it can be inferred that the person employed has been selected with reference to his individual skill, competency, or other personal qualification, can those duties be delegated to a third person?

Decision and Rationale: (Cockburn) No. Lea & Co. (D) relies upon, and we have previously approved, *Robson v. Drummond*, a case wherein the defendant could not be sued on a contract for the hire of a carriage to be kept in repair and painted once a year by the coachmaker, because the defendant might have been induced to enter into the contract by reason of the personal confidence which he reposed in the coachmaker. In like manner, where goods are ordered of a particular manufacturer, another, who has succeeded to his business, cannot execute the order, so as to bind the customer, who has not been made aware of the transfer of the business, to accept the goods. The latter is entitled to refuse to deal with any other than the manufacturer whose goods he intended to buy. We concur in the principle stated in *Robson v. Drummond*, namely, that where a person contracts with another to do work or perform service, and it can be inferred that the person employed has been selected with reference to his individual skill, competency, or other personal qualification, those duties may not be delegated to a third person. Personal performance is in such a case of the essence of the contract, which cannot in its absence be enforced against an unwilling party. In the present case, however, we cannot suppose that in stipulating for the repair of the waggons by the company, Lea & Co. (D) attached any importance to whether the repairs were done by the company, or by any one with whom the company might enter into a subsidiary contract to do the work. All Lea & Co. (D) cared for in this stipulation was that the waggons should be kept in repair; it was indifferent to them by whom the repairs should be done. [But Lea & Co. (D) argued to the contrary.] Therefore, the repair of the waggons, undertaken and done by the British Co. (P) under their contract with the Parkgate Co. (P) is a sufficient performance by the latter of their engagement to repair under their contract with Lea & Co. (D). Thus, so long as the Parkgate Co. (P) continues to exist, and through the British Co. (P) continues to fulfill its obligation to keep the waggons in repair, Lea & Co. (D) cannot be heard to say that the former company is not entitled to the performance of the contract on the ground that the companies have

incapacitated themselves from performing their obligations under it, or that, by transferring the performance thereof to others, they have absolved Lea & Co. (D) from further performance on their part. Judgment must be for Parkgate Waggon Co. (P) and British Co. (P) for the amount claimed.

Analysis:

This English Court case upheld the assignment and delegation of duties to repair the wagons. The court concludes, without any explanation, that Lea & Co. (D) was indifferent as to whom should make the repairs to the waggons, and thus it could not be considered a contract where personal performance was the essence of the contract. The court chooses to distinguish *Robson v. Drummond* while upholding its principle. However, *Robson* too involved the repair of a wagon, but included painting once a year by the coachmaker. Since the coachmaker was involved, it could be presumed that the defendant in that case might have been induced to enter into the contract because of the personal confidence he had in the coachmaker. It may have been that the coachmaker had *unique* skills, whereas in this case general repairs to wagons did not require such unique skills. If the performance of the original obligor is required, or the obligor's personal supervision, then the duties under the contract are not delegable. Personal performance will be implied as a term of the contract if the unique skills of the obligor are the essence of the contract.

FOR CONTRACT ASSIGNMENT AND DELEGATION OF PERFORMANCE, RELATIONSHIP OF ASSIGNEE TO OBLIGEE MUST BE CONSIDERED

Sally Beauty Co., Inc. v. Nexxus Prods. Co., Inc.

(Direct Competitor) v. (Hair Care Product Co.)
(1986) 801 F.2d 1001

M E M O R Y G R A P H I C

Instant Facts

Exclusive hair care products distributorship contract was assigned to competitor without consent of obligee.

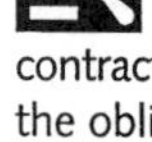

Black Letter Rule

Assignment of an exclusive distributorship contract, which delegates duty of performance, requires the obligee's consent.

Case Vocabulary

PER SE: Alone or by itself.

Facts: Sally Beauty Company, Inc. (Sally) (P) acquired Best Barber Beauty & Supply Company, Inc. (Best) and obtained the rights and interests in all of Best's contracts. Both companies were distributors of hair care and beauty products to retailers and hair salons. Prior to its merger with Sally (P), Best had entered into a contract with Nexxus Products (Nexxus) (D). The contract provided, among other things, that Best would be the exclusive distributor of Nexxus (D) hair care products in Texas. When Best merged into Sally (P), Nexxus (D) renounced its obligations under the contract with Best because Sally (P) was a direct competitor of Nexxus (D). Sally (P) was wholly owned by [big time hair care company] Alberto-Culver. Sally (P) sued Nexxus (D) for breach of contract and other claims. As a defense, Nexxus (D) contended that its contract with Best could not be assigned to Sally (P) without its consent [and it was not about to consent to such a thing!]. The district court entered summary judgment in favor of Nexxus (D). Sally (P) appealed. The court of appeal affirmed, but on different grounds. It held that assignment of the contract, which delegated the duty of performance to Sally (P), a direct competitor of Nexxus (D), required the consent of Nexxus (D).

Issue: Does the assignment of an exclusive distributorship contract, which delegates the duty of performance, require the obligee's consent?

Decision and Rationale: (Cudahy) Yes. An assignment of an exclusive distributorship contract that delegates the duty of performance requires the consent of the obligee. Nexxus (D) asserted that the contract was not assignable because it was one for personal services, based upon a relationship of personal trust and confidence between the President of Best and the Vice President of Nexxus (D). On the other hand, Sally (P) asserted that the contract was assignable because 1) it was between two corporations, not individuals, and 2) the character of performance would not be altered by the substitution of parties. The Vice-President of Nexxus (D) met personally with the President of Best for several days before entering into the contract. Best had been in the hair care business for 40 years and its President had extensive experience. It would be reasonable to conclude that Nexxus (D) developed personal trust and confidence in its relationship with Best. It is on this [obviously incorrect] reasoning that the district court granted Nexxus' motion for summary judgment, which denied Sally (P) the right to proceed to trial. However, we cannot affirm this summary judgment because these are issues for the trier of fact that preclude summary judgment. Nevertheless, we affirm summary judgment on a different ground. The exclusive distributorship agreement has as its dominant factor the sale of "goods," and thus is subject to the Uniform Commercial Code [governing the law of contracts of goods], as adopted by this State. Sally (P), which is wholly owned by Alberto-Culver, is a direct competitor of Nexxus (D). The distribution agreement requires performance in the form of using "best efforts" to sell and distribute Nexxus (D) products. The fact that Sally (P) is a direct competitor with Nexxus (D) precludes the delegation of duty of performance. Nexxus (D) did not bargain for this and should not be required to consent to that which it does not desire. Nexxus (D) contracted exclusively with Best for its best efforts in promoting the sale of Nexxus (D) products. Judgment affirmed.

Dissent: (Posner) The proper remedy is not to permit Nexxus (D) to cancel the contract because it has insecurity regarding the performance by Sally (P) of its obligation to use its best efforts to sell and distribute Nexxus (D) products. Rather, Nexxus (D) should have demanded assurance of due performance. A trial should be permitted on the issue of whether the merger of Best with Sally (P) so altered the conditions of performance under the contract as to permit Nexxus (D) to claim anticipatory repudiation by conduct and declare the contract broken. Judgment should be reversed and the case remanded for trial.

Analysis:

)elegating to a competitor the duty of performance of an exclusive distributorship contract will not be permitted absent the obligee's consent. 'he appellate court's ruling was based on the fact that Sally (P), being wholly owned by Alberto-Culver, was a direct competitor of Nexxus (D). 'erformance of the contract would involve using "best efforts" to distribute the products. There was no assurance that Sally (P) would always erform in the best interests of Nexxus (D). By delegating this duty to one controlled by a competitor would defeat the purpose of the contract. 'he court expressly did not address the situation where the assignee is not completely under the control of a competitor, such as, if Sally (P) were iot controlled by Alberto-Culver. The opinion fails to comment on Sally's (P) argument that the contract was assignable because it was between wo corporations. Instead, it focuses on Nexxus (D) contracting with Best for it to use its best efforts to distribute and sell Nexxus (D) products. f the contract were assigned to a non-competitor, the holding may have been different if there was no basis for Nexxus (D) to object to the ssignee. If, on the other hand, the contract had been assigned to a new start up company, with no experience in the field of hair care, the utcome would most likely be the same as the case at bar. It is important to consider the assignee's relationship to the obligee. The underlying acts show that there was reliance by Nexxus (D) on the experience of Best's President and the fact that the company had been in the business or 40 years. The law will protect the obligee from having to accept something for which he did not contract. To delegate the duty of erformance to a competitor was obviously not what Nexxus had bargained for.